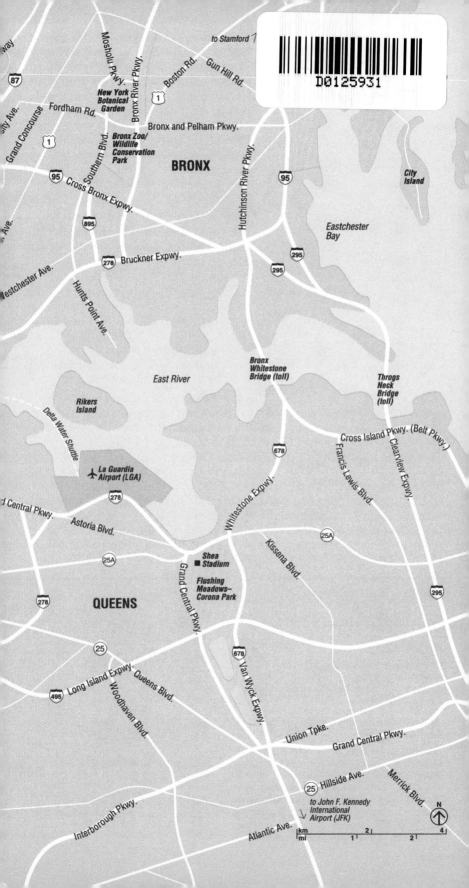

Orientation

MICHAEL STORRINGS

Sophisticated and brutal. Exhilarating and oppressive. Earthy and aloof. A thorough description of New York City might exhaus the largest vocabulary. New York is indeed city of dynamic contrasts, from the sleek granite high-rises of **Wall Street** and **Midtown** to the crumbling tenements of **Brooklyn** and the **Bronx**, from the bohemian spirit of **Greenwich Village** to the old-money atmosphere of **Upper Fifth Avenue**, and from the avant-garde art galleries of **SoHo** to the **Apollo Theater** and historic churches of **Harlem**.

Weighted down by wall-to-wall buildings and 7.4 million people, New York in its density may seem relentless and chaotic to first-time visitors. But it's essentially a city of small neighborhoods best explored one at a time. Don't exhaust yourself by trying to race from one end of the city to the other in the hopes of seeing "everything." Instead, make a list of must-sees in each neighborhood and enjoy all they have to offer before moving on to the next.

One of New York's chief attractions is the overwhelming number of places to visit. Every night on the town doesn't have to include dinner at a four-star restaurant and a Broadway show to be memorable, and you don't have to spend your days splurging in the expensive shops on **Fifth** or **Madison Avenues.** Some of New York's greatest pleasures are simple, and often inexpensive: sitting on the front steps of the **Metropolitan Museum of Art** and watching a mime while eating a hot dog; whiling away an hour in a cafe, sipping a cappuccino as the world goes by the window; walking through **Central Park** on a clear day and gazing up at the brilliant blue sky above the tall buildings; and, when you've said and done as much as you can, waving good-bye to the **Statue of Liberty** from the window of a departing plane, humming "New York, New York."

Area code 212 unless otherwise noted.

Getting to New York City

Airports

For convenient money-saving ways to get to the following airports, call **AIR RIDE** at 800/AIR.RIDE for information on buses and trains, and car, minivan, and limousine services.

John F. Kennedy International Airport (JFK)

The area's largest airport, almost always referred to simply as **JFK,** is located about 15 miles east of **Manhattan** in the borough of **Queens** and, depending on traffic, travel time can take anywhere from 35 to 90 minutes; average time is one hour. Most overseas flights, as well as many domestic flights, arrive and depart from **JFK.** Terminals are connected by free shuttle buses; if time is short, taxis are available.

How To Read This Guide

NEW YORK CITY ACCESS® is arranged by neighborhood so you can see at a glance where you are and what is around you. The numbers next to the entries in the following chapters correspond to the numbers on the maps. The text is color-coded according to the kind of place described:

Restaurants/Clubs: Red   **Hotels:** Blue

Shops/ Outdoors: Green   **Sights/Culture:** Black

& Wheelchair accessible

Wheelchair Accessibility

An establishment (except a restaurant) is considered wheelchair accessible when a person in a wheelchair can easily enter a building (i.e., no steps, a ramp, a wide-enough door) without assistance. Restaurants are deemed wheelchair accessible *only* if the above applies, *and* if the rest rooms are on the same floor as the dining area and their entrances and stalls are wide enough to accommodate a wheelchair.

Rating the Restaurants and Hotels

The restaurant star ratings take into account the quality, service, atmosphere, and uniqueness of the restaurant. An expensive restaurant doesn't necessarily ensure an enjoyable evening; however, a small, relatively unknown spot could have good food, professional service, and a lovely atmosphere. Therefore, on a purely subjective basis, stars are used to judge the overall dining value (see the star ratings at right). Keep in mind that chefs and owners often change, which sometimes drastically affects the quality of a restaurant. The ratings in this guidebook are based on information available at press time.

The price ratings, as characterized at right, apply to restaurants and hotels. These figures describe general price-range relationships between other restaurants and hotels in the area. The restaurant price ratings are based on the average cost of an entrée for one person, excluding tax and tip. Hotel price ratings reflect the base price of a standard room for two people for one night during the peak season.

Restaurants

★	Good
★★	Very Good
★★★	Excellent
★★★★	An Extraordinary Experience
$	The Price Is Right (less than $10)
$$	Reasonable ($10-$20)
$$$	Expensive ($20-$30)
$$$$	Big Bucks ($30 and up)

Hotels

$	The Price Is Right (less than $125)
$$	Reasonable ($125-$200)
$$$	Expensive ($200-$275)
$$$$	Big Bucks ($275 and up)

Map Key

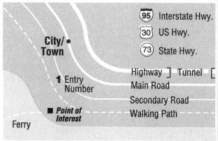

Airport Services

Airport Emergencies	718/244.4225/6
Currency Exchange	718/656.8444
Customs	718/553.1648
Ground Transportation	800/247.7433
Immigration	718/553.1688
Information	718/244.4444
Interpreters/Translators	Contact individual airline
Lost and Found	718/244.4225
Parking	718/244.4444
Police	718/244.4225/6
Traveler's Aid	718/656.4870

Airlines

American	800/433.7300
America West	800/235.9292
British Airways	800/247.9297
Delta	800/221.1212
El Al	768.9200, 800/223.6700
Northwest	
Domestic	800/225.2525
International	800/447.4747
TWA	
Domestic	800/221.2000
International	800/892.4141
United	800/241.6522
US Airways	800/428.4322

Getting to and from John F. Kennedy International Airport

By Bus New York Airport Service Express buses (718/706.9658) depart **JFK** daily every 15-30 minutes from 6AM to midnight for **Port Authority Bus Terminal** (Eighth Ave, between W 40th and W 42nd Sts) and **Grand Central Station** (Park Ave, between E 41st and E 42nd Sts). Buses to the airport from these two locations follow the same schedule. Tickets are available at the terminals' ground transportation desk. **Gray Line Air Shuttle** buses (315.3006) travel between the airport and nearly 50 hotels on the **East** and **West Sides** between **Battery Park** and **125th Street** in Manhattan daily every half-hour from 7AM to 11PM. The trip takes about an hour, though the hotel stops are time-consuming.

By Car The most direct way into and out of Manhattan is by car. From the airport, take the **Van Wyck Expressway** to the **Grand Central Parkway (GCP),** which connects with the **Long Island Expressway (LIE).** Those going to downtown Manhattan (or to Brooklyn) should exit the LIE onto the **Brooklyn-Queens Expressway (BQE).** The BQE, in turn, feeds into the **Williamsburg, Manhattan,** and **Brooklyn Bridges.** For Midtown destinations, continue on the LIE, which connects with the **Queens-Midtown Tunnel.** To get to the airport, reverse the directions.

Rental Cars

Most car-rental agencies offer free shuttles from the arrivals terminals to their airport locations.

Avis 718/244.5400, 800/331.1212
Budget 718/656.6010, 800/527.0700
Dollar 718/656.2400, 800/800.4000
Hertz............................718/656.7600, 800/654.3131
National 718/632.8300, 800/227.7368

By Limousine Car services and limousines provide transportation to, though not as frequently from, the airport. They're a good bet when you must leave for the airport during rush hour, when taxis usually can't be found. Rates are set in advance and are typically the same as—at times even less expensive than—a cab ride ($25 to $35 for a standard car, or $50 to $80 for a limousine). Many companies accept credit cards and offer standard as well as luxury cars and limousines. Here are some car service and limousine companies:

All City Transportation 718/402.4747
Ben's Luxury Transportation Services 645.9888
Carey 718/632.0500
Carmel..666.6666
City Ride 861.1000
Davel 645.4242
Fugazy 661.0100
Jerusalem....................996.6600, 888/JERUSALEM
Luxury Limo 800/LIMO.NEED

London Towncars 988.9700
Minute Man 718/899.5600
Olympic Limousine 995.1200, 800/872.0044
Tel Aviv 777.7777

By Taxi Taxis from the airport can be found outside all major arrivals buildings. An airport employee is usually on hand if you have any questions or need assistance. A cab ride from the airport for up to four people to anywhere in Manhattan costs a flat $30, plus tunnel or bridge tolls and a tip. From Manhattan, the cost is whatever the meter reads (usually approximately $30 to $35), plus tolls and tip. Not all taxi drivers will want to make the trip from Midtown (and should never ask to be compensated for their return trip into town), so allow yourself time to find one so inclined. See limousines (above) to reserve private car service for the same price, or less.

Subway/Bus This is the cheapest way to get into town; you'll need to catch a free shuttle bus marked **Howard Beach Station,** where you'll connect with the **A** train subway, making stops along **Eighth Avenue** at **West 34th, West 42nd,** and **West 59th Streets.** To coordinate your trip from Midtown, call 800/247.7433 for departure times for the bus from **Howard Beach Station** to the airport.

La Guardia Airport (LGA)

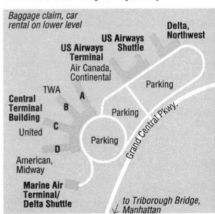

Located closer to Manhattan in northwest Queens, **La Guardia** is 8 miles northeast of Manhattan, or about a 30-minute drive. Most airlines serving other US cities use the two-level main terminal. **Delta Airlines** shares a terminal with **Northwest,** and **US Airways** has a shuttle terminal. Terminals are connected by free shuttle buses.

Airport Services

Airport Emergencies............................718/533.3900
Currency Exchange Information 718/533.3400
Customs/Immigration 718/476.4378,
....718/476.5211
Ground Transportation 800/247.7433,
....718/533.3705

nformation 718/533.3400

ost and Found....................................718/533.3988

arking..718/533.3850

....800/247.7433

olice 718/533.3935

irlines

ir Canada 800/776.3000

merican 800/433.7300

ontinental 800/525.0280

elta..800/221.1212

Midway..800/446.4392

Iorthwest..800/225.2525

WA 290.2121, 800/221.2000

Inited..800/241.6522

S Airways...800/428.4322

Getting to and from La Guardia Airport

Iy Boat Delta Water Shuttle (800/933.5935) is a igh-speed boat that departs from the **Marine Air erminal** several times weekday mornings and early venings. Travel time is approximately 25 minutes to ast **34th Street** and 40 minutes to Wall Street. Non-**elta** passengers can also use this service.

Iy Bus New York Airport Express buses 718/706.9658) depart **LaGuardia** daily every 20 ninutes from 6:40AM to 11:40PM for **Port Authority us Terminal** and **Grand Central Station**. Service uns daily from 6AM to midnight from these two ocations. Tickets are available at the ground ransportation desks in the terminals. **Gray Line Air huttle** buses (315.3006) leave the airport for nearly 0 Manhattan hotels daily every half-hour from 7AM o 11:30PM; buses depart hourly from these estinations to the airport. Travel time is about an our.

Iy Car If you're traveling to Manhattan by car, take he Grand Central Parkway to the **Triborough Bridge,** nen travel south on the **FDR Drive.** To save time and he toll, get off the Grand Central at the **21st Street** xit just before the Triborough Bridge, turn south on .1st Street, and take the **Queensboro Bridge (59th treet Bridge)** into Manhattan. To go downtown SoHo or Wall Street), take the Brooklyn-Queens xpressway to the Williamsburg Bridge, which exits t **Delancey Street**.

Iental Cars

he following companies have desks on the lower evel by baggage claim:

Ivis 718/507.3600, 800/331.1212

Iudget 718/639.6400, 800/527.0700

Iollar 718/779.5600, 800/800.4000

Iertz....................718/478.5300, 800/654.3131

Iational 800/227.7368, 800/227.7368

By Limousine Car and limousine services are also available, a standard car costing approximately $15-$20. See **JFK Airport** above for more information.

By Taxi Taxis depart from in front of **La Guardia**'s major terminals around-the-clock. The cost to Midtown is generally $15 to $25, plus bridge and tunnel tolls and tip.

Subway/Bus Buses include **Triborough Coach** (*Q33* or *Q47*; 718/335.1000), which runs a 24-hour bus service from **La Guardia**'s main terminal to the **Jackson Heights 74th Street** subway station (the **E, F, R,** and **7** all stop here) in Queens for connections into and out of Manhattan. The trip takes about 45 minutes. Another option is the *M60* bus running daily from 5AM to 1AM between La Guardia and **Morningside Heights** and Harlem in **Upper Manhattan.** The trip takes between 30 and 45 minutes.

Newark International Airport (EWR)

Local traffic snafus make **Newark** a popular choice, especially if your final destination is the West Side or downtown Manhattan. Located on Newark Bay, 16 miles southwest of Manhattan in New Jersey (30 minutes to an hour traveling time), it has one international and two domestic terminals, with a monorail that travels between terminals, shuttle bus connections, and easy public transportation options to and from Midtown.

Airport Services

Airport Emergencies...........................973/961.6633

Currency Exchange..............................973/961.4720

Customs..973/645.3409

Ground Transportation 800/247.7433

Immigration 973/645.3239

Information 973/961.6000

Lost and Found ....Contact individual airline

Parking...973/961.4751

Police 973/961.6230

Traveler's Aid 973/623.5052

Airlines

Air Canada 800/776.3000

America West 800/235.9292

American	800/433.7300
British Airways	800/247.9297
Continental	800/525.0280
Delta	800/221.1212
TWA	
Domestic	800/221.2000
International	800/892.4141
Virgin Atlantic	800/862.8621

Getting to and from Newark International Airport

By Bus New Jersey Transit (201/762.5100, 800/772.2222 in NJ) offers 24-hour bus service every 15 to 30 minutes to **Port Authority Bus Terminal**. Buses also go to Newark's **Penn Station** daily every 10 to 15 minutes from 6AM to 1AM, and every 30 to 60 minutes between 1AM and 6AM. **Olympia Trails** (964.6233) runs buses from the airport to **1 World Trade Center** every 30 minutes (Monday through Saturday from 6:45AM to 8:45PM; Sunday and holidays from 7:15AM to 8:15PM) and **Grand Central** and **Penn Station** (W 34th Street, at Eighth Ave) daily every 20 to 30 minutes from 6:15AM to midnight. The ride lasts from 30 to 45 minutes. **Gray Line Air Shuttle** buses (315.3006) run from the airport to nearly 50 hotels in Manhattan daily every 20 minutes from 7AM to 11PM, and hourly from Manhattan to the airport. Travel time is about an hour, mostly due to in-town hotel stops.

By Car The route to Manhattan by car is fairly straightforward. Take the **New Jersey Turnpike** and follow the signs to either the **Holland Tunnel** (downtown) or the **Lincoln Tunnel** (Midtown).

Rental Cars

The following are located in the baggage-claim area and are open daily from 7AM to midnight (the return lots are open 24 hours):

Avis	973/961.4300, 800/331.1212
Budget	973/961.2990, 800/527.0700
Dollar	973/824.2002, 800/800.4000
Hertz	973/621.2000, 800/654.3131
National	973/622.1270, 800/227.7368

By Limousine These services may be obtained at booths within individual terminals. To reserve in advance, see **JFK Airport** above.

By Taxi A cab to Manhattan will cost $25-$35; taxi stands are located in front of the arrivals building.

By Train There is currently no rail service between **Newark Airport** and Manhattan, though current negotiations are underway to create a monorail line, an extension of the one that connects the terminals.

Bus Station (Long-Distance)

The **Port Authority Bus Terminal** (Eighth Ave, between W 40th and W 42nd Sts) is the departure and arrival point for all long-distance buses, commuter buses, and bus links to the airports.

Train Station (Long-Distance)

Amtrak (582.6875, 800/872.7245) runs trains out of **Pennsylvania Station** (Madison Square Garden Center, Seventh Ave, between W 31st and W 33rd Sts) to most points in the US.

Getting around New York City—and Beyond

Perhaps the most crucial element of your stay is mastering the city's transportation services and routes. The five major ways of getting around are subway, bus, taxi, car service, and foot. Of these, walking is the most highly recommended, and sometimes the quickest. Manhattan is laid out in a rather easy-to-grasp grid of north/south avenues and east/west numbered streets. Fifth Avenue is the dividing line between east and west.

Bicycles Although plans to make New York a more bicycle-friendly city were in the works at press time, bicycle riding in Midtown is generally a hazardous art that should be left to the pot-hole–hardened bicycle messengers known for their derring-do.

Buses Crisscrossing town, New York City's network of buses may be slower than the subway, but you have the satisfaction of seeing where you're going and enjoying a more pleasant mode of travel. A sign on the front of each bus gives its route number and final destination, and stops are clearly marked on the street, sometimes with maps showing the route served (although not every bus serves every stop). During rush hours, buses marked "Limited" function like express subway lines and stop only at major intersections. In addition to the longer-distance routes that run on the north-south avenues, there are many crosstown bus routes. Exact change in coins, a token, or a "MetroCard" is required.

Subway riders using the MetroCard (see "Subway," below) can transfer free onto city buses within a two-hour time period. After your subway ride,

imply dip the card into the fare slot on the bus; it will egister "Xfer" and no additional amount will be educted. The same procedure is followed when you ransfer from one bus to another—the fare is educted only at the start of the trip.

Driving Think twice bout driving a car to get around Manhattan. Traffic is nightmarish, parking on he street is

mpossible, and parking garages are outrageously xpensive. If you must arrive by car, it's best to stash t away in a parking garage and then use alternative means of transportation. Hotels sometimes offer discounted parking rates to their guests (even the most expensive hotels charge extra). Parking tickets re given without mercy, so don't park at a meter that sn't working, and be sure you understand the estrictions posted on parking signs so your car isn't owed—something that happens all too frequently.

Car Service These so-called gypsy cabs (generally owner-operated and not as strictly controlled as icensed cabs) have sprung up in town simply because yellow cabs are sometimes scarce or will sometimes not go where you wish to go—particularly to the outer boroughs or to Harlem and **Washington Heights.** Or you may find yourself visiting until a late hour and wish to have a car at your door rather than trying to hail one on the venue. Car services and gypsy cabs are identified by heir "livery" license plates. Car services can be found in the *Yellow Pages* and gypsy cabs can be hailed on the street—if you have to. Confirm the fare n advance on the phone when reserving a car for a "drop off" or an hourly booking.

Ferries Ferries can be a good bet for crossing water. The **Staten Island Ferry** is still one of the thrills in New York City, running every 20 to 30 minutes 24 hours from the foot of **Whitehall Street** (next to **Battery Park**); you can stay on round-trip, and it's ree. Popular ferry services include:

Delta Water Shuttle..............................800/543.3779

Express Navigation
(Sandy Hook, New Jersey) 800/262.8743

Hoboken—World Financial Center Ferry......................
....201/420.6307

Port Imperial
(Weehawken, New Jersey) 800/533.3779

Staten Island Ferry.......................................225.5368

Parking Many hotels have either private parking or a special arrangement with a nearby lot, so check before arriving. Parking lots are not hard to come by, though they are expensive. Ask about daily rates or try to strike a deal if you'll be leaving your car there, unused, for more than 24 hours. If you opt to park on he street, make sure you understand the restrictions posted and the risk you run with frequent burglaries.

"Alternate side of the street parking" means you'll have to get there by 8AM the next day to move the car.

Subway It may be noisy and crowded, but the subway is the most efficient way to get around during rush hour and to conquer longer distances. Most of the trains have sleek, modern cars that are air-conditioned in the summer and heated in winter. The subway system is open 24 hours, although principal service is between 6AM and midnight. After hours, wait for your train in designated areas on the station platform.

The system is complicated and not always immediately decipherable. Entrance requires the purchase of a token or a prepaid "MetroCard," either of which allows you to travel its length and breadth. Tokens and MetroCards are available at token booths at all 469 stations as well as at some **McDonald's** restaurants, supermarkets, and newsstands. *Note:* At press time, the **MTA** was hoping to phase out tokens in favor of the "MetroCard." In any case, the pay-per-ride version of the MetroCard buys 11 rides for the price of 10, and allows a free bus-subway or subway-bus transfer within a two-hour period; while "unlimited" versions for periods of 1, 7, and 30 days can be used as often as you like (except that you must wait 18 minutes after entering one subway station before you can enter at another). One-day unlimited MetroCards are not available at some token booths.

Taxis They seem to rule the streets of New York City. In fact, there are nearly 12,000 licensed cabs—a meaningless number if you can't find one when you need one. Licensed cabs are bright yellow and signal their availability with a light on the roof. Cabs may be hailed anywhere on the street, except for crosswalks and intersections, and by law they are supposed to take you wherever you wish to go. But be forewarned—New York cab drivers are an independent bunch. The taxi rates are posted on the side of the cab; a 50¢ nighttime surcharge is applied from 8PM to 6AM. A cab ride in New York can be colorful, amusing, and efficient, or hellish and frustrating, depending on the traffic and the driver. Most cabbies are recently arrived immigrants and, though they must pass a language proficiency test, communication can occasionally be a problem; make sure the driver understands where you want to go.

Tours There's something here for everyone. Additional information on tours geared toward everything from architecture to history, culture, and the homes of the stars, is available at the **New York Convention & Visitors' Bureau** (see page 12). Here is a sampling of what's offered:

Adventure on a Shoestring (265.2663) celebrates everything that is wonderful and positive about the city. Walking tours include chats with members of the community toured. **Municipal Art Society** (935.3960) gives walking tours with an architectural orientation. **Urban Park Rangers** (427.4040) features walking tours of parks in all five boroughs, with an emphasis on botany, geology, and wildlife. The **Museum of the City of New York** (534.1672) provides walks of varying lengths geared to the museum's current exhibitions. Historian Joyce Gold of **History Tours** (242.5762) conducts walking tours of **Lower Manhattan,** Greenwich Village, **Chelsea,** Harlem, and other neighborhoods. **Heritage Trails New York** (269.1500) offers four self-guided walking tours in a 40-page book: Colored dots link some 50 historic sites in lower Manhattan.

Gray Line of New York (397.2600) offers two- to eight-and-a-half-hour Manhattan bus tours in English and a number of foreign languages.

Doorway to Design (221.1111) customizes a behind-the-scenes tour of the interior design, fashion, and art worlds as well as walking tours with an architectural historian. **92nd Street YM/YWHA** (996.1100) focuses on ethnic, cultural, architectural, social, and historical facets of New York and also offers bus tours to Manhattan environs. **Harlem Renaissance Tours, Inc.** (283.1297) provides visits to historic sites, gospel church services, soul food restaurants, and jazz clubs.

Cyclists can take a two-hour **Central Park Bicycle Tour** (541.8759), with bicycle provided, which explores one of the city's best green spaces. **Circle Line** (563.3200) and **Spirit Cruises** (727.2789) will whisk you to sail **New York Harbor** for a view of the breathtaking New York skyline.

Trains Grand Central Terminal (E 42nd St, between Lexington and Vanderbilt Aves) is the hub of the **Metro-North Commuter Railroad.** The **New Haven, Harlem,** and **Hudson Lines** service New York State and Connecticut.

Penn Station (Seventh Ave, between W 31st and W 33rd Sts) services the **Long Island Railroad** (718/558.7400) and **New Jersey Transit** (973/762.5100) commuter trains.

An underground train system called the **PATH** (800/234.7284) connects stations in Chelsea, Greenwich Village, and downtown's **World Trade Center** with Hoboken and Newark, New Jersey.

Walking To get a true sense of New York City, you're best off hitting the pavement, where one minute you'll find yourself dwarfed by Midtown skyscrapers and the next winding your way through narrow Greenwich Village streets. Most museums are conveniently close to one another, and parks and gardens offer good resting places for tired legs and aching feet. You can easily stroll from the Upper West Side to Midtown in about an hour; the most scenic route is along **Central Park West** to **Central Park South,** then on to Fifth Avenue. Warning: Beware bicycle messengers who have a habit of not yielding the right-of-way to pedestrians!

FYI

Accommodations New York City's hotels come in all sizes, locations, and prices. When booking ask if there are any special deals—Broadway tickets and breakfast, or special summer or weekend rates—that are not always publicized. With year-round conventions, trade fairs, and ever-growing numbers of tourists, never underestimate the importance of booking in advance: Even during slow months, hotels can be booked solid.

The **New York Convention & Visitors' Bureau**'s hotel hot line matches visitors with available accommodations in all price ranges, from 1 September through 31 December. Call this free service (212/582.3352, 800/846.ROOM) to make reservations at more than 80 hotels.

Climate The best months to visit New York are May, June, September, and October. July and August can be oppressively hot, with high humidity and temperatures hovering in the 90s. December through February are the coldest months, with blustery winds and temperatures in the 20s and below.

Months	Average Temperature (°F)
December-February	34
March-May	55
June-August	83
September-November	68

Drinking The legal drinking age in New York State is 21, and many bars, restaurants, and clubs require ID. Bar hours vary (all are closed before noon on Sunday), but the legal limit for closing is 4AM. On Sunday, restaurants may not serve alcohol until noon, and liquor stores are closed, but beer, which is sold in grocery stores, may be purchased after noon.

Hours It's a good idea to call ahead to find out if a particular restaurant, shop, or other attraction will be open the day and time you plan to visit. Keep in mind that hours may change substantially with the seasons, the economy, or even the whim of the owner.

Opening and closing times for shops, attractions, coffeehouses, tearooms, etc. are listed by day(s) only if normal hours (opening between 8 and 11 AM and closing between 4 and 7 PM) apply. In all other cases, specific hours will be given (e.g., 6AM-2PM, daily 24 hours, noon-5PM).

Money Most **Citibank, Chase,** and **American Express** branches will exchange foreign currency at current market rates. Most banks won't charge a fee if the amount changed is more than $200. Traveler's checks may be purchased at most banks, whose standard hours are Monday through Friday from 9AM to 3PM. Call **Chequepoint** (800/347.6027) for its different locations around town; all are open daily. **Thomas Cook**'s (800/287.7362) various locations often include Saturday and Sunday hours.

Personal Safety Cities attract every type of person, and that includes the worst. It is perhaps less a commentary about New York than about the times to say that you have to be alert on the street (and in buildings, the subway, etc.) and to try not to advertise helplessness, naiveté, or confusion, lest you risk attracting unsolicited assistance. Common sense dos and don'ts: Don't display your good jewelry on the subway. Don't make eye contact with people who impart a sense of danger or derangement, even though they may seem exotic to you. (View the scene, if you must, from a safe distance.) Carry your purse in front of you with the clasp side against your body. Don't carry your wallet in a back pants pocket or in a way that causes it to bulge. Don't let strangers carry packages for you and never leave your bag or bags unattended if even for a moment. If you see trouble coming, avoid it.

Publications There are three daily papers: *The New York Times,* the *New York Post,* and the *Daily News;* and a number of weekly publications, including *New York* magazine, *The New Yorker, Time Out, Variety, Backstage,* and *The Village Voice,* have excellent listings and information.

The biweekly tabloid *LGNY* and its newer, weekly competitor, the *New York Blade,* have local and national gay and lesbian news, commentary, and reviews.

Radio Stations

AM:

710	WOR	News/Talk
820	WNYC	National Public Radio
880	WCBS	News
1010	WINS	News
1130	WBB	News

FM:

88.3	WBGO	Jazz
93.9	WNYC	National Public Radio
95.5	WPLJ	Adult Contemporary
96.3	WQXR	Classical Music
110.3	WHTZ	Rock
102.7	WNEW	Classic Rock
105.1	WDBZ	Adult Contemporary

Restaurants Those restaurants garnering three- or four-star ratings usually warrant a reservation; when booking, check on their dress code. In the area of the **Theater District** and the blocks that surround it, restaurants often offer a pre-theater dinner (and recommend reservations to assure a seat). Other restaurants throughout the city offer prix-fixe meals during certain hours or at a particular time of the year.

Shopping The most varied shopping area in New York City is Fifth Avenue, with its stylish department stores, familiar chain outlets, and exclusive boutiques. Not far behind is **Madison Avenue,** well known for its high fashion and art galleries.
Each neighborhood may determine the hours certain stores follow, as will the season. The period between Thanksgiving and Christmas commonly sees extended hours; neighborhoods with a lot of foot traffic such as **Columbus Avenue** or areas of Greenwich Village may have longer hours. Stores may shut tight on Sunday on Madison Avenue, but it's a popular shopping day for SoHo's boutiques. If you're making a special trip during off hours, call first to verify the store's hours.

Smoking It is illegal to smoke on all public transportation, in the lobbies of office buildings, in enclosed public places, in taxis, in designated areas of theaters, and in most shops. Smoking in restaurants is limited to those establishments with fewer than 35 seats and the bar areas of certain larger restaurants if they are sufficiently separated from the main dining area.

"Something's always happening here. If you're bored in New York, it's your own fault."

Myrna Loy

Street Plan Manhattan is laid out in an easy-to-follow grid of north/south avenues and east/west numbered streets. Bear in mind that Fifth Avenue is the dividing line between east and west. Below **Houston Street,** the numbered streets end, and parts of downtown (Greenwich Village in particular) can get a little tricky.

Taxes There is an 8.25-percent sales tax on almost everything except supermarket food. The hotel tax is (gulp) 13.25 percent plus an occupancy charge of $2 per room/per night.

Telephones At press time it cost 25 cents to make a local call from a pay phone. Manhattan is in the 212 area code; calls to Brooklyn, the Bronx, Queens, and Staten Island require dialing 1, and then the 718 prefix. Two new overlay codes, which will also require dialing 1-plus-prefix, were added in late 1999: 646 for new numbers in the 212 area, and 347 for the 718 area; existing numbers will not change (except socially, as a 212 number begins to serve as a kind of status symbol). Response to advertisements with exchanges such as 394, 540, 550, etc. will cost you extra; the same goes for the 900 and 700 prefixes.

Tickets Theater tickets can be obtained at the box office, through ticket agencies (see the *Yellow Pages*), or at **TKTS** (W 47th St and Broadway, 768.1818). Tickets are not available for all shows; you may have a better chance close to curtain time, when producers release unused house seats. The same applies for music and dance tickets. For information on everything from show times and plot synopses to theater addresses, ticket prices, and a direct link to **Telecharge** or **Ticketmaster** to purchase tickets, call **The Broadway Line** (302.4111, 1/888.BROADWAY). Call **Telecharge** (239.6200) or **Ticketmaster** (307.4100) to buy tickets over the phone (with a surcharge).

Time Zone New York City is on Eastern Standard Time.

Tipping A 15- to 20-percent gratuity is standard. In restaurants, most people simply double the sales tax (8.25 percent). Taxi drivers are tipped a minimum 15 percent of the meter reading. Hotel bellhops and station porters expect a dollar for each bag they carry. A tip is a reward for service; if you don't get it, don't pay for it.

Visitors' Information Centers
The New York Convention & Visitors' Bureau maintains an information center (810 Seventh Ave, at W 53rd St, 484.1222, 800/NYC.VISIT) where you can get the lowdown on culture, dining, shopping, sightseeing, events, attractions, tours, and transportation. It is open daily. At the **Times Square Visitors Center** (1560 Broadway, between 46th and 47th Sts), you can buy tickets for Broadway shows, book sightseeing tours and airport transportation, get cash or exchange currency, surf the Net and obtain free brochures. The center is open daily 8AM-8PM.

There is also a free "Big Apple Greeter" program in which volunteer "greeters" take visitors on a four-hour walking tour of the five boroughs. Visitors pay their own subway/bus fares. Special language requirements or disability needs can be met. For an appointment, contact the **Office of the Manhattan Borough President** (669.2896) 48-72 hours in advance.

Phone Book

Emergencies
Ambulance/Fire/Police 911

Hospitals

   Bellevue Hospital Center 561.4141

   Mt. Sinai Medical Center 241.6500

   New York Presbyterian Hospital–
   Cornell Medical Center 746.5454

   NYU Medical Center 263.7300

   St. Luke's–
   Roosevelt Medical Center 523.4000

   St. Vincent's Hospital
   & Medical Center....................................604.7000

Pharmacy (24-hour) 604.8376

Police (Non-Emergency) 374.5000

Visitors' Information
AIDS Hotline 807.665

Amtrak 582.687

Convention and Visitors' Bureau 397.822

Disabled Visitors' Information....................397.822

Greyhound Bus 971.6300, 800/231.222

NYC Transit Authority

   Subway and bus information 718/330.123

   Lost and found and other services ....
   ....718/625.6200, 718/330.300

Time 976.161

US Customs...................................800/697.366

US Passport Office 206.350

Weather 976.121

Main Events

January
National Boat Show, Jacob Javits Center; **Winter Antiques Show,** Seventh Regiment Armory.

February
Chinese New Year, Chinatown; **New York International Motorcycle Show,** Jacob Javits Center; **Westminster Kennel Club/Westminster Dog Show,** Madison Square Garden; **Black History Month,** events all throughout the city.

March
Ringling Bros. and Barnum & Bailey Circus, Madison Square Garden; **St. Patrick's Day Parade,** Fifth Avenue; **Greek Independence Day Parade,** Fifth Avenue.

April
Easter Parade, Fifth Avenue; **Greater New York International Auto Show,** Jacob Javits Center; **Cherry Blossom Festival,** Brooklyn Botanic Garden; **Annual Flower Show,** Macy's; **New York City Ballet** (spring season) begins, State Theater, Lincoln Center; New York **Mets** (Shea Stadium) and New York **Yankees** (Yankee Stadium) open baseball season.

May
Washington Square Outdoor Art Show, University Place; **Rose Week/Orchid Show,** New York Botanical Garden, Bronx; **All** **City Beaches** open for the summer; **Memorial Day Parade,** Fifth Avenue; **Ninth Avenue International Festival,** between West 37th and West 57th Streets, is a weekend of food and fun.

June
Metropolitan Opera/New York Philharmonic concerts, city parks; **Belmont Stakes,** Belmont Park, Long Island.

July
Macy's Annual 4th of July Fireworks, East River; **American Crafts Festival,** Lincoln Center; **Shakespeare in the Park,** Delacorte Theater, Central Park.

August
US Open Tennis Championships, Flushing Meadows–Corona Park, Queens; **Harlem Week,** Upper Manhattan.

September
New York Philharmonic season opens, Avery Fisher Hall, Lincoln Center; **San Gennaro Festival,** Little Italy; **Washington Square Outdoor Art Show,** University Place; **New York Film Festival,** Alice Tully Hall, Lincoln Center; New York **Jets/Giants** season begins, Giants Stadium, Meadowlands, NJ; **New York is Book Country Fair,** Fifth Avenue, between 48th and 57th Streets; **Metropolitan Opera** opens, Metropolitan Opera House, Lincoln Center; **Caribbean Carnival,** Eastern Parkway, Brooklyn.

October
Ice skating begins at Rockefeller Center; **Halloween Parade,** Greenwich Village; **Columbus Day Parade,** Fifth Avenue; New York **Rangers** season begins, Madison Square Garden.

November
New York City Ballet (fall season) begins, State Theater, Lincoln Center; **New York City Marathon** begins at Verrazano-Narrows Bridge and ends in Central Park; **Macy's Thanksgiving Day Parade,** Broadway; **Veteran's Day Parade,** Fifth Avenue; **The Christmas Spectacular** featuring the Rockettes, Radio City Music Hall.

December
Lighting of the Christmas Tree, Rockefeller Center; **New Year's Eve** celebrations at Times Square; **Central Park Fireworks and Midnight Run,** Central Park.

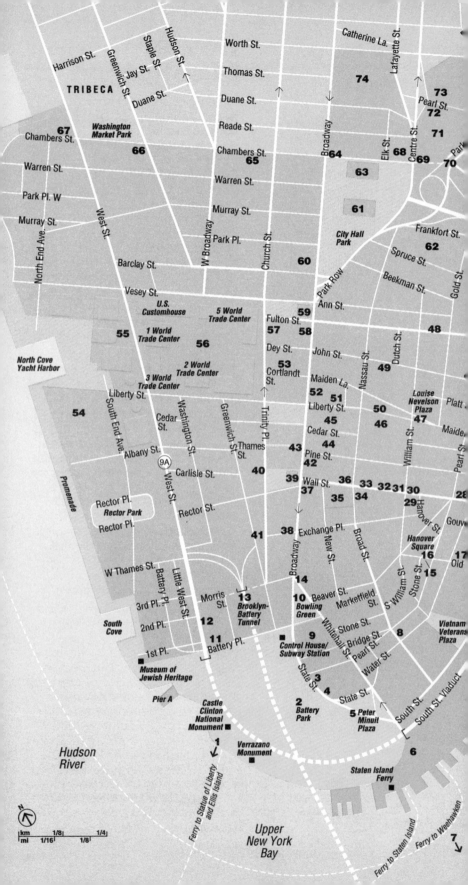

Mott St.

E Broadway

Catherine St.

Henry St.

Row

Oliver St.

St. James Pl.

Madison St.

Monroe St.

Market St.

Cherry St.

Water St.

South St.

' St.
lice
adquarters

. of
Finest

Robert F. Wagner Sr. Pl.

South St. Viaduct

Dover St.

21 Brooklyn
Bridge

22

23

Pearl St.

Water St.

Peck Slip

Front St.

Beekman St.

South St.

20

19

Fulton St.

4

Front St.

John St.

cher St.

5

Pier 18

Pier 17

Pier 16

Pier 15

18

Pier 14

7

Pier 13

Pier 11

Delta Water Shuttle to La Guardia Airport

Pier 9

all Street
eliport

Pier 6

East
River

Lower Manhattan

It all began on Lower Manhattan Island, bounded by **Chambers Street** and the **East** and **Hudson Rivers.** Here, at the confluence of these waterways, the earliest explorers—Giovanni da Verrazano, Esteban Gómez, and Henry Hudson—first touched land. And it was also here, in 1625, that the Dutch set up **Fort Amsterdam** to protect the southern perimeter of their settlement, called **Nieuw Amsterdam.** The skyscrapers and canyons of today's **Financial District** stand where the tiny Dutch settlement, and later the prime residential enclave of post-Revolutionary New York, once flourished.

The narrow alleys of the Financial District are a reminder of the scale of colonial America. But, except for a few fragments of old foundations, not a single building erected during the 40 years of Dutch rule remains. When the British Army withdrew in 1783 after 7 years of occupation, the village of New York—which covered 10 blocks north from what is now **Battery Park**—lay almost totally in ruins. But once New York City pulled itself together and began to push north, the city grew swiftly. Two blocks of low-rise commercial buildings from this early surge of development have survived: the **Fraunces Tavern** block and **Schermerhorn Row.**

When **City Hall**—the one still in use today—was being built in 1811 on the northernmost fringe of town, the north side of the building was covered with common brownstone instead of marble, because no one ever expected the building to be seen from that side. But by 1820, New York City had expanded another 10 to 15 blocks, and by 1850 the limits had pushed 2 miles north to 14th Street, and city planners with foresight began to assign numbers to the streets. A fire in 1835 leveled most of Lower Manhattan, but even that didn't halt the expansion of what had become the leading commercial center and port in the new country after the War of 1812. **Pearl Street** took its name from the iridescent shells that covered the beach at its location, the original shoreline of the East River. Landfill added **Water Street**, then **Front Street**, and finally **South Street**, where by the 1820s a thick forest of masts congested the port. The **South Street Seaport Museum** evokes that maritime era. By 1812, lawyers, insurance companies, merchants, and financiers were crowding out families in what quickly became the Financial District, whose symbolic and geographic center was the intersection of **Broad** and **Wall Streets** (named for the wooden wall that served as the northern fortification of Nieuw Amsterdam). The construction of the **Merchants' Exchange** in 1836 speeded up the area's transition to a commercial district.

Today you can visit the current stock exchanges, but in the limestone-and-glass caverns of Wall Street, only a few of the old public buildings remain: **Federal Hall**, the former **United States Custom House** on **Bowling Green**, the famous **Trinity Church** (an 1846 incarnation, several times removed from the original), and the less well known—but earlier—**St. Paul's Chapel**. A 20th-century masterpiece worth going out of your way to look at is the **Woolworth Building**, also located in this area.

The **Whitehall Building** is architecturally reminiscent of Dutch governor Peter Stuyvesant's mansion, which was on nearby **Whitehall Street**. **Bowling Green**, a cattle market in Dutch days and later a green for bowling and recreation at the center of a desirable residential area, is now an egg-shaped park at the foot of **Broadway**; its 1771 fence is still intact. And the **Civic Center**—the cluster of old and new government buildings, some handsome, some horrendous, just north of the Financial District—has become the western boundary of **Chinatown**.

Created by landfill, the present **Battery Park** offers cooling breezes, welcome greenery, and a panoramic view of **New York Harbor**. It's the jumping-off spot for the ferries to **Liberty Island**, **Ellis Island**, and **Staten Island**, the best sight-seeing buy for close-ups of the **Statue of Liberty** and the New York City skyline. The observation deck at the **World Trade Center** can't be beat for an aerial perspective of the Manhattan Island and its surroundings. Nearby, two massive developments, residential and commercial **Battery Park City** and the **World Financial Center**, symbolize Lower Manhattan's emergence as the epicenter of downtown activity. Developers have created new housing units by transforming abandoned office buildings—many featuring elegant lobbies with ornate ceilings and other architectural touches—into luxurious rentals and condominiums.

1 Ellis Island National Monument On 1 January 1892, when a boat carrying 148 steerage passengers from the SS *Nevada* pulled into the new pier on **Ellis Island,** Annie Moore, a 15-year-old Irish girl, became the first immigrant to set foot on the island. More than 12 million souls followed in her footsteps before the island was closed. In 1907, its peak year, 1,285,349 people were admitted. The original station burned to the ground in 1897, and what is now the **Ellis Island National Monument** was erected by **Boring & Tilton** in 1898. The present complex of buildings was already decaying during the World War II years when German aliens were imprisoned there. When it finally closed in 1954, vandals moved in and did their best to destroy what was left. In 1990, after 8 years of restoration (at a cost of $156 million, with much of the fund-raising spearheaded by Lee Iacocca), the main building opened as a museum. ◆ Ferry: fee includes visits to Ellis Island and the Statue of Liberty. Daily 9:30AM-3:30PM. Take Statue of Liberty Ferry from Castle Clifton in Battery Park. 269.5755

On Ellis Island:

Ellis Island Museum of Immigration Visitors can now follow the path their ancestors took upon arrival in the US: from the **Baggage Room,** where they dropped off what were often all of their worldly belongings, to the **Registry Room,** where they underwent 60-second medical and 30-question legal examinations, and on to the **Staircase of Separation,** which led to the ferryboats that transported the immigrants who were granted admittance (98 percent of those who arrived here) to either Manhattan, New Jersey, or points farther west. Also on view are exhibitions tracing the immigration experience: *Islands of Tears* is a poignant film that documents the voyage to America, and *Treasures from Home* contains personal property brought here by immigrants. The American Immigrant Wall of Honor is inscribed with the names of more than 500,000 immigrants who were commemorated by their descendants through a donation to the Statue of Liberty–Ellis Island Foundation (call 883.1986 for more information). In the **Oral History Studio** visitors are given the opportunity to listen to immigrants reminisce about their experiences here. The newest item, **The American Family Immigration History Center,** set to open in 2001, will provide state-of-the-art interactive computer access to the immigration records of anyone who came to this country in the past century. ♦ Free. Daily 9:30AM-3PM. 363.3200 ♿

1 Statue of Liberty National Monument
Officially named *Liberty Enlightening the World,* the figure alone (supported by a steel skeleton engineered by Gustave Eiffel) is 151 feet high, not counting the pedestal, which adds another 89 feet. It is a full 30 feet taller than the Colossus of Rhodes, one of the Seven Wonders of the Ancient World. French sculptor Frederic Auguste Bartholdi's original idea was to design a statue of a peasant woman holding the Lamp of Progress to Asia and place it at the entrance to the Suez Canal, an idea that was rejected by the sultan of Egypt. When Bartholdi came to the New World from France looking for a site for the statue, he traveled up and down the Eastern Seaboard and as far west as Salt Lake City, but he never for a moment seriously considered any place but Bedloe's Island, which he saw as his ship sailed into New York Harbor. It was finally placed on its pedestal, designed by **Richard Morris Hunt,** in 1886.

Bartholdi cleverly situated it so that when a ship rounds the Narrows between Brooklyn and Staten Island, the statue appears on portside, striding forward in a gesture of welcome. As the vessel passes directly in front of her, she seems suddenly erect and saluting. It is truly one of the most impressive optical illusions in the world.

The island, which was renamed Liberty Island in 1956, was used as a quarantine station in the early 18th century. After 1811, it was the

MICHAEL STORRINGS

site of **Fort Wood,** which is the star-shaped structure that forms the pedestal's base. In the years between, it was a popular place to hang pirates.

Since the statue's restoration (completed in 1986), climbing the spiral staircase to its crown is easier than it had been for the previous 100 years, but there are still 22 stories (300-plus steps) to climb, and in very close quarters. The windows at the crown are small but the view is worth it, although the panorama on the ground is impressive, too, as is the outlook from the open promenade around the top of the pedestal, just under Miss Liberty's feet. The line forms on the left to walk up to the crown; the line on the right is for the 10-story ascent by elevator to the top of the pedestal. Both lines can be quite long in the summer; you may be turned away if you arrive after 2PM, so plan to visit in the morning. ♦ Ferry: fee. Ferry: daily every 30 minutes in summer; every 45 minutes in winter. Ferry service from Castle Clinton in Battery Park. 269.5755

Within the Statue of Liberty:

The Statue of Liberty Museum
Beginning with the arrival of the Dutch, the museum chronicles the full history of immigration to the New World. It also contains exhibitions on the statue itself,

17

including the original torch, which was re-created and replaced during the 1986 restoration. ♦ Free. Daily. 363.3200

2 Battery Park The Dutch began rearranging the terrain the moment Peter Minuit bought Manhattan for trinkets valued at $24 from the Native Americans in 1626. When they dug their canals and leveled the hills, they dumped the dirt and rocks into the bay. Over the next 300 years or so, more than 21 acres were added to the tip of the island, creating the green buffer between the harbor and the dark canyons of the Financial District. The park takes its name from a line of British cannons that once overlooked the harbor in the late 1600s. Planted in 1992, the 100,000-rose **Hope Garden** is a living memorial to those who have died of AIDS. A **World War II Memorial** and **Korean War Memorial** stand in the park. Despite its bellicose moniker, the park has always been a place for those described by Herman Melville as "men fixed in ocean reveries" (Melville was born nearby at 17 State Street in 1819). ♦ Bounded by State and Whitehall Sts and the Hudson River, and Upper New York Bay and Battery Pl

Within Battery Park:

Staten Island Ferry This trip provides an excellent visual orientation to New York City. The ferry leaves from the southern tip of Manhattan, weaves through harbor traffic—from tug to sailboat, yacht to cruise ship—and travels past the **Statue of Liberty** and **Ellis Island** to the northeast edge of Staten Island, then back again. En route, passengers have a glorious view of the city's celebrated skyline. ♦ Free; fee for vehicles. Daily 24 hours. South St and Peter Minuit Plaza. 718/390.5253 &

Heroes have been honored with parades along lower Broadway since Colonial times. President Theodore Roosevelt was the first to be showered with ticker tape, as part of his welcome home from an African safari in 1910. Flags flew and paper cascaded from every window of every building, except one: The building at 26 Broadway, across from Bowling Green, didn't even raise a flag that day. It was the home of John D. Rockefeller, whose Standard Oil was involved in an antitrust suit instigated by the old "Rough Rider" himself. These days the tons of ticker tape that once filled the air have been replaced by shredded computer printouts.

Behind Trinity Church can be found the final resting place for such notable New Yorkers as Alexander Hamilton and Robert Fulton.

castle clinto

Castle Clinton National Monument Originally known as **Southwest Battery,** this structure served as a defense post housing 2 cannons within 8-foot-thick walls. It faced **Castle William** on Governors Island, and bot were fortified to block the harbor from enemy attack. In 1811, **John McComb Jr.** designed the original building, which fell into disuse when no enemy appeared. In 1946 the US Army gave the building to the city, which redesigned it to become the **Castle Garden** entertainment venue. The main hall was used for Swedish singer Jenny Lind's US premiere presented by showman P.T. Barnum. For several years, it was the Emigrant Landing Depot, processing more than seven million immigrants before giving up that role to **Ellis Island** in 1892. In one of its final incarnations from 1896 to 1941 the building housed the **New York Aquarium** (now at Coney Island in Brooklyn). Finally, as the need for repairs became apparent and its historical importanc was realized, the building was designated a National Historic Landmark in 1950. It has since been restored as a fort and is under the care of the National Park Service, with a bookstore and museum on site. It also serves as an information center and a ticket office fo the Statue of Liberty Ferry. ♦ Daily. Battery Pl (between State St and West Sts). 344.7220 &

Verrazano Monument During the 1909 Hudson-Fulton Festival, an extravaganza marking the 300th anniversary of Henry Hudson's trip up the river, New York's Italian Americans placed this heroic group by Ettore Ximenes at the edge of the harbor. The work commemorates their compatriot, Giovanni da Verrazano, who arrived here first in 1524. The female figure representing Discovery is trampling a book labeled History. ♦ Just sou of Castle Clinton National Monument

Battery Park Control House One of two surviving ornate entrances to the original **IRT** subway (the other is at West 72nd Street and Broadway), this structure was built in 1905 and was designed by **Heins & LaFarge.** The term "control house" was coined by enginee who designed them to control crowds comin and going in two directions at once. ♦ State S and Battery Pl

American Park at the Battery ★★$$ A spacious place filled with natural light, this restaurant right on the water has great views of the **Statue of Liberty** and Staten Island. In the summer, Happy Hour barbecues are hel on the large patio out back, with live music. The salmon tartare is delicious, as is the chicken with garlic mashed potatoes and the large rib-eye steak. ♦ American ♦ M-F lunch and dinner; Sa-Su brunch and dinner. Reservations recommended. 809.5508

Restaurants/Clubs: Red   Hotels: Blue
Shops/ ♥ Outdoors: Green   Sights/Culture: Black

3 New York Unearthed In 1990, a permanent archaeological display (administered by the **South Street Seaport Museum**) opened in a courtyard behind 17 State Street. Visitors enter at street level, where they view 10 dioramas, created by graphic designer Milton Glaser, that hold such items as medicine vials, crucibles, cannon balls, and bottles, all excavated on or near this site. On the **Lower Gallery,** a glass-enclosed space reveals archaeologists hard at work, while at the **Stratigraphy Wall,** visitors can view a three-dimensional cross-section of an archaeological site. Museumgoers may also board the **Unearthing New York Systems Elevator,** which takes them on a simulated dig, four centuries back into New York history. ◆ Free. M-Sa noon-6PM. 17 State St (at Pearl St). 748.8628 ♿

4 Church of Our Lady of the Rosary Originally designed in 1800 by **John McComb Jr.,** this pair of Georgian town houses was restored in 1965 as a shrine church dedicated to Elizabeth Ann Seton. Canonized in 1975 as the first US-born saint, Seton lived here with her family in the early 1800s. The exterior of each building, faithfully returned to its original condition with columns presumably cut from ship masts, provides a small reminder of the character of this fashionable residential neighborhood at the beginning of the 19th century. ◆ 7-8 State St (between Whitehall and Pearl Sts). 269.6865

5 Peter Minuit Plaza This small park honors the man who bought Manhattan from the Native Americans for a small price in 1626. Sent by the Dutch West India Company to oversee its holdings in the New World, Minuit eventually made Nieuw Amsterdam its center. He later died at sea. The flagpole is a memorial to the first Jewish settlers, who arrived in 1654. They had been expelled from Portugal to a Dutch colony at Recife in Brazil, but a Portuguese conquest drove them from there. On the way back to Holland, their ship was attacked by pirates, and the survivors were taken to the nearest Dutch colony, Nieuw Amsterdam, where they were allowed to stay. ◆ Between South and State Sts

6 Battery Maritime Building The sheetmetal-and-steel facade of this Beaux Arts ferry terminal has been painted green to simulate copper. Before the Brooklyn Bridge was built, there were 17 ferry lines between Lower Manhattan and Brooklyn. Until 1938, one of them operated out of this terminal, which was designed in 1906 by **Walker & Gillette.** Today it houses the small fleet of white ferries that serves Governors Island. ◆ 11 South St (at Battery Park)

7 Governors Island When the Dutch arrived here in 1624, they established their first toehold on what they called **Nut Island.** But even before the Dutch governor surrendered Nieuw Amsterdam to them in 1665, the British established their own governor here on the same island. In addition to the British **Governor's Mansion,** another historic landmark on the island is the 1840 **Admiral's Quarters,** home not of an admiral but actually of the commanding general of the army garrison stationed here from 1790 until 1966. For the next 31 years the Coast Guard headquartered their operations on the island. However, in 1997, it was decided that they should vacate this 173-acre jewel of the New York Harbor. Alas, it is also closed to the public. At press time, the future of the island was uncertain. ◆ Upper New York Bay

8 Fraunces Tavern This Georgian brick building (illustrated above), erected in 1719, became a tavern in 1762, and was made famous when George Washington said farewell to his officers here on the second floor on 4 December 1783. Washington returned six years later to the old **City Hall,** five blocks away, to take the oath of office as the first president of the new nation. The building was refurbished in 1907 in the spirit and style of the period rather than as an accurate restoration. ◆ 54 Pearl St (at Broad St)

Within Fraunces Tavern:

Fraunces Tavern Restaurant ★★$$$ Samuel Fraunces, George Washington's steward, opened this tavern in 1763. Now, Wall Streeters congregate here amid Colonial-era decor for such dependable fare as beef Wellington, Maryland crab cakes, herb-roasted Cornish hen, and New York sirloin steak. ◆ American ◆ M-F breakfast, lunch, and dinner. Reservations recommended. 269.0144

Fraunces Tavern Museum Above the restaurant, permanent and changing exhibitions of decorative arts, period rooms, paintings, and prints and manuscripts from 18th- and 19th-century America are on display. ◆ Admission. M-F; Sa-Su noon-4PM. 425.1778

United States Custom House

9 United States Custom House This 1907 building (illustrated above) by **Cass Gilbert** has been called one of the finest examples of the Beaux Arts style in New York City, and the reason is instantly apparent. The granite facade is surprisingly delicate, despite an ornate frieze and Ionic columns with Corinthian capitals along the face. Four seated female figures, representing Africa, Asia, Europe, and North America, are Daniel Chester French pieces. Reginald Marsh painted the murals in the wonderful oval rotunda. ♦ State St and Bowling Green. No phone

Within the United States Custom House:

National Museum of the American Indian The comprehensive collection of artifacts linked to the indigenous peoples of the Americas here is part of Washington, DC's Smithsonian Institution. The artifacts were assembled over a 54-year period by George Gustav Heye, a New York banker. Opened in 1994, this facility, which features changing displays of the one million objects in its collection, also stages educational workshops, film and video festivals, and performances of indigenous people's dance and theater. Among the permanent exhibits on display are Navajo weavings and blankets; stone carvings from the Northwest; basketry and pottery from the Southwest; gold from Colombia, Peru, and Mexico; and jade objects from the Olmec and Maya cultures. The museum collaborates with tribes from Tierra del Fuego to the Arctic Circle to present exhibitions that are characteristic of their traditions. ♦ Free. Daily. 514.3700 ♿

10 Bowling Green In 1734, a group of citizens leased the space facing the **Custom House** as a bowling green for an annual rent of one peppercorn. In the process it became the city's first park. In 1729, the park was embellished with an equestrian statue of England's King George III, which was demolished by a crowd that assembled here to listen to a reading of the Declaration of Independence on 9 July 1776 (the park's fence dates to 1771). The statue was melted down to make bullets that, according to some contemporary accounts, were responsible for the killing of 400 British soldiers during the war that followed. ♦ Broadway (at State St)

At Bowling Green:

The Charging Bull In response to the stock market crash of 1987, Arturo DiModica sculpted this 3.5-ton bronze bull to attest to the "vitality, energy, and life of the American people in adversity." It has been put up for sale; since the city is not allowed to buy work of art, they are half-heartedly looking for a patron.

11 Whitehall Building A 1930s real-estate guide said that the tenants of this 1903 building, which at the time included the Internal Revenue Service, Quaker Oats, and the Bon Ami Cleanser Co., had "an intimate relationship with the landlord," and no one ever moved out. There has been some turnover since the guide was written, but tenants are still (understandably) reluctant to give up offices boasting what may be the best views of New York Harbor. Originally designed by **Henry J. Hardenbergh**, its rear section was designed by **Clinton & Russell** 1910. ♦ 17 Battery Pl (at West St)

12 Downtown Athletic Club The arched ground-floor arcade and the window treatment of this Moorish-influenced Art Deco masterpiece, designed by **Starrett & Van Vleck** in 1926, are perfection itself, and the interior

Barnett-Phillips is even better. The rooms are reminiscent of a 1920s ocean liner. In addition to an enclosed roof garden, the building originally contained a miniature golf course. ◆ 19 West St (between Battery Pl and Morris St). 425.7000 &

13 Brooklyn-Battery Tunnel In the early 1930s, builder Robert Moses announced that he was going to construct a bridge between Lower Manhattan and Brooklyn to connect his Long Island parkway system with his West Side Highway, which reached a dead end at **Battery Park.** Preservationists were appalled. City officials, noting that the city would lose $29 million a year in real-estate taxes, also opposed it. The battle raged until 1939, when President Roosevelt stepped in and denied federal funds for the project. The bridge became a tunnel, and **Battery Park** was saved. When the tunnel—engineered by Ole Singstad in 1949—finally opened, it carried more than 15 million cars in its first year. ◆ Between the Gowanus Expwy, Brooklyn and West St

14 26 Broadway This graceful giant, built in 1885 and altered in 1922 by **Carrère & Hastings,** actually curves along to follow the street line. The most important business address in the world for half a century, this was where John D. Rockefeller said that he had revolutionized the way of doing business "to save ourselves from wasteful conditions and eliminate individualism." Undeniably he accomplished his goal, and at the same time built one of the world's greatest fortunes behind these walls, the headquarters of Standard Oil. When the Supreme Court dissolved the trust in 1911, the building became home to Socony Mobil, one of the new companies that rose from Standard Oil's ashes. ◆ At Beaver St

15 India House Richard J. Carman built this beautiful brownstone (one of the largest in the city) as headquarters for the Hanover Bank in 1854. In the decades that followed it was used as the New York Cotton Exchange and the main office of W.R. Grace and Co. It is now a private club. ◆ 1 Hanover Sq (between Pearl and Stone Sts)

16 Hanover Square Named for the English royal family of the Georges, this was once a small London-style park at the center of a residential neighborhood. Homeowners included Captain William Kidd, who was considered a solid citizen in New York but something quite different by the British, who hanged him for piracy in 1701. Captain Kidd has gone down in history as the most bloodthirsty of pirates, and even today people poke around beaches along the coast in hopes of finding the fabulous treasure he supposedly buried. The square was also the home of New York's first newspaper, the *New-York Daily Gazette,* established in 1725. George E.

Bissell's statue of *Abraham de Peyster,* a one-time mayor of the city, was moved here from Bowling Green. ◆ Between Pearl and Stone Sts

17 United States Assay Office Built in 1930 and designed by **James A. Wetmore,** this division of the United States Mint is used to refine gold and silver bullion and melt down old coins. It is also a storehouse that contains about 55 million troy ounces of gold, worth more than $2 billion at the official government price. ◆ Old Slip (between Front and Water Sts)

18 HRC (New York Health & Racquet Club) Tennis Nonmembers are allowed to reserve tennis courts here 24 hours in advance, but be prepared to pay high rates for the privilege—especially during the peak hours after 5PM weekdays. ◆ Charge for nonmembers. Daily 6AM-midnight. Piers 13 and 14, South St. 422.9300

19 South Street Seaport Back when sailing ships ruled the seas, New York's most active ports were along this stretch of the East River. With the coming of steamships, the deeper piers on the Hudson River attracted most of the seafaring traffic, and the East River piers fell into decline. In 1967, a group of preservation-minded citizens banded together to buy the rundown waterfront buildings and a collection of historic ships. Twelve years later, commercial interests moved in and provided funds to restore the old buildings and add some new ones. The result, thanks to the ingenuity of architects **Ben** and **Jane Thompson,** is a lively historic site that has revitalized a derelict neighborhood, transforming it into one of New York's most fascinating enclaves. Contributing to the historical air are the cobblestone streets paved with Belgian blocks. ◆ Daily. Bounded by the East River and Water St, and John and Dover Sts. 732.7678

Within South Street Seaport:

Titanic Memorial Lighthouse This structure originally overlooked the harbor from the Seamen's Church Institute on Water Street at Cuyler's Alley. A memorial to the 1,500 who died when the **White Star Line's** *Titanic* struck an iceberg in 1912, it was moved here in 1976 to mark the entrance to the seaport. ◆ Fulton and Water Sts &

South Street Seaport Museum The US's nautical heritage and the city's evolution are exhibited in three galleries, a children's center, crafts center, and library. The museum is housed in a former warehouse built in 1868. ♦ Museum: admission. Library: free. Museum: daily. Library: M-F. 213 Water St (between Fulton and Beekman Sts). Museum 748.8600, library 748.8648

Abercrombie & Fitch Sports clothing has kept this chain in business since 1892. ♦ Daily. 199 Water St (at Fulton St). 809.9000 ♿ Also at: 725 Fifth Ave (between E 56th and E 57th Sts, Fifth floor). 832.1001

Brookstone The ultimate hardware store, this place displays one of each tool or gadget in stock like an objet d'art next to a card describing its virtues. Each is the best in its class. Pick up a clipboard when you enter and write down your order as you go. At the end, the goods are delivered via a dumbwaiter from the loft above. ♦ Daily. 18 Fulton St (at Front St). 344.8108. Also at: 620 Fifth Ave (between W 49th and W 50th Sts). 262.3237

South Street Seaport Museum Shops This is New York's best source for fiction and nonfiction about ships of all kinds and the waters they sail. Also here are rare prints, ship models, and otherwise hard-to-find books on New York City and its history. ♦ Daily. 12-14 Fulton St (between South and Front Sts). 748.8663 ♿

Schermerhorn Row A row of Federal-style warehouses and countinghouses (shown above) built in 1812 by **Peter Schermerhorn** have been restored. At various times in their history, the buildings were used as stores, taverns, rooming houses, and hotels. Greek Revival cast-iron storefronts were added later when the Fulton Ferry brought more stylish customers into the area. The upper floors are the least altered from the original, but the mansard roof at the eastern end was added in 1868 when **2 Fulton Street** was the **Fulton Ferry Hotel.** The ground floor currently houses a variety of interesting shops, including **The Nature Company, The Body Shop,** and **The Sharper Image.** ♦ Fulton St (between South and Front Sts)

Fulton Market The 1882 building on this spot used to house a fresh produce and meat market, filled with merchandise brought from Long Island farms on the now-defunct *Fulton Ferry,* which connected Fulton Street in Manhattan with Fulton Street in Brooklyn. The reconstructed building (illustrated on page

23) now houses shops, restaurants, and stalls selling fresh food. Outlets in the market include **Zaro's Bread Basket,** the **Fulton Market Retail Fish Market,** and **Rocky Mountain Chocolate Factory** (for Italian pastries). ♦ Daily. 11 Fulton St (at Front St). 732.8257

The Ships Ships visiting **Piers 15, 16,** and **17** make this an ever-changing experience, but the seaport's permanent collection includes two tall ships open to the public: *Peking,* a steel-hulled, four-masted bark built in 1911 (and the second-largest sailing ship ever built), and *Wavertree,* a full three-masted iron-hulled ship built in 1885. Also here is *Ambrose,* the floating steel lighthouse that was anchored at the entrance to the harbor from 1908 until 1963, when she was replaced by a permanent tower. Tickets, available on **Pier 16** and at the **Visitors' Center** at Fulton and Water Streets, allow admission to the galleries of the **South Street Seaport Museum** (see above) and daily changing events. Other ships in the Seaport fleet include the working tugboat *W.O. Decker* and the schooner *Lettie G. Howard. Pioneer,* a former cargo schooner, makes 90-minute daytime and twilight sails in the harbor from late March to mid-November. Hours vary according to season. Reservations can be made within 14 days of a sail; unreserved tickets are sold each day starting at 10AM at **Pier 16** (669.9400). Special exhibits are scattered throughout the **Seaport;** two separate walking tours guide you to them. There are also special holiday events. ♦ Admission. Daily. Pier 16, South St. 748.8600, 748.8659

Seaport Liberty Cruises A number of 60-minute cruises of the harbor depart here March through December. In the warmer months there are longer cruises with music and live entertainment on Saturday nights. ♦ Fee. M-Tu, Sa-Su noon, 1:30, 3, 4:30, and 6PM; W-F noon, 1:30, 3, and 4:30PM. Tickets available at Pier 16 kiosk. Pier 16, South St. 630.8888

Pier 17 Modeled after the recreation piers of the 19th century, this development was built directly over the water. In good weather, it's packed with people enjoying the pleasures of the waterfront. Such shops and food stalls as **Cindy's Cinnamon Rolls, Minter's Ice Cream Kitchen, Bain's Deli,** and the Chinese fast-food **Wok & Roll** fill the inside. During the summer, the pier becomes a venue for concerts and other special activities. The many busy restaurants here offer spectacular scenery at spectacular prices, although the food is generally no better than average. ♦ Daily. South St. 732.8257 ♿

Within Pier 17:

Sequoia ★★$$ Outdoor dining on two levels overlooking the East River and Brooklyn Bridge is the draw here. Standard seafood

Fulton Market

MICHAEL STORRINGS

dishes, like salmon on lentils and mahimahi, are offered, and the prices aren't bad for the area. Be forewarned: It can get crowded with businesspeople at lunch. ♦ American ♦ Daily lunch and dinner. 732.9090

20 Fulton Fish Market Established in 1821, this venerable institution has been at this location since 1907. It was given the name **Tin Building** by old salts who still remembered the wooden structure it replaced. The market was located here to conveniently receive the daily haul from local fishing boats, but today the catch (from cleaner waters) arrives via refrigerated truck. Daytime visitors find the market a quiet place, but it is positively frantic between midnight and 8AM. Early risers can watch the activity wind down by taking guided tours at 6AM on the first and third Thursday of each month from May through October; reservations are required. ♦ Daily. South St (between Fulton and Beekman Sts). Tour information 669.9416

The site dug for the World Trade Center towers required the removal of 1.2 million cubic yards of earth, which was later used to create part of Battery Park City. It is estimated that on a clear day the twin towers of the World Trade Center can be seen from as far away as 53 miles. From the towers, one can, theoretically, see equally as far.

21 Brooklyn Bridge Built from 1869 to 1883, and designed by **John A. Roebling** and his son **Washington Roebling,** this milestone in civil engineering is an aesthetic, as well as a structural, masterpiece. The bridge gets its dynamic tension from the massive strength of its great stone pylons and Gothic arches contrasted with the intricate web of its woven suspension cables. In 1855, John Roebling's proposal for a bridge across the East River was met with derision, but far-sighted residents of Brooklyn (then a separate city) pushed the idea after the Civil War. The **Roebling** family's fate was inextricably tied up with that of the bridge. John died as the result of an accident on a Brooklyn wharf before work on the bridge began, but his son, Washington, carried on, even when he got the bends during construction and remained partially paralyzed for the rest of his life; his mother then took over the operation (plaques at both ends of the bridge commemorate the **Roebling** trio's dedication. The Brooklyn Bridge was the first to use steel cables. For 20 years it was the world's longest suspension bridge; for many more its span was the longest. The subject of many poems, paintings, paeans of praise, and bad jokes, the bridge still gives a special lift to the bicyclists, walkers, and runners who cross it. If you care to stroll across the bridge, the entrance is on Park Row: The left side is for pedestrians, the right for bikers. ♦ Between Adams St, Brooklyn and Park Row

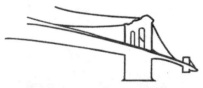

BRIDGE CAFE

22 Bridge Cafe ★★★$$ This aptly named place is located in the oldest wood-frame building south of Canal Street, under the Brooklyn Bridge. But don't be put off by the location—the menu, featuring such well-dressed staples as savory buffalo steak and fresh soft-shell crabs, is one of the best in the **Seaport** area. The whitewashed room with tin ceiling, brick walls, and burgundy tablecloths is cozy by day and romantically candlelit at night. ♦ International ♦ M-F lunch and dinner; Sa-Su brunch and dinner. Reservations recommended. 279 Water St (at Dover St). 227.3344 ๕

23 Seaport Inn $$ For the traveler who wants easy access to historic downtown Manhattan, or the businessperson who would rather walk to those early morning Wall Street appointments, this handsomely restored 19th-century building houses 72 tastefully decorated rooms offering a warm and comfortable refuge. Some rooms have terraces with views of the Brooklyn Bridge. There is no restaurant. ♦ 33 Peck Slip (at Front St). 766.6600, 800/HOTEL.NY ๕

24 127 John Street A huge electric display clock designed by Corchia–de Harak Associates, in addition to the nearby colorful steel patio furniture, add a touch of whimsy to the Water Street streetscape. ♦ View from Water St (between John and Fulton Sts)

25 Wall Street Plaza This 1973 white-aluminum–and-glass structure by **I.M. Pei & Associates** richly deserved the award it received from the American Institute of Architects for its classical purity, rather rare in the new buildings in this area. The 1974 sculpture in its plaza, by Yu Yu Yang, consists of a stainless-steel slab with an opening that faces a polished disk. It is a memorial to the **Cunard** liner *Queen Elizabeth*, whose history is outlined on a nearby plaque. ♦ 88 Pine St (at Front St)

26 Manhattan Seaport Suites $$$ Located in the heart of the historical district that harks

back to New York's early days, this suites-only hotel is just a two-minute walk from Wall Street. Suites come in four sizes, from an oversize double room to a miniature apartment that can sleep four people. All 49 suites have fully equipped kitchens, and many have a separate living room for business meetings. The **Rainbow Lounge** has a limited menu. A complimentary breakfast is served in the lobby. ♦ 129 Front St (between Wall St and Maiden La). 742.0003, 800/777.8483; fax 742.0124; www.seaportny.com/seaporthme.html ๕

St. MAGGIE'S CAFÉ

27 St. Maggie's Café ★$$ Young Wall Streeters come here for such light fare as the Mulberry Street grilled chicken salad, and for seafood dishes, including Maryland crab cakes or Norwegian salmon in a sesame and ginger sauce. ♦ American ♦ M-F lunch and dinner. Reservations recommended. 120 Wall St (at South St). 943.9050

28 74 Wall Street The nautical decoration around the arched entrance of this solid-looking 1926 building by **Benjamin Wistar Morris** is a reminder that it was built for the Seamen's Bank for Savings, the second-oldest savings bank in the city. It was chartered in 1829 as a financial haven for sailors, who usually arrived in the port with their pockets full of back pay accumulated while they were at sea. The official address of the property was 76 Wall Street, but it was changed because superstitious seamen refused to leave their money there—the numbers added up to 13. ♦ At Pearl St

29 55 Wall Street One of the first buildings in the area after the Great Fire of 1835 leveled 700 structures between South and Broad Streets, Coenties Slip, and Wall Street, this building was designed by **Isaiah Rogers** in 1836. It was built as a three-story trading hall for the **Merchants' Exchange** and later became the **Custom House.** In 1907, its height was doubled when it was remodeled and expanded by **McKim, Mead & White,** and it became the headquarters of First National City Bank, which still maintains an impressive-looking branch here under today's name, Citibank. ♦ At Hanover St

30 The Bank of New York The bank has occupied several buildings on this site since its founding by Alexander Hamilton in 1784. Commodore Vanderbilt used one of them as his banking headquarters. The present Georgian building, built in 1927 and designed by **Benjamin Wistar Morris,** is easily one of the most attractive in the area, with tall, arched windows and a broken pediment framing a handsome galleon lantern. ♦ 48 Wall St (at William St). 495.1784 ๕

31 Skyscraper Museum Curator and founder Carol Willis, an expert on finance and architecture, offers changing exhibits depicting the various aspects of the "business of buildings." Also on display at this museum, located in a former 1926 banking hall, are maps, period photographs, and construction records of New York's most famous gleaming towers of steel and glass. ♦ Free. Tu-Sa. 44 Wall St (at William St). 968.1961

32 40 Wall Street The tower was built in 1929, the same time as the **Chrysler Building** uptown, and was secretly designed by H. **Craig Severance** and **Yasuo Matsui** to be two feet higher, which would have made it the tallest in the world. (But the **Chrysler's** builders outfoxed the bankers with a secret plan of their own: They pushed a 123-foot stainless steel spire through a hole in their roof.) This was the headquarters of the Bank of the Manhattan Company, which eventually merged with Chase National Bank. The Manhattan Company was founded in 1799 by Aaron Burr, who was blocked by political rivals when he tried to charter a bank. Instead he received legislative permission to establish a water company. In the charter's fine print, he was granted the power to loan money to property owners who wanted to connect their buildings to his wooden water mains. Before he had dug up too many streets, Burr abandoned the water business and became what he had always wanted to be: a banker. ♦ Between William and Nassau Sts

33 30 Wall Street When this structure was built as the United States Assay Office in 1921 by architects **York & Sawyer,** the facade of its predecessor, the Bank of the United States, designed in 1826 by **Martin E. Thompson,** was dismantled and eventually reconstructed in the **American Wing** of the **Metropolitan Museum of Art.** Additions were made in 1955 by the firm of **Halsey, McCormack & Helmer.** ♦ Between William and Nassau Sts

33 Federal Hall National Memorial This Americanization of the Parthenon is one of New York City's finest examples of Greek Revival architecture and a fitting National Historic Landmark. At the front of the building, which was designed in 1842 by **Town & Davis,** John Quincy Adams Ward's statue of *George Washington* marks the spot where the Revolutionary War general became the country's first president. An early 18th-century building at this site (demolished in 1803) served as the United States governmental seat in the days when New York City was the nation's capital; it was here that the House of Representatives and the Senate first met. Today, Doric columns climbing 32 feet high extend across the building's face. Enter for a self-guided tour of the building's interior, which was designed by John Frazee and Samuel Thompson. ♦ M-F. 15 Pine St or 26 Wall St (at Nassau St). 825.6888 ♿

34 Morgan Guaranty Trust Company If ever a single man epitomized the American capitalist, J.P. Morgan (1837-1913) was that man. His son, John Pierpont Morgan Jr., took control of the empire in 1913, the year this building was built by **Trowbridge & Livingston.** Like his father, John Jr. was apparently not without enemies. On 16 September 1920, at the height of the lunch hour, a carriage parked on Wall Street suddenly exploded, killing 33 people and injuring 400. The marble walls of the building still have scars from the bomb, noticeable on the Wall Street side of the building. No reason was ever determined, and the owner of the carriage was never found. The bank survived unscathed, as did Morgan, who was out of town at the time. ♦ 23 Wall St (at Broad St)

35 New York Stock Exchange The **Exchange's** giant portico, colonnade, and sculptures express austerity and security—key design goals in 1903, when this building (pictured below) was designed by **George B. Post,** and when the upper section was designed in 1923 by **Trowbridge & Livingston.** The solemn facade masks the leading-edge technology that drives the exchange today. That technology, integrated with the judgment and skills of the trading floor's professionals, provides investors with the broadest, most

New York Stock Exchange

open, and most liquid equities market in the world. Before entering the gallery that overlooks the trading floor, visitors go through an exhibition area that includes video presentations and frequent lectures on the history and workings of the institution. A multilingual, prerecorded explanation of what's happening three floors below is provided from a glass-enclosed observation gallery overlooking the frenzied action on the trading floor. More than two thousand companies deal on the exchange; it is the world's largest, with stock valued at more than $3 trillion. The tickets for tours are dispensed at 20 Broad Street; there are a limited number for each session. ♦ Free. Visitors Gallery: M-F 9:15AM-2:45PM. Tours: M-F 9:15AM-3:45PM. Broad St (at Wall St), Third floor. 656.5168 ᶜ

36 Bankers Trust Building The pyramid on top of this 31-story tower, built in 1912 by **Trowbridge & Livingston,** became the corporate symbol of Bankers Trust and remained its logo even after the bank moved its main headquarters up to 280 Park Avenue in 1963. ♦ 16 Wall St (at Nassau St)

37 Irving Trust Company Building/The Bank of New York Ralph Walker's only skyscraper was built in 1932 on what was called the most expensive piece of real estate in the world in the 1930s. He said his design was one of superimposed rhythms, a steel frame draped outside with rippling curtains of stone. The gold, red, and orange Art Deco mosaics created by Hildreth Meière in the banking room off Wall Street make a visit rewarding even if you are not a depositor. ♦ 1 Wall St (at Broadway)

New York's first subway (one car, seating 22 passengers) was fueled by a blast of air from a huge steam-driven fan, which would suck the car back when it reached the end of the line. It traveled 10 miles an hour and ran under Broadway from Warren to Murray Streets, a distance of 312 feet. It was conceived and constructed in 1870 by Alfred Ely Beach, a publisher and the inventor of the typewriter.

During the peak years of immigration on Ellis Island, the record of languages spoken by a single official interpreter was 15. One interpreter was Fiorello La Guardia, who would later become the famous—and possibly the most beloved—mayor of New York City, responsible for cleaning up the corruption of Tammany Hall. He worked at Ellis Island for an annual salary of $1,200 from 1907 to 1910 and later was the first mayor to serve an until-then unprecedented three terms, from 1935 to 1945.

38 Waldenbooks The Lower Manhattan branch of the national chain is spacious, and many of its departments are separated by alcoves. Especially strong in business, the bookstore also offers wide selections in cooking, history and sports, with many remainder and sale books. ♦ M-F. 57 Broadway (at Exchange Alley). 269.1139

39 Trinity Church This historic architectural and religious monument has a strong square tower punctuated by an exclamation point spire, and the good fortune to stand at the head of Wall Street. The shaded grassy cemetery, a welcome open space in this neighborhood, offers a noontime haven for office workers. The cemetery came first, and such notables as Alexander Hamilton, William Bradford, and Robert Fulton are buried here (marked by placards that are especially helpful where gravestone inscriptions have worn away). This is the third church with this name on this site. The original was built in 1698, paid for by taxation of all citizens, regardless of religion, because the Church of England was the official religion of the colony. It burned in 1776. The second was demolished in 1839. A small museum behind the main altar documents the church's history.

The present structure (illustrated on the inside back cover of this book) was designed in 1846 by **Richard Upjohn;** Richard Morris Hunt's brass doors were added later. The **Chapel of All Saints,** designed by **Thomas Hash,** was built in 1913; and the **Bishop Manning Memorial Wing** by **Adams & Woodbridge** was erected in 1965. In 1993, work was completed on a time-consuming effort to restore the building to its original appearance. Workers steamed away a layer of paraffin that was applied to the building in the 1920s to keep it from crumbling; beneath the paraffin were layers of coal dust and pollutants that had made this building blacker than many other historic buildings. The result of the cleaning process—rosy sandstone as **Upjohn** had intended—was quite a surprise to Wall Streeters who, every day for years, had been walking past what they believed to be a very dark building. Classical concerts are often given here on Sunday during the winter months. ♦ Services: daily. Museum: M-F 9-11:45AM, 1-3:45PM; Sa 10AM-3:45PM; Su 1-3:45PM. Broadway (between Rector and Thames Sts). 602.0800 ᶜ

40 American Stock Exchange The building was known until 1953 as the "Curb Exchange" because before 1921 brokers stood at the corner of Wall and Broad Streets and communicated with one another through hand gestures. The present building was designed in 1930 by **Starrett & Van Vleck.** ♦ 86 Trinity Pl (between Rector and Thames Sts). 306.1000

Taking Stock of Wall Street

Wall Street's west end is marked by the spires of **Trinity Church**, with its newly cleaned, roseate facade and history-filled cemetery. Today's visitors, however, are far more intrigued with the less spiritual attractions of New York's Financial District. Whether the bulls (aggressive and expecting prices to rise) or the bears (more cautious, fearing falling prices) are in control, New York's various markets and halls of finance have become blue chip tourism magnets. Yet money had nothing at all to do with the founding of this world-famous bastion.

In 1653, a wooden wall was built as fortification against Indian and British attack, hence the name Wall Street. The wall was demolished at the end of the century, never having been tested in actual battle. By the late 1700s, Alexander Hamilton, the first Secretary of the Treasury, had issued bonds to pay off debts incurred by the US during the Revolutionary War. Some historians believe that the 1792 signing of the "Buttonwood Agreement" among 20 or so stockbrokers and merchants marked the beginning of the actual **New York Stock Exchange.** However, the formal **NYSE** was not inaugurated until 1817 when a group of brokers created a constitution and set down exacting membership requirements. The original name was **The New York Stock and Exchange Board.**

The latter part of the 19th century saw a boom in speculation, brought on by the specter of war and growing industrialism. By the 1870s, one could buy a seat on the Exchange for around $4,000 (a seat in 1996 cost $1,450,000). Though other exchanges emerged, they were eventually gobbled up by the mighty **NYSE.**

During most of its first century, the Exchange changed locations many times. But in 1901, at the height of industrialist J.P. Morgan's battle for control of the Northern Pacific Railroad, the **NYSE** moved into—and remained at—its current location, 10 Broad Street.

The number 29 seems to have been a jinx for the stock market, as has the month of October. The famous crash of 1929 took place on 29 October, when the market lost nearly a quarter of its value; many investors met with financial ruin, others leaped from the tops of the same buildings where they had created their fortunes. For the government's part, the crash precipitated the creation of the Securities and Exchange Commission (SEC), which enforced a set of rules on how stocks could be represented and traded. In 1971, the **NYSE** was incorporated as a nonprofit organization, and in 1975, the ruling on fixed commission regulations was repealed, paving the way for discount brokerage firms. Standardization, supposition, and superstition remain a part of Wall Street's roller coaster history. Right up to the present, both scandals and crashes continue to plague investors

large and small. Interestingly, the last major "correction," as noteworthy declines are delicately referred to today, occurred in 1987—once again in the month of October.

Today many of the most powerful investment firms, banks, exchanges, and other financial institutions have opened their public spaces to visitors. The former New York Chamber of Commerce at **65 Liberty Street,** now the International Commercial Bank of China, has a dramatic **Great Hall** with an ornate, carved ceiling and a breathtaking skylight. Art Deco devotees should head to **1 Wall Street,** now home to The Bank of New York, and **70 Pine Street,** headquarters of the American International Group. The interiors and facades of these structures are nearly as elegant as those of the **Chrysler** and **Empire State Buildings.** In contrast, **1 Chase Manhattan Plaza,** with its Isamu Noguchi rock formation and lively Jean Dubuffet sculpture, brings an element of modern airiness and whimsy to this vast outdoor space.

The **Alliance for Downtown New York** (212/566.6700) is a good starting point for information about the ins and outs of New York's Financial District.

Some of Wall Street's most impressive sights, some of which can be viewed only by special arrangement, are best seen on the new **Heritage Trails World of Finance** walking tour. Stops include the **Federal Reserve Bank,** where billions of dollars in gold bricks are on display. Call 888/487.2457 for information about times, dates, and cost of the tour.

Financial Must-Sees

New York Mercantile Exchange Visitors' Center and Galleries. The new hi-tech trading floor opened in July 1997. Visitors can learn about trading through a series of dioramas and electronic maps, and then look down at the actual spectacle from overhanging galleries. One North End Ave (just south of Vesey St). For information call 212/299.2000.

Nasdaq's MarketSite. A 55-foot wall with 100 monitors that display real-time stock data. 33 Whitehall St (between Pearl and Bridge Sts), Ninth floor. For information call 212/709.2471.

The Museum of American Financial History. This is the only American museum focusing on the country's financial development. Here you can see many unique artifacts, such as a bond signed by George Washington. Admission is free. 28 Broadway (between Beaver St and Exchange Pl). Call 212/908.4519 for information.

The Skyscraper Museum. This is where you can learn about the history and construction of Wall Street's towering icons of wealth and power. Admission is free. 44 Wall St (at William St). Call 212/968.1961 for information.

SYMS

AN EDUCATED CONSUMER
IS OUR BEST CUSTOMER®

41 Syms Located in the heart of the Financial District, this famous discount house is primarily for men and women with conservative tastes. Sizes range from lean and trim to portly, at discounts of 30 to 50 percent. Unlike in some discount stores, here you'll find the original labels on the stock. Selections include double-breasted and single-breasted suits in conservative pinstripes, herringbones, and Harris tweeds, as well as double-pleated slacks, jeans, and all the accessories to go with them. But the greatest strength of this store is the shirt department, which takes up nearly the entire second floor. On the third and fourth floors are the women's departments. ♦ Daily. 42 Trinity Pl (between Edgar and Rector Sts). 797.1199. Also at: 400 Park Ave (at E 54th St). 317.8200

42 Bank of Tokyo Trust Alterations from 1975 by **Kajima International** have modernized **Bruce Price**'s 1895 building. The eight Greek ladies by J. Massey Rhind still guard the building from their perch on the third floor. Look farther up and you'll find more of them on an even higher level. ♦ 100 Broadway (at Pine St). 766.7916 &

43 Trinity and US Realty Buildings The **Trinity Building** by **Francis H. Kimball** replaced **Richard Upjohn**'s five-story 1840 building of the same name, which was the first office building in the city. After the present Gothic structure was built in 1906, its developer, US Realty Company, acquired a similar 50-foot plot next door and constructed an identical 21-story building for their own use, with a shared service core along Thames Street. Fantastic creatures sporting lions' heads and eagles' wings watch as you approach the entrance to the **Trinity Building**. ♦ 111 and 115 Broadway (at Thames St)

On 16 December 1835, fire engulfed Lower Manhattan, scorching everything south of Wall Street and east of Broadway. Over 650 buildings were burned. The flames took nearly 20 hours to bring under control; property damage was some $20 million.

The South Street Seaport Museum is home to the nation's largest private collection of historic vessels.

The World Trade Center has more than a half-million square feet of glass.

44 Equitable Building The massive structure is noteworthy not for any particular stylistic qualities but for its size, which changed the history of building in New York. This 40-story block contains 1.2 million square feet of office space on a site of slightly less than an acre. The public outcry when it was completed in 1915 by **Ernest R. Graham** led to the creation of the 1916 zoning laws, the first in the country, to ensure a minimum of light and air on city streets in the future. ♦ 120 Broadway (between Pine and Cedar Sts)

45 Marine Midland Bank One of Lower Manhattan's more successful modern-style steel-and-glass high-rises, this one was designed in 1967 by **Skidmore, Owings & Merrill.** The sleek black building is of an appropriate scale, largely due to a spandrel design that helps it fit into its older, more ornate surroundings. A vermilion cube by sculptor Isamu Noguchi enlivens the plaza. ♦ 140 Broadway (at Liberty St). 658.1641 &

46 Chase Manhattan Bank Built in 1960 as a catalyst to revitalize the aging Wall Street area the bank's aluminum-and-glass face rises an impressive 813 feet, and it is still a fittingly imposing base for the Rockefeller banking empire. The designers, **Skidmore, Owings & Merrill,** gave the tower a trend-setting feature its large plaza, which is home to *A Group of Four Trees* by Jean Dubuffet and a sunken sculpture garden by Isamu Noguchi. ♦ 1 Chase Manhattan Plaza, Liberty St (between William and Nassau Sts). 552.2222 &

47 Louise Nevelson Plaza This small triangular park with large steel sculptures created by the late Louise Nevelson is a popular lunch spot. ♦ Bounded by Liberty St, Maiden La, and William St

48 Strand Bookstore "Miles and miles of books" is the trademark description of this epic store, and its vast collection includes thousands of review copies of new books, hundreds of coffee-table books, and tables full of mass-market and trade paperbacks, all sold at a generous discount. ♦ Daily. 95 Fulton Street (between Gold and William Sts). 732.6070. Also at: 828 Broadway (at E 12th St). 473.1452

49 John Street United Methodist Church Home to the oldest Methodist society in the US, this Georgian-style building, designed by **William Hurry** in 1841, was erected on the site of a "preaching house" built by the congregation in 1766. On the lower level is a museum containing such relics as a clock, an altar rail, and foot warmers. ♦ Museum: M, W F noon-4PM. 44 John St (between William and Nassau Sts). 269.0014

50 Federal Reserve Bank of New York This is the banker's bank, where the nations of the world maintain the balance of trade by the storage and exchange of gold, which is housed on five underground floors that occupy an entire city block. The unimaginable riches inside this Fort Knox are reflected in the building's exterior, modeled after a 15th-century Florentine palazzo, with Samuel Yellin's finely detailed ironwork adding to the serene beauty of the limestone-and-sandstone facade (designed by **York & Sawyer** in 1924). Free one-hour tours of the building and gold vaults are available Monday through Friday on a limited basis. Reservations are required at least one week in advance. ◆ 33 Liberty St (between William and Nassau Sts). 720.6130 &

51 Chamber of Commerce of the State of New York Designed by **James B. Baker** in 1901, this ornate Beaux Arts edifice is ponderous from its heavy stone base to its massive top, with Ionic columns adding to its almost predatory look. ◆ 65 Liberty St (at Liberty Pl)

52 McDonald's $ Despite the tuxedo-clad doorman, glass-and-wood dining room, and pianist serenading diners, this is the home of the golden arches. With the exception of imported Illy espresso and cappuccino and pastries from real bakeries, neither deep-fried nor microwaved, the food is standard McDonald's fare. Investors will appreciate the Dow Jones ticker tape, informing them of market fluctuations as they munch their Big Macs. ◆ Fast food ◆ Daily breakfast, lunch, and dinner. 160 Broadway (between Liberty St and Maiden La). 227.3828; fax 227.7916; mcdonalds160broadwayny.com &

department store

53 Century 21 A larger version of the Brooklyn discount department store, this place has three bustling floors of top-quality merchandise—everything from designer clothes and accessories for men and women, to housewares and appliances. While some of the fashions may be from a season ago the prices make them perennials. ◆ M-Sa. 22 Cortlandt St (between Broadway and Church St). 227.9092. Also at: 472 86th St (between Fifth and Fourth Aves), Bay Ridge, Brooklyn. 718/748.3266

54 Battery Park City When this eclectic complex of 14,000 rental apartments and condominiums is finally complete, it will support a population larger than that of Bozeman, Montana (the residential population will be approximately 25,000). The total development cost of this 92-acre landfill site adjacent to the Financial District is estimated at $4 billion, including the privately financed

$1.5-billion **World Financial Center.** The master plan devised in 1979 by **Cooper, Eckstut Associates** divides the blocks into parcels, with individual developers for each one, thus avoiding a superblock appearance. About 30 percent of the site is open parkland with parks linked by the 1.2-mile landscaped waterfront. **The Esplanade** was designed by landscape architects Stanton Eckstut between Liberty and West Thames Streets; Eckstut, Susan Child Associates, and artist Mary Miss at the South Cove; and Carr, Lynch, Hack & Sandell between North Cove Yacht Harbor and Chambers Street; it extends the entire length of the site, providing a perfect place to relax and watch the river traffic. Access for people with disabilities has been incorporated into the overall design.

The first completed section was **Gateway Plaza** (1982), a trio of 34-story towers and three 6-story buildings that provide 1,712 residential units. The structures, designed by **Jack Brown** and **Irving Gershorn,** were begun before the current plan was established.

The architects who worked on **Rector Place** (1988), the second phase of residential construction, included **Charles Moore; James Stewart Polshek; Gruzen Samton Steinglass; Ulrich Franzen & Associates; Conklin Rossant; Mitchell/Giurgola;** and **Davis, Brody & Associates.** Developed under the master plan, this 9-acre plot contains 2,200 apartments grouped around 1-acre **Rector Park,** designed by landscape architects Innocente & Webel.

The third phase, **Battery Place,** consists of 2,800 residential units on 9 parcels located between **Rector Place** and Pier A. The architects involved in the initial three buildings are **The Ehrenkrantz Group & Eckstut, Gruzen Samton Steinglass,** and **James Stewart Polshek & Partners.** The southern end of this area will include a **Ritz-Carlton** hotel; two more residential buildings; and the three-acre **South Gardens** park designed by landscape architect Hanna Olin. ◆ Bounded by West St and the Hudson River, and Pier A and Chambers St. 416.5300 &

Within Battery Park City:

Museum of Jewish Heritage Located in a dignified, tiered pyramid facing the water, this museum, designed by **Kevin Roche John Dinkeloo & Associates,** examines Jewish culture from the end of the 19th century to the present. The exhibits, featuring films, photographs, videotapes, and artifacts, give prominence to the Holocaust and its survivors and also include musicians, actors, writers, and philosophers. ◆ Admission. M-W, Su; Th 9AM-8PM; F and holiday eves 9AM-2PM. 18 First Pl (off West St). 968.1800 &

Restaurants/Clubs: Red   Hotels: Blue

Shops/ ♥ Outdoors: Green   **Sights/Culture:** Black

55 World Financial Center More than eight million square feet of office, retail, and recreational space have been created on landfill produced by the construction of the **World Trade Center** across West Street. Designed by **Cesar Pelli & Associates** and completed in 1981, the complex includes four 33- to 50-story office towers, two 9-story buildings designated as gatehouses, a four-acre plaza, and a vaulted and glass-enclosed **Winter Garden,** whose most dramatic feature is 15 Washington robusta palm trees. The only ones of this size in the city, they are each a uniform 45 feet high. Tenants include **Bally of Switzerland, Caswell-Massey, Godiva Chocolatier, Manufacturers Hanover Trust, Rizzoli International Bookstore, and Plus One Fitness Clinic.** The **Courtyard,** a two-level outdoor piazza, houses four international restaurants and cafes. The **World Financial Center Plaza** is a stellar example of public space design: 3.5 beautifully landscaped acres of parkland on the Hudson River with twin reflecting pools. The center presents an ongoing series of music, dance, and theater events as well as visual arts installations, and is world headquarters for such companies as American Express, Merrill Lynch, and Dow Jones. ◆ Daily. West St (between Albany and Vesey Sts). 945.0505 &

Within the World Financial Center:

Coco Marina ★★$$ This former **Sfuzzi** is now part of Pino Luongo's empire (**Coco Pazzo, Coco Opera, Le Madri,** and **Tuscan Square**). While diners take in a view of the marina, chef Claudio Leone indulges their tastes of the sea with such offerings as skate marinated in lime and cilantro, seared tuna steak with warm fennel and sun-dried tomatoes, and a perfectly tasty grilled lobster. End the meal with a refreshing parfait of lemon frozen yogurt. ◆ Italian ◆ Daily lunch and dinner. Winter Garden Atrium. 385.8080 &

Hudson River Club ★★★★$$$$ Chef Matthew Maxwell has created an entire new cuisine within these walls. Featuring foods from the Hudson River Valley, the portions are large and calorie-laden, but infused with such subtle flavors that dishes come off as delicacies. The menu changes seasonally, but traditional standouts are foie gras, tuna steak, rabbit confit, and grilled bass. The magnificent desserts are as appealing to the eye are they are to the palate. The extensive wine list gives special attention to affordable New York State wines. ◆ American ◆ M-F lunch and dinner; Sa dinner; Su brunch. Reservations recommended; jacket required. 4 World Financial Center, Upper level (enter at North End Ave). 786.1500 &

Johnney's Fish Grill ★★$$ The dark green walls mounted with stuffed fish and black-and-white photos of fishermen plying their nets make you feel as if you were in a New England seafood house. The very fresh fish offered here reinforces this impression, and the rich New England clam chowder is nothing short of spectacular. Clams on the half shell, Maryland crab cakes, grilled swordfish, and the fresh and artistically designed sushi are all worth a taste. ◆ Seafood ◆ M-F lunch and dinner. 4 World Financial Center. 385.0333 &

Au Mandarin ★★$$ The authentic Mandarin menu served here—particularly the diced chicken marinated with minced garlic, ginger, and peppercorns; beef tangerine; and Peking duck—is especially popular among businesspeople seeking something a little different at lunchtime. ◆ Mandarin ◆ Daily lunch and dinner. 3 World Financial Center, Courtyard. 385.0313 &

Donald Sacks ★★$$ Chef Kurt Sippel offers three affordable specials each day and six freshly made salads, including the signature curried chicken salad. Duck-confit quesadilla and grilled rack of lamb served with roasted-garlic mashed potatoes and Port wine sauce are samples of the heartier fare served. ◆ American ◆ Daily lunch and dinner. 2 World Financial Center, Courtyard. 619.4600 &

Tahari The designer's full line of sophisticated clothing for women, including scarves, jewelry, and handbags, is stocked here. The shop is decorated with antiques (not for sale) from Ellie Tahari's private collection. ◆ Daily. 2 World Financial Center, Upper Level. 945.2450 &

56 World Trade Center (WTC) Seven buildings, including the **New York Marriott World Trade Center** and the two landmark towers, make up this massive complex set on a semicircle around a five-acre plaza. Designed by **Minoru Yamasaki & Associates** and **Emery Roth & Sons,** WTC was begun in 1962 and finished in 1977. At 110 stories, the monolithic twin towers are the tallest in the city (shown on page 4). All the structures are connected underground by the concourse—a vast pedestrian mall filled with shops, banks, public spaces, and restaurants, including branches of **Au Bon Pain** and **Ben and Jerry's.** Beneath it all are parking garages, where on 26 February 1993, a terrorist bomb went off in **1 World Trade Center,** killing six people, injuring many more, and causing millions of dollars of damage. ◆ Church St (between Liberty and Vesey Sts). 435.4170

Within the World Trade Center:

The Observation Deck Take the quarter-mile, 58-second elevator ride from the mezzanine level to the 107th floor where the observation deck affords the best views in town—especially on a clear day. There are 24 multilingual video kiosks that chronicle New York City facts in a flash, as well as nighttime laser light rooftop shows. A Central Park–themed food court will satisfy hungry explorers. ♦ Admission; buy tickets on the mezzanine level. Daily 9:30AM-9:30PM. 2 World Trade Center. 323.2340 &

Windows on the World ★★$$$ After a $25-million renovation, this elegant 107th-floor restaurant seems even more spectacular than at its debut in 1976: a sleek, multitiered dining room washed in pastel tones and a carpet emblazoned with patterns of street maps from cities around the world. Appetizers include Asian seafood broth with crab dumpling, and portobello mushroom filled with snails in green-garlic butter. Among the innovative entrées are roasted veal shank sealed in parchment with cumin, garlic, and Mexican spices; broiled Atlantic cod in herb sauce; and rack of lamb with stuffed grape leaves. Save room for the luscious desserts—the frozen nougat with raspberry coulis, praline raspberry-mango napoleon, and Big Apple crisp in phyllo with applejack ice cream are memorable. The wine list is extensive, with over 700 selections. ♦ International ♦ M-F lunch and dinner; Sa-Su brunch and dinner. Reservations recommended; jacket required. 1 World Trade Center. 524.7011

The Greatest Bar on Earth $$ This is a great spot to sip a cocktail and marvel at the views to the south and west. The bar boasts 16 kinds of vodka and a menu that includes sushi, sashimi, open-faced sandwiches, and burgers. Also here is the cigar-friendly **Skybox** lounge. On the weekend there's live music for those who want to dance the night away. ♦ International ♦ Cover charge Th-Sa after 10PM. Bar: M-Sa lunch and dinner; Su brunch. Music: Th-Sa 10PM-2AM. 1 World Trade Center. 524.7011

Wild Blue ★★$$$ Formerly Cellar in the Sky, this casual, soothingly hued restaurant on high features stellar harbor views from floor-to-ceiling windows and chef Michael Lomonaco's regionally inspired American dishes. Try the panroasted New Bedford cod with bacon and cockles, Colorado lamb T-bone chops, or anything from the daily market menu. The wine list is extensive, including almost 50 served by the glass. ♦ American ♦ M-Sa dinner. Reservations recommended. 1 World Trade Center. 524.7107

TKTS Half-price day-of-performance tickets are available here for evening performances of Broadway and Off-Broadway shows. Wednesday, Saturday, and Sunday matinee tickets are sold from 11AM to closing the day before the performance. ♦ M-F 11AM-5:30PM; Sa 11AM-3:30PM. 2 World Trade Center, Mezzanine. 768.1818. Also at: W 47th St and Broadway &

 Austin J. Tobin Plaza This 5-acre space between the towers is graced with a fountain that surrounds a 25-foot bronze construction by Fritz Koenig. The granite pyramid at the entrance is by Masyuki Nagare, and the stainless steel abstract sculpture is by James Rosati. Also note the Alexander Calder stabile just outside on Church Street. Other sculpture is often temporarily displayed on the windy plaza, which is frequently used as a setting for concerts and other events. Other works of art commissioned for the **World Trade Center** include Louise Nevelson's *Sky-Gate New York* on the mezzanine of **1 World Trade Center,** and a three-ton tapestry by Joan Miró, which hangs in the mezzanine of **2 World Trade Center.**

NEW YORK Marriott. WORLD TRADE CENTER

New York Marriott World Trade Center $$$$ Sleek yet welcoming, this 818-room hotel affords views of the Hudson River from its highest floors. Designed in 1981 by **Skidmore, Owings & Merrill,** it is packed during the week with businesspeople who want proximity to Wall Street and the **World Trade Center;** on the weekend, visitors come to experience the sights and charms of Old New York. Free weekend shuttle buses uptown make it a pleasure to venture out of the neighborhood, too. A fitness center provides a free indoor swimming pool, jogging track, sauna, and exercise rooms (fee for racquetball and massage), along with spectacular views of the harbor. The business center offers secretarial services, personal computers, and cellular phones. The **Executive Floors** boast a special lounge with complimentary cocktails, breakfast, and other perks. The adjacent concourse of the **World Trade Center** is a bazaar of stores and restaurants. And there's a comfortable spot in the lobby for express breakfast or lunch. ♦ 3 World Trade Center. 938.9100, 800/469.8478; fax 444.3444 &

Within the New York Marriott World Trade Center:

Greenhouse Cafe ★$$ This gardenlike, sun-drenched cafe has a skylight roof that gives an unusual view of the **Twin Towers**

soaring above. Executive chef Walter Plendner's eclectic menu features such dishes as panfried mozzarella in a basil crust with stewed plum tomatoes, in addition to daily curries and a buffet featuring roasted meats and an antipasto that changes daily.
♦ American ♦ Daily breakfast, lunch, and dinner. Plaza level. 444.4010 &

Tall Ships Bar & Grill ★$$ As befits the name, the decor is strictly nautical, with canvas sails draped overhead, polished mast-worthy woods, and stripes on the walls. The food is simple—blackened or broiled swordfish steak with grilled vegetables, chicken fingers with plum sauce, and freshly baked pies for dessert.
♦ American ♦ M-F lunch and dinner; Sa-Su dinner. Lobby level. 938.9100

Borders Books and Music If you can't find it here, it's probably out of print. This store carries over 100,000 book titles and an impressive music and video collection, along with an extensive selection of periodicals and newspapers. ♦ Daily. 5 World Trade Center. 839.8049. Also at: 550 Second Ave (at E 32nd St).685.3938; 461 Park Ave (at E 58th St). 980.6785

57 The Millenium Hilton $$$$ Fifty-five stories high, this sleek lodging has overlooked downtown New York since it was built in the shadow of the **World Trade Center** in 1992. It offers 561 nicely appointed guest rooms and suites, an indoor pool and health center, an executive business center, and other amenities. The hotel's restaurants include the casual Grill. ♦ 55 Church St (between Dey and Fulton Sts). 693.2001, 800/752.0014; fax 571.2316

Within the Millenium Hilton Hotel:

Taliesin ★★$$$ This formal, pretty room with wood paneling and etched glass is the setting for ambitious food, some of which succeeds. Try the clam and corn chowder with thyme, pancetta, and sage-wrapped swordfish medallions with saffron risotto, or panroasted wild boar in tamarind.
♦ American ♦ M-F breakfast, lunch, and dinner. 312.2000 &

58 195 Broadway There are more columns on the facade of this building than on any other building in the world, with even more inside (the lobby is like an ancient Athenian temple). It was designed in 1917 by **William Welles Bosworth** as headquarters for the American

Telephone & Telegraph Company. The ornamental panels over the Broadway entrance, as well as the bronze seals on the lobby floor and the other interior decorative elements, are by Paul Manship, whose best-known work in New York is the *Prometheus* fountain in **Rockefeller Plaza.** ♦ Between Dey and Fulton Sts

59 St. Paul's Chapel Built in 1766 by **Thomas McBean,** this is Manhattan's only remaining pre-Revolutionary War church—it even survived 1776's Great Fire—making it the oldest public building in continuous use. The chapel is not only a rare Georgian architectural gem; it is also historically important. Said to be the most impressive church in the colony when built, its grandeur loses nothing in the shadow of that neighboring temple of commerce, the **World Trade Center.** It's humbling to remember that in 1750 this site was a wheat field; the cemetery once extended to the Hudson River; and George Washington came here to pray after his inauguration as the country's first president on 30 August 1789. **McBean**'s plan for the edifice was much influenced by St. Martin-in-the-Fields in London, designed by his teacher, **James Gibb.** The interior, lit by Waterford crystal chandeliers, is one of the city's best. Come here for the concerts of classical and church music Monday and Thursday at 12:10PM (donation requested), or for services Sunday at 8AM. ♦ Broadway (between Fulton and Vesey Sts). 602.0800 &

60 Woolworth Building One of the city's most dramatic skyscrapers and one of the world's most ornate commercial buildings, it was designed by **Cass Gilbert** in 1913 as the headquarters of Frank W. Woolworth's chain of five-and-dime stores. The building, known in its day as a "cathedral of commerce," is a Gothic celebration inside and out, with picturesque details enhancing the forceful massing and graceful vertical thrust, which culminates in a perfectly composed crown. Inside, the lobby features a soaring glass mosaic ceiling and marble walls awash with more Gothic detail. An added surprise are the caricature bas-reliefs, including one of **Gilbert** himself with a model of the building and another of Frank Woolworth counting nickels and dimes. The Woolworths were so pleased with **Gilbert**'s work that they paid for it in cash ($1.5 million); they still maintain an office here. It's well worth a visit. ♦ 233 Broadway (between Barclay St and Park Pl)

The first slaves brought from Africa arrived in New York in 1625. The practice grew, and the first slave market was established at the foot of Wall Street in 1711; it was not until 1827 that slavery was abolished in New York.

61 City Hall New York City is still doing business (with a little help from the nearby **Municipal Building**) in the same structure that was its headquarters in 1811 when the building was completed. This elegant scaled-down palace by **Mangin and McComb,** a winning entry in a design competition, successfully combines the Federal style with French Renaissance details. The central hall has a sweeping twin-spiral marble staircase under a splendid dome, making it the perfect setting for public functions and grand entrances. Kings, poets, and astronauts have been received here. Upstairs, the grand **City Council Chamber** (also used by the Board of Estimate) and the **Governor's Room**—now a portrait gallery with paintings by Sully, Trumbull, Inman, and others—are worth a visit. There are always exhibits with historical or artistic themes. Interiors were restored and refurbished between 1902 and 1920, and the exterior was restored and repaired by **Shreve, Lamb & Harmon** in 1959. What is known today as **City Hall Park** has always been the city's village green or town common; equally grand in scale, the park sets off the mass of **City Hall.** ◆ M-F. City Hall Park, Broadway (between Park Row and Chambers St)

62 Pace University Originally founded as an accounting school, this university now offers courses in the arts and sciences as well as business, education, and nursing. The welded copper sculpture on the facade, by Henri Nachemia, represents *The Brotherhood of Man.* The building itself was designed by **Eggers & Higgins** in 1970. ◆ 1 Pace Plaza, Nassau St (between Spruce and Frankfort Sts). 346.1200 ♿

63 New York City Courthouse The building was known as the **Tweed Courthouse** because Tammany Hall chieftain William Marcy Tweed escalated its cost to 52 times the appropriated amount, most of which went into his own bank account. Because of the scandal, the building became a symbol of graft and has always been something of a municipal stepchild. Recent attempts to restore it have been halfhearted, but it has been saved from destruction. The original building, designed by **John Kellum** and constructed in 1872, had a grand staircase in front; the staircase was removed in 1955 to make room for the widening of Chambers Street, leaving a blank space that ruins the facade. ◆ 52 Chambers St (between Park Row and Broadway)

64 Ellen's Cafe and Bake Shop ★$ Ellen Hart Sturm, a former Miss Subway beauty queen, runs this bustling upscale cafe and bakery across from **City Hall,** where the walls are lined with photos of former Miss Subways (Ellen, who also runs a diner in the Theater District, see page 152, sponsors yearly reunions). Try the "Mayor's Special" (toasted Thomas' English Muffin halves layered with tuna salad and tomato slices and topped with melted cheese). Be sure to save room for Ellen's pecan pie. ◆ American ◆ M-Sa breakfast, lunch, and early dinner. 270 Broadway (at Chambers St). 962.1257 ♿

65 Ecco ★$$ Carved mahogany, beveled mirrors, and a two-story-high tin ceiling provide a clubby "old saloon" atmosphere at this dining spot. The waiters bustle through the crowd that's equal parts Wall Streeters and art dealers. Pasta dishes are especially good: Try the *farfalle alla zingara* (butterfly-shaped pasta with hot Italian peppers and plum tomatoes) and *penne baresi* (with fresh broccoli rabe and sweet sausage). ◆ Italian ◆ M-F lunch and dinner; Sa dinner. Reservations required. 124 Chambers St (between Church St and W Broadway). 227.7074

66 P.S. 23 Too bad all schools aren't as well designed (some of the architectural elements seem to come straight out of a child's imagination) or as nicely sited as this one, which was built in 1988 by architect **Richard Dattner.** Though the school is not open to the public, be sure to study the fanciful fence by artist Donna Dennis that encloses the schoolyard. ◆ 292 Greenwich St (at Chambers St). 233.6034

67 Stuyvesant High School Built in 1991 by **Alexander Cooper & Partners,** this is the most recent location of one of the country's most prestigious and progressive public high schools. Since the difficult-to-earn Westinghouse science scholarships were first awarded, this school's students have routinely finished the competition among the top 10 from all over the US. Graduates include Nobel laureates Joshua Lederberg and Raoul Hoffman. The building is not open to the public. ◆ 345 Chambers St (at West St). 312.4800

68 Surrogate's Court Monumental sculptures, including a pair by Philip Martiny at the entrance—one representing *Britannia* (an English soldier and a maiden), the other *America* (a Native American and a Pilgrim)—along with an array of cherubs, eagles, festoons, ship prows, and shields, let you know something important is going on here. The French Empire facade, reminiscent of the

Paris Opéra, is only the beginning. The interior has an Egyptian-tile mosaic ceiling with the 12 signs of the zodiac by William de Leftwich Dodge, as well as marble walls and floors and allegorical reliefs. The huge double stairway is yet another touch borrowed from the Opéra. Intended to be the last resting place of important city records, the building, which was designed in 1911 by **John Rochester Thomas** and **Horgan & Slattery,** also serves as the Surrogate's Court. Over the years this became its primary function, as the need grew for more space to probate wills and administer guardianships and trusts. ♦ 31 Chambers St (at Centre St). 374.8233

69 Municipal Building McKim, Mead & White created this Neo-Classical skyscraper (illustrated below) in 1914 to house city government offices. The building straddles Chambers Street and coexists quite happily with neighboring, smaller **City Hall** without

Municipal Building

MICHAEL STORRINGS

upstaging it. The almost Baroque confection is topped with a fanciful cluster of colonnaded towers capped by Adolph Weinman's gilded statue. ♦ 1 Centre St (at Chambers St)

70 Police Plaza At three full acres, this is the largest public plaza in New York. On the south side is a prison window from the 1763 **Rhinelander Sugar Warehouse,** which was on this site until 1895. (The original building was used by the British to house American prisoners of war during the Revolution.) The five interlocking oxidized-steel disks, a 1974 creation by Bernard Rosenthal, represent the five boroughs of the city. Just beyond, an eight-foot waterfall marks the entrance to a multilevel parking garage under the plaza, which was designed in 1973 by **M. Paul Friedberg.** ♦ Park Row and Chambers St

71 St. Andrew's Church The Roman Catholic church was established here in 1842 to minister to the needs of Irish immigrants. Its mission has changed along with the neighborhood. The present church was designed in 1939 by **Maginnis & Walsh** and **Robert J. Reiley.** ♦ 20 Cardinal Hayes Pl (off Pearl St, between Park Row and Centre St). 962.3972

72 United States Courthouse Here's another Lower Manhattan structure trying to be a temple. Designed in 1936 by **Cass Gilbert** and **Cass Gilbert Jr.,** this civic building presents a traditional, stately image with rows of Corinthian columns as a base for a tower crowned with a gold pyramid. ♦ 40 Centre St (at Pearl St)

73 New York County Courthouse A National Historic Landmark, this hexagonal building was designed by **Guy Lowell** in 1926. The Roman style of the building—particularly the Corinthian portico—works much better here than at the neighboring **United States Courthouse.** ♦ 60 Centre St (at Pearl St)

74 Jacob K. Javits Federal Building The smaller building on the left houses the **US Customs Court,** and the taller one with the strange windows is filled with government offices. Both buildings were designed by **Alfred Easton Poor** and **Kahn & Jacobs** in 1967. ♦ 26 Federal Plaza, Broadway (between Duane and Worth Sts)

Fitness à la Carte

New York City offers so many culinary delights that it's easy to let your willpower wander while you spoon up that last delicious bite of cranberry-pear crumble. If you want to eat your cake and keep your figure too, consider working out. Many of the city's deluxe hotels offer their guests gyms with up-to-the-minute fitness equipment. New York City also has some of the best workout centers in the country—it's possible to swim in Olympic-size pools, climb simulated mountains, go cross-country biking, and even play team volleyball on a year-round basis. Although most health and fitness clubs require a minimum annual membership, the ones listed below do sell single-day passes. "Ys" are generally less expensive than private clubs, though they do have some restrictions, such as showing proof of nonresidency.

At press time, prices ranged from a reasonable $15 to a muscle-cramping $50; higher doesn't always mean better, either. Also, most facilities ask for a photo ID. Some allow you to take group classes on an availability basis. Spa treatments such as massage and facials are always extra, as is personal training. It's a good idea to call ahead for schedules.

Some of the bigger clubs have numerous locations throughout the city, so when you call, ask which is nearest to your hotel.

Asphalt Green Housed in what was an actual asphalt plant on the **East River,** this is perhaps Manhattan's finest swim facility. Although it has private memberships, it's become a popular community center, organizing team sports and swim meets. Besides the two indoor pools, there are two equipment-filled gyms and an outdoor track. Day passes for either the pool or gym alone are $15; $25 buys a pass to both. ♦ Call 369.8890 for information.

Crunch This group of five clubs has a hip sensibility—their local TV commercials feature people dressed as animals or men talking about working out in women's clothing (their slogan is "no judgments"). A one-day pass costs $20. Locker room facilities are a bit more spartan than at other clubs. Call 614.0120 for information.

Equinox Another chain with a "downtown" attitude. You'll find more hardbody types sporting black workout gear at these five locations than you will elsewhere. The branch at the **Barbizon Hotel** features a pool and spa facility. A one-day pass costs $26 and allows you to take classes, and use the aerobic and weight equipment, or buy a single personal training session for $95. ♦ Call 721.4200 for information.

New York Health & Racquet Club One of the first health clubs in New York, this chain has a preppie atmosphere at most of its branches that's reflected in the price of a day pass—$50. There's also a chain-wide policy of charging extra for towels, and having locker room attendants who may expect tips. The aerobics and calisthenics classes can be topnotch, but some branches have somewhat shoddy equipment, and the pools generally do not match the quality of those in other, less expensive clubs. Still,

they're all over town and are one of the few clubs to offer tennis facilities (which cost extra, of course). ♦ Call 797.1500 for information.

New York Sports Club With nearly 30 locations within Manhattan, this is one of the city's fastest-growing fitness centers. The cost for a one-day pass is $25 at all branches. The best one, in terms of facilities and size, is at the **Holiday Inn Crowne Plaza Hotel,** where's there's a lap pool and oversize exercise studio. Most have complimentary steam and sauna in the locker rooms. ♦ Call 246.6700 for information about locations and passes.

92nd Street Y (Young Men's/Women's Hebrew Association) This "Y" has a large pool and fitness equipment area, along with an elevated indoor track. Day passes are $20 for all facilities. There are locker rooms with steam and sauna. One caveat: the "Y" closes for many Jewish holidays, so it's best to call in advance. ♦ Call 427.6000 for information.

The Sports Center at Chelsea Piers This state-of-the-art facility is among New York's largest. Passes cost $31 per day on weekdays and $50 on weekends. Facilities include a 25-yard indoor pool, a fitness center with aerobic equipment and weights, and a quarter-mile indoor track. There's also boxing, volleyball, and other activities. Rock climbing is available for an extra fee, and guests can use the cafe. There's a spa run by the Origins cosmetic company. ♦ Call 336.6000 for information.

Vanderbilt YMCA One of several Manhattan "Ys," this facility is part of an inexpensive residence not far from the **United Nations.** Cost for a nonresident day pass is $15. There's a good-size indoor pool, a relatively small indoor track and cardiac/aerobic machine area, weights, and a basketball court. Locker rooms are basic but have steam rooms and saunas. Call 756.9600 for information. The "Y" on West 63rd Street has a nicer pool and the same admission price, but you'll have to show proof of out-of-state residence to obtain a day pass. ♦ Call 787.1301 for information.

World Gym At the two local branches of this popular club, you can pump iron round the clock—they're open 24 hours on weekdays. Extensive cardiovascular equipment, a full range of exercise classes, steam rooms, massages, a juice bar, and a pro shop are available. Mini memberships are offered by the day, week, or month; the 10-visit card may be the best deal. ♦ Call 874.0942 for the West Side branch; 780.7407 for the Greenwich Village location.

YWCA This facility has an outstanding, regulation indoor pool, a warmer, smaller (and older) pool, an indoor track, basketball court, a small weight and equipment room, dance studios, and decent, if not plush, showers and lockers. Its **Midtown** location makes it convenient to many hotels, and its $15 day-pass charge makes year-round swimming a reality for New York's residents and visitors alike. Sometimes swim meets are held, so it's best to check ahead of time. ♦ Call 755.4500 for information.

Chinatown/Lower East Side/
Little Italy

In New York's early days, the swampy territory just northeast of **City Hall** was considered worthless. But as waves of immigrants began arriving in the middle of the 18th century, the former marshes became valuable to the real-estate developers who packed the newcomers into crowded tenements. The distinct ethnic flavors of Chinatown, the Lower East Side, and Little Italy were

established as each immigrant group settled the area roughly bounded by the **East River** and **Lafayette, Chambers,** and **Houston Streets.**

Nearly every part of New York has metamorphosed several times during the last two centuries. But in this area, it's mainly the populace, rather than the architecture, that has changed. During the 1860s, thousands of Germans arrived, forcing the long-settled Irish farther uptown. Between 1881 and 1910, 1.5 million Jews fled Romania, Hungary, and Russia, creating the largest Jewish settlement in the world on Manhattan's Lower East Side. Italians, Greeks, Poles, and Turks were among the other settlers. The neighborhood continues to be a first stop for newly arrived immigrants; today's predominantly Hispanic population fills streets that still carry the legacy of the earlier Jewish residents.

The southwestern portion of this area is a magnet for Chinese immigrants, who began arriving from San Francisco during the 1870s. Since immigration laws were changed in the mid-1960s, the neighborhood has welcomed more of them than ever. Once covering 3 square blocks and now 40 square blocks and growing, the area's more than 150,000 Chinese residents make Chinatown the largest Chinese community outside of Asia. The need for more living space has caused new arrivals to cross **Canal Street** into the enclave once traditionally occupied almost exclusively by immigrants from Naples and Sicily. The result is that the neighborhood called Little Italy is now filled with hundreds of small, crowded factories and other businesses identified by Chinese ideograms. (Distressed about this new ethnic incursion, Italian community leaders have requested that signs along **Mulberry Street** be posted only in Roman letters, so that the neighborhood retains what little character is left despite ambitious Chinese landlords.)

New York City's Chinatown is a neighborhood that thrives on street life, but except for pagoda telephone booths, don't expect quaintness. What you will find is a warren of shops selling exotic vegetables and bargain-basement Chinese clothing and housewares, along with Formica- and vinyl-filled restaurants, many of

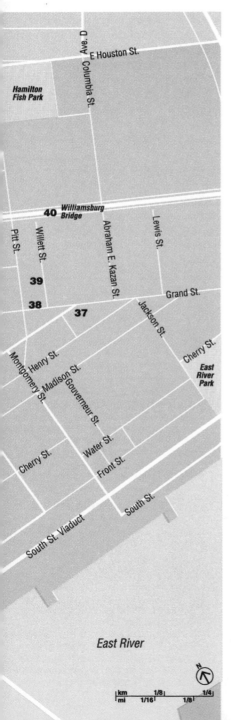

which prepare wondrous dishes. The largest crowds appear on Chinese New Year, which occurs in late January or early February.

The Lower East Side is roughly the area below East Houston Street, from the East River to the **Bowery**. During the 1880s and 1890s, immigrants from Eastern Europe flooded into the cramped redbrick tenements. At the turn of the century, this was the world's largest Jewish settlement, a slum that later became a center of culture and community (documented by, among others, critic Irving Howe in his 1976 study, *World of Our Fathers*) that spawned many writers, businesspeople, and intellectuals. Most of the upwardly mobile Jewish immigrants left as quickly as possible; now the Lower East Side is home to Chinese, Latin Americans, and African-Americans. However, although many synagogues remain empty, the old crowd still comes back for a steak at **Sammy's Famous Roumanian Jewish Steakhouse** or to shop: **Orchard Street**, though not the bargain bonanza it once was, remains a good discount destination for everything from fabrics to designer dresses. In observation of the Sabbath, most nonreligious sites on the Lower East Side are closed Friday afternoon and all day Saturday.

Mulberry Street is the main drag of Little Italy (bounded by the Bowery, Lafayette, Canal, and East Houston Streets), a bustling residential area filled with neighborhood stores and old Italian social clubs. The area was settled mainly between 1880 and 1924 by immigrant families, many of whom have moved on. But they too always come back—especially for the Feast of San Gennaro, a weeklong religious celebration held each September that is famous for its eating, drinking, and merrymaking.

1 Criminal Courts Building Called the "Tombs" after its Egyptian Revival ancestor across the street, this giant ziggurat is the third Manhattan jail, the last built before prisoners were housed at Riker's Island. Designed by **Harvey Wiley Corbett** in 1939, it is an elegant Art Moderne structure (you'll recognize **Corbett**'s hand in **Rockefeller Center**). In its day, the Tombs' 835-cell jail set a standard for penal reform: Each cell housed only one prisoner. ◆ 100 Centre St (between Hogan Pl and White St). 374.5880

At the corner of Washington Place and Greene Street, a plaque commemorates the deaths of 146 people in a fire at the Triangle Shirtwaist Company. The victims were predominantly Jewish and Italian immigrant women. When the fire broke out, the workers were unable to escape because the owners locked them in the building during shifts, a common practice. The fire brought attention to the despicable conditions of employment in the sweatshop industry, and the state enacted many reforms in the fire code and workplace safety regulations. The owners of the Triangle Shirtwaist Company were absolved of any responsibility for the deaths in a court of law.

Restaurants/Clubs: Red   Hotels: Blue

Shops/ ♥ Outdoors: Green   Sights/Culture: Black

2 Columbus Park The only real open space in Chinatown provides a setting for ballplaying and outdoor entertainment and is a staging area for the dragon dancers during Chinese New Year. It replaces Mulberry Bend, once a red-light district and part of the 19th-century slum neighborhood known as Five Points. ◆ Bounded by Mulberry, Baxter, Worth, and Bayard Sts

3 Thailand Restaurant ★★$$ Some of the best and least expensive Thai food Chinatown has to offer is served here. All of the dishes are reliable, but a specialty is koong kratiam (garlic shrimp and peppers). Vegetarian dishes are also available. ◆ Thai ◆ Daily lunch and dinner. 106 Bayard St (at Baxter St). 349.3132 ఉ

4 Shanghai Cuisine Restaurant ★★$ A relative newcomer that caters to the City Hall crowd, this place offers inexpensive lunch specials. The dinner menu is a bit more exotic, featuring soup dumplings, braised pork in brown sauce, and other Shanghai specialties. ◆ Shanghainese ◆ Daily lunch and dinner. 89-91 Bayard St (at Mulberry St). 732.8988

5 Museum of Chinese in the Americas Begin your visit to Chinatown by exploring this small museum founded in 1980, or join one of their walking tours, organized for groups of 20 or more. The museum houses the nation's largest research collection of oral histories, photographs, and artifacts relating

to the Chinese-American experience.
♦ Nominal admission. Tu-Sa noon-5PM. 70 Mulberry St (at Bayard St). 619.4785

6 Bo Ky Restaurant ★$ The specialty of this popular restaurant, owned by ethnic Chinese Chaozhou people from Vietnam, are the big bowls of steaming hot rice noodles topped with shrimp, fish, shrimp balls, or sliced roasted duck. ♦ Vietnamese ♦ Daily breakfast, lunch, and dinner. No credit cards accepted. 80 Bayard St (between Mott and Mulberry Sts). 406.2292

7 Mandarin Court ★★$ Sisters Kitty and Carol Chan from Hong Kong offer such well-prepared dishes as shrimp baked with spicy salt, clams with black-bean sauce, and pork chops Hong Kong–style. Dim sum is especially good and served without the bustle of larger nearby dim sum palaces. ♦ Hong Kong ♦ Daily breakfast, lunch, and dinner. 61 Mott St (between Bayard and Canal Sts). 608.3838

8 Tai Hong Lau ★$ This is a great place for authentic and inexpensive Cantonese cooking. Try the Winter Melon Treasure, a curved piece of white melon atop a mixture of mushrooms, roasted duck, chicken, pork, and shrimp, surrounded by broccoli florets. The baby clams with lettuce leaves are good, too. ♦ Cantonese ♦ Daily breakfast, lunch, and dinner. 70 Mott St (between Bayard and Canal Sts). 219.1431

8 Eastern States Buddhist Temple of America, Inc. The sparkling gold mountain of Buddhas in the window beckons you into this temple with more than a hundred statues of Buddhas and other religious articles in the back. Neighborhood worshipers come here to pay their respects and light incense. ♦ Daily. 64 Mott St (between Bayard and Canal Sts). 966.4753 ♿

9 Lung Fong Bakery Most of the beautiful sweets offered here, like black-bean doughnuts, are acquired tastes, and this is the best bakery in Chinatown to start garnering them. For the less adventurous, the huge, meltingly good almond and walnut cookies are a sure bet. ♦ Daily. 41 Mott St (between Mosco and Bayard Sts). 233.7447 ♿

10 Hunan Garden ★★$ The large and interesting menu at this friendly restaurant features spicy Hunan specialties and other Chinese favorites, among them Peking duck, spicy lobster in Hunan sauce, and sautéed chicken and shrimp in a taro "bird's nest." ♦ Hunan/Cantonese ♦ Daily lunch and dinner. 1 Mott St (at Worth St). 732.7270 ♿

11 20 Mott Street ★★$ This is as close to the Hong Kong dining experience as you'll find in New York. Specialties include baked conch stuffed in its own shell, fried squab, and salt-baked shrimp. The dim sum is among the best in the neighborhood. ♦ Cantonese ♦ Daily

breakfast, lunch, and dinner. 20 Mott St (between Park Row and Pell St). 964.0380

11 Peking Duck House ★★$ As the name suggests, this is the place to come for Peking duck. The thoroughly crisped delicacy is carved tableside in what is called home-style (with the flesh clinging to the skin), rather than the usual banquet style (skin only), and is served with traditional accompaniments: thin pancakes in which to roll the duck, slivered cucumbers, and a scallion brush to swab the duck with hoisin sauce. Also great as an appetizer, one order serves six hearty diners. Or get steamed pork dumplings to munch on while you wait. ♦ Beijing/Szechuan ♦ Daily lunch and dinner. 22 Mott St (between Park Row and Pell St). 227.1810

12 Nam Wah Tea Parlor ★$ After 78 years, this is the oldest and most colorful Hong Kong dim sum parlor in the area. The lure here is the funky atmosphere rather than the food, which is not as good as at other restaurants in Chinatown. ♦ Dim sum ♦ Daily breakfast, lunch, and early dinner. No credit cards accepted. 13 Doyers St (between Bowery and Pell St). 962.6047

12 Vietnam ★★★$ Chef/owner Minh Ly offers diners over 200 menu choices including *cha gio* (Vietnamese spring roll), *mon canh* (soups), *do bien* (seafood dishes), and beef or chicken with lemongrass. Wash it all down with Hue beer from Hue City, the ancient capital of Vietnam. ♦ Vietnamese ♦ Daily lunch and dinner. 11 Doyers St (between Bowery and Pell St). 693.0725

13 Edward Mooney House Built in 1789, the oldest Federal-style house in Manhattan was modified in 1971 to become a busy branch of the New York Off-Track Betting Corp., which has since moved on to larger quarters. The building is now occupied by a mortgage bank. ♦ 18 Bowery (at Pell St)

14 Chatham Square The monument in the center of the square is the Kim Lau Memorial, designed by Poy G. Lee in 1962 and dedicated to Chinese-American war dead. ♦ Park Row (at Bowery)

15 Mariners' Temple Designed in 1842 by **Minard Lafever,** this brownstone Greek temple was originally called the **Oliver Street Church** and served sailors based at the nearby East River piers. It is now a Baptist church whose worshipers include a widely varied community. ♦ 12 Oliver St (at Henry St). 233.0423

Bagels, from the Yiddish word *beygel*, are traditional Jewish rolls made from a yeast-based dough in the shape of a doughnut. Label Vishinsky, inventor of an early automatic bagel maker, claimed that the first New York bagel emerged from 15 Clinton Street in 1896.

16 First Shearith Israel Cemetery Located near Chatham Square, which it once covered, this is the surviving fragment of the Congregation Shearith Israel's first burial ground (there are two more), the oldest Jewish cemetery in Manhattan. The earliest gravestone is dated 1683. Shearith Israel was founded by early Portuguese and Spanish settlers in 1654 and is now located uptown at a synagogue on Central Park West. ♦ 55 St. James Pl (between James and Oliver Sts)

17 St. James Roman Catholic Church This Greek Revival–style church built in 1837 is an interesting neighbor to the nearby **Mariners' Temple**; both were designed by **Minard Lafever.** ♦ 32 James St (between Madison St and St. James Pl). 223.0161

18 William Clark House Originally built in 1824, this house—and especially the entrance—would appear to epitomize all the elegance of the Federal style. But there is a twist: It is one of the few known to have four floors (two or three were preferred). ♦ 51 Market St (between Monroe and Madison Sts)

19 Long Shine Restaurant ★★$ The cuisine here is Fujianese, a more recent import from one of China's southern provinces, and well worth trying. Don't miss the soups, particularly the savory fish *mein* soup, with shredded pork, shrimp, and Chinese cabbage. For those who want more traditional fare, there's also an extensive Cantonese menu. ♦ Fujianese/Cantonese ♦ M-Sa breakfast, lunch, and dinner; Su dinner. No credit cards accepted. 47 E Broadway (between Market and Catherine Sts). 346.9888 ⅃

THE NICE RESTAURANT
麗 晶 大 酒 樓
紐約華埠東百老滙大道三十五號

20 Nice Restaurant ★★$ One of Chinatown's better Cantonese restaurants, this place serves excellent barbecued duck and minced squab wrapped in lettuce leaves. For dessert, try the cold melon and tapioca. ♦ Cantonese ♦ Daily breakfast, lunch, and dinner. 18 E Broadway (at Catherine St), Second floor. 941.0911 ⅃

21 Golden Unicorn ★★★$$ This place is decorated in sleek black and peach with mirrors everywhere. Always bustling, it is popular with families who come to sample the amazing variety of dim sum, so be sure to arrive early. Dinner is equally good, and interestingly enough, the nonspicy dishes are better than the hot ones. Start with tasty fried dumplings, then move on to egg foo yong,

salt-baked shrimp, and chicken with black-pepper sauce. ♦ Cantonese ♦ Daily breakfast, lunch, and dinner. 18 E Broadway (at Catherine St), Second floor. 941.0911 ⅃

22 Triple 8 Palace Restaurant ★$$ It helps to be Chinese in this large, garish restaurant—the staff can be a bit surly to outsiders. If you can get your waiter's attention, try the steamed dumplings, fresh oyster pancakes, moist and tender soy chicken and abalone, and vegetable soups. Hordes of workers stop by at lunch, and it's crowded on weekends as well. ♦ Hong Kong ♦ Daily breakfast, lunch, and dinner. 88 E Broadway, Top floor (under the Manhattan Bridge). 941.8886

23 Canton ★★$$ Have the owner, Eileen, order for you at this favorite, upscale restaurant that attracts celebrities, including architect **I.M. Pei.** Special dishes on the fairly small menu include squab wrapped in lettuce. ♦ Cantonese ♦ W-Su lunch and dinner. No credit cards accepted. 45 Division St (between Market St and Bowery). 226.4441

24 Great Shanghai ★★$ This restaurant has been here forever—though you wouldn't guess it from the modern pink, gray, and neon decor—and the food remains pure Chinatown. Recommended are the steamed vegetable dumplings and the prawns in ginger sauce with carrots and scallions. ♦ Shanghainese ♦ Daily lunch and dinner. 27 Division St (between Market St and Bowery). 966.7663

25 N.Y. Noodletown ★★$ Ever since the *New York Times* rhapsodized about the salt-baked crabs here, it's been virtually impossible to get a seat—which is not to imply that it was easy to get one before. The noodles with beef are deservedly popular, as are the various crisp roasted meats—such as the pig—and the soft-shell crabs in season. ♦ Cantonese ♦ Daily breakfast, lunch, dinner, and late-night meals. No credit cards accepted. 28 Bowery (at Bayard St). 349.0923

26 Confucius Plaza Designed in 1976 by **Horowitz & Chun** and at odds with its smaller 19th-century neighbors, this huge, chunky building solves a pressing need for more living space. It also houses a public school whose population is almost entirely first- and second-generation Chinese. ♦ Bowery (between Division St and the Manhattan Bridge)

27 New Good Taste ★★★$$ Sushi and sashimi have recently become something of a fad in New York's Chinese community, and although this dining spot serves predominantly Chinese food, its sushi and tempura are very palatable, along with a few Japanese appetizers that aren't half bad. Dinnertime is busy but the friendly staff does its best to accommodate everyone. The spicy duck in noodles is a favorite. ♦ Cantonese ♦ Daily lunch and dinner. 65 Bayard St (between Bowery and Mott St). 928.6890 ⅃

28 Oriental Garden Seafood ★★$$ Don't be surprised: The staff often seats strangers together at one table to accommodate the crowds, which seem to be ever-present. But the seafood, particularly the golden walnut prawns, is good enough to make diners forget the feeling of being packed in like sardines. ◆ Cantonese/Seafood ◆ Daily breakfast, lunch, and dinner. 14 Elizabeth St (between Bayard and Canal Sts). 619.0085 &

28 Lin's Sister Associates Corp. Herbs, vitamins, and various traditional medicines are carried in this drugstore. If you're feeling poorly, stop in for a detailed consultation and prescription from an herbalist, who might recommend a tea, capsules, or a poultice. ◆ Daily. 18A Elizabeth St (between Bayard and Canal Sts). 962.8083. Also at: 4 Bowery (between Doyers and Pell Sts). 962.5417

28 Jing Fong ★★$$ This place is a combination of every Chinese restaurant you've ever been to, replete with lanterns, lions on pedestals, fan-shaped windows, and dragons. The food is excellent and beautifully presented. Try the baked chicken with garlic, the paper-thin beef with Mongolian hot pot, and the baked pork chops with black beans. ◆ Cantonese ◆ Daily breakfast, lunch, and dinner. 20 Elizabeth St (between Bayard and Canal Sts). 964.5256 &

29 Silver Palace ★★$$ Some of the best dim sum in the city is served in this bustling dining room. Regulars get preference when the line grows long, especially on Sunday. Popular choices include shrimp rolls, steamed dumplings, and sweet buns. ◆ Dim sum ◆ Daily breakfast, lunch, and dinner. 50 Bowery (between Bayard and Canal Sts). 964.1204

29 Hee Seung Fung (HSF) ★$$ Long lines are common here because these folks are especially welcoming to Westerners. It's easier than usual to order dim sum here, as the restaurant offers a photographic guide to the 75 available varieties. The *ha gow* (steamed shrimp dumpling) is always a winner. A full menu is offered at dinner but isn't especially recommended; the Chinese community flocks here at night for steamboat—a huge array of immaculately fresh seafood, meats, vegetables, beancurd, and rice noodles that you cook for yourself in a wokful of boiling water at your table, flanked by a variety of dipping sauces. ◆ Dim sum ◆ Daily breakfast, lunch, and dinner. 46 Bowery (between Bayard and Canal Sts). 374.1319

30 Manhattan Bridge The elaborate approach to the bridge from Canal Street is a shadow of its former self, but the quality still shows. Originally known as the **Court of Honor,** the bridge—a 1905 work by **Gustav Lindenthal**—was designed so that vehicles would pass under a triumphal arch designed by **Carrère &**

Hastings. Brooklyn-bound streetcars were forced to go around the arch, and the subway was hidden underneath it. The Daniel Chester French sculptures (representing Manhattan and Brooklyn) that flanked the arch were moved to the front of the **Brooklyn Museum** in 1963. ◆ Between Flatbush Ave Ext, Brooklyn and Canal St

31 Eldridge Street Synagogue The congregation of K'hal Adath Jeshurun Anshe Lubz built this as the first Orthodox synagogue in the area at a time when other congregations were transforming Christian churches for their own use. Constructed in grand scale in 1887 by **Herter Bros.,** the main sanctuary was an opulent room with brass chandeliers and an ark imported from Italy. The building fell into disrepair—although the congregation has never missed a Sabbath—and is currently being restored to its original splendor by the Eldridge Street Project, which offers tours of the building, now a National Historic Landmark with a center for the celebration of American Jewish history. Comedian Eddie Cantor spent his boyhood in a building across the street (he answered to the name Edward Iskowitz back then). ◆ Admission for tours. Tours: Tu, Th 11:30AM, 2:30PM; Su 11AM-4PM. 12 Eldridge St (between Forsyth and Canal Sts). 219.0888

32 Harry Zarin Co. Fabric Warehouse Decorator fabrics at super prices are sold at this second-floor source—everything from opulent silk brocades to mattress ticking. This is one of the few spots in the area open on Saturday. ◆ Daily. 72 Allen St (at Grand St). 226.3492 &

32 Fishkin Women's sportswear by Adrienne Vittadini and Liz Claiborne, sweaters by Pringle, handsome boots and shoes by Via Spiga and Nickels, and silk and cashmere are sold at a 20-percent discount. ◆ M-F, Su. 314 Grand St (at Allen St). 226.6538

33 Leslie's Originals This is the place for fashionable footwear at a 30-percent (or more!) discount. Women's shoes include sandals, espadrilles, pumps, and quality leather shoes and boots, depending on the season. The men's stock includes loafers, wingtips, and sport shoes. ◆ M-F, Su. 319 Grand St (between Orchard and Allen Sts). 431.9196

41

34 A.W. Kaufman Luxurious lingerie from a variety of designers, including Christian Dior, Mary McFadden, and Lejaby, are packed into this narrow shop, along with imports from Belgium and Switzerland. ♦ M-F, Su. 73 Orchard St (between Grand and Broome Sts). 226.1629

35 Seward Park Two blocks of tenement buildings were removed in 1900 to make way for this three-acre breathing space (named for William H. Seward, who was governor of New York, a US senator, and Lincoln's secretary of state). In its early days, the park was a gathering place for immigrants looking for daily work. The southern and western edges are the site of a regular Sunday flea market, during which elderly people sell tchotchkes (knickknacks). The prices are good, and the bargaining is entertaining in itself. ♦ Canal and Essex Sts

36 Educational Alliance Built in 1891 by **Arnold W. Brunner,** this is the United States's first settlement house, founded in 1889 by so-called "uptown Jews," who felt an obligation to help fellow Jews in the downtown ghetto and to stem possible anti-Semitism. It held classes to Americanize youngsters, provided exercise and bathing facilities, and gave assistance to women whose husbands had deserted them, which was common among immigrant families. Among the young people the organization served was Arthur Murray, who learned how to dance here. ♦ 197 E Broadway (at Jefferson St)

37 Ritualarium In 1904, the former **Arnold Toynbee Hall** of the Young Men's Benevolent Association was converted to a mikvah, a ritual bath for Orthodox Jewish women, who are required to attend in preparation for marriage and on a monthly basis after that. Because the Scriptures command that the water be pure, rainwater is collected in cisterns. ♦ Tours given by appointment. For information call Mrs. Bormiko (674.5318). 313 E Broadway (at Grand St). 475.8514

38 Abrons Arts Center This complex for the performing and visual arts, built by **Prentice and Chan, Ohlhausen** in 1975, is part of the Henry Street Settlement, a social service agency that has operated on the Lower East Side since 1893. Its programs include arts workshops, professional performances, and exhibitions—all meant to help participants develop self-expression through the arts and an appreciation of the cultural diversity of New York City. The complex contains three theaters: the **Recital Hall,** the **Experimental Theater,** and the **Harry DeJur Playhouse.** ♦ 466 Grand St (between Willett and Pitt Sts). 598.0400 ♿

39 Bialystoker Synagogue Built in 1826 as the **Willett Street Methodist Episcopal Church,** it was purchased by the Congregation Anshei Bialystok in 1905 and is the oldest

structure housing a synagogue in New York. ♦ 7 Willett St (between Grand and Delancey Sts). 475.0165

40 Williamsburg Bridge Built in 1903 by **Leffert L. Buck,** this is the second bridge to span the East River. Its construction changed Williamsburg in Brooklyn from a resort area to a new home for immigrants from the Lower East Side. The bridge is unusual in that there are no cables on the land side of the steel towers, robbing it of some of the soaring grace of a full suspension span. ♦ Between Broadway, Brooklyn and Delancey St

41 Ratner's ★$$ Its glory days behind, this New York institution is now more a cultural, rather than a gustatory, destination. A traditional dairy restaurant, all the standard Jewish dairy dishes are served here. It's best, however, to soak in the *Yiddishkeit* over a bowl of soup, a plate of panfried blintzes (with pot-cheese or potato filling), or the deep-fried pierogi. ♦ Eastern European/Jewish ♦ M-Th, Su breakfast, lunch, and dinner; F breakfast and lunch; Sa dinner. 138 Delancey St (between Suffolk and Norfolk Sts). 677.5588

42 Streit's Matzoth Company This is the only Manhattan producer of the unleavened bread used during Passover. Watch the huge sheets of matzos as they pass by the window on conveyor belts, and buy some samples on your way out. ♦ M-F, Su. 150 Rivington St (at Suffolk St). 475.7000

43 Tonic Formerly the **Kedem Kosher Wine Factory,** this oddly-shaped, loft-like performance space was recently turned into one of the Lower East Side's hottest new spots to hear live music, mostly of the alternative and experimental variety. Currently expanding their schedule to include a New Music Series, a Sunday Night Songwriters Circle, and Monday night movies, what has put **Tonic** on the map is not their evening shows, but their Klezmer Sunday Brunch series, curated by former Klezmatics clarinetist David Krakauer. Playing to standing-room only crowds, bands like Eve Sicular's critically-acclaimed Metropolitan Klezmer draw audiences that include everyone from eighteen-year-old pierced punk-rockers, to lesbian and gay families, to older Jewish and non-Jewish couples. There's a full bar on the first floor, so arrive half an hour before show time to secure a seat; then grab a bagel with whitefish salad from the bar before the show starts. A peek into the basement during intermission is worth the look: the old floor-to-ceiling wine casks still stand, like ghosts from another time. ♦ Cover. Hours vary for shows;

call in advance. 107 Norfolk St (between Delancey and Rivington Sts). 358.7501; www.tonic107.com

44 Schapiro's House of Kosher and Sacramental Wines Take a tour of the only winery still operating in the city. Wines are also available for purchase here. ♦ Nominal fee. M-F by appointment only; Su 11AM-4PM. 126 Rivington St (between Norfolk and Essex Sts). 674.4404

45 Economy Candy Company People with a longing for old-fashioned penny candy will find it in this store, which has been selling candy of all kinds, as well as dried fruits, nuts, coffees, teas, and other delicacies, since 1937. Though the prices are good, a penny just doesn't go as far as it used to. Be sure to ask for the mail-order catalog. ♦ Daily. 108 Rivington St (between Essex and Ludlow Sts). 254.1832 ♿

46 Orchard Street The old pushcarts are gone, but bargain hunters still flock to this street, a seething indoor-outdoor bazaar of discount dresses, coats, shoes, linens, fabrics, and accessories. More than 300 stores line this and surrounding thoroughfares from East Houston to Canal Streets on the Lower East Side. On Sunday, many of the streets are closed to traffic, and the latest from Ralph Lauren to Christian Dior is hawked from the sidewalks. These are mostly Hong Kong–produced knock-offs. The stores carry a wide array of well-known and secondary lines of discounted fashion. This kind of shopping is not for the faint of heart, but if you go prepared for the rough and tumble of bartering and remember that not all stores take credit cards or have gracious salespeople, you can turn up some jewels among the schlock—and have fun, too. Go during the week if you can. Sunday is insane, and many stores close early on Friday and all day Saturday. ♦ From Canal to E Houston Sts

46 Beckenstein Discounted home furnishing fabrics are sold here, though this old-time family name is best known for the enormous and excellent collection of men's fabrics across the street, including shirting of pure cotton, cashmere, mohair, and fine wools—most discounted 15 percent. ♦ M-F, Su. 130 Orchard St (between Delancey and Rivington Sts). 475.4887. Also at: 125 Orchard St (between Delancey and Rivington Sts). 475.7575 ♿

47 Lower East Side Tenement Museum This small, fascinating museum—now a National Historic Landmark—is visited predominantly by the curious descendants of immigrants who fled to the US at the end of the 19th and beginning of the 20th centuries. The grim reality of the appalling hardships they faced is palpable here, where visitors on guided tours see cramped living spaces in recreated tenement apartments and learn about the lives of actual residents: the Gumpertz family, German Jews of 1878; the Confino family, Sephardic Jews of 1916; and the Baldizzi family, Italian Catholics of 1935. Imaginative programs that focus on all facets of the immigrant experience include one-hour weekend walking tours of the historic Lower East Side, photographic and art exhibits, media presentations, dramatic readings from immigrant literature, plays, films, and lectures. ♦ Nominal admission. Tu-F, Su. 97 Orchard St (between Broome and Delancey Sts). 431.0233

48 Fine & Klein An extensive collection of high-end handbags, briefcases, and accessories includes the latest from Carlos Falchi, Enny, and Lisette (sometimes Valentino and Givenchy, too). You'll find good discounts and gracious service at this Orchard Street institution. Upstairs at **Lea's** (677.7637) enjoy a 30-percent discount on women's clothing from such designers as Albert Nippon and Louis Féraud. ♦ M-F, Su. 119 Orchard St (between Delancey and Rivington Sts). 674.6720

GISELLE SPORTSWEAR

49 Giselle Sportswear Better American sportswear for women, including warm, woolly alpaca jackets and soft leather jackets and pants, is sold at 25 percent off. ♦ M-F, Su. 143 Orchard St (between Delancey and Rivington Sts). 673.1900

49 Anna Z High-fashion European clothing for women includes designs by Bill Kaiserman and Malisy Gilbert Basson at 20 percent off retail. ♦ M-F, Su. 143½ Orchard St (at Rivington St). 533.1361

One man's junk is another man's treasure, and you can find examples of both along Canal Street between Broadway and Sixth Avenue. The selections range from used clothing to seemingly useless pieces of electronic equipment, plumbing supplies, and other assorted gadgets and hardware. It costs nothing to look, and very little to buy the myriad (possibly) fascinating things you see here. The street was originally a wide drainage ditch carrying polluted water from the Collect Pond (eventually filled to become the Foley Square area) over to the Hudson River. Citizen complaints about the stench and the mosquito problem led to the filling of the ditch—which the city preferred to call a canal—in 1820.

49 Tobaldi European high-fashion men's clothes are discounted 20 percent. Merchandise includes tweed jackets, leather jackets, pure cotton shirts, silk ties, and bikini underwear. ◆ M-F, Su. 83 Rivington St (at Orchard St). 260.4330

50 Congregation Adath Jeshurun of Jassy Synagogue This 1903 building was also the home of the First Warsaw Congregation. Now abandoned, it still projects a rich and distinctive image with its collage of architectural styles. ◆ 58-60 Rivington St (between Allen and Eldridge Sts)

51 The Hat/El Sombrero $ You won't find the best Mexican food here, but this popular neighborhood eatery has its defenders. Try the *nachos tradicionales* (topped with beef, beans, cheese, and salsa), wash it down with a margarita, and soak in the local color. ◆ Mexican ◆ Daily lunch and dinner. No credit cards accepted. 108 Stanton St (at Ludlow St). 254.4188

52 Katz's Delicatessen ★★$ This well-known delicatessen was made even more famous by the memorably orgasmic deli scene shot for the 1989 movie, *When Harry Met Sally.* Sit at a table and enjoy the whole experience, but only if you're not in a hurry. While you wait, take in the old advertising signs hanging from the ceiling, including the famous "Send a Salami to your Boy in the Army." For the pinnacle of Jewish deli food, try the delectable hot pastrami piled high on thin-sliced rye bread; Specials (oversized hotdogs served with beans); a side of kosher pickles; and wash it all down with a can of Dr. Brown's Cream Soda or Celery Tonic. ◆ Deli ◆ Daily breakfast, lunch, and dinner. No credit cards accepted. 205 E Houston St (at Ludlow St). 254.2246 &

53 Russ & Daughters A shopping mecca for serious connoisseurs of bagels and lox with a schmear of cream cheese, this establishment is also not bad for take-out golden smoked whitefish, sweet pickled herring, salads, dried fruits, nuts, and other items that belong to a category of food some native New Yorkers call "appetizing." ◆ Daily. 179 E Houston St (between Orchard and Allen Sts). 475.4880 &

54 Idlewild Here's a retro bar with a twist: It resembles the inside of a chic 1960s jet. Cool as the concept is, this place can get plenty crowded on board. Those lucky enough to check in early have a better chance of nabbing one of the 24 airplane seats in the "nose." ◆ Tu-Su from 8PM. 145 E Houston St (between Forsyth and Eldridge Sts). 477.5005 &

55 Yonah Schimmel ★$ Jewish specialties, including 12 varieties of their legendary knishes, clabbered milk (yogurt), and borscht have been dished up in this old downtown storefront since the turn of the century. ◆ Eastern European/Jewish ◆ M-F, Su breakfast, lunch, and early dinner. 137 E Houston St (at Forsyth St). 477.2858

56 Puck Building The Romanesque Revival building (pictured at left) reflects the influence of the Chicago School in its bold and vibrant use of brickwork. It was once the home of the humor magazine, Puck, whose spirit remains in the two larger-than-life statues perched on third-floor ledges at the northeast corner. The interior of this great building, constructed in 1885 to the designs of **Albert Wagner,** has been renovated as commercial condominium for art galleries, workshops, and design offices. The opulent rooms are also rented out for weddings and other celebrations. ◆ 295 Lafayette St (at E Houston St). 274.8900 &

57 Urban Archaeology Owner Gil Shapiro has moved his seemingly infinite collection of architectural ornaments and artifacts, display cases, lighting fixtures, and more into the immense quarters of a four-story former candy factory. Interior designer Judith Stockman revamped all 50,000 square feet, a process that included sandblasting candy off the walls. Two lovely skylit areas show off cast-iron furniture and garden accessories. The stock is sold wholesale and retail. ◆ M-Sa. 285 Lafayette St (between Prince and Jersey Sts). 431.6969. Also at: 143 Franklin St (between Varick and Hudson Sts). 431.4646

Puck Building

MICHAEL STORRINGS

58 Do Kham Sold here are clothing, jewelry, and accessories from Tibet and elsewhere in the Himalayas, some designed by the amiable store owner, Phelgye Kelden, a former Tibetan monk. Check out his chic fake and genuine fur hats. ♦ Daily. 51 Prince St (between Mulberry and Lafayette Sts). 966.2404

59 Old St. Patrick's Cathedral When the new cathedral at Fifth Avenue and 50th Street was consecrated in 1879, this became a Roman Catholic parish church serving a predominantly Irish neighborhood. Originally built by **Joseph Mangin** in 1815, it was New York's first Gothic Revival building. The church was restored in 1868 by **Henry Engelbert** after its historic facade was badly damaged in an 1866 fire. ♦ 264 Mulberry St (between Prince and E Houston Sts). 226.8075

60 Old St. Patrick's Convent and Girls' School Built in 1826, the beautiful Federal doorway framed with Corinthian columns makes this unusually large Federal-style building a treasure. ♦ 32 Prince St (at Mott St)

61 Just Shades In stock are window shades made of string, parchment, rice paper, silk, and burlap; others can be custom-ordered. ♦ M-Tu, Th-Su. 21 Spring St (between Elizabeth and Mott Sts). 966.2757

Star Discoveries

New York's attractions make it a glittering magnet for the rich and famous, and with more films than ever being made in the city, star-struck visitors are likely to strike it rich here. Celebrities—many of whom have residences in town—don't only shop at **Armani** and dine at **Le Cirque 2000,** they also browse the museums and art galleries, soak up ballet and opera, go to jazz clubs and Broadway shows, and jog in **Central Park**. In fact, one of the charming aspects of New York City life is that you might unexpectedly glimpse a famous face almost anywhere—Paul Newman dining at a local Upper East Side restaurant, **Sarabeth's**; Liza Minelli chatting outside the General Motors Building on Fifth Avenue; Patricia Neal buying supplies at her local stationery store on York Avenue; John Malkovitch shopping at **Fairway** market on the West Side; and former New York City major John V. Lindsay waiting for a subway train at **Grand Central**.

Here are some of the best sites for celebrity sightings. Note that New Yorkers are fairly low-key when they come face-to-face with a well-known personality—a quick, appreciative glance is the sophisticated response.

Morgans, Royalton, and **Paramount Hotels** are favorites of the hip and famous. The **Royalton's 44** restaurant draws top publishing types at lunch. Stevie Wonder has been known to entertain evening guests with an impromptu concert. Across the street, the venerable **Algonquin** appeals to British actors and followers of cabaret. The **Oak Room** remains one of the city's best rooms to see and hear top-flight singers. When Julie Wilson or Andrea Marcovicci are in the spotlight, the audience will probably be star-studded, too.

The **Four Seasons** is the hottest haven for show business on parade. It's not unusual to see actor Tommy Lee Jones running between the bar and the public pay phones in the lobby on the same night you might catch a glimpse of a Spice Girl refusing to give an autograph.

The **Regency** has long been the favorite breakfast place of powerful business moguls. And in 1997, it gained national notoriety as Frank Gifford's scene of marital infidelity. Other stars, like Harrison Ford, praise the hotel's more family value–oriented perks—like the in-house laundry that is willing to do diapers.

Venerable theater district restaurants such as **Sardi's** and **Gallagher's** are often where many opening-night parties take place. And it's possible to catch a famous actor or actress eating a pre- or post-performance dinner at these spots or others in the neighborhood.

Restaurants near **Carnegie Hall** and **Lincoln Center** are good bets for the same reason. Reserve early or late for the best chance to catch a dining diva.

SoHo and **TriBeCa** are popular neighborhoods with night owls from the worlds of entertainment and fashion. The later the closings, the more daring the behavior of stars like Drew Barrymore and Brad Pitt. And where there's a piano to be played or a microphone to be held, Billy Joel and Liza Minnelli might just take up the cause.

Elaine's (Upper East Side) celebrity cachet means you'll probably be unable to get a table in the front room—the place to be—unless you're someone notable yourself. Nurse a beer at the bar and act cool; usually someone interesting and familiar, such as Woody Allen, will show up.

If you jog or racewalk around the **Reservoir** in **Central Park**, you might find yourself in step with Madonna. A number of show business folks and their families live uptown, and when the weather is good, they come out to play with their kids and walk their dogs.

When Broadway actors take the night off, many of them spend it checking out the competition. If you spring for orchestra seats, your fellow *Playbill* reader might be someone you'll be seeing on the other side of the footlights the next night. Off-Broadway is even trendier. Established rockers often drop in at less pricey venues to see what their next chart challenger might sound like. Comedy clubs, though not as numerous as they were a decade ago, are also people watching places. Even Janeane Garofalo has been known to stop in for a few laughs.

Klezmer: More than Just a Shtetl of Mind

Klezmer, an amalgamation of stirring traditional Jewish music from Eastern Europe (Poland, Hungary, the Ukraine, Russia), also includes strains of Middle Eastern, Greek, Balkan, and North African musical influence. Arising originally in the shtetls (the small, Jewish-populated rural towns that spotted the countryside around cities like L'vov and Czernowitz), klezmer found its way to Manhattan's Lower East Side in the early 1900s; there the brilliant clarinetists Dave Tarras and Naftule Brandwein did much to remind homesick Jewish residents of the family and towns they left behind. The music has recently seen a major revival, oddly among the young, hip, downtown New York jazz-loving music fans who cram into darkened clubs like **Tonic** (see page 42) to hear music that was arranged nearly a century ago.

Instantly recognizable by the whine of the soprano clarinet, the accordion, the violin, and the trumpet, klezmer has often been referred to as Jewish bluegrass—it is so foot-stompingly fun that not even the most conservative music fan will be able to sit still while listening to it. Some of klezmer's popular contemporary bands include Andy Statman's Klezmer Orchestra (with legendary bluegrass/jazz mandolinist David Grisman often sitting in); and the Klezmatics, whose more modern take on the style has led them to the stage of the **Brooklyn Academy of Music,** among other well-known halls.

However, for a taste of more traditional klezmer, one must either listen to the pre–World War II recordings of the great clarinetist Naftule Brandwein; or the contemporary New York–based band, Metropolitan Klezmer, whose talented bandleader, arranger, and drummer, Eve Sicular, has assembled some of the finest classical- and jazz- trained musicians to play this historical music including young twentysomething violinist and cutting-edge composer Harris Wulfson, and Ishmail Butera, the latter of whom lends a decidedly Balkan influence to the tunes. When asked what it is that makes klezmer music so popular in this day and age, lifetime New Yorker, klezmer fan extraordinaire and expert on *Yiddishkeit* Shmuel ben Tzvi replied, "Klezmer is like borscht: there's a little of everything mixed in; nothing clashes, nothing fights. Klezmer is deliciously fun, musically sophisticated, ethnically rich, and everyone has a good time."

62 Off SoHo Suites $$ The 38 suites are large and tastefully furnished, and the prices are rock bottom. What's the snag? This isn't exactly Park Avenue, and the 10 least expensive suites share a bath and kitchen. But very few others are recommended in this area east of SoHo (hence the name), with easy access to all mass transit. Most suites have color TV, marble bathtubs, air-conditioning, a gourmet eat-in kitchen, and access to a fitness center. ♦ 11 Rivington St (between Chrystie St and Bowery). 979.9808, 800/633.7646; fax 979.9801

63 Sammy's Famous Roumanian Jewish Steakhouse ★★$$ People laugh, talk, kibbitz (joke), and hug all night long (when they're not grabbing the mike for an impromptu comedy set) at this New York institution. For a main course, try the Roumanian tenderloin steak, fried breaded veal chop, or boiled beef with mushroom-barley gravy. Mashed potatoes with fried onions, and kasha *varnishkes* (buckwheat groats with bow-tie macaroni) are old standards to order on the side. The food is authentically rich; enjoy it with an egg cream, the classic New York *digestif*. But don't drink what's in the pitcher that stands on every table: it's schmaltz—rendered chicken fat—meant to be poured onto their fabulous chopped liver, or spread on challah instead of butter, and guaranteed to harden your arteries even as you look at it. ♦ Eastern European/Jewish ♦ Daily dinner; entertainment nightly. Reservations required. 157 Chrystie St (between Delancey and Rivington Sts). 673.0330

64 Mazer Store Equipment Co. Mimi Sheraton, Lauren Bacall, and Stockard Channing shop here for their restaurant-quality Garland stoves, which come with porcelain-coated oven walls, back, and roof. Service is what distinguishes this store from others of its kind. ♦ M-F. 207 Bowery (between Delancey and Rivington Sts). 674.3450

65 New York Gas Lighting Company This lighting store, one of the many concentrated in this neighborhood, takes its name from its authentic open-flame gaslights. It also offers an array of handsome fixtures, including opalescent chandeliers from the Czech Republic, lamps made from antique ginger jars, and the Hunter wood ceiling fan. ♦ Daily 145 Bowery (between Grand and Broome Sts). 226.2840 &

66 Greenpoint Bank The 1894 building designed by **McKim, Mead & White** is the former **Bowery Savings Bank.** Outside, the Roman columns attached to a Renaissance facade are somehow apropos on the edge of Little Italy. Inside, take a look at the opulent detailing. ♦ M-Th 9AM-3PM; F; Sa 9AM-noon. 130 Bowery (between Grand and Broome Sts)

67 Road to Mandalay ★★$$ All the food is good, but the noodle dishes are special. Don't miss the shrimp fritters and the grilled tiger prawns in lemongrass sauce. ♦ Thai/Burmese ♦ M-F dinner; Sa-Su lunch and dinner. 380 Broome St (between Mott and Mulberry Sts). 226.4218

68 Caffè Roma ★$ Knowledgeable New Yorkers favor this lovely Old World bakery over all others. No redecorating was ever necessary to make this place look authentic—it just is. The cannoli, whether plain or dipped in chocolate, are perfect. ♦ Bakery/Cafe ♦ Daily. No credit cards accepted. 385 Broome St (at Mulberry St). 226.8413

69 Grotta Azzurra ★★$$ Another downtown dining institution, this eatery features food that is, if not extraordinary, familiar and consistent. The meat and poultry dishes, like chicken cacciatore, are more tastily prepared than the seafood selections. The portions are ample, and dining in the cavernous environs is fun. ♦ Neapolitan ♦ Tu-Su lunch and dinner. No credit cards accepted. 387 Broome St (at Mulberry St). 925.8775

70 The Police Building A commanding presence with an imposing dome as a symbol of authority, this 1909 building by **Hoppin & Koen** was the main headquarters of the New York City Police Department for nearly 65 years. The new copper dome was crafted by French artisans brought here to restore the Statue of Liberty's copper flame, and the 1988 restoration was the work of **Ehrenkrantz Eckstut & Kuhn Architects.** The interior, by dePolo/Dunbar, has been converted into 55 cooperative apartments. ♦ 240 Centre St (between Grand and Broome Sts)

71 Italian Food Center The De Mattia family has run this one-stop shopping emporium—filled with domestic and imported Italian foodstuffs—for nearly 30 years, to the great delight of Italophiles. More than a dozen kinds of breads are baked on the premises daily, and the vast array of Italian cold cuts is mouth-watering. Try the New York Special hero sandwich, a fresh pizza, focaccia, *bruschetta,* or one of the temptingly displayed spinach or sausage rolls. ♦ Daily. 186 Grand St (at Mulberry St). 925.2954 ♿

72 Benito I and Benito II ★$ The original owners of this pair of small trattorie sold out and moved to Los Angeles. The restaurants are no longer related, except by name, but either one is a good choice for a hearty low-cost meal. ♦ Neapolitan ♦ Daily lunch and dinner. Benito I: 174 Mulberry St (between Grand and Broome Sts). 226.9171. Benito II: 163 Mulberry St (between Grand and Broome Sts). 226.9012 ♿

73 Da Nico ★★$ The decor is more stylish—terra-cotta floors, hanging copper pots, brick walls lined with shelves of olive oil and wine bottles, a marble bar with antipasto platters—and the atmosphere less raucous here than at surrounding neighborhood eateries. And a new backyard garden adds a romantic touch. This is an excellent place for coal-fired–brick-oven pizzas, lobster, veal chops, and tons of pasta dishes, which are cooked fresh daily and in full view. ♦ Neapolitan ♦ Daily lunch and dinner. 164 Mulberry St (between Grand and Broome Sts). 343.1212 ♿

74 Alleva Dairy Founded in 1892, the oldest Italian cheese store in the US is still family owned. Not a day goes by without a proud Alleva on hand to tend to the regular customers who come from far and near to shop for the mozzarella (fresh and smoked) made daily. There's also a small selection of noncheese items, including dried pasta, an excellent fresh tomato sauce packaged to go, and several types of smoked and cured meats. ♦ Daily. 188 Grand St (at Mulberry St). 226.7990

74 Piemonte Ravioli Company Since 1920, the same family has been churning out freshly made pasta from old family recipes in this modest-looking store that is, in fact, one of America's major suppliers. The refrigerator and counter are freshly stocked with pasta of all types, colors, shapes, and fillings. The filled pastas, such as ravioli and cannelloni, are favorites. Try the plump ravioli stuffed with cheese, spinach, or porcini mushrooms. ♦ Tu-Sa; Su hours vary. 190 Grand St (between Mott and Mulberry Sts). 226.0475

75 Pearl River Chinese Products Any Sinophile's passion for clothing and housewares can be satisfied in this store. Choose from cotton T-shirts, silk jackets, pillowcases, sheets, and bedspreads in pastel pinks, blues, and yellows, embroidered with flowers and animals. For Chinese cooking, an easy-to-use wok with a wooden handle is another find. ◆ Daily. 200 Grand St (at Mott St). 966.1010 &

76 Ferrara A slick emporium, this cafe includes an extensive take-out department, featuring a wide variety of Italian pastries, cookies, and candies. The espresso bar is one of the city's more popular places for cappuccino and the like. In nice weather, the bar extends onto the sidewalk, where a counter dispenses Italian gelati. ◆ Daily. 195 Grand St (between Mott and Mulberry Sts). 226.6150. Also at: 201 W 42nd St (at Seventh Ave). 398.6064; 1700 Broadway (between W 53rd and W 54th Sts). 581.3335

76 E. Rossi & Co. This old-fashioned, crowded, family-run store sells bocce balls, pasta machines, cookbooks in both Italian and English, and a variety of kitchen gadgets, such as cheese graters. ◆ Daily. 191 Grand St (at Mulberry St). 966.6640

77 Angelo's of Mulberry Street ★★$$ An old Little Italy standby that is still a favorite for tourists, this restaurant can be counted on for such consistently decent entrées as veal *valdostana* (stuffed with cheese and ham) or veal parmigiana. ◆ Southern Italian ◆ Tu-Su lunch and dinner. 146 Mulberry St (between Hester and Grand Sts). 966.1277

78 Ristorante Taormina ★$$ With its blond wood and peach furnishings, exposed brick walls, large windows, and graceful tall plants, this is not the typical Little Italy restaurant. The stuffed artichokes are excellent, and the veal entrées are also quite good, as are most items on the Neapolitan menu. ◆ Neapolitan ◆ Daily lunch and dinner. 147 Mulberry St (between Hester and Grand Sts). 219.1007 &

79 Sal Anthony's S.P.Q.R. ★★$$ The multilevel room is grand and gorgeous and the food is classic Italian. Good menu choices include *linguine veronelli* (seafood in tomato sauce), broiled veal chops, and shell steak sautéed with mushrooms. ◆ Neapolitan ◆ Daily lunch and dinner. 133 Mulberry St (between Hester and Grand Sts). 925.3120

Giovanni da Verrazano, an Italian-born navigator sailing for France, was the first European to see New York when he discovered New York Bay in 1524. Henry Hudson, an Englishman employed by the Dutch, reached the bay and sailed up the river now bearing his name in 1609, the same year that northern New York was explored and claimed for France by Samuel de Champlain.

80 Forzano Italian Imports Inc. This is the place to buy a souvenir of Little Italy. Italian music is piped onto the street to lure customers inside, where they'll find a large selection of all things Italian, including records and tapes; espresso makers in every shape; a variety of meat grinders; and T-shirts celebrating Italy. ◆ Daily. 128 Mulberry St (at Hester St). 925.2525

80 Caffè Napoli It feels like a sidewalk cafe even inside this *pasticceria*. Take a cue from the locals, who have dessert here rather than at the more famous **Ferrara**. The cannoli is a definite star among the many marvelous-looking pastries. ◆ Daily. 191 Hester St (at Mulberry St). 226.8705

80 Puglia Restaurant ★$ Come here for the generous portions of home-style cooking like rigatoni in vodka sauce and veal parmigiana—just two of the many dishes served at this rambling restaurant. The mostly young crowd sits at communal tables and sings along with the waiters to the live music, which adds to the festive *ambiente*. ◆ Southern Italian ◆ Tu-Su lunch, dinner, and late-night meals. No credit cards accepted. 189 Hester St (between Mott and Mulberry Sts). 966.6006 &

81 Vincent's Clam Bar ★★$ Choose the fresh seafood with a choice of mild, medium, or hot marinara sauce at this neighborhood institution. Hot is for serious Italian pepper lovers, so beware. An expanded menu offers a variety of meat entrées, chicken, salads, coffee, and dessert. ◆ Seafood ◆ Daily lunch, dinner, and late-night meals. 119 Mott St (entrance on Hester St). 226.8133 &

81 Pho Bâng Restaurant ★$ Come here for authentic Vietnamese cooking, especially the excellent whole shrimp summer rolls. A plate of exotic lettuces and an array of sauces accompany the meal. ◆ Vietnamese ◆ Daily lunch and dinner. 117 Mott St (between Canal and Hester Sts). 966.3797. Also at: 6 Chatham Sq (between Doyers and Mott Sts). 587.0870; 3 Pike St (at Division St). 233.3947

82 Wong Kee ★$ The good, fresh food offered at ridiculously low prices makes one wonder how they stay in business. Try the wonton-cabbage soup, any of the wide rice noodles, boiled chicken breast, roasted duck, or scrambled eggs with pork. Skip the chef's suggestions. ◆ Cantonese ◆ Daily lunch and dinner. No credit cards accepted. 113 Mott St (between Canal and Hester Sts). 226.9018

82 New Chao Chow ★$ This place serves up Chaozhou dishes, including what is perhaps the best *lo soi* duck in New York. The bird is cooked in a rich sauce flavored with cinnamon, eight-star anise, and nutmeg. ◆ Southern Chinese ◆ Daily breakfast, lunch and dinner. No credit cards accepted. 111 Mott St (between Canal and Hester Sts). 226.2590

83 Oriental Pearl ★$ Suggested items on the extensive menu at this large, plain restaurant are Peking spare ribs, steamed flounder, or shrimp with walnuts. Also recommended is Peking-style chicken in bird's nest (not the famous swallow's saliva, but a kind of edible bowl of delicious deep-fried taro). ♦ Cantonese ♦ Daily breakfast, lunch, and dinner. 103 Mott St (between Canal and Hester Sts). 219.8388 &

84 Luna ★$$ A century old and still going strong, this traditional Italian restaurant feels more like an oversized kitchen than the requisite tourist stop it is. The hallway that leads to the dining room gives you a full view of the bustling kitchen. Despite, or perhaps because of, the haphazard mix of tables and booths, propped-up photographs, and occasionally gruff service, the experience feels authentic, and the food is predictably

filling. ♦ Southern Italian ♦ Daily lunch, dinner, and late-night meals. No credit cards accepted. 112 Mulberry St (between Canal and Hester Sts). 226.8657

85 Il Cortile ★$$$ The lines to get in may be too long, the rooms too noisy, and the waiters too harried, but the fresh food at this dining spot is well prepared and the room beautifully decorated. ♦ Northern Italian ♦ M-Th, Su lunch and dinner; F-Sa lunch, dinner, and late-night meals. 125 Mulberry St (between Canal and Hester Sts). 226.6060

86 Holiday Inn Downtown $$ The only hotel in Chinatown has very little Asian detail in either the public areas or the 223 guest rooms to distinguish it from any other contemporary hotel in Manhattan. Its Hong Kong–style restaurant, **Pacifica**, is very good, but with the plethora of less expensive and often more authentic restaurants within blocks of the hotel, it would be a shame to eat in. ♦ 138 Lafayette St (at Howard St). 966.8898, 800/HOLIDAY; fax 966.3933

Bests

Howard J. Rubenstein
President, Rubenstein Associates, Inc.

Running around the **Central Park Reservoir** at sunrise with the morning glow of the sun peeking out behind New York's skyscrapers.

Savoring the steak at **Peter Luger**'s in **Brooklyn**—the nation's best steak house!

Cheering for the New York **Yankees** at **Yankee Stadium** on a warm summer night.

Enjoying a leisurely lunch at the **Hemsley Park Lane Hotel** while overlooking **Central Park.**

Ice skating at **Rockefeller Center** with your family.

Reading the delicious gossip in the newspaper columns of the *New York Post*—including Page Six, Cindy Adams, Neal Travis, and Liz Smith.

Posing for a photo "ape-ortunity" with King Kong on the observation deck of the **Empire State Building.**

Watching the latest work of the Bard performed during **Shakespeare in the Park.**

Being as awestruck as your children (or grandchildren) by touring the **Museum of Natural History** and coming upon Tyrannosaurus rex looking for a snack.

Enjoying the fabulous music and the rich history of **The Apollo** theater in **Harlem.**

Isabelle Stevenson
President, American Theater Wing

Fairway market: Because it's next door to **Citarella's** and because it has everything from radicchio to rye bread.

Theater: Any and all—live.

No. 30 bus: Good for people watching and talking while getting there.

Bloomingdale's!

Theater: Off-Broadway, Off-Off Broadway, and Broadway. The **American Theater Wing Seminars**—free on CUNY-TV, Channel 75.

Henny Santo
Co-owner, The Sign of the Dove, Arizona 206, Arizona Cafe, Contrapunto, and Yellowfingers

Going to watch the penguins in **Central Park**'s **Zoo** during the summer. You feel cool and refreshed watching them in their icy, water home. During the winter, it's the **Zoo's Rain Forest.** With birds flying overhead and the humid temperature of the tropics, you can truly forget that winter is outside this tropical haven.

Sitting by the pool at the **Frick Museum** also defies the weather outside. This tranquil setting is cool and relaxing during the heat of summer and feels like a wonderful spring day throughout the rest of the year.

Sitting in **Bryant Park** almost any season, but especially in the summer. It's a wonderful peaceful getaway where you can read, talk with friends, and listen to free jazz.

Riding the **Roosevelt Island** tram has an amazing view. Followed by an "ultimate" margarita just down the street at **Arizona 206.** If it's summer relax at a sidewalk cafe table, or during the winter snuggle inside by the fireplace.

Finding and taking a fabulous backstage tour offered by **The New School.**

SoHo/TriBeCa

The name SoHo was coined to define the district **South of Houston Street**, not to honor the neighborhood in London. Combined with the wedge-shaped territory known as TriBeCa (the abbreviated description of **Triangle Below Canal Street**), it includes the area bounded by **Lafayette Street**, the **Hudson River**, and **Chambers** and Houston Streets.

The area was occupied by Native Americans during the 17th century, then by farms and estates spread between old New York and the outlying suburb of Greenwich Village. Houses were built here in the early part of the 19th century (the oldest one still standing, at **107 Spring Street**, dates from 1806), and from the 1840s to 1860s this was the center of the city, boasting the major department store **Lord & Taylor**, on **Grand Street**, as well as the city's principal hotel, **The American House**, at **Spring Street** and **West Broadway**.

The architectural period referred to as American Industrial flourished in this area from 1860 to 1890. Businesses opened in prefabricated cast-iron buildings fashioned to look literally like temples of commerce. By the 1960s, light industry had moved on to new areas, and Robert Moses, the city's master planner, viewed SoHo as an industrial wasteland that he wanted to level and replace with the Lower Manhattan Expressway. When that plan was abandoned in the mid-1960s, artists looking for large, cheap studio space discovered SoHo. With the artists came avant-garde galleries, one-of-a-kind boutiques, and expensive nouvelle cuisine restaurants. The entire area was declared a Historical District in 1973. Today, SoHo is saturated with an artistic mix of original ideas and junk, sheer exuberance and exhibitionism, a funky alternative to the art world of Madison Avenue or 57th Street. (Keep in mind that many of the area's shops, restaurants, and galleries don't open until 11AM or noon and are closed on Monday and often during the month of August.)

TriBeCa, unlike SoHo, retains much of the bohemian quality that characterized the entire complex of cast-iron architecture between Chambers and Houston Streets before it went upscale. Because this neighborhood overlaps the City Hall area, with its enormous daytime working population, it has been more successful in resisting the tide of fad enterprise. Greek coffee shops, shoe repairs, pet shops, and appliance and camera stores enliven commercial streets little changed since the 1930s. Art and commerce have, of course, transformed TriBeCa to a certain degree, but they have not overwhelmed it. With easy access to Chinatown and Lower Manhattan, it remains a unique, artistic, and ethnic New York neighborhood.

1 Washington Market Park Progress has reduced the former **Washington Market** to this little park. In its day the market extended up along the river from Fulton Street into this neighborhood. Even Washington Street, which once formed its spine, is now just a one-block thoroughfare between Vesey and Barclay Streets. (Though many New York households stocked their larders with goods from the old market, it was essentially a wholesale produce exchange—now centered at Hunt's Point in the Bronx.) The park that remains is one of Manhattan's better play areas for young children. It is clean, safe, and, from a kid's point of view, great fun. Look for outdoor music concerts in warm weather. ◆ Chambers and Greenwich Sts

2 Duane Park Cafe ★★★$$$ This comfortably elegant restaurant offers relative quiet in a pretty room with cherry-wood accents. Standouts include miso-marinated duck breast with arugula; crispy skate with ponzo and tempura vegetables; panseared yellowfin tuna and roast garlic potato gratin with eggplant caponata; and a delicious chocolate hazelnut strudel with homemade banana ice cream. ◆ Continental ◆ M-F lunch and dinner; Sa dinner. Reservations recommended. 157 Duane St (at W Broadway). 732.5555

3 The Odeon ★★$$ Manhattan meets the Left Bank at this neon-lit space, a hot brasserie for the downtown art crowd since it first opened in 1980. Try the filet mignon

L+S Collection
494 Broome (#71 is 453)

Fists Eddy 889 Bway

au poivre with creamy potatoes dauphinois or homemade spinach and ricotta ravioli. Recommended on the lower-priced brasserie menu are the crab cakes and the steak *frites* (with french fries). For dessert, the delectable profiteroles or cranberry-apricot bread pudding can't be beat. ♦ American/French ♦ M-F lunch, dinner, and late-night meals; Sa-Su brunch, dinner, and late-night meals. Reservations recommended. 145 W Broadway (at Thomas St). 233.0507 &

4 Secondhand Rose Antiques dealer Suzanne Lipshutz (aka "Secondhand Rose") features primarily 19th-century treasures, with an emphasis on Moorish designs, in this 5,000-square-foot space. Her impressive stock ranges from custom-made leather furniture to antique wallpaper and linoleum. ♦ M-F; Sa-Su by appointment only. 138 Duane St (between Church St and W Broadway). 393.9002 &

ROJEMARIE'J

5 Rosemarie's ★★★$$$ An attractive display of Italian plates that decorates the bare brick walls and the warm and romantic ambience add to the pleasures of the nuova cucina at this dining spot. Ravioli filled with spinach is exceptional, and trifolata (wild mushrooms with polenta, pancetta, and sage) is a fine first-course choice. Favorite entrées include an authentic osso buco and pollo arrosto (roasted farm-raised chicken), as well as a black squid tortellini with lobster sauce. Another plus: The service is outstanding. ♦ Northern Italian ♦ M-F lunch and dinner; Sa dinner. Reservations recommended. 145 Duane St (between Church St and W Broadway). 285.2610

6 American Telephone & Telegraph Long Lines Building Designed by **John Carl Warnecke & Associates** and built in 1974, this almost windowless (except for the high, squared portholes) edifice houses a wealth of impressive electronic wizardry for communications. Texturized pink Swedish granite contrasts with vertical stripes of a beige granite used for decoration. ♦ Church St (between Thomas and Worth Sts)

7 Knitting Factory An impressive, somewhat avant-garde weekly roster of performances—everything from jazz to poetry readings to the latest performance art—are held in this lively two-level venue. ♦ Cover. Shows: daily; call for schedules. 74 Leonard St (between Broadway and Church St). 219.3055

Restaurants/Clubs: Red   **Hotels:** Blue
Shops/ 🌳 Outdoors: Green   **Sights/Culture:** Black

8 The Sporting Club Bar & Grill ★$ Up to 15 different events can be beamed in by 5 satellites at one time onto screens (7 of which are 10-footers) in every corner of this high-energy, sports fanatic's dream. There's a full menu featuring burgers, chicken and pasta dishes, and the like. ♦ American ♦ M dinner; Tu-Sa lunch and dinner; Su brunch and dinner. Reservations required for major sporting events. 99 Hudson St (at Franklin St). 219.0900

9 Chanterelle ★★★★$$$$ Acclaimed chef/owner David Waltuck and his wife, Karen, provide an exquisite dining experience in this pretty space designed by Bill Katz. Bedecked with prints, drawings, and lithographs, as well as stunning floral arrangements, the restaurant's decor complements its original, artfully presented, and always delicious cuisine. Try the signature seafood sausage to start, followed by noisettes of venison or breast of moulard duck with citrus marmalade. Perfect endings include such one-of-a-kind creations as orange spiced crème brûlée with blood orange–Cointreau ice cream. The wine list is good—and affordable. ♦ French ♦ M dinner; Tu-Sa lunch and dinner. Reservations required. 2 Harrison St (at Hudson St). 966.6960 &

9 New York Mercantile Exchange Built in 1884, this is another headquarters, like the one at 628 Broadway, for the big dealers in dairy and poultry products. The main offices used to be uptown, but this great old building, closer to the actual markets, is where the action was at the turn of the century. ♦ 6 Harrison St (between Hudson and Greenwich Sts).

10 Puffy's Tavern Retaining the atmosphere of a speakeasy, which it was during Prohibition, this pre-TriBeCa bar pulls you in from the street to have a beer, hang out, and listen to the jukebox with the after-work crowd and neighborhood regulars. ♦ M 4PM-4AM; Tu-S noon-4AM. No credit cards accepted. 81 Hudson St (at Harrison St). 766.9159

11 A.L. Bazzini Company The delicious aroma of nuts being honey-roasted fills the shop and even wafts into the street. A full array of gourmet treats, including breads, vinegars, preserves, pesto sauces, great coffee beans, and exotic condiments and spices, is here for the buying. There are also a few tables at which to enjoy such homemade prepared foods as overstuffed peanut butter–and–jelly sandwiches (among others), pastries, cookies, cakes, and muffins. ♦ M-Sa 339 Greenwich St (at Jay St). 334.1280

12 Independence Plaza Built in 1975 by architects **Oppenheimer, Brady & Vogelstein** and **John Pruyn**, this 40-floor middle-income housing project is a little off the beaten path and has great views of the river. ♦ Greenwich St (between Chambers and N Moore Sts)

13 Harrison Street Row Originally built in 1828 and restored in 1975 by **Oppenheimer, Brady & Vogelstein,** this row of impeccably restored Federal houses acts as an antidote to the massive apartment houses above it. ♦ 37-41 Harrison St (between Greenwich and West Sts)

14 Tribeca Grill ★★★$$$ In 1990, Drew Nieporent teamed up with several celebrity partners, including actor Robert DeNiro, to open this loftlike restaurant in the former Martinson Coffee Building. Enhancing the space are original artworks by DeNiro's late father, Robert Sr., and custom-designed Tiffany chandeliers by David Rockwell. The menu changes frequently but might include such contemporary offerings as pan-seared ruby red trout served with roast purple potatoes and citrus beurre blanc; herb fettuccine with caramelized cauliflower, wild mushrooms, and light parmigiano cream; and roasted pheasant with chestnut stuffing and lingonberry sauce. For dessert, try a classic crème brûlée or the banana tart with milk chocolate–malt ice cream. ♦ American ♦ M-F lunch and dinner; Sa dinner; Su brunch and dinner. Reservations required. 375 Greenwich St (at Franklin St). 941.3900 ♦

15 TriBakery Fresh breads baked daily and fine pastries are sold retail to local customers as well as wholesale to the finest restaurants in the city. Bread doughs are hearth baked and rolled into shapes that include a special Italian olive, crispy French baguette, and wholesome country white sourdough. A full line of delicious American and Italian pastries is also available. ♦ M-Sa breakfast. No credit cards accepted. 186 Franklin St (between Hudson and Greenwich Sts). 431.1114 ♦

riverrun
RESTAURANT & BAR

15 Riverrun ★$ Opened in 1979, this is one of TriBeCa's pioneer restaurants and pubs. It serves 15 microbrews on tap and remains a neighborhood staple for chicken potpie and meat loaf. It's also a comfortable place to eat, drink, and talk without feeling rushed. ♦ Continental ♦ M-F lunch and dinner; Sa-Su brunch and dinner. 176 Franklin St (between Hudson and Greenwich Sts). 966.3894

16 Nobu ★★★★$$$$ Another venture by Drew Nieporent and Robert DeNiro, this spot is a wonderland of out-of-this-world sushi overseen by Los Angeles's star chef, Nobu Matsuhisa. The million-dollar fairy-tale forest setting features a copper-leaf ceiling, wooden floors with stenciled cherry blossoms, birch trees, and a wall of 50,000 black river pebbles. The food is as innovative as the decor. Try the Matsuhisa Specialty—black cod with miso, or the squid "pasta" (strips of seafood with mushrooms and asparagus in a garlic-flavored red-pepper oil). Desserts include a trio of pot de crème (green tea, ginger, and coffee custard) and the Bento Box, a warm chocolate soufflé cake with shiso syrup and green-tea ice cream. If you can't get a reservation, the restaurant's new annex, **Next Door Nobu** (105 Hudson St, at Franklin St, 334.4445), which doesn't take reservations, will seat you sooner or later and may feed you even better, according to the word on the street. ♦ New Japanese ♦ M-F lunch and dinner; Sa-Su dinner. Reservations required. 105 Hudson St (at Franklin St). 219.0500 ♦

17 Commodities A natural-foods supermarket, this place carries a large stock of organic and otherwise healthful comestibles, as well as body-care products, cookbooks, and health food for pets. There's an extensive variety of flour, rice, cereal, beans, and pasta sold in bulk. ♦ Daily. 117 Hudson St (at N Moore St). 334.8330 ♦

18 Montrachet ★★★$$$ It's a family venture back here where it all started for brothers Drew and Tracy Nieporent. The low-key setting created by **Spanier & Daniels** is stylish, and the contemporary French cuisine, artfully prepared by Remi Lauvand, always excellent. Favorite entrées include roasted wild bass with flageolet beans and tomatoes and truffle-crusted salmon prepared with a red-wine fumet. Desserts are also exceptional, especially the passion fruit Bavarian with warm berries and banana-and-chocolate gratin on linzer crust. ♦ French ♦ M-Th dinner; F lunch and dinner; Sa dinner. Reservations recommended. 239 W Broadway (between White and Walker Sts). 219.2777

18 White Street An eclectic range of styles reflects the history of the TriBeCa cast-iron district. There are more attractive streets nearby, but none more typical. Contrast the authentic Federal details of **No. 2,** which was originally built as a liquor store in 1809; the artful stonework of **No. 10,** which was designed by **Henry Fernbach** in 1869; and the mansard roofline of **No. 17.** The upper stories of **Nos. 8** and **10** are shorter than the lower floors—a favorite Renaissance Revival device that makes the buildings appear taller. ♦ Between Sixth Ave and W Broadway

19 SoHo Photo Gallery Here you'll find the oldest and largest cooperative gallery for photographers in New York. ♦ Th 6-8PM; F-Su 1-6PM. 15 White St (between Sixth Ave and W Broadway). 226.8571

20 El Teddy's ★$$ Inside this three-story building topped with a life-size replica of the **Statue of Liberty**'s crown are old-fashioned booths, vintage 1940s wallpaper, and a neon fish tank, among other varied and unusual touches. The cuisine is creative Mexican—goat-cheese quesadillas and the like—and the margaritas are reputed to be among the best in town. ♦ Mexican ♦ M-Th lunch and dinner; F lunch, dinner, and late-night meals; Sa dinner and late-night meals; Su dinner. 219 W Broadway (between Franklin and White Sts). 941.7070 &

20 Layla ★★★$$$ Drew Nieporent and partners have transformed this into a fantasy straight out of the *Arabian Nights,* complete with Casbah motifs and belly dancers. The innovative menu features a combination of cold and hot *mezze* (appetizers) including hummus, roasted beets, tender grilled octopus salad, and goat cheese–crusted black-olive ravioli with a tomato-fennel sauce—all served with house-baked pita bread and grilled *zaatar* bread. For entrées, try the grilled monkfish kabob or Moroccan couscous royale (Gulf shrimp, clams, mussels, chickpeas and *merguez* sausage in a seafood broth). Don't miss the chocolate-and-pomegranate napoleon or orange-blossom crème brûlée for dessert. ♦ Middle Eastern ♦ M-F lunch and dinner; Sa-Su dinner. Reservations recommended. 211 W Broadway (at Franklin St). 431.0700

21 Franklin Station Cafe ★★★$$ Edith Piaf croons in the background and a continuous slide show of artsy photographs runs on the wall in this airy, refreshing space. Highlights of the delightfully illustrated menu include vegetable curry with coconut sauce, *rendang* chicken with roasted coconut and ginger, and seafood *laksa* (fish, shrimp, and red clams in a coconut curry soup). Such simple dishes as mango curry shrimp and noodles in peanut satay sauce with pineapple, romaine lettuce, and tofu are equally flavorful. Icy fresh fruit shakes (try the mango) and homemade tarts add to the appeal. The Southeast Asian theme is less evident in the breakfast menu, which consists mainly of omelets. ♦ Malaysian ♦ Daily breakfast, lunch, and dinner. 222 W Broadway (at Franklin St). 274.8525

22 Arqua ★★$$$ The poor acoustics in this pretty, peach-colored dining room with white, flying saucer–shaped light fixtures make conversation difficult. Concentrate instead on the food, especially the *pappardelle* with duck-and-mushroom sauce, gnocchi with tomatoes, and rabbit braised in white wine and herbs. ♦ Italian ♦ M-F lunch and dinner; Sa-Su dinner. Reservations recommended. 281 Church St (at White St). 334.1888

Until the late 1700s the western area of what is today called TriBeCa was owned by Trinity Church (Broadway, between Rector and Thames Sts). Its most prominent parishioners, who were probably also those with the most generous wallets, had streets named after them: (John) Chambers, (James) Duane, and (Joseph) Reade.

23 Let There Be Neon Founded by Rudi Stern, one of America's foremost neon artists, this gallery features clocks, chairs, windows, signs, stage sets, and interiors, all in neon. ♦ M-F. 38 White St (between Broadway and Church St). 226.4883

24 Barocco ★★$$$ People don't seem to mind that they are seated close together in this lively trattoria. Try the spinach ravioli filled with ricotta and Swiss chard and topped with a basil-tomato sauce; rigatoni with pureed eggplant, peppers, and tomato; risotto with seafood; or the delicious rack of lamb. During the week, these or other meals can be purchased to go from the shop next door. ♦ Italian ♦ M-F lunch and dinner; Sa-Su dinner. Reservations recommended. 301 Church St (at Walker St). 431.1445

25 Jan Weiss Gallery Weiss, a quantitative investment analyst–turned–art collector, shows the work of contemporary American, Australian, and European artists. ♦ Th-Sa and by appointment. 68 Laight St (at Greenwich St). 925.7313

26 Tribeca Potters Watch potters create in this working studio and gallery. All of the wares are lead-free and microwave- and dishwasher-safe. ♦ M-F; call for Saturday and Sunday hours. 443 Greenwich St (between Vestry and Desbrosses Sts) 431.7631 &

27 F.illi Ponte ★★★$$$ The once famous **Ponte's Steak House** is now an Italian showplace, complete with downstairs bar, upstairs cigar lounge, wood-burning oven, French rotisserie, and a dining room that offers a panoramic view of the Hudson River. Main course selections inspire and satisfy: Choose from a sumptuous roasted suckling pig, flavorful veal chop with Marsala and black truffles, or a classic grilled yellowfin tuna. All pastas are homemade. Desserts are rich, and the wine list is formidable. ♦ Italian ♦ M-F lunch and dinner; Sa dinner. Reservations required. 39 Desbrosses St (at West St). 226.4621 &

Capsouto Frères

28 Capsouto Frères ★★★$$$ This dining spot's calm and inviting setting—a spacious multilevel room bedecked with green potted plants—provides the perfect backdrop for chef Eric Heinrich's contemporary French cuisine. Choose from among such entrées as ravioli *St-Jacques aux champignons* (homemade ravioli with scallops and mushrooms); roasted duckling with a ginger and black-currant sauce; or red snapper in a *nage* of star-anise broth and a confetti of vegetables. The soufflés here are legendary, but all the desserts are excellent, including the profiteroles, raspberry-laced napoleon, and an "overstuffed" *tarte tatin* (apple tart) with crème fraîche. An impressive wine list emphasizes French and California wines and features the hard-to-find white Beaujolais. ♦ Contemporary French ♦ M dinner; Tu-F lunch and dinner; Sa-Su brunch and dinner. Reservations recommended. 451 Washington St (at Watts St). 966.4900

29 Holland Tunnel Built in 1927, this was the world's first underwater tunnel for vehicles, dipping nearly a hundred feet below the surface of the Hudson River. The tunnel is about 29 feet wide with a 12-foot ceiling. Its north tube is 8,558 feet long, and its south tube stretches 8,371 feet. Clifford M. Holland was the man who masterminded this engineering marvel, and the feat secured his name in New York—and American—history. ♦ Between Watts St and Boyle Plaza, Jersey City, New Jersey

30 Triplet's Old New York Steak House ★$$$ As the name suggests, this place is owned and run by identical triplets, brothers who were separated at birth and reunited at age 19. The old-fashioned steak-house fare comes with a Jewish twist. For appetizers try the chopped liver with grated radish and raw onion or homemade creamed spinach, then move on to such mainstays as grilled lamb or the signature Romanian tenderloin steak, rubbed with fresh garlic. The *Kishka Cabaret* performs lighthearted show tunes and such nightly. ♦ American/Jewish ♦ W-Su dinner. Reservations required. 11-17 Grand St (between Sixth Ave and Varick St). 925.9303 ♿

31 The Screening Room ★★$$ This innovative spot takes the concept of "dinner and a movie" to a whole new level. Treat yourself to first-rate contemporary American cooking in the sleek, yet retro-style setting. Start with panfried artichokes, followed by the cedar-planked salmon. After the meal, take in the *film du jour* in one of the two movie theaters right on the premises. Sunday brunch is followed by screenings of *Breakfast at Tiffany's.* ♦ American ♦ M, Sa dinner; Tu-F lunch and dinner; Su brunch and dinner. 54 Varick St (at Canal St). 334.2100

32 Café Noir ★★$$ A relaxed European vibe, funky music, and late-night hours are the draws at this little bar-restaurant on the southern fringes of SoHo. The eats are okay but come for the fun of it. ♦ French ♦ Bar: daily 11AM-4AM. Restaurant: M-F lunch and dinner; Sa-Su brunch and dinner. 32 Grand St (at Thompson). 431.7910

33 Ronald Feldman Fine Arts Inc. The gallery's eclectic and challenging stable includes American, European, and Russian artists. ♦ Tu-Sa; Monday by appointment. 31 Mercer St (between Canal and Grand Sts). 226.3232

34 443 Broadway In a neighborhood of iron buildings pretending to be stone, this five-story building, designed by **Griffith Thomas** in 1860, is the real thing, and it's a real beauty, once you get past the altered ground floor. ♦ Between Howard and Grand Sts

35 L'Ecole ★★$$ This handsome restaurant with soft lighting and high ceilings is run by the students of the famed **French Culinary Institute.** Alain Sailhac (formerly the chef at **Le Cirque** and **Le Cygne**) oversees as head chef and does double duty as Dean of Culinary Studies. The reasonably priced, three-course lunches and four- or five-course dinners change daily; selections might include classic French onion soup, country-style pâté, marinated venison stew, and sage-roasted rack of lamb. A short selection of wines by the glass is available. ♦ French ♦ M-F lunch and dinner; Sa dinner. 462 Broadway (at Grand St). 219.3300

36 478 Broadway Of all the cast-iron buildings in New York, this was the one that the magazine *Architectural Record* hailed, built in 1874 and designed by **Richard Morris Hunt,** as the "most serious attempt to utilize the almost unlimited strength of the material." ♦ Between Grand and Broome Sts

37 486 Broadway Built in 1883 by **Lamb & Rich,** this titanic former home of the Mechanics Bank combines Romanesque and Moorish elements in brick, stone, and terra-cotta. Look up at the mansard roof with its projecting windows and small cupolas. ♦ At Broome St

38 Alice Underground An eclectic mix of inexpensive, wearable separates and outerwear for men and women can be found here. Many of the unisex fashions are from the 1950s to the 1970s. ♦ Daily. 481 Broadway (at Broome St). 431.9067

39 Haughwout Building Famous as the building that contained New York's first elevator (a reminder of which is a small rusting sign over the door just to the left of the main entrance), this cast-iron Italian palazzo was designed by **John Gaynor** and erected in 1857. The edifice now houses **Staples**

downstairs and the **SoHo Mill Outlet** upstairs. In its former life, it was E.V. Haughwout's cut-glass and silver store. ♦ 490 Broadway (at Broome St)

40 L'Orange Bleue ★★$$ "The earth is blue like an orange" wrote the French poet Paul Eluard (in French, of course) and his rather luscious observation applies as much to this romantically charged, appealingly louche, edge-of-SoHo watering hole and eatery as it does to the planet at large. For here you'll find a Gallic-exotic ambience—faintly lit deep orange walls and gorgeous North African lighting fixtures—and a French-Moroccan menu in uncommon harmony. The *tagine* (stew) and couscous dishes are prepared with the requisite succulence, while the more complex fish and seafood dishes (which change frequently) have it in abundance. Portions are uniformly generous and served in thickly glazed ceramic earthenware.
♦ French/Moroccan ♦ M-F dinner; Sa-Su brunch and dinner. 430 Broome St (at Crosby St). 226.4999

41 Canal Jean Co. The original home of surplus chic has much more than jeans. Shop here for the SoHo look without flattening your wallet. ♦ Daily. 504 Broadway (between Broome and Spring Sts). 226.1130

42 521-523 Broadway Nothing but this section remains of the luxurious **St. Nicholas Hotel,** which was built in 1854 and once extended along Broadway, Mercer, and Spring Streets. Its original frontage on the three streets was 750 feet. Inside, the rugs, tapestries, crystal chandeliers, and beveled mirrors made it a tourist attraction even among visitors who couldn't afford to stay there. The bridal suite, filled with satin, lace, rich rosewood, and crystal, was considered the best place to begin a happy marriage. **Long Island Fabrics** (925.4488), on the ground floor of No. 521, stocks a good selection of African prints.
♦ Between Broome and Spring Sts

43 495 Broadway Proof that hope springs eternal, this handsome brick-and-stone structure with fine iron panels, designed by **Alfred Zucker** in 1893, replaced an 1860 cast-iron building at almost the same time the district began its decline. ♦ Between Broome and Spring Sts

44 SoHo Antiques Fair and Flea Market This weekend flea market takes advantage of those who've made brunch or lunch, gallery hopping, and window shopping in SoHo part of their weekend. It's not half as big as the Annex Antiques Fair and Flea Market (see page 117), but you might uncover a real find from dealers who prefer the smaller scale of this corner parking lot. ♦ Free. Sa-Su. Broadway and Grand St. 682.2000 ♿

45 Ted Baker Comfortably stylish menswear is on sale at the New York outpost of this British designer. Cool shirts with innovative fabrics are a Ted Baker trademark, but there are great trousers, sportcoats, and accessories, too. ♦ Daily. 107 Grand St (at Mercer St). 343.8989 ♿

Yohji Yamamoto

46 Yohji Yamamoto Themes of recent collections by this talented Japanese designer have included turn-of-the-century Eastern Europe and haute couture with an asymmetrical twist. The prices are high, but the shop is worth a visit even if only to see the iron, rolled-steel, and bronze fixtures designed in London by Antony Donaldson. ♦ M-Sa. 103 Grand St (at Mercer St). 966.9066 ♿

47 Niall Smith Antiques This is a popular haunt for designers and collectors from all over the world in search of Neo-Classical European furniture dating from the late 18th and early 19th centuries. ♦ M-Sa. 96 Grand St (between Mercer and Greene Sts). 941.7354

47 If Inside this cavernous space is a range of fashionable clothing for men and women, from the likes of designers Martin Margiela, Ivan Grundahl, Dries Van Noten, Comme des Garçons, and Vivienne Westwood. ♦ Daily. 94 Grand St (between Mercer and Greene Sts). 334.4964

48 Greene Street These five cobblestoned blocks are in the heart of the SoHo Cast-Iron Historic District (designated in 1973), an area taken over by textile manufacturing and other light industry after the retail and entertainment center of the city moved north in the mid-19th century. The 50 cast-iron buildings still intact here were built between 1869 and 1895. Functionally, cast iron anticipated modern steel-frame building techniques, but decoratively, it was used to imitate styles and manners of traditional masonry construction. Designers particularly loved ornate Renaissance and Neo-Classical motifs, which they altered with a free and fantastical hand. The two outstanding buildings on this street—which are in excellent condition—are both by **J.F. Duckworth: No. 28-30** (1872), a magnificently mansarded representative of the Second Empire style with leafless Corinthian columns, and **No. 72-76** (1873), also Corinthian, but here treated in an Italianate manner with a pedimented porch and porticoes all the way up the projecting center bays. This building was erected for the Gardner Colby Company, whose initials appear on the pilasters. Also noteworthy are the arched lintels and columns, with their egg-and-dart motifs, of **No. 114-120,** designed in

1882 as a branch of a department store; the Ionic capitals turned sideways at **Nos. 132-134, 136,** and **138** (1885); and all of the extraordinarily ornate **No. 31** (1876). Of course, not all of the buildings on Greene Street are cast iron. Several masonry buildings of the same period sport decorative ironwork as well—**Nos. 42-44** and **84-86,** for example—and one is, well, paint: The brick side wall on the corner is graced by Richard Haas's trompe l'oeil mural (1975) that mimics the cast-iron facade of the building. Many interior spaces remain intact as well. Perhaps the easiest to visit are buildings that best demonstrate the expansive qualities of a loft space and have been turned into galleries, such as the one at **No. 142.** ◆ Between Canal and W Houston Sts

ARTISTS SPACE

48 Artists Space One of the most original and certainly one of the most successful of the alternative space galleries, this perennial springboard for new talent maintains a file of about 4,000 artists from New York State and New Jersey, which is used by collectors, curators, and architects in search of an artist who falls into a specific category: conceptual, feminist, under 35, etc. ◆ Tu-Sa. 38 Greene St (between Grand and Broome Sts). 226.3970 ♿

49 The Drawing Center Designed by **James Stewart Polshek** in 1986, this elegant space is an important nonprofit exhibition space for unaffiliated artists, as well as for exceptional scholarly shows of works on paper from historical and contemporary periods. ◆ Tu-Sa. 35 Wooster St (between Grand and Broome Sts). 219.2166 ♿

49 Performing Garage The **Wooster Group,** one of America's oldest experimental theater companies—founded in 1967 by director Richard Schechner—is housed in this space. Under the direction of Elizabeth LeCompte, it redefines traditional notions of story line, thematic content, and performance structure. ◆ 33 Wooster St (between Grand and Broome Sts). 966.3651

50 La Jumelle ★$ This place must have been separated at birth from its twin (the name in French) **Lucky Strike,** just two doors down (see below). Both are charmingly frumpy bars-cum-restaurants with bistro menus written on blackboards. Try the steak au poivre or chicken Dijon. ◆ French ◆ Daily dinner and late-night meals. Reservations recommended. 55 Grand St (between Wooster St and W Broadway). 941.9651

50 Lucky Strike ★$ People come to this very popular, late-night hangout to sit, talk, smoke, and eat. Such bistro bites as steak *frites* or lentil salad over arugula are served. ◆ French ◆ M-F lunch, dinner, and late-night meals; Sa-Su brunch, dinner, and late-night meals. 59 Grand St (between Wooster St and W Broadway). 941.0479

51 Asian Opera Owners Gitu and Bina Ramani and Belle MacIntire draw on the work of artisans and designers from Indonesia, Thailand, and India to create an appealing melange of goods that's meant to enhance both home and wardrobe. The result is a sort of upmarket bazaar where you can peruse exotic armoires and other home furnishings as well as jewelry, hand-knit shawls, tapestries, and clothing. ◆ M-Sa. 62 Grand St (between Wooster St and W Broadway). 625.2521

52 SoHo Grand Hotel $$$$ This stylish 15-story **William Sofield**–designed hotel is a welcome addition to the area. The interior lobby and public areas reflect the art-influenced neighborhood with its combined Art Deco and modern design. Note the intricate work on the elaborate wrought-iron and glass stairway in the lobby. The 367 rooms are small, but boast Midtown amenities, including color TV and fax and computer hookups. Top-floor rooms are more spacious and offer memorable skyline views. The **Grand Bar,** opposite the lobby lounge, is a popular watering hole. The hotel, owned by Hartz Mountain Industries, is pet-friendly—guests can have a complimentary pet black goldfish for the length of their stay. A **TriBeCa Grand** nearby at 2 Sixth Avenue is scheduled to open in spring 2000. ◆ 310 W Broadway (between Canal and Grand Sts). 965.3000, 800/965.3000; fax 965.3200 ♿

Within The SoHo Grand Hotel:

Canal House ★★★$$ American fare at its finest is served at this sedately decorated restaurant off the hotel's chic lobby. Oversized floor lamps, beige walls, old-fashioned ceiling fans, and upholstered chairs make dining here a perfectly tranquil experience. Starters include excellent rock-shrimp risotto with butternut squash and apple-smoked bacon, a tangy Caesar salad, or the hearty, scrumptious macaroni and cheese. Among entrées, standouts include jumbo lump crab cakes; panroasted organic chicken breast with crushed potatoes and roasted-garlic sauce; and winter vegetable casserole with fennel-and-beet coulis. ◆ American ◆ Daily breakfast, lunch, and dinner. Reservations recommended. Parlor floor. 965.3588 ♿

53 Felix ★★$$$ Another player in the see-and-be-seen intersection of Grand Street and West Broadway, this place, like **Lucky Strike** and **La**

Jumelle (see page 57), attracts a cross section of models, downtown hipsters, and trendy professionals who dine on such bistro fare as *moules du Père Tin-Tin* (steamed mussels in white wine), cassoulet, roasted chicken, and steak *frites*. The outdoor cafe is a good place to people watch. ♦ French ♦ M dinner; Tu-Su lunch and dinner. 340 W Broadway (between Grand and Broome Sts). 431.0021

54 Alison on Dominick ★★★$$$$ Owner Alison Becker Hurt has created one of the most romantic spots in town with this pretty, whitewashed candlelit room where chef Daniel Silverman offers hearty French food. The menu, which changes seasonally, features such appetizers as goat cheese–and–black truffle raviolo, roast portobello–and–leek terrine, and creamless Maine shrimp bisque. Among the main courses might be roast Florida red snapper with fingerling potatoes, braised fennel, and roast garlic; panseared filet mignon with a potato, leek, and roquefort tart; and sautéed Arctic char with asparagus, oyster mushrooms, and salsify. For dessert don't miss the white chocolate–and–coffee ice cream coupe, with almond praline and warm chocolate sauce; or the bourbon vanilla crème brûlée with candied citrus rind. The wine list is first-rate. ♦ French country ♦ Daily dinner. Reservations recommended. 38 Dominick St (between Varick and Hudson Sts). 727.1188

55 Bell Caffè $ The neighborhood artists who hang out here want to keep this place a secret, lest the crowds that choke the streets east of Sixth Avenue begin to encroach. The food is decent (homemade breads, soups, and vegetable pies), but the scene is more the point. The decor is eclectic and fun: an assemblage of stuff saved from the garbage dump by co-owner Kurt, obviously a skillful scavenger. Check out the bathrooms, where the decor reaches its zany apex. There's live music every night and never a cover. ♦ Cafe ♦ Daily lunch, dinner, and late-night meals. 310 Spring St (between Renwick and Greenwich Sts). 334.2355

56 Castillo Cultural Center This progressive, independent cultural center encompasses a performance space, gallery, publishing house, photo lab, and video lab. One notable performance included a live hair montage—three-dimensional environments created on top of peoples' heads. ♦ Gallery: free. Theater: admission. M-Sa 10AM-10PM; Su noon-6PM. 500 Greenwich St (between Canal and Spring Sts). 941.5800, 941.1234 for information ♿

57 The Ear Inn $ The building that houses this dark and dusty 1817 bar/restaurant near the river has been designated a landmark. Back then, the shoreline was only five feet from the entrance, and the place was filled with seafaring rowdies. Today, it serves crowds of landlubbers decent pub food, including burgers and sandwiches. ♦ American ♦ M-Sa lunch, dinner, and late-night meals; Su brunch, dinner, and late-night meals. 326 Spring St (between Greenwich and Washington Sts). 226.9060

58 New York City Fire Museum The Fire Department's own collection of apparatuses and memorabilia dating back to colonial times is combined here with that of the Home Insurance Co. This is the largest exhibition of its kind in the country, and if you have youngsters in tow they won't complain a bit about the long walk west when they discover this is the destination. ♦ Admission suggested. Tu-Su. 278 Spring St (between Varick and Hudson Sts). 691.1303 ♿

59 Veruka ★★★$$$ Named for the little girl in *Willy Wonka and the Chocolate Factory* who "wanted the world and wanted it now," this downtown ultra hot spot offers food and libations for the famous and rich. The velvet rope out front is designed to keep stargazers and the unstylishly clad out of the chic ground-level lounge, but don't be intimidated, especially if you have a reservation for the downstairs dining room. Here chef Anthony Walton turns out eclectic, pricey, and frequently delectable fare. To start, dive into the warm artichoke dip with assorted breads, crispy calamari which is cooked to perfection and served with a roasted garlic sauce, or splurge on caviar. The entrée menu is limited, but several of its shining stars, including sesame-crusted tuna with pickled carrot, cucumber, and a spicy soy drizzle; and grilled center-cut shell steak with portobello, fingerling potatoes, and tarragon aioli, show up on the "assortments" menu, three-tiered culinary flights of fancy with price tags that spell sharing. ♦ New American ♦ Daily dinner. Reservations required. 525 Broome St (at Sixth Ave). 625.1717

60 Ceramica Classic Italian patterns appear on imported linens, mosaics, and earthenware—the Rafaelesco, a dragon pattern Raphael used on many of his frames, is particularly beautiful. Everything is handmade, most of it hailing from Italy. ♦ Daily. 59 Thompson St (between Broome and Spring Sts). 941.1307

61 Country Cafe ★★$ The rustic decor starts with the rooster sign outside and continues inside with pale yellow walls dotted with illustrations of farm animals, wood pumpkins on shelves, and dried flowers scattered artfully about. Just as earthy is the delicious food. Try the wild-mushroom casserole, onion tart, Cornish hen with tarragon juice, hanger steak with shallot sauce, and the rich *tarte tatin*. There's also a good, inexpensive wine list. ♦ French ♦ M-F lunch and dinner; Sa-Su brunch and dinner. No credit cards accepted. 69 Thompson St (between Broome and Spring Sts). 966.5417

62 Il Bisonte These fine hand-crafted leathergoods are known for their casual style: Handbags, portfolios, luggage, and accessories come straight from Florence. ♦ Daily. 72 Thompson St (between Broome and Spring Sts). 966.8773. Also at: 22 E 65th St (between Madison and Fifth Aves). 717.4771 ♿

63 Barolo ★★$$$ In inclement weather, the dining room provides a sophisticated setting; but once the weather warms up, the scene moves to the charming back garden. There's excellent pasta made daily on the premises— a different ravioli dish appears every day. Standout main courses include a delicious grilled chicken breast stuffed with goat cheese; savory breaded veal chop topped with fresh tomato and arugula; and whole sea bass baked in salt. ♦ Italian ♦ M-Th, Su lunch and dinner; F-Sa lunch, dinner and late-night meals. Reservations recommended. 398 W Broadway (between Broome and Spring Sts). 226.1102 ♿

64 O.K. Harris Works of Art A SoHo landmark for 20 years, this gallery is a record-setter, with more than 60 artists represented and an average of 50 exhibitions each year in its 11,000-square-foot spread. Ivan Karp, an early champion of Pop Art, is the gallery's founder and chief point man. ♦ Tu-Sa; closed in August. 383 W Broadway (between Broome and Spring Sts). 431.3600

64 Gemini GEL at Joni Weyl New and vintage prints from the venerable LA workshop, including editions by Ellsworth Kelly, Roy Lichtenstein, and Robert Rauschenberg, are on view. ♦ Tu-Sa. 375 W Broadway (between Broome and Spring Sts), Second floor. 219.1446 ♿

64 Betsy Senior Gallery Senior maintains a select inventory of contemporary prints and drawings, as well as new editions by rising stars. ♦ Tu-Sa. 375 W Broadway (between Broome and Spring Sts), Second floor. 941.0960 ♿

65 The Cupping Room Cafe ★$$ This charming neighborhood restaurant is where locals go for a great Sunday brunch. Everything from waffles, giant muffins, bagels with the fixings, and terrific coffees make a visit here worthwhile. Noteworthy lunch and dinner selections from chef Tomas Zavala

include shrimp quesadilla and black-pepper fettuccine with homemade chicken sausage. There's live jazz every Wednesday and Friday night. ♦ Continental ♦ M-F breakfast, lunch, and dinner; Sa-Su brunch and dinner. Reservations recommended for dinner. 359 W Broadway (between Grand and Broome Sts). 925.2898

66 59 Wooster Street Originally a warehouse, this six-story building, designed by **Alfred Zucker** in 1890, dominates the corner where it stands. Its mass is relieved by arched, iron-rimmed windows on its Broome Street facade, and by highly sculptural reliefs scattered over its surface. The seemingly random play between the rough-hewn masonry, smooth brickwork, and crenellated roofline (look hard and you'll see hand-size human faces way up top) somehow pulls the building together and gives it an oddly noble presence. It's best seen from the south side of Broome Street. ♦ At Broome St

Within 59 Wooster Street:

Brooke Alexander In luxurious quarters designed by the English architect **Max Gordon,** Carolyn and Brooke Alexander feature painting and sculpture by some of the most vigorous talents, including Jane Dickson, Yvonne Jacquette, and Tom Otterness. Also featured are American prints since 1960 by such contemporary masters as Johns, Lichtenstein, and Judd, as well as a selective inventory of works by younger artists and also Europeans. ♦ W-Sa. Second floor. 925.4338 ♿

67 Printed Matter Inc. This nonprofit art center specializes in books made by artists. The average price per book is $10 to $15— choose among 5,000 titles by 2,500 artists— making them one of very few bargains in the art world. ♦ Tu-Sa. 77 Wooster St (between Broome and Spring Sts). 925.0325 ♿

68 Craft Caravan, Inc. Traditional African handicrafts are the draw, and some interesting household items are displayed in a case up front—Beauty Pageant talc powder and Elephant Powder laundry detergent, for instance. ♦ Daily. 63 Greene St (between Broome and Spring Sts). 431.6669 ♿

68 Heller Gallery One of the most important representatives of the modern glass movement, this always interesting gallery usually has two solo shows and a monthly overview. ♦ Tu-Su. 71 Greene St (between Broome and Spring Sts). 966.5948

69 The King of Greene Street Greene Street offers a concentration of the best of SoHo's remaining cast-iron architecture, but even here this industrial palace is a stand-out. It is one of four on this street designed by **Isaac Duckworth** in 1873 and was called the "King of Greene Street" (the faded blue "Queen" is at **No. 28**). It is actually two buildings that pass as one, whose five-floor columned, cast-iron facade is a masterpiece of French Second Empire. ♦ 72-76 Greene St (between Broome and Spring Sts)

70 Friends of Figurative Sculpture Bronze sculptures of the human figure in a variety of sizes are featured in this welcoming gallery. ♦ Sa-Su. 53 Mercer St (between Grand and Broome Sts). 226.4850

71 Gourmet Garage This produce emporium offers a wide variety of goods at decent prices. Whether you're looking for a supply of crusty breads, blood oranges, portobello mushrooms, sun-dried tomatoes, kalamata olives, *parmigiano reggiano,* English farmhouse cheddar, or one of several chutneys, this store probably has it. ♦ Daily. 453 Broome St (at Mercer St). 941.5850. Also at: 301 E 64th St (at Second Ave). 535.5880; 2567 Broadway (at W 97th St). 663.0656

72 The Enchanted Forest This bewitching shop looks like a miniature set for a fantasy adventure. Beasts, books, and handmade toys are part of the celebration. ♦ Daily. 85 Mercer St (between Broome and Spring Sts). 925.6677

72 Bar 89 ★★★$ This is one of New York's more interesting watering holes. The clean white space is predictably SoHo but the immense curved bar and skylit cathedral ceiling lend a dramatic sense of place to a surprisingly low-key atmosphere. Have a Manhattan or order a light meal from the casual American menu. Incidentally, the high-tech, second-floor bathrooms here are not to be missed: it seems like the doors of the stalls are transparent, but thanks to some artful lighting, they aren't. ♦ American ♦ Daily lunch and dinner. 89 Mercer St (between Broome and Spring Sts). 274.0989

73 Spring Street Natural ★$ The health-oriented menu here is mostly vegetarian, but almost any appetite can be satisfied in this airy place filled with greenery. Line-caught fish and free-range poultry—especially stir-fry and the roasted chicken with honey-mustard glaze—are among the best nonveg choices. ♦ American ♦ M-Th lunch and dinner; F lunch, dinner, and late-night meals; Sa brunch, dinner, and late-night meals; Su brunch and dinner. 62 Spring St (at Lafayette St). 966.0290

74 Portico Owner Steven Werther travels far and wide to find craftspeople who meet his meticulous standards of construction. Among the pieces he has chosen are handmade reproductions of Shaker furniture, Argentine antiques, and dishes and glassware from Italy. In the middle of the store—it's a historical landmark building that stretches all the way to Wooster Street—is a pleasant cafe where you can sit and relax with a cappuccino or a cup of tea (try one from the United Society of Shakers in Maine). ♦ Daily. 72 Spring St (between Crosby and Lafayette Sts). 941.7800. Also at: Portico Bed, 139 Spring St (at Wooster St). 941.7722

75 Balthazar ★★$$$ Even if celebrity restaurateur Keith McNally's brasserie wasn't filled with famous faces and designer-clad denizens, it would still merit a visit because of the picture-perfect Paris bistro decor and surprisingly good food. Such French classics as onion soup and escargot share the menu with updated comfort cuisine like duck shepherd's pie and rabbit rillette with apricots. Only one caveat—stay away from the overpriced, and undersized, desserts and cheese plate. There's a good selection of well-priced wines, along with draft beers and traditional French aperitifs like Cynar (distilled from artichokes). Save room for the rich desserts, some of which can be bought at their adjacent bakery. If your name isn't Iman, Uma or Keanu, you probably won't get one of the cozier booths or window tables, but the equalizing, frenetic bar at the entrance provides a perfect vantage point for star-spotting. ♦ French ♦ Restaurant: daily lunch and dinner. Bakery: daily breakfast. Reservations recommended well in advance. 80 Spring St (between Crosby St and Broadway) 965.1414

76 New York Open Center Each year this education center offers hundreds of workshops, courses, lectures, and performances that explore spiritual and social issues, psychology, the arts—in short, all aspects of traditional and contemporary world culture. Check out the bookstore for the latest literature on all of the above. ♦ Bookstore: daily. 83 Spring St (between Crosby St and Broadway). 219.2527

77 P.P.O.W. The adventuresome young partners, Penny Pilkington and Wendy Olsoff (hence the name), pride themselves on their preference for individuals over trends. They show David Wojnarowicz and Erika Rothenberg as well as installation work (built environments) by TODT. ♦ Tu-Sa. 532 Broadway (between Spring and Prince Sts), Third floor. 941.8642 &

78 101 Spring Street Designed by **N. Whyte** in 1871, this building displays a sensitive approach to the use of cast iron as complex ornament. The ground floor is completely unchanged. ♦ At Mercer St

79 Penang ★★$$ A fancier version of its sister restaurant in Flushing, Queens, this place looks a little like Walt Disney's idea of Malaysia: a straw roof, strings of white lights, a waterfall, and waitresses wrapped in sarongs. The food is authentic and reasonably priced. Try the beef *rendang* (strips cooked until tender with ground onions, chili peppers, coconut, and lemongrass) and the noodle, vegetable, and shrimp soup. ♦ Malaysian ♦ Daily lunch, dinner, and late-night meals. Reservations recommended. 109 Spring St (between Mercer and Greene Sts). 274.8883. Also at: 240 Columbus Ave (at W 71st St). 769.3988; 38-04 Prince St (between 39th and 37th Aves), Flushing, Queens. 718/321.2078

80 SoHo Kitchen and Bar ★$ Pizza, grilled fish, and such basic pasta dishes as fettuccine with sun-dried tomatoes are the menu's mainstays. But the food takes second place to the theatrical interior designed by owner Tony Goldman—dramatic lighting, immense canvases, a black ceiling, and suspended airplanes. ♦ American ♦ M-Th, Su lunch and dinner; F-Sa lunch, dinner and late-night meals. 103 Greene St (between Spring and Prince Sts). 925.1866

80 Zona One of the very best reasons to visit SoHo, Louis Sagar's high-ceilinged, wonderfully airy space is as much a gallery as a store: Paolo Soleri's bells, garden tools, furniture of the Southwest, terra-cotta, and other well-designed, earth-conscious housewares from the Great American Desert (and all over the world) are displayed with great care and imagination—qualities every store should aim for. It's worth buying something just to get it gift-wrapped. ♦ Daily. 97 Greene St (between Spring and Prince Sts). 925.6750 ь

81 Platypus All sorts of upscale housewares are available here, from designer kettles and flatware by Alessi, Michael Graves, and Aldo Rossi to 18th-and 19th-century pine armoires, cupboards, and cribs. Godiva chocolates are sold as well. ♦ Daily. 128 Spring St (at Greene St). 219.3919

81 Peter-Roberts Antiques This upscale antiques shop specializes in American Arts and Crafts furniture and accessories. ♦ Daily. 134 Spring St (between Greene and Wooster Sts), Ground floor. 226.4777

81 Laurence Miller Gallery Rotating works by such photography greats as Helen Levitt hang in this gallery beside those of younger shutterbugs, all chosen with Miller's customary discretion. ♦ Tu-Sa. 138 Spring St (between Greene and Wooster Sts), Third floor. 226.1220

82 Manhattan Bistro ★★$$ The charming French bistro look of Marie DeGrossa's restaurant complements chef Xavier Mayonove's creative cuisine. For starters try the salmon combo (cured, smoked, and poached). Entrées might include monkfish *choucroute* (with a cabbage-stuffed pastry shell and vegetable breadcrumbs) and rack of lamb with braised fingerling potatoes. For dessert, indulge in the "chocolate molten" with homemade chocolate ice cream or a made-to-order soufflé. The wine list is good. ♦ French ♦ M-F lunch and dinner; Sa-Su brunch and dinner. Reservations recommended for dinner. 129 Spring St (between Greene and Wooster Sts). 966.3459

83 Boom ★$$$ Innovative creations at this popular SoHo spot for "world cuisine" range from sesame-crusted rare tuna to avocado blinis with lobster, osetra caviar, and crème fraîche. The candlelit setting is eclectic yet romantic. ♦ International ♦ M-F lunch and dinner; Sa-Su brunch and dinner. 152 Spring St (between Wooster St and W Broadway). 431.3663

84 Tennessee Mountain ★$$ The smells wafting down Spring Street will whet your appetite for ribs, fried chicken, and vegetarian chili—but the aromas can be better than the actual food. The frozen margaritas are sure to elevate your mood. ♦ American ♦ M-F lunch and dinner; Sa-Su brunch and dinner. Reservations recommended. 143 Spring St (at Wooster St). 431.3993

84 Putumayo Fashions from developing countries around the world—Thailand, Peru, Guatemala—are here in vivid, eye-appealing colors. Create complete outfits of chiffonlike skirts and crisp linen blouses and shirts, or use one piece, such as the classic llama sweaters, to match any wardrobe. ♦ Daily. 147 Spring St (between Wooster St and W Broadway). 966.4458

84 Morgane Le Fay The window at this women's clothing boutique is always austere and monochromatic. Featured inside is clothing designed by Liliana Ordas—flowing dresses, coats, capes, and skirts in a wide range of wool flannels, wool crepes, jerseys, and velvets. ♦ Daily. 151 Spring St (between Wooster St and W Broadway). 925.0144. Also at: 746 Madison Ave (between E 64th and E 65th Sts). 879.9700 &

85 Tootsi Plohound You would probably never guess that a store with a name like this sells unusual and well-made men's and women's shoes. ♦ Daily. 413 W Broadway (between Spring and Prince Sts). 925.8931 & Also at: 137 Fifth Ave (between E 21st and E 22nd Sts). 460.8650

85 415 West Broadway There are eight galleries in this impressive six-story building with a simple cast-iron storefront. ♦ Between Spring and Prince Sts

Within 415 West Broadway:

Witkin Gallery The focus is on vintage and contemporary photography by such artists as Evelyn Hofer, George Tice, and Jerry N. Uelsmann. Also available are new, rare, and out-of-print books on photography. ♦ Tu-Sa. Fourth floor. 925.5510

86 Beau Brummel Ralph Lauren began his career designing ties for this store. Today, most of the men's clothing and accessories sold here are by European designers. ♦ Daily. 421 W Broadway (between Spring and Prince Sts). 219.2666

86 Detour The accent is on a European sensibility in this collection of clothing for men. The women's collection is sold at 472 West Broadway. ♦ Daily. 425 W Broadway (between Spring and Prince Sts). 219.2692

87 Joovay Fine cotton and silk lingerie, sleepwear, and a good selection of toiletries are featured in this boutique. ♦ Daily. 436 W Broadway (between Spring and Prince Sts). 431.6386 &

88 420 West Broadway Two of SoHo's most prestigious galleries, **Leo Castelli** and **Sonnabend,** as well as several others, are housed in this heavy-hitter building. ♦ Between Spring and Prince Sts

Within 420 West Broadway:

Charles Cowles Gallery Contemporary painting joins sculpture and ceramics by a wide-ranging stable that includes many West Coast artists. ♦ Tu-Sa. Fifth floor. 925.3500

Leo Castelli Gallery A must-see on anyone's SoHo circuit, Castelli's extraordinary gallery features a veritable *Who's Who* of Abstract Expressionist and Pop artists, many of whom have shown their work with Castelli since the early 1960s. Jasper Johns, Ellsworth Kelly, and Ed Ruscha are but a few of the gallery regulars. ♦ Tu-Sa. Second floor. 431.5160

Sonnabend Gallery Ileana Sonnabend's celebrated and highly respected eye has drawn in such Americans as Robert Morris, who shares the floor with an ever-growing list of distinguished Europeans, including Jannis Kounellis, Gilbert & George, and Anne and Patrick Poirier. ♦ Tu-Sa. Third floor. 966.6160

89 Paracelso A moderately priced source for women's clothes made from natural fibers, this store features styles—many from India—that are casual and loose-fitting. ♦ Daily. 414 W Broadway (between Spring and Prince Sts). 966.4232

90 Ad Hoc Softwares Owners Julia McFarlane and Judith Auchincloss scour the marketplace for a wide range of bed and bath items, including unbleached, chemical-free linen and cotton sheets from Austria and West Germany, Italian and French waffle towels, and high-quality blankets from Europe. Also stocked are bath and beauty accessories and small gift items. ♦ Daily. 410 W Broadway (at Spring St). 925.2652 &

90 Spring Street Books In addition to a top-notch selection of books, this store features a good selection of newspapers, foreign magazines, and remainders. The late hours are a boon to last-minute gift shoppers. ♦ M-Th 10AM-11PM; F 10AM-midnight; Sa 10AM-1AM; Su 11AM-10PM. 169 Spring St (between W Broadway and Thompson St). 219.3033

90 Kin Khao ★★$ Still the trendiest around for Thai fare, this cavelike setting offers decent versions of such traditional dishes as pad thai and *por pia sod* (vegetable spring rolls). Flavorful *massaman kari* (beef, coconut curry, and potatoes with peanut sauce), *kwaytio ki mow* (sautéed spicy rice noodles with basil and tomatoes), and fresh *pla pow* (whole grilled fish in banana leaves) are great main dishes. ♦ Thai ♦ Daily dinner. 171 Spring St (between W Broadway and Thompson St). 966.3939

91 Spring Street Garden The always charming window displays show off just some of the exotica within—unusual varieties of tulips (the French parrot tulip is stupendous), miniature roses, and all sorts of dried flowers. Delivery within Manhattan is available. ♦ Tu-Sa. 186½ Spring St (between Thompson and Sullivan Sts). 966.2015

92 Mezzogiorno ★★$$$ Designed by architect and interior designer **Roberto Magris,** this airy restaurant opens onto the sidewalk during the warmer months. Highlights include wood-burning–oven pizzas (served at lunchtime and after 8PM), vibrant salads, and wholesome, homemade pasta specials. For starters try the fresh tuna carpaccio or the eggplant croquettes. Then follow with a hearty entrée of *taglierini alla ciociara* (pasta with cherry tomatoes, prosciutto, peas, and mozzarella) or the pasta of the day. ◆ Italian ◆ Daily lunch, dinner, and late-night meals. No credit cards accepted. 195 Spring St (between Thompson and Sullivan Sts). 334.2112

93 Blue Ribbon ★★$$ The kitchen of this bustling spot stays open very late, which is one reason it's a favorite stop for chefs who arrive after their own shifts end. The other incentive is the eclectic menu, featuring such dishes as duck breast with orange sauce, *paella basquez* (with seafood and chicken), and shrimp *Provençale.* The wine list is small but well chosen, and desserts, such as the banana split, will transport you back to your childhood. ◆ Eclectic ◆ Tu-Su dinner and late-night meals. 97 Sullivan St (between Spring and Prince Sts). 274.0404

94 Erbe All-natural herbal products from Italy for the face, body, and hair are sold in this intimate shop. A variety of beauty services are available by appointment. ◆ Tu-Sa. 196 Prince St (at Sullivan St). 966.1445

95 Raoul's ★★$$$ This lovely old-fashioned bistro has wooden floors, an Art Deco bar, leather booths, and an antique stove in the center of the room. In pleasant weather, diners can sit in the garden room behind the kitchen. Try the panseared foie gras, steak au poivre, and rare breast of duck with green apples. The extensive wine list (120 selections) includes French, Italian, Spanish, American, and Australian wines. ◆ French ◆ Daily dinner and late-night meals. Reservations recommended. 180 Prince St (between Thompson and Sullivan Sts). 966.3518

95 Hans Koch Ltd. Fine belts and handbags are featured in this shop. If nothing suits your fancy, Mr. Koch will whip up something that does. ◆ Daily. 174 Prince St (between Thompson and Sullivan Sts). 226.5385

96 Omen ★★$$ Quiet and attractive, this restaurant with exposed brick walls, light fixtures wrapped in filmy white fabric, and gleaming dark tables has cultivated a loyal following. The namesake dish, *omen* (Japanese noodles served with a variety of toppings and flavorings), is a perfect introduction to the extensive menu, which includes a tuna steak with ginger, oysters-in-miso casserole, raw tuna with mountain yam and quail eggs, yellowtail and string bean teriyaki sautéed with sake, and seafood tempura. ◆ Japanese ◆ Daily dinner. Reservations recommended. 113 Thompson St (between Spring and Prince Sts). 925.8923

96 Peter Fox Shoes All Peter Fox designs, inspired by Victorian and medieval styles, are handmade (except for the stitching of the sole to the leather) in Italy. Bridal customers have included supermodel Paulina Porizkova and model-turned-actress Phoebe Cates. ◆ Daily. 105 Thompson St (between Spring and Prince Sts). 431.6359. Also at: 806 Madison Ave (between E 67th and E 68th Sts). 744.8340 ♿

97 Peter Hermann Leather Goods This shop provides the finest handbags, belts, and luggage in the world, mostly from Europe. It's also one of the few places in the US where you'll find Mandarina Duck, a hi-tech luggage line from Italy. ◆ Daily. 118 Thompson St (between Spring and Prince Sts). 966.9050

98 Milady's ★$ This neighborhood bar is frequented by locals who come for beer and good conversation. The simple entrées include great burgers and zesty salads. ◆ American ◆ Daily lunch and dinner. 162 Prince St (at Thompson St). 226.9340

98 Vesuvio Bakery A SoHo landmark, this charming storefront has been selling chewy loaves of bread, breadsticks, and addictive pepper biscuits since 1928. ◆ M-Sa. 160 Prince St (between W Broadway and Thompson St). 925.8248

99 The Work Space The law firm of Dolgenos Newman & Cronin maintains this contemporary art exhibition space in the same building as their offices. With the assistance of a professional curator, they show the work of emerging and contemporary artists that might not make it into a commercial gallery due to lack of mainstream marketability. ◆ Tu-Sa. 101 Wooster St (between Spring and Prince Sts), Eighth floor. 219.2790 ♿

100 130 Prince Street Designed in 1989 by **Lee Manners & Associates,** this new "PoMo" (Postmodern) building is home to English jewelry designer **Stuart Moore**'s shop (see below) of sophisticated *bijoux,* plus a number of art galleries—**Lohring Augustine, Perry Rubenstein, Christine Burgin, Andrea Rosen, Petersberg, Victoria Munroe,** and **Tony Shafrazi**—each of which commissioned its own architect to design the space according to its specifications. ◆ At Wooster St

100 Stuart Moore Visit this jewelry shop if you are in the market for exceptionally well-made (expensive) jewelry in 18K gold or platinum. Custom work is the specialty, and the mark-up on gemstones exceeding $6,000 in cost is only 20 percent—a bargain, if you can afford it. ◆ Daily. 128 Prince St (between Greene and Wooster Sts). 941.1023

Hollywood on the Hudson

New York was a thriving film production city long before the sunny skies of Hollywood began to lure producers and filmmakers west in the early 1900s. D.W. Griffith loved to shoot here, and Mack Sennett's *Keystone Cops* ran rampant through Coney Island.

The city goes out of its way to court the film industry: There's a special mayor's office to act as an industry liaison, to provide police protection for stars and production crews, and even to help arrange scenes ranging from helicopter chases to historical location settings. The number of feature films shot here has quadrupled since 1977, and movie, TV, and commercial production ranks among the city's top five growth industries.

It's no wonder then that many visitors to movieland's Gotham get a feeling of déja vu. Here are a few of the movies and locations you may remember:

America, America(1963), Elia Kazan's portrayal of his own family's immigration to the US, incorporates **Ellis Island** locales.

Arthur(1981), in which Dudley Moore questions his date's (Liza Minnelli) profession just a bit too loudly in the **Oak Bar** at the **Plaza Hotel.**

Big(1988) stars Tom Hanks and Robert Loggia performing a charming impromptu musical number at **FAO Schwarz.**

Bonfire of the Vanities(1990), based on Tom Wolfe's novel, captures Sherman McCoy's world of **Upper East Side** privilege and debauchery. Courtroom scenes were filmed on location in the **Bronx.**

Breakfast at Tiffany's(1961) Audrey Hepburn and George Peppard find love on **Fifth Avenue.**

Bright Lights, Big City(1988) finds Michael J. Fox in the fast lane in the film adaptation of Jay McInerney' best-selling novel.

Crocodile Dundee(1987) Paul Hogan checks in at the **Plaza** while visiting from Down Under.

Desperately Seeking Susan(1984) portrays Rosanna Arquette as a suburban housewife and her unexpected adventures with Madonna in **Battery Park.**

Die Hard with a Vengeance(1995) Bruce Willis and Samuel L. Jackson track down a mad bomber (Jeremy Irons) on the streets of New York.

Dog Day Afternoon(1975) stars Al Pacino and two cohorts who turn a simple **Brooklyn** bank robbery into chaos.

First Wives Club(1996) Goldie Hawn, Diane Keaton and Bette Midler wreak havoc and revenge on their ex-husbands in such places as **Café des Artistes** and **Barneys New York.**

Fort Apache, The Bronx(1981) Paul Newman fights the bad guys in this crime-ridden part of the Bronx.

The French Connection(1971) casts Gene Hackman as the unforgettable cop Popeye Doyle as he tracks drug smugglers in a spectacular car chase along Brooklyn's **Stillwell Avenue.**

Funny Girl(1968) Barbra Streisand shares the spotlight with the **Statue of Liberty.**

Ghostbusters(1984) Bill Murray, Dan Aykroyd, and Harold Ramis move into (and blow the roof off of) the **No. 8 Hook and Ladder Firehouse** in TriBeCa and finally come to terms with these supernatural beings at **55 Central Park West.**

The Godfather (1972) is the first of a trilogy staring Marlon Brando, James Caan, Diane Keaton, Robert Duvall, and Richard Castellano in Mario Puzo's look at the mob.

The Godfather, Part II (1974) returns to **Little Italy** where Robert De Niro plays young mob boss Don Corleone.

GoodFellas (1990) Robert DeNiro, Ray Liotta, and Joe Pesci rise in the mob ranks in this Martin Scorsese film.

Hannah and Her Sisters (1986) Carrie Fisher, Diane Wiest, and Sam Waterston star in Woody Allen's Manhattan-based family drama. Mia Farrow, Barbara Hershey, and Michael Caine add to the angst.

The Lost Weekend (1945) Ray Milland suffers the DTs at **Bellevue Hospital** after a three-day bender.

Manhattan Murder Mystery (1993) features Woody Allen as a New York book editor, with Dianne Keaton, as his wife, delving into the mysterious disappearance of their neighbor.

Mean Streets (1973) Martin Scorsese's slice of life in Little Italy starring a young Robert De Niro and Harvey Keitel.

Midnight Cowboy (1969) Dustin Hoffman and Jon Voight stop traffic at **West 58th Street** and **Sixth Avenue.**

Miracle on 34th Street (1947) is the classic tale that proves there really is a Santa Claus. A young Natalie Wood co-stars with Maureen O'Hara.

Moonstruck (1987) Cher finds love at the **Metropolitan Opera.**

Night Falls on Manhattan (1997) Director Sidney Lumet's drama about police corruption starring Andy Garcia takes its cast to the **Municipal Building,** the **U.S. Customs House,** and **Bowling Green.**

On the Town (1949) This musical by Leonard Bernstein, Betty Comden, and Adolph Green is the quintessential New York picture with Frank Sinatra, Gene Kelly, and Ann Miller dancing from **Wall Street** to **Rockefeller Center.**

The Pawnbroker (1965) is Sidney Lumet's film of a Jewish concentration camp survivor (Rod Steiger) running a pawnshop in **Harlem.**

Prince of Tides (1991) A New York psychiatrist (Barbra Streisand) helps high school football coach (Nick Nolte) to uncover his darkest secrets.

Ransom (1996) Ron Howard directs Mel Gibson as a distraught father trying to save his kidnapped son. Scenes include **Central Park**'s **Bethesda Fountain,** and the **Heliport** at **61st Street** and the **FDR Drive.**

Rosemary's Baby (1968) highlights the **Dakota Apartments** (West 72nd St and Central Park W) in Roman Polanski's film starring Mia Farrow and John Cassavetes.

Saturday Night Fever (1977) shows John Travolta's life as he tries to escape his dead-end career as a disco king. His identity crisis reaches a climax atop the **Verrazano-Narrows Bridge** when a friend falls to his death.

Serpico (1974) Al Pacino fights corruption in the NYPD, with location shots at **New York University.**

Sophie's Choice (1982) stars a very Victorian-looking Meryl Streep and Kevin Kline who reside in **Flatbush** at 101 Rugby Road.

Superman (1978) finds Clark Kent, the mild-mannered reporter for the Daily Planet, saving the world—and Lois Lane. The former **Daily News Building** is featured.

The Taking of Pelham One Two Three (1974) finds subway riders at the mercy of extortionists on the No. 6 train.

Taxi Driver (1976) Robert De Niro discovers his talents for cleaning up New York's crime-ridden streets in this Martin Scorsese film.

A Tree Grows in Brooklyn (1945), based on Betty Smith's novel, stars Dorothy McGuire and Joan Blondell in the depiction of a troubled family.

West Side Story (1961) pits two street gangs on the **West Side.** Director Robert Wise's opening scene takes place between Amsterdam and West End Avenues at West 68th Street.

When Harry Met Sally (1989) Meg Ryan demonstrates to Billy Crystal the art of sexual deception as they share a meal at **Katz's Delicatessen** on the **Lower East Side.** A memorable scene.

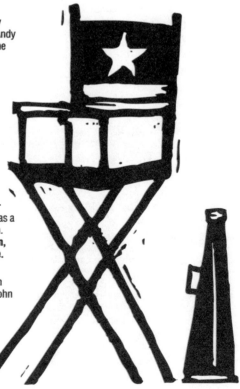

100 Harriet Love Originally the shop that made antique clothes fashionable, today it's one of the best in the business of new clothing with a vintage feel. (The owner is the author of *Harriet Love's Guide to Vintage Chic.*) Almost all of the clothes here are vintage-inspired, mostly from the styles of the 1940s and 1950s. Vintage jewelry and alligator- and crocodile-skin bags are also in stock. ♦ Daily. 126 Prince St (between Greene and Wooster Sts) 966.2280 ♿

100 Reinstein/Ross This is a shop devoted entirely to the exquisite jewelry created by Susan Reinstein, namely, multicolored sapphires and 22K gold, often alloyed in subtle colors, most of which she has developed herself. ♦ Tu-Su. 122 Prince St (between Greene and Wooster Sts). 226.4513 ♿ Also at: 29 E 73rd St (between Madison and Fifth Aves). 772.1901

agnès b.

100 agnès b. Classics for men, women, and children—such as V-necked sweaters and cotton T-shirts—are made modern with a twist by this French designer with a loyal following. ♦ Daily. 116-118 Prince St (between Greene and Wooster Sts). 925.4649 ♿ Also at: 1063 Madison Ave (between E 80th and E 81st Sts). 570.9333

101 David Beitzel Gallery Owner Beitzel's eye takes in a broad range of styles, and he tends to favor emerging artists who work in highly individual idioms. ♦ Tu-Sa. 102 Prince St (at Greene St). 219.2863

101 Fanelli Cafe ★$ A holdover from the days when SoHo was a neighborhood of factories, this cafe has a tavernlike atmosphere. The ambience is a greater draw than the only adequate food—except for the terrific hamburgers and fries—and more-than-surly service. ♦ American ♦ Daily lunch, dinner, and late-night meals. No credit cards accepted. 94 Prince St (at Mercer St). 226.9412

102 110 Greene Street The sign says this is "The SoHo Building," but long before anyone ever thought of calling this neighborhood

SoHo, it was an annex of the **Charles Broadway Rouss Department Store** that thrived over on Broadway. It was designed by **William J. Dilthy** and built in 1908. ♦ Between Spring and Prince Sts

102 A Photographer's Place The shop buys and sells photographic books, antiques, and prints. ♦ Daily. 133 Mercer St (between Spring and Prince Sts). 431.9358 ♿

103 Zoë ★★★$$$ The food is ever-changing and consistently improving at Thalia and Stephen Loffredo's stylish restaurant, where the crowd is the perfect mix of uptown types meeting downtowners. Don't pass up the crispy calamari with Vietnamese dipping sauce. For a hearty main course, choose from char-grilled Argentine natural beef with Linzano-glazed vegetable skewers and chimichurri sauce, lightly smoked Chilean sea bass on grilled asparagus, endive and trevisano salad with roasted grapefruit vinaigrette, and other savory surprises. The brunch menu is highly recommended. ♦ Contemporary American ♦ M-F lunch and dinner; Sa-Su brunch and dinner. Reservations recommended. 90 Prince St (between Broadway and Mercer St). 966.6722

104 Little Singer Building In a letter to the *Sun* in 1904, when he designed this 12-story building for the Singer Sewing Machine Co., **Ernest Flagg** said, "I believe tall buildings will shortly become unsafe. As an architect, I will never have anything to do with buildings of this kind." A year later he began work on the big Singer Building, a 41-story, 612-foot tower on Broadway at John Street, which was demolished in 1967, leaving this as a monument to what was lost. ♦ 561-563 Broadway (between Spring and Prince Sts)

105 SoHo 20 Gallery The gallery is a cooperative of women artists with group and individual shows. ♦ Tu-Sa. 545 Broadway (between Spring and Prince Sts), Third floor. 226.4167

106 560 Broadway This is a fine old brick structure that holds its own in a sea of cast-iron neighbors. It was remodeled to house several distinguished art galleries. ♦ At Prince St

Within 560 Broadway:

Dean & DeLuca The ultimate and original high-tech gourmet grocery is housed here in 9,700 square feet of space. Wonderful kitchenware, cookbooks, and samplings from the world's gastronomic centers are displayed with extraordinary panache. Added bonuses: a coffee/espresso bar, butcher, fishmonger, and a full range of prepared take-out dishes. This place is a must for anyone passionate about food. ♦ Daily. Ground floor. 226.6800 ♿

106 Duggal Downtown Professional photographers in the neighborhood come to this extension of the West 20th Street branch for their film and processing needs. It's a huge space with a continually changing photography exhibition along the right-hand wall and windows through which you can watch the technicians work. ♦ M-Sa. 560 Broadway (between Spring and Prince Sts). 941.7000. Also at: 9 W 20th St (between Fifth and Sixth Aves). 924.7777

06 Zero This is a showroom for the eponymous Italian high-tech modular display system. ♦ By appointment only. 560 Broadway (between Spring and Prince Sts). 925.3615

07 Savoy ★★★$$$ Run by chef/owner Peter Hoffman and his wife, Susan Rosenfeld, this cozy place features an eclectic menu that follows the seasons. A second floor contains a comfortable bar and lounge area. The creative menu may include such popular choices as salt-crusted baked duck with braised kale, blood oranges, and black olives; and monkfish with chick-pea fritters, bacon-braised collard greens, and green-peppercorn bordelaise. The dessert menu might feature warm chocolate cake with clementine sorbet and orange sauce; coconut pana cotta with rum-roasted pineapple; or a coffee hazelnut napoleon. The carefully chosen wine list also spotlights artisan vintners. ♦ Continental ♦ M-Sa lunch and dinner; Su dinner. Reservations recommended. 70 Prince St (at Crosby St). 219.8570 &

08 Stark Gallery Current works by contemporary American and European artists are exhibited at this gallery, which features avant-garde abstractionists. ♦ Tu-Sa. 113 Crosby St (between Prince and E Houston Sts). 925.4484 &

09 280 Modern Decorative arts are this gallery's draw, with an emphasis on designer furniture from the 1920s to the 1960s. There is also a small selection of original works by the late Piero Fornasetti of Milan. ♦ M-Sa; Su

by appointment. 280 Lafayette St (between Prince and Jersey Sts). 941.5825 &

110 568-578 Broadway A boon for art lovers is the proliferation of gallery clusters in fine old Broadway buildings, making life easy for the browser, rain or shine. This dual-entry structure now houses so many galleries that it has been dubbed **The Mall** by art-world locals. ♦ Between Prince and E Houston Sts

Within 568-578 Broadway:

Curt Marcus Gallery Contemporary American and European artists in all media are exhibited here. ♦ Tu-Sa. 578 Broadway, 10th floor. 226.3200 &

110 Academy of American Poets For more than a half-century this little-known academy has been the city's—and the nation's—headquarters for American poets. It sponsors an annual grant to assist American poets at all stages of their careers, and organizes a Poetry Reading Series at points around the city to further public interest and recognition. Since the society's beginning in 1934, events have centered around such literary lights as Long Island–born Walt Whitman. Call or write for a reading schedule. ♦ M-F. 584 Broadway (between Prince and E Houston Sts), Suite 1208. 274.0343 &

110 Alternative Museum Two spacious galleries house a museum founded and operated by well-known artists for unrecognized artists. Poetry readings and concerts—folk, jazz, traditional—take place, with the emphasis on the international and unusual. ♦ Donation suggested. Tu-Sa. 594 Broadway (between Prince and E Houston Sts). 966.4444 &

111 The Cockpit Re-creations of the vintage goatskin and horsehair jackets preferred by those daring young men in their flying machines are available here, along with what the store calls "current issue." Everything to do with flying—from B-17 flight bags and shorts made from Flying Tigers briefing maps, to books, watches, patches, gloves, and boots—is here. ♦ Daily. 595 Broadway (between Prince and W Houston Sts). 925.5455, 800/354.5514 &

111 Museum for African Art This vibrant museum is one of only two in the country specializing in sub-Saharan art (the other is part of the Smithsonian). Painted wooden masks, life-size carved figures, vivid textiles, and architectural sculptures all contribute to the complex and interesting rotating exhibits mounted by founder/director Susan Vogel. Behind an 1860s cast-iron facade, **Maya Lin** designed the striking galleries, which opened in 1993. (As the **Center for African Art,** the museum was on East 68th Street for a decade before moving to these expanded quarters.) The museum gift store is an interesting stop in itself. ♦ Donation suggested. Museum: Tu-F. Gift store: M-F. 593 Broadway (between Prince and W Houston Sts). 966.1313 &

TheNewMuseum
OF CONTEMPORARY ART

111 The New Museum of Contemporary Art Founder/director Marcia Tucker is the force behind this unique institution. She not only shows artists who have trouble getting a foot in the museum establishment's door, but also exhibits all aspects of their work. ♦ Donation requested. W-Su. 583 Broadway (between Prince and W Houston Sts). 219.1222 &

112 Guggenheim Museum SoHo Further enhancing this area's status as a mecca for contemporary art lovers is the downtown branch of the uptown museum with one of the world's preeminent collections of modern and contemporary art. Within a landmark 19th-century loft building, architect **Arata Isozaki** designed the 30,000 square feet of galleries, which opened in 1992. The six-story brick structure, with its cast-iron storefronts and detailed cornice, was designed in 1881 by **Thomas Stent** for John Jacob Astor III, and in its early days housed garment manufacturers and stores. Inside, the flexible and modern exhibit spaces retain the original cast-iron columns. The **Guggenheim Museum Store** is definitely worth a visit. At press time, plans were in the works for a new restaurant serving American fare to replace the defunct **Monzù.** ♦ Admission. Museum: M, Th-Su. Store: daily. 575 Broadway (at Prince St). 423.3878

113 Match ★★$$ Late in the evening, the velvet rope comes out, and a discriminating doorperson selects which souls are hip enough to enter the crowded bar. But even during dinner hour, this place is a scene: Tables are jammed and the staff exudes attitude. There's an extensive sushi list, including the elegantly wrapped Match roll (shrimp, cucumber, and eel). Other popular picks include spit-roasted duck with potato dumplings and wok-seared bluefin tuna with warm *soba* (buckwheat) noodle salad. The dessert samplers offer everything from chocolate cake to lemon tart, and a well-chosen wine list is fairly priced. Downtown, bands provide live music on Sunday and Monday nights. ♦ Fusion ♦ M-F lunch, dinner, and late-night meals; Sa-Su brunch, dinner, and late-night meals. Reservations required. 160 Mercer St (between Prince and W Houston Sts). 343.0020. Also at: 33 E 60th St (between Park and Madison Aves). 906.9173

114 Distant Origin A clone of the incomparable Zona around the corner on Wooster Street, this shop stocks an impressive selection of Southwestern paintings, pillows, pottery, and furniture. ♦ Daily. 153 Mercer St (between Prince and W Houston Sts). 941.0025

114 After the Rain The sister store of **The Enchanted Forest,** this is a grown-up's fantasy of kaleidoscopes, art glass, tapestries and handmade jewelry. ♦ Daily. 149 Mercer St (between Prince and W Houston Sts). 431.1045 &

115 Jerry's ★★$$ Owner Jerry Joseph has been serving SoHo's local businessfolk—especially the gallery crowd—eclectic American fare for over a decade. Fresh soups, salads, and sandwiches are served, with lunch and brunch times bustling. Rigatoni with braised lamb, Jodi's pot roast, and seared Atlantic salmon are popular favorites. Try the lemon or pecan tart for dessert. A short wine list is available. ♦ American ♦ M-F breakfast, lunch, and dinner; Sa brunch and dinner; Su brunch. 101 Prince St (between Mercer and Greene Sts). 966.9464

115 Edward Thorp Gallery Owner Thorp's affinity for slightly offbeat landscape painting is clear in the work of artist April Gornik. He also represents Deborah Butterfield, who sculpts horses out of found objects. ♦ Tu-Sa. 103 Prince St (between Mercer and Greene Sts). 691.6565

116 Phyllis Kind Gallery An eclectic collection of contemporary paintings and "outsider" art by American and international artists is shown. ♦ Tu-Sa. 136 Greene St (between Prince and W Houston Sts). 925.1200

116 John Weber A longtime art world fixture, Weber has supplemented his distinguished roster of minimal and conceptual artists, including Sol LeWitt and the estate of Robert Smithson, with some bright new—and offbeat—talent. ♦ Tu-Sa. 142 Greene St (between Prince and W Houston Sts), Third floor. 966.6115 &

116 Sperone Westwater The New York home to many of Italy's most innovative artists, including Mario Merz, "the three C's"(Sandro Chia, Francesco Clemente, Enzo Cucchi), and Susan Kothenberg, this gallery also boasts an impressive roster of other European and American talents. ♦ Tu-Sa. 142 Greene St (between Prince and W Houston Sts), Second floor. 431.3685. Also at: 121 Greene St (between Prince and W Houston Sts). 431.3685 &

116 The Pace Gallery The downtown branch of the blue-chip gallery is located in a vast space that provides a dramatic backdrop for large-scale paintings and sculpture. ♦ Tu-Sa. 142 Greene St (between Prince and W Houston Sts), Ground floor. 431.9224. Also at: 32 E

57th St (between Park and Madison Aves). 421.3292

116 Space Untitled The space may be untitled but it's far from nondescript. Despite a tucked-away feel, this is one cavernous cafe, where an array of decidedly modern art adorning the otherwise white walls reminds you where you are. Take time to look around; there's usually some offbeat installation artwork in the back and changing exhibits in the big room behind the ordering area. The coffees and cakes aren't quite as impressive as the setting, but this is still a very atmospheric place to take a respite from shopping or strolling. ◆ Daily. 133 Greene St (between Prince and W Houston Sts). 260.6677

117 Kelley and Ping ★★$ The atmosphere is pure Southeast Asian noodle shop, with bare hanging light bulbs, floor-to-ceiling wooden cases filled with Thai herbs and ingredients, and an open kitchen that allows full view of the chef at work. Owned by Brad Kelley of **Kin Khao** (see page 62), this informal spot has been a neighborhood favorite since it opened. Try *yam woosen* (clear noodles with chicken, shrimp, scallions, and red onion); Malaysian curried noodles; and lemongrass chicken. ◆ Asian ◆ Daily lunch and dinner. 127 Greene St (between Prince and W Houston Sts). 228.1212

117 Back Pages Antiques An impressive collection of classic Wurlitzer jukeboxes, working slot machines, Coca-Cola vending machines, Seeburg nickelodeons, pool tables, and advertising signs is available here. If you need to furnish a party room, look no further. ◆ M-Sa; call for Sunday hours. 125 Greene St (between Prince and W Houston Sts). 460.5998

118 Whole Foods A full selection of everything you need for a sound body and soul is available here: vitamins, grains, fresh fish, organic vegetables, kosher chicken and turkeys, cosmetics, and an impressive assortment of books to explain what to do with all those things. ◆ Daily. 117 Prince St (between Greene and Wooster Sts). 982.1000. Also at: 2421 Broadway (at W 89th St). 874.4000 ⑮

118 Prince Street Bar & Restaurant ★$ The faithful clientele come as much for the lively bar scene as for the fairly standard burgers,

salads, and sandwiches. On a more interesting note, there also are Indonesian specialties, including *gado gado* salad (with peanut sauce and shrimp chips), spicy shrimp Jakarta (jumbo shrimp with brown rice and broccoli), and beef *rendang*. ◆ Eclectic ◆ M-Sa lunch and dinner; Su brunch and dinner. 125 Prince St (at Wooster St). 228.8130 ⑮

119 Betsey Johnson For more than two decades, designer Johnson's fashion statements have been providing the youthful with a statement of their own. ◆ Daily. 138 Wooster St (between Prince and W Houston Sts). 995.5048. Also at: 251 E 60th St (between Second and Third Aves). 319.7699; 1060 Madison Ave (at E 80th St). 734.1257; 248 Columbus Ave (between W 71st and W 72nd St). 362.3364 ⑮

120 Casa La Femme ★★★$$ From the sidewalk in front of this terminally hip SoHo standby, the spectacle of a string of floor-bound cocktail-sippers nestled among piles of silken embroidered pillows is arresting. Enter and the magic continues: a row of Berber-style linen tents, the color of which rotates every six months, presides over a complement of regular tables. In order to be seated at a table under a tent you must order the prix-fixe menu and be amenable to sitting on the floor—adorned with fresh sod in season—as the tables are low in traditional Middle Eastern style (pillows make this a more palatable choice). Popular appetizers include Egyptian grape leaves and *tamaya* (sautéed chick-pea dumplings with fava beans and coriander). Don't-miss entrées include the succulent *tagine khodar* (roasted vegetables and dried fruits with couscous) and *samek mashwy* (a grilled whole striped sea bass with pickled baby eggplant and tahini dip.) ◆ Egyptian ◆ Daily dinner. Reservations recommended. 150 Wooster St (between Prince and W Houston Sts). 505.0005 ⑮

121 147 Wooster Street Designed in 1876 by **Jarvis Morgan Slade,** this arched storefront decorated with bands of fleur-de-lis and other floral motifs is all hand-carved in marble. Only the cornice is iron. ◆ Between Prince and W Houston Sts

121 Dia Center for the Arts For over 20 years, **Dia** (from the Greek word meaning "through") has played a vital role among art institutions both locally and internationally by producing projects in every artistic medium. Three locations (two in SoHo, the third in Chelsea) present pop, minimal, and conceptual works. ◆ Admission. W-Sa. 141 Wooster St (between Prince and W Houston Sts). 473.8072. Also at: 393 W Broadway (between Broome and Spring Sts). 925.9397; 548 W 22nd St (between 10th and 11th Aves). 989.5566

122 Susan P. Meisel Decorative Arts
Twentieth-century decorative arts are exhibited here, including hand-painted English pottery created by Clarice Cliff between 1928 and 1938, 1950s Mexican sterling silver jewelry, and vintage watches. ◆ Tu-Sa. 133 Prince St (between Wooster St and W Broadway). 254.0137 &

122 Louis K. Meisel Owner Meisel championed the photorealists back in the 1970s and has stuck to his convictions despite the art world's ever-changing tides. ◆ Tu-Sa. 141 Prince St (between Wooster St and W Broadway). 677.1340 &

123 SoHo Wine & Spirits Welcome to what may very well be the most civilized, not to mention the best-stocked, small wine store in town. You won't encounter any wine snobbery in this well-organized, well-designed outlet, which also carries the city's most extensive selection of single-malt Scotch whiskies. ◆ M-Sa. 461 W Broadway (between Prince and W Houston Sts). 777.4332

123 I Tre Merli ★★$$ The exposed brick walls and high ceiling give this restaurant with a wine bar a quiet charm. The food—especially the large selection of homemade pastas—is quite good. The seasonal menu might include garden vegetable salads; carpaccio (raw fish and meat varieties); veal scallopini sautéed with lemon and artichokes; grilled swordfish with red peppers and capers; and the fish of the day. Desserts are homemade and also delicious. ◆ Italian ◆ M-F lunch, dinner, and late-night meals; Sa-Su brunch, dinner, and late-night meals. Reservations recommended. 463 W Broadway (between Prince and W Houston Sts). 254.8699

124 Amici Miei ★★$$$ Another SoHo venue to eat and be seen at, this place features a wood-burning oven that turns out good pizza, focaccia, and grilled shrimp. The pastas are popular, particularly the gnocchi, spaghetti with Manila clams, and homemade black squid-ink pasta with spicy tomato sauce. ◆ Northern Italian ◆ M-F lunch and dinner; Sa-Su brunch and dinner. 475 W Broadway (at W Houston St). 533.1933 &

Restaurants/Clubs: Red   Hotels: Blue
Shops/ ❦ Outdoors: Green   Sights/Culture: Black

125 Can ★$$ Stylish presentations of French-Vietnamese fare are served at this attractive restaurant, designed to resemble an art gallery. Try the Vietnamese pâté (barbecued beef in vine leaves), lemongrass duck, grilled squid stuffed with pork, and Vietnamese curried chicken. ◆ French/Vietnamese ◆ Daily lunch and dinner. Reservations recommended for dinner. 482 W Broadway (at W Houston St). 533.6333

126 Rizzoli Bookstore of SoHo Though half the size of its uptown location, this shop is worth a stop to peruse one of the city's best selections of fine art books, foreign magazines, and music recordings. ◆ M-Th 11AM-11PM; F-Sa 11AM-midnight; Su noon-8PM. 454 W Broadway (between Prince and W Houston Sts). 674.1616. Also at: Winter Garden Atrium, World Financial Center, West St (between Albany and Vesey Sts). 385.1400; 31 W 57th St (between 5th and 6th Aves). 759.2424

127 Buffalo Chips Bootery Choose from a fashionable line of podiatrist-approved cowboy boots with steel-reinforced arches and low, tapered heels for proper support. If you can't find a pair that you like among the 50 or so on display, they'll be glad to do a custom design. ◆ Daily. 131 Thompson St (between Prince and W Houston Sts). 253.2228 &

128 Sean Chic but unpretentious casual and informal menswear is sold at this shop featuring French designer Emile Lafaurie. ◆ Daily. 132 Thompson St (between Prince and W Houston Sts). 598.5980

129 Eileen Lane Antiques Scandinavian, Biedermeier, and Art Deco furniture and lighting are the specialty of this antiques shop. ◆ Daily. 150 Thompson St (between Prince and W Houston Sts). 475.2988

130 Quilty's ★★★$$$ One of SoHo's shining stars, the interior of this dining spot is elegantly plain with white walls decorated with prints of butterflies, and flowers set on every table. Chef Katy Sparks's menu is just as straightforward, with an emphasis on American cuisine with Mediterranean influences. Try the pork tenderloin with Port-plumped prunes, country salad with grilled pears and Maytag blue cheese, or the pan-roasted Scottish salmon with brulèed clementines. Desserts are just as fine—

especially the Black Mission fig and
raspberry strudel with Armagnac ice cream.
♦ American ♦ Daily lunch and dinner.
Reservations recommended. 177 Prince St
(between Thompson and Sullivan Sts).
254.1260

131 Depression Modern Owner Michael Smith
likes to redecorate his shop, and does so
every Saturday with the Moderne furniture of
the 1930s and 1940s that he spends the rest
of the week restoring to its original condition.
♦ W-Su. 150 Sullivan St (between Prince and
W Houston Sts). 982.5699 &

131 Joe's Dairy Today, only about three
storefronts remain of the old Italian-American
enclave along Thompson and Sullivan Streets.
This store, with its checkered tile floor and
sweating glass cases, is one of them; it
specializes in creamy, delectable housemade
cheese. *Parmigiano reggiano* is hewn from
fragrant wheels, and sweet ricotta is drawn
from moist, cool containers. Smoke pours
from the basement door a few times a week,
when *mozzarella affumicato* (smoked) is
made. ♦ Tu-Sa; call ahead for weekend hours.
156 Sullivan St (between Prince and W
Houston Sts). 677.8780

132 Cub Room ★★★$$$ Chef/owner
Henry Meer, formerly of **Lutèce,** creates
upscale cuisine without unnecessary
formality. Appetizers such as salmon *tartare,*
pressed vegetable terrine, and Maine crab
cakes are a treat. Sesame-crusted grilled
yellowfin tuna; wood-grilled lobster
fricassee; and chateaubriand (for two) with
wild mushrooms and shallot Burgundy sauce
are adeptly prepared. End the meal with a
superb poached pear or crème caramel. The
wine list leans toward American varietals.
♦ American ♦ M dinner; Tu-F lunch and
dinner; Sa-Su brunch and dinner.
Reservations required. 131 Sullivan St (at
Prince St). 677.4100 &

FRONTIÈRE

132 Frontière ★★$$$ The name of this
romantic spot refers to the French and Italian
border—the region that also influences the
kitchen. Old-fashioned stone walls, fireplace,
and intimate lighting create a thoroughly
inviting experience. The food is sophisticated
but earthy; try the terrine of duck made with
foie gras, prunes, and Armagnac; bowtie
pasta with fresh seafood in garlic-and-saffron
broth; and grilled *poussin* (squab) with lemon,
mustard, and rosemary. ♦ Southern
French/Northern Italian ♦ M-Sa lunch and
dinner. Reservations recommended. 199
Prince St (between Sullivan and MacDougal
Sts). 387.0898

PROVENCE

132 Provence ★★★$$ From its slate-blue,
rustic wooden facade to its charming back
garden, Michel and Patricia Jean's Provençal
bistro is a sheer delight. The dining room is
simple and warm, with ocher walls, columns,
wood accents, and dried flower
arrangements—*très romantique.* Start with
chef Pablo Trobo's creamy fish soup with
gruyère *rouille* or *pissaladière* (onion and
anchovy tart). Follow with monkfish with
saffron rice and ratatouille, steamed vegetables
with cod and mussels, or braised rabbit with
olives and fava beans. Top off the meal with a
fruit tart or a perfectly charred crème brûlée.
The wine list is diverse and, appropriately,
spotlights selections from Provence. ♦ French
♦ Daily lunch and dinner. Reservations
required. 38 MacDougal St (between Prince
and W Houston Sts). 475.7500

133 Film Forum The intriguing space of this art
house featuring independent American and
foreign films and retrospectives was designed
by **Stephen Tilly** and **Jay Hibbs.** ♦ 209 W
Houston St (between Sixth Ave and Varick St).
727.8110 &

134 S.O.B.'s Sounds of Brazil ★★$$
Specializing in Bahian and other Brazilian
food, this casual restaurant is better known
for its late-evening showcase of salsa, samba,
reggae, and whatever else is currently being
imported from the Caribbean, South America,
and Africa. The *caipirinhas* (Brazil's favorite
cocktail, a blend of crushed limes, sugar and
sugarcane liquor) keeps them coming back.
♦ Brazilian ♦ Cover for music. M-Sa lunch,
dinner, and late-night meals. Reservations
required for dinner. 204 Varick St (at W
Houston St). 243.4940

135 Culture Club Girls who just wanna have fun
and all those who still want to party like it's
1999 won't have to fight for the right at this
fun nightspot for reluctantly aging Gen-Xers.
Sink a drink—a Devo or Purple Rain, for
starters—and feel the noise. ♦ Cover. Th-Su.
179 Varick St (between King and Charlton
Sts). 243.1999

136 375 Hudson Street Say the word
"advertising" and Madison Avenue naturally
comes to mind. But many advertising
agencies and related businesses have
relocated downtown, including the branch of
Saatchi & Saatchi, the marketing
communications giant, occupying this
building. Check out the inspiring modern art,
including works by Frank Stella, in the lobby.
Most of the building's neighbors are printing
companies. ♦ At W Houston St

Greenwich Village

Radical and old guard, quaint and glitzy, authentic and ersatz, Greenwich Village is anything but a homogenous neighborhood. Bounded by **Broadway**, the **Hudson River**, and **West Houston** and **14th Streets**, America's birthplace of the bohemian spirit is home to students of **New York University (NYU)**, actors in Off-Broadway theaters, jazz musicians, and an assortment of other residents who work uptown.

Greenwich Village's eccentric personality starts with the layout. In the 1790s, the area's country estates were sold off in lots or subdivided and developed by large landholders. Weavers, sailmakers, and craftspeople moved into rows of modest homes along streets that followed the boundaries of the old estates and travelers' paths.

New Yorkers fleeing epidemics of smallpox, yellow fever, and cholera that ravaged the city in the 1790s and early 1800s settled in Greenwich Village, which was far removed from the congested city center. Hastily built houses and hotels arose to accommodate the newcomers. **Bank Street** is named for Wall Street banks that opened here along with other commercial ventures during the severe epidemic of 1822.

In the 1830s, prominent families began to build town houses at **Washington Square**, which had become a public park in 1828. New York society took over **Fifth Avenue** and the side streets from **University Place** to **Sixth Avenue** (more formally known as **"Avenue of the Americas"**). But the fashionable Washington Square elite soon gravitated to **Gramercy Park, Madison Square**, and upper Fifth Avenue, so that by the late 1850s the Village had turned into a quiet backwater of middle-class, old-line Anglo-Dutch families. Warehouses and industrial plants proliferated along the Hudson River, and commercial development began to the east and north. But the Village always retained its residential character. In the 1880s and 1890s, Irish and Chinese immigrants moved in, while Italians populated the tenements built south of Washington Square.

Houses from all periods coexist in the Village, but only one of the many brownstones still stands; they once lined Fifth Avenue from Washington Square to **Central Park** in what was called "Two Miles of Millionaires." One of the first brownstone mansions designed in the Italianate style, this lone survivor was built in 1853 at 47 Fifth Avenue for Irad Hawley, president of the Pennsylvania Coal Company. The **Salmagundi Club,** the city's oldest club for art and artists (founded in 1870), moved into the brownstone in 1917 and still opens its doors for exhibitions from time to time.

As the high rollers moved out, their large houses were divided into flats and studios and their stables transformed into homes. The cheap rents appealed to such writers as Edgar Allan Poe, Horace Greeley, Walt Whitman, Mark Twain, and Edna St. Vincent Millay, who at one time occupied the narrowest house in the city at **75½ Bedford Street.** The influx of creative energy continued, and Greenwich Village established itself as the seat of bohemia in the United States before World War I.

After the war, the Village continued to be a magnet for those looking for sexual freedom, radicalism, and revolt in politics and the arts. Upton Sinclair founded the Liberal Club on **MacDougal Street;** the **Washington Square Players** (later renamed the **Theater Guild**) came into being in 1917; and the following year, the **Provincetown Players,** the company that gave Eugene O'Neill his first chance, opened in the Village (the company still puts on plays at the **Provincetown Playhouse** on MacDougal Street).

Sharing the Village's streets with bohemians in the 1930s were families who had been here for generations, white-collar workers, and Irish and Italian blue-collar workers. After World War II, the Beat generation and then the hippies in the 1960s discovered the Village, as did entrepreneurs and developers. Although residents have fought hard to keep the community the way it was, apartment houses and high-rises have made inroads. Some of the development, such as **Westbeth,** a Bell Telephone Laboratories building recycled as housing for artists, has been architecturally sensitive. One of the Village's largest landowners, Sailors' Snug Harbor, however, has been criticized for some of the decisions it has made for its 21 acres of leased land near Washington Square. In 1801, Captain Robert Richard Randall deeded this land and a small cash gift for the purpose of establishing a home for retired seamen (now located in North Carolina and financed by the returns on the Greenwich Village holdings). Trinity Parish, the other large landowner with deeds from the same period, is usually given high marks for helping to maintain the ambience of the Village.

Today every style of 18th- and 19th-century architecture, culture, and history intermingles in Greenwich Village, from the gracious classical houses on the north side of Washington Square, where writers Henry James and Edith Wharton lived, to converted stables in **MacDougal Alley** behind them, where in the 1900s sculptors Jo Davidson and Gertrude Vanderbilt Whitney and actor Richard Bennett occupied houses. **Judson Memorial,** a square-towered church designed in the Romanesque style by **McKim, Mead & White,** is as well known for its experimental dance and theater productions as for its historical or architectural value. **NYU** now has colleges and schools at its Washington Square campus. **The New School for Social Research,** America's first university for adults, is still championing social causes and offering a dazzling variety of night-school courses. In 1970, the **New School** and **Parsons School of Design** formed a partnership that broadened the excellent curricula of both schools.

History is everywhere—in such places as the **Minetta Tavern** on MacDougal Street, filled with photos and memorabilia from earlier days, and the **Cedar Tavern** on University Place, where Abstract Expressionists Jackson Pollock, Franz Kline, and Larry Rivers used to hang out. At the **Gansevoort Market,** the city's wholesale meat market, you can envision what the area was like when Herman Melville worked as a customs inspector for 19 years at what was then the **Gansevoort Dock.**

---

1 Brother's Bar-B-Q ★★$ From the deep South, through New Orleans, to Southwestern cuisine that can rival Santa Fe's finest, the word "barbecue" means many things, and this place deals in them all. The colorfully modern space is equipped with an African mahogany bar and lounge. Try the North Carolina hickory-smoked pulled pork, char-grilled chicken breast, or shredded smoked beef brisket sandwiches.
♦ Southern Barbecue ♦ M-F lunch and dinner; Sa-Su brunch and dinner. 225 Varick St (at Clarkson St). 727.2775

The residents of Greenwich Village named Waverly Place after Sir Walter Scott's novel *Waverley* to honor him the year after his death, though they failed to spell the name right.

---

2 Restaurant Boughalem ★★$$ The defining color at this trendy spot—black—is softened by the muted lemony yellow lighting and low-volume techno music. For a delicious appetizer, try the steamed dumplings with goat cheese, potatoes, and leeks in an herb broth. Entrées are light, and include Dijon-mustard–crusted grilled salmon with red bliss potato puree and citrus sauce; panroasted grouper with stewed cabbage in a lobster broth; and farfalle (butterfly-shaped pasta) with black olives, tomatoes, broccoli rabe, and parmesan. On the downside, some of the tables are too close together and the dessert menu is limited. ♦ French/New American ♦ M-Sa dinner; Su brunch and dinner. Reservations recommended. 14 Bedford St (between Houston and Downing Sts). 414.4764 &

3 **Cent' Anni** ★★$$$ A lively crowd gathers to enjoy the large portions of first-rate Northern Italian cuisine offered at this popular Village trattoria. The menu features an exceptional minestrone and a few outstanding pasta dishes—try penne with sun-dried tomatoes or fettuccine with rabbit. There's a delicious red snapper roasted in garlic and oil; and a popular, cooked-to-order porterhouse steak as well. ♦ Italian ♦ M-Sa lunch and dinner; Su dinner. Reservations recommended. 50 Carmine St (between Bedford and Bleecker Sts). 989.9494 ♿

4 **House of Oldies** Here is an incredible collection of rare and out-of-circulation rock 'n' roll and R&B LPs, including 10,000 rock 'n' roll 78s and over a million 45s. Additional stock is sent up from the basement via a dumbwaiter. ♦ M-Sa. 35 Carmine St (between Bedford and Bleecker Sts). 243.0500

5 **Tutta Pasta Ristorante** ★$ An outgrowth of the store next door, this cafe serves its pasta and sauces freshly made, with above-average results. Fettucine Alfredo, tortellini bolognese, and gnocchi with pesto are tops here. There are about 20 appetizers and 10 variations on thin-crust, brick-oven pizzas to choose from, so *mangia, mangia!* ♦ Italian ♦ Daily lunch and dinner. 26 Carmine St (between Bedford and Bleecker Sts). 463.9653. Also at: Numerous locations throughout the city

6 **Church of Our Lady of Pompeii** The gilded marble interior of this 1927 church designed by **Matthew Del Gaudio** gives the impression that this structure might have been moved intact from the hills of Italy. Some services are still conducted in Italian. ♦ 25 Carmine St (between Bedford and Bleecker Sts). 989.6805

7 **Marys** ★$ An 1820 town house is the setting for this restaurant featuring such seasonal eclectic American fare as crispy sweetbread salad frisée, crab cakes with mustard sauce, and pan-roasted chicken breast with apple-leek stuffing. The roaring fireplaces and Federal-style drapes are, however, still in place. ♦ American ♦ M-Sa dinner; Su brunch and dinner. 42 Bedford St (between Carmine and Leroy Sts). 741.3387

8 **New York Public Library, Hudson Park Branch** The original 1905 building by **Carrère & Hastings**, who also designed the main branch up on Fifth Avenue, was expanded in 1935. **The Early Childhood Resource and Information Center,** a facility for parents, teachers, and caregivers, is located here; call for their special hours. ♦ M-Tu, F 1-6PM; W 10AM-6PM; Th 1-8PM. 66 Leroy St (at Seventh Ave S). 243.6876

9 **Anglers & Writers** ★$ Literary Paris of the 1930s is recaptured in this cozy, unpretentious cafe/tearoom owned by mother-and-son team Charlotte and Craig Bero. It's filled with charmingly mismatched English and Austrian china, turn-of-the-century American country furniture, and shelf after shelf of books—with an emphasis on Hemingway, Fitzgerald, and fly-fishing guides. The food is hearty and all-American—beef stew, chicken potpie, open-face turkey sandwich, and sensational pies and cobblers for dessert. ♦ American ♦ M-F breakfast, lunch, and dinner; Sa-Su brunch and dinner. 420 Hudson St (at St. Luke's Pl). 675.0810

10 **Village Atelier** ★$$ Like a small country inn in southwestern France, this romantic hideaway boasts antique and cherry-wood furniture and fresh flowers on the tables. The country setting is an appropriate backdrop for the well-prepared, rustic French food served. Try the roasted pheasant with venison or grilled salmon with horseradish butter. ♦ French ♦ M-F lunch and dinner; Sa-Su dinner. Reservations recommended. 436 Hudson St (at Morton St). 989.1363 ♿

11 **75½ Bedford Street** Built in 1873, this 9.5-foot-wide building is thought to be the narrowest in the city and was the last New York City residence of Edna St. Vincent Millay and her husband, Eugen Boissevain. **No. 77** next door, built in 1800, is the oldest house in the Village. ♦ Between Morton and Commerce Sts

11 **Cherry Lane Theater** Built as a brewery in 1846, this building was converted to a 184-seat theater (founded in 1924 by Edna St. Vincent Millay) for avant-garde productions. *Godspell* had its world premiere here. ♦ 38 Commerce St (between Bedford and Barrow Sts). 989.2020

12 **The Grange Hall** ★$ A former tavern, this restored Art Deco restaurant boasts a beautiful mahogany bar and soaring columns. The raucous Generation-X scene is hip and fashionable. Grazers can choose from a large variety of organic meat and grain dishes, such as warm orange beets, available in appetizer portions. Main courses include herb-crusted organic chicken breast with honey-glazed carrots, grilled lamb steak with rosemary red cabbage, and a platter of oven-roasted seasonal farm vegetables. The farm theme is carried through to the decor: A mural of farmers graces the wall. ♦ American ♦ M-F lunch and dinner; Sa-Su brunch and dinner. Reservations recommended. 50 Commerce St (between Bedford and Barrow Sts). 924.5246

13 39 and 41 Commerce Street This well-preserved pair of mansard-roofed houses with a central garden dates to 1831. An apocryphal but oft-repeated tale is that they were built by a sea captain for his two unmarried daughters, who were not on speaking terms. ♦ Between Bedford and Barrow Sts

14 St. Luke-in-the-Fields James N. Wells designed this simple Federal-style building in 1822. Restored after a 1981 fire, it still has the feeling of a country church. St. Luke's School, one of the city's most highly respected Episcopal parochial schools, was established in 1945. The thrift store next door is a tad more expensive than you'd expect, but it's well stocked. ♦ 487 Hudson St (between Barrow and Christopher Sts). 924.0562

15 Grove Court Between 10 and 12 Grove Street, at the middle of what some consider to be the most authentic group of Federal-style houses in America, you can find one of the most charming and private enclaves in Manhattan. These six brick-fronted buildings were built in 1854 as houses for working men when the court was known as "Mixed Ale Alley." ♦ Between Bedford and Hudson Sts

16 Chumleys $$ A speakeasy during the 1920s, this signless building has a convenient back door on Barrow Street, still used by regulars. Cozy and convivial, with working fireplaces and wooden benches deeply carved with customers' initials, the place has atmosphere aplenty, but the food isn't terrific. Nevertheless, it's a great place to stop for a drink, especially if you like ghost stories. According to local legend, the long-departed Mrs. Chumley comes back and rearranges the furniture in the middle of the night. ♦ American ♦ Daily dinner. 86 Bedford St (between Barrow and Grove Sts). 675.4449

17 Twin Peaks In 1925, **Clifford Reed Daily** transformed this very conventional 1830 residence into a fairy-tale fantasy as a reaction against undistinguished Village architecture. Pseudo-Tudor details trim the stucco facing, and an unorthodox flap acts as a front cornice (there's an attic room behind it). It's not great architecture, but it's great fun. ♦ 102 Bedford St (between Grove and Christopher Sts)

18 Lucille Lortel Theatre Formerly the **Theatre De Lys,** this 299-seat house was a major boost to Off-Broadway in the 1950s, when a revival of the Brecht-Weill classic *The Threepenny Opera* was staged here. It was later renamed for its distinguished owner, Lucille Lortel, who produced *Brecht on Brecht* and John Dos Passos's *USA.* In recent times, it was home to the hugely successful *Steel Magnolias* during its 2.5-year run. ♦ 121 Christopher St (between Bleecker and Hudson Sts). 924.2817 ⅊

Mc Nulty's
Tea & Coffee Co., Inc.
Established in 1895

19 McNulty's Tea and Coffee Company In business since 1895, this place has been quietly selling exotic coffees (from China, Sumatra, and Indonesia) long before the trend for specialty coffees began in this country. The shop also stocks more than 250 varieties of tea. ♦ Daily. 109 Christopher St (between Bleecker and Hudson Sts). 242.5351

20 David's Pot Belly Stove ★$ This tiny, dimly lit place is better than most when it comes to satisfying an uncontrollable urge for a hamburger with any conceivable topping, an omelette, or a salad—even at three in the morning. Believe it or not, the eggs are a signature dish. ♦ American ♦ Daily 24 hours. 94 Christopher St (between Bleecker and Bedford Sts). 242.8036

Grove
Restaurant & Garden

21 Grove ★★$$ Whether you choose the pale yellow dining room—with wooden floors and softly lit oil paintings—or the 70-seat garden in back, you'll find this a quiet, civilized place to dine. The food is hearty and well prepared, with some unusual touches. Offerings include panroasted monkfish served with leeks and potato hash; hearty hanger steak prepared with shallots and white wine and served with french fries; and slow-roasted ratatouille with bulgur, pine nuts, and dried fruit. ♦ American ♦ M-F dinner; Sa-Su brunch and dinner. Reservations recommended. 314 Bleecker St (at Grove St). 675.9463

21 Surya ★★$$ Subdued lighting and trendy Indian techno music provide the postmodern backdrop for inventive offerings that draw on the spicy culinary traditions of Chettinand, the region of southern India around Madras. Try such fish dishes as fenugreek-scented salmon in a curry-leaf, onion, tomato, and tamarind sauce or sautéed halibut with ginger and coconut cream sauce. Most main courses are served with mint rice. The vegetarian menu is extensive. ♦ Indian ♦ M-F dinner; Sa-Su brunch and dinner. Reservations recommended. 302 Bleecker Street (between Grove St and Seventh Ave). 807.7770 &

22 Grove Street Cafe ★$$ Convenient to the Village theaters, this quaint dining room is stylish and bohemian, with exposed-brick walls and recessed lighting. Its nouvelle Italian cuisine is very good. Top choices are the creative pasta dishes or *risotto del giorno,* and grilled salmon with marinated garden vegetables. ♦ Italian ♦ M-Th dinner; F lunch and dinner; Sa-Su brunch and dinner. Reservations recommended. 53 Grove St (between Bleecker St and Seventh Ave S). 924.8299

23 Christopher Park Until the Parks Department put a sign near the entrance, everyone thought this was Sheridan Square. The confusion began when the **IRT Sheridan Square** subway stop was opened in 1918, and was compounded when Joseph Pollia's statue of the Civil War general was placed here (possibly by mistake) in 1936. ♦ Seventh Ave S (at Christopher St)

24 Sheridan Square Because **Christopher Park** is closer to the **Sheridan Square** subway stop, which is around the corner, Sheridan Square is at the same time one of the best-known and hardest to find spots in all of Greenwich Village. The community garden in the center yielded rare archaeological treasures when it was created in the early 1980s. It was the only spot in Manhattan that hadn't been disturbed since Indians lived here. ♦ Bounded by Barrow and W Fourth Sts and W Washington Pl

25 Jekyll and Hyde $ The atmosphere is dark and reminiscent of a typical 19th-century pub, except that it's cluttered with mad-scientist paraphernalia and such assorted grotesquerie as a roaring dinosaur head. The menu includes a standard range of pastas, salads, and burgers, and the bar offers an amazing selection of beer—over 250 varieties—served in authentic English yard glasses and traditional pints. ♦ American ♦ Daily lunch, dinner, and late-night meals. 91 Seventh Ave S (between Barrow and Grove Sts). 255.5388. Also at: 1409 Sixth Ave (between W 57th and W 58th Sts). 541.9517 &

26 One If By Land, Two If By Sea ★★★★$$$$ The onetime home of Aaron Burr, this romantic candlelit restaurant boasts a working fireplace, a large bar, and a pianist who plays romantic tunes nightly. Chef Thomas Donnelly creates a seasonal array of dishes that may include warm lobster medaillons and shrimp poached in chervil broth with leek fondue and Champagne, panseared tuna steak, and grilled rack of lamb served with Yukon gold potatoes and mint jus. For dessert, don't miss the bittersweet chocolate mousse torte with roasted and caramelized banana. ♦ Continental ♦ Daily dinner. Reservations required. 17 Barrow St (between Seventh Ave S and W Fourth St). 255.8649

27 Sweet Basil The giants of the jazz world perform here regularly. Most people come to listen to music and have a drink, but the club also offers food, including good salads and stir-fry dishes. ♦ Cover. Shows: daily 9, 11PM. 88 Seventh Ave S (between Barrow and Grove Sts). 242.1785

28 Ottomanelli's Meat Market For years, the window display of stuffed rabbits and game birds here gave pause to even the least repentant of carnivores. Fortunately, this shop's reputation for very fresh game is such that there is no longer a need to advertise quite so explicitly. All the meat is cut to order, and fans of the veal roast stuffed with prosciutto are legion. ♦ M-Sa. 285 Bleecker St (between Jones St and Seventh Ave S). 675.4217. Also at: Macy's Herald Square, The Cellar, Broadway (between W 34th and W 35th Sts). 695.4400

29 John's Pizzeria ★★$ Arguing about the best pizza in New York is something of a local sport, and this place, established in 1934, deserves at least honorable mention. The thin-crust pies are made in a coal oven—one reason they're so good. Another is the delicious toppings—fresh mushrooms, spicy sausage, or whatever you like. ♦ Italian ♦ Daily lunch and dinner. 278 Bleecker St (at Morton St). 243.1680 & Also at: 48 W 65th St (between Central Park W and Broadway). 721.7001; 408 E 64th St (between York and First Aves). 935.2895; 260 W 44th St (between Broadway and Eighth Ave). 391.7560

30 Cucina Stagionale ★$ The prices are low, and the menu gives a twist to basic Italian fare at this ever-popular, homey pasta place. Try the eggplant manicotti, vegetable lasagna, or any pasta with fresh seafood. But don't arrive too hungry; there's almost always a line of people waiting for a table, bottles of wine in hand (there's no liquor license). ♦ Italian ♦ Daily lunch and dinner. No credit cards accepted. Reservations recommended. 275 Bleecker St (at Jones St). 924.2707

31 Aphrodisia Whether seeking remedies or flavors, scoop your choice from among the 800 herbs and spices into a small paper bag and label it with the name and price. Those ready to turn over a new leaf could consult the wide selection of books for healthful living. ♦ Daily. 264 Bleecker St (between Sixth Ave and Seventh Ave S). 989.6440 &

31 Trattoria Pesce Pasta ★★$$ Beginning with the bright red entrance and the windows displaying the catch of the day with an array of antipasti, this is one of the neighborhood's more welcoming places. Start with a fresh antipasti selection—marinated peppers, grilled fennel, marinated white beans, mozzarella—or *pasta e fagioli* (a broth rich with beans, vegetables, and macaroni). The fish specialties change according to market availability, but keep an eye out for the excellent *zuppa di pesce* (an Italian bouillabaisse) or the mixed seafood grill. ♦ Italian ♦ Daily lunch and dinner. 262 Bleecker St (between Leroy and Morton Sts). 645.2993. Also at: 1079 First Ave (at E 59th St). 888.7884

32 A. Zito & Sons Bakery For over 50 years the authentic Italian bread's crunchy crusts and delicate inside texture have lured devoted notables: There's a photo on the wall of Frank Sinatra, who is pictured admiring a loaf. These breads, fresh from the oven, are easy to love; the whole wheat is a standout. ♦ M-Sa; Su until 2PM. 259 Bleecker St (between Cornelia and Jones Sts). 929.6139

32 Murray's Cheese Shop Nearly 200 varieties of cheeses, many from Italy, France, and Spain, are sold here at competitive prices. Superior service keeps satisfied customers coming back. Grocery items, salads, meats, and delicacies are also offered at this self-styled "mini-**Balducci's.**" ♦ Daily. 257 Bleecker St (at Cornelia St). 243.3289 &

Pó

32 Pó ★★★$$ Chef Mario Batali and partner Steve Crane change the menu seasonally, but whenever you visit this tiny, romantic place, you can count on such inventive, flavorful dishes as tomato ravioli filled with white beans in balsamic vinegar or marinated brown-butter quail with pomegranate molasses on a salad of *frisée* (curly endive). If you're having trouble making up your mind about which of the tempting Mediterranean-inspired dishes to select, a tasting menu is the way to go. ♦ Mediterranean ♦ Tu dinner; W-Su lunch and dinner. Reservations recommended. 31 Cornelia St (between Bleecker and W Fourth Sts). 645.2189

32 The Cornelia Street Café ★★$$ Started by artists nearly 23 years ago, this cafe has always been charming, with whitewashed brick walls, a fireplace, and glass-paneled doors that in summer open onto the quiet street for alfresco dining. The menu changes seasonally and includes a tasty, crisp salmon

with paella; zesty pepper-crusted yellowfin tuna with sweet garlic risotto cake; and grilled double-ribbed pork chop with spinach. Save room for one of the desserts baked on the premises—banana *tarte tatin* (caramelized upside-down tart) with cocoa sorbet, for example. There's also live music that changes weekly. ♦ Bistro/Cafe ♦ M-F breakfast, lunch, and dinner; Sa-Su brunch and dinner. Reservations recommended. 29 Cornelia St (between Bleecker and W Fourth Sts). 989.9319 &

33 Home ★★$$ This dining place was named in appreciation of the James Beard quote: "American food is anything you eat at home." Former Midwesterners David Page and Barbara Shinn have created a cozy spot, best described as an urban farmhouse, where they offer heartwarming entrées of peppered Newport steak, cumin-crusted pork chops, and grilled New York trout. Also memorable are the homemade ketchup, barbecue sauce, and thyme-mustard dressing. For dessert try the creamy dark chocolate pudding. ♦ American ♦ M-F breakfast, lunch, and dinner; Sa-Su brunch and dinner. 20 Cornelia St (between Bleecker and W Fourth Sts). 243.9579

33 Le Gigot ★★$$$ The perfect spot for a wintry Sunday night's supper, this tiny, 25-seat restaurant offers a menu composed largely of country French standbys. Senegalese chef Alioune Ndiaye prepares such outstanding dishes as *blanquette de veau; boeuf bourguignon* so rich with red wine that you'll be tempted to drink from the serving bowl after you finish the succulent and tender chunks of beef; the perfectly-cooked namesake leg of lamb; and a rich and garlicky seafood stew. Long unnoticed in the New York restaurant scene, dining at this beautifully lit and friendly bistro requires reservations. But even if you arrive without them, relax in the bar's window seat with a glass of wine: it's worth the wait. ♦ French ♦ Tu-F lunch and dinner; Sa-Su brunch and dinner. 18 Cornelia St (between Bleecker and W Fourth Sts). 627.3737

34 The Bagel ★$ The Village Breakfast—strawberry pancakes—is the big draw at this tiny restaurant and deli. It's also known for such standard deli fare as pastrami and corned beef sandwiches. ♦ American/Deli ♦ Daily breakfast, lunch, and dinner. No credit cards accepted. 170 W Fourth St (between Cornelia and Jones Sts). 255.0106

35 Caffè Vivaldi ★$ This Old World Village favorite always pleases with its relaxed and cozy atmosphere—it offers Manhattan a taste of turn-of-the-century Vienna, with dramatic arias playing in the background. Come here on a cold winter's day for a light lunch or sweets. ♦ Cafe ♦ Daily lunch, dinner, and late-night meals. 32 Jones St (between Bleecker and W Fourth Sts). 929.9384

36 St. Joseph's Church The oldest Roman Catholic church building in Manhattan, this Greek Revival temple was built in 1834 by **John Doran**. It has a gallery inside as well as delicate crystal chandeliers and a gilded sanctuary that contrasts with the simplicity of the Greek Revival exterior. The outside wall on Washington Place is made of Manhattan schist, the extremely hard stone that underlies the whole island. ◆ 371 Sixth Ave (at W Washington Pl). 741.1274

37 Gus' Place ★$$ Gus Theodoro's casual and gracious eatery specializes in Mediterranean—predominantly Greek—cuisine. The *mezedes* (a platter of assorted appetizers) is enough to send you away satisfied and mighty happy, but if you stopped there you'd miss Gus's specialty—lamb shank—and that would be a shame. ◆ Greek/Mediterranean ◆ M-Sa lunch and dinner; Su brunch and dinner. Reservations required. 149 Waverly Pl (between Gay and Christopher Sts). 645.8511 &

37 Gay Street Thought to be named after a family who lived here in the mid- to late-18th century, the block contains a well-preserved group of Greek Revival houses on the east side and Federal row houses on the west. **No. 14** is the location of the basement apartment that was the setting for Ruth McKenney's play *My Sister Eileen*, which later was made into the musical *Wonderful Town*. ◆ Between Waverly Pl and Christopher St

38 Oscar Wilde Memorial Bookshop This small shop offers a tasteful selection of books on gay and lesbian subject matter, including literary classics, rare editions, legal guides, sociology, and periodicals. ◆ Daily. 15 Christopher St (between Greenwich Ave and Waverly Pl). 255.8097

39 Three Lives & Company A wonderful collection of fiction and specialty books is carried in this store. Readings occasionally take place here on Thursday nights. The owners are knowledgeable and helpful. ◆ Daily. 154 W 10th St (at Waverly Pl). 741.2069

40 Crystal Gardens This shop for the spiritually inclined offers quartz, minerals, medicine jewelry, seminars, consultations, and an interesting newsletter written by co-owner Connie Barrett. ◆ Daily. 21 Greenwich Ave (between Christopher and W 10th Sts). 727.0692

41 Patchin Place Like Milligan Place around the corner on Sixth Avenue, this cluster of small houses constructed in 1848 by **Aaron D. Patchin** was built as rooming houses for waiters and other personnel from the now-departed **Brevoort Hotel** over on Fifth Avenue. It became famous in the 1920s as the home of poet e.e. cummings, among others. ◆ Off W 10th St (between Sixth and Greenwich Aves)

41 Cafe Asean ★★$ This warm and romantic cafe (named in recognition of the Association of South East Asian Nations), features foods from Malaysia, Thailand, Vietnam, Indonesia, and Singapore. Start with *cha glo* (Imperial rolls with shrimp, chicken, and mushrooms); *sup mang cua* (crabmeat with asparagus soup); or Malaysian salad with squid, pineapple, and cucumber. Continue the feast with Singaporean fried rice noodles with shrimp and Chinese sausage, *bo lui* (Vietnamese beef rolls with garlic and onions), or *kari kapitan* (coconut curry chicken with potatoes). It's all well prepared and the prices are very affordable. ◆ Asian ◆ Daily lunch and dinner. No credit cards accepted. 117 W 10th St (between Sixth and Greenwich Aves). 633.0348

42 New York Public Library, Jefferson Market Branch Frederick Clarke Withers and **Calvert Vaux** modeled this 1877 structure, built on the site of the old **Jefferson Market** and originally used as the **Third Judicial District Courthouse,** after Mad King Ludwig II of Bavaria's castle Neuschwanstein. It is the epitome of Victorian Gothic, with steeply sloping roofs, gables, pinnacles, sets of variously shaped arched windows, and stone carvings all set off by a rather unusual clock tower that served as a fire lookout. After the occupants moved out in 1945, the building sat idle until citizens pressured the city government to find a new user, and the public library agreed to move in. **Giorgio Cavaglieri** handled the 1967 remodeling. ◆ M-Sa. 425 Sixth Ave (at W 10th St). 243.4334 &

In the 1790s, 22,000 victims of yellow fever were buried in what is now Washington Square Park. The park was later the site of a huge celebration in 1824 when 20 highwaymen were hanged from an elm tree in the park's northwest corner.

In 1942, distressed by commercial publishers' lack of interest in her work, writer Anaïs Nin borrowed $175 and, with a friend, rented a loft at 144 MacDougal Street, purchased a used printing press, and went on to print three of her books.

Restaurants/Clubs: Red   Hotels: Blue
Shops/ ♥ Outdoors: Green   Sights/Culture: Black

43 Balducci's This is the grocery ne plus ultra in Greenwich Village. It began humbly many years ago as a produce stand across the street from the present site, and today the family-run store is one of the grandest and best-stocked specialty shops in New York City. Not only is the produce still top-notch, but the cheese selection is first-rate too, as are the fish, meat, cold cuts, and take-out dishes (try Mama's delicious sun-dried tomato sauce over spaghetti—created by the late, beloved Mama Balducci), and everything from the bakery department. The shelves hold packaged products from all over the world, but specialize in delicacies from Italy and France. ◆ Daily. 424 Sixth Ave (at W Ninth St). 673.2600 ሌ

44 Jefferson Market Devoted customers of this market enjoy its spacious aisles brimming with quality fresh produce, meats, cheeses, and other grocery items. Don't miss the famous rotisserie chickens. ◆ Daily. 450 Sixth Avenue (at W 10th St). 533.3377 ሌ

45 Gran Caffè Degli Artisti ★$ Ask for a table in the back, where it's cozy and filled with funky antiques. Don't bother with the Italian entrées; go directly to the iced mochaccino and one of the more decadent pastries or cakes. ◆ Cafe ◆ Daily lunch and dinner. 46 Greenwich Ave (between W 10th St and Seventh Ave S). 645.4431

46 Village Vanguard This world-famous basement jazz club also features Dixieland, blues, avant-garde, and folk music. Pop singers, comedians, and poets have appeared. ◆ Cover. Shows: M-Th, Su 9:30PM and 11:30PM; F-Sa 9:30PM, 11:30PM, and 1AM. Reservations recommended. 178 Seventh Ave S (at Perry St). 255.4037

47 Riviera Cafe $$ The people watching here is probably the best in the Village and better than the casual menu, which includes burgers and salads. Sip some wine and watch the ongoing parade passing by your table. ◆ American ◆ Daily lunch, dinner, and late-night meals. 225 W Fourth St (between Christopher and W 10th Sts). 929.3250

48 La Metairie ★★$$$ The Village is known for its romantic restaurants, and this rustic, candlelit place, with a white picket fence and hand-painted duck sign, is one good reason why. The menu is chef Jose Pichareo's take on Provençale cooking—duck with orange and balsamic-vinegar sauce, and sautéed salmon with a garlic-mustard crust—with the addition of lobster risotto, or some equally unexpected dish. ◆ French ◆ M-F dinner; Sa-Su brunch and dinner. Reservations recommended. 189 W 10th St (at W Fourth St). 989.0343 ሌ

The annual Halloween parade in Greenwich Village is the nation's largest night parade.

49 Pierre Deux Stop here for Provençale furniture, china, and accessories. ◆ M-Sa. 369 Bleecker St (at Charles St). 243.7740. Also at: 870 Madison Ave (at E 71st St). 570.9343

50 Biography Bookshop As the name implies, this bookstore has the best selection of biographies anywhere. Feel free to browse. ◆ Daily. 400 Bleecker St (at W 11th St). 807.8655

51 Taylor's This snug gourmet takeout is run by Cindi Taylor. The onion-poppy hot dog buns—with Pommery mustard mixed into the dough—give you a good reason to eat hot dogs, and the triple-fudge brownies will throw off your calorie count for the week. ◆ Daily. 523 Hudson St (between W 10th and Charles Sts). 645.8200. Also at: 156 Chambers St. 962.0546.

52 Sazerac House ★★$$ The building alone makes it worth a visit to this nearly 40-year-old restaurant. Part of an 18th-century farm purchased from the Earl of Abingdon, this place was renovated in 1826 by a local carpenter who made it his home. A knowing crowd, homesick New Orleanians among them, continue to come here for gumbo, jambalaya, and the perennially popular crab cakes. ◆ Cajun/Creole ◆ M-F lunch and dinner; Sa-Su brunch and dinner. Reservations recommended. 533 Hudson St (at Charles St). 989.0313

53 Caribe ★$ West Village meets West Indies at this fun and funky eatery where Jamaican food is offered in a junglelike setting. Start with a handsome bowl of black bean soup or bujol (dried codfish simmered with chopped onions, red peppers, garlic, and spices). For the brave-at-heart (-burn), try a spicy picadillo (Cuban-style pork cubes sautéed with green peppers, onions, pimentos, and olives); or ropa vieja ("old clothes"— shredded flank steak sautéed in a spicy sauce). ◆ West Indian ◆ Daily lunch and dinner. 117 Perry St (at Greenwich St). 255.9191

54 White Horse Tavern $ Come here for the sense of history, the food is not the feature— with the exception of relatively good burgers and okay fries. The poet Dylan Thomas drank himself to death in the corner of the bar, and the apocryphal story still circulating is that his last words were: "I've had 19 straight whiskeys. I believe that's the record." ◆ American ◆ M-Sa lunch, dinner, and late-night meals; Su brunch, dinner, and late-night meals. 567 Hudson St (at W 11th St). 243.9260

55 Burgundy Wine Company The finest wines of Burgundy and the Rhône are this shop's specialty. Be sure to ask for the mail-order catalog: It's an informative brochure filled with vignettes about wine merchant Al Hotchkin's travels through the vineyards, including his thoughts on wines he's discovered. ◆ M-Sa. 323 W 11th St (between Greenwich and Washington Sts). 691.9092

56 Westbeth Built in 1897 by Bell Telephone Laboratories (then Western Electric), this was where the transistor was invented and the first TV pictures were transmitted. When Bell Labs moved to the suburbs in 1965, **Richard Meier Associates** renovated the 1900 **Cyrus Eidlitz**–designed building and turned it into a nonprofit residential building exclusively for artists of all kinds (pictured below). Envisioned as a center for the arts with galleries and dance and sculpture studios, it is, in fact, merely subsidized apartments for anyone who happens to be an artist. ◆ 463 West St (at Bank St)

57 Tortilla Flats ★$ This popular West Village eatery is known for its noisy atmosphere and inexpensive Tex-Mex eats—chicken, shrimp, or steak fajitas, *enchiladas verdes* (in a green-chili salsa), and chicken and bean chimichangas—made from natural ingredients. Monday and Tuesday are big-prize bingo nights but don't bring along your mild-mannered grandma. ◆ Tex-Mex ◆ Daily lunch, dinner, and late-night meals. 767 Washington St (at W 12th St). 243.1053 &

58 Kelter/Malce Beautiful antique quilts from the early 1800s are on sale at this store, as well as a good selection of Amish and other patchwork quilts, Beacon and Pendleton blankets, Navajo weavings, folk art, and antique Christmas ornaments. ◆ M-Sa by appointment. 74 Jane St (between Greenwich and Washington Sts). 989.6760

59 Restaurant Florent ★★$$ A former diner turned hip bistro, this is a welcome late-night spot for those seeking a complete meal. Given the number of meat-packing plants in the neighborhood, meat entrées are, of course, specialties of the house. The *boudin noir* (blood sausage) appetizer and the steak *frites* (with french fries) are both popular. Any of the fish dishes are also worth trying. After midnight on weekends there's an all-night breakfast menu. Tibor Kalman's M & Co. is responsible for the very stylish design, and to some extent, the layout of the restaurant itself. ◆ Continental ◆ M-Th, Su breakfast, lunch, dinner, and late-night meals; F-Sa open 24 hours. No credit cards accepted. 69 Gansevoort St (between Ninth Ave and Washington St). 989.5779 &

60 Gansevoort Market The city's wholesale meat district is housed in this collection of old brick buildings. The action intensifies in the early morning hours before sunrise, when people from restaurants all over New York converge to find the best meat. ◆ Bounded by Ninth Ave and West St, and Gansevoort and W 14th Sts

61 Mother This smallish club on the edge of the meat-packing district attracts a loyal following for its special theme nights, which have ranged from Fang Club (vampire gothic) to Click & Drag ("cyber slut" dress code strictly enforced); not to mention theatrical spectacles of uncertain taste such as *A Very Jackie Christmas*. ◆ Call for schedule. 432 W 14th St (at Washington St). 366.5680; www.mothernyc.com

62 Patisserie J. Lanciani Magnificent French, Italian, and Viennese cakes, tarts, brownies, and croissants are offered both wholesale and retail at this bakery. ◆ Daily. 414 W 14th St (between Ninth Ave and Washington St). 989.1213 &

Westbeth

MICHAEL STORRINGS

Child's Play

1 Feel like a shrimp under the 10-ton blue whale or watch lasers dance against a night sky. Or perhaps you'd rather travel the earth with T. Rex in the **Dinosaur Halls**. All are at the **American Museum of Natural History**.

2 Kids can indulge their dreams of being firefighters at the **New York City Fire Museum**.

3 The **New York City Ballet**'s *Nutcracker Suite* brings dancing toy soldiers, evil mice, and sugarplum fairies to **Lincoln Center**.

4 The **New York Philharmonic**'s Young People's Concerts at **Avery Fisher Hall** include talks to introduce kids to classical music.

5 Getting into the **Brooklyn Children's Museum** through a 180-foot tunnel and waterway is half the fun.

6 You can climb up on a mushroom and join Alice, the Cheshire Cat, and the Mock Turtle at José de Creeft's statue overlooking **Central Park**'s **Conservatory Water**.

7 One of the best ways to enjoy **Lower Manhattan** is with a view from the deck of a 19th-century three-master on the river at the **South Street Seaport**.

8 Learn about the laws of physics in the futuristic playground of mazes and climb-friendly structures at the **New York Hall of Science** in Flushing Meadows–Corona Park.

9 Create your own animated cartoon, or pretend you're a famous movie star by looking into a "magic mirror" at the **American Museum of the Moving Image** in Astoria.

10 Produce your own newscasts and public affairs programs at the **Time Warner Center for Media** at the **Children's Museum of Manhattan**.

63 El Faro ★$$ A dark, minimally decorated den of a restaurant, this place has been around forever serving good-quality, full-flavored Spanish food. You can't go wrong with the rich and fragrant paella, seafood stew, or other fish dishes. ♦ Spanish ♦ Daily lunch and dinner. 823 Greenwich St (at Horatio St). 929.8210

64 Peanut Butter & Jane This children's clothing store stocks more than 200 brands, from basics to one-of-a-kinds by local artists, as well as toys and accessories. ♦ Daily. 617 Hudson St (between W 12th and Jane Sts). 620.7952

65 La Ripaille ★★$$ The cozy, warm atmosphere, much like a French farmhouse, makes this one of the most romantic dining spots in a neighborhood full of romantic dining spots. Chef/owner Alain Laurent takes pride in serving such *Provençale*-style dishes as duck *magret* (breast) with red currants and Port, shell steak in green peppercorn sauce, and Norwegian salmon in a light Champagne *velouté* (white sauce), all of which are consistently quite good. ♦ French ♦ M-Sa dinner. Reservations recommended. 605 Hudson St (between Bethune and W 12th Sts). 255.4406

66 Abingdon Square The square is named for Charlotte Warren, Countess of Abingdon and daughter of Sir Peter Warren, whose estate once covered this area. The statue at the uptown entrance, placed here in 1921, is a memorial to the American dead of World War I. ♦ Bounded by Bleecker St, Eighth Ave, and Hudson St, and W 11th and W 12th Sts

67 Casa di Pré ★$$ The honest, home-style food at this place that has been a fixture in the neighborhood for quite some time is cooked with a sure, light hand. Try veal *sorrentino* (cooked in a Marsala sauce with prosciutto and mozzarella) or sole *francese* (dipped in a flour-and-egg batter and sautéed in lemon butter). ♦ Italian ♦ Tu-F lunch and dinner; Sa dinner; Su brunch and dinner. Reservations recommended for three or more. 283 W 12th St (at W Fourth St). 243.7073 &

68 Corner Bistro $ If strolling around the Village has whetted your appetite for a fat, juicy burger, this neighborhood standby is the place to go. You'll have plenty of time to check out the locals in this dark, cozy pub because the service is extremely slow. ♦ American ♦ Daily lunch, dinner, and late-night meals. No credit cards accepted. 331 W Fourth St (at W 12th St). 242.9502

69 Tavern on Jane ★$$ This favorite Village gathering spot serves such basic tavern fare as fish and chips, homemade chili, burgers, pastas, salads, steaks and seafood, and daily specials. ♦ American ♦ M-F lunch and dinner; Sa-Su brunch and dinner. 31 Eighth Ave (at Jane St). 675.2526 &

70 Nell's The doormen are less choosy these days, now that the club is less in vogue. But you might still spy hip literary types and the occasional celeb lounging on one of the cushy couches. The club's main claim to fame among younger patrons is that its owner, Nell, costarred in *The Rocky Horror Picture Show.* ♦ Cover. M-Tu, Su 10PM-3AM; W-Sa 10PM-4AM. 246 W 14th St (between Seventh and Eighth Aves). 675.1567

70 Jerry Ohlinger's Movie Material Store The collection includes innumerable posters and thousands of stills in both color and black and white, including some 10,000 from Disney films alone. ♦ Daily 1-7:45PM. 242 W 14th St (between Seventh and Eighth Aves). 989.0869

71 Integral Yoga Institute All aspects of yoga are presented: meditation, breathing, relaxation, diet and nutrition, stress management, Hatha for pregnant women, video classes, chanting. The institute's store next door sells all kinds of macrobiotic essentials as well as natural cosmetics and remedies. Vitamins, minerals, herbs, and homeopathic remedies are for sale across the street at the **Natural Apothecary** (No. 234). ♦ M-Sa. 227 W 13th St (between Seventh and Greenwich Aves). 929.0586 ♿

72 Café de Bruxelles ★$$ A sophisticated bar scene is the real attraction at this lovely spot, which made a name for itself as the first Belgian restaurant in the downtown area. Don't miss the rich *waterzooi* (Belgian stew) or ever-popular *moules* (mussels). ♦ French/Belgian ♦ M-Sa lunch and dinner; Su brunch and dinner. Reservations recommended. 118 Greenwich Ave (at W 13th St). 206.1830

73 Tea and Sympathy ★$ Those enamored of bangers and mash, shepherd's pie, and other English specialties flock here. For traditionalists, there's a Sunday dinner of roast beef and Yorkshire pudding. ♦ English ♦ M-F lunch and dinner; Sa-Su breakfast, lunch, and dinner. 108 Greenwich Ave (between W 12th and 13th Sts). 807.8329 ♿

74 Benny's Burritos ★$ After sipping one of Benny's high-octane margaritas, you'll understand why it gets so rowdy here. Any one of the footlong burritos with a tempting choice of fillings at bargain prices is worth trying. So are the nachos, enchiladas, quesadillas, and chili. Expect a long wait. ♦ Tex-Mex ♦ M-F lunch, dinner, and late-night meals; Sa-Su brunch, dinner, and late-night meals. No credit cards accepted. 113

Greenwich Ave (at Jane St). 727.0584. Also at: 93 Ave A (at E Sixth St). 254.3286 ♿

75 Ye Waverly Inn ★$$ Longtime Village residents don't seem to care that the quality of the food served here—chicken potpie, Southern fried chicken, and peasant meat loaf (wrapped in homemade dough)—is not as good as it could be. They continue to flock to this handsome 150-year-old dining spot for its authentic Early American charm—irregularly shaped rooms with low ceilings, lace curtains, flowered wallpaper, and in winter, roaring fireplaces. ♦ American ♦ M-F lunch and dinner; Sa-Su brunch and dinner. Reservations required. 16 Bank St (at Waverly Pl). 929.4377

76 Chez Brigitte ★$ Come to this counter-only eatery for inexpensive French food. Friendly chef Rose Santos took over the kitchen from the late Brigitte and continues to cook simple, homey dishes such as a rich *boeuf bourguignon* and a hearty veal stew. ♦ French ♦ M-Sa lunch and dinner. No credit cards accepted. 77 Greenwich Ave (between W 11th and Bank Sts). 929.6736

77 St. Vincent's Hospital The largest Catholic hospital in the United States, built in 1977 by **Ferrez & Taylor,** this modern monstrosity is the main building and proof that not every Village community protest is successful. But the medical facility now has a physician referral service (800/999.6266) and has served the community well in every other way since it was founded by the Sisters of Charity in 1849. ♦ Seventh Ave S (between W 11th and W 12th Sts). 604.7000

78 West 14th Street Best known as a magnet for bargain-hunters, this street is also home to a number of noteworthy loft buildings. Walk on the north side of the street and look across at **Nos. 138-146** (1899), an ostentatious confection that drew on the 1893 Chicago World's Fair for its inspiration; and **Nos. 154-160** (1913), **Herman Lee Meader**'s colorful glass-and-tile design that is literally grounded in Art Nouveau and aspiring to Art Deco. ♦ Between Sixth and Seventh Aves

79 Salvation Army Centennial Memorial Temple This 1930 building by **Voorhees, Gmelin & Walker** is one of the best Art Deco extravaganzas around, with an overblown entrance and unrestrained interiors that capture the exuberance and color of the era. Not open to the public, the building houses the executive offices and programs of the Salvation Army. ♦ 120 W 14th St (between Sixth and Seventh Aves). 337.7200 ♿

80 Bar Six ★★$ With its aged, yellow ocher walls and mirrors, this bistro looks like it's been here forever. The French, American, and Moroccan food is first-rate. Best bets are the grilled spicy shrimp with warm lentil salad, lamb kabobs with lemon couscous, and chicken *tajine* (stew). ♦ Bistro ♦ M-F lunch and dinner; Sa-Su brunch and dinner. 502 Sixth Ave (between W 12th and W 13th Sts). 645.2439

81 Cafe Loup ★★$$ Cozy and comfortable, this French bistro, in business for more than 20 years, serves solid fare. Chef/owner Lloyd Feit offers tasty grilled escargots for an appetizer. Smoked brook trout, Colorado lamb chops in a Cabernet sauce, grilled skirt steak in shallot sauce, and other classically prepared French dishes are among the excellent entrées. Desserts—rice pudding with Tahitian vanilla sauce, Valrhona double chocolate pudding, wedges of intense chocolate fudge, and lemon crepes—are luscious. ♦ French ♦ M-F lunch and dinner; Sa dinner; Su brunch and dinner. Reservations recommended. 105 W 13th St (between Sixth and Seventh Aves). 255.4746 &

ZINNO 🎹

82 Zinno ★$$ Occupying the ground floor of a town house, this sleek bar and restaurant offers chamber jazz and some good food. Stick to the pastas; a good choice is homemade linguine with pancetta, porcini mushrooms, and tomatoes. ♦ Italian ♦ M-F lunch and dinner; Sa-Su dinner. 126 W 13th St (between Sixth and Seventh Aves). 924.5182 &

83 Village Community Church This abandoned gem is thought by architectural historians to be the best Greek Revival church in the city. The original design, dating to 1846, is attributed to **Samuel Thompson** and based on the Theseum in Athens. But the materials are the antithesis of the Doric model: The six huge columns and the pediment are of wood, and the walls are brick and stucco. ♦ 143 W 13th St (between Sixth and Seventh Aves)

84 James Beard House ★★★★$$$$ Major chefs from New York and around the country prepare special dinners almost nightly here, which are open to members and the public. Although it's pricey, considering the five or six courses that are served with almost as many wines, diners get their money's worth and more. Call ahead for a schedule and membership information. ♦ Eclectic ♦ Call for schedule; there is normally a single dinner seating at 7PM. Reservations required. 167 W 12th St (between Sixth and Seventh Aves). 675.4984; www.jamesbeard.org

85 Famous Ray's Pizza ★$ Though a number of impostors have tried to claim title to the name "Famous Ray the Pizza King," this Village institution is the only real heir to the throne, serving more than 2,000 loyal customers a day. Expect a line for pizza that's hardly as good as it used to be but is, at least, still fresh out of the oven. Ray's "Famous Slice" has *all* the toppings, but purists opt for the traditional "Red, White, and Green" (tomato sauce, mozzarella, basil, and parsley). ♦ Pizza ♦ Daily lunch, dinner, and late-night meals. No credit cards accepted. 465 Sixth Ave (at W 11th St). 243.2253

86 Butterfield House The 1962 edifice by **Mayer, Whittlesey & Glass** is an unusually sensitive apartment block. The fine 7-story, bay-windowed section on 12th Street is an in scale counterpoint to a series of row houses. Beyond an interior courtyard, the wing on 13th Street is taller, adapting to the stronger, larger scale of that block. ♦ 37 W 12th St (between Fifth and Sixth Aves)

87 Kate's Paperie All sorts of *papier* is found here, from gift wraps and marbleized papers to printmaking and handmade papers, Noguchi paper lamps, and Samurai-inspired dolls constructed with different textures of handmade grass papers. Make your own beautiful gifts or choose from the fine selection of journals, photo albums, and pens. Printing and engraving services are also available. ♦ M-Sa. 8 W 13th St (between Fifth and Sixth Aves). 633.0570 & Also at: 561 Broadway (between Spring and Prince Sts). 941.9816

88 East West Books A wide range of books on Eastern philosophy, religion, cooking, medicine, and New Age lifestyles are sold at this shop. ♦ Daily. 78 Fifth Ave (between W 13th and W 14th Sts). 243.5994 &

89 Parsons School of Design This college holds a unique place in American education. Here, art and industry were for the first time firmly linked on a large institutional level, even before Walter Gropius and the Bauhaus school. Founded as the **Chase School** in 1896 by painter/art teacher William Merritt Chase, the institution was spurred to its current high position in the world of art and design education by the leadership of Frank Alvah Parsons. Parsons arrived in 1907 and as the school's president implemented his vision of art and directly influenced both industry and everyday life. Under his direction the school changed its name to the **New York School of Fine and Applied Arts** and added programs such as interior architecture and design, fashion design and illustration, and advertising art. In 1940, the name was changed to honor President Parsons. In 1970 the school again took an innovative step in art education, joining with the **New School for Social Research** to broaden the scope of both institutions. **Parsons** moved to this site within the **New School** campus in 1972. Here, nearly 7,000 full- and part-time students can utilize the city's vast cultural and professional resources. The staff is made up primarily of professionals working in New York's vibrant art and design industry. In 1977, the school added a Garment District extension, the **David Schwartz Fashion Center,** at West 40th Street and Seventh Avenue. Work by students is shown from March through June at the exhibition centers at 2 West 13th Street and 66 Fifth Avenue. ♦ 66 Fifth Ave (between W 12th and W 13th Sts). 229.8910; www.parsons.edu ♿

89 Forbes Building The heart of the Forbes publishing empire is located in this 1925 **Carrère & Hastings** building. What's best here is the **Forbes Magazine Galleries** on the main floor. The collection includes more than 500 toy boats, displayed along with Art Deco fittings from the liner *Normandie* and models of the late Malcolm Forbes's private yachts. There is a collection of 12,000 toy soldiers and 250 trophies awarded for every accomplishment from raising Leghorn chickens to surviving a working lifetime in the corporate battlefields. American history is represented in a collection of presidential papers, historical documents, and model rooms. But the best part, for many, is a display of 12 Fabergé Easter eggs, the world's largest private collection of these priceless objects created for the czars of Russia. Admission is limited to 900 tickets a day and is reserved for group tours and advance reservations on Thursday. ♦ Free. Tu-W, F-Sa; call ahead to verify days and hours. 62 Fifth Ave (between W 12th and W 13th Sts). 206.5548 ♿

90 First Presbyterian Church Joseph C. Wells modeled this fine Gothic Revival church with an imposing tower after the one at Magdalen College at Oxford. The south transept, an 1893 addition by **McKim, Mead & White,** includes an outdoor pulpit overlooking the inviting garden. The **Church House,** which adjoins the church on the uptown side, was designed in 1960 by **Edgar Tafel** to perfectly match the 1846 building.
♦ 12 W 12th St (at Fifth Ave). 675.6150 ♿

91 Gotham Bar and Grill ★★★★$$$$ In this impressive, multilevel loft space—accented with massive overhead lights draped in white fabric, mustard-colored columns, and a statue of Lady Liberty—the master chef Alfred Portale continues to be in top form. His menu is superb: Try the striped bass with Manila clams, spinach, couscous, and *merguez* sausage; or rack of lamb with Swiss chard, roast shallots, and garlic mashed potatoes. Be sure to save room for one of the devastating desserts: warm chocolate cake served with toasted almond ice cream; apple *tarte tatin*; or bittersweet chocolate tiramisù. ♦ American ♦ M-F lunch and dinner; Sa-Su dinner.

Reservations required. 12 E 12th St (between University Pl and Fifth Ave). 620.4020

92 Asti $$$ Enjoy the singing waiters and professional opera singers while you eat standard Southern Italian fare. Go for the fun, which begins nightly at 6:30PM. ♦ Italian ♦ Tu-Su dinner. 13 E 12th St (between University Pl and Fifth Ave). 741.9105

93 Bowlmor Lanes The Nieuw Amsterdam Dutch introduced bowling to America, but their legacy seems to be unappreciated in Manhattan, where there are only a handful of places to play the game. This one includes a bar and grill and a pro shop. ♦ M-Th, Su 10AM-1AM; F-Sa 10AM-4AM. 110 University Pl (between E 12th and E 13th Sts). 255.8188 ♿

93 Japonica ★★★$$ Friendly service, spectacular specialty rolls, and an unusual assortment of sushi—baby yellowtail, giant clam, spicy smelt caviar, and baby octopus, all rolled with white or brown rice—draw diners from all over the city to this very small place. Those who are feeling experimental (and have some money to play with) should let the chef put a sushi assortment together—the artistry is extraordinary. ♦ Japanese ♦ Daily lunch and dinner. 100 University Pl (at E 12th St). 243.7752

94 The Cast Iron Building Designed by **John Kellum** in 1868, this building was converted from the **James McCreery Dry Goods Store** into apartments by **Stephen B. Jacobs** in 1973. In a city known for outstanding cast-iron structures (particularly in the SoHo neighborhood), this is one of the most representative examples, sporting layers of Corinthian columns topped by arches. Unfortunately, the uppermost story added later is an insensitive mismatch. ♦ 67 E 11th St (at Broadway)

95 Cedar Tavern ★$ This old, tavern-style restaurant with a beautiful back bar (over 120 years old) serves decent hamburgers, steaks, and pork chops. It has also long been a hangout for artists. ♦ American ♦ Daily lunch, dinner, and late-night meals. 82 University Pl (between E 11th and E 12th Sts). 929.9089

They're all over New York, but rooftop water tanks seem more visible in the Village than anywhere else. Their average height above sea level is about the same as a five-story building, and any building higher than that needs to pump water to its upper floors. The tanks are made of western yellow cedar and have a life expectancy of about 30 years. The two-inch boards, which are as strong as 14 inches of concrete, are held together with steel bands around the outside, and the water inside swells the wood to a tight fit. The insulating properties of wood prevent freezing in winter and keep the water cool, if not cold, in summer.

96 Il Cantinori ★★$$$ Country antiques from Italy set the stage for an authentic Tuscan meal at one of Pino Luongo's many restaurants. Begin with the assortment of grilled vegetables, then move on to *tonno al pesto* (grilled tuna steak sliced and served with pesto vinaigrette and diced tomatoes). For dessert, good luck trying to choose among the apple tart, double-layer chocolate cake, various gelati, and tiramisù. ♦ Italian ♦ Daily lunch and dinner. 32 E 10th St (between Broadway and University Pl). 673.6044

97 Knickerbocker Bar & Grill ★$$ Fascinating 19th-century artifacts and posters fill this casual yet classy bar and restaurant. T-bone steak, pork chops, and panroasted chicken are among the more popular dishes. But the subdued atmosphere and live jazz (Wednesday through Sunday starting at 9:45PM)—often featuring name performers—are the main draws. There's a small cover charge added to meals during the shows. ♦ American ♦ M-Sa lunch and dinner; Su brunch and dinner. Reservations recommended. 33 University Pl (at E Ninth St). 228.8490 &

98 The Rose Cafe ★★$$ Not surprisingly, the glassed-in sidewalk cafe is a favorite place to sit at this elegant restaurant—the windows offer a moving tableau of passersby strolling down Fifth Avenue to **Washington Square Park**. But the sophisticated dining room, with beige walls accented with mirrors and whimsical yellow, white, and green striped lighting fixtures, is also a good place to enjoy poached salmon salad, an assortment of gourmet sandwiches, pizzas with ingredients that include grilled chicken and smoked salmon, carrot ravioli in pepper-coriander sauce, grilled chicken paillard with ratatouille, and pepper-crusted loin of pork with cider sauce. ♦ American bistro ♦ M-F lunch and dinner; Sa-Su brunch and dinner. Reservations recommended. 24 Fifth Ave (at W Ninth St). 260.4118

99 Marylou's ★★$$$ Skip the appetizers and soups here and go directly to the generous main courses, particularly the perfectly broiled fresh fish, of which there are usually at least a half-dozen choices. And given the

graceful, traditional appointment in each of the four dining rooms—pleasant wood-framed paintings, fireplaces, library walls—and the friendly service, this can be considered one of the best seafood restaurants in the Village. ♦ Seafood ♦ M-Sa dinner; Su brunch and dinner. Reservations recommended. 21 W Ninth St (between Fifth and Sixth Aves). 533.0012

100 Eighth Street Since the 1960s the stretch of Eighth Street between Sixth Avenue and Broadway has been the shopping district for suburban raffish types who want the Village look, whatever that may be. The selection of stores—mostly shoes and accessories—has spilled over to Broadway, where secondhand reigns. ♦ Between Broadway and Sixth Ave

101 MacDougal Alley Like Washington Mews, this is a street of converted stables, with the advantage of trees but the same disadvantage of parked cars. **No. 7,** on the north side, was built in 1899 as a studio for a stained-glass artisan. **No. 17½** was converted to a home for Gertrude Vanderbilt Whitney, founder of the **Whitney Museum,** in 1934. **No. 19,** on the south side, was built in 1901 as an automobile stable, and the 1854 stable that is **No. 21** was reconstructed in 1920 by architect **Raymond Hood.** ♦ Off MacDougal St (between Washington Sq N and W Eighth St)

102 New York Studio School of Drawing, Painting & Sculpture The Whitney Museum was established here in 1931. Tradition was already evident on the block, which was the heart of the Village art scene at the time. It began with the conversion of a stable at 4 West Eighth Street by **John Taylor Johnston** as a gallery for his private art collection. His friends were so impressed that they got together and founded the **Metropolitan Museum of Art** in 1870. ♦ 8 W Eighth St (between Fifth and Sixth Aves). 673.6466

103 Patricia Field Trendsetting fashions for women and men are this store's forte, great for those who live by their own dress code. Unless you work in a most uncorporate job or as a bartender in a club, you probably won't get a chance to wear most of what's for sale here to the office. Still, the music's great and the clientele colorful. ♦ Daily. 10 E Eighth St (between University Pl and Fifth Ave). 254.1699

104 Clementine ★★★$$$ Understated drama defines the dining experience at this new restaurant. Start off with a cocktail (many of which feature clementine juice) at the 30-foot bar. Move into the dining room where a pool of gurgling water, complete with rock garden, dominates. But what clearly takes center stage here is chef John Schenk's innovative, flavorful cooking, which leans, in his own words, more toward funk than finesse. Try the roasted cod with balsamic reduction, mashed potatoes, and sweet roasted carrots; delectable Buffalo mahimahi; or chili-rubbed pork loin with mustard greens, cheddar-coriander custard, and barbecued onions, and you'll see what he means. For dessert? The baked hot fudge or anything else with chocolate. **Kumquat,** the restaurant's delivery service, features a lower-price menu for those who want to try Schenk's fare at home. ♦ American ♦ Daily dinner and late-night meals. Reservations recommended. 1 Fifth Ave (at E 8th St). 253.0003

105 Washington Mews Some of these charming buildings behind the town houses on Washington Square North were stables in the early 1900s. But those on the south side of the alley, more uniform because they were all stuccoed at the same time, date from the 1930s. Most are now used by **NYU.** Their size and quaintness contribute to the small-scale, congenial atmosphere of the neighborhood. ♦ Between University Pl and Fifth Ave

MICHAEL STORRINGS

106 Washington Square Village life centers around this square. Joggers, children, university students, and Village matrons provide the local color; flea markets and fairs occupy the grounds on weekends. The area was a marsh, a potter's field, a venue for public hangings, and a military parade ground before it was claimed as a public park in 1828. Elaborate, fashionable houses soon appeared around it, and **NYU** appropriated the east side in the late 1830s. The **Memorial Arch** (pictured above), designed by **Stanford White** of **McKim, Mead & White,** was originally a wooden monument built in 1889 for the centennial celebration of George Washington's inauguration. It became so well liked that private funds were raised to rebuild it permanently in stone. The sculpture,

Washington, on the west pier was created by Alexander Stirling Calder, father of Alexander Calder. By the 1950s the park had seriously decayed. The city transit authority was using the arch as a bus turnaround, and there was a proposal to run Fifth Avenue underneath it. Popular outrage blocked the tunnel, put a halt to the buses, and gave momentum to the movement to redesign the park—a community effort that was realized in the 1960s. The park has become haven to a variety of street types—performers, wanderers, and chess-players—but the local community has made a concerted effort to keep it safe. Weekend afternoons in warm weather still bring out a wild mix. ♦ Bounded by Washington Sq E and Washington Sq W, and Washington Sq S and Washington Sq N

107 Washington Square North At one time there were 28 of these exemplary Greek Revival row houses—home to the cream of New York society when they were built in 1831 and later the center of an artistic community. The first six constructed, **Nos. 21 to 26,** by **Martin E. Thompson,** remain intact. **Nos. 7 to 13** were gutted in the late 1930s, and the facades alone are left, fronts for an apartment complex owned by **NYU.** Of those demolished, **No. 1** was at one time or another the home of Edith Wharton, William Dean Howells, and Henry James, who set his novel *Washington Square* at **No. 18,** his grandmother's house; **No. 3** was where John Dos Passos wrote *Manhattan Transfer;* and **No. 8** was once the residence of the mayor. To the west of Fifth Avenue, the mock-Federal wing of the apartment tower at 2 Fifth Avenue was a compromise by the builder, **Samuel Rudin,** in response to community objection to the original plan, which had the tower on the square. ♦ Between University Pl and MacDougal St

108 Washington Square Hotel $ In 1961, this was called the **Hotel Earle** and was the first New York residence of Bob Dylan, who played bars and coffeehouses in the neighborhood. Today its modest accommodations are popular with dollar-conscious graduate students and young Europeans. Nearly all 170 rooms have been renovated; ask for one overlooking Washington Square. A complimentary breakfast is served at **C3 Restaurant & Lounge** (see below) and an exercise room is available for guests' use. The location is perfect if you plan to spend a lot of time in the Village. ♦ 103 Waverly Pl (at MacDougal St). 777.9515, 800/222.0418; fax 979.8373; wshotel@ix.netcom.com; www.wshotel.com

Within the Washington Square Hotel:

C3 Restaurant & Lounge ★★$ This restaurant with burgundy leather booths and beaded lamps features a relaxing atmosphere and friendly service. There's also some very earthy, satisfying food that chef John McGrath prepares with a sophisticated twist. His signature dish, plaintain-crusted snapper with roasted corn salad and red pepper pesto, is just one example of the crosscultural menu offerings. The good-quality wine list is very affordable. The **Lounge** is a good place for a quiet drink; jazz is played here on Tuesday nights. ♦ American ♦ M-F breakfast, lunch, afternoon tea, and dinner; Sa-Su brunch, afternoon tea, and dinner. 254.1200

109 Babbo ★★★$$$ Refined Italian regional cooking prepared with an uncommon flair is what packs them in nightly here at one of the Village's most exciting new restaurants. Chef Mario Batali changes the menu according to what's freshest at the market, but you can always expect innovation in every bite. Antipasti might include organic lettuces with a black olive blood orange citronette or sweet pea "flan" with sweet pea shoots and a carrot marinade. Try one of the sublime pasta dishes—goat cheese tortellini with dried orange and wild fennel pollen (it's delicious) or *spaghettini* with spicy artichokes, sweet garlic, and a one-pound lobster. Follow with the spicy two-minute calamari or any of the savory grilled meat or game dishes. Desserts are the stuff sweet dreams are made of: saffron *panna cotta* with blood oranges and blood orange sorbet and a devilishly divine chocolate pistachio *semifreddo* (soft ice cream) are standouts. The prix-fixe tasting menus are a good deal, and the extensive all-Italian wine list is sure to please even the most discriminating oenophiles. ♦ Italian ♦ Daily dinner. 110 Waverly Pl (between Washington Sq W and Sixth Ave). 777.0303

110 Antique Boutique The city's largest used-clothing store boasts more than 30,000 pieces, including leather jackets, men's oversize cashmere coats, and gabardine shirts. It's not unusual to see some of New York's top designers shopping here for ideas they'll take home in their minds if not in a shopping bag. ♦ Daily. 712-714 Broadway (between W Fourth St and Washington Pl). 460.8830 &

111 Bottom Line Theater Cabaret This small cabaret-style nightclub with a superlative sound system was the model for Boston's Paradise and LA's Roxy. Best known as the launching pad for Bruce Springsteen and Patti Smith, among others, its days as an industry showcase are long gone. But the club still continues a remarkably consistent booking policy, which includes jazz groups, comedy, drama, and assorted special presentations. The place is comfortable, clean, and efficient. A bar menu is available. Call for changing show schedules. ♦ Cover, drink minimum. ♦ Shows: daily 7:30 and 10:30PM. 15 W Fourth St (at Mercer St). 228.7880

112 New York University (NYU) More than 15,000 full-time students study at the Washington Square campus of New York's largest private university, composed of 14 schools, including the **Tisch School of the Arts** and the highly regarded **NYU School of Business and Public Administration.** The campus extends beyond the classroom and dormitory buildings and into the converted lofts and Greek Revival row houses common in Greenwich Village. When the old University Heights campus in the Bronx was sold to the **City University of New York** in 1973, the focus shifted here.

Architects **Philip Johnson** and **Richard Foster** were commissioned to make a master plan that would unify the disjointed collection of buildings and enable the campus to handle the increased activity. Their plan called for rebuilding some of the older structures, refacing the existing ones with red sandstone, and establishing design guidelines for future construction. Only three buildings were refaced before the plan was abandoned. ♦ Bounded by Mercer and Macdougal Sts, and W Third and E Eighth Sts. 998.4636

Within New York University:

Elmer Holmes Bobst Library Designed by **Philip Johnson** and **Richard Foster** to be the architectural focal point of the university, this stolid-looking cube is 150 feet high and clad in Longmeadow redstone (in the tradition of Washington Square), with a 12-story interior atrium around which the stacks and reading rooms are organized. Chevronlike stairways with gold anodized aluminum railings provide scale, and the design of the marble floor, influenced by Palladio's piazza for Venice's San Giorgio Maggiore, adds to the decorative interior detail that is the antithesis of the austere exterior. The building is not open to the public. ♦ Washington Sq S and La Guardia Pl. 998.2505 &

Judson Memorial Baptist Church This Romanesque church, erected in 1892 by **McKim, Mead & White** was built as a bridge between the poor to the south of the square and the rich above it and has always had a full program of social activities in addition to its famous performance schedule, from avant-garde theater and concert music in the 1960s to dance and performance art today. The best part is inside, where you can appreciate the fine stained-glass windows by John LaFarge. The church was named for Adinoram D. Judson, the first Baptist missionary to Burma. **Judson Hall** and the bell tower above it functioned until recently as **NYU** dormitories. ♦ 55 Washington Sq S (between Thompson and Sullivan Sts). 477.0351

Hagop Kevorkian Center for Near Eastern Studies Designed in 1972 by **Philip Johnson** and **Richard Foster,** this huge granite building fits snugly into its corner site and is highlighted by an interesting array of angled corner windows. ♦ 50 Washington Sq S (at Sullivan St). 998.8877 &

13 Le Frite Kot ★$ Come here when you crave french fries the way the Belgians make them: twice fried in peanut oil and served with a variety of sauces, the best of which is garlic mayonnaise. You won't be sorry; this authentic dive serves nothing but the Belgian trinity of *frites,* mussels, and beer, but what more could you possibly want? ♦ Belgian fast food ♦ Daily lunch and dinner.148 W 4th St (between MacDougal St and Sixth Ave). 979.2616

14 Blue Note Jazz Club Top jazz artists perform here nightly at 9 and 11:30PM (and sometimes again at 1AM), and on the weekend for a jazz brunch and matinee at 1PM and 3:30PM. A reasonably priced continental menu is available. Grover Washington Jr., the Modern Jazz Quartet, and Oscar Peterson all make appearances. ♦ Cover, drink minimum. Daily. Reservations recommended. 131 W Third St (between MacDougal St and Sixth Ave). 475.8592

15 Bleecker Bob's Golden Oldies The selection of records and CDs is voluminous, grouped according to genre (everything except classical and opera), not artist, but the knowledgeable staff knows the location of every last recording, and late-night browsing is an encouraged Village tradition. You might find yourself elbow-to-elbow with rock stars themselves. ♦ M-Th, Su noon-1AM; F-Sa noon-3AM. 118 W Third St (between MacDougal St and Sixth Ave). 475.9677 &

15 Caffè Reggio Home since 1927 to one of New York City's oldest cafes, this fabulously bleak place was built around 1785. It's a great spot for deep conversation or journal writing. Sip your coffee outside in nice weather. ♦ Daily lunch and dinner; M-Th, Su until 2AM; F-Sa until 4AM. No credit cards accepted. 119 MacDougal St (at W Third St). 475.9557

15 Players Theatre When the **Shakespeare Wright Company** first opened this 248-seat theater in 1959, they mainly performed works by the Bard. Today they rent out the space for a variety of performance types: music, drama, comedy, one-person shows. ♦ 115 MacDougal St (at Minetta La). 254.5076

16 La Bohème ★$$ With its open kitchen, floral arrangements, and dim lighting, this bistro is a cozy spot to enjoy specialties from Provence—confit of duck with orange and pear sauce and herb-crusted grilled chicken served with mashed potatoes and caramelized garlic. In warmer months, the room opens onto Minetta Lane, a charming, quiet street—something of a rarity in noisy Manhattan. ♦ French ♦ Tu-F dinner; Sa-Su brunch and dinner. 24 Minetta La (between MacDougal St and Sixth Ave). 473.6447

116 Minetta Lane Theatre This Off-Broadway theater presents revues as well as new plays in a more comfortable setting than many. It has 378 seats. ♦ 18 Minetta La (between MacDougal St and Sixth Ave). 420.8000 &

117 1 Minetta Street DeWitt Wallace and his wife, Lila Acheson, published the first issue of the *Reader's Digest* from a basement apartment here in 1922. ♦ At Sixth Ave

118 Minetta Tavern ★$$ The caricatures and murals behind the old oak bar and elsewhere around this Italian restaurant will take you back to the Village of the 1930s. The menu offers standard Italian fare, which is nicely prepared, if not very exciting. ♦ Italian ♦ Daily lunch and dinner. 113 MacDougal St (at Minetta La). 475.3850 &

119 Porto Rico Opened in 1907, this old-time coffee store isn't even one of the Village's oldest, but the long lines of caffeine-oholics on Saturday mornings are evidence that it's the uncontested favorite. Two reasons: the quality of the beans and the price. ♦ Daily. 201 Bleecker St (between MacDougal St and Sixth Ave). 477.5421

120 Caffè Dante Although Italian is spoken here, this place is really made authentic by the strong coffee and the let-them-sit-as-long-as-they-want attitude. Treat yourself to the cheesecake. ♦ M-Th until 2AM; F-Su until 3AM. No credit cards accepted. 79 MacDougal St (between W Houston and Bleecker Sts). 982.5275

121 Da Silvano ★★$$ An interesting menu at this dining spot features Tuscan fare. Start with chicken-liver *crostini* (toasts), followed by *rigatoni focaccia* (in a sauce of butter, cream, garlic, sage, rosemary, tomato, and double-smoked bacon) or quail in a Barolo wine sauce with radicchio. The elegantly rustic rooms attract a handsome, affluent clientele. The service is correct, and the wine list well chosen. ♦ Italian ♦ M-Sa lunch and dinner; Su dinner. Reservations recommended. 260 Sixth Ave (between W Houston and Bleecker Sts). 982.2343 &

122 Aggie's ★$ It looks like an LA diner, but the attitude is pure New York, and you'll find the home-style cooking hearty no matter where you're from. The signature chili con carne and meat loaf with mashed potatoes are favorites. ♦ American ♦ M-Sa breakfast, lunch, and dinner; Su lunch. No credit cards accepted. 146 W Houston St (at MacDougal St). 673.8994 ᕃ

122 Raffetto's Fresh pasta is made daily (witness the alchemy next door), and it's cut into a variety of widths before your eyes. Stuffed versions—including ravioli and tortellini—are also for sale, as are imported Italian products that will help you create first-rate dishes. ♦ Tu-Sa. 144 W Houston St (between Sullivan and MacDougal Sts). 777.1261 ᕃ

123 MacDougal-Sullivan Gardens Historic District These 24 houses date from 1844 to 1850. To attract middle-class professionals, **William Sloane Coffin** (heir to the W.J. Sloane furniture fortune) modernized them in 1920 and combined their gardens to make a midblock private park. ♦ Sullivan and MacDougal Sts (between W Houston and Bleecker Sts)

Within the MacDougal-Sullivan Gardens Historic District:

Chez Jacqueline ★★$$ Owned and run by lively Jacqueline Zini, this popular bistro specializes in dishes from her native Provence, including one of the best fish soups in town and a delicious beef stew cooked in red wine. Other winners are the rack of lamb with fresh herbs and sautéed veal kidneys with braised onion. Try the *tarte tatin* for dessert. ♦ French ♦ M-F lunch and dinner; Sa-Su dinner. Reservations required. 72 MacDougal St. 505.0727 ᕃ

"I should have been born in New York, I should have been born in the Village, that's where I belong."

John Lennon

Edna St. Vincent Millay gained her middle name by virtue of being born in St. Vincent's Hospital.

In the 1820s, a stagecoach ride from the Battery to Greenwich Village took one hour. By 1830, horse-drawn trolleys had reached 15th Street.

It is rumored that during World War II a man secretly lived within the Washington Square Memorial Arch for seven months and was discovered when he hung his wash out to dry.

Restaurants/Clubs: Red   **Hotels:** Blue

Shops/♥ Outdoors: Green   **Sights/Culture:** Black

124 Sullivan Street Playhouse This 153-seat theater has long been home to the longest-running production in American history, *The Fantasticks*, which opened in May 1960. In honor of this feat, Sullivan Street along this block has been dubbed "Fantasticks' Lane" by the city. ♦ 181 Sullivan St (between W Houston and Bleecker Sts). 674.3838

125 Le Figaro Café $ In the old days, this place was a Beat hangout, with underground shows downstairs. But that, as they say, is history. Today this high-volume beanery caters to the weekend blitz of young tourists on Bleecker Street. ♦ Bistro/Cafe ♦ M-F lunch and dinner; Sa-Su brunch, dinner, and late-night meals. No credit cards accepted. 184 Bleecker St (at MacDougal St). 677.1100 ᕃ

126 Caffè Borgia This old-world coffeehouse is authentic right down to the smoke-dulled mural. It's a perfect place to spend an afternoon sipping cappuccino and reading a good book. For the hungry, there are sandwiches, quiches, and pastries as well. ♦ M-Th, Su 10AM-2AM; F 10AM-4AM; Sa 10AM-5AM. 185 Bleecker St (at MacDougal St). 674.9589. Also at: 161 Prince St (between W Broadway and Thompson St). 677.1850

127 Il Mulino ★★★★$$$ Behind the unassuming facade lies one of the best and most popular Italian restaurants in the city. Once seated in the cozy dining room with its exposed-brick walls, begin with something from the delightful antipasto table—carpaccio, clams casino, or the crispy fried zucchini. Follow with one of the delicious entrées: chicken braised in wine and artichokes; fillet of beef in caper sauce; rolled veal with wine, cream, and wild mushrooms; or salmon with porcini mushrooms. For dessert try the sinfully rich chocolate mousse (this wicked concoction is prepared daily); if it seems overindulgent, then settle for juicy poached pear topped with fresh cream. There's an extensive wine list. ♦ Italian ♦ M-F lunch and dinner; Sa dinner. Reservations required. 86 W Third St (between Thompson and Sullivan Sts). 673.3783

128 Classic Toys Put together your own private army, create a miniature zoo, or mount a wee Wild West show from this imaginative collection. Collectors and commercial photographers, as well as local children, shop here for tin soldiers and matchbox cars, circus sets, and stuffed dinosaurs. ♦ Tu-Su noon-6:30PM. 218 Sullivan St (between Bleecker and W Third Sts). 674.4434

128 Science Fiction Shop Although New York's sci-fi fans may miss the otherworldly atmosphere of the old shop on Bleecker Street, they're still hooked on the excellent stock of new, out-of-print, and used books and periodicals sold here. ♦ Daily. 214

Sullivan St (between Bleecker and W Third Sts). 473.3010

29 Nostalgia and All That Jazz II Here's an impressive selection of vintage records with an emphasis on jazz, as well as one of New York's best selections of early radio programs and film soundtracks. ◆ Daily. 217 Thompson St (between Bleecker and W Third Sts). 420.1940 &

30 Village Chess Shop You can play chess from noon to midnight with another expert like yourself or buy unique chess sets made from materials ranging from nuts and bolts to ivory and onyx. ◆ Daily noon-midnight. 230 Thompson St (between Bleecker and W Third Sts). 475.8130 &

30 Grand Ticino ★★$$ A neighborhood favorite since 1919, this small Italian restaurant will satisfy the most romantic notions of an evening in Greenwich Village—forest-green walls and burnished wood, muted wall sconces and linen tablecloths. Among the tasty choices on the menu are *stracciatella alla Romana* (Italian egg drop soup with spinach) and *vongole reganate* (baked clams), and a flavorful *risotto piemontese* (with mushrooms). For a dramatic dessert, order the hot zabaglione to be flambéed tableside. ◆ Northern Italian ◆ Daily lunch and dinner. 228 Thompson St (between Bleecker and W Third Sts). 777.5922

31 Stella Dallas The shop is a good source for reasonably priced men's and women's retro rags from the 1930s to 1950s, collected by a fashion stylist and a clothing designer. ◆ Daily. 218 Thompson St (between Bleecker and W Third Sts). 674.0447

32 Il Ponte Vecchio ★$$ This bustling white dining room decorated with posters is one of the old reliable Italian places in the neighborhood, and it offers a large, traditional menu. Try the calamari with marinara sauce; asparagus topped with parmesan; *spaghetti amatriciana;* rigatoni with sausage and cream; fettuccine with sun-dried tomatoes and arugula; chicken with white wine, artichokes, mushrooms, and peppers; and old-fashioned cheesecake. ◆ Italian ◆ M-Sa lunch and dinner; Su dinner. Reservations recommended. 206 Thompson St (between Bleecker and W Third Sts). 228.7701 &

33 Bitter End Once a springboard for numerous musical careers, this small room now features mostly once-famous folkies and/or young hopefuls performing rock, folk, country, and occasionally comedy. ◆ Cover, drink minimum. Daily 7:30PM-4AM. 147 Bleecker St (between La Guardia Pl and Thompson St). 673.7030

33 Peculier Pub More than 250 brands of beer from 35 countries are served here to students from almost as many American colleges. ◆ M-Th, Su 4PM-2AM; F 4PM-4AM; Sa 2PM-4AM. 145 Bleecker St (between La Guardia Pl and Thompson St). 353.1327

Ennio & Michael

134 Ennio & Michael ★★$$$ Welcome to a well-run, cheerfully bustling trattoria. The large, airy dining room features photographs taken by New York radio personality Cousin Brucie, as well as paintings by local artists. Among the hearty offerings are a fried zucchini appetizer and such satisfying main courses as *spaghetti puttanesca* (with tomatoes, capers, and olives) and *rigatoni matriciana* (with fresh tomato sauce, prosciutto, and onions). ◆ Italian ◆ Daily lunch and dinner. 539 La Guardia Pl (between Bleecker and W Third Sts). 677.8577 &

135 University Village This 1966 high-rise housing complex is noteworthy in a city where high-rises are the norm, thanks to **I.M. Pei & Partners'** deft handling of scale, a result of the well-articulated facade. The concrete framing and recessed glass clearly define each apartment unit and provide a straightforward, unadorned exterior pattern. Because of a pinwheel apartment plan, the inner corridors are short, and apartments are unusually spacious. Two towers are owned by **NYU;** the third is a co-op. A 36-foot-high sculpture in the plaza between the towers is an enlargement of a cubist piece by Picasso. **I.M. Pei & Partners** used the same exterior treatment in the **Kip's Bay** housing project (Second Ave and W 30th St). ◆ 100 and 110 Bleecker St (between Mercer St and La Guardia Pl); 505 La Guardia Pl (at Bleecker St)

136 Cable Building McKim, Mead & White designed this building in 1894. It was once the headquarters and powerhouse of the Broadway Cable Traction Company, which operated streetcars propelled by underground cables in the 19th century. ◆ 611 Broadway (at W Houston St)

Within the Cable Building:

Angelika Film Center Big commercial hits as well as a selection of independent and foreign films are shown in this six-screen cinema. The cafe, a good spot for reading the paper or writing in a journal, serves snacks until midnight. ◆ Mercer and W Houston Sts. 777.FILM

East Village

The East Village is counterculture central, where shaved heads, tattoos, and various pierced body parts are as common as is the designer-clad crowd on Madison Avenue. In this neighborhood bounded by the **East River, Broadway,** and **East Houston** and **East 14th Streets,** many of the galleries, boutiques, clubs, and restaurants represent the cutting edge of what's next in downtown.

This last bastion of bohemia was once the grandest part of Greenwich Village. Governor Peter Stuyvesant's estate originally covered the area from the present **Fourth Avenue** to the East River and from **East Fifth** to **East 17th Streets.** He is buried beneath his chapel, now the site of **St. Mark's-in-the-Bowery Church** (built in 1799), today known as much for its ministry to the disadvantaged and its far-out religious services as for its historical significance. In the 1830s, the houses of the Astors, Vanderbilts, and Delanos lined **Lafayette Street** from **Great Jones Street** to **Astor Place.** Almost

nothing is left from those times except the **Old Merchants' House** on **East Fourth Street** near Lafayette Street and the remaining homes of **Colonnade Row** (also known as "LaGrange Terrace"), where John Jacob Astor and Warren Delano, FDR's grandfather, lived.

Astor Place was once the scene of the **Vauxhall Gardens,** where people went in the summer to enjoy music and theater. It was replaced by the popular **Astor Place Opera House,** which is remembered chiefly for the 1849 riot between rival claques (hands hired to applaud a certain performer or act) of the British actor William Macready and the American Edwin Forrest, in which 34 people were killed (or 22, depending on which account you read) before the militia brought the crowd under control. Astor Place was named for the first John Jacob Astor, who arrived from Germany in 1789 at the age of 21 with $25. Before his death at the age of 85, he had made a fortune in fur trading and Manhattan real estate.

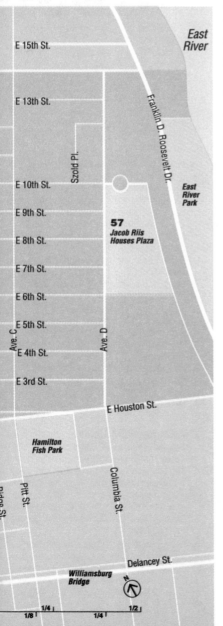

The **Astor Library,** built with a bequest from John Jacob Astor, is now the home base of the **New York Shakespeare Festival** at the **Public Theater,** an enterprise where something exciting is always on the boards or on the screen. Other architectural survivors from the 1850s are the Italianate **Cooper Union,** the country's first coeducational college and the first open to all races and creeds.

For at least 30 years, the East Village has been an enclave of counterculture; in the 1960s, hippies crowded into Day-Glo–painted "digs," spending nights with the Grateful Dead or Iron Butterfly at such clubs as the **Fillmore East** and the **Electric Circus.** Though geographically connected to its gentrified western neighbor, Greenwich Village, the East Village is a younger, less manicured community. But things aren't as gritty as they once were. Even the streets of the so-called "Alphabet City" (**Avenues A, B, C, and D**), once seedy and drug-infested, are now lined with restaurants and boutiques.

The East Village is more than ever a melting pot. The Italian influence is still visible in the old-fashioned *pasticcerie* (pastry shops). **Little India,** the stretch of **East Sixth Street** between **First** and **Second Avenues,** contains at least 20 Indian and Pakistani restaurants, with another half-dozen spilling over onto the avenues. Near Astor Place at **Cooper**

Square (Third Avenue) and **East Seventh Street** is **Little Ukraine**—a world of Byzantine churches with onion domes, shops with Slavic music and painted eggs, and restaurants serving piroshki and stuffed cabbage. Multiethnic, yes. Flamboyant, absolutely. Happily, everyone seems to coexist peacefully in what is one of the most colorful niches of New York City today.

---

1 Louisiana Community Bar and Grill ★$$ Come here for the food: crawfish boil, red beans and rice with andouille sausage and cornbread, and Cajun chicken wings in a jalapeño-garlic-pepper sauce are genuinely down-home and prepared by chef Salvador Garcia, who was trained by Paul Prudhomme. There's live music nightly. ♦ Cajun ♦ Daily dinner. Reservations recommended. 622 Broadway (between E Houston and Bleecker Sts). 460.9633

2 New York Mercantile Exchange In 1882, **Herman J. Schwartzmann** designed this cast-iron jungle with bamboo stems, lilies, and roses complemented with Oriental motifs. The **Exchange**, obviously no longer here, was once headquarters for all the big butter-and-egg men and wholesale dealers in coffee, tea, and spices. The ground floor is currently occupied by **Urban Outfitters**, clothier to many a university student. ♦ M-Sa 10AM-10PM; Su noon-8PM. 628 Broadway (between E Houston and Bleecker Sts). 475.0009

3 Bayard Condict Building The only **Louis Sullivan** building in New York is hidden among the industrial high-rises on Bleecker Street. The structure (formerly the **Condict Building**) was already an anachronism when it was completed in 1898, because the Renaissance Revival style that followed the 1893 Chicago World's Fair turned popular taste away from the elegant, quintessentially American designs of **Sullivan** and the Chicago School. The intricate cornice filigree and soaring vertical lines of the terra-cotta–clad steel piers are **Sullivan** trademarks; the six angels at the roofline were applied under pressure from the client. ♦ 65 Bleecker St (between Lafayette St and Broadway)

4 Sphere Whether you're looking for a slightly unusual outfit or something that screams "downtown," chances are you'll find the clothes that fit the bill here. The womens- and menswear in this funky, attractive NoHo boutique are the products of such cutting-edge yet affordable designer companies as Onyx Noir, Nero Bianco, and Bill Hallman. ♦ Daily. 357 Lafayette St (between Bleecker and Bond Sts). 673.8850

5 Bouwerie Lane Theatre In 1874, when the lower end of the Bowery was a theater district, **Henry Engelbert** built this fanciful cast-iron building as a bank. Today, it is the home of the **Jean Cocteau Repertory,** an unusual company of resident actors that often

performs several works in the same week. Its presentations are usually classical plays or plays by writers better known for other literary genres. ♦ 330 Bowery (at Bond St). 677.0060

6 CBGB and OMFUG Long after everyone has forgotten what the initials of this Bowery dive stand for (Country, BlueGrass, Blues, and Other Music For Uplifting Gourmandisers), they will remember it as the birthplace of punk rock. Here, as it has since 1974, this long, dark bar illuminated by neon beer signs still plays host to an array of groups under a wide banner of styles. ♦ Cover. Daily 8PM-3AM. 315 Bowery (between E First and E Second Sts). 982.4052

7 New York Marble Cemetery Located on the inside portion of the block (enter from an alley on Second Street), this early 1800s cemetery was one of the first built in the city and is one of the very few left in Manhattan. The burial vaults are underground, and the names of those interred are carved into marble tablets set into a perimeter wall that surrounds a small grassy area. Down the block (52-74 E Second St) is the **New York City Marble Cemetery,** started in 1831 along the same nonsectarian lines but with aboveground vaults and handsome headstones. Genealogists can trace New York's early first families—the Scribners, Varicks, Beekmans, Van Zandts, Hoyts, and one branch of the Roosevelts—from tombstone information. Burial here is restricted to the descendants of the original vault owners, but no one has applied since 1917. ♦ E Second St (between Second Ave and Bowery)

8 Anthology Film Archives Located in the **Second Avenue Courthouse** building, this center for the preservation and exhibition of film and video works holds daily screenings that are open to all. Only students, scholars, museums, and universities have access to the archives and library. ♦ Admission. Daily; call for schedules. 32 Second Ave (at E Second St). 505.5110

9 Irreplaceable Artifacts of North America Evan Blum salvages buildings, so on any given day you're likely to find saloon bars, lighting fixtures, antique architectural ornaments, neon marquees, or stained-glass windows in his showrooms. There are seven floors chockablock with fascinating collectibles from Europe, Canada, South America, and the United States. ◆ Daily. 14 Second Ave (between E Houston and E First Sts). 473.3300

10 Chez Es Saada ★★★$$$ Androgynous pretty boys lounging in Middle Eastern garb and rose petals strewn about the floor contribute to a decadent atmosphere that's heightened by delicious hummus, *baba ganooj*, and other Middle Eastern grazing grub. Pricey but good. ◆ Middle Eastern ◆ Daily dinner. Reservations recommended. 42 E 1st St (between First and Second Aves). 777.5617

11 Style Swami Colorful women's and men's African clothing designed by Alpana Bawa is showcased in this shop, along with a selection of home furnishings. ◆ Tu-Su. 70 E First St (between First and Second Aves). 254.1249

11 City Lore In a gentrified brownstone just off First Avenue, a group of serious folklorists explore New York cultural traditions through photo and tape archives, oral histories, discussion groups, music and film festivals, and concerts. ◆ Call for an appointment M-F. 72 E First St (between First and Second Aves). 529.1955

12 Boca Chica ★$$ This place used to have wild dancing on weekends and nights, but has tamed down of late. Discerning patrons now come to enjoy delicious and fresh Pan-Latin cuisine: coconut shrimp, plantains, various curry-infused fish dishes, seviche, and such. The main room is understated and pleasant. Best of all, the food is a real bargain. ◆ Pan-Latin ◆ M-Sa dinner; Su brunch and dinner. 13 First Ave (at E First St). 473.0108

13 Lucien ★★$$ Small and cozy, this place has closely set tables that would spell crowded in a less appealing restaurant. There are daily fish specials as well as such French classics as coq au vin. The service is excellent. ◆ French ◆ M-Sa dinner; Su brunch and dinner. 14 First Ave (at E First St). 260.6481

14 Lucky Cheng's ★★$$ At this trendy Asian spot, the waitresses in their tight silk dresses are not what they seem—they're actually men in a sort of lighthearted version of *M. Butterfly*. The food is as dramatic as the servers: Indonesian chicken or beef satay, grilled mahimahi in a tangy Vietnamese sauce, Chinese five-spice chicken with roasted chestnut–scallion pancakes, and spicy

Japanese pepper sirloin with sun-dried shiitake mushrooms should pique any appetite. ◆ Pan-Asian ◆ Restaurant: daily dinner. Drag shows: nightly. 24 First Ave (between E First and E Second Sts). 473.0516

15 Esashi ★★$$ A low-key sushi place that won't charm you into sitting and lingering over sake, but this place won't empty your wallet either. Decent sashimi and a good selection of beers make for a pleasant evening. ◆ Japanese ◆ Daily dinner. 32 Ave A (between E Houston and E Second St). 505.8726

16 Two Boots ★$ For 15 years, this family-oriented original has served Louisiana cuisine with an Italian twist—the boots refer to the shape of both state and country. Salad, pizza, and sandwich delivery are available at **Two Boots to Go** (42 Ave A, 254.1919). ◆ Creole/Italian ◆ M-F dinner; Sa-Su brunch and dinner. 37 Ave A (between E Second and E Third Sts). 505.2276 &. Also at: 74 Bleecker St (between Lafayette St and Broadway). 777.1033; 75 Greenwich Ave (at Seventh Ave S). 633.9096

17 Great Jones Cafe ★$ Blackened fish, sweet-potato fries, gumbo, and other decent, reasonably priced eats are served in this cozy but lively neighborhood cafe. The daily specials are probably a lot like your mom used to make. ◆ Cajun/American ◆ M-F dinner; Sa-Su brunch and dinner. No credit cards accepted. 54 Great Jones St (between Bowery and Lafayette St). 674.9304

18 376-380 Lafayette Street This richly ornamented yet somewhat uncomfortable warehouse is most notable because it was designed by **Henry J. Hardenbergh** in 1888, several years after he designed the **Dakota** apartments uptown on West 72nd Street. ◆ At Great Jones St

18 Time Cafe ★$$ Trendy crowds populate this spot from breakfast until late at night. They come not only to talk on their cellular phones and be seen, but to dine on an extensive menu of delicious dishes that includes an assortment of large salads, sesame-coated salmon, and a unique pistachio-encrusted chicken with red grape sauce. Within the cafe is a bilevel Moroccan club called **Fez**, which offers music, poetry readings, theater, and film. Call ahead for cover and schedule. ◆ American ◆ M-F breakfast, lunch, dinner, and late-night meals; Sa-Su brunch, dinner, and late-night meals. Reservations recommended. 380 Lafayette St (at Great Jones St). 533.7000

Restaurants/Clubs: Red   **Hotels:** Blue
Shops/ ♥ Outdoors: Green   **Sights/Culture:** Black

19 Tower Records The ultimate store for the listener comprises a main building on Broadway and East Fourth Street for pop, jazz, R&B, and dance; a classical annex next door (on Lafayette Street); and video and electronic annexes in between. If they don't have it, chances are it's going to be tough to find. Bibliophiles can visit **Tower Books** down the block at 383 Lafayette Street. ♦ Daily 9AM-midnight. 692 Broadway (at E Fourth St). 505.1500. Also at: 1977 Broadway (between W 66th and W 67th Sts). 799.2500; Trump Tower, 725 Fifth Ave (between E 56th and E 57th Sts). 838.8110

20 Marion's Continental Restaurant and Lounge ★★$$ This was the supper club during the 1950s, when senators, presidents, and movie stars were all regulars. It closed in the early 1970s, but Marion's son and a business partner reopened it in 1990 with much of its signature decor intact. The food is good, with such favorites as Caesar salad and steak au poivre topping the menu. Come for the inexpensive vodka Gibsons, old-fashioneds, and Manhattans. ♦ Continental ♦ Daily dinner. 354 Bowery (between Great Jones and E Fourth Sts). 475.7621

21 B Bar & Grill ★$$ A former gas station, the dining room flaunts its roots with a haute garage motif—from photos of car engines to displayed truck parts. Food is secondary here—getting the chance to furtively gawk at such celebrities as Cindy Crawford and Donna Karan is more the point. However, you can get a perfectly acceptable grilled salmon, roasted free-range chicken, seared yellowfin tuna, and for dessert, the banana split or brownie with ice cream. ♦ American ♦ M-F lunch and dinner; Sa-Su brunch and dinner. Reservations recommended. 40 E Fourth St (at Bowery). 475.2220 ⑆

22 Phebe's Place During the 1960s this was a popular hangout among Off-Broadway playwrights Sam Shepard, Robert Patrick, and Leonard Melfi. Today it continues to attract the East Village arts crowd, as well as a lot of off-duty police officers. Cheap pitchers of domestic beer and burgers pull in the college students, too. ♦ M-F 4PM-4AM; Sa 5PM-4AM. 361 Bowery (at E Fourth St). 473.9008

La MaMa etc.

23 La MaMa E.T.C. First called **Cafe La MaMa,** this theater has been in the vanguard of the Off-Broadway movement since 1961. Under the direction of Ellen Stewart, it has been instrumental in presenting both American and international experimental playwrights and directors to this country. Stewart nurtured playwrights Sam Shepard, Lanford Wilson, Ed Bullins, Tom Eyen, Israel Horovitz, and Elizabeth Swados, among others. Directors Tom O'Horgan, Marshall Mason, Wilford Leach, Andrei Serban, and Peter Brook have helped to stage many extraordinary productions here. ♦ 74A E Fourth St (between Second Ave and Bowery) 475.7710

24 Cucina di Pesce ★$$ For more than 10 years, this friendly restaurant with a huge bar has been serving reasonably priced Italian dishes. Try the spinach penne with asparagus and sun-dried tomatoes in cream sauce; or the tuna steak grilled with sautéed sweet peppers, capers, olives, and onions. There's outdoor garden dining during the warmer months and, to accommodate the crowds, the same management opened **Frutti di Mare,** an annex across the street (84 E Fourth St, 979.2034) that serves both lunch and dinner ♦ Italian ♦ Daily dinner. No credit cards accepted. 87 E Fourth St (between Second Ave and Cooper Sq). 260.6800 ⑆

25 Merchants' House & Museum This outstanding example of an 1830s Greek Revival town house remains intact with interiors and furnishings just the way they were when wealthy merchant Seabury Tredwell and his family lived here, thanks to Tredwell's daughter, Gertrude. Rumor has it Gertrude was the inspiration for Henry James's novel, *Washington Square,* although museum staff staunchly deny any such connection. Paintings, furniture, china, and books reflect their tasteful and conservative style. ♦ Admission. M-Th, Su 1-4PM. Call for information about group tours. 29 E Fourth St (between Bowery St. and Lafayette St). 777.1089

26 Bayamo ★$$ Although the menu is slightly gimmicky, the food is consistently good at this place that's one of the better eateries on the lower Broadway strip. The inventive appetizers include fried or grilled chicken wings and fried wontons. Happy Hours and late nights tend to get a little crowded; the mob at the bar clamoring for frozen margaritas can be six deep. If that's not your speed, maybe lunch or an early evening dinner on the balcony would be best ♦ Cuban/Chinese ♦ M-Th, Su lunch and dinner; F-Sa lunch, dinner, and late-night meals. Reservations recommended. 704 Broadway (between E Fourth St and Astor Pl). 475.5151

27 Shakespeare & Co. Though not related to its Paris namesake, this bookstore is a favorite among New Yorkers. ♦ M-Th, Su 10AM-11PM; F-Sa 10AM-midnight. 716 Broadway (between E Fourth St and Washington Pl). 529.1330. Also at: 939 Lexington Ave (at E 69th St). 570.5148; 1 Whitehall St (at Broadway). 742.7025

28 Astor Place Hairstylists Considering all there is to do in New York, it may seem strange that watching haircuts has become a spectator sport on Astor Place, but look at the pictures in the window and on the walls of the far-out styles and you'll understand why. The prices are extremely low, too. (One of the signs in the window says they also do regular haircuts, but don't count on it.) ◆ Daily. 2 Astor Pl (at Broadway). 475.9854 ♿

29 Astor Wines and Spirits A large selection and generally good prices are the draws of this spacious wine and liquor shop, but sometimes the staff is less than thoroughly knowledgeable. ◆ M-Sa. 12 Astor Pl (at Lafayette St). 674.7500

BLUE MAN GROUP

30 Astor Place Theatre Across the street from the more artistically ambitious **Public Theater,** this 298-seat off-Broadway venue has spent nine years as home to the not very cerebral but very weird comedy of *Blue Man Group.* ◆ 434 Lafayette St (between E Fourth St and Astor Pl). 254.4370

31 Colonnade Row The city's business and social leaders—the Astors, Vanderbilts, Delanos—once occupied the homes along this row, also known as "LaGrange Terrace." Only four of the nine built in 1833 by **Seth Greer** remain. The streetfront Corinthian colonnade was used to give the row a sense of unity and solidity. Despite designation as a New York City Landmark, these unique and historic structures remain in disrepair. ◆ 428-434 Lafayette St (between E Fourth St and Astor Pl)

Within Colonnade Row:

Indochine ★★★$$ This trendy spot boasts excellent French/Vietnamese food, which is served in a softly lit tropical-themed room, filled with an attractive, well-dressed crowd. Try the delicate spring rolls, a spicy salad of fillet of beef with Asian basil and shallots, crispy duck with ginger, and a delicious whole sea bass with lemongrass. ◆ French/Vietnamese ◆ Daily dinner. Reservations recommended. 430 Lafayette St. 505.5111

Toast ★★$$$ Large overhead fans and palm trees lend a decidedly tropical feel to this space, where the food features such delicacies as squid-ink pasta, Louisiana crab cakes, and other multicultural seafood dishes. ◆ International ◆ Daily dinner. Reservations recommended. 428 Lafayette St. 473.1698

THE PUBLIC THEATER

32 Public Theater The landmark home of the **New York Shakespeare Festival (NYSF)** has six theaters. Between **Newman** (seats 299), **Anspacher** (seats 299), **Martinson** (seats 1,650), **LuEster** (seats 135), **Susan Stein Shiva** (seats 100), and the **Little Theater** (seats 90), there's space for over 2,500 people. The Romanesque Revival buildings were designed for John Jacob Astor by **Alexander Saeltzer** (south wing, 1853), **Griffith Thomas** (center, 1859), and **Thomas Stent** (north wing, 1881). Originally New York City's first free library, the buildings later served as the Hebrew Immigrant Aid Sheltering Society. These structures were on the verge of being demolished in the mid-1960s, when that dynamic man of the theater Joseph Papp came to the rescue with the **NYSF** and architect **Giorgio Cavaglieri.** Today, the **NYSF** not only manages to continually mount superb presentations but always seems to find the money needed to avert financial crises. The list of extraordinary shows that originated here and went on to Broadway includes *Hair* by Gerome Ragni and James Rado, *That Championship Season* by Jason Miller, Michael Bennett's *A Chorus Line* (which won three Pulitzers), David Rabe's *Sticks and Bones,* Caryl Churchill's *Serious Money,* and Rupert Holmes's *The Mystery of Edwin Drood.* About 25 theatrical productions are mounted each year. Film viewings were introduced in 1981. **Cavaglieri**—who also renovated the **Jefferson Market Courthouse**—did an admirable job salvaging much of the interior: Many of the theater spaces are impressive, and the entrance and lobby still include the original Corinthian colonnade. ◆ Quiktix (half-price tickets for performances) are available two hours before curtain. 425 Lafayette St (between E Fourth St and Astor Pl). 260.2400

33 Riodizio ★★$$ Everything about this place is larger than life—from the lofty space it occupies next to the **Public Theater,** to the pitchers of *caipirinha* (the Brazilian national drink). Try the all-you-can-eat rotisserie offering an unlimited amount of a variety of grilled meats, seafood, and vegetables. Don't miss the "Rainforest" dessert with layers of passion fruit and white chocolate mousse in a toasted lime meringue. ◆ Brazilian ◆ Daily dinner. Reservations required. 417 Lafayette St (between E Fourth St and Astor Pl). 529.1313 ♿

Cooper Union

MICHAEL STORRINGS

34 Cooper Union Founded by multimillionaire Peter Cooper in 1859, this is a full-tuition-scholarship private college (illustrated above). The inventor and industrialist, so brilliant with problems of application in the country's young iron and rail industries, spent his entire life ashamed of his less-than-minimal education, and the opening of this school was his attempt to help underprivileged young men and women get the education they deserved but couldn't afford. It was the first coeducational college, the first open to all races and creeds, and the first to offer free adult education courses—several are offered at night to accommodate those working in the daytime.

Architect **Frederick A. Petersen** used the rails Cooper produced in his ironworks in the college's construction (a grid of T-shaped rails was used to transmit loads to the walls). This building is considered by some to be the oldest extant building in America framed with steel beams, and was declared a National Landmark in 1962. Two other breakthroughs in the building were the use of an elevator and the placing of vents under each of the 900 seats in the **Great Hall** auditorium—in the basement—through which fresh air was pumped. The **Great Hall** has, since the school's founding, been the scene of open expression on crucial issues of the day, from suffrage to civil rights. Abraham Lincoln delivered one of his most eloquent speeches here shortly before he was nominated as a presidential candidate. Both the NAACP and the American Red Cross were started

in the building. The college still sponsors provocative lectures and many other events under its Great Hall Programs, which are open to the public. When architect **John Hejduk** gutted and renovated the building in 1974, he provided pristine classrooms, offices, and exhibition space—all with a high-modern Corbusian vocabulary. Augustus Saint-Gaudens, Adolph A. Weinman, and Leo Friedlander were graduates of the art school. More recent alumni include Milton Glaser, Alex Katz, and Seymour Chwast. ♦ Administrative offices: 30 Cooper Square (between E Fourth St and Astor Pl). 7 E Seventh St (between Third and Fourth Aves). 353.4100

35 Cooper Square The statue of inventor and industrialist Peter Cooper seated in this triangular park is by Augustus Saint-Gaudens, a Cooper Union graduate. Its base is by **Stanford White**, who spent his boyhood in this neighborhood. Cooper, born 1791, was a self-made man who used the profits from a small grocery store to buy a glue factory up on 34th Street. He then invented a way to make better glue and became the biggest manufacturer in the country. Cooper invested the profits from that enterprise in Manhattan real estate and branched out to Baltimore, where he made a fortune selling land. He later designed and built the first American steam locomotive (the "Tom Thumb"), contributed to the development of technology for the iron industry, took an active part in progressive politics (for the abolition of slavery and for public education), and founded the **Cooper Union** (see above). ♦ Bounded by Third Ave and E Fourth and E Seventh Sts

36 Global 33 ★★$ This neighborhood favorite showcases food and drink from all over the world. The lighting is subdued, courtesy of beams filtering through holes in ceiling panels, and the overall ambience resembles that of an international airport lounge, circa 1960. Try the couscous with fennel, orange, mint, and onion; fried zucchini polenta with roasted-pepper cream sauce; or grilled pork kabobs with Moorish seasoning. Global drinks include Brazilian *caipirinhas,* Jamaican dark-and-stormys, and British Pimms. ♦ International ♦ Daily dinner and late-night meals. Reservations recommended. 93 Second Ave (between E Fifth and E Sixth Sts). 477.8427

37 Circa ★★$$$ The adobe-style interior of this restaurant is as appealing as its Mediterranean menu. There are zesty pizzas, hearty soups, including lentil with morels and chestnuts, and cornmeal-crusted fried calamari for appetizers. Those with more robust appetites can choose from smoked pork chops with mashed yams and apple, black pasta with mussels, and pumpkin gnocchi and chanterelles in cream with toasted pecans. ♦ Mediterranean/American ♦ M-Th lunch and dinner; F lunch, dinner, and late-night meals; Sa brunch, dinner, and late-night meals; Su brunch and dinner. Reservations recommended. 103 Second Ave (at E Sixth St). 777.4120 &

38 Back From Guatemala A unique collection of clothing, jewelry, artifacts, and music celebrating tribal arts from the Andes to the Himalayas is found here. Established in 1975, this store embodies the freewheeling ethnicity of the East Village. ♦ Daily noon-11:30PM. 306 E Sixth St (between First and Second Aves). 260.7010 &

38 Passage to India ★$ With more than 20 Indian restaurants in the area, competition is heavy, but this small spot is among the better ones. The freshly baked breads and tandoori specials are highlights. What really stands out from the rest of the neighborhood is the small selection of Indonesian chicken, lamb, and shrimp dishes, including satays and *nasi goreng,* Indonesian-style fried rice. ♦ Indian/Indonesian ♦ Daily lunch, dinner, and late-night meals. 308 E Sixth St (between First and Second Aves). 529.5770

39 Mitali ★★$$ The running gag about the Indian restaurants on and around Sixth Street is that one central kitchen supplies them all. However, the meals prepared at this dimly lit eatery are a standout. Try the *murgha tikka*

muslam (chicken barbecued over charcoal and then cooked in a sauce of cream and almonds) or any of the tandoori specialties. ♦ Indian ♦ M-Th lunch and dinner; F-Su brunch and dinner. Reservations recommended. 334 E Sixth St (between First and Second Aves). 533.2508. Also at: 296 Bleecker St (at Seventh Ave S). 989.1367

40 Opaline ★★$$ Large and airy, this East Village hideaway is the place to be. The menu strikes a balance between tradition and innovation. Baked oysters Opaline and mussels steamed with Champagne and cream are two of the delectable appetizers. On the classic side, crisp duck breast, salmon Wellington, and braised lamb shank are some of the favorites. Save room for the creamy citrus tart. There's an excellent wine list. ♦ French/American ♦ Daily dinner. 85 Ave A (between Fifth and E Sixth Sts). 475.5050

41 Pisces ★★$$ As the name might suggest, this handsome place with wood beams and exposed brick walls is known for very fresh, well-prepared fish, some of it smoked in-house. While certain items (grilled tuna, mesquite smoked trout, and sautéed skate) are always available, the presentation, sauces, and side dishes change seasonally. The seafood paella is highly recommended. ♦ Seafood ♦ M-F dinner; Sa-Su brunch and dinner. Reservations recommended. 95 Ave A (at E Sixth St). 260.6660

42 7A Cafe ★★$$ A very modern atmosphere—defined by copious quantities of metal, aluminum, and post-industrial fixtures—attracts a young crowd to this eatery, who also appreciate the diner prices and late-night hours. The great sandwiches, burgers, and breakfasts alone are worth a stop here. ♦ American ♦ Daily breakfast, lunch, dinner, and late-night meals. 109 Ave A (at Seventh St). 475.9001

43 Miracle Grill ★★$$ Grilled chicken with soy ginger sauce, New York steak with *chipotle* (smoked jalapeño-pepper) butter, and vanilla-bean flan are just a few of the inventive specialties served at this tiny and casual restaurant. Dine alfresco in the garden when the weather is fine. ♦ Southwestern ♦ M-F dinner; Sa-Su brunch and dinner. 112 First Ave (between E Sixth and E Seventh Sts). 254.2353 &

44 Caffè della Pace This warm and unpretentious little cafe, a few steps up from the street, has good cappuccino and a very rich tiramisù. ♦ Daily. No credit cards accepted. 48 E Seventh St (between First and Second Aves). 529.8024

45 Kiev ★$ A better buy, not to mention better borscht, would be hard to find in New York. This is one of the best Eastern European places around. The cheese blintzes, pierogi (filled with cheese or potato), fried veal cutlets, and all of the soups are very satisfying. ♦ Ukrainian/Polish ♦ Daily 24 hours. No credit cards accepted. 117 Second Ave (at E Seventh St). 674.4040 ♿

46 St. George's Ukrainian Catholic Church An Old World cathedral with modern touches, this 1977 church designed by **Apollinaire Osadea** is the anchor of a Ukrainian neighborhood of more than 1,500 people. ♦ 16-20 E Seventh St (at Taras Shevchenko Pl). 674.1615

47 Fragrance Shop NY, Inc Owner Lalita Kumu and her congenial staff love to get to know their customers and share their knowledge of fragrance and body-care products. They'll introduce you to the store's own line, which includes facial and skincare products, body oils, and shampoos, and show you the products they import from other companies. ♦ Daily. 21 E Seventh St (between Second and Third Aves). 254.8950 ♿

47 McSorley's Old Ale House Not so long ago, this saloon, which has been here since 1854, had a men-only policy; not surprisingly, it was among the first targets of the feminist movement in 1970. The current clientele, which includes women, is made up mostly of college students, but except for that, the place hasn't changed much since its early days. ♦ Daily 11AM-1AM. No credit cards accepted. 15 E Seventh St (between Second and Third Aves). 473.9148

47 Surma This Ukrainian shop has Slavic cards, books, videos, and records, plus egg-decorating kits and honey. ♦ M-Sa. 11 E Seventh St (between Second and Third Aves). 477.0729 ♿

Inside the doorway of the Public Theater are two white columns. "May Peace Prevail on Earth" is written on each in Japanese and English. The columns were sent to the late Joseph Papp by the Society of Prayer for World Peace, an organization that does not aim to convert lost souls, but is dedicated to planting as many peace poles as possible.

You've seen them in every movie about New York, from *Breakfast at Tiffany's* to *Taxi Driver*. The yellow Checker cab, with an ocean of leg room and two jump seats, and passengers sitting high above the potholes and surrounding traffic, will forever be nostalgically associated with bygone New York City, but you won't see one in the city any more: the last Checker driver, Earl Johnson, retired his car in August 1999.

Restaurants/Clubs: Red   Hotels: Blue
Shops/ ♟ Outdoors: Green   Sights/Culture: Black

48 St. Mark's Place In the 1960s, this extension of Eighth Street from Third Avenue to **Tompkins Square Park** was the East Coast capital of hippiedom. The sidewalks were crowded with flower children, and the smell of marijuana was everywhere. Among the shared interests of the street's denizens was the famous rock club **The Electric Circus**, which was in a former Polish social club at **No. 23**. Then, in the 1970s, the street became the punk boardwalk, and multicolored Mohawks predominated. It is quieter these days— witness the corner of Second Avenue, where the old **St. Mark's Cinema** has been converted into co-op apartments, and retail stores have been taken over by **The Gap.** But the crowds are still colorful, proving that the street's far from dead. ♦ Ave A to Third Ave

48 St. Mark's Sounds A true music-lover's store, this place doesn't have the conveyor-belt feeling of **Tower Records.** The store also sells and trades used records in excellent condition. ♦ Daily 11AM-11:30PM. 20 St. Mark's Pl (between Second and Third Aves). 677.3444

48 Dojo ★$ Students of nearby **New York University** and local residents seem to depend on the food that has been served here for more than 25 years. Try the chicken sukiyaki salad or the incredibly inexpensive soy burger with tahini sauce. In nice weather you can dine on the outdoor porch. ♦ Japanese/American ♦ Daily breakfast, lunch, dinner, and late-night meals. No credit cards accepted. 24 St. Mark's Pl (between Second and Third Aves). 674.9821. Also at: 14 W Fourth St (at Mercer St). 505.8934

49 Khyber Pass Afghani Restaurant ★★$ A former judge of the Supreme Court in Afghanistan runs this authentic Afghan restaurant boasting handsome antiques and offering native music. Knowing you're in good hands, just sit back on a throw pillow and get ready to enjoy *aushak* (scallion dumplings) as an appetizer, and such tasty entrées as chicken kabob with *kabuli palow* (carrots, raisins, almonds, and rice). ♦ Afghan ♦ Daily lunch and dinner. 34 St. Mark's Pl (between Second and Third Aves). 473.0989

50 B & H Dairy and Vegetarian Cuisine Restaurant ★$ Once upon a time the initials "B & H" stood for owners Bergson and Heller, and the clientele comprised the cast and crew of the Yiddish theater productions along Second Avenue. The restaurant has been refurbished several times since then, as has the menu—it includes tasty offerings in a lighter vegetarian style—but thank goodness the challah recipe is still the same. The French toast here is heavenly. ♦ Vegetarian ♦ M-F lunch and dinner; Sa-Su brunch and dinner. 127 Second Ave (between E Seventh St and St. Mark's Pl). 505.8065

East Village

51 Orpheum Theatre This refurbished theater has been around since 1908, when it was the scene of many Yiddish theater hits. *Little Mary Sunshine* had a long run here. In recent years, it's hosted such winners as *Little Shop of Horrors,* the comedienne Sandra Bernhard's one-woman show, and *Stomp!,* the high-energy percussion performance from England. ♦ 126 Second Ave (between E Seventh St and St. Mark's Pl). 477.2477

52 Cafe Mogador ★$$ Moroccan cuisine is prepared here without fanfare. Lamb, beef, and *merguez* (sausage) kabobs, and several varieties of couscous follow a selection of appetizers brought to your table on an enormous tray. The spicy carrots are out of this world, and the steaming *bastilla* (fresh chicken and herbs in a puff pastry) is one of the best entrées on the menu. Top it off with tea or authentic Turkish coffee for dessert. ♦ Middle Eastern/Moroccan ♦ M-F lunch and dinner; Sa-Su brunch, dinner, and late-night meals. No credit cards accepted. 101 St. Mark's Pl (between Ave A and First Ave). 677.2226

53 Stingy Lulu's ★★$ This campy dive has been around for years. Customers don't come for the decor (plastic booths, tacky pieces of Americana on the walls), the food (good but not outstanding burgers, fries, salads and the occasional vegetarian-friendly pasta dish) or the entertainment (your "waitress" suddenly drops her tray and gyrates next to a boom-box for five painfully lip-synched minutes), but for the overall effect, which is friendly, noisy, kitschy, and cheap. The lounge next door serves lovely cocktails that can cost twice that elsewhere in the city. Nightly drag shows are performed by the waitstaff. ♦ American ♦ M-F lunch, dinner, and late-night meals; Sa-Su brunch, dinner, and late-night meals. No credit cards accepted. 129 St. Mark's Place (between Ave A and 1st Ave). 674.3545

54 Flea Market ★★$$ French Bistro fare, from steak *frites* (with French fries) and duck confit to rabbit and sometimes even wild boar, are served in a setting apropos to the name. The *raviolio* is sublime, which bodes well for vegetarians. This dining spot is a good choice when you want a relief from the overly funky food that defines so many of the neighborhood's eateries. ♦ French ♦ M-F lunch and dinner; Sa-Su brunch, dinner, and late-night meals. 131 Avenue A (between St Marks Pl and Ninth Sts). 358.9280

55 Tompkins Square Park The original plan for this 16-acre park called for extending it all the way east to the river. It was to be a farmers' market, and part of the plan was to cut a canal through the middle to give easy access to Long Island farmers. But the land became a parade ground instead in the 1830s. In 1874, it was the site of America's first labor demonstration, when a carpenters' union clashed with club-wielding police. Among the injured was Samuel Gompers, who later became president of the American Federation of Labor. The little Greek temple near the center covers a drinking fountain placed there by a temperance organization in 1891. The park gained its modern-day notoriety during hippiedom, when it served as the grounds for "love-ins" and "be-ins," and more recently when it was the site of a violent confrontation over real-estate speculation in the area and unsuccessful efforts to enforce a nighttime curfew. ♦ Bounded by Aves B and A, and E Seventh and E 10th Sts

56 Mesopotamia ★★★$$ The menu at this romantic spot couples Chef Peter Pluymers's Flemish culinary gusto and appetite for invention. His finesse translates into such appetizers as smoked salmon rolls filled with diced vegetables, sour cream, and horseradish; and a honey-baked goat cheese salad topped with nuts and a raspberry dressing. For entrées, best bets are the grilled mahimahi on a bed of caramelized turnips and chicken *waterzooi*. Beer lovers will be heartened by the extensive selection of hard-to-find gourmet Belgian brews. ♦ Belgian/International ♦ M-F dinner; Sa-Su brunch and dinner. 98 Avenue B (between E Sixth and E Seventh Sts). 358.1166

57 Jacob Riis Houses Plaza The large number of people who actually use this park is a tribute to **M. Paul Friedberg**'s careful and creative 1966 plan. Both adults and children find it a pleasant alternative to the streets, with its amphitheater, clever playground furniture, and plenty of room in which to roam. ♦ Bounded by Franklin D. Roosevelt Dr and Ave D, and E Sixth and E 10th Sts

58 Cafe Margaux ★★$$ Don't let the location keep you away from this oh-so-French eatery, where the Gallic charm of the waitstaff seems to work its way into the food, too. Try any of the succulent grilled fish dishes, all very reasonably priced. ♦ French ♦ Daily dinner. 175 Ave B (at E 11th St). 260.7960

RUSSIAN & TURKISH BATHS

59 Russian & Turkish Baths The last remaining bathhouse in a neighborhood that once was full of them still gets its steam heat the old-fashioned way: Enormous boulders are heated up in the subbasement and when they're red-hot, water is thrown on them,

101

All That Jazz

Jazz may have been born in New Orleans, but New York City was its ultimate destination. In the heyday of jazz during the 1940s and 1950s, musicians knew they hadn't really made it until they played the Big Apple. And play they do: Everything from fusion to Dixieland continues to flourish in locations throughout the city. Even **Lincoln Center for the Performing Arts,** that highly conservative mecca of music, produces a year-round program of jazz concerts of the highest caliber.

Jazz and Blues Clubs

The well-known clubs listed below regularly host big names in the jazz world. Cover charges vary, depending on the club and the performer, but you can almost always lessen the bite by listening from the bar.

Birdland Having enjoyed its heyday in the 1940 to 1950s, when such luminaries as Charlie Parker and Dave Brubeck ignited the stage, this **Theater District** club no longer hosts stars of that same caliber, but devotees still say it's well worth the trek to relive a transcendent moment in music history. ♦ 315 W 44th St (between Eighth and Ninth Aves). 581.3080

Blue Note Big names appear regularly at this premier jazz showcase, a must for jazz buffs. There are usually two shows on weeknights and three on weekend nights, in addition to tunes provided by the talented house trio. Look for jazz brunches and matinees on Saturday and Sunday as well. ♦ 131 W Third St (between MacDougal St and Sixth Ave). 475.8592

Cajun Dixieland jazz and occasional serious blues are played nightly in a New Orleans atmosphere, accompanied by Creole/Cajun food. There's a popular jazz brunch on Sunday. ♦ 129 Eighth Ave (between W 16th and W 17th Sts). 691.6174

Iridium Located across from **Lincoln Center,** this is one of the city's newest venues to feature well-known talent. The cozy basement has two sets on weekdays; three sets on weekends. On the ground floor is the innovative restaurant **Merlot.** ♦ 44 W 63rd St (between Broadway and Columbus Ave). 582.2121

Sweet Basil This small wood-and-brick space fills early, and when well-known musicians appear, reservations can be hard to come by. Weekend matinees have no cover charges; weekend jazz brunches are a **Village** ritual. ♦ 88 Seventh Ave S (between Barrow and Grove Sts). 242.1785

Village Gate 52 After more than four decades, the "Gate" has moved uptown and is still packing 'em in. Within its new quarters, performers range from up-and-coming to world-class personalities, covering every angle of jazz as well as other types of music. ♦ 240 W 52nd St (between Broadway and Eighth Ave). 307.3232

Village Vanguard For more than 50 years, this landmark club has hosted mostly mainstream jazz. Large bands and combos are often the nightly attractions, with two sets Monday through Thursday, and three sets Friday through Sunday. ♦ 178 Seventh Ave S (at Perry St). 255.4037

Visiones A small, intimate venue in the midst of the Village's jazz enclave, this place presents good though little-known combos twice nightly and three times on weekends, and decent Spanish and American bistro fare. ♦ 125 MacDougal St (at W Third St). 673.5576

Zinno Unlike most music-oriented clubs, this place gives its menu of noteworthy Italian food more than ample attention. Blues or mainstream jazz is offered nightly by duos and trios in a lovely, informal setting. ♦ 126 W 13th St (between Sixth and Seventh Aves). 924.5182

Some Other High Notes

Meanwhile, rock and pop musicians know they've arrived when they land gigs at the following venues. Some of them are major institutions, others newer on the scene.

Avery Fisher Hall, Lincoln Center for the Performing Arts ♦ Broadway and W 65th St. 875.5030

Bottom Line ♦ 15 W Fourth St (at Mercer St). 228.6300

CBGB ♦ 315 Bowery (between E First and E Second Sts). 982.4052

Radio City Music Hall ♦ 1260 Sixth Ave (at W 50th St). 247.4777

S.O.B.'s Sounds of Brazil ♦ 204 Varick St (at W Houston St). 243.4940

Supper Club ♦ 240 W 47th St (between Broadway and Eighth Ave). 921.1940

Tramps ♦ 51 W 21st St (between Fifth and Sixth Aves). 727.7788

Webster Hall ♦ 125 E 11th St (between Third and Fourth Aves). 353.3243

Wetlands ♦ 161 Hudson St (at Laight St). 966.4225

releasing what the owners claim is true, penetrating wet heat—not mere steam heat. And if you've never had a *platza* rub, try it. Softened oak branches are tied together in the old Russian style to form a natural loofalike scrub, soapy and tingly and very refreshing. There's also a Turkish bath (sauna). Upstairs are cots if you're overwhelmed, and a small food and drink bar. ◆ Daily 9AM-10PM (coed: M-Tu, F-Sa; women: W; men: Th, Su). 268 E 10th St (between Ave A and First Ave). 473.8806

60 DeRobertis Pastry Shop ★$ If you can get past the display counters filled with traffic-stopping cheesecakes, pies, cakes, and biscotti (among the best in the city), you'll find a wonderfully tiled coffeehouse that hasn't changed a bit since it began serving frothy cappuccino back in 1904. ◆ Bakery/Cafe ◆ Tu-Su. 176 First Ave (between E 10th and E 11th Sts). 674.7137

61 Theater for the New City Now located in what used to be an indoor market, this offbeat, roots-in-the-1960s troupe has managed to keep its old ambience and point of view. The productions are hit-and-miss. Each of the four theaters seats between 60 and 100. ◆ 155 First Ave (between E Ninth and E 10th Sts). 254.1109 ♿

62 Enchantments Local and visiting witches stop here regularly for the tools of their craft: herbs, oils, tarot cards, caldrons, and ceremonial knives (used to cut air and create a sacred space), plus jewelry, books, and calendars. ◆ Daily. 341 E Ninth St (between First and Second Aves). 228.4394

63 Veselka ★$ An amazing array of Eastern European fare—pierogi, kielbasa, blintzes, and stuffed cabbage—is turned out at bargain-basement prices in this unadorned yet cozy establishment. ◆ Ukrainian ◆ Daily 24 hours. 144 Second Ave (at E Ninth St). 228.9682

63 Ukrainian ★$ Located within the **Ukrainian National Home** community center, this place serves such wonderful Eastern European specialties as pierogi, blintzes, and stuffed cabbage. The combination platter gives a sampling of all three. ◆ Ukrainian ◆ Daily lunch and dinner. No credit cards accepted. 140 Second Ave (between St. Mark's Pl and E Ninth St). 529.5024 ♿

After numerous attempts at private incorporation to build a city subway system, the city secured the passage of the Rapid Transit Act in 1891, under which the system was finally built.

The New York City Transit Authority provides nearly 40 percent of America's total mass transit with a fleet consisting of 5,917 subway cars.

64 New York Public Library, Ottendorfer Branch Anna Ottendorfer, patron of the German-language newspaper *New York Staats Zeitung,* founded this beautiful terra-cotta building, which was built by **William Schickel** in 1884. Before becoming a branch of the **New York Public Library,** it was the home of the **Freie Bibliothek und Lesehalle,** a German-language library and reading room. ◆ M-Sa. 135 Second Ave (between St. Mark's Pl and E Ninth St). 674.0947

65 Cloisters Cafe ★$ At this most delightful spot in the neighborhood for escaping the city, the inside is dark and encrusted with stained glass, while the outside is a beautiful grapevine-canopied bower. Gigantic salads, good challah French toast, and fresh fish entrées are featured. In hot weather, the yogurt ambrosia (made with fresh fruits and nuts) and a refreshing glass of iced mint tea are the next-best thing to air-conditioning. ◆ American ◆ M-F lunch, dinner, and late-night meals; Sa-Su brunch, dinner, and late-night meals. No credit cards accepted. 238 E Ninth St (between Second Ave and Stuyvesant St). 777.9128

66 St. Mark's Bookshop This popular bookstore remains a good source for journals on African culture, feminist issues, socialism, and cultural theory. ◆ Daily. 31 Third Ave (at Stuyvesant St). 260.7853 ♿

67 Bussola ★★$$$ In honor of the card game *briscola* played in Italy, the walls here are decorated with cards. But who cares about playing cards when you can feast on such authentic Sicilian specialties as artichokes with mint; tagliatelle with sausage, peas, and cream; *bucatini* with sardines; and swordfish carpaccio. ◆ Italian ◆ M-Sa dinner. 65 Fourth Ave (between E Ninth and E 10th Sts). 254.1940

68 Grace Church The fascinating spire atop this white marble church, which is sited at a bend of Broadway, provides a focal point for any southern approach. James Renwick Jr. won the right to design the Episcopal church in a competition. He worked with copybooks of the Pugins, the English theorists, to produce a Gothic Revival structure in 1846 that many consider to be the city's best. **Heins & LaFarge** designed an enlargement for the chancel in 1900. **Renwick**'s rectory, next door at 804 Broadway, is another marvel—a restrained foil for the more fanciful church. ◆ 800 Broadway (between E 10th St and E 12th Sts). 254.2000

69 St. Mark's-in-the-Bowery Church Erected in 1799 on the site of a garden chapel on Peter Stuyvesant's estate, this church has always been held in high regard as a neighborhood church, and its stately late-Georgian style encourages this congenial attitude. As the membership grew, a Greek

Revival steeple designed by **Ithiel Towne** was added in 1828, giving the church a more urban image; and a cast-iron Italianate portico was added to the entrance in 1854. This mélange does not mesh successfully, but it does reflect the parishioners' concerns about preserving the church's early history. A fire nearly destroyed the building in 1978. Architect **Herman Hassinger** took charge of the restoration, which included rebuilding the steeple according to the original design. The interior was gutted and redesigned in a simple and straightforward manner, typical of the pre- and post-Revolutionary War period. The stained-glass windows on the ground floor, newly designed by Hassinger, use themes similar to the original windows. The building is also home to the **Poetry Project, Inc.** (674.0910), **Danspace** (674.8112), and **Ontological Hysterical Theatre** (533.4650). ♦ 131 E 10th St (at Second Ave). 674.6377

70 2nd Avenue Deli ★$$ Ask to be seated in the **Molly Picon Room** in this very famous and popular deli where the wealth of Yiddish theater memorabilia will certainly enhance the dining experience. As for the food, certain Jewish specialties are very good. Try the superb chopped liver (passed out on bits of rye bread to placate the hungry crowds when lines get long on weekends), stuffed breast of veal, Romanian tenderloin steak, boiled beef, or kasha varnishkes (with bowtie macaroni). ♦ Jewish ♦ Daily lunch, dinner, and late-night meals. 156 Second Ave (at E 10th St). 677.0606 ♿

71 Tenth Street Lounge A severe metal facade and forbidding steel doors give way to this popular neighborhood watering hole. The interior is warmed up with votive candles, a hodgepodge of overstuffed couches, and, for a curious touch of academia, school desks used as tables. ♦ Daily 5PM-3AM. 212 E 10th St (between First and Second Aves). 473.5252 ♿

72 Veniero's Pasticceria & Cafe ★$ Mirrors and chandeliers decorate this century-old bakery/cafe. But customers generally don't notice the decor; they're hypnotized by all the desserts. Try the biscotti (cookies); creamy pastries; fluffy, golden ricotta cheesecakes; and fabulous fruit-topped custard tortes and tarts. There's also a seating area that is often crowded with locals and tourists, where cappuccino goes well with a *sfogliatelle* (a flaky cheese-filled pastry). ♦ Bakery/Cafe ♦ Daily. No credit cards accepted. 342 E 11th St (between First and Second Aves). 674.7264

73 Angelica Kitchen ★$ Named after an herb believed to bring good luck, a place like this could only exist in the East Village. The seasonal vegetarian macrobiotic menu (no dairy products or sugar) changes with the solstice and equinox. The delicious fare, such

as lentil-walnut pâté, norimaki (rolled vegetable sushi), or three-bean chili (lentils, kidney, and black beans), and all of the homemade breads, spreads, and salads are made with organically grown ingredients. ♦ Organic vegetarian ♦ Daily lunch and dinner. 300 E 12th St (between First and Second Aves). 228.2909

73 John's of Twelfth Street ★$$ This place could have been the model for every little Italian restaurant that was ever lit by candles stuck in wine bottles. It's one of the city's oldest and was once a favorite of Arturo Toscanini. The menu is red-sauce traditional and the special salad is outstanding. ♦ Italian ♦ Daily dinner. Reservations recommended. No credit cards accepted. 302 E 12th St (between First and Second Aves). 475.9531

74 Immaculate Conception Church Now a Roman Catholic church, this 1894 building designed by **Barney & Chapman** was originally an Episcopal mission of **Grace Church**, which included a hospital and social service facilities arranged in a cloisterlike setting punctuated by the elaborate tower. ♦ 414 E 14th St (between Ave A and First Ave). 254.0200 ♿

75 Kiehl's Located at the historical **Peter Stuyvesant Pear Tree Corner** since 1851, this vintage establishment produces handmade cosmetics and 118 essences (including 4 kinds of patchouli oil), using natural ingredients and extracts according to centuries-old formulations. The white-coated staff is extremely helpful and generous with samples. On display is an impressive collection of new and vintage motorcycles. All in all, it's an East Village must. ♦ M-Sa. 109 Third Ave (between E 13th and E 14th Sts). 677.3171

76 Footlight Records Collectors of vintage LPs rejoice! Here is the world's largest selection of film soundtracks and original Broadway cast albums as well as top vocalists (Sinatra, Crosby, Merman), jazz greats (Django Reinhardt, Bix Beiderbecke), and out-of-print records of all sorts. In most cases, you may listen before buying. ♦ Daily. 113 E 12th St (between Third and Fourth Aves). 533.1572

77 Utrecht Art & Drafting Supplies Excellent prices are offered here by this major manufacturer of professional art and drafting supplies. Mail-order catalogs are available at the store or by calling 800/223.9132. ♦ Daily. 111 Fourth Ave (between E 11th and E 12th Sts). 777.5353 ♿

78 Forbidden Planet This is the city's headquarters for science fiction, horror, and fantasy books, comics, and related merchandise. ♦ Daily. 840 Broadway (at E 13th St). 473.1576 ♿

Bests

Gerry Frank
Author, *Where to Find It, Buy It, Eat It in New York*

Taking in an afternoon game at **Yankee** or **Shea Stadiums** on a warm summer day.

Looking out over the **East River** at the Manhattan skyline from **Lighthouse Park** on **Roosevelt Island**.

Visiting the **Museum of Immigration** on **Ellis Island**.

Taking a ride on one of the 388 elevators in **Rockefeller Center** (preferably to the top).

Sitting on one of the 7,674 benches in **Central Park** on a glorious spring day.

Wandering through the **Frick Collection**.

Looking down one of the open grates that expose 238 miles of subway tracks below the city streets.

Visiting the Romanesque/Byzantine–style **St. Bartholomew's Church**.

Gawking at the Fabergé eggs at the **Forbes Magazine Galleries**.

Sampling Martine's chocolates at **Bloomingdale's**.

Enjoying a leisurely and luxurious weekend at the new **Four Seasons Hotel**.

Taking in the farmers' market on Monday, Wednesday, Friday, and Saturday at **Union Square**.

Tuning in to **Joan Hamburg** for great consumer advice (WOR—710 AM radio—weekdays from 10AM to noon).

Sipping an espresso or cappuccino in **Little Italy**.

Watching a favorite episode of a favorite TV show at the **Museum of Television and Radio**.

Getting up as early as 4AM to witness the activity at the **Fulton Fish Market**.

Visiting the **Federal Hall National Memorial** (26 Wall St), where George Washington took oath as the first US president.

Relaxing in the **Ford Foundation**'s garden atrium.

Taking the kids to see **The Cloisters**.

Taking a **Circle Line** cruise.

Visiting the **United Nations**.

Taking a boat trip on the lake in Central Park on a summer day (**Loeb Boathouse**).

Taking a bargain ride on the **Staten Island Ferry**.

Riding through **Central Park** in a hansom cab.

Gallery hopping in **SoHo** on a Saturday afternoon.

Dancing at the **Rainbow Room**.

Attending the flea market and antiques sale on Sunday at Sixth Avenue and West 26th Street.

Exploring the towering beauty of the **Cathedral Church of St. John the Divine**.

Watching the lights on the **Statue of Liberty** while walking along the promenade at **Battery Park**.

Securing a bargain ticket for a Broadway matinee at the **TKTS** booth in **Times Square**.

Watching the **Rockettes** at **Radio City Music Hall**.

Getting into a political discussion with a cab driver.

Browsing the **New York Is Book Country** book fair on Fifth Avenue in September.

Getting pampered at **Elizabeth Arden**.

Having one of the finest French dinners anywhere at **La Réserve**.

Visiting **Theodore Roosevelt's birthplace** and George Washington's headquarters (65 Jumel Terr).

Taking home fresh fruit and vegetables from **Grace's Marketplace**.

Linda Fairstein
Prosecutor and Crime Novelist

Like my fictional counterpart in my series of murder mysteries—Alexandra Cooper—when I am not at work in the **Criminal Courthouse,** I am happiest spending time in my favorite places on Manhattan's **Upper East Side.**

I love to wander through the **Frick Collection** to see which paintings are on display, or study the fascinating exhibits at the **Metropolitan Museum of Art's Costume Institute**. If kids are along for the day, the **Met**'s collections of mummies and armor keep them riveted.

If it's a beautiful afternoon, pick up a novel at **The Corner Bookshop** and walk over to one of the city's best-kept secrets, **Central Park**'s **Conservatory Garden**, for a quiet read.

Then, wander down the length of **Madison Avenue**, and daydream at the magnificent window displays—everything from antiques to paintings to jewels to the chicest clothes in town. Stop in at **E.A.T. Zabar's**, where I promise you can find some whimsical gift for everyone on your list.

Marie Wilson
President, Ms. Foundation for Women

A Day Uptown: Start at the **Metropolitan Museum of Art**'s **Egyptian Galleries,** spending time at the **Temple of Dendur**. And don't forget the wonderful costume exhibit there. The gift shop is also a must for its variety of books and jewelry.

Walk south through **Central Park,** stopping at **The Carousel** if it is summer, or at **Wollmann Rink** for ice- or roller skating. At lunch or teatime, try the **Plaza Hotel,** then stroll down **Fifth Avenue** window shopping (or more).

Walk a few blocks to **Times Square,** buy half-price tickets at the **TKTS** booth, then eat at **Jezebel,** whose lackluster exterior hides the charms of the American South, with shawls, porch swings, and chandeliers abounding. In the summer months, you might consider the **Bryant Park Cafe** in back of the library—great food and a great view. After the theater, have a quick snack at **Joe Allen,** or a drink at **B. Smith's.**

Union Square/ Gramercy/ Murray Hill

Both Union Square, formerly known as **Stuyvesant**, and Murray Hill were named for farms, while Gramercy inherited its name from an early–19th-century housing development that lured the rich by offering them access to their own private park. Together these three dynamic neighborhoods cover **14th to 39th Streets**, from **Sixth Avenue** to **Franklin D. Roosevelt Drive** on the **East River**. Publishers, ad agencies, architectural firms, photography studios, and other upscale companies running from high uptown rents now inhabit these areas. Mostly residential since the commercial center of the city moved north in the 19th century, the district once again features loft dwellers lured by the neighborhood's newfound energy and a host of fashionable stores to accommodate them.

Gramercy Park, the centerpiece of the Gramercy area, was established in the 1830s by lawyer and landowner Samuel Ruggles. To make one of his tracts

more valuable, he sacrificed 42 potential building lots to create this London-style park. Then he set aside more land for a wide avenue north of the park (which he named **Lexington**, for the Revolutionary War battle) and for **Irving Place** south of it (which he named for his friend Washington Irving, who created "Father Knickerbocker," one of the symbols of New York).

The land that Ruggles owned was once part of a huge estate that belonged to Peter Stuyvesant, the last Dutch governor-general of Nieuw Amsterdam, who retired there after the British took over. His original 1651 deed noted a valley created by a creek called Crommessie, a combination of two Dutch words meaning "crooked little knife" (for the shape of a nearby brook). The name was eventually altered to "Gramercy" to fall more easily off English-speaking tongues.

Stuyvesant's name lives on in the neighborhood east of Gramercy, and in another London-style park, **Stuyvesant Square**, that straddles **Second Avenue**. After the Stuyvesant family sold part of their estate to the Delanceys in 1746, it was developed into a working farm known as **Rose Hill**. It is a quiet residential area today, but through the beginning of the 20th century the notorious Gas House Gang ruled the neighborhood, averaging an estimated 30 hold-ups every night on East 18th Street alone.

The original Gas Housers' territory included another residential neighborhood, Murray Hill, which extends north from **34th** to **39th Streets**, and east from Sixth Avenue. The gang took its name from factories along the East River that produced gas to illuminate the city in the 19th century. The stretch between 23rd and 34th Streets is often called **Kips Bay**, after a farm established by Jacobus Kip in 1655.

By the end of the 19th century, when J. Pierpont Morgan moved to Kips Bay, a gentlemen's agreement had been established restricting the streets of Murray Hill to private houses. Until the invasion of high-rise hotels and apartments in the 1920s, it was a neighborhood of elegant mansions, many of which still stand.

Today, where gas storage tanks once sprouted east of Stuyvesant Square, thousands of people occupy middle-class apartments in the **Stuyvesant Town** and **Peter Cooper Village** rental complexes (both built in the late 1940s and attacked for being purely functional and without ornamentation), and in **Waterside** (high-rises built in 1974 on the East River between **East 25th** and **East 30th Streets**). Visible from the FDR Drive is **Bellevue Hospital Center**, which originated as a six-bed infirmary on the site of the present **City Hall** in a building that it shared with a poorhouse and a jail.

---

1 Union Square In 1811, when the city fathers decreed that all of Manhattan's streets should follow a rigid grid pattern, Broadway was already in place, cutting an angle from southeast to northwest. Rather than change it, they turned it to the city's advantage by creating squares wherever Broadway crossed a north-south avenue. What may have inspired them was this already existing square, which grew up around the meeting point of Broadway, the post road to Albany, and Boston Post Road, which later became Third Avenue. In the years before the Civil War, it was the heart of a fashionable residential neighborhood, surrounded by prestigious stores and theaters. When fashion moved uptown, the square became a center for labor demonstrations and rallies. It was landscaped and altered in 1936, when it was also raised a few feet above ground level to allow for the subway station under it. The pavilion at the north end, sometimes used for summer concerts, was added at the same time. The redesign also forced Broadway to make a left turn at East 17th Street and share its right-of-way with Park Avenue South before getting back on course at East 14th Street. The landscapers came back almost 50 years later to begin a multiphase renovation (phase one began in 1984) to transform the area once again. (The park had become a gloomy hangout for drug pushers and derelicts.) Among their accomplishments to date is the replacement of the magnificent

Independence Flagstaff at the center of the park, originally donated by Tammany Hall. The face-lift also includes new Art Deco–style subway kiosks, which flank the equestrian statue of *George Washington,* the masterpiece of sculptor John Quincy Adams Ward, which was placed there in 1856. Ward's collaborator was Henry Kirke Brown, who was responsible for the figure of *Abraham Lincoln* at the other end of the park. Nearby is a representation of the *Marquis de Lafayette,* created in 1876 by Frederic Auguste Bartholdi, who gave us the Statue of Liberty 10 years later. ♦ Bounded by Union Square E and Union Square W, and E 14th and E 17th Sts

On Union Square:

Union Square Greenmarket This location is the largest and arguably the most interesting of the city's greenmarkets. In addition to a huge variety of fresh, seasonal, and organic fruits and vegetables sold here (a regulation stipulates that all perishables must be sold within 24 hours of harvesting), fish, cheese, eggs, baked goods, honey, and plants are offered. Some locals make a beeline for the fresh flowers, and at Christmastime, for the freshest trees, wreaths, and garlands. ♦ M, W, F-Sa. Union Sq W and E 17th St. 477.3220 &

2 **Zeckendorf Plaza** There are more than 670 cooperative apartments in this 1987 building by **Davis, Brody & Associates.** Four illuminated pyramids sit atop the sprawling complex. Life here is self-contained, with such amenities as a health club and shopping facilities. At 108 East 15th Street is the 225-seat **Gertrude and Irving Dimson Theater,** the permanent home of the **Vineyard Theater Company.** The development is often cited as a key to the gentrification of the Union Square neighborhood. ♦ Bounded by Irving Pl and Union Sq E, and E 14th and E 15th Sts. 826.2900

3 **Consolidated Edison Building** This massive structure, completed in 1929 by **Henry J. Hardenbergh,** has its critics, but everyone loves its clock tower built in 1926 by **Warren & Wetmore.** It is softly lit at night, as it should be, considering that its owner is the electric company. The building, which fills nearly the whole block, replaced two structures that each had an impact on the city. Tammany Hall, which controlled City Hall for more than 100 years, was headquartered here

in a large but unassuming brick building that had a spacious auditorium for public meetings, and a smaller one that became a profit center as **Tony Pastor's Music Hall,** which, in 1881, was the birthplace of American vaudeville. It was next door to a jewel box of a building known as the **Academy of Music,** the predecessor of the **Metropolitan Opera,** which in its decline became the scene of anti-Tammany rallies. ♦ 4 Irving Pl (between E 14th and E 15th Sts). 460.4600 &

4 **Con Edison Energy Museum** The age of electricity, brought to New York in 1882 by Thomas Edison, is chronicled with exhibitions, artifacts, and imaginative displays that extend from the present into the future. A representation of today's New York at night is reached through a long passageway that is a tour of underground New York, complete with a passing subway. ♦ Free. Tu-Sa. 145 E 14th St (between Third Ave and Irving Pl). 460.6244 &

5 **Stuyvesant Town** There are 8,755 moderately priced rental apartments in this complex, which looks forbidding from the street (when it was built in 1947, Lewis Mumford called it "police state architecture"). The roadways within the complex are virtually free of cars. The tenants, many of whom are senior citizens and young families, live a carefree existence, thanks to good security and careful maintenance provided by the landlord, the Metropolitan Life Insurance Company. In the blocks between East 20th and East 23rd Streets, the development is known as **Peter Cooper Village,** an upscale version of this complex, with larger apartments and higher rents. ♦ Bounded by Ave C and First Ave, and E 14th and E 20th Sts

6 **Stuyvesant Square** Created in 1836 at the edge of the Gas House District (one of the city's poorest neighborhoods), this four-acre oasis, donated to the city by the Stuyvesant family, was the dividing line between rich and poor. In the center of the western half is a 1936 sculpture of *Peter Stuyvesant* by Gertrude Vanderbilt Whitney, founder of the **Whitney Museum.** ♦ Bounded by Nathan D. Perlman and Rutherford Pls, and E 15th and 17th Sts

7 **Friends' Meeting House** The simple, two-story Greek Revival structure, built in 1860 by **Charles T. Bunting,** reflects the peaceful nature of the Society of Friends, whose meetings for worship are held here. ♦ 15 Rutherford Pl (at E 15th St). 777.8866

8 **216 East 16th Street** Part of a row of striking Italianate houses built in the early 1850s, this building is still a joy to behold. The lower stories are brownstone, but brick is used on the upper floors, which, along with the wonderful windows, makes the building stand out. ♦ At Rutherford Pl

9 St. George's Episcopal Church It's easy to believe that this solid brownstone, vaguely Romanesque church was where financier J.P. Morgan attended services. Dating from 1846, it was the design of **Otto Blesch** and **Leopold Eidlitz.** ◆ E 16th St and Rutherford Pl. 475.0830

9 St. George's Chapel Built in 1911 by **Matthew Lansing Emery** and **Henry George Emery,** this Romanesque companion sits in the shadow of the massive church—most certainly one of New York's overlooked treasures. ◆ Rutherford Pl (between E 16th and E 17th Sts)

10 Washington Irving High School Though originally a girls' technical high school, the school expanded its curriculum to include a full range of subjects when it moved here from Lafayette Street in 1912. The huge bust of Irving at the East 17th Street corner was created in 1885 by Friedrich Baer. ◆ 40 Irving Pl (between E 16th and E 17th Sts). 674.5000

11 Guardian Life Insurance Company In 1911, when this building was designed, there was a new architectural movement away from flat-topped buildings with cornices, which were beginning to bore many corporate clients. **D'Oench & Yost** responded by producing a four-story mansard roof for the top of this lavish tower. Not satisfied that it was unusual enough to become their symbol, the insurance company added a huge electric sign that would soon work against them. Their name was "Germania Life," which set them apart as pariahs when World War I broke out. They solved the problem by changing their name. The 1961 extension behind the building, which adds little more than space, was designed by **Skidmore, Owings & Merrill.** ◆ 201 Park Ave S (at E 17th St). 598.8000

12 Rothman's Union Square For nearly seven decades, this discount retailer has been outfitting men in the know with labels from Canali, Hickey-Freeman, and Valentino. They stock a good selection of casual and dress shirts, as well as various accessories. ◆ Daily. 200 Park Ave S (at E 17th St). 777.7400

THE CITY BAKERY

13 The City Bakery ★★$ Fresh ingredients from the **Union Square Greenmarket** just a half-block away are turned into tasty dishes at this bakery/cafe/salad bar. Such hearty soups as lentil or potato with cumin, served with warm focaccia, are made on the premises each morning, as are the heavenly sweets, for which the bakery is well known. The tart-as-art follows the fruits of the season. ◆ American ◆ M-Sa breakfast, lunch, and early dinner.

22 E 17th St (between Union Sq W and Fifth Ave). 366.1414 ₺

14 Union Square Cafe ★★★★$$$ The jewel in the crown of Danny Meyer's restaurant empire, this very light, welcoming, airy modern space has rich cherry-wood floors and beige walls, wainscoted with hunter green and dotted with small brightly colored paintings. Chef Michael Romano's inventive dishes include gazpacho risotto with shrimp, cucumber, tomatoes, and peppers; and grilled marinated filet mignon of tuna. Be sure to save room for one of the delectable desserts. ◆ American ◆ M-Sa lunch and dinner; Su dinner. Reservations required. 21 E 16th St (between Union Sq W and Fifth Ave). 243.4020

15 Coffee Shop ★★$$ In pleasant weather, trendy "club kids" spill into the sidewalk cafe of this slick diner with a Brazilian flair. The menu includes the Sonia Braga chicken salad sandwich (rolled with papaya and cashews in a flour tortilla) and a traditional Brazilian *feijoada* (pork and bean stew) served on Saturday. ◆ International ◆ Daily breakfast, lunch, dinner, and late-night meals. 29 Union Sq W (at E 16th St). 243.7969

16 Richard Stoddard Performing Arts Books Here you'll find mostly out-of-print books plus ephemera relating to the performing arts—playbills, autographs, and periodicals. ◆ M-Tu, Th-Sa. 18 E 16th St (between Union Sq W and Fifth Ave), Room 305. 645.9576 ₺

17 Steak Frites ★$$ Steak and fries are the meat and potatoes at this spot off Union Square, but there also are tasty soups, hearty sandwiches, and interesting pasta specials. It's dimly lit and romantic, but service could be improved. ◆ Bistro ◆ M-F lunch and dinner; Sa-Su brunch and dinner. Reservations recommended. 9 E 16th St (between Union Sq W and Fifth Ave). 463.7101 ₺

One year after New York City became the first capital under the Constitution in 1788, an official census of Manhattan's population registered 33,000. Exactly one hundred years later, the surrounding four boroughs joined Manhattan to create the world's largest city, with a population of 3 million. Today, the city is home to a whopping 7.4 million people.

Restaurants/Clubs: Red   **Hotels:** Blue
Shops/ ▼ Outdoors: Green   **Sights/Culture:** Black

Paul Smith

18 Paul Smith Rock stars and Wall Street bankers have been found here shopping for classic clothing with style. This is the eccentric Englishman's only US outlet—he has 45 stores in Japan and 7 in London—for his handsomely made suits, sports jackets, and slacks, plus wacky playclothes, occasionally. ◆ Daily. 108 Fifth Ave (at W 16th St). 627.9770

18 Mesa Grill ★★★$$$ With its spacious setting and soaring ceilings, this upscale Southwestern restaurant draws a crowd for famous chef/owner Bobby Flay's cooking. The menu includes such innovative dishes as goat cheese and fresh basil quesadilla; tomato-tortilla soup with avocado, white cheddar cheese, and cilantro; red snapper wrapped in a blue corn tortilla with fire-roasted *poblano* chili vinaigrette; and grilled baby lamb chops served with a preserved jalapeño sauce and sweet potato tamale. Save room for the blueberry cobbler with pecan biscuit and buttermilk custard sauce or banana ice-cream cake with pecan butter crunch. ◆ Southwestern ◆ M-F lunch and dinner; Sa-Su brunch and dinner. 102 Fifth Ave (between W 15th and W 16th Sts). 807.7400 &

19 The YIVO Institute for Jewish Research (Yidisher Visnschaftlekher Institut) The world's largest collection of books, letters, and manuscripts in Hebrew and Yiddish—including rabbinical works from as far back as the 16th century—are housed in these new quarters after a relocation from the Theater District. Covering all aspects of Jewish life, its extensive library is open for browsing. ◆ M-Th. 15 W 16th St (between Fifth and Sixth Aves). 246.6080

20 St. Francis Xavier Church This Baroque Roman Catholic monument to the Jesuit missionary would be right at home in his native Spain. The interior is the sort of thing American tourists go out of their way to see in Europe. ◆ 45 W 16th St (between Fifth and Sixth Aves). 627.2100

21 Flowers ★★★$$$ The decor is haute farmhouse, with rough-hewn beams, artistic-looking lanterns suspended from the walls, and hanging baskets of dried flowers. Although the loud music and crush at the front bar may be somewhat off-putting, the menu more than compensates. Changing seasonal offerings might include tequila-marinated salmon with *frisée* and a dill crème fraîche to start, and such main dishes as grilled loin of pork, truffled whipped potatoes, and *haricots verts* (French green beans) in a Port-and-mustard sauce;

grilled mahimahi, mushroom-artichoke couscous, and papaya-mango salsa with plaintain chips; or pan-roasted Chilean sea bass with a salad of shaved fennel, basil, orange, and olives with a beet-and-horseradish sauce. Those having a sweet tooth will be amply satisfied with the baked Alaska with frozen yogurt and bittersweet chocolate sauce. ◆ International ◆ M-F lunch and dinner; Sa dinner; Su brunch and dinner. Reservations recommended for dinner. 21 W 17th St (between Fifth and Sixth Aves). 691.8888 &

22 Siegel-Cooper & Company Originally **Siegel-Cooper Dry Goods Store,** this garish white brick and terra-cotta retail temple (fashioned by **DeLemos & Cordes** under the influence of the Chicago World's Fair of 1893) lived up to its slogan "The Big Store—A City In Itself" with 15.5 acres of space, 17 elevators, a tropical garden, and a smaller version of Daniel Chester French's monument *The Republic,* which had graced the Fair. (The fountain at the base of the statue became a favorite rendezvous for New Yorkers.) The store was located in the fashionable shopping district called "Ladies' Mile," but when **Macy's** and **B. Altman** moved uptown, it sold its inventory to **Gimbels** and the statue to Forest Lawn Cemetery in Los Angeles. The building was converted into a military hospital during World War I, and in recent years it has served as construction space for television scenery and home to garment manufacturing firms, as well as such stores as **T.J. Maxx** and **Filene's Basement.** ◆ Sixth Ave and W 18th St

23 Books of Wonder If there are no children in your life, this store will make you wish there were—or at least make you fondly remember when you were a child yourself. Authors and illustrators make frequent appearances to read from their books and to sign copies. There is a half-hour storytime every Sunday at 11:30AM (except between Thanksgiving and New Year's). ◆ Daily. 16 W 18th St (between Fifth and Sixth Aves). 989.3270 &

23 Academy Books and Records You'll find a good selection of out-of-print, used, and rare books and records here, as well as used CDs. ◆ Daily. 10 W 18th St (between Fifth and Sixth Aves). 242.4848

24 Barnes & Noble Originally a purveyor of textbooks with branches at most major local colleges, this store has branched out all over town (and the nation) in recent years. There are two here, the main store on the southeast corner and the Sale Annex across the street. You can still buy and sell textbooks, but the selection of books and records beyond that is almost overwhelming, at prices that are surprisingly low. ◆ Daily. 105 Fifth Ave (at E 18th St). 807.0099. Also at: Numerous locations throughout the city &

25 Daffy's Imagine three floors of designer clothes and accessories for men and women of every age group at discount prices. We're not talking Calvin and Giorgio, but those with a discerning eye will always find some good pieces. ♦ Daily. 111 Fifth Ave (at E 18th St). 529.4477. Also at: Numerous locations throughout the city &

26 Paragon This gigantic sporting goods store has an extensive sportswear collection. Its sales often have spectacular bargains. ♦ Daily. 867 Broadway (at E 18th St). 255.8036

27 MacIntyre Building Built in 1892 by **R.H. Robertson,** this Romanesque office building has obviously seen better days, but it hasn't lost its pride. You can tell by the way those beasts at the corners are sticking their tongues out at you. ♦ 874 Broadway (at E 18th St)

28 Old Town Bar ★$ The popularity of this century-old tavern may be sufficient to keep it in business for another hundred years. Sit in the time-worn wooden booths and enjoy the famous chicken wings, a burger (served with fried onions on an English muffin), and an icy mug of draft beer. ♦ American ♦ Daily lunch and dinner. 45 E 18th St (between Park Ave S and Broadway). 529.6732

29 Sal Anthony's ★$$ The hearty Italian menu is predictable but reliable; a huge bay window in front adds cheer. Try the chicken in olive oil and garlic or the linguine with white clam sauce. During the summer, tables are set out on the sidewalk for alfresco dining. ♦ Italian ♦ Daily lunch and dinner. Reservations required. 55 Irving Pl (between E 17th and E 18th Sts). 982.9030

30 Inn at Irving Place $$$ One of the city's intimate hotels, this one is a gem, with 12 rooms handsomely appointed in *Age of Innocence* trappings in a 19th-century town house. Tastefully chosen period pieces might include big brass beds or oversized Victorian armoires—the kind of furniture seldom found on this side of the Atlantic. The inn's discreet albeit casual appeal extends to the lack of sign or awning or uniformed doorman. ♦ 54 Irving Pl (between E 17th and E 18th Sts). 533.4600; fax 533.4611

Within the Inn at Irving Place:

Verbena ★★★$$$ At a time when most restaurants try to double as designer showrooms, this small but elegant dining room is a welcome change. Try not to fill up on the freshly baked bread—save room for the autumn mushrooms with angel-hair pasta in truffle mushroom broth; butternut-squash ravioli flavored with roasted oranges and sage; seared venison chop with twice-baked sweet potatoes, chestnuts, and pomegranate seeds; or succulent beer-braised ribs of beef with root vegetables and horseradish dumplings. Desserts are uniformly excellent—especially the rum-soaked savarin filled with warm bittersweet chocolate and crème brûlée with lemon verbena. ♦ American ♦ M-Sa dinner; Su brunch and dinner. Reservations required. 260.5454 &

31 Friend of a Farmer ★$$ The country cooking and on-the-premises baking might well take you back to your grandma's kitchen. The Long Island duckling and Cajun-style chicken are always good. ♦ American ♦ M-F breakfast, lunch, and dinner; Sa-Su brunch and dinner. 77 Irving Pl (between E 18th and E 19th Sts). 477.2188

31 Choshi ★★$$ The fresh and well-prepared sushi and sashimi here are great buys at lunch. Prix-fixe dinner menus are another terrific deal. Choose between indoor and outdoor dining. ♦ Japanese ♦ M-F lunch and dinner; Sa-Su brunch and dinner. 77 Irving Pl (at E 19th St). 420.1419

32 Pete's Tavern ★$$ One of several saloons that claim to be the oldest in town, this place also boasts that O. Henry did some of his writing in a corner booth. If the bar was as busy then as it is now, his powers of concentration must have been incredible. The food, which runs from standard Italian specialties to hamburgers, isn't exceptional, but the atmosphere is great, and the sidewalk cafe sits on one of the city's more pleasant streets. ♦ Italian/American ♦ M-F lunch and dinner; Sa-Su brunch and dinner. 129 E 18th St (at Irving Pl). 473.7676

33 Manhattan Doll House This shop has the largest collection of new and antique dolls, doll houses, and doll accessories in the city—all for sale. ♦ M-Sa. 236 Third Ave (between E 19th and E 20th Sts). 253.9549 &

34 Police Academy and Museum The movie version of it notwithstanding, this academy takes its job very seriously. The building has a swimming pool and a gymnasium, as well as a museum that shows how the city's police officers came to be called New York's Finest, with displays that help you understand what they've been through to earn the title. Visitors are welcome, but call first since they close when meetings are scheduled. ♦ Free. M-F 9AM-3PM. 235 E 20th St (between Second and Third Aves). 477.9753

35 Gramercy Park/Gramercy Park Historic District Established by Samuel Ruggles in 1831, this former marshland became the model of a London square ringed by proper 19th-century Neo-Classical town houses. It is the sole surviving "private park" in New York City—only surrounding residents have keys to get in—but the perimeter is well worth a stroll. Many notables have lived in this neighborhood, including James Harper, the mayor of New York City (1844), and Samuel J. Tilden, governor of New York State (1874-86), who was an unsuccessful presidential candidate; his home (15 Gramercy Park S) is now the **National Arts Club.** The statue in the park is of actor Edwin Booth, who lived at **No. 16** Gramercy Park South until he had the building remodeled by **Stanford White** in 1888 for The Players Club. **Numbers 34** and **36** on the east side are among the city's earliest apartment buildings, designed in 1883 by **George DaConha** and in 1905 by **James Riles,** respectively. Note the magnificent ironwork on **Nos. 3** and **4** Gramercy Park West, attributed to **Alexander Jackson Davis,** one of the city's more individualistic and energetic architects. The Gramercy Park Historic District extends in an irregular area out from the park, including all of the west and south frontages and part of the east, the park itself, and Irving Place almost to East 19th Street on the west side and to East 18th Street on the east, as well as parts of East 20th and East 21st Streets west of the park. Of particular interest is the beautiful block between Irving Place and Third Avenue on East 19th Street (remodeled as a group by **Frederick J. Sterner**). ♦ Bounded by Gramercy Park E and Fifth Ave, and E 18th St and Gramercy Park N

Within the Gramercy Park Historic District:

The Brotherhood Synagogue This austere brownstone cube was designed in 1859 by **King & Kellum** as a Friends' meetinghouse, and was remodeled in 1975 by **James Stewart Polshek** as a synagogue. ♦ 28 Gramercy Park S (between E 20th St and Irving Pl). 674.5750

The Hampden-Booth Theatre Library In 1888, founder Edwin Booth charged The Players Club with the task of creating "a library relating to the history of the American stage and the preservation of pictures, bills of the play, photographs, and curiosities." Small group tours and use of the library, which includes four major collections (from Edwin Booth, Walter Hampden, the **Union Square Theatre,** and William Henderson), are granted by appointment only. ♦ 16 Gramercy Park S (at Irving Pl). 228.7610

National Arts Club Built in 1845 by **Calvert Vaux,** this building has housed the National Arts Club since 1906, but its colorful history began when politician Samuel J. Tilden, who gained fame by destroying the Tweed Ring, used the coup to become governor of New York. To protect himself in the topsy-turvy days of early unions and political machinery, Tilden installed steel doors at the front of this Victorian Gothic home and had a tunnel dug to East 19th Street as an escape route. ♦ 15 Gramercy Park S (between Irving Pl and E 20th St). 475.3424

36 L'Express ★★$$ Perfectly capturing the ambience of a French bistro, this charming cafe is one of the best places for friendly welcomes and hearty food. The 24-hour menu includes an omelette with gruyère and ham, eggs Benedict, breast of duck with tomato chutney, and grilled salmon with lentils and mustard sauce. ♦ Bistro ♦ Daily 24 hours. 249 Park Ave S (at E 20th St). 254.5858 &

37 Patria ★★★$$$ The handsome bilevel room, decorated with golden columns and earthy paintings of avocados, draws a fashionable crowd for the Latin-inspired food of Miamian chef Douglas Rodriguez. Among the outstanding culinary favorites are Honduran seviche (a vibrant combination of tuna marinated in chilies, ginger, and coconut milk), crispy red snapper with coconut-conch rice, spicy seafood *chupe* (a stew of lobster, clams, shrimp, calamari, and scallops), and the sugarcane tuna. The chocolate cigar with spun-sugar matches brings a whimsical and tasty conclusion to a meal. Such specialty drinks as *mojito* (rum, sugarcane juice, lime juice, and mint), *manguini* (Champagne and fresh mango juice), and the Patria colada (a variation of the piña, with passion fruit and shaved coconut) receive the same high marks as the food. ♦ New Spanish ♦ M-F lunch and dinner; Sa-Su dinner. Reservations required. 250 Park Ave S (at E 20th St). 777.6211

GRAMERCY

TAVERN

38 Gramercy Tavern ★★★$$$ In a *New York Magazine* cover story that preceded the restaurant's opening, owner Danny Meyer (of **Union Square Cafe** fame) stated his "modest ambition: to reinvent the four-star restaurant. Together with chef Tom Colicchio, he comes close. Superb selections from the seasonal menu include tuna *tartare,* crispy sweetbreads, roasted cod with zucchini confit, loin of lamb with lemon confit, and roasted Scottish venison. Excellent endings include baked chocolate mousse cake, orange-laced cannoli, and buttermilk *panna cotta.* For those who want a less formal dining experience, the tavern room at the front of the restaurant offers more reasonable—but still delicious—fare.♦ American ♦ M-Sa lunch and dinner; Su dinner. Reservations required. 42 E 20th St (between Park Ave S and Broadway). 477.0393 ᕃ

39 Theodore Roosevelt Birthplace Teddy Roosevelt was born here in 1858 and lived in a house on the site until he was a teenager. The original house was destroyed in 1916, but was faithfully reconstructed seven years later by **Theodate Pope Riddle** as a memorial to the 26th president. The National Historic Site incorporates 26 East 20th Street, once the home of Roosevelt's uncle. The restoration contains five rooms of period furniture and an extensive collection of memorabilia, including teddy bears. ♦ Nominal admission; seniors, children free. W-Su. 28 E 20th St (between Park Ave S and Broadway). 260.1616

40 Goelet Building Chicago architects developed steel-framed office buildings with highly ornamental exteriors, and in the 1880s, firms such as **McKim, Mead & White** began developing their own variations on the theme, which they called "New York Style." This is a prime example. ♦ 900 Broadway (at E 20th St)

41 Campagna ★★$$$ Owner-chef Mark Strausman's Tuscan-style trattoria is comfortably decorated with white walls, Italian country antiques, and abstract paintings. Excellent selections include fried calamari, six-layer lasagna, and Florentine rib steak. Desserts are more opulent here than at most Italian restaurants, especially the three-layer torte with chocolate cake, mascarpone, and chocolate mascarpone mousse. ♦ Italian ♦ M-F lunch and dinner; Sa-Su dinner. Reservations recommended. 24 E 21st St (between Park Ave S and Broadway). 460.0900 ᕃ

42 901 Broadway Originally **Lord & Taylor Dry Goods Store,** this 1869 **James H. Giles** building displays a romantic cast-iron facade with echoes of Renaissance castle architecture as a monument to the glories of this formerly fashionable shopping neighborhood before **Lord & Taylor** moved uptown along with its neighbors **W&J Sloane** and **Arnold Constable.** Industrial tenants have occupied it ever since, and the remodeled mundane ground floor has no connection with the fanciful upper ones. ♦ At E 20th St

43 ABC Carpet The original owner of this 1882 building was **W&J Sloane,** which moved uptown and became one of the city's leading furniture dealers. It specialized in carpets and rugs when it was here, and the tradition is continued by one of Sloane's former competitors. Founded in 1987, this floor-covering emporium is one of New York's more reasonably priced sources of carpets of every description, from wall-to-wall carpeting to area rugs of every design, quality, and price, as well as various remnants and tiles. Across the street, at **No. 881,** are six floors of merchandise, including antique and reproduction rugs and furniture, plus bed, bath, linen, and lighting departments. The floor displays are so tasteful that apartment dwellers flock here on weekends just to look for ideas. ♦ Daily. 888 Broadway (at E 19th St). 473.3000

44 Arnold Constable Dry Goods Store Building A glorious two-story mansard roof tops this skillful marriage of Empire and Italianate styles, designed by **Griffith Thomas** in 1877. Note the rare combination of marble and cast iron in the facade—the city's first use of cast-iron construction for retail space. ♦ 881-887 Broadway (between E 18th and E 19th Sts)

45 News Bar ★$ The fresh pastries and sandwiches are great, but the espressos, cappuccinos, and steamed milks are superlative. Pull up a chair at the counter and immerse yourself in your favorite periodical, which is likely to be found among the several hundred newspapers and magazines offered. ♦ Cafe ♦ Daily. 2 W 19th St (at Fifth Ave). 255.3996. Also at: 366 W Broadway (at Broome St). 343.0053; 107 University Pl (between E 12th and E 13th Sts). 260.4192

46 Revolution Books Before you start your revolution, stop here for inspiration from the masters of the art. The books cover political science with an emphasis on the radical. ♦ Daily. 9 W 19th St (between Fifth and Sixth Aves). 691.3345 ᕃ

Getting to the top is the literal object of the annual Empire State Building Run Up, a marathon race of unusual proportions. Entrants must negotiate the building's 1,575 steps. People from around the globe enter the event, held each February. Average winning time is 12 to 14 minutes, with winners and losers alike earning a splendid view from the 86th floor and an elevator ride down.

Tin Pan Alley, once located on West 28th Street between Broadway and Fifth Avenue, was the heart of the world-famous music publishing industry.

NYC: Past and Present

Battery Park

Past: Located at the tip of Manhattan, this was a fortification used to block enemy attack. Later, it housed the **New York Aquarium.**

Present: Castle Clinton, with walls eight feet thick, still stands; this is where tickets can be purchased for the ferry to the **Statue of Liberty/Ellis Island**. The area is one of the prettiest promenades on the city's waterfront.

City Hall Park

Past: Once the **Old Negro Burial Ground,** this park also served as a parade ground, a prison, and site of public executions.

Present: Between **Park Row** and **Broadway,** the beautiful grounds facing **City Hall** now serve as the site of many official city ceremonies—and more than a few demonstrations.

Flushing Meadows–Corona Park

Past: Nearly one-and-a-half times larger than Central Park, this was little more than a tidal marsh and garbage dump made famous by F. Scott Fitzgerald's *The Great Gatsby* as "the valley of ashes." In 1939 and again in 1964 the site was home to the World's Fair.

Present: One of the city's largest parks, it offers a wide range of activities including golf, ice-skating, and roller-skating. Also here are the **Hall of Science, Carousel, Queens Wildlife Center,** and **Queens Theater-in-the-Park.**

Fort Schuyler

Past: Located at the tip of **Throgs Neck** in the **Bronx,** it once housed a lighthouse to guide ships through the passage between **Long Island Sound** and the **East River.**

Present: A refurbished Fort Schuyler is now the home of the **United States Maritime College,** a branch of the **State University of New York.**

Mulberry Street

Past: The center of the Italian section of the **Lower East Side,** this area teemed with pushcarts, wagons, and tenements. Fire escapes were used for the storage of household goods and for drying clothes.

Present: The colorful, lively Italian influence can still be felt here, although the growth of **Chinatown** has made the neighborhood more diverse, with Chinese shops and restaurants.

Rockefeller Center

Past: This area was the city's first botanical garden.

Present: Today a city within a city, it boasts flora along the Channel Gardens (one side representing England, the other France). Its annual flower show, in April, features the artistic designs of area horticulturists; the lighting of its towering, sparkling Christmas tree officially marks the start of the holiday season every year.

Park Avenue

Past: During the 1800s the New York and Harlem Railroad used the stretch from 46th to 96th Streets (then called **Fourth Avenue**) as a north-south rail link; it was named Park Avenue in 1888. The avenue was lined with brick and brownstone residences.

Present: The railroad tracks were covered and now run underground. Today, modern glass-and-steel office buildings line the avenue. To the north, many elegant dowager apartment buildings lend touches of class; at the southern end is the **MetLife Building** silhouetting the sky.

Castle Clinton

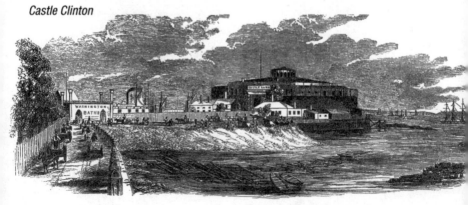

47 Caffe Bondì ★★$$$ What began as a small neighborhood cafe and *pasticceria* has grown into a full-blown restaurant, complete with an outdoor patio. Try any of the simple yet delicious pastas, which include *taglierini* (thin noodles) with tomatoes, mushrooms, and rosemary cream, or one of the Sicilian specialties, such as caponata. ♦ Italian ♦ M-F lunch and dinner; Sa-Su brunch and dinner. 7 W 20th St (between Fifth and Sixth Aves). 691.8136

48 Periyali ★★★$$$ The friendly staff at this top-notch taverna is unabashedly proud of its traditional Greek menu. Giant white beans with garlic sauce, char-grilled octopus or shrimp, lamb chops with rosemary, anything in phyllo pastry, and fresh whole fish are all good picks. For dessert there's homemade baklava and wonderful *diples* (thin strips of deep-fried dough dipped in honey). The extensive wine list includes a good selection of Greek wines. White stucco walls, wooden floors, and soft Greek music complete the experience. ♦ Greek ♦ M-F lunch and dinner; Sa dinner. Reservations recommended. 35 W 20th St (between Fifth and Sixth Aves). 463.7890

49 Limelight Inside an alluringly forbidding deconsecrated church is Peter Gatien's revamped nightclub of 1980s notoriety that once again offers one of New York's more distinctive after-hours scenes. The main dance floor takes on an added measure of drama by being so far away from the lofty cathedral ceilings. Two sets of elevated catwalks afford patrons a view of the stained-glass windows or the ground-floor action from almost dizzying heights, and access to a warren of bars and special VIP rooms. The most unusual of these is the grotesque, but chic, **Giger Room,** designed by the artist who brought us those ill-mannered creatures in the *Aliens* movies. The action starts late here. Note: Be sure to call ahead to find out about times, special events, and cover charges. ♦ Sixth Ave (at W 20th St). 358.5915

50 Cal's Restaurant & Bar ★★$$ The dining room here is reminiscent of a Parisian grand cafe: soaring ceilings, a large carved-wood bar, and massive columns. The menu is varied and well executed, featuring such dishes as oven-roasted beet and endive salad; saffron *risotto primavera;* roasted stuffed quail with dates and onions; house-cured salmon with grapefruit and star anise; roasted chicken with wild-mushroom sauce, and a honey herb-glazed duck. Desserts too good to miss include bananas in a chocolate cookie crust, and a brownie ice-cream sandwich. ♦ American ♦ M-F lunch and dinner; Sa-Su dinner. Reservations recommended. 55 W 21st St (between Fifth and Sixth Aves). 929.0740 ♿

51 Lola ★$$$ Simply and attractively decorated, this restaurant serves authentically spiced and curried foods from the Caribbean, along with some familiar Italian fare. Try Lola's fried chicken or grilled snapper, and don't forget the onion rings. During weekday lunches, the private dining room becomes the less expensive **Lola Bowla,** which serves all entrées—mainly soups, pastas, and salads—in bowls. ♦ Caribbean/Italian ♦ M-F lunch and dinner; Sa dinner; Su brunch and dinner. Reservations recommended. 30 W 22nd St (between Fifth and Sixth Aves). 675.6700

52 Stern's Dry Goods Store This restoration of **Henry Fernbach**'s 1878 building is possibly the most sensitive of any cast-iron building in New York. ♦ 32-36 W 23rd St (between Fifth and Sixth Aves)

53 Western Union Building A reflection of the city's Dutch origins, this building was created by **Henry J. Hardenbergh** in 1884, the same year as his **Dakota** apartment house overlooking **Central Park.** ♦ 186 Fifth Ave (at W 23rd St)

54 Flatiron Building In 1902, when **Daniel H. Burnham** (of Chicago World's Fair fame) filled the triangular site where Broadway crosses

Flatiron Building

MICHAEL STORRINGS

Fifth Avenue in a most reasonable but unconventional manner—with a triangular building—he raised many eyebrows and made history. This limestone-clad Renaissance palazzo was one of the city's first skyscrapers, at 285 feet high, and it is one of **Burnham**'s best. At the juncture between traditionalism and modernism, the structure, with its articulated base and strong cornice, looks like an ocean liner in a column's clothing. Built as the **Fuller Building**, people soon dubbed it the "Flatiron" for its shape, once they stopped calling it "Burnham's Folly." ♦ 175 Fifth Ave (between E 22nd and E 23rd Sts)

55 Bolo ★★$$$ The decor is a manifestation of the vibrant energy at work here: vivid greens, reds, and golds, as well as collaged graphic images. This is the place where Bobby Flay takes on Spanish food and makes it hum. Try the warm octopus and sweet-onion salad with sage-and-lemon vinaigrette; tenderloin of pork with walnut romesco and caramelized-date shallot sauce; or curried shellfish-and-chicken paella. ♦ New Spanish ♦ M-F lunch and dinner; Sa-Su dinner. Reservations recommended. 23 E 22nd St (between Park Ave S and Broadway). 228.2200 ♿

ALVA

56 Alva ★★$$$ The black walls of this small, narrow restaurant are mirrored, adorned with photos of Thomas Alva Edison, and illuminated by light bulbs. Clearly, owner Charlie Palmer—also of **Aureole**—hopes to capture the spirit of genius, or at least invention. The earthy and flavorful fare includes grilled salmon in a grainy mustard Riesling sauce, and double-garlic roasted chicken. ♦ American ♦ M-F lunch and dinner; Sa-Su dinner. Reservations recommended. 36 E 22nd St (between Park Ave S and Broadway). 228.4399 ♿

57 Space Kiddets This lively boutique features moderate to expensive clothing and accessories for boys and girls with an emphasis on trendiness and practicality. There's also a selection of toys and games, along with colorful "play" jewelry that fashion-conscious moms will borrow from their daughters. ♦ M-Sa. 46 E 21st St (between Park Ave S and Broadway). 420.9878

58 Calvary Church Designed in 1846 by **James Renwick Jr.**, the architect of **St. Patrick's Cathedral**, this Protestant Episcopal church once had steeples. **Renwick** had them removed in 1860 because, some critics said, they embarrassed him. If the exterior was less

than perfect, the architect made up for it inside the church with the nave, which is exquisite. The Sunday-school building on the uptown side, also a **Renwick** design, was added in 1867. ♦ 61 Gramercy Park N (at Park Ave S). 475.1216

59 Russell Sage Foundation Building The foundation that set out to dispense $63 million for good works in 1906 did much of its own good work in this 1912 building by **Grosvenor Atterbury** before selling the building to Catholic Charities, which in turn sold it for development as apartments. ♦ 4 Lexington Ave (at E 22nd St)

60 Gramercy Park Hotel $$ This 1927 edifice by **Thompson & Churchill** was **Stanford White**'s last home and is a favorite of European travelers who fancy the relaxed Old World style and sensible prices. The choice rooms face the park (guests have access), which is ringed with historic landmarks and turn-of-the-century brownstones. The 380 rooms vary (some have been renovated), so ask to see a few of the others if you're not satisfied with yours. ♦ 2 Lexington Ave (at Gramercy Park N). 475.4320, 800/221.4083; fax 505.0535

61 Rolf's Restaurant ★$$ New York was once famous for its German restaurants, and this is one of the very few still operating. The walls and ceilings are covered with art, stained glass, and carved wood. Try the veal shank, shell steak, and excellent potato pancakes. For desert, there's apple strudel and Black Forest cake. ♦ German ♦ Daily lunch and dinner. 281 Third Ave (at E 22nd St). 473.8718

62 Asser Levy Recreational Center In 1906 right-thinking architects **Arnold W. Brunner** and **William Martin Aiken** finally used the overappropriated style of the Romans in its original manner—for baths (like those of Caracalla or Diocletian). Formerly called the **Public Baths,** this formal structure now houses a fitness center with indoor and outdoor swimming pools; membership required. ♦ E 23rd St (at Asser Levy Pl). 447.2020

School of VISUAL ARTS

63 School of Visual Arts Working professionals teach more than 5,500 students the fundamentals of illustration, photography, video, film, animation, and other visual arts in buildings throughout the neighborhood. Frequent exhibitions in the main building on East 23rd Street are free to the public. The luminary faculty includes Milton Glaser, Eileen Hedy-Schultz, Ed Benguiat, and Sal DeVito. ♦ 209 E 23rd St (between Second and Third Aves). 679.7350 &

64 Live Bait ★$$ An extremely popular after-work destination, the bar is packed sardine-style, with a crowd downing oysters from shot glasses and sipping Rolling Rocks from bottles. The decor is pure fishing shack, and although a cheeky sign above the bar says, "If you want home cooking, stay home," the food is definitely Carolina home-style. The menu includes smothered pork chops; fried chicken; and plantation gumbo with andouille sausage, shrimp, and chicken served over creole rice. For dessert try the Mississippi mud, Key lime, or pecan pie. ♦ Southeastern ♦ Daily lunch, dinner, and late-night meals. Reservations recommended. 14 E 23rd St (between Park Ave S and Broadway). 353.2400

65 Metropolitan Life Insurance Company Originally, the 700-foot marble tower (adjacent to the main building) was decorated with 200 carved lions' heads, ornamental columns, and a copper roof. But its four-sided clock, which at 26.5 feet is 4.5 feet taller than Big Ben, hasn't changed since 1909, when the tower was built. The north building, across East 24th Street, was designed in 1932 by **Harvey Wiley Corbett** and **E. Everett Waid** and is surprisingly light for all its limestone mass. Note the sculpted quality of the polygonal setbacks, the vaulted entrances at each of the four corners, and the Italian marble lobby. This block was the site of the **Madison Square Presbyterian Church.** Completed by **Stanford White** in 1906, it was his last, and many say his finest, building. ♦ 1 Madison Ave (at E 23rd St). 578.2211 &

66 Madison Square What once was a swampy hunting ground, then a pauper's graveyard, is now a quiet refuge in the midst of madness. The square dates from 1847, when it was a parade ground and only a small part of a proposed park that was laid out in the Randell Plan of 1811—the plan that created the city's grid street pattern. Like other squares in this part of town, it was the focus of a fashionable residential district that flourished in pre–Civil War days. After the war, the fancy **Fifth Avenue Hotel**, the **Madison Square Theater,** and the second home of **Madison Square Garden** all faced the square. This incarnation of the **Garden** will always be remembered because **Stanford White,** who designed the building, was shot and killed in its roof garden by

Harry K. Thaw, the jealous husband who thought **White** was paying too much attention to his wife, Evelyn Nesbit. Today, the square is ringed by mostly public and commercial buildings, but manages to retain its air of serenity. ♦ Bounded by Madison and Fifth Aves, Broadway, E 23rd St, and Madison Sq N

67 200 Fifth Avenue This is the center of America's wholesale toy business, which extends into several nearby buildings. Its 15 floors are a dreamland for children, who, alas, are not allowed to browse. But the lobby is open to the public and not to be missed. ♦ Between W 23rd and W 24th Sts

F O L L O N I C O

68 Follonico ★★$$$ The open kitchen and wood-burning oven add to the feeling of Old World warmth at this dining spot. Try calamari roasted with garlic; ravioli filled with rabbit, veal, and pork in a butter-and-sage sauce; seafood stew; smoked goose breast with white beans and pomegranate seeds; osso buco; roasted chicken; or baked salt-crusted red snapper. Top the meal off with an apple tart baked in the wood-burning oven. The wine list is filled with unusual Italian selections that are affordably priced. ♦ Italian ♦ M-F lunch and dinner; Sa dinner. Reservations recommended. 6 W 24th St (between Broadway and Sixth Ave). 691.6359 &

69 Worth Monument This richly ornamented obelisk in a plot separating Broadway and Fifth Avenue marks the grave of Major General William Jenkins Worth, for whom the street in Lower Manhattan and the city of Fort Worth, Texas, were named. After fighting the Seminole in Florida, he went on to become a hero of the Mexican War in 1846. The monument was designed in 1857 by **James C. Batterson.** ♦ W 25th St and Fifth Ave

70 Serbian Orthodox Cathedral of St. Sava Built in 1855 by **Richard Upjohn** for **Trinity Church,** this chapel became a cathedral of the Eastern Orthodox faith in 1943. The beautiful altar and reredos inside are by **Frederick Clarke Withers.** The parish house was designed in 1860 by **Jacob Wrey Mould.** ♦ 15 W 25th St (between Broadway and Sixth Ave). 242.9240

71 Annex Antiques Fair and Flea Market Commonly referred to as the "26th Street Flea Market," this is the city's original, largest, and most popular weekly antiques and flea market (though **GreenFlea** creates some competition uptown). Treasures can be found amid eclectic and fascinating trash year-round, as more than 500 vendors congregate in this parking lot in the middle of the Flower District. You'll find everything from Tiffany silver to bentwood chairs and 1950s collectibles. The **Chelsea Antiques Annex** (not to be confused with the **Chelsea Antiques Building,** see page 134), with an entrance at 122 West 26th Street (between Sixth and Seventh Aves), follows the same hours. ♦ Nominal admission. Sa-Su. Sixth Ave (between W 24th and W 27th Sts). 243.5343

72 Center for Book Arts This organization offers a gallery and teaching and work space for hand-producing and publishing books, including bookbinding, papermaking, and letterpress printing, all by hand. ♦ Gallery: M-Sa. 28 W 27th St (between Sixth Ave and Broadway), Third floor. 481.0295; fax 481.9853

73 New York Life Insurance Company This 1928 Gothic masterpiece was designed by **Cass Gilbert** the architect of the **Woolworth Building** and New York's **Federal Courthouse.** The square tower topped by a gilded pyramid—a style Gilbert called "American Perpendicular"—is dramatically lighted at night. Its lobby is a panorama of detail, from polychromed coffered ceilings to bronze elevator doors, and ornate grilles over the subway entrances. ♦ 45-55 Madison Ave (between E 26th and E 27th Sts). 576.7000

74 Tabla ★★★$$$ Few new restaurants in town have generated as much buzz—or praise—as this innovative Indian spot owned by Danny Meyer. The space may not exactly exude warmth, but Chef Floyd Cardoz prepares such inventive dinner entrées as coconut-spiced organic chicken with bok choy, watermelon radish, and kohlrabi; taro-crisped red snapper with white beans, a trio of mustard greens, and ambot-tik sauce, and braised Nova Scotia lobster with toasted couscous, green beans, and coriander-coconut curry. Be sure to leave room for dessert—the vanilla bean kulfi with blood-orange rosewater and pistachio crisp is a winner. The breads are wonderful. Those wishing a quick bite can stop at the cafe on the ground floor. ♦ New Indian ♦ M-F lunch and dinner; Sa dinner. Reservations recommended. 11 Madison Ave (at E 25th St). 889.0667 ♿

The Empire State Building is one of the world's eight wonders—and the only one constructed in the 20th century.

75 Appellate Division of the Supreme Court of the State of New York Here, in the busiest appellate court in the world, nine justices hear most appeals in civil and criminal cases arising in New York and surrounding counties. The building, designed by **James Brown Lord**—murals, statuary, and all—was finished in 1900 at $5,000 under budget, with a final price tag of just under $644,000. It is one of the city's treasures. Stop in and be impressed. The building is open to the public when court is not sitting. ♦ M-F. 27 Madison Ave (at E 25th St). 340.0400 ♿

76 69th Regiment Armory Designed in 1905 by **Hunt & Hunt,** this is where the infamous Armory Show introduced modern art to New York in 1913—the most famous work in the show was Marcel Duchamp's *Nude Descending a Staircase*. Note the gun bays overlooking Lexington Avenue, with the barrel-vaulted **Drill Hall** behind it. ♦ 68 Lexington Ave (between E 25th and E 26th Sts). 889.7249

77 La Colombe d'Or ★★★$$$ The piquant cuisine of Provence, deftly prepared with a light touch, is served in a rustic, romantic setting. Start with eggplant carpaccio with warm goat cheese, sliced tomatoes, and basil; or escargots au roquefort (snails simmered with shallots, white wine, and roquefort cheese in flaky pastry). Next move on to the aioli, a *Provençale* specialty of cod and seasoned vegetables steamed with aromatic herbs; or a traditional cassoulet. Good bets for dessert include a lemon tart and *le fondant au chocolat* (flourless Belgian chocolate cake with crème anglaise). ♦ French ♦ M-F lunch and dinner; Sa-Su dinner. Reservations recommended. 134 E 26th St (between Third and Lexington Aves). 689.0666

78 I Trulli ★★★$$$ Nicola Marzovilla tried to re-create the trattorie of his childhood in Southern Italy's Puglia when he opened this warm, simple place. The dining room is dominated by a glassed-in fireplace and a whitewashed wood-burning oven that mirrors the distinctive beehive shape of *trulli*—ancient Pugliese houses. From here and from the kitchen emerge wonderfully earthy dishes, such as the clay casserole of potatoes, portobello mushrooms, and herbs; baked oysters with pancetta; ricotta dumplings with tomato sauce; spicy chicken with vinegar and garlic; grilled free-range chicken; and stewed baby octopus. For dessert, try the fruit poached in wine. There's also an extensive wine list with good choices at all price levels. In nice weather, sit in the lovely garden out back. ♦ Italian ♦ M-F lunch and dinner; Sa dinner. Reservations recommended. 122 E 27th St (between Lexington Ave and Park Ave S). 481.7372

79 Bellevue Hospital Center Established in 1736, this municipal hospital cares for some 80,000 emergency cases per year. Its services are available to anyone, with no restrictions, including ability to pay. The medical center was a pioneer in providing ambulance service, in performing appendectomies and Caesarean sections, and in developing heart catheterization and microsurgery. It is not, as is often believed, solely a psychiatric hospital. The administration building was designed in 1939 by the prestigious architectural firm **McKim, Mead & White**. ♦ 462 First Ave (between E 25th and E 30th Sts). 562.4141

80 Waterside There are 1,600 apartments in these brown towers built by **Davis, Brody & Associates** in 1974 on a platform over the East River. They are a world apart, reached by a footbridge across the FDR Drive at East 25th Street, or by the riverfront esplanade to the north. The river views here are spectacular. ♦ At the eastern end of E 25th St. 725.5374

81 The Water Club ★★★★$$$ Inside the glass-enclosed, sky-lit former barge, which is anchored at the river's edge, landlubbers are treated to views that are among the best in town—the cocktail lounge opens into a terraced dining room with a panorama of the East River. Naturally, seafood is the best choice (the monkfish medallions with zucchini chips is highly recommended), but Chef Gary Coyle has added his spin on American cuisine with a variety of meat dishes, such as pork tenderloin with orange-rosemary marinade, wood-grilled filet mignon, and rack of lamb with sweet garlic. Desserts range from a milk chocolate torte to the classic crème brûlée to handmade sorbets and ice creams. ♦ American ♦ M-Sa lunch and dinner; Su brunch and dinner. Reservations required. At the eastern end of E 30th St (access from E 34th St). 683.3333

82 Kips Bay Plaza These twin 21-story slabs facing an inner, private park were the first

exposed concrete apartment houses in New York. The complex, completed in 1965, was designed by **I.M. Pei & Associates** and **S.J. Kessler**. ♦ Bounded by First and Second Aves, and E 30th and E 33rd Sts

83 Marchi's ★★$$$ Not much has changed since this elegant restaurant opened in 1930. "No sign outside—no menu inside," is still the motto. The Marchi family has served the same fixed menu with a European flair for nearly that long: an antipasto platter, homemade lasagna, deep-fried whiting with cold string beans and beets in vinaigrette, roasted veal and roasted chicken with mushrooms and tossed greens, and dessert. ♦ Northern Italian ♦ M-Sa dinner. Reservations recommended. 251 E 31st St (between Second and Third Aves). 679.2494

84 Manhattan Fruitier Owner Jehv Gold fills stupendous baskets with a varied selection of exotic seasonal fruits from all over the world. He can supply the appropriate arrangement, according to your needs, and will deliver your order throughout Manhattan. In addition to the beautiful fruit baskets, other exquisite food gifts include jars of fruit in maple syrup, chocolate truffles in beautiful boxes, European cookies, and New Hampshire honey. ♦ M-F. 105 E 29th St (between Lexington Ave and Park Ave S). 686.0404

85 Les Halles ★$$ A re-creation of the type of hangouts that once surrounded the great wholesale food market in Paris, this place has been a success since it opened in 1991. Some of its loyal customers patronize the butcher shop in front; others go to the often noisy dining room in back for onion soup, garlicky sausage, steak served with *pommes frites* (french fries), or cassoulet. ♦ French ♦ M-F lunch and dinner; Sa-Su brunch and dinner. Reservations recommended. 411 Park Ave S (between E 28th and E 29th Sts). 679.4111 &

86 Park Bistro ★★★$$$ Black-and-white photos of Paris in the 1950s line the walls at this friendly bistro. Specialties include a warm

119

potato salad topped with goat cheese and served with a small green salad; roasted muscovy duck breast in shallot sauce; wild mushroom ravioli in Port sauce; sautéed skate in a red wine vinegar sauce with white beans; fresh cod with onion sauce and fried leeks; and *onglet*, known here as hanger steak (the prime section of beef that French butchers usually keep for themselves), served with green-peppercorn sauce. For dessert, try the decadent warm chocolate torte or the thin apple tart with Armagnac. There's also a good selection of mostly French wines. ◆ French ◆ M-F lunch and dinner; Sa-Su dinner. Reservations recommended. 414 Park Ave S (between E 28th and E 29th Sts). 689.1360 &

87 Church of the Transfiguration/The Little Church Around the Corner When actor George Holland died in 1870, a friend went to a nearby church to arrange for the funeral. "We don't accept actors here," he was told, "but there's a little church around the corner that will." They did, and the **Church of the Transfiguration**—an Episcopal church built in 1849 and later expanded—got both a new name and a new reputation among actors, some of whom, including Edwin Booth, Gertrude Lawrence, and Richard Mansfield, are memorialized among the wealth of stained glass and other artifacts inside. During World War I and in the years following, it was the scene of more wedding ceremonies than any other church in the world. ◆ 1 E 29th St (between Madison and Fifth Aves). 684.6770 &

88 Marble Collegiate Church This Gothic Revival church has not been changed since the day it was built in 1854 by **Samuel A. Warner** The clock is still wound by hand every eight days, and the cane racks behind the pews are still waiting to receive your walking stick. A Dutch Reform church (the oldest denomination in the city), established here by Peter Minuit in 1628, it has served under the flags of Holland, England, and the US. The most famous minister to use its pulpit was Dr. Norman Vincent Peale, author of *The Power of Positive Thinking*. ◆ 272 Fifth Ave (at W 29th St). 686.2770

HOTEL WOLCOTT

89 Hotel Wolcott $ Popular with the young and young-at-heart because of its near-hostel prices, this 300-room hotel is efficiently run. The facade and lobby are turn-of-the-century, but the rooms have simple, contemporary

decor meant to withstand heavy traffic: The hotel is always close to full. ◆ 4 W 31st St (between Fifth Ave and Broadway). 268.2900; fax 563.0096

90 Greeley Square Alexander Doyle's statue of *Horace Greeley*, founder of the *New York Tribune*, was donated by members of the newspaper unions—which says something about Greeley's management style. The area around the square offers the best buys in cameras and related merchandise. The site across Sixth Avenue, now the home of the **Stern's** department store, is where Gimbels kept its secrets safe from **Macy's**, which is only a block away on **Herald Square**. ◆ Bounded by Broadway and Sixth Ave, and W 32nd and W 33rd Sts

91 Stanford $ This small hotel with 130 rooms is renovating in stages. It's convenient to the **Empire State Building** and **Madison Square Garden** and shopping and has color TVs in all rooms. ◆ 43 W 32nd St (between Fifth Ave and Broadway). 563.1480, 800/365.1114; fax 629.0043

92 Grolier Once an exclusive hideaway for the bibliophiles of the **Grolier Club**, then a private home, and most recently **The Madison**, a private club, this turn-of-the-century landmark building now hosts and caters private parties. The building is closed to the public. ◆ 29 E 32nd St (between Madison and Fifth Aves). 679.2932

93 The Empire State Building Yes, Virginia, this is the once-upon-a-time World's Tallest Building (after the two Petronas Towers in Malaysia, the Sears Tower in Chicago, and the twin towers of the **World Trade Center** it currently ranks sixth), famous in fact and fiction, icon of New York City, and the first place from which to study the city. It has an impressive collection of statistics: 1,250 feet to the top of the (unsuccessful) dirigible mooring mast; 102 floors; 1,860 steps; 73 elevators; 60 miles of water pipes; 5 acres of windows; 365,000 tons of material—and it was under construction for only 19 months. Built by **Shreve, Lamb & Harmon** in 1931, during the Depression, it was known for many years as the "Empty State Building," and the owners relied on income from the **Observation Deck** to pay their taxes. Oh yes—on a good day you can see for at least 50 miles.

The architects must be lauded for the way in which they handled the immense and potentially oppressive bulk of this building. The tower is balanced, set back from the street on a five-story (street-scale) base. The subtly modulated shaft rises at a distance, terminating in a conservatively geometric crown. The limestone-and-granite cladding, with its steel mullions and flush windows, is restrained, with just a touch of an Art Deco air (compared to the exuberant ornamentalism of the **Chrysler Building,** for example). This is *dignity.* Belying the fears of the general public, the tower has not yet cracked or toppled, although it does sway quite a bit in high winds, and only once has a plane crashed into it (in 1945, when a bomber broadsided the 79th floor). There have been a few suicides, and a lot of birds have been knocked out of the sky during their migrating season, one of the reasons it always stays illuminated.

The site, too, has a lively history. Between 1857 and 1893 it was the address of a pair of mansions belonging to members of the Astor family and the center of New York social life. In the early 1890s a feud erupted, and William Waldorf Astor, who had the house on West 33rd Street, moved to Europe and replaced the house with a hotel—the **Waldorf.** His aunt across the garden, Mrs. William Astor, moved within the year, and had a connecting hotel— the **Astoria**—completed by 1897. The **Waldorf** and **Astoria Hotels** immediately

The Empire State Building

MICHAEL STORRINGS

became a social center and operated together as one hotel for many years, under the agreement that Mrs. Astor could have all connections between them closed off at any time. When the original structures were demolished in 1929, the **Waldorf-Astoria** moved uptown to Park Avenue. ◆ 350 Fifth Ave (at W 34th St)

Within The Empire State Building:

Empire State Observatory There is an open platform on all four sides of the 86th floor, well protected with heavy mesh and metal bars. A few steps above it is a glass-enclosed area with food service and a souvenir shop. An elevator takes you higher, to the all-enclosed 102nd-floor lookout, where the view, surprisingly, is slightly different. It's the quintessential not-to-be-missed way to end your evening on the town. Tickets are available on the concourse, one level below the street. ◆ Admission (combination tickets include *Skyride* admission). Daily 9:30AM-midnight; last elevator at 11:30PM. Enter on W 34th St. 736.3100 &

Skyride You won't have to leave the building's second floor to experience some of the city's other celebrated attractions. This simulated-flight sight-seeing tour guides a helicopter under, between, and over sites like the Brooklyn Bridge, the **World Trade Center,** and Coney Island's **Cyclone** roller coaster; it even crashes through the window of **FAO Schwarz.** And all this in seven minutes. ◆ Admission (combination tickets include the nonsimulated observation deck upstairs). Daily. Second floor. 279.9777

94 **New York Public Library, Science, Industry, and Business Branch** The newest addition to the city-wide system, this extensive library is located on several floors of the former **B. Altman** department store. The branch accommodates more than 16,000 square feet of space in this Renaissance Revival building designed in 1906 by **Trowbridge & Livingston.** The expansion helped to relieve the overcrowded main research library (on 42nd Street) of more than two million books and periodicals. ◆ M-Sa. 188 Madison Ave (between E 34th and E 35th Sts). 592.7000

95 **Astro Gallery** With a collection of minerals and gems from 47 countries, ranging from amethyst crystals to zircons, this is a paradise for collectors and a good source of fine jewelry at low prices. ◆ Daily. 185 Madison Ave (at E 34th St). 889.9000

96 **Complete Traveller Bookstore** This small store has an amazingly large selection of books and maps—enough to satisfy even the most jaded traveler. ◆ Daily. 199 Madison Ave (at E 35th St). 685.9007

97 **Church of the Incarnation Episcopal** Built in 1864 by **Emlen T. Littel,** this modest

church seems to be trying to hide the fact that it contains windows by Louis Comfort Tiffany and John LaFarge, sculpture by Daniel Chester French and Augustus Saint-Gaudens, and a Gothic-style monument designed by **Henry Hobson Richardson**. Fortunately, the church provides a folder for a self-guided tour. ♦ 209 Madison Ave (between E 35th and E 36th Sts). 689.6350

98 Dolci On Park Café ★$$ You can make a satisfying meal here of linguine with sausage, penne with four cheeses, tortellini with ham, fettuccine with smoked salmon, chicken Marsala, or salmon with mushrooms and cream sauce. But a high point of the meal has to be the dessert. Indulge in a cannoli, chocolate eclair, smooth mocha sponge cake, fresh fruit tart, creamy cheesecake, or delightful tiramisù—with a cup of espresso or cappuccino. In fair weather, sit at one of the sidewalk tables. ♦ Italian ♦ M-Sa breakfast, lunch, and dinner. 12 Park Ave (between E 34th and E 35th Sts). 686.4331 ♦

99 2 Park Avenue This better-than-average office building is particularly stunning at the top, where the basic structural pattern gives way to some jazzy, colorful Art Deco tile. **Ely Jacques Kahn** designed the building in 1927, with Leon Solon as color consultant. ♦ Between E 32nd and E 33rd Sts

100 1 Park Avenue When Fourth Avenue below East 34th Street had its designation upgraded to "Park Avenue South," this and **2 Park Avenue** across the street kept their original addresses. Until 1925, when **York & Sawyer** built on this site, the area wasn't considered upscale. In the 19th century, it was the location of Peter Cooper's glue factory and later of barns for the livestock and horsecars of the **New York and Harlem Railroad**. ♦ Between E 32nd and E 33rd Sts

101 3 Park Avenue This brick tower structure is turned diagonally against its companions and the city. Compare this straight-up tower, built in 1976, and its stylized mansard roof with the careful, soaring composition of the Empire State Building two blocks away—they were designed by the same firm, **Shreve, Lamb & Harmon**. A plaque on the terrace wall at East 33rd Street marks this as the site of the 71st Regiment Armory. ♦ Between E 33rd and E 34th Sts

102 Dumont Plaza Hotel $$$ All the 250 rooms—be they studios or 1- and 2-bedroom suites—have their own kitchens. There's also a restaurant, **Harold's**. ♦ 150 E 34th St (between Third and Lexington Aves). 481.7600, 800/637.8483; fax 889.8856 ♦

103 Nicola Paone ★★$$$ Designed to resemble an Italian marketplace, this place has a serious Northern Italian menu that is enlivened by such imaginative offerings as artichokes stuffed with bread crumbs and anchovies, shrimp with basil, smoked salmon and white wine, the whimsical Nightgown (sliced veal and eggplant topped with mozzarella), *baci baci* (boneless chicken breast, spinach, and prosciutto), and shrimp *tritone* (with smoked salmon and basil in a white-wine sauce). Service is courtly and helpful, and the wine list boasts a 400-bottle selection. ♦ Italian ♦ M-F lunch and dinner; Sa dinner. Reservations recommended. 207 E 34th St (between Tunnel Exit St and Third Ave). 889.3239

104 St. Vartan Cathedral This is the seat of the Armenian Orthodox Church in America, with a Romanesque design inspired by churches in Asia Minor. It was built in 1967 by **Steinman & Cain**, and its dome was re-covered in 18-karat gold leaf in 1993. ♦ 630 Second Ave (between E 34th and E 35th Sts). 686.0710

105 El Parador ★★$$$ Opened long before Mexican food came into vogue, this spot remains popular among Mexican food aficionados as well as those looking for a good time. Among many estimable selections are the chicken Parador (marinated and steamed), grilled sirloin fajitas, and *chilaquiles verdes* (stewed chicken with sour cream and green-tomatillo sauce). ♦ Mexican ♦ Daily lunch and dinner. Reservations recommended. 325 E 34th St (between First Ave and Tunnel Entrance St). 679.6812

106 Quark International Discover gadgets and hi-tech surveillance equipment galore, from Swiss army knives, folding bicycles, and talking translators to video camera tie clips. ♦ M-F; Sa by appointment. 537 Third Ave (between E 35th and E 36th Sts). 889.1808 ♦

107 Sniffen Court This charming and unusually well-preserved mews of 10 carriage houses was built shortly before the Civil War (1850-60) and was designated a Historic District in 1966. ♦ 150-158 E 36th St (between Third and Lexington Aves)

108 Shelburne Murray Hill $$$ Each of the 258 rooms in this all-suite hotel has a kitchen. ♦ 303 Lexington Ave (at E 37th St). 689.5200, 800/637.8483; fax 779.7068

109 Doral Court Hotel $$$ The 190 rooms here are sunny and quiet, and the staff is enthusiastic. Kitchenettes are available on request. You can visit the nearby fitness center or even have a stationary bike brought to your room. The **Courtyard Cafe and Bar** is always a pleasure. ◆ 130 E 39th St (between Lexington and Park Aves). 685.1100, 800/223.6725; fax 889.0287 ⑆

09 Doral Tuscany Hotel $$$ The refrigerators in the 120 rooms here are stocked with refreshments, and if you run out, room service will replenish them. Leave your shoes outside your door at night and they'll be shined by morning. And when you rise and shine, you can visit the hotel's squash club and sports training institute. The **Time and Again** restaurant serves breakfast, lunch, and dinner. ◆ 120 E 39th St (between Lexington and Park Aves). 686.1600, 800/223.6725; fax 779.7822

10 Rossini's ★$$$ The hot antipasto Rossini—clams *oreganata,* shrimp scampi, and *mozzarella in carrozza* (cheese wrapped in bread and fried)—is a specialty at this casual, friendly restaurant. Entrées include chicken *romano* (stuffed with spinach and roasted veal). A pianist performs on Monday and Friday, an electric keyboard player plays Tuesday through Thursday, and an opera trio serenades on Saturday. ◆ Italian ◆ M-F lunch and dinner; Sa-Su dinner. Reservations recommended. 108 E 38th St (between Lexington and Park Aves). 683.0135

10 Church of Our Savior A perfect example of Romanesque Gothic architecture, this church was built by **Paul C. Reilly** in 1959, at a time when architects were tossing off glass boxes with the excuse that there were no craftspeople left to do this kind of work. The interior of this Roman Catholic church proves that there must have been at least a few in New York in the 1950s. ◆ 59 Park Ave (at E 38th St). 679.8166 ⑆

11 Sheraton Russell $$$ This 146-room hotel was named for Judge Horace Russell, who once had a home on this site. An oak-paneled lobby, mahogany floors, Oriental rugs, spacious rooms decorated with antiques, and the attentive service make it seem like a private club or country estate. The **Club Lounge** offers a complimentary breakfast buffet and, in the evening, complimentary hors d'oeuvres. In addition, there's a 24-hour fitness center. ◆ 45 Park Ave (at E 37th St). 685.7676, 800/325.3535; fax 889.3193 ⑆

112 Doral Park Avenue Hotel $$$ Here's an Old World–style hotel with modern touches, including access to a fitness center up the street on Park Avenue. The 188 rooms are well furnished, the atmosphere gracious and traditional. ◆ 70 Park Ave (at E 38th St). 687.7050, 800/223.6725; fax 973.2497 ⑆

Within the Doral Park Avenue Hotel:

Saturnia Restaurant ★$$$ The atmosphere is warm and candlelit. In season, service extends out to a sidewalk cafe. ◆ American ◆ Daily breakfast, lunch, and dinner. Reservations recommended. 687.7050

113 The Kitano New York $$$$ Designed with the business traveler in mind, this understated and contemporary hotel offers guests peace and quiet on the southern cusp of Midtown. There are 157 soundproofed guest rooms (including 8 suites), complete with mahogany and cherry furniture, and an authentic Japanese tatami suite with a tea ceremony room. The bathrooms are exceptionally clean and modern. Japanese fare is served at the **Nadaman Hakubai Restaurant,** which has three private tatami rooms. ◆ 66 Park Ave (at E 38th St). 885.7000, 800/457.4000; fax 885.7100; www.kitano.com ⑆

114 Jolly Madison Towers Hotel $$ Completely modernized, this comfortable hotel offers meeting facilities and 240 rooms. A small fee gives guests access to an in-house health club with sauna and gym. Ask for a room with a view of the **Empire State Building.** The **Whaler Bar** is a favorite meeting place. ◆ 22 E 38th St (at Madison Ave). 802.0600, 800/225.4340; fax 447.0747

115 Morgans $$$ Former discotheque owner Ian Schrager runs this trendy hotel (he also refurbished the **Royalton** and the **Paramount**), with rooms and furnishings created by French designer André Putman. The hotel prides itself on getting you whatever you want—if the urge for sushi strikes at midnight, no problem. All 112 refurbished rooms have VCRs, stereos, blackout shades on the windows, and phones in the bedrooms and bathrooms. Guests have access to a sports club facility nearby. There's also a Philippe Starck–designed restaurant on the premises, **Asia de Cuba,** featuring Asian and Cuban cuisine. ◆ 237 Madison Ave (between E 37th and E 38th Sts). 686.0300, 800/334.3408; fax 779.8352

116 231 Madison Avenue This 45-room freestanding brownstone mansion, built in 1852 for banker Anson Phelps Stokes, was

Restaurants/Clubs: Red   Hotels: Blue
Shops/ ♟ Outdoors: Green   Sights/Culture: Black

bought by J.P. Morgan for his son in 1904. In 1944, it became the property of the Evangelical Lutheran Church, which is responsible for the architecturally sacrilegious brick addition on the East 37th Street side. It has been restored and incorporated into the **Pierpont Morgan Library**; the museum's book store is also located here. ♦ Tu-Su. At E 37th St. 685.0610

117 The Pierpont Morgan Library Financier J.P. Morgan began collecting books, manuscripts, and drawings in earnest in 1890, and eventually had to construct this magnificent small palazzo to house his treasures. It was designed in 1906 by **Charles Follen McKim** of **McKim, Mead & White**. The building itself is a treasure, and the 1928 annex on the Madison Avenue side complements it perfectly. Inside, Morgan's library and office have been preserved exactly as they were when he died in 1913. The collection includes more than 1,000 illuminated medieval and Renaissance manuscripts, the finest in America. It also contains the country's best examples of printed books, from Gutenberg to modern times, as well as an extensive collection of fine bookbinding. And its collection of autograph manuscripts, both literary and musical, is considered one of the best in the world. Art historian Kenneth Clark summed it all up perfectly when he said, "Every object is a

treasure, every item is perfect." On your way out, visit the bookshop, where you'll find wonderful books, toys, and cards. ♦ Donatio requested. Tu-Th, Sa; F 10:30AM-8PM; Su noon-6PM. 29 E 36th St (between Park and Madison Aves). 685.0610

Within The Pierpont Morgan Library:

Morgan Cafe ★$ A refined place indeed f the true lady's (or perfect gentleman's) lunch this elegant skylit cafe is located near the bookshop. Sandwiches, salads, and afternoc tea are among the appropriately light and delicate offerings. ♦ Cafe ♦ Tu-Su breakfast, lunch, and afternoon tea. 685.0008

118 Lord & Taylor This store has made a specialty of stocking clothing by American designers. Its shoe department is legendary as is the caring quality of its sales help, whi is quite a rarity these days. The department store is also justly famous for its Christmas window displays, without which the holiday in New York wouldn't be the same. The stor was the first in the history of retailing to devote its window displays to anything but merchandise during the holiday season. The custom began during the unusually warm December of 1905, when customers didn't seem to feel Christmasy. The management got them into the proper mood by filling the store's windows with a snowstorm the

The Pierpont Morgan Library

likes of which New Yorkers hadn't seen since the famous Blizzard of '88. If you arrive 15 minutes before the store opens in the morning, seating, free coffee (there are also three restaurants within the store), and music are provided just inside the front door. ◆ Daily. 424 Fifth Ave (between W 38th and W 39th Sts). 391.3344 &

119 West Marine Most of the stores on this block sell trimmings and ribbons, but if you need a stout coil of rope, you'll find it at this amazing emporium (formerly **E & B Goldbergs'**, now under new ownership). New York is America's biggest seaport, but it still comes as a surprise to discover a place selling anchors, depth finders, fishing equipment (including the tournament reels that are so much more expensive in Europe), and other gear for yacht enthusiasts and sailors. It is a perfect store for the shoes and foul-weather

clothes and other outfits you need if you want to look like you belong to the yacht club set. ◆ Daily. 12 W 37th St (between Fifth and Sixth Aves). 594.6065 &

120 M&J Trimming Though this well-known chockablock trimmings store looks like the kind traditionally open to the trade only, it has always been a retail-shopper's dream. Countless buttons, tassles, piping, frogs, and decorative borders will transform the most nondescript garment into an award-winner. Aspiring and professional designers come here for inspiration, resourcefully using buttons and beads for everything from jewelry to shoe decoration, kitsch to elegant. A newer **M&J Decorator Collection** next door at 1014 Sixth Avenue makes the same treasure trove of braiding and trimming available for home design. ◆ M-Sa. 1008 Sixth Ave (between W 37th and W 38th Sts). 391.9072

Bests

Geraldine Ferraro
Former Co-host of CNN *Crossfire*

Find out that New York City is more than just Manhattan by:

Taking a ride on the **Staten Island Ferry.**

Visiting the **Bronx Zoo.**

Catching the R subway to the **American Museum of the Moving Image** in Queens.

Enjoying the beauty of the **Brooklyn Botanic Garden.**

Dining at the **Rainbow Room** on a clear night.

Attending early morning Mass at **St. Patrick's Cathedral** (you needn't be Catholic).

Watching a parade (any parade) on **Fifth Avenue.**

Taking a car ride across the **59th Street Bridge** from Queens to Manhattan to see the most beautiful skyline in the world.

Eating your way through a street fair.

Riding the tram to **Roosevelt Island.**

Taking a toddler to the **Children's Museum of Manhattan** to meet the Cat in the Hat.

Bringing a blanket and enjoying **Shakespeare in the Park** at the **Joseph Papp Theater.**

Sitting in on an auction at **Christie's.**

Visiting **Ellis Island** and listening to the taped voices of those who came to this great country around the turn of the century.

Seeing a **Knicks** game at **Madison Square Garden** (if you can get tickets!).

Watching the opening of the **New York Stock Exchange.**

Joining the early morning crowd at **Rockefeller Center** and appearing on *The Today Show.*

Food cruising on **Broadway** and stopping at **H&H Bagels** for the best bagels in the "bagel capital of the world" and **Zabar's,** the quintessential deli!

Anne Rosenzweig
Chef/Owner, Lobster Club

An unusual perspective of Manhattan begins with an early-morning breakfast at **Sylvia's** (salmon cakes, grits, deep-fried slab bacon, and biscuits). This is the perfect start to a walking day.

Then a stroll through the marvelous but crumbling architecture of Harlem, especially around **Mount Morris Park** . . . Then down to the **Conservatory Garden** at Fifth Avenue and 105th Street. The gardens are completely transformed every season. In spring, huge lilac bushes create an intoxicating aroma under which one can read the Sunday papers. During the summer, they are the setting of some of the most beautiful weddings in New York.

Sitting in the upper decks of **Shea Stadium** on a hot, hot summer night just to catch a good breeze.

On the rare occasions when the city is under a deep, fresh blanket of snow—cross-country skiing in **Central Park** and getting hot roasted chestnuts afterward.

The Indian restaurants on **East Sixth Street** in summer—eating outside in back with a gang of friends on picnic tables for the cheapest sums possible.

Buying bags of flattened fortune cookies at one of the many bakeries in **Chinatown**—they're the ones that didn't make it.

Jazz cruises at night up the **Hudson River** and being able to see the skyline at twilight.

Chelsea

Named for the estate acquired by Captain Thomas Clarke in 1750, Chelsea was originally bounded by **West 14th** and **West 25th Streets**, and **Eighth Avenue** and the **Hudson River.** Today, the Chelsea area, which extends farther north to **West 34th Street** and east to **Sixth Avenue**, is quite a mixed bag. Clement Clarke Moore, who had inherited his grandfather's land—and is best known as the author of the poem *Visit from St. Nicholas*—divided his family estate and laid out the neighborhood's original building lots in 1830, some of which he donated to the General Theological Seminary. The surrounding area was a flourishing middle-class suburb that never quite made it as a desirable address. Once the **Hudson River Railroad** opened on **11th Avenue** in 1851, it attracted breweries and slaughterhouses and their workers' shanties and tenements,

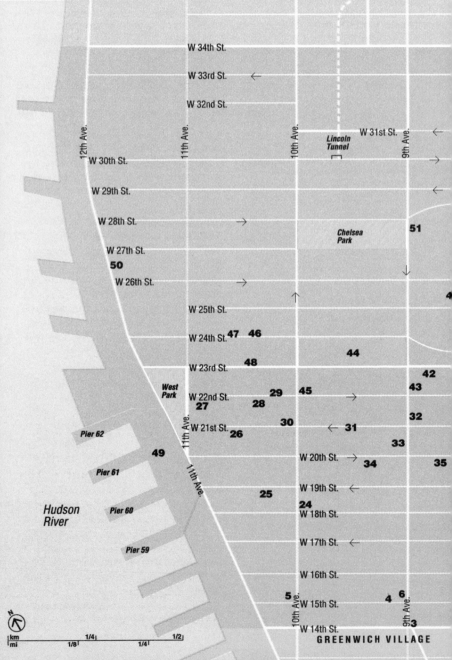

which marked the beginning of the area's aesthetic decline. In the 1870s, the remaining town house blocks were invaded by the city's first elevated railroad, on **Ninth Avenue.**

Despite its industrial image, Chelsea became a creative retail center. A flurry of theatrical activity took over **West 23rd Street** in the 1880s, but by 1892 the theater world had moved uptown, leaving behind the artists and writers who eventually departed for the newer bohemia of Greenwich Village. The funky **Hotel Chelsea**, on West 23rd Street, is a remnant of Chelsea's theatrical heyday, when actors and playwrights lodged there. In the 1960s, Andy Warhol's superstars Viva and Edie Sedgewick lived there, and his film *Chelsea Girls* documented a chapter in the renaissance of the old survivor.

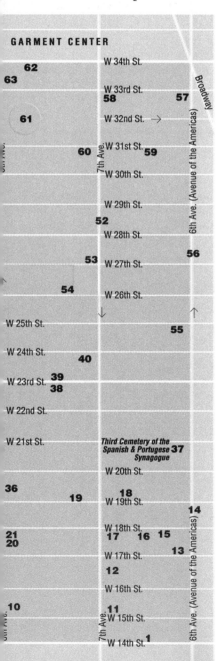

GARMENT CENTER

W 34th St.
62
63
W 33rd St.
58   57   Broadway
61   W 32nd St. →
60 7th Ave. W 31st St. 59
W 30th St.
W 29th St.
52
W 28th St.   6th Ave. (Avenue of the Americas)
53 W 27th St.   56
54   W 26th St.
W 25th St.
55
W 24th St.
40
W 23rd St. 39
38
W 22nd St.
W 21st St.   Third Cemetery of the
Spanish & Portugese 37
Synagogue
W 20th St.
36   18
19   W 19th St.
14
W 18th St.
21   17   16 15
20   W 17th St. 13
12   6th Ave. (Avenue of the Americas)
W 16th St.
10   11
7th Ave. W 15th St.
W 14th St. 1

The country's motion picture industry started in Chelsea in 1905, and for a decade it flourished in old lofts and theaters used as studios. Adolph Zukor's **Famous Players Studio**, which employed Mary Pickford and John Barrymore, produced films here. But the Astoria Studios in Queens built a better facility, and eventually balmy Hollywood beckoned. The film business also moved on.

In the 1930s, new industry found quarters in the area near the piers. The 11th Avenue railroad was replaced by a less objectionable elevated train, and the Ninth Avenue line shut down. The clean sweep of 1950s and 1960s urban renewal replaced slum housing with housing projects, and renovation started on desirable Federal and Greek Revival town houses. Today, Chelsea is a pastiche of town houses, housing projects, industrial buildings, tenements, secondhand office-furniture stores, and a large number of churches.

Chelsea's retail career was also short-lived. As the gentry pursued their determined course uptown, so did fashionable stores. By the 1870s, West 23rd Street blossomed, and the blocks on Sixth Avenue south of it became known as the "Ladies' Mile." During the latter part of the century, giant dry-goods stores of limestone and cast iron lined Sixth Avenue (now officially **Avenue of the Americas**) and **Broadway.** Many of the buildings that still stand, reminders of past retail glories, are used as lofts and offices. By the early part of the 1900s, the fashion action had moved to West 34th Street, and by the 1930s, West 23rd Street was a has-been.

But Chelsea has been discovered—again—thanks to an overflow of residents, stores, and restaurants fleeing Greenwich Village's escalating rents. In the late 1970s and 1980s, Chelsea came to be the destination of a northward immigration of Greenwich Village's gay community, with Eighth Avenue supplanting the Village's Christopher Street as the main gay thoroughfare in New York. Myriad shopping possibilities run the gamut from the antiques shops on Ninth Avenue between **West 20th** and **West 22nd Streets** to the **Flower District** on the blocks between **West 27th** and **West 30th Streets** on Sixth Avenue.

Today Chelsea wears an artistic hat, encouraged by the arrival of SoHo's respected **Dia Center for the Arts** and a crop of cutting-edge galleries that have opened on West 22nd Street and neighboring blocks. One of Chelsea's— and the city's—last undesirable pockets is reinventing itself, with **Chelsea Piers Sports & Entertainment Complex** and **Chelsea Market** making an economic impact along the riverfront.

1 New York State Armory The 42nd Infantry Division of the New York National Guard is headquartered in this building, designed by **Charles S. Kawecki** in 1971 to make its members feel warlike. ♦ 125 W 14th St (between Sixth and Seventh Aves)

2 319 West 14th Street A 20-year-old Orson Welles and his first wife, Virginia Nicholson, lived in a basement apartment here between 1935 and 1937, during which time he directed the famous all-black *Macbeth* for Harlem's **Negro Theater.** ♦ Between Eighth and Ninth Aves

3 Old Homestead ★★★$$$ Established in 1868, this is the oldest steak house in Manhattan, and huge steaks and prime ribs are served here the way they always have been. Those who prefer to cook their own can buy fresh cuts of beef (including one-inch-thick steaks) at the **Old Homestead Gourmet** shop (807.0707) next door, which also stocks various sauces and gourmet items, including the crème de la crème of chocolates, the French Valrhona and the Belgian D'Orsay. ♦ American ♦ Daily lunch and dinner. Shop: M-Sa. Reservations recommended. 56 Ninth Ave (between W 14th and W 15th Sts). 242.9040 ♿

4 Markt ★$$ This upscale and surprisingly spacious Belgian bistro (its name means "market" in Flemish) is the place for those with hearty appetites. Seafood is the draw here: Start off at the sizeable raw bar, or order mussels steamed in white wine or genuine Hoegaaden (the Belgian white beer), or lobster stewed in a fennel and cream sauce from the menu. The *waterzooi*, a traditional Belgian stew with either fresh fish or chicken and vegetables, offers a pleasant change. There's an extensive range of Belgian beers

as well as a French wine list. Note: Come early on the weekend to avoid the higher noise level. ♦ Belgian ♦ M-F dinner; Sa-Su lunch, brunch, and dinner. Reservations recommended. 401 W 14 St (at Ninth Ave). 727.3314

Frank's

5 Frank's ★★$$$ In the Molinari family since 1912, this restaurant still serves some of the best steaks around to the people who work in the business and know what's good. Always extraordinary are the dry-aged shell steaks, a filet mignon weighing nearly a pound, and the loin lamb chops. All the pastas are made from scratch: Try the fettuccine bolognese or the *paglia e fieno* ("straw and hay"—green and white flat noodles in a sauce of cheese, cream and prosciutto). Basic, good-quality desserts include giant slabs of cheesecake. ♦ American ♦ M-F lunch and dinner; Sa-Su dinner. Reservations recommended. 85 10th Ave (at W 15th St). 243.1349 ♿

6 Chelsea Market This early–20th-century structure was once a Nabisco factory churning out cookies and crackers. Today, with much of its interior of overhead pipes and exposed brick walls still intact, it's Manhattan's newest marketplace. Here shoppers can purchase a variety of goodies from a variety of merchants: **The Cleaver Company**, caterers with a small shop/cafe; **Manhattan Fruit Exchange**, a wholesale/retail produce market; **The Lobster Place**, for seafoods of every description; **Amy's Bread**, haven for incredibly tasty breads, pastries, and sandwiches; and **Buonitalia**, an importer of select Italian pastas, cheeses, and olive oil. It's one-stop shopping—Manhattan style. ♦ Daily. 75 Ninth Ave (between W 15th and W 16th Sts). 243.5678 &

7 El Cid ★★$ With blue tablecloths and mirrored walls, this small and cheerful tapas bar is an informal, fun place to come with a group to sample from among 32 varieties of tapas. The handful of meat and fish dishes include a hearty *paella valenciana* (with chicken, Spanish sausages, shellfish, and saffron rice). The wine list showcases good, inexpensive Spanish wines. ♦ Spanish ♦ Tu-Su dinner. 322 W 15th St (between Eighth and Ninth Aves). 929.9332

8 Port of New York Authority Commerce Building/Union Inland Terminal No. 1 The organization now known as the Port Authority of New York and New Jersey had its headquarters in this blockbuster, designed in 1932 by **Abbott, Merckt & Co.,** before moving down to the **World Trade Center.** The top floors were designed for manufacturing, but the elevators can carry a 20-ton truck to any floor. ♦ 111 Eighth Ave (between W 15th and W 16th Sts)

9 Cajun ★$$ The honky-tonk atmosphere and live Dixieland music (nightly at 8PM) are fun, and the creole-Cajun food, which comes in hearty portions, doesn't disappoint. ♦ Creole/Cajun ♦ M-F lunch and dinner; Sa dinner; Su brunch and dinner. Reservations recommended for five or more. 129 Eighth Ave (between W 16th and W 17th Sts). 691.6174

10 Chelsea Trattoria ★$$ This pretty trattoria with peach walls and exposed brick is a reliable place for standard Italian fare. The osso buco and the fettuccine with artichokes, mushrooms, and tomatoes are especially recommended. ♦ Italian ♦ Daily lunch and dinner. 108 Eighth Ave (between W 15th and W 16th Sts). 924.7786

11 Jensen-Lewis Two floors of creative, colorful merchandise, from sofas and beds to lamps and luggage (even bean-bag chairs), can be found here. This store is especially known for its selection of director's chairs. ♦ Daily. 89 Seventh Ave (at W 15th St). 929.4880

12 Loehmann's Don't expect much plushness or service on the inside. Instead, you'll find 60,000 square feet filled with discounted merchandise—mostly for women. The best clothes are in the "Back Room" on the fourth floor, with names like Bally, Donna Karan, and Kenneth J. Lane. As with all quality discounters, the labels and stock are constantly changing. One feature that hasn't changed is the communal dressing rooms. ♦ Daily. 101 Seventh Ave (between W 16th and W 17th Sts). 352.0856. Also at: Numerous locations throughout the city

13 Da Umberto ★★$$$ This casual and restful trattoria specializes in Tuscan dishes, especially wild game (hare, pheasant, and venison). The veal chop with Cognac sauce is a favorite, and the antipasti selections are worth a try. ♦ Italian ♦ M-F lunch and dinner; Sa dinner. Reservations required. 107 W 17th St (between Sixth and Seventh Aves). 989.0303

14 Sixth Avenue Although **Barneys New York** has vacated its downtown location, this area continues to be a vital center for shopping. Bargain hunters flock to **620 Sixth Avenue,** a Victorian-pillared landmark built in 1896 as the **Siegel-Cooper Dry Goods Store** (see **Siegel-Cooper & Company** on page 110), where such popular emporia as **T.J. Maxx** and **Filene's Basement** discount fashions and accessories. Also here is **Bed, Bath & Beyond**'s flagship megastore that features 80 patterns of bed linens, 132 colors and patterns of bath towels, and 218 styles of place mats, as well as gadgets galore. The area's side streets are also treasure troves of poster and art shops. ♦ Between W 18th and W 19th Streets

15 Two World Arts This store is the direct importer of the antiques and unique decorative objects that are sold here. Paintings and custom artwork from well-known artists are also available. ♦ M-Sa. 122 W 18th St (between Sixth and Seventh Aves). 633.1668

16 Movie Star News Millions of head shots, stills, and lobby cards fill the filing cabinets in this garage space, a popular source for collectors, newspapers, magazines, and TV. Paula Klaw and her family also stock movie posters, as well as a selection of books on theater and film. ♦ M-Sa. 134 W 18th St (between Sixth and Seventh Aves). 620.8160 &

16 Poster Gallery The selection of vintage posters from 1910 to 1965, most of which are original lithographs from Europe and the US, is among the best you'll find on either side of the Atlantic. ♦ Tu-Su. 138 W 18th St (between Sixth and Seventh Aves). 206.0499

17 Le Madri ★★★$$$ Pino Luongo's stylish restaurant turns out Tuscan-style specialties for the illustrious crowds that flock to his doorstep. Order roasted vegetables for the whole table and any of the homemade pastas, which include a signature gnocchi of the day and *cavatelli* (short, curled pasta) with broccoli rabe. Wood-oven–roasted chicken and panseared veal chop with roasted scallions are also treats. On summer weekends the restaurant hosts an alfresco film series; Italian movies are shown on a screen in the parking lot next door, while the crowd munches on salads, pizzas, and pastas. ♦ Italian ♦ M-Sa lunch and dinner; Su brunch and dinner. Reservations recommended. 168 W 18th St (at Seventh Ave). 727.8022

18 A Different Light Bookstore Confirming that the ever-growing gay community is well-established in the Chelsea neighborhood, this book shop moved here when it outgrew its Greenwich Village quarters. It remains undoubtedly the best bookstore of its kind in the city. Stocking some 180,000 titles, it is an excellent place to find literature on a wide variety of gay- and lesbian-related topics and issues. The staff is friendly and helpful, and there's a full schedule of readings and popular events such as the Sunday night free-movie-and-popcorn series. ♦ Daily 10AM-midnight. 151 W 19th St (between Sixth and Seventh Aves). 989.4850

19 Bessie Shonberg Theater Operated by the **Dance Theater Workshop (DTW)**, this 160-seat theater (named after the dancer, choreographer, and teacher) is one of the most active dance, mime, and poetry houses in the city and offers young performing artists a variety of support services. Famous clown/dancer/mime Bill Irwin has often played here. **DTW** also runs the picture gallery in the lobby of the theater. ♦ 219 W 19th St (between Seventh and Eighth Aves), Second floor. 691.6500

20 Cola's ★★$ You'll find a casual mix of Northern and Southern Italian cuisine served at this cozy restaurant. Hand-painted walls lend a gentle ambience to the small room, where a lively downtown crowd comes to sample such pasta dishes as penne with goat cheese and eggplant and heartier fare like pork chops in balsamic vinegar. The wine list offers many fine selections. ♦ Italian ♦ Daily dinner. 148 Eighth Ave (between W 17th and W 18th Sts). 633.8020

Only a handful of all the semiactuated signals (those chest-high buttons that pedestrians push to make the light change to green) installed on lightpoles around Manhattan actually work; most are located along 12th Avenue.

Restaurants/Clubs: Red   **Hotels:** Blue
Shops/ 🌳 Outdoors: Green   **Sights/Culture:** Black

21 Gascogne ★★$$ Chef Alain Eigenmann re-creates the rich, hearty foods from the southwest region of France, including a superb fish soup, foie gras, roasted duck, and an excellent cassoulet. Also featured are wines from the same region. ♦ French ♦ M-F lunch and dinner; Sa dinner; Su brunch and dinner. Reservations required. 158 Eighth Ave (between W 17th and W 18th Sts). 675.6564

21 Viceroy ★$$ The dining room, with its tin ceiling, plants, and metallic blinds, is a favorite among Chelsea's gay community, who come to table-hop and be served hearty food by muscle-bound young waiters. Aside from being a "happening" place, the restaurant also offers some very good food. Offerings include Aegean salad (arugula, tomatoes, feta, scallions, roasted peppers, cucumber, and olives tossed with balsamic vinaigrette and croutons), seared peppered tuna with stir-fried Asian greens, roasted chicken, and steak *frites* (with french fries). For dessert, don't miss the chocolate mousse cake. Be sure to come early—by 7:30PM it's mobbed. ♦ American/Continental ♦ M-Sa lunch, dinner, and late-night meals; Su brunch, dinner, and late-night meals. 160 Eighth Ave (at W 18th St). 633.8484 ♿

22 Eighteenth and Eighth ★$ The cozy dining room is decorated with dried leaves, eccentric teapots, and drawings of the male anatomy. Come here for large portions of such creative comfort food as roasted loin of pork stuffed with herbs; grilled leg of lamb with sun-dried tomatoes and black olives; roasted chicken with lemon, garlic, and rosemary; and a very satisfying meat loaf. The place is extremely popular among locals, so expect a wait. ♦ American ♦ M-F breakfast, lunch, and dinner; Sa-Su brunch and dinner. 159 Eighth Ave (at W 18th St). 242.5000

J ● Y C L

23 The Joyce Theater Renovated in 1981 by **Hardy Holzman Pfeiffer Associates,** this is a theater *for* dancers and the people who love dance; it's elegant, intimate, and deep in the heart of Chelsea. The building was once the decrepit and infamous **Elgin** movie house, but a 1981 remodeling resulted in the current 474-seat venue, completely replacing the building's interior and re-Deco-izing the exterior. The theater is named for the daughter of the principal donor. ♦ 175 Eighth Ave (at W 19th St). 242.0800 ♿

24 La Lunchonette ★$$ The homey bar and open kitchen in this bistro seem familiar enough, but the free-range chicken with mustard, lamb sausage with sautéed apples, and panfried whole trout with wild mushrooms add interesting variations to a time-honored cuisine. ♦ French ♦ M-F lunch and dinner; Sa dinner; Su brunch and dinner. Reservations recommended. 130 10th Ave (at W 18th St). 675.0342

THE KITCHEN

25 The Kitchen This veteran space for experimental performing and visual arts presents the works of artists pushing the boundaries of their forms in dance, film, video, music, performance art, and literature. Programs are scheduled most evenings, and generally require that tickets be purchased in advance. Call for the current performance schedule. ♦ Box office: M-F or call Ticketmaster. 512 W 19th St (between 10th and 11th Aves). 255.5793 &

26 Paula Cooper Gallery A pioneer in the area nearly two decades ago, owner Cooper has built a stable of remarkable winners, including Jennifer Bartlett, Jonathan Borofsky, and Elizabeth Murray. ♦ Tu-Sa. 534 W 21st St (between 10th and 11th Aves). 255.1105 &

27 Dia Center for the Arts Since branching out here in 1985 to secure additional space for its changing exhibitions, this SoHo gallery was the first to stake out a presence in Chelsea, spawning an artistic movement "uptown" that continues to flourish. Works by contemporary artists—including John Chamberlain, Walter De Marie, and John Beuys—are mounted in this four-story space. ♦ Admission. Th-Sa noon-6PM; closed July-Aug. 548 W 22nd St (between 10th and 11th Aves). 989.5566. Also at: 141 Wooster St (between Prince and W Houston Sts). 473.8072; 393 W Broadway (between Broome and Spring Sts). 925.9397

28 Comme des Garçons Rei Kawakubo's cutting-edge clothes for men and women are for sale in this suitably stunning showcase. Merchandise is displayed in a warren of whitewashed, interconnected rooms, which you enter via a futuristic ramp fashioned of brushed aluminum. The overall effect is at once disconcerting and playful, and totally in tune with the avant-garde artistic spirit of the neighborhood. ♦ Daily. 520 W 22nd St (between 10th and 11th Aves). 604.9200

29 Max Protetch Gallery The primary commercial outlet in New York for drawings by such distinguished architects as Louis I. Kahn, Frank Lloyd Wright, Michael Graves, Aldo Rossi, and Rem Koolhaas, the gallery also exhibits painting, ceramics, and sculpture. It's well worth a visit to these spacious quarters. ♦ Tu-Sa. 511 W 22nd St (between 10th and 11th Aves). 633.6999 &

30 Guardian Angel Church This little complex of Italian Romanesque buildings, designed in 1930 by John Van Pelt, surrounds what is known as the **Shrine Church of the Sea.** The name reflects the one-time presence of the busiest piers in the Port of New York, a short walk to the west. The church's Renaissance interior is even more impressive than the redbrick-and-limestone facade. The priest in charge of this Roman Catholic church is designated Chaplain of the Port, with duties that include assigning chaplains to ships based here. ♦ 193 10th Ave (at W 21st St). 929.5966

31 West 21st Street Almost all the 19th-century houses on this block follow Clement Clarke Moore's requirement of front gardens and street trees. In its earliest years as a residential community, all of Chelsea looked much like this. The building with the unusual peaked roof on the Ninth Avenue corner was built in the 1820s by **James N. Wells** and is the oldest house in the neighborhood. ♦ Between Ninth and 10th Aves

32 Somethin' Else! Dozens of antiques shops are scattered around this neighborhood, some authentic, some dubious, all of them browsers' delights. But this one is, indeed, something else, with its collection of old toys, quilts, jewelry, and an entire wall of crystal glasses. ♦ Daily. 182 Ninth Ave (between W 21st and W 22nd Sts). 924.0006 &

33 General Theological Seminary You're welcome to enter this oasis through the library building on Ninth Avenue during public hours or, in summer, to take the free "Grand Design" tour. Land for the Episcopal Seminary was donated by Clement Clarke Moore in 1830, on the condition that the seminary should always occupy the site. The **West Building,** built in 1835, is the oldest building on campus, as well as New York's oldest example of Gothic Revival architecture. It predates **Charles C. Haight**'s renovation (1883-1900), which includes all the other Gothic buildings. In the center is the **Chapel of the Good Shepherd,** with its outstanding bronze doors and 161-foot-high square bell tower. **Hoffman Hall,** at the 10th Avenue end, contains a medieval-style dining hall complete with a barrel-vaulted ceiling, walk-in fireplaces, and a gallery for musicians. The other end is dominated by the new and very much out-of-place **St. Mark's Library,** built in 1960 by **O'Connor & Kilhan,** containing some 170,000 volumes, along with one of the world's largest collections of Latin Bibles. ♦ M-F noon-2:30PM; Sa 11AM-3:30PM; closed to the public when school is not in session and on religious holidays. 175 Ninth Ave (between W 20th and W 21st Sts). 243.5150 &

34 406-424 West 20th Street This row of extremely well-preserved Greek Revival houses was built by Don Alonzo Cushman, a dry-goods merchant who, in 1837, developed much of Chelsea and built these as rental units. The attic windows are circled with wreaths, the doorways framed in brownstone. Even the newel posts, topped with cast-iron pineapples, are still intact. ♦ Between Ninth and 10th Aves

35 St. Peter's Episcopal Church The church and its rectory and parish hall are outgrowths of Clement Clarke Moore and James W. Smith's 1838 plan to build them in the style of Greek temples. The traditional explanation is that the plan was changed when one of the vestrymen came back from England with tales of the Gothic buildings at Oxford. The congregation decided to switch styles, even though the foundations were already in place. The fence that surrounds this charming complex was brought here from **Trinity Church** on lower Broadway, where it had stood since 1790. Renovations are under way to replace the roof, repoint and preserve the masonry, and repair or replace all of the woodwork in the tower and window and door openings. ♦ 346 W 20th St (between Eighth and Ninth Aves). 929.2390

TROIS CANARDS

36 Trois Canards ★★★$$ Chef and co-owner Alonzo Tello turns out impressive French bistro fare in this elegant restaurant. The romantic interior is accented with dark wood paneling, beautifully etched glass walls, and earth-toned banquettes. The soups are excellent, and the risotto with duck confit and oyster mushrooms is a classic. Tello prepares a perfect rack of lamb with roasted vegetables, a specialty. Crispy roasted duckling with long-grain rice gets a zing from mixed vegetables and fruit sauce. Also getting high marks is the homemade porcini ravioli in wild-mushroom cream sauce. Save room for the superb dessert soufflé. ♦ French ♦ M-F lunch and dinner; Sa-Su brunch and dinner. Reservations recommended. 184 Eighth Ave (between W 19th and W 20th Sts). 929.4320

37 Third Cemetery of the Spanish & Portuguese Synagogue Enclosed on three sides by painted brick loft buildings, this private enclave is the third cemetery established by the first Jewish congregation in New York; tombstones date from 1829 to 1851. The second cemetery is in Greenwich Village, the first (see page 40) on the Lower East Side. ♦ W 21st St (between Sixth and Seventh Aves)

38 Hotel Chelsea When the hotel was first built in 1884 by **Hubert, Pirrson & Co.**, Chelsea was the heart of the Theater District, attracting creative people just as Greenwich Village would a decade later. In its early days

the hotel was home to such writers as William Dean Howells and O. Henry, and later to Thomas Wolfe, Arthur Miller, Mary McCarthy, Vladimir Nabokov, and Yevgeny Yevtushenko. Sarah Bernhardt once lived here, and this is where Dylan Thomas spent his last days. In the 1960s and 1970s, it was a favorite stopping place for visiting rock stars, who shared the atmosphere with modern classical composers George Kleinsinger and Virgil Thomson. Originally designed as an apartment building, it was the first in New York to have a penthouse. The **Chelsea** was converted to a hotel in 1905, but although it has had an interesting past, it is not currently recommended as a lodging place, since the premises are somewhat dingy. ♦ 222 W 23rd St (between Seventh and Eighth Aves). 243.3700; fax 243.3700 ext 2171

38 Manhattan Comics & Cards Here is an extensive collection of new and old comic books and baseball cards. ♦ Daily. 228 W 23rd St (between Seventh and Eighth Aves). 243.9349

39 Unity Book Center "For books that matter" is their tagline; topics include Marxism-Leninism, socialism, African-American literature, and women's equality. ♦ M-Sa. 23 W 23rd St (between Seventh and Eighth Aves). 242.2934

40 McBurney YMCA $ One of the first social workers to deal with the problems of foreign-born New Yorkers, Robert Ross McBurney ran a Y at East 23rd Street and Fourth Avenue in the 1870s. This YMCA branch, built in 19?? by **Parish & Schroeder**, is its successor. The building contains 240 basic rooms (all with shared baths), a track, a pool, a gymnasium, and a rooftop sundeck. The maximum stay here is 25 days. ♦ 206 W 24th St (between Seventh and Eighth Aves). 741.9210; fax 741.0012

41 Penn Station South This 12-square-block complex of 2,820 apartments was built in 1962 by **Herman Jessor** as middle-income housing for the International Ladies' Garment Workers Union. ♦ Bounded by Eighth and Ninth Aves, and W 23rd and W 29th Sts

42 Chelsea Bistro and Bar ★★★$$ A carved wood bar, floral borders, Impressionist prints on white walls, and a working exposed-brick fireplace adorn this warm, elegant, and authentically Parisian bistro. Try such dishes salmon *tartare*, escargots *Provençale*, house-smoked salmon with horseradish sauce, grilled sea scallops and shrimp with wild mushroom polenta and lemon-chive sauce, and braised lamb shank with slow-roasted tomatoes and vegetables. A rich *tarte tatin* (apple tart) and a glass of prune Armagnac are the perfect endings to a meal. ♦ French ♦ M-Sa dinner; Su brunch and dinner. Reservations recommended. 358 W 23rd St (between Eighth and Ninth Aves). 727.2026 ♦

42 Negril Island Spice ★★$$ The downtown branch of its namesake in the Theater District, the decor of this place attempts to whisk you away to the island of Jamaica. Try the codfish fritters with avocado salsa; ginger-lime chicken; a whole, fried red snapper with onions, peppers, scallions, tomatoes, and thyme; the callaloo (Jamaican greens with onions and tomatoes); or any of the rotis. For dessert, the bread pudding in caramelized raisin sauce is hard to resist and even harder to forget. ◆ Jamaican ◆ M-Sa lunch and dinner; Su brunch and dinner. Reservations required for dinner. 362 W 23rd St (between Eighth and Ninth Aves). 807.6411 ᴥ Also at: 402 W 44th St (between Ninth and 10th Aves). 765.1737 ᴥ

43 Siena ★★★$$ Popular chef Scott Bryan reopened the former **Luma**, with its Asian-influenced American menu, as a space bathed in warm brown hues and serving updated Tuscan fare that changes seasonally. For an interesting appetizer, try the warm dandelion salad with pancetta, wild mushrooms, and a white truffle essence. Signature entrées include Barolo braised pork with mushrooms, aromatic vegetables, smoked bacon, and mascarpone polenta; rabbit *pappardelle* (wide pasta) with wild mushrooms, roasted shallots, sage, and black pepper; and panroasted codfish with roasted onions, sautéed greens, pancetta, and balsamic vinegar. The affordable wine list features selections from all the regions of Italy. ◆ Northern Italian ◆ Daily dinner. Reservations recommended. 200 Ninth Ave (between W 22nd and W 23rd Sts). 633.8033 ᴥ

44 London Terrace Apartments This double row of buildings with a garden in the center contains 1,670 apartments. It was built in 1930 by **Farrar & Watmaugh** at the height of the Depression and stood virtually empty for several years, despite such lures as an Olympic-size swimming pool and doormen dressed as London bobbies. It is the second complex by that name on the site. The original, built in 1845, was a row of Greek Revival buildings with wide front lawns on West 23rd Street. ◆ Bounded by Ninth and 10th Aves, and W 23rd and W 24th Sts

EMPIRE

45 Empire Diner ★$ Refurbished in 1976 by designer Carl Laanes, this 1930s-style diner has retained the classic trappings of the original establishment—the Art Deco aluminum-winged clock near the entrance and the baked-enamel finish outside. Open around the clock, it has a bar and is a favorite among late-night/early-morning patrons, who come for one of the best diner breakfasts in town: try the omelette with salsa or smoked mozzarella, fajitas, or burgers. Don't miss the signature Empire chocolate pudding for

dessert. ◆ American ◆ Daily 24 hours. 210 10th Ave (at W 22nd St). 243.2736

46 Barbara Gladstone Gallery Gladstone's space allows her to mount dual exhibitions from an ever-increasing stable of European and American artists. Vito Acconci, Anish Kapoor, Rosemarie Trockel, and Jenny Holzer are part of her distinguished roster. ◆ Tu-Sa. 515 W 24th St (between 10th and 11th Aves). 206.9300 ᴥ

47 LiebmanMagnan Gallery Although it's in an offbeat location—next to a car repair garage and above a *halal* meat restaurant—this is one of Chelsea's best small galleries. The artists represented are a varied bunch, but their work tends to touch on issues of identity—be it of personal or cultural nature. ◆ Tu-Sa. 552 W 24th St (between 10th and 11th Aves). 255.3225

48 WPA Theater Under the impressive artistic direction of Kyle Renick, such productions as *Steel Magnolias, Little Shop of Horrors,* and *The Whales of August* have blossomed into memorable Off-Broadway hits and feature films. The theater seats 122. ◆ 519 W 23rd St (between 10th and 11th Aves). 206.0523 ᴥ

49 Chelsea Piers Sports & Entertainment Complex With city officials and entrepreneurial visionaries talking about the island's glorious future of waterfront parklands, this is the first major development whose ship has come in. The historic **Piers 59, 60, 61,** and **62** are fully in service, housing an ambitious $100-million sports facility with a golf driving range (**Golf Club,** 336.6400); a vast sports-fitness center, including an indoor running track, a spa, rock climbing, and 25-yard swimming pool (**Sports Center,** 336.6000); two outdoor regulation-size roller-skating venues (**Roller Rinks,** 336.6200); twin indoor ice-skating rinks (**Sky Rinks,** 336.6100); a marina (336.6600); and a 40-lane bowling complex (**AMF Chelsea Piers Bowl,** 835.2695). In addition, there are several restaurants and for all those sports enthusiasts, the **New York–Cornell Special Surgery Sports Medicine Center** (336.5100) can help alleviate all sprains and pains.

Originally built in 1910 by **Warren & Wetmore,** the architects of **Grand Central Terminal,** as docks for the era's grand ocean liners, it was refitted by **Butler Rogers Baskett** for its new role as the West Side's luxury playground. ◆ Daily. 11th Ave (between W 14th and W 23rd Sts). 336.6666

"There are two million interesting people in New York—and only 78 in Los Angeles"
Neil Simon

New York Bay is really a tidal estuary and the world's southernmost fjord.

50 Starrett-Lehigh Building A pacesetter in its day, this Art Deco collection of glass, concrete, and brown brick with rounded corners was built over the yards of the **Lehigh Valley Railroad,** and had elevators powerful enough to lift fully loaded freight cars onto its upper warehouse floors. It was designed in 1931 by **Russell G.** and **Walter M. Cory** and **Yasuo Matsui.** ♦ 12th Ave (between W 26th and W 27th Sts)

51 Church of the Holy Apostles The slate-roofed spire of this Episcopal church makes it a standout among the huge brick apartment houses all around it. Built in 1848 by **Minard Lafever** with 1858 transepts by **Richard Upjohn,** it's an unusual feature of the view to the west from the **Observation Deck** of the **Empire State Building.** ♦ 296 Ninth Ave (between W 26th and W 28th Sts). 807.6799 &

52 Fur District Yes, that man you just passed did have a silver fox cape over his arm. No, he didn't steal it, and chances are that no one will steal it from him. It's commonplace in the Fur District for thousands of dollars' worth of merchandise to be delivered in such a casual way. It's all in a day's work for the people who make and sell fur garments in this neighborhood. ♦ Bounded by Sixth and Eighth Aves, and W 27th and W 30th Sts

53 Fashion Institute of Technology (FIT) If there were a competition for the ugliest block in Manhattan, the center of this complex on West 27th Street would win easily. All the buildings, built between 1958 and 1977, are by the same firm, **De Young & Moscowitz,** but obviously not by the same hand. The prestigious school, part of the **State University of New York,** was created by New York's garment industry to train young people in all aspects of the fashion business. ♦ Seventh Ave and W 27th St. 217.7999

William Marcy "Boss" Tweed began his political career in 1848 as the organizer of the Americus Volunteer Fire Company, whose unusually large fire engine was painted with the head of a tiger. The fire company was associated with Tammany Hall (the Democratic political machine), and it was an easy step from one to the other. By 1853 Tweed had become a congressman; by 1867 he was powerful enough to overthrow Reform mayor Fernando Wood and put his own man, George Opdyke, in charge at City Hall. In 1868, he became Grand Sachem of Tammany Hall, which gave him backroom control over the state as well as the city. Attacks by cartoonist Thomas Nast in *Harper's Weekly* led to his downfall in 1873. He was convicted, but jumped bail and slipped away to Spain, where he was captured by police who recognized him from the Nast cartoons. He died in prison three years later.

54 221 West 26th Street This building was originally an armory. It was also once the **Famous Players Studio,** where, in 1915, Adolph Zukor paid Mary Pickford an unprecedented $2,000 per week as one of his most famous players. ♦ Between Seventh and Eighth Aves

55 Chelsea Antiques Building If the hundreds of dealers at the weekend **Annex Antiques Fair and Flea Market** a block away don't satisfy you, this antiques cove is wonderfully convenient and considerably calmer. Twelve floors are filled with quality dealers of art, antiques, and estate treasures, from collectibles to serious museum pieces. ♦ Daily. 110 W 25th St (between Sixth and Seventh Aves). 929.0909 &

56 Flower District The best time to smell the flowers here is the early morning, when florists from all over the city arrive to refresh their stock. If you're in the market for a large plant or a small tree, you'll find it here on the sidewalk soaking up the sun. ♦ Sixth Ave (between W 26th and W 29th Sts)

57 Manhattan Mall With eight floors of shops plus a food court, this place will make you feel like you're in a mall in the 'burbs. **Stern's** (department store), **The Body Shop** (skin-care products), **Accento** (handknit sweaters), and **Cartoons & Friends** (clothes and accessories adorned with favorite cartoon characters) are of particular interest, but two other reasons to visit this vertical mall, designed in 1989 by Baltimore-based **RTKL Associates,** are the clean bathrooms and the **Visitors' Center** on the seventh floor; stop in if you need tourist brochures, transportation information, or assistance in getting theater tickets or making restaurant reservations. ♦ W 33rd St and Sixth Ave. 465.0500 &

58 New York Hotel Pennsylvania $$ Originally designed in 1918 by **McKim, Mead & White,** this hotel was named for the nearby **Pennsylvania Station.** In the 1930s, it was a hot stop for the Big Bands: Glenn Miller immortalized its phone number with his "Pennsylvania 6-5000." All 1,700 rooms have been renovated; its **Globetrotter** restaurant serves breakfast only. ♦ 401 Seventh Ave (between W 32nd and W 33rd Sts). 736.5000, 800/223.8585; fax 502.8798

59 Schoepfer Studios Carrying on an 85-year-old family business started by his grandfather, taxidermist Jim Schoepfer stocks a veritable zoo, including zebras, armadillos, anteaters, birds, and fish. A sign on the door welcomes customers, not browsers; fortunately, there's a lot to see in the window display. ♦ M-F. 138 W 31st St (between Sixth and Seventh Aves). 736.6939

60 St. John the Baptist Church Designed in 1872 by **Napoleon LeBrun,** this Roman Catholic church is noted for its white marble

General Post Office

MICHAEL STORRINGS

interior. ♦ 210 W 31st St (between Seventh and Eighth Aves). 564.9070 ⑆

61 Madison Square Garden Center
America's premier entertainment facility, designed by **Charles Luckman Associates** in 1968, hosts more than 600 events for nearly 6 million spectators each year. Within the center are the 20,000-seat **Arena,** the 5,600-seat **Theater at Madison Square Garden,** and the **Exposition Rotunda** with a 20-story office building. It is home to the **New York Knicks** and the **New York Rangers.** Throughout the year, the facility hosts exhibitions and trade shows; boxing; rodeos; dog, cat, and horse shows; circuses; graduations; rock concerts; tennis; track and field, and gymnastics events; and an occasional presidential convention.
♦ Seventh Ave (between W 31st and W 33rd Sts). 465.6741 ⑆

Within Madison Square Garden Center:

Pennsylvania Station Make connections here for Long Island via the **Long Island Railroad** and for points north, south, and west via **Amtrak.** ♦ Amtrak 800-USA-RAIL; Long Island Railroad 718/217.5477

62 1 Penn Plaza In 1972, **Charles Luckman Associates** designed this, the tallest of the complex of buildings that replaced the late, great **Pennsylvania Station.** ♦ 250 W 34th St (between Seventh and Eighth Aves). 239.7400 ⑆

63 Tir Na Nog ★$$$ This lively newcomer to a restaurant-starved area is a good place to come for hearty portions of such dishes as shepherd's pie; Clonakilty roasted black

pudding; or Irish salmon with warm corn blinis, dill crème fraîche, and baby greens. On the American contemporary side, try the grilled mahimahi with artichoke-potato puree and tomato confit or the Tir Na Nog burger, made with Ballycashel Irish Cheddar. One warning: the bar's popularity as an after-work hangout can make early evening dining during the week a noisy experience. ♦ Irish/American ♦ Daily breakfast, lunch, and dinner. 5 Penn Plaza (Eighth Ave, between W 33rd and W 34th Sts). 630.0249

UNITED STATES POSTAL SERVICE®

64 General Post Office The monumental stairway and columned entrance (shown above) were designed by **McKim, Mead & White** in 1913 to match their design for the splendiferous old **Pennsylvania Station,** sadly demolished in 1963. Look up for that famous inscription about rain, snow, and the gloom of night that made it the first attraction of visitors arriving by train. At press time, plans were in the works to relocate **Penn Station** underneath the post office, so that New Yorkers will be able to boast a **McKim, Mead & White** train terminal once again.
♦ Daily 24 hours. Eighth Ave (between W 31st and W 33rd Sts). 967.8585

"New York is a city of dreams."
Isaac Bashevis Singer

Restaurants/Clubs: Red   **Hotels:** Blue
Shops/ ⑆ Outdoors: Green   **Sights/Culture:** Black

135

Theater District/ Garment Center

The Theater District and the Garment Center may well be considered the pulse of the city's economy; New Yorkers take their tourism and fashion industries very seriously. For those who love "street theater," no part of town is more entertaining than the Garment Center, which has more than a slight influence over what Atlanta, Kansas City, and Pittsburgh are wearing. Then there's **Broadway**, which has no equivalent in any other American—or foreign—city. This crucible of fashion design and theater fits in a relatively small area—**West 34th** to **West 59th Streets**, from **Sixth Avenue** (officially, **Avenue of the Americas**) to the **Hudson River**.

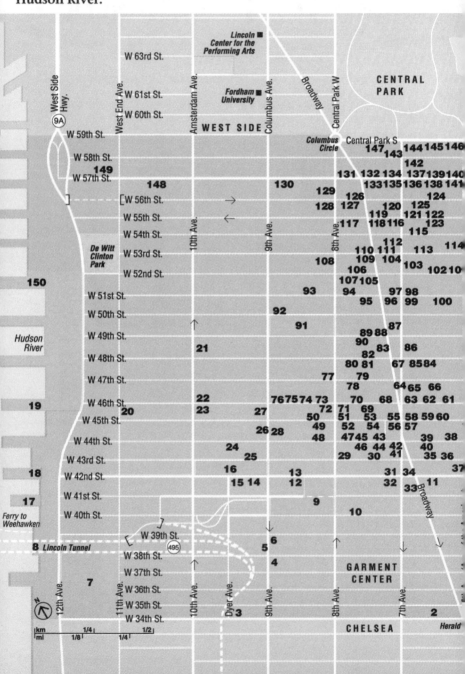

Before 1900, the garment trade was centered below East 14th Street on the Lower East Side, then home to the Eastern European Jewish community. By 1915, it had moved north along Broadway and Sixth Avenue as far as West 30th Street, replacing part of the rough-and-tumble **Tenderloin District.** The merchant princes who were establishing their fine department stores along Fifth Avenue were distressed to find garment workers mingling with their affluent customers and formed a committee to put a stop to it. The committee's solution was to order the construction of two garment work-shop buildings, **Nos. 498** and **500 Seventh Avenue**, at **West 37th Street**, a comfortable distance away. Not long after the 1921 completion of the loft buildings, Seventh Avenue came to be synonymous with American fashion and New York city's "rag trade": Street signs today read "Fashion Avenue." Specialists in various parts of the clothing business (apparel, accessories, jewelry, textiles, or trimming) tend to gather together; apparel showrooms, for example, are generally grouped along Seventh Avenue and Broadway, between **West 35th** and **West 42nd Streets.**

When the **Metropolitan Opera House** opened at **West 39th Street** and Broadway in 1883, the **Floradora Girls** were already packing them in at the **Casino Theater** across the street. In 1902, the first portion of **Macy's** was built at West 34th Street and Broadway where it replaced, among other buildings, **Koster & Bial's Music Hall**, where Thomas Edison first demonstrated moving pictures.

As the city's center moved uptown, the theaters followed. The theatrical quarter moved north across West 42nd Street in the early 1900s. Theater owners banded together in a syndicate to gain more control over the artists they booked. This gave them control over the competition that remained downtown as well, and those theatrical enterprises were effectively put out of business. The syndicate's power increased greatly in 1916, when the three Shubert brothers began to build new theaters in the **Times Square** area, which the subway had put within easy reach of the entire city. Other entrepreneurs joined the rush, and their legacy is still with us.

In 1876, an elevated railroad was built along **Ninth Avenue**, and thousands of immigrants, chiefly from Ireland, moved to the neighborhood from downtown. Work was plentiful in the sawmills, warehouses, stone yards, and stables along the Hudson River. Around this time, the area bordered approximately by West 30th and West 59th Streets and **Eighth** and **12th Avenues** evolved into one of America's toughest neighborhoods: **Hell's Kitchen,** named for the gang that ruled here, thriving on hoodlumism, extortion, and highway robbery. Well into the 20th century—long after gang wars in New York were officially declared over—merchants and property owners west of Eighth Avenue continued to pay "tribute" to the Hell's Kitchen Gang; they had no choice, until the gang finally disappeared. Today, although the occasional porn theater stands next to Broadway theaters, and the crowds in the streets include the odd hustler or petty criminal, the area is chiefly inhabited by aspiring actors yearning to be near the stage. In the past decade, an explosion of fine restaurants has taken place, providing an affordable alternative for the before- and after-theater crowds.

Today the neon-lit area surrounding Times Square (predominantly West 42nd between Seventh and Eighth Avenues and Eighth Avenue between West 42nd and **West 44th Streets**) still has its share of adult movie houses, peep shows, and other dens of iniquity, but it is undergoing radical change once again. The Walt Disney Company spearheaded a renewal of this area with a $40-million renovation of the 92-year-old **New Amsterdam Theater**. Other major entertainment companies that have committed to the area include **Madame**

Tussaud's, London's high-tech **Wax Museum;** and Livent, a Toronto company that has combined the **Lyric** and **New Apollo Theaters** into the **Ford Center for the Performing Arts.** Future projects include the renovation and reconstruction of the **Harris, Liberty,** and **Empire** theaters; the opening of **E Walk,** an 860-room hotel/entertainment complex; and several theme-oriented restaurants.

1 Herald Square During the 1880s and 1890s, this was the heart of the Tenderloin, an area of dance halls, bordellos, and cafes adjacent to Hell's Kitchen. New York City's theater and newspaper industries were once headquartered here. The square—which, like most of the squares in New York, is anything but—was named for the *New York Herald,* which occupied a Venetian palazzo, completed in 1921 by **McKim, Mead & White,** on the north end. Greeley Square, to the south at West 33rd Street, was named for the founder of the *New-York Tribune.* Note the **Crossland Savings Bank** by **York & Sawyer**—it has lots of columns inside and out. ♦ Bounded by Sixth Ave and Broadway, and W 34th and W 35th Sts

2 Macy's The Broadway building of this New York institution was built in 1901 by **DeLemos & Cordes;** the Seventh Avenue building was built in 1931 by **Robert D. Kohn.** Although it has always seemed to have more of everything than any other department store, it didn't have a compelling fashion image until 1974, when Ed Finkelstein, who had been president of the San Francisco store, took charge of the New York branch. Today it is both extensive and stylish. The haven for children on the fifth floor contains a vast selection of imported and domestic clothing. Fragrance fans can sniff themselves into a stupor at the main floor's perfume arcade. The ninth-floor **Corner Shop** includes a dazzling array of fine antiques. **The Cellar** turns shopping for the kitchen into a heady experience, and even includes fine food to go with the fine kitchenware (branches of familiar shops like **William Greenberg Jr. Desserts** and **Ottomanelli's Meat Market** are here). You can eat breakfast, lunch, and dinner, get a facial, mail a letter, have your jewelry appraised, buy theater tickets, and convert foreign currency into dollars—without ever leaving the store. Perhaps above all else, the department store is known for its special events including the Thanksgiving Day Parade, elaborate Christmas displays, Spring Flower Show, and the Fourth of July Fireworks display. ♦ Daily. Bounded by Broadway and Seventh Ave, and W 34th and W 35th Sts. 695.4400 ᴸ

3 The Original Improvisation Although it was relocated here in 1992, this is the original, the place that marked the start on the road to stardom for talents like Richard Pryor, Robin Williams, Stiller & Meara, and Rodney Dangerfield. Light meals are served in casual surroundings. ♦ Cover, drink minimum.

Shows: W-Sa. Reservations recommended. 433 W 34th St (between Ninth and Dyer Aves). 582.7442 ᴸ

4 Hero Boy ★$ According to the Manganaro family, who established this enterprise as a satellite of their grocery store next door, the sandwich term "hero" (variously known in other parts of the country as "grinder," "po'boy," or "submarine") was coined at this stand. The Manganaros also claim to be the first to sell these by the foot. The hot meals— lasagna, baked ziti—are good too. ♦ Italian ♦ M-Sa breakfast, lunch, and dinner. 492 Ninth Ave (between W 37th and W 38th Sts). 947.7325 ᴸ

5 Guido's ★$$ In the rear of the Supreme Macaroni Co.—a store that leads you back to a time before the words "gourmet" or "nouvelle cuisine" were ever uttered—is a restaurant serving the best macaroni this side of Naples. The prices are moderate and the service straightforward. ♦ Italian ♦ M-F lunch and dinner; Sa dinner. Reservations recommended. No credit cards accepted. 511 Ninth Ave (between W 38th and W 39th Sts). 564.8074 ᴸ

6 Cupcake Cafe Loyal customers consider Ann and Michael Warren's cakes to be works of art. Not coincidentally, the Warrens and their team of assistants are all artists in other media— painting, sculpture, photography—who transfer those talents to a baked and frosted canvas. Wedding and birthday cakes are specialties. Even if you don't need a fanciful cake, stop by for a great muffin (especially corn), a doughnut, fruit pie, or cup of soup du jour. ♦ Daily. 522 Ninth Ave (at W 39th St). 465.1530

7 Jacob K. Javits Convention Center This huge facility—made almost entirely of glass—covers 22 acres between West 34th and West 39th Streets, making it the largest exposition hall under one roof in North America and one of the biggest buildings in the world. It has 900,000 square feet of exhibition space. The lobby, called the **Crystal Palace,** is 150 feet high. Designed by **I.M. Pe**

& Partners, it was called "the center at the center of the world" when it opened in 1986, and events are already scheduled into the 21st century. Oddly, the building appears opaque during the day, while at night the interior lighting makes the structure glow. ♦ 655 W 34th St (between 11th and 12th Aves). 216.2000

8 Lincoln Tunnel The tunnel, which is 97 feet below the Hudson River, connects Manhattan with Weehawken, New Jersey, and more than 36 million vehicles use it every year. The 8,216-foot center tube was the first to be built. **Aymar Embury II** was the architect; Ole Singstad completed the engineering in 1937. It was joined by the 7,482-foot north tube in 1945, and the 8,006-foot south tube in 1957, making it the only 3-tube vehicular tunnel in the world. ♦ Between Dyer Ave and Rte 495, Weehawken, New Jersey

9 Port Authority Bus Terminal Erected in 1950, the terminal was expanded in 1963 and again in 1982 by the **Port Authority Design Staff.** This is the largest and busiest bus terminal in the world, with three levels of platforms serving all of New York's long-distance bus lines and most of the commuter buses between New York and the New Jersey suburbs. A special section on the West 42nd Street side also serves all three metropolitan airports. For people who prefer driving into Manhattan but not through it, a rooftop parking garage connects directly by ramp to the Lincoln Tunnel. As in any major transportation hub, exercise caution inside the terminal—be aware of your belongings at all times, and avoid isolated areas, particularly the restrooms. ♦ Daily 24 hours. Bounded by Eighth and Ninth Aves, and W 40th and W 42nd Sts. Bus info 564.8484

10 B&J Fabrics, Inc. At the heart of New York's Garment Center, this store has been in business since 1940 (and at this address since 1954). Its three floors contain 8,000 square feet of space dedicated to the finest European and American fashion fabrics, offered at discount rates. ♦ M-Sa. 263 W 40th St (between Seventh and Eighth Aves). 354.8150 ♿

11 Hotalings News Agency This is *the* stand in New York City for out-of-town and international newspapers and magazines. ♦ Daily. 142 W 42nd St (between Sixth Ave and Broadway). 840.1868 ♿

12 Health Insurance Building Better known as the original **McGraw-Hill Building,** this 35-story tower was commissioned when growth was expected in this area. Green and glorious, it still stands alone. Built in 1931 by **Hood, Godley & Fouilhoux,** it has the distinction of being the only New York building mentioned in *The International Style,* the 1932 book by Hitchcock and Johnson that codified modern architecture. In fact, this tower is not strictly glass-and-steel aesthetics but an individual composition with Art Deco detailing. Eminent architectural historian **Vincent Scully** called it "Proto-jukebox Modern." ♦ 330 W 42nd St (between Eighth and Ninth Aves)

13 Church of the Holy Cross Although this was built in 1870 by **Henry Engelbert** as the parish church of a poor neighborhood, it has several windows and mosaics designed by Louis Comfort Tiffany. Father Francis P. Duffy, chaplain of the famous Fighting 69th Division in World War I, fought from the pulpit of this church to break up the gangs of Hell's Kitchen. He served here until his death in 1932. ♦ 329 W 42nd St (between Eighth and Ninth Aves). 246.4732 ♿

14 Chez Josephine ★★$$$ In 1986, the ebullient Jean Claude Baker launched this unique restaurant as a tribute to his late adoptive mother, cabaret legend Josephine Baker. Fittingly, the place is a great hit with critics and the public alike. Featured on the menu are lobster bisque, goat-cheese ravioli, and roasted duck à l'orange. A pianist playing bluesy tunes adds to the atmosphere. ♦ French ♦ M-Sa dinner. Reservations recommended. 414 W 42nd St (between Ninth and Dyer Aves). 594.1925

15 Theater Row Beginning with the former **West Side Airlines Terminal,** which now houses video recording studios and the **National Spanish Television Network,** this ambitious project, begun in 1976 by **Playwrights Horizons** (416 W 42nd St), includes a dozen Off-Broadway theaters and a revitalized street scene that gives new life to the Lincoln Tunnel exit that cuts the block in half. Tickets for all theaters are available at **Ticket Central** located at **Playwrights Horizons.** ♦ Box office: daily 1-8PM. W 42nd St (between Ninth and 10th Aves). 279.4200

16 Manhattan Plaza These towers, built in 1977 by **David Todd & Associates,** provide subsidized housing for performing artists, whose rent for the 1,688 apartments is based on their income. Their presence pays dividends in the vitality they bring to the neighborhood. ♦ Bounded by Ninth and 10th Aves, and W 42nd and W 43rd Sts

Within Manhattan Plaza:

Restaurants/Clubs: Red	**Hotels:** Blue
Shops/♟ Outdoors: Green	**Sights/Culture:** Black

WEST BANK CAFE

West Bank Cafe ★$$ The tables at the upstairs dining room are covered with butcher paper, which can be graced with an assortment of pasta dishes, such seafood specials as seared tuna steak with coriander, various salads, and burgers. After dinner (or before), head downstairs to the cabaret and enjoy a musical comedy or a group of short plays. ♦ American ♦ Restaurant: M-Sa lunch and dinner; Su brunch and dinner. Cabaret: Tu-Sa 8PM, 10:30PM. Reservations recommended. 407 W 42nd St. 695.6909

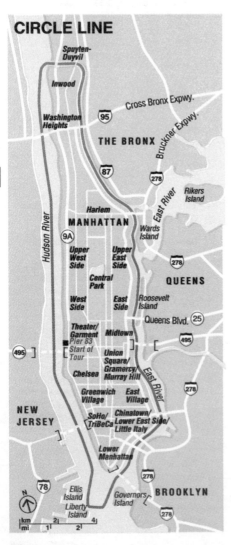

CIRCLE LINE

Little Pie Company The aromas here are glorious and the all-natural pies are just like Mom used to make. Fresh fruit pies predominate in summer, sour cream–apple and pumpkin pies are highlights in fall. ♦ Daily. 424 W 43rd St. 736.4780 ᵫ

17 **World Yacht Cruises** ★★$$$$ This five-yacht fleet offers romantic year-round dinner cruises—including dancing—around New York harbor. The food (four courses, usually featuring a salmon or beef entrée) is good; the scenery, better. ♦ Continental ♦ Daily dinner. Reservations required; jacket required. Pier 81 12th Ave (just south of W 42nd St). 630.8100

18 **Circle Line** There is simply no better way to orient yourself to Manhattan's wonders. This well-narrated tour heads down the Hudson River, past the **Statue of Liberty,** up the East River to the Harlem River, through Spuyten-Duyvil, and back down the Hudson. The eight vessels are converted World War II landing craft or Coast Guard cutters. When you get on board, try to sit on the port side (left as you face forward and head south). That way, all your views are of Manhattan. During the summer, there are 12 three-hour cruises a day starting at 9:30AM. ♦ Fee. Daily. Complimentary shuttle service from Midtown available. Pier 83, 12th Ave (just north of W 42nd St). 563.3200

19 **Intrepid Sea Air Space Museum** The veteran World War II and Vietnam War aircraft carrier *Intrepid* is now a technological and historical museum. Other than the Air and Space Museum in Washington, DC, no other institution gives such a thorough picture of the past, present, and future of warfare and technology in air, space, and sea. The tamer **Pioneers Hall** features mock-ups, antiques, and film clips of flying machines from the turn of the century through the 1930s. Insights into the future as well as contemporary exploration of the ocean and space are shown in **Technologies Hall,** along with the artifacts of 20th- and 21st-century warfare: jumbo jets, mammoth rockets, and complex weaponry. More aircraft can be inspected on the *Intrepid* 900-foot flight deck. The most recent acquisitions are the guided missile submarine *Growler* and the Vietnam-era destroyer *Edson.* Visitors can climb through the control bridges and command centers of the carrier, but spaces are cramped, and there is often a wait. Dress warmly in winter months. ♦ Admission; children under age six and uniformed military free. Daily Memorial Day–Labor Day; W-Su Labor Day–Memorial Day. Pier 86, 12th Ave (four blocks north of W 42nd St). 245.0072

20 **Landmark Tavern** ★$$ An old waterfront tavern, this once-rowdy place now offers modern-day diners a cleaner and more refine version of its 19th-century rooms, where foo is still served from antique sideboards. The Irish soda bread, baked every hour, is a gem.

The fish-and-chips, shepherd's pie, prime rib, and hamburgers are all good. ♦ American ♦ M-Sa lunch and dinner; Su brunch and dinner. Reservations recommended. 626 11th Ave (at W 46th St). 757.8595 &

21 Peruvian Restaurant ★$ Ignore the fluorescent lighting and Formica tables; instead concentrate on what is probably the best and most authentic Peruvian cuisine in New York: terrific baked fish, hearty stews, and delicious *papas asadas* (potatoes boiled in broth). The pleasant service is another plus. ♦ Peruvian ♦ Daily lunch and dinner. No credit cards accepted. 688 10th Ave (between W 48th and W 49th Sts). 581.5814

22 Mud, Sweat & Tears This is a cheerful, neat pottery studio for beginning and expert potters. The facilities include 10 electric wheels, spacious tables, hand-building supplies, glazes, a kiln where firings are done frequently, and a small retail area where the potters sell their wares. ♦ M-F 11AM-8PM; Sa-Su noon-7PM. Call for information on classes. 654 10th Ave (at W 46th St). 974.9121

23 Mike's American Bar and Grill ★$$ Faithfuls claim that this place has the best enchiladas in town. Other good picks include spinach fettuccine with spicy shrimp, and chicken stewed with prunes, onions, thyme, and tomatoes. Don't miss the killer hot chili or the grilled specials. ♦ American/Mexican ♦ M-F lunch and dinner; Sa-Su brunch and dinner. Reservations recommended. 650 10th Ave (between W 45th and W 46th Sts). 246.4115 &

24 The Actors Studio It was in this former Greek Orthodox church that Lee Strasberg trained such stars as Marlon Brando, Dustin Hoffman, Al Pacino, and Shelley Winters. It seats 125 people. ♦ 432 W 44th St (between Ninth and 10th Aves). 757.0870

24 The New Dramatists This company, which offers free readings, was founded in 1949 by a group of Broadway's most important writers and producers in an effort to encourage new playwrights; alumni include William Inge, John Guare, and Emily Mann. The nonprofit organization took occupancy of the building, formerly a Lutheran church, in 1968. ♦ 424 W 44th St (between Ninth and 10th Aves). 757.6960

25 Le Madeleine ★★$$$ Salads, pastas, fish, and such light meat dishes as grilled chicken breast with a Pommery mustard sauce are featured in this charming French bistro. There's also a beautiful skylit, brick-walled garden room that serves outdoor meals year-round and is always booked up for brunch. ♦ French ♦ M-F lunch and dinner; Sa-Su brunch and dinner. Reservations recommended. 403 W 43rd St (between Ninth and 10th Aves). 246.2993

25 Westside Theater For more than 20 years the two theaters in this converted Episcopal church have presented award-winning productions such as *A Shayna Maidel* and *Extremities*. They seat 210 and 190. ♦ Call for performance schedule. 407 W 43rd St (between Ninth and 10th Aves). 315.2244

26 Rudy's Bar This is one of the area's few remaining neighborhood bars. Locals come for light snacks, conversation, and good drinks. ♦ Daily till 4AM. 627 Ninth Ave (between W 44th and W 45th Sts). 974.9169

26 Poseidon Greek Bakery The Fable family has been turning out paper-thin phyllo-dough pastries in this tiny shop for 75 years. Try the sweet baklava, spinach pies, and tempting cinnamon-and-sugar almond cookies. For those who want to make their own delicacies, phyllo is for sale. ♦ Tu-Su. 629 Ninth Ave (between W 44th and W 45th Sts). 757.6173 &

27 Bruno The King of Ravioli This shop sells a vast selection of fresh pastas and sauces, including ravioli, manicotti, cannelloni, lasagna, stuffed shells, and gnocchi, all made in its New Jersey factory. ♦ M-Sa. 653 Ninth Ave (between W 45th and W 46th Sts). 246.8456. Also at: Numerous locations throughout the city

27 Zen Palate ★★★$$ A vegetarian oasis, this place serves excellent cuisine in an upscale, minimalist setting. It's a bit pricey, but worth the culinary cultural adventure for such dishes as basil *moo shu* rolls (with nuts and vegetables), Zen Retreat (a squash shell stuffed with vegetables, beans, and tofu), Dreamland (panfried spinach noodles with shiitake mushrooms and ginger), and Mushroom Forest (an exotic combination of fungi, pine nuts, and vegetables on a bed of Boston lettuce). Alcoholic beverages are not served, but you can bring your own. ♦ Asian/Vegetarian ♦ Daily lunch and dinner. Reservations recommended. 663 Ninth Ave (at W 46th St). 582.1669. & Also at: 34 Union Sq E (at E 16th St). 614.9345; 2170 Broadway (between W 76th and W 77th Sts). 501.7768 &

28 Film Center Building The pink and black marble in the lobby and the pattern of the orange and blue tiles on the walls helped attract some 75 motion picture distributors, who made this 1929 building by **Buchman & Kahn** their headquarters. The stores on this block rent out moviemaking equipment. ♦ 630 Ninth Ave (between W 44th and W 45th Sts). 757.6995

28 Jezebel ★★$$$ The nondescript exterior doesn't prepare you for the dramatic interior, which suggests nothing less than a New Orleans bordello. The lavish setting provides the perfect counterpoint to owner Alberta Wright's soul food—she-crab soup, smothered chicken, oxtail stew, garlic shrimp, broiled seafood platter (lobster tails, scallops, and shrimp), and shrimp creole. And don't forget the corn bread. Finish with pecan or sweet potato pie. The extensive wine list concentrates on French varieties. ♦ Soul food ♦ M-Sa dinner. Reservations required. 630 Ninth Ave (at W 45th St). 582.1045

29 Ben & Jerry's Drop in to this popular shop for a scoop of the famous Vermont ice cream in such exotic flavors as Cherry Garcia, Cookie Dough, or Rainforest Crunch. Even dieters can indulge—low- or no-fat yogurts and sorbets are also offered. This shop's profits go to a community group that provides permanent, affordable homes for single adults in the Times Square area. ♦ M-Sa 11AM-midnight; Su noon-10PM Apr–mid-Sept; M-Sa noon-11PM, Su noon-8PM mid-Sept–Mar. 680 Eighth Ave (at W 43rd St). 221.1001 ᒼ Also at: Numerous locations throughout the city ᒼ

30 The New York Times In 1913, less than 10 years after moving to Times Square, the *Times* had grown so much that this annex was built by **Ludlow & Peabody** around the corner on West 43rd Street. Its size was doubled in 1924. The building was expanded again in 1945, and the original tower was eventually abandoned. The newspaper discontinued printing at this location in 1997; it now utilizes more modern and expanded facilities in nearby Queens. ♦ 229 W 43rd St (between Broadway and Eighth Ave). 556.1234

31 Ford Center for the Performing Arts After years of neglect, two classic theaters— the **Lyric** and **New Apollo**—were resurrected by the Toronto-based Livent, Inc., and are now a single 1,830-seat state-of-the-art complex. The **Lyric**, designed by **V. Hugo Koehler,** opened in 1903, while the **New Apollo,** designed by **De Rosa & Pereira,** made its debut in 1930. Much of the original ornate plaster work was restored and remounted for the debut production of *Ragtime.* ♦ 213-15 W 42nd St (between Seventh and Eighth Aves). 582.4100

31 New Victory Theater New York's oldest active theater was built in 1900 by Oscar Hammerstein as a venue marking 42nd Street as the new theater district. Created by **J.B. McElfatrick and Sons,** its impressive interior boasted a large dome with plaster angels around its rim. Two years later, David Belasco

completely renovated the theater, adding his own imprint. Since then, the **New Victory** has run the theatrical gamut: from burlesque shows to second-run films. In 1995, it reemerged as the first theater to herald the "New 42nd Street." Much of the original interior has been restored by **Hardy Holzman Pfeiffer Associates**; the dome remains intact, and the grand Venetian staircase leading to the theater was reconstructed. Family-oriented productions—including vaudeville, featuring jugglers and clowns; classical ballet and modern dance; puppet shows, mimes, and circuses; and films for young audiences—are offered year-round. **The Flying Karamozov Brothers, Le Carrousel Theatre Company,** and **Children's Television Workshop** are just a few of the headliners to be seen here. ♦ 209 W 42nd St (between Seventh and Eighth Aves). Telecharge 239.6200

32 New Amsterdam Theater Disney's much-heralded reopening of this 1903 showplace— originally designed by **Henry B. Herts** and **Hugh Tallant**—reflects the architectural talents of **Hardy Holzman Pfeiffer Associates,** who restored and refurbished the elaborate interior to its original splendor replete with ornate Art Nouveau–style flora and fauna. While it retains the best of its turn-of-the-century grandeur, the theater also sports a new high-tech sound system. The **New Amsterdam** is now the home of Disney theatrical productions; at press time, the megahit *The Lion King* was still running. ♦ 214 W 42nd St (between Seventh and Eighth Aves). Ticketmaster 307.4100

33 XS New York This Times Square newcomer, best visited during the day and early evening, claims to be the place where virtual space meets cyberspace. The multilevel entertainment complex features virtual-reality games and interactive experiences that will leave you craving more. Play a round of virtual-reality golf, ski down the slopes on the Alpine Surfer, or feel like Top Gun in the F-1 flight simulator. If all this leaves you breathless, take a break at the cafe. There's a gift shop, too. ♦ Fee for games. Daily. 1457 Broadway (between W 41st and W 42nd Sts). 398.5467, 888/XS2.PLAY

34 Times Square In April 1904, almost a year before the *New York Times* moved into what had been called Longacre Square, the mayor and the board of aldermen passed a resolution naming the area, bounded by Broadway, Seventh Avenue, and West 42nd and West 47th Streets, after the newspaper. It quickly became known as "The Crossroads of the World," partly in deference to the *Times,* which certainly could claim that title. Today, it is the heart of the Theater District and the site of some of the most spectacular electric advertising signs ever created. The square is one of a series of open spaces created as

Broadway crosses the straight north-south avenues, in this case Seventh Avenue. When you stand at the base of the old *Times* tower and look uptown, Broadway comes into the square on your left, and leaves it behind you on your right, having cut across Seventh Avenue at the intersection of West 45th Street. ◆ Bounded by Broadway and Seventh Ave, and W 42nd and W 47th Sts

34 1 Times Square When this building was under construction as headquarters for the *New York Times*, even the *Times*'s arch rival, the *Herald,* grudgingly ran a story under the headline "Deepest Hole in New York a Broadway Spectacle," which said that the new *Times* tower was the most interesting engineering feat to be seen anywhere on Manhattan Island. Designed by **Eidlitz & MacKenzie,** it was completed in 1904. The newspaper's pressroom was in the tower's basement, but because the building was being built over the city's biggest subway station, the basement had to be blasted out of solid rock 55 feet down. The presses began printing the *Times* down there on 2 January 1905, after the new year had been welcomed with the dropping of a lighted ball down the flagpole on the roof. The celebration has been repeated every year since, although in 1966 the *Times* sold the building to Allied Chemical Co., which stripped it bare and refaced it with marble. Recently, Warner Bros. took ownership of this building, and one can only anticipate that a legendary mouse will have to share the spotlight with a familiar rabbit. ◆ Seventh Ave (between W 42nd and W 43rd Sts)

35 Casablanca Hotel $$$ This hotel achieves the near impossible: It's an oasis of calm and character just footsteps from Times Square. The 48 rooms and suites exude the updated colonial flavor in evidence when you first walk in: rich wood paneling, exotic antiques, and antique French architectural prints. Guest refrigerators are stocked with complimentary iced tea, mineral water, and Callebaut chocolates. The second floor is home to the cozy **Rick's Cafe**, where guests can have a complimentary continental breakfast or afternoon wine and cheese. There's also a computer with Internet hook-up here, and a tiny outdoor terrace in the back. The staff is charming and capable. ◆ 147 W 43rd St (between Broadway and Sixth Ave). 869.1212, 888/922.7225; fax 391.7585; casahotel@aol.com; www.casablancahotel.com ৬

Times Square

MICHAEL STORRINGS

36 The Town Hall The work of **McKim, Mead & White,** this 1921 landmark is an elegant building with excellent acoustics. Joan Sutherland made her New York debut here. Today, the hall is constantly in use for concerts and cultural events. ◆ 123 W 43rd St (between Sixth Ave and Broadway). 840.2824 ৬

When revelers ring in the New Year, they're watching the newly refurbished ball in Times Square, which now glitters with 12,000 rhinestones, 180 halogen lights, and 144 bright strobes.

The Ziegfeld Follies, the most beloved and long-lived of Broadway's musical revues, originated in Paris with the Follies of 1907 (patterned after the French Folies Bergère of the late 19th century). The Broadway extravaganza was named after its famed American producer, Florenz Ziegfeld Jr.

37 National Debt Clock In a frighteningly rapid-fire frenzy, this billboard records our national debt by the megasecond as we sink deeper into the red. In addition to displaying the ever-changing national share, it also shows the average family's share. Best not to look. ♦ Sixth Ave (between W 42nd and W 43rd Sts)

38 Belasco The eccentric David Belasco, whose preferred style of dress was a priest's frock, wrote and produced *Madame Butterfly* and *The Girl of the Golden West* here. Both were later adapted into operas by Giacomo Puccini. Belasco's ghost is said to continue to visit backstage. This theater, dating to 1907, was a creation of **George Keister.** ♦ 111 W 44th St (between Sixth Ave and Broadway). Telecharge 239.6200

38 Cafe Un Deux Trois ★$$ Crayons for doodling on the paper-covered tables provide a charming bit of bohemia for those who never venture downtown. The gimmick isn't really necessary, however, as the place delivers satisfaction with such simple but good food as scallops *Provençale* and steak *frites* (with french fries). ♦ French ♦ Daily lunch and dinner. 123 W 44th St (between Sixth Ave and Broadway). 354.4148

MILLENNIUM
BROADWAY · NEW YORK

39 Millennium Broadway $$$ This sleek and handsome executive-style hotel offers such business-minded amenities as 2 dual-line speaker phones in each of the 627 rooms, phone mail in 4 languages, and television access to Macktel, an interactive communication system that allows guests to preview restaurant menus, order sporting event and theater tickets, and even check out. A **Club Floor** affords guests a private lounge (where a complimentary continental breakfast, as well as evening cocktails and hors d'oeuvres, are served) and such other upscale conveniences as a concierge for **Club** guests and private check-in and check-out. In addition, there is a fitness center staffed with private trainers. At the 650-seat **Hudson Theatre,** a 1902 landmark next door, the hotel maintains a full-service auditorium and 35mm and 70mm screening facilities. ♦ 145 W 44th St (between Sixth Ave and Broadway). 768.4400, 800/934.9953; fax 789.7688 ♿

Within the Millennium Broadway:

Restaurant Charlotte ★★$$$ An informal yet elegant room reflects chef Rhys Rosenblum's creative flair for incorporating traditional American and Southwestern

cuisines. Menu favorites include seared scallops and creamy mashed potatoes studded with bits of lobster, braised lamb shank with saffron risotto, and grilled salmon. Save room for the classic crème brûlée or silk chocolate cake. ♦ American/Southwestern ♦ M-F breakfast, lunch, and dinner; Sa-Su brunch and dinner. 789.7508

40 Virgil's ★$$ The place mats at this mammoth barbecue restaurant detail the search for perfect versions of each dish—Texas for sliced brisket, North Carolina for pulled pork. The walls are a source of more information—a history of barbecue in articles and pictures. Although authenticity, by its very definition, can't be copied, this place does a pretty good job—especially when it comes to ribs, pulled pork, mashed potatoes, and greens. The portions here are huge, including such desserts as butterscotch and lemon cheese pies. ♦ Barbecue ♦ Daily lunch and dinner. 152 W 44th St (between Sixth Ave and Broadway). 921.9494

41 Paramount Building The bank on the corner of West 43rd Street replaced the entrance to the famous **Paramount Theater,** built in 1926 by **Rapp & Rapp.** The great glass globe on its pinnacle and the four-sided clock make the building an attraction, as does its lavish lobby. Before the theater closed in 1964 its stage had been graced by such stars as Mae West, Pola Negri, Tommy Dorsey, Bing Crosby, and, of course, Frank Sinatra. ♦ 1501 Broadway (between W 43rd and W 44th Sts)

42 Ollie's Noodle Shop ★$ Cold sesame noodles; scallion pancakes; and vegetable, pork, and shrimp dumplings are all favorites at this bargain-priced Chinese restaurant. ♦ Chinese ♦ Daily lunch, dinner, and late-night meals. 200 W 44th St (at Broadway). 921.5988. Also at: 2315 Broadway (at W 84th St) 362.3712 ♿; 2957 Broadway (at W 116th St). 932.3300

42 Carmine's $$ Come hungry and bring at least one friend to share the huge portions of Southern Italian fare; all meals are meant for two or more. ♦ Italian ♦ Daily dinner. 200 W 44th St (between Broadway and Eighth Ave). 221.3800. Also at: 2450 Broadway (between W 90th and W 91st Sts). 362.2200

43 Shubert Alley The stage doors of the **Shubert Theater** (on West 44th Street) and of the **Booth** (on West 45th) open onto this space. So does the entrance to the offices of the Shubert Organization, making this a favorite spot for Broadway hopefuls to casually stroll up and down hoping to be noticed by the right people. A gift shop, **One Shubert Alley** (M-Sa 9AM-11:30PM; Su noon-7PM; 944.4133, 800/223.1320), specializes in merchandise related to Broadway shows. ♦ Between W 44th and W 45th Sts

43 Shubert It will be hard to imagine anything but *A Chorus Line* here, but that's what they said about Katharine Hepburn in *The Philadelphia Story,* and Barbra Streisand in *I Can Get It for You Wholesale.* The theater itself was built in 1913 by **Henry B. Herts.** ♦ 225 W 44th St (at Shubert Alley). Telecharge 239.6200 &

44 Sardi's ★★$$$ For more than 75 years this restaurant has been synonymous with Theater District dining. French chef Patrick Pinon produces such dishes as a delicious roasted free-range chicken with garlic. Sentimental favorites, however, such as cannelloni, are still available. Once in a while, you can spot a celebrity; otherwise, stargazers can content themselves with identifying famous customers who are immortalized in the numerous caricatures gracing the walls. ♦ Continental ♦ M-Sa lunch, dinner, and late-night meals. Reservations recommended; jacket required. 234 W 44th St (between Broadway and Eighth Ave). 221.8440

44 Helen Hayes This theater was constructed in 1912 by **Ingalls & Hoffman.** In 1965, when it was known as the **Little Theatre,** it became home to the *Merv Griffin* and *David Frost* shows. It reopened as a Broadway theater in 1974. In 1983, it was dedicated to the "First Lady" of the theater. ♦ 240 W 44th St (between Broadway and Eighth Ave). 944.9450; Ticketmaster 307.4100 &

45 Broadhurst It was here, in this 1918 work of **Herbert J. Krapp,** that Humphrey Bogart picked up his credentials as a tough guy when he appeared with Leslie Howard in *The Petrified Forest.* ♦ 235 W 44th St (between Shubert Alley and Eighth Ave). Telecharge 239.6200

46 St. James At this 1927 work of **Warren & Wetmore,** Rodgers and Hammerstein's *Oklahoma!* was followed by *Where's Charley?* with Ray Bolger, which in turn was followed by, among others, the original productions of *The King and I, The Pajama Game,* and *Tommy.* ♦ 246 W 44th St (between Broadway and Eighth Ave). Telecharge 239.6200 &

47 Majestic *The Music Man, Carousel, A Little Night Music,* and *The Wiz* helped this theater, built in 1927 by **Herbert J. Krapp,** live up to its name. *The Phantom of the Opera,* which has been playing since 26 January 1988, is carrying on the tradition. ♦ 247 W 44th St (between Shubert Alley and Eighth Ave). Telecharge 239.6200 &

47 Milford Plaza Ramada $$ Built in 1928 by **Schwartz & Gross,** this 1,300-room hotel was originally known as the **Lincoln.** It was built and first operated by the United Cigar Stores Co., which said it catered to the better element of the masses. There are two restaurants and a complete fitness center. ♦ 700 Eighth Ave (at W 44th St). 869.3000, 800/221.2690; fax 944.8357

48 Birdland ★$$ Live jazz is featured nightly at this jazz club and restaurant. ♦ American ♦ Cover; drink minimum. Daily dinner and late-night meals. Call for changing schedule of shows. Reservations recommended. 315 W 44th St (between Eighth and Ninth Aves). 581.3080

49 Martin Beck The famed Theatre Guild Studio used this 1924 house, a work of **G. Albert Lansburgh,** in the 1930s. Great performances echo from the stage, including those of the Lunts in Robert Sherwood's *Reunion in Vienna,* Katharine Cornell in *The Barretts of Wimpole Street,* and Ruth Gordon in *Hotel Universe.* In the 1950s, Arthur Miller's *The Crucible* and Tennessee Williams's *Sweet Bird of Youth* played here. In 1965, Peter Brook's production of *Marat/Sade* gave Broadway audiences a look at a new avant-garde. Liz Taylor came here for her Broadway debut in Lillian Hellman's *The Little Foxes.* ♦ 302 W 45th St (between Eighth and Ninth Aves). Telecharge 239.6200 &

50 Triton Gallery You'll find theater posters and show cards for current and past performances on Broadway and elsewhere in this shop that provides custom framing and mail order, too. Ask for a catalog. ♦ M-Sa. 323 W 45th St (between Eighth and Ninth Aves). 765.2472 &

51 Frankie and Johnnie's ★★$$$ A former speakeasy and onetime celebrity hangout for the likes of Al Jolson and Babe Ruth, this joint is still popular and tends to get busy (and loud) at dinner. But the crowds continue to get a hearty meal along with nostalgia for their money—this old Broadway chophouse still turns out great steak, veal, and lamb chops. ♦ Steak house ♦ M dinner; Tu-Sa lunch and dinner. Reservations required. 269 W 45th St (at Eighth Ave). 997.9494. Also at: 194-05 Northern Blvd (between 195th and 194th Sts), Flushing, Queens. 718/357.2444

51 Sam's ★$$ A popular hangout for theater people, this rustic place has exposed brick walls and very reasonable prix-fixe dinners, featuring such standards as ribs, shell steak, and grilled Cajun chicken. Although stars sup here occasionally, its most devoted fans are the "gypsies," members of the chorus lines. There's piano entertainment Wednesday through Saturday nights. ♦ American ♦ M-Sa lunch, dinner, and late-night meals; Su brunch and dinner. Reservations recommended. 263

W 45th St (between Broadway and Eighth Ave). 719.5416

52 Golden One of the longest-running shows in history, *Tobacco Road* (1933), played this 1927 house, another work of **Herbert J. Krapp**. *A Party with Comden and Green, At the Drop of a Hat, Beyond the Fringe,* and Victor Borge kept audiences laughing here. ♦ 252 W 45th St (between Shubert Alley and Eighth Ave). Telecharge 239.6200 &

52 Royale Actress Mae West kept house here for three years as the title character in *Diamond Lil.* The theater was used as a radio studio by CBS from 1936 to 1940. Laurence Olivier dazzled audiences with his appearances in *The Entertainer* and *Becket. Grease,* which was Broadway's longest-running musical at the time, settled here during its last years. ♦ 242 W 45th St (between Shubert Alley and Eighth Ave). Telecharge 239.6200 &

53 Imperial *Rosemarie* and *Oh, Kay!* set the tone for this theater, which was built by **Herbert J. Krapp** in 1923. Hit musicals have always found a home here: *Babes in Toyland, Jubilee, Leave It to Me, Annie Get Your Gun,* and the incomparable Zero Mostel performing "If I Were a Rich Man" in *Fiddler on the Roof. Les Misérables,* based on Victor Hugo's novel set in 19th-century France, is currently in its thirteenth year. ♦ 249 W 45th St (between Broadway and Eighth Ave). Telecharge 239.6200 &

53 Music Box Composer Irving Berlin built this charming theater to accommodate his *Music Box Revue of 1921.* Also presented here were the first musical to win a Pulitzer Prize, George Gershwin's *Of Thee I Sing;* John Steinbeck's *Of Mice and Men;* Kurt Weill's last musical, *Lost in the Stars;* and Kim Stanley in *Bus Stop.* ♦ 239 W 45th St (between Broadway and Eighth Ave). Telecharge 239.6200 &

54 Plymouth *Abe Lincoln in Illinois,* with Raymond Massey, opened not long after John and Lionel Barrymore appeared here together in *The Jest.* The theater was built in 1917 by **Herbert J. Krapp.** ♦ 236 W 45th St (between Shubert Alley and Eighth Ave). Telecharge 239.6200 &

54 Booth Although this 1913 theater, created by **Henry B. Herts,** was named for Edwin Booth, Shirley Booth also made a name for herself here with Sidney Blackmer in *Come Back, Little Sheba.* ♦ 222 W 45th St (at Shubert Alley). Telecharge 239.6200 &

55 Marriott Marquis $$$ This hotel boasts the world's tallest atrium, through which its glass-enclosed elevators zip up and down, serving 47 floors and 1,911 rooms! It has a Broadway theater on the third floor, New York's largest ballroom, and its highest lobby (reached by a chain of escalators passing through floor after quiet floor of meeting rooms). The two on-site gyms have Nautilus,

sauna, Jacuzzi, and a trainer, if you need a push. Valet parking, concierge, and several restaurants and lounges are also available in this 1985 creation of **John Portman.** ♦ 1535 Broadway (between W 45th and W 46th Sts). 398.1900, 800/228.9290; fax 704.8930 &

Within the Marriott Marquis:

Marquis Many expected it to suffer from its somewhat untheatrical surroundings—and the bad press caused by the demolition of several old theaters to make way for it. The ill will seems to have been forgotten, however, during the almost four-year run of the theater's first production, *Me and My Girl.* ♦ Ticketmaster 307.4100

The View ★$$$$ This is New York's only revolving restaurant: It has a limited view, as do the revolving lounges above it, but when the turntable takes you past **Rockefeller Center** and the skyline to the east and uptown you'll be glad you took a ride in that glass elevator. ♦ Continental ♦ Tu-Sa dinner; Su lunch and dinner. Reservations required; no sneakers or jeans permitted. 704.8900

56 Minskoff In 1973, Debbie Reynolds opened this house with a revival of *Irene.* Capacious and modern, it has housed more technically extravagant productions since then, including *Sunset Boulevard* by Andrew Lloyd Weber. ♦ 200 W 45th St (at Broadway). 869.0550; Ticketmaster 307.4100 &

57 Roundabout Theatre This theater was built in 1928 by **Thompson, Holmes & Converse.** Under the leadership of producing director Todd Haimes, the **Roundabout** has won recognition as one of the city's finest theatrical organizations. It remains committed to producing classics by the world's greatest playwrights—Ibsen's *Ghosts,* Pirandello's *Enrico IV,* Carson McCullers's *Member of the Wedding*—at affordable prices. ♦ 1530 Broadway (between W 44th and W 45th Sts). 869.8400 &

58 Official All Star Cafe ★★$$ Fans of all seasons will cheer for this trilevel restaurant offering a state-of-the-art sports experience that will entertain as well as satisfy. Once seated in the baseball-glove–shaped banquettes, sports buffs can enjoy giant hamburgers, ball-park hot dogs, spicy Buffalo shrimp, egg rolls served with a red chili sauce and Chinese mustard, chili, meat loaf with mashed potatoes, and fried chicken with pepper gravy. Sports memorabilia, viewing screens, huge scoreboards, and overhead "blimp" all score a hit. ♦ American ♦ Daily lunch and dinner. 1540 Broadway (at W 45th St). 840.8326 &

58 Virgin Megastore Modeled after its London flagship sister, this perpetually mobbed multilevel store boasts more than 150,000 music titles (on CD and cassette), 15,000 video titles, and a well-stocked bookstore.

Listening stations with headphones allow customers to hear before they buy. ♦ Daily. 1540 Broadway (between W 45th and W 46th Sts). 921.1020. Also at: Union Square South (corner of 14th St and Broadway). 947.5010

59 Lyceum Producer Daniel Frohman built this theater in 1903. Now a city landmark, it is the oldest New York house still used for legitimate productions. It opened with *The Proud Prince.* In 1947, Judy Holliday and Paul Douglas wise-cracked through *Born Yesterday.* The **A.P.A.–Phoenix Repertory** made this home base for several seasons, and in 1980, *Morning's at Seven* by Paul Osborn was revived here. A lyric, Neo-Baroque structure with banded columns and undulating marquee, it was the first theater designed by **Herts & Tallant,** undisputed kings of theater architecture. Frohman was such a theater fan that he had his apartment above the theater fitted with a trapdoor through which he could see the stage. ♦ 149 W 45th St (between Sixth Ave and Broadway). Telecharge 239.6200 ♿

59 Hamburger Harry's ★$ In addition to the 16 varieties of major-league burgers served at this casual grill, the mesquite-grilled seafood and steaks lure connoisseurs of the rare and well done. A Mexican accent adds color to the menu—the Ha-Ha Burger comes freighted with chilies, guacamole, *salsa verde,* and cheddar cheese. ♦ American ♦ M-Sa lunch and dinner. 145 W 45th St (between Sixth Ave and Broadway). 840.2756. Also at: 157 Chambers St (between Hudson and Greenwich Sts). 267.4446

60 Cabana Carioca ★★$$ The narrow, flamboyantly painted staircase leads to several different floors, but wherever you decide to sit, you can count on seriously large servings of Brazilian food. Don't miss the suckling pig, steak dishes, and *feijoada,* a traditional Brazilian Sunday afternoon dish of black beans and pork, served here every day. If you really want to get into the spirit, try a potent *caipirinha* (a drink made from a sugarcane-derived spirit, crushed lemon, ice, and sugar). ♦ Brazilian ♦ Daily lunch and dinner. 123 W 45th St (between Sixth Ave and Broadway). 581.8088

61 American Place Founded with the intention of providing a forum for living American playwrights, this theater opened originally at **St. Clement's Church** in 1964 with two memorable plays: Robert Lowell's *Old Glory* and William Alfred's *Hogan's Goat.* In 1971, a brand new theater with a modified thrust stage

was built, adding another dimension to the quality productions. ♦ 111 W 46th St (between Sixth Ave and Broadway). 840.3074 ♿

62 Actor's Equity Building This is the union for all stage actors in America—from the virtually unknown to the most famous. It was founded in 1913 by 112 actors to protect the rights and establish good working conditions for professional stage performers and stage managers. If you're into stargazing, keep your eyes peeled. ♦ 165 W 46th St (between Sixth Ave and Broadway)

63 I. Miller Building Almost hidden behind advertising signs, on the facade of the building, are sculptures of great women of the theater: Marilyn Miller, Rosa Ponselle, Ethel Barrymore, and Mary Pickford, none of whom would have thought of appearing on stage in anything but I. Miller shoes. The figures are by Alexander Stirling Calder, whose son, Alexander Calder, invented the mobile. The shoe store is gone, but the ladies are still here, at least for now. ♦ W 46th St (at Broadway)

64 Duffy Square World War I chaplain of the Fighting 69th, Father Francis P. Duffy served as pastor of nearby **Holy Cross Church** and is honored in this triangle with a 1937 sculpture by Charles Keck at West 46th Street. He shares the honor with a 1959 statue by George Lober of *George M. Cohan,* the actor/producer/writer who wrote "Give My Regards to Broadway," among hundreds of other songs. ♦ Bounded by Seventh Ave and Broadway, and W 46th and W 47th Sts

64 TKTS The Theater Development Fund, housed in this 1973 work of **Mayers & Schiff,** sells tickets to Broadway and Off-Broadway shows and **Lincoln Center** productions; tickets are sold at half-price (plus a service charge) for performances on the day of sale. Tickets are not available for every show, but a board tells you what is on sale. A better selection is sometimes available close to curtain time, when producers release unused house seats, and during bad weather, when fewer people venture out. Also try Monday and Tuesday evenings, when most theaters alternate closing. ♦ Tickets go on sale 10AM for matinees, 3PM for evening performances. No credit cards or personal checks accepted. W 47th St and Broadway. 768.1818 ♿ Also at: 2 World Trade Center, Church St (between Liberty and Vesey Sts). Same phone number ♿

65 Times Square Visitors Center In this bright, capacious space you can purchase tickets for Broadway shows (at the **Broadway Ticket Center**), book sight-seeing tours and airport transportation, get cash or exchange currency, surf the Net, and obtain free brochures. There's also a video history of Times Square. ♦ Daily 8AM-8PM. 1560 Broadway (between W 46th and W 47th Sts). No phone

65 Palace Theater "Playing the Palace" was the dream of every vaudeville performer from the theater's 1913 opening well into the 1930s. The advent of movies brought hard times, but the theater was renovated and reopened as a showcase for big musicals in 1966. *Sweet Charity, Applause, La Cage aux Folles,* and *The Will Rogers Follies* were among its long-running hits; its newest arrival, *Aida,* is an extravagant musical featuring songs by Elton John & Tim Rice. ♦ 1564 Broadway (between W 46th and W 47th Sts). 730.8200; Ticketmaster 307.4100 ♿

65 Doubletree Guest Suites $$$ This modern 460-suite hotel is within easy walking distance of **Rockefeller Center,** Fifth Avenue shopping, **Lincoln Center,** and Broadway theaters. There's also a restaurant, the **Center Stage Cafe.** ♦ 1568 Broadway (at W 47th St). 719.1600, 800/222.8733; fax 921.5212 ♿

66 Portland Square Hotel $ This was once home to James Cagney, Lila Lee, and John Boles. Today, the renovated budget-priced hotel features 136 attractive rooms. ♦ 132 W 47th St (between Sixth and Seventh Aves). 382.0600, 800/388.8988; fax 382.0684 ♿

67 Renaissance New York $$$ Opened in 1992, this Marriott-owned property boasts a Postmodern structure by **Stephen B. Jacobs** in the heart of Times Square. All 305 rooms, including 10 one-bedroom suites, feature richly furnished accommodations that include such amenities as 3 telephones in each room, call waiting, fax ports, voice mail, and VCRs. There's also the added benefit of a 24-hour concierge service that will secure theater tickets in no time. The top three **Club Floors** offer additional personal services. ♦ 714 Seventh Ave (between W 47th and W 48th Sts). 765.7676, 800/228.9898; fax 765.1962 ♿

Within the Renaissance New York:

Foley's Fish House ★★$$ For more than 90 years, the Foleys have been purveyors of the freshest seafood sold to the finest US restaurants. Now they're lending their name to this hotel dining room. Try the fried shrimp with seaweed and sesame salad, mahimahi with river-harvested roasted shallots, or seared shark with warm white-bean salad and marinated arugula. A must for any seafood lover are the great choices of chowders. ♦ Seafood ♦ Daily lunch and dinner. Reservations recommended. 261.5200

68 Lunt-Fontanne Mary Martin and Theodor Bikel appeared here in *The Sound of Music,* and Marlene Dietrich performed here alone not long afterward. The theater, a work of **Carrère & Hastings,** dates to 1910. ♦ 205 W 46th St (between Broadway and Eighth Ave) 575.9200; Ticketmaster 307.4100 ♿

69 Richard Rodgers Gwen Verdon appeared here in *Damn Yankees, Redhead,* and *New C in Town.* It is also where Olsen & Johnson began the long-running *Hellzapoppin'.* Formerly the **46th Street Theater,** built in 1925 by **Herbert J. Krapp,** it was dedicated Richard Rodgers in 1990. ♦ 226 W 46th St (between Broadway and Eighth Ave). 221.1211; Ticketmaster 307.4100 ♿

70 Paramount Hotel $$$ This venture from hotelier Ian Schrager and French designer Philippe Starck is more affordably priced tha its sister, the **Hotel Royalton** (see page 174) The 610-room hotel, in a building erected in 1928 by **Thomas W. Lamb,** is reminiscent of movie set, with a large gray staircase that loc as though it could lead up to a spaceship but goes only as far as the mezzanine, where foo is served. Elevators are illuminated in differe colors: purple and orange, for example; and bathrooms in the smallish rooms (the less expensive rooms can be downright tiny) contain some futuristic Starck designs like silver cone-shaped sinks and lamps that resemble stethoscopes. Amenities include fitness and business centers, VCRs and fres flowers in every room, a **Dean & DeLuca** gourmet shop, the popular **Whiskey** bar, anc children's playroom. ♦ 235 W 46th St (betwe Broadway and Eighth Ave). 764.5500, 800/225.7474; fax 354.5237

Within the Paramount Hotel:

The Mezzanine ★★$$$ Though you'll b able to watch the comings and goings of people down in the lobby from this perch, th food will make a bid for your attention, too. The varied menu ranges from light grilled-chicken and wild-mushroom salad to the more substantial mustard-glazed salmon fil and roasted loin of lamb in a red-wine sauc It's also a good place to come for dessert— the banana splits and ice-cream sodas are great. ♦ American ♦ Daily breakfast, lunch, and dinner. 764.5500

Coco Pazzo Teatro ★★$$$ Pino Luong owner of such culinary hot spots as **Le Mad** and **Mad 61,** opened this more informal, Broadway version of his uptown **Coco Pazz** featuring plenty of banquettes and mirrors s that diners can see and be seen. The menu splendid mix of Italian with Asian overtones that's pleasing to the eyes as well as to the palate. Good choices include pasta specials braised lamb spiced with orange zest, olives and fava beans; and calf's liver with sautéed onions and polenta. Desserts are heavenly– especially the tangy cool watermelon parfai

♦ Italian ♦ Daily lunch and dinner. Reservations recommended. 827.4222

71 Broadway Inn $$ Located in the heart of Times Square, this is one of the smaller guest houses in the city (40 rooms, each with private bath), and its intimate surroundings make it truly a home away from home. The inn's interiors are contemporary, with exposed brick walls in the lobby, modern furnishings, and foliage throughout. A complimentary breakfast is served daily. ♦ 264 W 46th St (at Eighth Ave). 997.9200, 800/826.6300; fax 768.2807

72 Orso ★★$$$ It's easy to relax at this Northern Italian bistro serving pasta, seafood, veal, and wonderful pizzas—try the pie topped with roasted peppers, sun-dried vegetables, provolone, and sage. The handsome marble bar is an inviting place to unwind either before or after the theater. ♦ Italian ♦ Daily lunch and dinner. Reservations recommended. 322 W 46th St (between Eighth and Ninth Aves). 489.7212

72 Joe Allen ★$$ Here is an opportunity to gaze upon posters of Broadway shows, handsome waiters, a stagestruck clientele, and occasionally the stars themselves. A blackboard menu lists the basic fare—salads, chili, or grilled fish—but the place is famous for its hamburgers, meat loaf, and fries. ♦ American ♦ M-F lunch and dinner; Sa-Su brunch and dinner. 326 W 46th St (between Eighth and Ninth Aves). 581.6464

Since 1906

73 Barbetta ★★★$$$ Owner Laura Maioglio oversees every detail of this splendid Italian restaurant, first established by her father over 90 years ago. The two-story interior has been skillfully refurbished with 18th-century Piemontese and American antiques. The menu is as classic as the decor: Examples include *linguine al pesto* with Yukon gold potatoes, roasted organic rabbit in white wine with savoy cabbage, and char-grilled squab with cranberry beans and foie gras. Always a sensation are the truffles that are used in a number of the dishes. Classic desserts—try the zuppa inglese— are superb, and the extensive wine list boasts many Italian varieties. ♦ Northern Italian ♦ M-Sa lunch and dinner. Reservations recommended. 321 W 46th St (between Eighth and Ninth Aves). 246.9171

74 Becco ★★$$ The Bastianich family, who own the felicitous **Felidia** restaurant on the East Side, are also the proprietors of this informal spot on Restaurant Row. A wide variety of flavorful Italian dishes, such as wild-mushroom risotto and roasted suckling pig, are featured. The prix-fixe lunch and daily menus are both good values. ♦ Italian ♦ Daily lunch and dinner. 355 W 46th St (between Eighth and Ninth Aves). 397.7597

74 Lattanzi ★★$$$ Enjoy a taste of the Roman Jewish Quarter in a casual atmosphere. Baby artichokes sautéed in olive oil, homemade pastas, and grilled fish are all made to order. ♦ Italian ♦ M-F lunch and dinner; Sa dinner. Reservations recommended. 361 W 46th St (between Eighth and Ninth Aves). 315.0980

75 Firebird ★★★★$$$ Within two adjacent Restaurant Row brownstones is a luxe Imperial Russian flight of fantasy that's as much about theater as cuisine—perhaps more. Dining here is like eating inside the Hermitage in St. Petersburg, circa 1912, with its pricey paintings, elegant chandeliers, original costumes from Diaghilev's famed Ballets Russes, and museum-caliber Russian artifacts. The menu features such czarist savories as buttered buckweat blini and sevruga caviar with sour cream, seared Karski shashlik, and marinated boneless lamb with fruit and almond pilaf and red pepper salad. Even if this kind of food doesn't appeal to you, consider stopping by for a vodka-laced libation pre- or post-theater. ♦ Russian ♦ Daily dinner. Reservations recommended. 365 W 46th St (between Eighth and Ninth Aves). 586.0244

76 Hour Glass Tavern ★$$ Believe it or not, there's a homey, old-fashioned, laid-back feeling here, despite the hourglass above the table that gives customers exactly 60 minutes to savor the reasonably priced, 3-course prix-fixe dinner. Tasty entrées include a spicy grilled blackened shrimp or salmon fillet; homemade lamb sausage; and penne with hot sausage, chicken, and spinach. ♦ American ♦ M-Tu, Sa-Su dinner; W-F lunch and dinner. No credit cards accepted. 373 W 46th St (between Eighth and Ninth Aves). 265.2060 ♿

77 Koyote Kate's ★$$ If you've got a hankering for honky-tonking, this is the place. The Tex-Mex menu here includes a good 10-ounce burger and jalapeño shrimp (the peppers are stuffed with whole shrimp, breaded, and deep-fried). Dip these in sour cream to put out the fire, or better yet, order a frozen margarita or two and go hog wild. There's live country and blues music Tuesday through Saturday evenings. ♦ Tex-Mex ♦ M-F lunch and dinner; Sa-Su dinner and late-night meals. 307 W 47th St (between Eighth and Ninth Aves). 956.1091

On 13 May 1890, Mrs. Andrew Carnegie laid the cornerstone for the new Carnegie Music Hall. Amazingly, it was opened one year later.

77 B. Smith's ★★$$$ Like its owner, former model/actress Barbara Smith, this restaurant is sleek, elegant, and contemporary. The entrées are creatively presented and intriguingly prepared. Try Caribbean-style tournedos of tuna with pigeon peas and rice in a coconut milk–curry sauce or a grilled mango-glazed spiced scampi. Sweet potato–pecan pie and profiteroles are the favorite desserts. ◆ Continental ◆ M-F lunch and dinner; Sa-Su brunch and dinner. Reservations recommended. 771 Eighth Ave (at W 47th St). 247.2222

78 Brooks Atkinson The former **Mansfield**, designed by **Herbert J. Krapp** in 1926, was renamed in 1960 in honor of the *Times* critic. *Come Blow Your Horn*, the first in a series of Neil Simon comedy hits, opened here. Charles Grodin and Ellen Burstyn performed here for three years in *Same Time Next Year*. ◆ 256 W 47th St (between Broadway and Eighth Ave). 719.4099; Ticketmaster 307.4100 ♿

78 Pierre au Tunnel ★★$$$ A good Theater District standby, this place serves excellent bistro fare, especially such Old World specialties as *tripes à la mode de Caen* (calf's stomach lining, in a consommé with white wine, apple brandy, potatoes, carrots, and white turnips) and *tête de veau vinaigrette* (calf brains, tongue, and cheek in a thick mustard vinaigrette with capers). ◆ French ◆ M-Sa lunch and dinner. Reservations required. 250 W 47th St (between Broadway and Eighth Ave). 575.1220

Macy's, which claims to be "The World's Largest Store," boasts over two million square feet of floor space.

On 19 June 1997, when the Winter Garden theater production of *Cats* set its records as the longest-running show in Broadway history, it had been seen by 8 million people, employed 231 actors, sold 390,000 T-shirts, and contributed an estimated $3.12 billion to the New York City economy. When Andrew Lloyd Webber decided to close the show in Summer 2000, it was still drawing an audience of nearly 9,000 people every week.

Which US city has the most historical places? No, it's not Washington. According to the National Register of Historic Places, New York has the most—624 officially registered spots. Philadelphia is second with 470, and Washington comes in third with 335.

Restaurants/Clubs: Red **Hotels:** Blue
Shops/ ▾ Outdoors: Green **Sights/Culture:** Black

79 Barrymore One of the great artists of her era, Ethel Barrymore opened this theater (designed by **Herbert J. Krapp**) in 1928 in *Kingdom of God.* The stage has seen the start of many illustrious careers: Fred Astaire danced his way to stardom in Cole Porter's *The Gay Divorce* (filmed as *The Gay Divorcée*); Walter Huston introduced the haunting standard "September Song" in *Knickerbocker Holiday;* and Marlon Brando first achieved prominence when he costarred with Jessica Tandy in *A Streetcar Named Desire*. ◆ 243 W 47th St (between Broadway and Eighth Ave). Telecharge 239.6200 ♿

80 Pong Sri ★$$ This place has long received high marks for being among the city's most authentic Thai restaurants (although some Thai food fanatics complain that the usual fiery spices have been toned down to accommodate the American palate), alongside Chinatown's **Thailand Restaurant** (see page 38), which is under the same management. Dishes include lobster stir-fry with basil leaf and chili paste, whole deep-fried red snapper with a hot and spicy sauce, and assorted vegetables with bean curd in red curry and coconut milk. ◆ Thai ◆ Daily lunch and dinner. 244 W 48th St (between Broadway and Eighth Ave). 582.3392.

81 Longacre In the 1930s, **The Group Theater** premiered three Clifford Odets plays: *Waiting for Lefty, Paradise Lost,* and *Till the Day I Die*. Julie Harris appeared in *The Lark* and *Little Moon of Alban*. In 1960, theater of the absurd invaded Broadway with the brilliant Zero Mostel in *Rhinoceros* by Eugene Ionesco. In 1980, *Children of a Lesser God* won a Tony. The 1913 building is the work of **Henry B. Herts**. ◆ 220 W 48th St (between Broadway and Eighth Ave). Telecharge 239.6200 ♿

82 Walter Kerr It took precisely 66 days for the Shubert Organization and eminent theater designer **Herbert J. Krapp** to build the former **Ritz Theatre** in 1921. It opened with Clare Eames in John Drinkwater's *Mary Stuart* and left audiences spellbound in 1924 with Sutton Vane's eerie *Outward Bound*, starring Alfred Lunt and Leslie Howard. After years of being used for live radio and TV broadcasts, the theater underwent restoration and returned to legitimacy in 1971 with the rock opera *Soon*. Heavily restored again in 1983, the house easily ranks as one of Broadway's most beautiful theaters and authentically executed restorations, a showcase of Italian Renaissance detail. It was the home of Tony Kushner's unqualified hit *Angels in America*, a two-part AIDS epic (*Millennium Approaches* and *Perestroika*) that many claim brought integrity back to Broadway drama. ◆ 219 W 48th St (between Broadway and Eighth Ave). Telecharge 239.6200 ♿

83 Holiday Inn Crowne Plaza $$$ The 1989 arrival of the ultracontemporary chain's crown jewel gave a major boost to the ongoing effort to revamp the Times Square area. The 770 rooms are ideally situated for sight-seeing and theatergoing. For a view of Broadway, book a room on the east side; to see the Hudson River, book the west side. The **Club Floor** features a lounge and complimentary beverages with snacks. Indulge in one of the popular restaurants—**Broadway Grill, Samplings,** or **The Balcony**—and work off those calories at the pool or fitness center. ♦ 1605 Broadway (between W 48th and W 49th Sts). 977.4000, 800/243.NYNY; fax 333.7393 &

84 Cort Many fine plays have opened on this stage, including *The Swan, Merton of the Movies, Charley's Aunt,* and *Lady Windermere's Fan.* But one of the most poignant was *The Diary of Anne Frank,* by famed Hollywood writers Frances and Albert Hackett, which won a Pulitzer in 1955. The theme of children living under political oppression returned here in the 1980s with *Sarafina!* In 1990, *The Grapes of Wrath* took the Tony for best play. ♦ 138 W 48th St (between Sixth and Seventh Aves). Telecharge 239.6200 &

85 Sam Ash Music Store For decades this block of West 48th Street has been a musicians' mecca. Orchestral and rock 'n' roll musicians—from those struggling at the bottom of the heap to those celebrating at the top of the charts—come here for state-of-the-art supplies and equipment. Wander in just to see who's buying. ♦ M-Sa. 160 W 48th St (between Sixth and Seventh Aves). 719.2661 &

The Drama Book Shop
Since 1923

86 Drama Book Shop Established in 1923, this is one of the city's most comprehensive sources of books on the dramatic arts (the **Library and Museum of Performing Arts at Lincoln Center,** see page 264, is another). Subject areas include domestic and foreign theater, performers, music, dance, makeup, lighting, props, staging, and even puppetry and magic. ♦ Daily. 723 Seventh Ave (between W 48th and W 49th Sts), Second floor. 944.0595 &

87 Caroline's Comedy Club This upscale venue is a major stop on the comedy club circuit for up-and-coming talent. Jerry Seinfeld, Jay Leno, and Billy Crystal all cut their teeth here. Dinner is served, but you can just order drinks. ♦ Cover; drink minimum. Shows M-Th,

Su 8PM; F-Sa 8PM, 10:30PM. Reservations required. 1626 Broadway (between W 49th and W 50th Sts). 757.4100 &

88 The Brill Building At the turn of the century, publishers of popular songs were all located on 28th Street west of Broadway. The noise of pianos and raspy-voiced song pluggers gave the name "Tin Pan Alley" to the street. When the action moved uptown, the publishers moved to this building and brought the name with them. The bust of the young man over the door is a memorial to the son of the building's original owner, who died just before construction began. ♦ 1619 Broadway (between W 49th and W 50th Sts)

Within The Brill Building:

Colony Records An institution for recordings and sheet music for soundtracks, shows, and jazz, this is a fun stop for post-theater browsing. ♦ Daily 9:30AM-1AM. 265.2050 &

89 Ambassador Built in 1921, this is another work of **Herbert J. Krapp.** In 1939, Imogene Coca, Alfred Drake, and Danny Kaye began their careers here in the *Strawhat Review.* ♦ 215 W 49th St (between Broadway and Eighth Ave). 735.0500; Telecharge 239.6200

90 Eugene O'Neill This 1925 work of **Herbert J. Krapp** was the site of Arthur Miller's first major success, *All My Sons,* which opened here in 1947 with Ed Begley and Arthur Kennedy. The revival of *Death of a Salesman* was garnering rave reviews here at press time. ♦ 230 W 49th St (between Broadway and Eighth Ave). Telecharge 239.6200 &

90 The Time $$$ Downtown funk meets Times Square madness at this new and decidedly unconventional hotel, where each guest room is done up in a primary color—red, yellow or blue. In a blue room, for example, you'll find not only blue furnishings but an artfully displayed blue fruit for the tasting and a "blue" inspired scent in the bathroom. Reserve a room according to your mood (or the mood you think you'll be in when you arrive). The hotel's public spaces have hardly any color at all. This wonderfully wacky stuff is the brainchild of dashing young hotelier (and former *Vogue* model) Vikram Chatwal. The gifted, Transylvanian-born Adam D. Tihany is responsible for the creative concept and interior design of this luxury property, which has 164 rooms and 28 suites, as well as the hotel's high-profile restaurant **Palladin.** ♦ 224 W 49th St (between Broadway and Eighth Ave). 320.2925, 877/TIME.NYC; fax 320.2926; www.thetimeny.com

91 Worldwide Plaza Changes in zoning laws encouraged the construction of this mixed-use complex of residences and offices on the site of the second **Madison Square Garden** (1925-66). The apartment towers were designed by **Frank Williams;** the office tower by **Skidmore, Owings & Merrill.** Both were built in 1989 in a slow but successful attempt to bring commercial activity to this area of Eighth Avenue. Commercial occupants include Ogilvy & Mather and Polygram Records. ◆ Bounded by Eighth and Ninth Aves, and W 49th and W 50th Sts

92 Chez Napoléon ★★$$ Tucked away at the edge of the Theater District is this intimate bistro, where the menu features such classic French dishes as onion soup, escargots, steak au poivre, *choucroute garni* (sauerkraut garnished with potatoes and pork), and chocolate mousse, and the kitchen does them all justice. ◆ French ◆ M-F lunch and dinner; Sa dinner. Reservations recommended. 365 W 50th St (between Eighth and Ninth Aves). 265.6980

93 Café Des Sports ★$ Although regular customers would no doubt prefer that this dining spot remain one of New York's better-kept secrets, the staff ensures that all newcomers are warmly welcomed. The menu features such traditional French dishes as roasted breast of chicken and grilled steak. ◆ French ◆ M-F lunch and dinner; Sa-Su dinner. 329 W 51st St (between Eighth and Ninth Aves). 974.9052

93 René Pujol ★★$$ A truly old-fashioned bistro, this town house dining room is filled with French country atmosphere and decor, including an exposed brick wall and pottery on display. Try the lobster bisque, roasted breast of duck, grilled steak, or rack of lamb. The crème brûlée and any of the soufflés are highly recommended. ◆ French ◆ M-Sa lunch and dinner. Reservations recommended. 321 W 51st St (between Eighth and Ninth Aves). 246.3023

94 Les Pyrénées ★★$$$ The working fireplace at this casual country restaurant makes it a cozy spot, especially in winter. Recommended dishes include rack of lamb, escargots, cassoulet, grilled Dover sole, thin apple tart, and chocolate mousse. ◆ French ◆ M-Sa lunch and dinner; Su dinner.

Reservations recommended. 251 W 51st St (between Broadway and Eighth Ave). 246.0044

95 Gershwin Formerly the **Uris Theater,** the structure—built in 1972 by **Ralph Alswang**—presents lavish revivals of such well-loved musicals as *Showboat* and *Candide.* ◆ 222 W 51st St (between Broadway and Eighth Ave). 586.6510; Ticketmaster 307.4100 ♿

96 Ellen's Stardust Diner ★$ The burgers here won't win any awards, but they're delivered to the shake, rattle, and roll of 1950s music. The menu gets as fancy as grilled swordfish, but your best bet is a Velveeta cheeseburger and an ice-cream sundae for dessert. Be prepared to wait. ◆ American ◆ Daily breakfast, lunch, dinner, and late-night meals. 1650 Broadway (at W 51st St). 956.5151

96 Winter Garden This beautiful theater, designed by **W.A. Swasey,** opened with Al Jolson in 1911. The Shuberts produced 12 annual editions of their revue *The Passing Show.* Fanny Brice, Bob Hope, and Josephine Baker were featured in the *Ziegfeld Follies.* Other hits were *Plain and Fancy, West Side Story, Funny Girl,* and the record-shattering 18-year run of *Cats* which finally closed in June of 2000. ◆ 1634 Broadway (between W 50th and W 51st Sts) Telecharge 239.6200 ♿

97 Sheraton Manhattan $$$ A heated indoor swimming pool, a sun deck, and a gym with modern equipment are features of this conveniently located 660-room hotel. Rates are slightly more expensive here than across the street. Children stay free if no extra bed is required. ◆ 790 Seventh Ave (between W 51st and W 52nd Sts). 581.3300, 800/325.3535; fax 315.4265 ♿

98 Equitable Center A huge mural created by Roy Lichtenstein for this 1985 building by **Edward Larrabee Barnes** brings you in off the street. Inside are other works of art to be seen, but the famous Thomas Hart Benton murals, painted in 1930, have been moved one block east on 51st Street to 1290 Sixth Avenue, where they can be viewed to better advantage in the lobby. Also off the building's lobby are the **Equitable Gallery** and the **Brooklyn Museum Shop.** ◆ Gallery and shop: M-Sa. 787 Seventh Ave (between W 51st and W 52nd Sts). 554.4818

Within the Equitable Center:
Le Bernardin ★★★★$$$$ The elegant wood-paneled room with a collection of maritime art is a gracious setting in which to appreciate the heady cooking of chef Eric Ripert, protégé of late owner Gilbert Le Coze. If you love seafood you can't go wrong on the near-poetic menu, but you might start with the crab and shrimp bouillabaisse aioli (crab cake melting in a rich saffron lobster broth,

with poached shrimp and croutons), or the now classic tuna carpaccio, and follow with the panroasted loin of monkfish studded with roasted garlic and rosemary, with lemon tagliatelle, toasted pine nuts, aged parmesan, and parsley oil; or a whole red snapper baked in rosemary and thyme salt crust (a dish with a two-person minimum that requires 24 hours' notice). Pastry chef Florian Bellanger works his own kind of magic to create a frozen tangerine parfait on a meringue with nougat and tangerine sauces, a warm chocolate tart with melting whipped cream and dark chocolate sauce, homemade ice creams and sorbets and more. Service is as flawless as the food. ♦ French/Seafood ♦ M-F lunch and dinner; Sa dinner. Reservations required. 155 W 51st St (between Sixth and Seventh Aves). 489.1515

Palio ★★★$$$$ Named for a horse-racing festival in the Italian town of Siena, Maria Pia Hellrigl's restaurant is worth a visit if only to see the stunning interior designed by **Skidmore, Owings & Merrill.** The lovely table appointments are by Vignelli Associates, and a wraparound Sandro Chia mural surrounds the ground-floor bar, where the Bellinis (an apéritif of peach nectar and Champagne) are a delight. The upstairs dining room delivers luxury in every detail—from the fine crystal to each perfect rose. Another reason to visit is the menu of delectable treats like homemade ravioli stuffed with foie gras and duckling, *spaghettini con frutti di mare* (pasta with seafood), and *branzino ai sapori d'autunno* (sea bass with herbs and seasonal vegetables). For dessert, try the black-polenta *timbale* (molded dessert) with marinated grapes. ♦ Italian ♦ M-F lunch and dinner; Sa dinner. Reservations recommended; jacket and tie recommended, even at the bar. 151 W 51st St (between Sixth and Seventh Aves). 245.4850 &

99 Michelangelo $$$ Some of the space of the old **Taft Hotel** has gotten a new lease on life in the form of this 178-room marble-and-crystal palace that belongs to the Star Italian chain of hotels—hence its name and the large number of Italian guests. Amenities include 24-hour room service, a concierge, a complimentary 24-hour fitness center, and access (for a fee) to a health club across the street. The larger-than-average rooms have TVs in hand-inlaid armoires (and smaller TVs in the bathrooms). Valet parking is available. Another plus (for families): The management *likes* children. ♦ 152 W 51st St (at Seventh Ave). 765.1900, 800/237.0990; fax 541.6604 &

Within the Michelangelo:

Limoncello ★★★$$$ Owner Romeo DeGobbi's intimate establishment boasts simple decor, polished walls, and beautiful hand-painted Art Nouveau watercolors and murals—a serene setting for chef Sal Musso's creations. Select from any of the homemade pastas and risottos or try confit of duckling, or veal medaillons sautéed with Marsala and walnuts. Top off the meal with a fruit tart, tiramisù, or an excellent sorbet. ♦ Italian ♦ M-F breakfast, lunch, and dinner; Sa breakfast and dinner; Su breakfast. Reservations recommended. 777 Seventh Ave (between W 50th and W 51st Sts). 582.1310

100 Cité ★★★$$$ Designed to resemble a grand Parisian cafe, this elegant restaurant is filled with artifacts imported from that city: floral-pattern Art Deco grillwork from the original Au Bon Marché department store and intricate crystal chandeliers from an old Parisian cinema. It's a gracious space in which to enjoy simple, top-quality food. Chef David Amorelli prepares some dishes with a Mediterranean slant, including the excellent grilled-corn chowder, grilled tuna with ginger chutney and wild rice croquettes, and herb-crusted salmon steak with braised cabbage and horseradish beurre blanc. However, for a truly Parisian experience, order the shrimp or lobster cocktail, followed by a fine roasted prime rib or filet mignon au poivre. The extensive wine list is expertly employed in a promotion that's become popular all over town: Four excellent wines are included with the prix-fixe dinner after 8PM. For more casual tastes, the less expensive but equally high quality **Cité Grill** is right next door. ♦ French ♦ M-F lunch and dinner; Sa-Su brunch and dinner. Reservations recommended. 120 W 51st St (between Sixth and Seventh Aves). 956.7100 &

101 Looking Toward the Avenue Installed in 1989, the three enormous bronze *Venuses* (ranging in height from 14 to 23 feet) by artist Jim Dine are a humanizing presence amid the impersonal towers that surround them. ♦ 1301 Sixth Ave (at W 52nd St)

The New York City Council passed a bill requiring that photographic records be made of any building about to be razed. The photos become part of the municipal archives. Councilman Harry Stein, sponsor of the bill, said his only regret was that no one had thought of the idea 150 years before.

102 Ben Benson's Steakhouse ★★★$$$$
This classic-style New York restaurant serves massive portions of meat—including T-bones, aged sirloins, and triple-cut lamb chops—that few will be able to finish in one sitting. Other dishes, some meatless, are also impressive: Maryland crab cakes, Maine lobster, whole roasted chicken, and broiled fillet of sole are all superb. If you have any room left for dessert, try the cheesecake. The latest addition, a charming, flower-framed outdoor cafe, offers lighter fare—soups, sandwiches, salads, and pasta dishes—as well as a petite filet mignon au poivre, English-cut prime rib, and grilled pork tenderloin. Alfresco diners can also select items from the regular menu. ♦ American ♦ M-F lunch and dinner; Sa-Su dinner. Reservations recommended. 123 W 52nd St (between Sixth and Seventh Aves). 581.8888

103 Sheraton New York Hotel & Towers $$$
This efficient, modern, 1,700-room hotel has excellent convention facilities for the mainly corporate clientele. Guests have use of the indoor swimming pool across the street at the pricier **Sheraton Manhattan**. There are several restaurants and lounges, and room service is available until 1AM. ♦ 811 Seventh Ave (between W 52nd and W 53rd Sts). 581.1000, 800/325.3535; fax 841.6496 &

104 Martini's ★$$ Come here for grilled fish, including charred tuna with green mango, tomato, and onion sauce, and fabulous desserts—try the lemon tart. Order the namesake drink, a martini, which comes in a designer glass. ♦ American/Mediterranean ♦ Daily lunch and dinner. Reservations recommended. 810 Seventh Ave (at W 53rd St). 767.1717

104 Visitors' Information Center This 2,200-square-foot space is New York City's official source for information on culture, dining, shopping, sight-seeing, events, attractions, tours, and transportation. There are multilingual tourism information counselors on hand as well as electronic information kiosks. ♦ Daily. 810 Seventh Ave (at W 53rd St). 484.1222

105 Novotel $$$ Part of the large French chain, the hotel begins on the seventh floor of this 1984 building by **Gruzen & Partners,** and many of its 474 rooms and suites look down into the heart of Times Square. Room service runs until midnight. **Cafe Nicole** offers dazzling views and nightly entertainment. ♦ 226 W 52nd St (between Broadway and Eighth Ave). 315.0100, 800/221.3185; fax 765.5369

105 Gallagher's Steak House ★★★$$$ Even confirmed carnivores may flinch as they pass the glass-walled meat locker (also visible from the street) filled with raw slabs of beef, but it's been there since the restaurant first opened in 1927. Oak floors and knotty-pine walls confirm that you're in one of New York's very serious steak joints. In fact, management claims that the original "New York strip" (prime sirloin on the bone) was first served here. The dry-aged prime sirloin, filet mignon and prime ribs are all satisfying and delicious. ♦ Steak house ♦ Daily lunch and dinner. Reservations recommended. 228 W 52nd St (between Broadway and Eighth Ave). 245.5336 &

106 Roseland The legendary ballroom, which opened in 1919, still plays host to big bands and aspiring Fred Astaires and Ginger Rogerses (as well as rock, salsa, and world music bands), although only two days a week now: Thursday there is a DJ; Sunday there is live music. ♦ Admission. Th, Su 2:30-11PM. 239 W 52nd St (between Broadway and Eighth Ave). 247.0200 &

106 Virginia Formerly called the **ANTA,** this theater was built in 1925 by **Howard Crane** for the **Theatre Guild.** Pat Hingle and Christopher Plummer starred here in Archibald MacLeish' *J.B.,* which won the Pulitzer Prize in 1959. Sir Thomas More was brilliantly played by Paul Scofield in Robert Bolt's *A Man for All Seasons* in 1961. *No Place To Be Somebody* moved here from the **Public Theater** after its author, Charles Gordone, won the Pulitzer in 1969. ♦ 245 W 52nd St (between Broadway and Eighth Ave). Telecharge 239.6200 &

107 Neil Simon When this theater was erected in 1927 by **Herbert J. Krapp,** Fred and Adele Astaire were in the first production, George and Ira Gershwin's *Funny Face.* A more recent hit was *Annie,* which arrived here exactly 50 years later. ♦ 250 W 52nd St (between Broadway and Eighth Ave). 757.8646; Ticketmaster 307.4100 &

108 Bangkok Cuisine ★★$$ The food is excellent, and among the best dishes are the seafood soups spiced with pepper and lemongrass, any of the satays, *mee krob* (crisp noodles tossed with pork, shrimp, and bean sprouts), chicken *masaman* (with coconut milk, peanuts, avocado, and curry), and baked fish smothered with hot spices. It's crowded in the early evening but becomes increasingly peaceful as the night wears on. ♦ Thai ♦ M-Sa lunch and dinner; Su dinner. Reservations recommended. 885 Eighth Ave (between W 52nd and W 53rd Sts). 581.6370 &

109 Broadway Ethel Merman filled this theater with sound and ticketholders as the star of *Gypsy.* Built in 1924 by **Eugene De Rosa,** this is also where Barbra Streisand performed in *Funny Girl,* and where Yul Brynner gave his final performance in *The King and I.* *Miss Saigon* opened here in 1991 and was scheduled to close at press time. ♦ 1681 Broadway (between W 52nd and W 53rd Sts). Telecharge 239.6200 &

10 Ed Sullivan This landmark theater, which was built by **Herbert J. Krapp** in 1927 and is full of Gothic details inside and out, has showcased vaudeville, music hall, stage shows, radio, and TV. It was a casino-style nightclub in the 1930s, then became the broadcast home of the Fred Allen radio show, and, from 1948 to 1971, the "Ed Sullivan Show." Under its vaulted cathedral ceiling, American audiences got their first look at the Beatles, Elvis Presley, and Rudolf Nureyev. CBS bought and restored the theater in 1993; it is now home to the ever-popular David Letterman's "Late Show." ♦ 1697 Broadway (between W 53rd and W 54th Sts). Ticket information 975.2476

11 Au Cafe ★$$ This coffee bar with a variety of sandwiches, salads, soups, pastas, burgers, and pastries is an ideal place to relax with your thoughts or a newspaper. Soft background jazz and small marble pedestal tables create an airy, laid-back environment. There's also a spacious palm-lined outdoor seating area that is delightful in nice weather. ♦ American ♦ Daily breakfast, lunch, and dinner. 1700 Broadway (between W 53rd and W 54th Sts). 757.2233

12 Stage Delicatessen ★$$ Since 1937, this local spot for Damon Runyon characters has been a classic Jewish delicatessen serving enormous sandwiches to locals, celebrities, and tourists alike. Most famous are the pastrami and corned beef, but don't overlook the cheese blintzes or chicken in the pot. ♦ Deli ♦ Daily breakfast, lunch, dinner, and late-night meals. 834 Seventh Ave (between W 53rd and W 54th Sts). 245.7850

13 Remi ★★$$$ Fresh antipasti, Venetian-style ravioli filled with fresh tuna and crispy ginger in a light tomato sauce, and a selection of grilled meats and fish please the deal makers from nearby Time-Warner, who lunch here, as well as some of the city's esteemed chefs, who reserve tables here on their nights off. The desserts are worth the splurge, especially the *cioccolatissima* (a warm chocolate soufflé cake with a cappuccino parfait) and the *zabaglione sarah venezia* (broiled zabaglione with fruit and vanilla ice cream). For those who like grappa, there are 45 varieties from which to choose. ♦ Italian

♦ M-F lunch and dinner; Sa-Su dinner. Reservations recommended. 145 W 53rd St (between Sixth and Seventh Aves). 581.4242

114 New York Hilton and Towers $$$ The quintessential luxury convention hotel in town is this tower of more than 2,000 well-appointed rooms, each with a small private bar, and offering such services for businesspeople as quick checkout, a copy center, rental pocket beeper phones, and a multilingual staff. **Executive Tower** rooms offer a refrigerator, radio alarm, electric shoe polisher, and a free copy of *USA Today* with breakfast. A battery of restaurants and cocktail lounges includes **Sports Bar and Grill 53,** a fine restaurant. ♦ 1335 Sixth Ave (between W 53rd and W 54th Sts). 586.7000, 800/HILTONS; fax 315.1374 &

115 Rhiga Royal Hotel $$$$ All rooms are spacious in this 54-story, 214-room luxury hotel, though 30 suites define indulgence. There are great views; amenities include VCRs and two independent phone lines; most rooms have computer and fax ports. There's 24-hour room service. ♦ 151 W 54th St (between Sixth and Seventh Aves). 307.5000, 800/937.5454; fax 765.6530 &

Within the Rhiga Royal Hotel:

Halcyon ★★★$$$ Executive chef John Halligan turns out some intriguing food combinations at this elegant dining room. Outstanding menu choices change seasonally but may include roasted rack of lamb served with rosemary-mascarpone risotto. Chocolate fans will enjoy the Valhrona chocolate mousse cake. ♦ American ♦ Daily breakfast, lunch, and dinner. Reservations recommended. 468.8888 &

116 Carnegie Delicatessen ★★$$ Indulge yourself at *the* classic kosher-style deli, a New York legend that became famous for sandwiches named after other New York legends. The menu may seem a bit pricey at first, but wait until you see the size of the sandwiches—massive affairs that inevitably provide enough to share or cart home. Leave room, if you can, for the cheesecake. The downside: Getting people in and out—which translates into not providing gracious service or comfort—is the goal here, and after so many years it's become an honored tradition. ♦ Deli ♦ Daily breakfast, lunch, dinner, and late-night meals. No credit cards accepted. 854 Seventh Ave (at W 55th St). 757.2245 &

117 Siam Inn ★★$$ Spicy, authentic, and delicious fare is offered in this popular Thai restaurant. Fish and seafood dishes are best, especially the Bangkok jumbo shrimp with fresh herbs and garlic sauce. Expect to see executives at lunch and theatergoers in the evening. To accommodate them, service is quick and dependable. ♦ Thai ♦ M-F lunch and dinner; Sa-Su dinner. 916 Eighth Ave (between W 54th and W 55th Sts). 974.9583

118 Broadway Diner ★$ This hip, upscale, 1950s-style diner is replete with period white tile and a neon clock, along with lots of tables and counter space. Traditional diner fare includes a wide variety of good daily specials—salads, steaks, and fish—plus a tasty grilled chicken salad, hearty burger deluxe, and trendy portobello mushroom sandwich. ♦ American ♦ Daily breakfast, lunch, dinner, and late-night meals. No credit cards accepted. 1726 Broadway (at W 55th St). 765.0909. Also at: 590 Lexington Ave (at E 52nd St). 486.8838 &

119 MONY Tower When built in 1950 by **Shreve, Lamb & Harmon,** this was the headquarters of the insurance company known as Mutual of New York, which has since become MONY Financial Services. The mast on top of the tower is all about change of another kind: If the light on top is green, look for fair weather; orange means clouds are coming, and flashing orange signals rain; when it flashes white, expect snow; if the lights on the mast itself are rising, so will the temperature, and when they descend, it is going to get cold. ♦ 1740 Broadway (between W 55th and W 56th Sts)

120 The Park Central Hotel $$ When the 1920s roared, a lot of the sound and fury echoed through these halls, which were a meeting place for bootleggers and small-time gangsters. The ghosts have all been exorcised, and the 1927 hotel by **Groneburg & Leuchtag** has a new lease on life. The 1,055 reasonably priced rooms attract groups and airline crews. There's also a breakfast bistro and lounge. ♦ 870 Seventh Ave (between W 55th and W 56th Sts). 247.8000, 800/346.1359; fax 484.3374 &

121 Wellington Hotel $$ This 1930s property is often overlooked, even though it has 700 rooms featuring phones with voicemail, two restaurants including the fine **Molyvos** (see below), cocktail lounge, and e-mail kiosk. Rates have gone up somewhat since renovation of all rooms was completed in early 1993, but the hotel is still a find. ♦ 871 Seventh Ave (between W 55th and W 56th Sts). 247.3900, 800/652.1212; fax 581.1719 &

Within the Wellington Hotel:

Molyvos ★★★$$$ Cast aside all thoughts of soggy spinach pie and sticky-sweet baklava, for this large, lively dining room elevates Greek food to its rightful place in the pantheon of gastronomy. The mood of generosity and intense, sunny flavors begins with the appetizers, including a wonderful sampler plate of traditional Greek spreads—smoky eggplant, tangy fish roe, and pungent garlic yogurt—and perfect wood-grilled octopus. Entrées include heroic portions of lamb shank baked in a clay pot, rabbit stew, and impeccable grilled whole fish. Attention to detail here ranges from making tender phyllo dough in-house for desserts (don't miss the custard filled pastry called *bogatsa*, or the definitive baklava) to offering some 30 Greek wines on the well-chosen list—they're as good as they are unknown. Warm, enthusiastic service and a reasonable noise level all make this a most welcome addition to the Midtown scene. ♦ Greek ♦ Daily lunch and dinner. Reservations recommended. 871 Seventh Ave (between W 55th and W 56th Sts). 582.7500

christer's

122 Christer's ★★$$$ The rustic decor of split logs and plaid-covered banquettes centers around a stone fireplace, and a number of fish paintings grace the walls. Chef Christer Larsson's menu, American with Scandinavian leanings, highlights fresh fish and seafood; don't miss the gravlax; house-smoked Serrano salmon with black beans, corn, avocado, and tomatillo salsa; or salmon barbecued on an oak board with bacon and tamales. Desserts include a chocolate cake with an almond crust and peach sauce, apple leaf (apples baked in phyllo dough topped with vanilla ice cream), and a lingonberry compote with chocolate ice cream. ♦ American/Scandinavian ♦ M-F lunch and dinner; Sa dinner. Reservations recommended. 145 W 55th St (between Sixth and Seventh Aves). 974.7224

122 City Center Theater This somewhat unlikely Moorish fantasy was built as a Shriners' temple in 1924 by **H.P. Knowles** and converted to a theater in 1943. It was the home of the **New York City Opera** and the **New York City Ballet** before they moved to **Lincoln Center.** Splendidly renovated, the 2,731-seat theater has raking and improved sightlines, so audiences no longer have to strain their necks to see. Regular performers include the **Alvin Ailey, Martha Graham,** and **Merce Cunningham** dance companies. ♦ Box office daily noon–8PM. 131 W 55th St (between Sixth and Seventh Aves). 581.7907 &

123 Castellano ★★$$$ The peach-colored dining room is a re-creation of Harry's Bar in Venice, but the food is authentic Tuscan cuisine, although a few dishes from other regions make an appearance. Try the green-and-white fettuccine with cream and ham, or any of the grilled fish entrées. ♦ Italian ♦ M-F lunch and dinner; Sa-Su dinner. Reservations required. 138 W 55th St (between Sixth and Seventh Aves). 664.1975

123 Gorham Hotel $$$ First opened in 1929, this 120-room hotel was renovated to the tune of $16 million in 1993. It's a lovely and convenient Midtown choice for visitors and particularly families, since contemporary-style rooms are large and come with a compact although fully equipped kitchenette—and there's no charge for children under 16. If you've opted for one of the 45 suites, you can look forward to a whirlpool bath at the end of a long day. ♦ 136 W 55th St (between Sixth and Seventh Aves). 245.1800, 800/735.0710; fax 582.8332 &

124 The Mysterious Bookshop If you want to know *whodunit,* the amazingly well-informed staff here won't spoil the fun by telling you, but they will guide you to the exact book that you're looking for. There are thousands of mystery books, both new and out of print, in this two-level shop. Sherlock Holmes fans: Take note that members of the Baker Street Society regularly meet here. ♦ M-Sa. 129 W 56th St (between Sixth and Seventh Aves). 765.0900

125 Joseph Patelson Music House Musicians, from beginners to world-renowned maestros, have been coming to this former carriage house for their music needs (sheet music and books, orchestral and opera scores) ever since it opened in 1920. With the widest selection of music (mostly classical, with some jazz, pop, and Broadway) in New York, it's no surprise that this shop receives orders from as far away as Japan. ♦ M-Sa. 160 W 56th St (between Sixth and Seventh Aves). 582.5840 &

126 Lee's Studio Sleek, contemporary lighting fixtures and table and floor lamps like those you'd expect to find in Milan or at the **Museum of Modern Art,** as well as a carefully chosen selection of chairs, sofas, and accessories, fill this shop. ♦ Daily. 1755 Broadway (at W 56th St). 581.4400. Also at: 1069 Third Ave (at E 63rd St). 371.1122 &

127 Baluchi's ★$ Come here for the best chicken *tikka* (marinated in yogurt and cooked dry—a boneless tandoori) and curries in the neighborhood, and save yourself a trip downtown to Little India on East Sixth Street. ♦ Indian ♦ M-F lunch and dinner; Sa-Su dinner. 240 W 56th St (between Broadway and Eighth Ave). 397.0707 &

128 Bricco ★★★$$ The captivating aromas from the wood-burning oven alone would lure passersby into this chic restaurant, and the well-prepared Neapolitan food lives up to the scent: broiled calamari with sautéed mushrooms; clams with white wine and garlic; veal chop with portobello mushrooms; and outstanding pastas including *linguine puttanesca* (with olives, capers, and anchovies). Desserts are just as tempting, with a selection of sorbets and tiramisù topping the list. ♦ Italian ♦ M-F lunch and dinner; Sa-Su dinner. Reservations recommended. 304 W 56th St (between Eighth and Ninth Aves). 245.7160

129 Hearst Magazine Building Architect **Joseph Urban**'s bizarre 1928 concoction is reminiscent of the Viennese Secession, with strange obelisks standing on a heavy base and rising over the roof of the six-story pile. Apparently, this was intended to be the plinth for another seven stories; it would have remained a folly nonetheless. The building is not open to the public. ♦ 959 Eighth Ave (between W 56th and W 57th Sts). 649.2000

130 Parc Vendome Apartments This was one of the sites considered for a second **Metropolitan Opera House.** The scheme died when opera patrons were told that a skyscraper would be built to help support it. "We don't need that kind of help," they sniffed and took their money elsewhere. The 570-unit apartment house, a 1931 creation of **Henry Mandel,** contains a private dining room, a gymnasium and pool, music room, and terraced gardens. ♦ 340 W 57th St (between Eighth and Ninth Aves). 247.6990

131 Coliseum Books Here you'll find a huge mix of both general interest and scholarly books: academic, trade, and mass-market paperbacks; sports; how-to books; scholarly journals; and oversize paper and hardcover remainders. Computer reference, a helpful staff, and late hours are also pluses. ♦ M 8AM–10PM; Tu-Th 8AM–11PM; F 8AM–11:30PM; Sa 10AM–11:30PM; Su noon–8PM. 1771 Broadway (at W 57th St). 757.8381

132 Hard Rock Cafe ★$$ The tail end of a 1958 Cadillac is the marquee of this mecca for young tourists. Inside, check out the guitar-shaped bar and rock memorabilia that includes dozens of gold records, the purple jacket of the rock star formerly known as Prince, and Jimi Hendrix's guitar. The sandwiches and burgers are decent. Requisite

Hard Rock T-shirts and sweatshirts are for sale in the gift shop next door. ♦ American ♦ Daily lunch, dinner, and late-night meals. 221 W 57th St (between Seventh Ave and Broadway). 459.9320

133 Lee's Art Shop, Inc. "The Department Store for Artists" is appropriately located directly across the street from the Art Students League. The extensive materials department attracts artists and architects, and the pens, stationery, and picture frames make great gifts. ♦ Daily. 220 W 57th St (between Seventh Ave and Broadway). 247.0110 ᘯ

134 Art Students League The three central panels on this French Renaissance palace represent the Fine Arts Society, the Architectural League, and the **Art Students League**, all of which originally shared this facility and made it the scene of nearly every important exhibition at the turn of the century. Dating to 1892, this is a work of **Henry J. Hardenbergh**. ♦ 215 W 57th St (between Seventh Ave and Broadway). 247.4510

134 The Osborne Except for the removal of its front porch and the addition of retail stores, this wonderful apartment building has hardly changed since it was built by **James E. Ware** in 1885. Unfortunately not open to the public, the opulent lobby was designed by Louis Comfort Tiffany. ♦ 205 W 57th St (at Seventh Ave)

134 Cafe Europa ★$ Bright and pretty, with dreamy trompe l'oeil ceilings, this cafe is a convenient spot to have a sandwich (made with very fresh ingredients) or such hot dishes as pizza and pasta. The muffins, tarts, and cakes accompanied by full-flavored coffees make great snacks. ♦ Cafe/Takeout ♦ Daily breakfast, lunch, dinner, and late-night meals. 205 W 57th St (between Seventh Ave and Broadway). 977.4030 ᘯ

135 Trattoria Dell'Arte ★★$$$ According to the proud management of this colorful restaurant opposite **Carnegie Hall,** the world's largest antipasto bar resides here. Choose from the impressive assortment, which includes sun-dried tomatoes, roasted fennel, fresh mozzarella, various seasonal vegetables, and a separate seafood bar with lobster, shrimp and scallop salad, calamari, and smoked salmon. ♦ Italian ♦ M-F lunch and dinner; Sa-Su brunch and dinner. Reservations recommended. 900 Seventh Ave (between W 56th and W 57th Sts). 245.9800 ᘯ

136 Carnegie Hall This landmark was built in 1891 by **William B. Tuthill; William Morris Hunt** and **Dankmar Adler** served as consultants. Peter Ilyich Tchaikovsky conducted at the opening concert, and during the next 70 years, the **New York Philharmonic** played here under such greats as Gustav Mahler, Bruno Walter, Arturo Toscanini, Leopold Stokowski, and Leonard Bernstein. Considered to have acoustics matched by few others in the world, the hall has attracted all of the 20th century's great musicians, and not just the classical variety; W.C. Handy brought his blues here in 1928, and was followed by

Carnegie Hall

MICHAEL STORRINGS

Count Basie, Duke Ellington, Benny Goodman, and others. Nowadays, conductor Skitch Henderson and the **New York Pops** call it home. When it was announced in the 1950s that the **New York Philharmonic** would be moving to **Lincoln Center,** the landmark was put up for sale. Violinist Isaac Stern and a group of concerned music lovers waged a successful campaign to save it. Their efforts eventually resulted in a restoration, completed in 1986 by **James Stewart Polshek & Partners,** which rendered it as glorious visually as it is acoustically. The corridors are lined with scores and other memorabilia of the artists and composers who have added to the hall's greatness. The space above the auditorium contains studios and apartments favored by musicians and artists. Another part of the space is occupied by the **Weill Recital Hall,** used by soloists and small chamber groups. In 1991, **The Rose Museum at Carnegie Hall** took over yet another part of the building. The basement was recently renovated to house a new high-tech performance space. ♦ Free. Tours: M-Tu, Th-F 11:30AM, 2PM, and 3PM. Museum: M-Tu, Th-Su 11AM-4:30PM. 154 W 57th St (at Seventh Ave). 247.7800 ♦

137 Uncle Sam's Umbrella Shop Since 1892, this shop has been protecting New Yorkers from the elements, with umbrellas in all different sizes, shapes, and prices, and repairs while you wait. They also carry a collection of elegant wooden walking sticks with whimsical handles. All of the umbrellas for the 1993 revival of the musical *My Fair Lady* (inspired by the paintings of René Magritte, it was a virtual forest of parasols) were made here. ♦ M-Sa. 161 W 57th St (between Sixth and Seventh Aves). 582.1977 ♦

138 Planet Hollywood ★$$ Owned (though not managed) by a trio of celluloid powerhouses (Sylvester Stallone, Bruce Willis, and Arnold Schwarzenegger), this hot eatery is forever loud and packed. It's also fun: The interior, a veritable museum of movie memorabilia, was created by the set designer for the first *Batman* film. The pizza and burger selections are good, but remember to leave room for the apple strudel, made from Arnold's mother's secret recipe. A gift shop next door sells souvenirs that no trendy diner should be without. ♦ American ♦ Daily lunch, dinner, and late-night meals. 140 W 57th St (between Sixth and Seventh Aves). 333.7827

138 Le Parker Meridien $$$$ The hotel's main entrance is on West 56th Street, but an attractive corridor leading to the other side gives it a more uptown address. When making a reservation, ask for an odd-numbered room above the 26th floor for a wonderful view of **Central Park.** The 42-story hotel has 700 rooms, 2 restaurants, a rooftop swimming pool with a jogging track, and racquetball and squash courts. The 24-hour room service has a European flair, as does everything else about the hotel. ♦ 118 W 57th St (between Sixth and Seventh Aves). 245.5000, 800/543.4300; fax 307.1776 ♦

Within the Parker Meridien:

Norma's ★★★$$ This sleek, airy, and immaculately clean restaurant offers the most creative breakfast menu in New York—and possibly anywhere. Each meal begins with one of chef David Rangel's signature "smoothie shots" such as pineapple-cantaloupe-honeydew or plum-watermelon-pineapple. Follow that with an egg-white frittata of shrimp, oven-roasted roma tomato and spinach, red berry risotto "oatmeal" in a crispy wafer bowl, or the totally decadent and delicious molten chocolate French toast with pineapple compote. Another legend in the making is the new-fangled old-fashioned silky berry breakfast puddin'. Portions are uncommonly generous. Breakfast is served all day long, but there's a terrific "later than breakfast" menu, too. Another plus is the authentic French coffee served. ♦ Breakfast ♦ Daily breakfast until midnight. 708.7460

Seppi's ★★★$$ An upscale midtown crowd enjoys a downtown vibe and the creations of an innovative kitchen at this atmospheric bistro opened by the owners of **Raoul's** in Soho. There are faithfully recreated pressed-tin ceilings, framed old French beer ads, cushy booths—and an in-house tarot card reader. The menu draws on that of countries once traversed by the *Orient-Express* (France, Switzerland, Austria, Italy, and Turkey), and changes seasonally, but it might include grilled daurade with cumin-scented root vegetables and red beet-sumac sauce, and Ottoman vegetable rice with grilled vegetables and tomato coulis, as well as such staples as steak au poivre. Desserts run the gamut from assorted homemade sorbets to such treats as a white chocolate souffle with Kirsch-marinated cherries. ♦ French/Mediterranean ♦ M-F lunch and dinner; Sa-Su brunch and dinner. 708.7444

139 Salisbury Hotel $$ This originated as one of New York's apartment hotels, for permanent residents, so that the 201 available rooms here, most of which have serving pantries and individual safes, are extra-large. Guests are served a complimentary continental breakfast, and an ice-cream shop is open during the summer. A floor-by-floor renovation has been in progress for some time. ♦ 123 W 57th St (between Sixth and Seventh Aves). 246.1300, 800/223.0680; fax 977.7752 ♦

140 Steinway Hall Look through the concave window into the showroom of this prestigious piano company, housed, appropriately, in a domed hall with a huge crystal chandelier. The 12-story building, built in 1925, with a 3-story

Greek temple on the roof, also includes a recital salon. The relief of *Apollo* over the central arch is by Leo Lentelli; the building is by **Warren & Wetmore.** ♦ Daily. 109 W 57th St (between Sixth and Seventh Aves). 246.1100

141 Motown Cafe ★$$ Located in the former **Automat,** this eatery is filled with Motown memorabilia and sounds of such legends as The Supremes, The Four Tops, and The Temptations. Behind glass doors that once dispensed food are gold records, and album covers serve as menus. The food can be hit-and-miss, though the dishes with a Southern bent are the best bets. Try the crispy chicken fingers served with a honey-mustard sauce or the very spicy Buffalo chicken wings. There's a gift shop located downstairs. ♦ American/Southern ♦ Daily lunch, dinner, and late-night meals. 104 W 57th St (between Sixth and Seventh Aves). 581.8030

142 Alwyn Court The terra-cotta dragons and other decorations that cover every inch of this 1909 apartment house by **Harde & Short** are in the style of the great art patron of the Renaissance, Francis I. His symbol, a crowned salamander, is displayed above the entrance at the West 58th Street corner. Although it's not open to the public, almost no one ever passes by without stopping for a lingering look. ♦ 180 W 58th St (at Seventh Ave)

142 Petrossian ★★★$$$$ Whether you're in Paris or New York, this restaurant is *the* place to go for caviar. Many varieties of precious roe are offered at this high-class, Art Deco influenced marble and mink-trimmed room, with ornate gilded statuettes and enlarged etchings of Erté drawings. Try the sevruga, osetra, and beluga, foie gras terrine, or the sampling of salmon—marinated, smoked, and spiced. Chef P.G. Gustafsson's innovative and delicious dishes include roasted lobster with winter vegetables, potato puree, and mushroom truffle sauce; and halibut with shrimp aioli. Desserts are similarly hard to pass up—especially the lemon tart with lemon custard and caramel. The wine list is excellent and the very best Champagnes can be ordered by the glass. There's a sublime prix-fixe brunch and surprisingly affordable prix-fixe lunches and dinners. Take-home delicacies are available in the adjoining shop. ♦ Continental ♦ M-F lunch and dinner; Sa-Su brunch and dinner. Reservations required; jacket required. 182 W 58th St (at Seventh Ave). 245.2214

143 Freed of London Best known to beginning and professional ballet dancers for their handmade shoes from England and Spain, the store also sells tap, ballroom, and theatrical shoes, plus dancewear. ♦ M-Sa. 922 Seventh Ave (at W 58th St). 489.1055

144 The New York Athletic Club This 22-story building, designed by **York & Sawyer** in 1930, houses handball and squash courts as well as other exercise facilities, including a swimming pool. The club itself was founded in 1868 and has sent winning teams to many Olympic Games. There are guest rooms, but visitors who want to begin their day running in **Central Park** are not permitted to go through the lobby in jogging outfits. ♦ Daily for members only: M-F 6:30AM-9PM; Sa 9AM-7PM; Su 10AM-6PM. 180 Central Park S (at Seventh Ave). 247.5100

144 The Essex House, a Westin Hotel $$$ The original 1930 grand hotel by **Frank Grand** greets the new millennium as a renovated Westin hotel within the Starwood Hotels & Resorts chain. The Art Deco details of the facade and the artful use of setbacks, however, still make it one of Manhattan's more pleasing towers. The hotel boasts a European-style health spa and two restaurants, including the **Cafe Botanica** (see below). A third of the 597 rooms and suites have **Central Park** views. ♦ 160 Central Park S (between Sixth and Seventh Aves). 247.0300, 800/WESTIN.1; fax 315.1839 &

Within the Essex House:

Cafe Botanica ★★★$$$ This delightful dining spot features such flavorful and creative food as herbed *pappardelle* (thick pasta) with Great Northern beans and black truffle oil, grilled calamari with roasted red-pepper coulis, wood-grilled Maine lobster with pumpkin risotto, and roasted rack of lamb with eggplant gratin. For dessert, there are excellent fruit tarts, mango mousse, and chocolate truffle cake. There are also good prix-fixe lunches and dinners, as well as a spectacular Sunday brunch. ♦ International ♦ M-Sa breakfast, lunch, and dinner; Su brunch and dinner. Reservations recommended. 484.5120 &

145 Hampshire House A hotel converted to elite cooperative apartments, this building, a work of **Caughey & Evans,** has a peaked roof of copper that has turned a marvelous shade of green, one of the highlights of the skyline bordering **Central Park.** Its lobby is a joy; when the cornerstone was put in place, it was filled with the best books and music of 1931. ♦ 150 Central Park S (between Sixth and Seventh Aves)

Within the Hampshire House:

Churrascaria Plantation ★★$$ Begin your journey into the tangy, hearty world of Brazilian barbecue at this palm-tree–studded spot with a *caipirinha,* Brazil's national cocktail. Then head to the world-class salad bar, where among other things you can sample *bacalhaoada* (a savory codfish stew). Back at the table, flip your coaster over so the green side faces up—a signal for the server to bring on the barbecue. And it comes in abundance, from garlic beef and short ribs to crispy chicken thighs and flank steak. When you've had your fill, flip the coaster so the red side's up (you know what that means). Both the lunch and dinner menus are reasonably priced, all-you-can-eat prix-fixe. A Brazilian guitarist strums his stuff Tuesday, Friday, and Saturday nights. ◆ Brazilian ◆ Daily lunch and dinner. Reservations recommended. 489.7070

146 Central Park Inter-Continental $$$$ Formerly the famous **Ritz-Carlton,** this upscale hotel is now part of the Inter-Continental chain. It was known as the **Navarro** until its 1982 refurbishing by **Parrish-Hadley,** which included the charming bow to another era of putting awnings over the windows. Whatever it is called, the hotel continues in the tradition of the great Cesar Ritz, who opened his first hotel in London in 1898. The design of the 207-room hotel is in the style of a luxury European home. Amenities include 24-hour room service, robes, twice-daily housekeeping, turndown service, refrigerators upon request, no fewer than three phones in every room, and a fitness center. ◆ 112 Central Park S (between Sixth and Seventh Aves). 757.1900, 800/241.3333; fax 757.9620; newyork.interconti.com &

Within Central Park Inter-Continental:

Fantino Grill ★★★$$$ This elegant room of soft peach hues, chandeliers, and oil paintings adorning the walls is as beautiful as it was when it was an Italian restaurant, but the menu is now mostly steak house, with some refined touches under the guidance of chef de cuisine Michael Walsh. Try the seafood hot pot or beef carpaccio with white-truffle oil as starters, and note that the entrée list always includes several seafood dishes, pasta, and risotto. There is a fairly extensive list of wines by the glass. ◆ Steak house ◆ Tu-Sa breakfast, lunch, and dinner; M, Su breakfast and lunch. Reservations recommended; jacket required. 757.1900

147 Gainsborough Studios In 1908, **Charles W. Buckham** designed this apartment building—now one of the oldest in the city—as an artists' cooperative. It is worth passing by for a look at the frieze by Isadore Konti across the second floor—a festival procession with a bust of Gainsborough at the center enlivening the fine facade. ◆ 222

Central Park S (between Seventh Ave and Columbus Cir)

147 San Domenico ★★★★$$$$ After captivating the palates of international food critics for 18 years in a suburb of Bologna, Gianluigi Morino transplanted his labor of love to New York in 1988, and began dazzling food critics here. Today, the same standards for Italian *"alta cucina"* are maintained under the watchful eye of owner Tony May and his daughter, Marisa. The marble bar, terra-cotta floor imported from Florence, and smooth, ocher-tinted stucco walls applied by artisans from Rome provide a lovely, subdued environment. The meals—prepared at the artful hands of chef Odette Fada—are equally delightful. Don't miss the meltingly rich soft egg yolk–filled ravioli with truffle butter; it's a taste experience that you'll never forget. End your repast with any of the innovative desserts—hazelnut chocolate soufflé, caramel mousse with sesame seeds, or the napoleon made with orange *tuiles* (French cookies) layered with lime parfait—but don't overlook the quintessential tiramisù. The sensational yet affordable prix-fixe dinner is a wonderful bargain for those who don't mind eating early. ◆ Italian ◆ M-F lunch and dinner; Sa-Su dinner. Reservations required; jacket required. 240 Central Park S (between Seventh Ave and Columbus Cir). 265.5959 &

148 CBS Broadcast Center Currently operating as a TV production center and the headquarters of "CBS News," this was originally the headquarters of a dairy, and CBS old-timers still refer to it as the "Cowbarn." ◆ 524 W 57th St (between 10th and 11th Aves). 975.4321

149 Copacabana In the 1940s and 1950s, you could be thrilled here by the Copa Girls and entertained by such personalities as Sammy Davis Jr. and Jerry Vale. Although nightclub shows like those are a thing of the past, this club is still a bright spot on Tuesday night, when Latin music is the lure, and Friday and Saturday nights, when the Latin beat is augmented by an upstairs disco. Shows usually begin around midnight. The rest of the time it is used for private parties. ◆ Cover. Tu 6PM-3AM; F 6PM-4AM; Sa 10PM-4AM; Su 6PM-2AM. 617 W 57th St (between 11th and 12th Aves). 582.2672

150 Passenger Ship Terminal The last of the great ocean liners (also known as the "Cunard Queens"), the SS *France* and the USS *United States,* used piers in this neighborhood. But by the time this terminal complex was finished in 1976, except for the *QE2,* only cruise ships called here regularly. Most arrive Saturday morning and leave the same afternoon. The facility is used at other times as exhibition space. ◆ 711 12th Ave (west of De Witt Clinton Park). 246.5451

Midtown

A sense of power pervades Midtown, the heart of Manhattan. Giant high-rises stand shoulder to shoulder, creating solid walls of concrete and glass that seem to stretch to the sky. The area's weighty importance begins with a concentration of office buildings around **Grand Central Terminal**, touches on **Rockefeller Center** to the west, encompasses the headquarters of the **United Nations** to the east, and extends to the border of **Central Park** to the north. On **Fifth Avenue**, the tote of choice is more often a classy shopping bag than a briefcase. The street is home to some of the world's most exclusive stores, including **Saks, Henri**

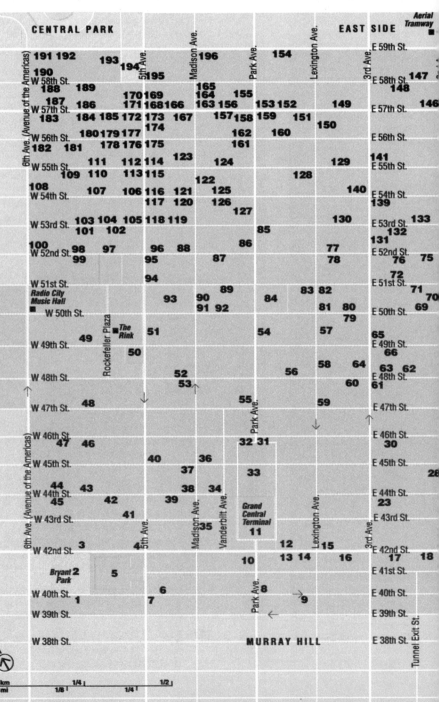

endel, **Cartier**, **Tiffany**, and **Bergdorf Goodman**. Also within Midtown's oundaries (roughly **40th** and **59th Streets**, the **East River**, and **Sixth venue**) are world-class hotels (**The Plaza**, the **Waldorf-Astoria**, the **Four easons**, **The Pierre**, **The St. Regis**), the many art galleries of **East** and **West 7th Street**, and the incomparable **Museum of Modern Art**.

's a good bet that 90 percent of the people who jam Midtown's streets live lsewhere. But the area is actually a great place to live. The possibilities include he huge **Tudor City** complex overlooking the UN; **Turtle Bay**, with its blocks f brownstone houses in the 50s east of **Third Avenue**; and dozens of prewar apartment buildings standing proud throughout. **Beekman Place**, two blocks of town houses between the East River and **First Avenue**, is a hidden treasure. **Sutton Place**, a longer residential street above **East 53rd Street** along the river, was part of a plan for English-style houses for the well-to-do developed in 1875 by Effingham B. Sutton. Morgans, Vanderbilts, and Phippses, among other notables, lived here.

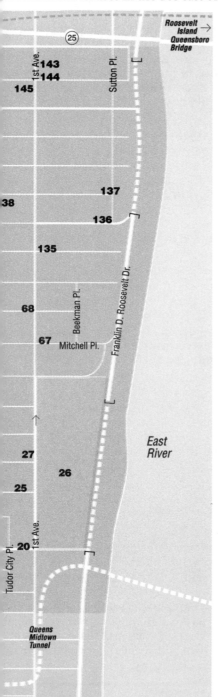

But it wasn't always that way. When Sutton Place was built, it was in wild territory overlooking what was then called **Blackwell's Island** (now **Roosevelt Island**) in the East River, where the city maintained an almshouse, workhouse, prison, and insane asylum. Although a horsecar line ran along **Second Avenue** between Fulton and 129th Streets, Sutton's riverfront property was a long way from the mainstream. The neighborhood didn't become "acceptable" until J.P. Morgan's daughter moved here in 1921.

Before then, society generally stayed west of **Park Avenue**. In fact, in the 19th century anyone who suggested that **Fourth Avenue** would one day be called Park Avenue would have been laughed out of the city. In 1832, a railroad line was built in the center of the dirt road, and steam trains huffed and puffed their way in and out of New York past squatters' shacks with goats in the front yards and pigs out back.

Little by little, roofs were constructed over the tracks, but it wasn't until the present **Grand Central Terminal** was designed in 1903 that anything was done about covering the railroad yards that had grown up between

Lexington and **Madison Avenues** from **East 42nd** to **East 45th Streets.** When the UN moved into the area in 1947, the cattle pens disappeared and **Midtown East** became a neighborhood in its own right.

From the day Fifth Avenue was first established in 1837, the rich and famous began to arrive. Railroad tycoon Jay Gould was one of the first. He built a mansion at **47th Street** and Fifth Avenue and began taking important friends like Russell Sage, Morton F. Plant, and William H. Vanderbilt to business dinners at the nearby **Windsor Hotel.**

By the late 1800s, Vanderbilt had built three mansions on the west side of Fifth Avenue at 51st Street. His son, William K. Vanderbilt, built a fourth palace a few doors uptown. Another son, Cornelius II, tried to upstage them with an even grander house at **58th Street.** In their quest to outdo one another, they ended once and for all the idea of the traditional New York row house with a brownstone front. Who would have thought of living anywhere but on Fifth Avenue in the blocks between 40th and 59th Streets?

Mrs. Astor, that's who. When her husband's nephew, William Waldorf Astor, built a hotel **(The Waldorf)** next to her house on Fifth Avenue at West 33rd Street, she retaliated by tearing down the house and building another hotel next to his **(The Astoria).** Then she built a Renaissance *palazzo* for herself at Fifth Avenue and **East 65th Street.** After her inaugural ball there in 1896, "Millionaire's Row," as Fifth Avenue was called, began moving uptown. (Both of the hotels were eventually destroyed to make room for the **Empire State Building,** and the **Waldorf-Astoria** reopened in its present site at Park Avenue and East 49th Street.)

Only a few reminders of the 19th-century mansions remain on Fifth Avenue, including two that house **Cartier** and **Versace** at **East 52nd Street.** Houses of worship include such landmarks as **St. Thomas Church, St. Patrick's Cathedral,** the Romanesque **St. Bartholomew's Church,** and the vaguely Moorish **Central Synagogue**—the oldest building in the city in continuous use as a synagogue. Secular monuments also remain, such as the vast **New York Public Library** and, of course, **Grand Central Terminal,** which was saved after a long, citizen's battle spearheaded by the late Jacqueline Onassis.

Except for **St. Bartholomew's Church,** the **Waldorf-Astoria Hotel,** and a few more holdouts, today Park Avenue north of **Grand Central Terminal** is wall-to-wall office buildings, including important examples of the "glass box" genre built in the 1950s: the **Seagram Building** by **Ludwig Mies van der Rohe** and **Philip Johnson,** and the **Lever House** by Skidmore, Owings & Merrill. On Park Avenue north of East 57th Street, things turn decidedly residential.

Impressive office buildings and complexes on the other avenues range from the 19 buildings that comprise the Art Deco–period **Rockefeller Center** to the contemporary **Olympic Tower, Citicorp, Sony Plaza,** and **IBM** buildings. Madison Avenue above East 50th Street has seen an office-building boom, but it's Third Avenue in the 20-block strip from **39th Street** to 59th Street that has had the real mega–office building explosion.

Unexpected pockets of distinctive apartment buildings and town houses continue to cling to the side streets of Midtown (**West 54th Street** near the **Museum of Modern Art,** for example). In combination with small parks such as **Greenacre** and **Paley,** they bring greenery and human scale to what might seem at first glance to be a solid concentration of masonry. Nevertheless, despite the relief the parks provide, Midtown will always be the place where New York puts all its strength and energies on display.

1 American-Standard Building Originally known as the **American Radiator Building,** this 1923 tower was **Raymond Hood**'s first major project in New York City (he had just won the *Chicago Tribune* commission). He later had his hand in the **McGraw-Hill, Daily News,** and **Rockefeller Center** buildings. This 21-story midblock high-rise is a stylized variation of the *Tribune* design, with Gothic details tempered by Art Deco lines. Hood used black brick so that the window holes would fade into the sculpted mass, and the gold ornamented top would be that much more spectacular. When lit, it has been compared to a glowing coal. The plumbing showroom in the lobby is not part of the original design. ♦ 40 W 40th St (between Fifth and Sixth Aves)

2 Bryant Park The only park in the city designed like a formal garden was named for the poet William Cullen Bryant, a prime mover in the campaign to establish **Central Park** and a champion of the Hudson River School of painters, which established the fashion for wild, naturalistic parks. Before becoming a park, the land was a potter's field, and in 1853 it was the site of America's first **World's Fair,** held in a magnificent domed pavilion of iron and glass known as the **Crystal Palace.** The building stood here until 1858, when it burned to the ground. After the ruins were cleared, the space was used as a parade ground for troops getting ready to defend the Union in the Civil War. When the war was over, it was dedicated as a public park.

In 1934, as the result of a competition to aid unemployed architects, the park was redesigned by **Lusby Simpson,** whose plan was executed under the direction of urban planner Robert Moses. In the Depression years, the area was a gathering spot for the unemployed, and in the 1960s it became a retail space for marijuana peddlers. In 1980, the Bryant Park Restoration Corporation (Hanna/Olin Ltd.) began a massive restoration program, and today the park is a safer, handsomer, and friendlier spot, with new landscaping and lighting, restored monuments, footpaths and benches, food service, and a host of public events. A $4.2-million glass-and-steel pavilion designed by **Hardy Holzman Pfeiffer Associates** houses the **Bryant Park Grill** and the more informal **Cafe,** which serves seasonal American fare. ♦ Bounded by the New York Public Library and Sixth Ave, and W 40th and W 42nd Sts

3 43 West 42nd Street Some people actually like this former **W.R. Grace Building** with its sloping, ski-jump, wind-loading facade, but it is generally considered a poor interruption of the street wall. Designed in 1974 by **Skidmore, Owings & Merrill,** it has a

barren little plaza on the corner of West 43rd Street and Sixth Avenue—an alleged public amenity in exchange for which the developers were allowed extra floors. The architects built an identical structure for a different client at **9 West 57th Street** at the same time. ♦ Between Fifth and Sixth Aves

4 Nat Sherman's The tobacconist to the stars, his specialty is the pure tobacco cigarette wrapped in brown or in such trendy colors as shocking pink, turquoise, or scarlet. He also stocks cigars and Dunhill lighters. ♦ Daily. 500 Fifth Ave (at W 42nd St). 246.5500

43 West 42nd Street

MICHAEL STORRINGS

5 New York Public Library Center for the Humanities Treat your soul to one of New York's greatest experiences, the sight of the front of this library's **Center for the Humanities,** designed in 1911 at a cost of $9 million by **Carrère & Hastings.** The familiar lions, *Patience* and *Fortitude,* are the work of Edward Clark Potter. But there is much more to see: the bases of the 95-foot-high, tapered steel flagposts (by Thomas Hastings) on the terrace; the lampposts; the balustrades; the urns; the sculpture high above by Paul Bartlett, George G. Barnard, and John Donnelly; and the fountains in front, both by Frederick MacMonnies (the one on the right represents *Truth,* the other *Beauty*). The library was built with the resources of two privately funded libraries, combined in 1895 with the infusion of a $2-million bequest from New York Governor Samuel J. Tilden. John Jacob Astor's library, the first general reference library in the New World, was enhanced by James Lenox's collection of literature, history, and theology. (In 1891, Andrew Carnegie donated $52 million for the establishment of 80 more branches in the New York Public Library system.) This grand building is completely dedicated to research, and none of its more than six million books or 17 million documents can be checked out; so vast is the collection that the original four floors of stacks beneath the building and behind the reading rooms have been supplemented by a space underneath **Bryant Park,** which can hold up to 92 miles of stacks.

Considered the repository of one of the largest research collections in the world, the building remains one of the finest examples of Beaux Arts architecture. The main lobby, **Astor Hall,** contains the information desk, the bookshop, and an exhibition area. Marble from floor to ceiling, the hall is lavishly decorated with carved garlands, ribbons, and rosettes. The room directly behind **Astor Hall** is the **Gottesman Exhibition Hall,** which has the most beautiful ceiling in the city. The hall's changing exhibitions are thematic, covering a variety of subjects such as urban history, architecture, and photography. The exhibitions are based on materials drawn from the library's own holdings, demonstrating the richness of the research collections.

The **Third Floor Hall** and the rooms it serves are rich with carved wood panels and vaulted ceilings. The murals, by Edward Lanning, were executed as part of a WPA project. The library's art collection, including paintings by Gilbert Stuart, Sir Joshua Reynolds, and Rembrandt Peale, is displayed in the **Edna B. Salomon Room.** Directly across the hall is **Room 315,** the catalog room, where you can request books; it leads into the **Main Reading Room,** 51 feet high and one-and-a-half blocks long, filled with massive oak tables (with power points where you can plug in a laptop) and surrounded by reference works. The catalog and reading rooms reopened in 1999 following extensive restorations.

The **Celeste Bartos Forum,** beautifully restored by the firm **Davis, Brody & Associates,** is distinguished by its 30-foot-high glass dome, which rests on steel pillars adorned with Corinthian ornamentation. It is used for lectures, concerts, films, and special events. ♦ Main Reading Room: M-Sa. Tours: M-Sa 11AM, 2PM. Free tours meet at the front desk; call ahead for schedule. Fifth Ave (between W 40th and W 42nd Sts). 661.7220, 930.0800

6 Quality Inn by Journey's End Hotel $$ Ten of this hotel's 189 rooms are designed for disabled guests. Priced at the low end of this category, the inn offers amenities that include complimentary morning coffee and newspaper, in-room movies, and laundry and dry-cleaning services. ♦ 3 E 40th St (between Fifth and Madison Aves). 447.1500, 800/221.2222; fax 213.0972 ♿

7 New York Public Library, Mid-Manhattan Branch This branch, redesigned in 1981 by **Giorgio Cavaglieri,** once housed **Arnold Constable,** the department store that provided trousseaux for fashionable brides in the 1890s (you can see pictures of the brides in the library's collection of microfilm editions of old newspapers). This library has the largest circulating collection of any of the branch libraries. The ground floor includes an outlet of the **Metropolitan Museum of Art** gift shop. Free tours meet at the ground-floor information desk. ♦ Collections: M-Sa. Tours: M, W, F 2:30PM. 455 Fifth Ave (at E 40th St). 340.0833 ♿

8 101 Park Avenue Designed in 1983 by **Eli Attia & Associates,** this speculative tower of black glass rises, angled and tucked, above a granite plaza on an awkward corner. Its slick outline and sheer height, which may be fun from the inside, are somewhat disturbing from the outside. ♦ At E 40th St

9 New York Astrology Center The country's largest source of astrology books, healing books, and tarot cards can be found here. The center also offers computerized and one-on-one horoscope interpretations. ♦ M-Sa. 124 E 40th St (between Lexington and Park Aves). 949.7211

10 Philip Morris Headquarters Ulrich **Franzen & Associates'** light gray granite-clad building, designed in 1983, is a glass box hiding behind a postmodernist/historicist appliqué of Palladian patterns. The main facade, rather oddly, faces the Park Avenue viaduct. The enclosed garden and lobby of the building contain an espresso bar, a gift shop featuring contemporary Native American art, a chocolate shop, a magazine stand, and the **Whitney Midtown,** a satellite exhibition space of the **Whitney Museum of Modern Art.** The museum showcases a permanent sculpture exhibition in a vast, high-ceilinged area, while a smaller, more intimate space houses changing exhibits of 19th- and 20th-century American art, sometimes relating to Midtown life (paintings by the Ashcan School depicting New York street life, for instance). Gallery talks take place Monday, Wednesday, and Friday at 1PM. The site was originally the home of the Art Moderne **Airlines Building** (built in 1940 by **John B. Peterkin**). ♦ Museum: free. M-F. 120 Park Ave (between E 41st and E 42nd Sts). 878.2550 &

11 Grand Central Terminal This extraordinary complex (illustrated below) is a true jewel made even brighter with the long-awaited and extensive renovations completed in 1998. In 1913, **Reed & Stem**'s designs for the new terminal to replace the **New York Central** and **Hudson River Railroads' Grand Central Station** were chosen in a competition that included submissions by **Daniel H. Burnham** and **McKim, Mead & White.** The firm of **Warren & Wetmore** was hired as the associate architect and was largely responsible for the

design of the elaborate public structure. **Reed & Stem** and railroad engineer William Wilgus devised the still-efficient multilayered organization of the immense amount of traffic that flows through the terminal: trains (on two levels), subways, cars, and people.

The main, southern facade of the terminal is dominated by Jules Coutan's sculptures of Mercury, Hercules, and Minerva *(Glory of Commerce, Moral Energy,* and *Mental Energy).* At the center of the facade is a bronze figure of Commodore Cornelius Vanderbilt, founder of the railroad. The building's other major facade fronts Vanderbilt Avenue and what was a genteel residential neighborhood to the west; the tenements to the east were disregarded. In building the terminal, 32 miles of new tracks were laid, 18,000 tons of steel were used, and 2.8 million cubic yards of earth excavated.

The inner workings of the terminal are organized around the impressive **Main Concourse.** When entered by way of the arcades from Lexington Avenue, the soaring vault is particularly striking. But the space may be better appreciated as a whole from the marble stairs at the Vanderbilt Avenue end. The hall is 160 feet wide, 470 feet long, and 150 feet high at its apogee—larger than the nave of Notre Dame in Paris. The ceiling, a plaster vault suspended from steel trusses, is decorated with a zodiac representing the constellations of the winter sky, featuring 2,500 lit stars, designed by Paul Helleu. The floors of the **Main Concourse** are Tennessee marble, and the trim is Italian Bottocino marble. The great arched windows are 60 feet tall and 33 feet wide; recently cleaned and

Grand Central Terminal

MICHAEL STORRINGS

restored, they now let in massive amounts of light that augment the artifical light from enormous egg-shaped chandeliers.

The terminal was the centerpiece of a gigantic real-estate development that included eight hotels and 17 office buildings by 1934. When the railroad was forced to electrify, engineer Wilgus realized that if the trains were run underground and the tracks covered over, the air rights could be leased to developers. Thus Park Avenue was born. **Metro North** operates from here. The new additions include a grand staircase at the east end of the concourse (it was part of the original plans), an updated climate control system, and a new liquid crystal arrivals/departures display. The famous sky is more sparkling than ever, thanks to fiber optics, and new restaurants (including the first **Michael Jordan's The Steakhouse,** 655.2300) and shops have opened. ♦ Tours are conducted by the Municipal Art Society for a small fee (883.0009); they meet at the Chase Manhattan Bank in the Main Concourse on Wednesday at 12:30PM. E 42nd St (between Lexington and Vanderbilt Aves). Train information: 532.4900

Within Grand Central Terminal:

OYSTER
BAR⋮RESTAURANT

Oyster Bar and Restaurant ★★$$$
Looking much like what it is—a railroad station with tables—this place offers nicely prepared and absolutely fresh seafood, including, of course, a large variety of oysters. Although the daily menu reflects the fresh catches of the day, you can count on delicious chowder and excellent oysters panroasted or fried, as well as smoked salmon, rice-battered shrimp, and a selection of clams on the half shell. Due to the tiled, vaulted ceilings, however, the lunch-hour crowd generates megadecibels. ♦ Seafood ♦ M-F lunch and dinner. Reservations recommended. Lower level. 490.6650 ♿

Transit Museum Gift Shop The perfect way to while away a minute or an hour between trains, this modern gift shop celebrates something most Americans and certainly most Manhattanites take for granted: transportation. A host of subway and train-related souvenirs are handsomely displayed beneath a contemporary mural by Brian Cronin. ♦ M-F; Sa mornings. 682.7572

12 Grand Hyatt Hotel $$$ The 1934 **Warren & Wetmore**–designed **Commodore Hotel** was remodeled in 1980 by **Gruzen & Partners,** and is now a bustling commercial hotel reminiscent of Las Vegas with waterfalls and a soaring atrium. Glamorous dining and watering holes

are visible from the lobby, including the **Sun Garden,** which is cantilevered over East 42nd Street. **Trumpets** is now an elegant cigar bar. The 1,400 rooms are attractive, although some are small, and the hotel is affiliated with a nearby health club, which guests can use for a moderate fee. ♦ E 42nd St (between Lexington and Vanderbilt Aves). 883.1234, 800/223.1234; fax 697.3772 ♿

13 Home Savings of America Resembling a Roman basilica, the main banking room is 160 feet long, 65 feet high, and definitely worth a visit. The walls are limestone and sandstone, and the mosaic floors are French and Italian marble. The building was designed in 1923 by **York & Sawyer.** ♦ 110 E 42nd St (between Lexington and Park Aves). 953.8330

14 Chanin Building The headquarters of the Chanin real-estate empire is an Art Deco triumph built in 1929 by **Sloan & Robertson.** At the third-floor level is an exuberant terra-cotta frieze. The detailing of the lobby is extraordinary, particularly the convector grilles and elevator doors. ♦ 122 E 42nd St (between Lexington and Park Aves). 697.2200

15 Chrysler Building Built by **William Van Alen** in 1929 for the Chrysler Automobile Company, this tower (illustrated at right), which many consider the ne plus ultra of skyscrapers, is an Art Deco monument. The building has many car-oriented decorative elements: abstract friezes depicting automobiles, flared gargoyles at the fourth setback resembling 1929 radiator hood ornaments, and the soaring

Chrysler Building

spire modeled after a radiator grille. The lobby, decorated with African marble and once used as a car showroom, is another Deco treasure. Use the Lexington Avenue entrance and look up at the representation of the building on the ceiling of the lobby (made brighter by major renovations completed in 1999), and be sure to peek into an elevator cab. The lighting of the spire at night—with specially fitted lamps inside the triangular windows—was an idea of **Van Alen**'s that was rediscovered and first implemented in 1981. The edifice was briefly the tallest building in the world until surpassed by the **Empire State Building** in 1929. ♦ 405 Lexington Ave (at E 42nd St)

16 Mobil Building The self-cleaning stainless-steel skin on this monolith is 37 thousandths of an inch thick—self-cleaning because the creased panels create wind patterns that scour them. The building was designed by **Harrison & Abramovitz** in 1955. ♦ 150 E 42nd St (between Third and Lexington Aves)

17 New York Helmsley Hotel $$$ This 788-room property is geared towards the business traveler, and room service is available around the clock. Other niceties include **Harry's New York Bar** for drinks and **Mindy's Restaurant** for dining. ♦ 212 E 42nd St (between Second and Third Aves). 490.8900, 800/221.4982; fax 986.4792 &

18 The News Building The former home of New York's most successful tabloid, *The New York Daily News* (relocated in 1995 to larger quarters at 450 West 33rd Street) is a clean, purely vertical mass that was designed in 1930 by **Howells & Hood**, the pair responsible for the Chicago Tribune Tower (in all its Gothic wonder). The stringent composition even has a flat top—a bold step in 1930. The building tells its own story in the frieze over the entrance and in the lobby, where a globe is the center of an interplanetary geography lesson. (When the globe was first unveiled, it was spinning the wrong way.) The 1958 addition on Second Avenue, by **Harrison & Abramovitz**, is not up to the original. ♦ E 42nd St (between Second and Third Aves)

19 The Crowne Plaza at the United Nations $$$ This renovated property (once notorious for having the smallest rooms in the city) now boasts 303 expanded rooms, each with a marble bathroom, two-line telephones, and fax and PC ports. Within the hotel are a restaurant, a bar and lounge, meeting rooms, conference and banquet facilities, a business center, and a small health club facility. ♦ 304 E 42nd St (between First and Second Aves). 986.8800, 800/879.8836; fax 986.1758 &

20 Tudor City Soaring over East 42nd Street, this Gothic development on its own street was built in 1925 by the **Fred F. French Company** and **H. Douglas Ives**. It comprises 11 apartment buildings, a hotel, shops, a restaurant, a church, and a park. The complex's orientation toward the city seems ill-considered today, but when this enclave was planned, the East River shore below was a wasteland of breweries, slaughterhouses, glue factories, and gasworks. At the turn of the century, the bluff, known as Corcoran's Roost, was the hideout of the infamous Paddy Corcoran and the Rag Gang. Now it provides a good vista of the nearby **UN**. ♦ Bounded by First and Second Aves, and E 40th and E 43rd Sts

21 Ford Foundation Building This 1967 design by **Kevin Roche John Dinkeloo & Associates** is probably the oldest and certainly the richest and least hermetic re-creation of a jungle in New York City. Though the building is small with a rather typical entrance on East 43rd Street, the East 42nd Street side is much more extroverted. It appears as if a container had been opened, leaving the black piers barely restraining an overflowing glass and Cor-Ten steel box of offices that contains a luxuriant park inside a 12-story atrium. Although economically foolhardy and somewhat noisy, this building is handsome and very definitely not to be missed. ♦ 320 E 43rd St (between Tudor City Pl and Second Ave). 573.5000 &

22 Sichuan Pavilion ★★$$$ The Chinese menu here is one of the most interesting in the city and popular with **United Nations** delegates. During lunch, regular customers tend to get preferential treatment, so be prepared. Chicken with mixed mushrooms, lemon chicken, ginger-and-scallion shrimp, scallops with peppercorn sauce, and crispy fish are all good choices. ♦ Chinese ♦ Daily lunch and dinner. Reservations required for lunch, recommended for dinner. 310 E 44th St (between First and Second Aves). 972.7377

23 East ★★$$ Part of a city-wide chain, the service, prices and quality of food is consistently good at all locations. Early dinner specials are unbeatably cheap—there isn't a Japanese place in town that can match these prices. ♦ Japanese ♦ Daily lunch and dinner. No credit cards accepted. 210 E 44th Street (between Second and Third Aves). 687.5075. Also at: 251 W 55th Street (between Broadway and Eighth Ave). 581.2240

24 UNICEF House The exhibitions here illustrate the international children's operation

United Nations

MICHAEL STORRINGS

in action, highlighting the importance and potential of global cooperation among all races. **The Danny Kaye Center,** housed in the same building, runs *Within Our Reach,* a film about the challenges that face children all over the world. The center's retail shop has an extensive collection of UNICEF cards and gifts. ♦ Free. M-F. 3 UN Plaza, E 44th St (between First and Second Aves). 326.7000

25 United Nations Plaza This combination office building, apartment house, and hotel with a striking glass-curtain wall was designed by **Kevin Roche John Dinkeloo & Associates** in 1976. It was so successful that it was duplicated in 2 UN Plaza, adjoining it to the west, in 1980. ♦ E 44th St (at First Ave)

Within 1 United Nations Plaza:

United Nations Plaza Park Hyatt $$$$
Beginning on the 28th floor of 1 UN Plaza, this contemporary hotel includes 428 rooms, a lounge and restaurant, an indoor tennis court, and a swimming pool and health club with a dazzling view. Complimentary limousine service to Wall Street, the Garment District, and theaters is also available, though the majority of diplomat guests need only stroll

across the street for their day's business appointments. ♦ 758.1234, 800/228.9000; fax 702.5051 ₺

Within the United Nations Plaza Park Hyatt:

Ambassador Grill Restaurant ★★$$$
Chef Jamie Sanders has revitalized this old-fashioned mirrored dining room with such dishes as Dover sole, grilled double lamb chops with rosemary *jus,* steak frites with au poivre sauce and grilled monkfish. On Sundays, stop in for the all-you-can-eat brunch. ♦ American ♦ M-Sa lunch and dinner; Su brunch and dinner. Reservations recommended. 702.5014

26 The United Nations (UN) This complex (illustrated above) was designed in 1952 by an international committee of 12 globally renowned architects that included **Le Corbusier** of France, **Oscar Niemeyer** of Brazil, and **Sven Markelius** of Sweden; the committee was headed by American **Wallace K. Harrison.** The site—once the actual Turtle Bay where the Saw Kill ran into the East River—was a run-down area with slaughterhouses, light industry, and a railroad barge landing when John D. Rockefeller Jr. donated the money to purchase the land for the project. The complex, an enclave apart from the city (it is considered international and not American territory) and in formal contrast to it, has had tremendous influence on its surroundings as well as on the direction of architecture.

Housing the staff bureaucracy, the 39-story **Secretariat** was New York's first building with all-glass walls (these are suspended between side slabs of Vermont marble), and is the only example that approaches the tower-in-the-park urban ideal of the 1940s. (To make way for the **UN** building, the city diverted the traffic on First Avenue into a tunnel under UN Plaza and created a small landscaped park, **Dag Hammarskjold Plaza**.) Measuring 544 feet high and 72 feet wide, this anonymously faced building is a remarkable sight seen broadside from East 43rd Street, where it was set in deliberate opposition to the city grid. The General Assembly meets in the limestone-clad, flared white building to the north under the dome.

Visitors enter through the north side of the **General Assembly Building** across from East 45th Street. Outside, flags of all 188 member nations fly in alphabetical order at equal height, the same order in which delegates are seated in the General Assembly. More than a million visitors come here every year to see the physical presence of this forum of nations, but also in search of the elusive spirit of peace it symbolizes. Taking a tour is a good idea if you want to explore more than the grounds (don't miss the gardens) and the Chagall stained-glass windows in the lobby of the **General Assembly Building**. But don't expect to witness more than real estate if the General Assembly isn't in session (regular sessions are from the third Tuesday in September through mid-December).

Tours, conducted by young people from around the world, steer large groups through the elegant **Assembly Hall** (note the Léger paintings on the walls); the **Secretariat Building**; and the **Conference Building**, which houses media, support systems, and meeting rooms, including the **Security Council Chamber** (donated by Norway), the **Trusteeship Council Chamber** (donated by Denmark), and the **Economic and Social Council Chamber** (donated by Sweden). But you can find out more about how the organization actually functions by witnessing the public part of the UN's business as it takes place in the **General Assembly.** Tours of the General Assembly end at the basement **UN Gift Shop,** a great souvenir source with interesting hand-crafted gifts representing all 188 member nations. ♦ Admission. Tours daily 9:15AM-4:45PM. First Ave (between E 42nd and E 48th Sts). General information: 963.1234; group tours: 963.4440; tours: 963.7713; gift shop: 963.7700

Within The United Nations:
Delegates' Dining Room ★★$$$ The **UN** dining room is open to the public for lunch during the week. It offers a very good international luncheon buffet with a choice of 22 dishes, in addition to an à la carte menu that includes asparagus with lemon vinaigrette, lobster salad, barbecued salmon with ginger-honey sauce, loin of venison, and steak with shallot sauce. Try the chocolate terrine or frozen-raspberry soufflé for dessert. The view of the East River is the best offered by any restaurant in Manhattan. ♦ Continental ♦ M-F lunch. Reservations required; jacket required. UN Conference Building. 963.7625

27 International Education Information Center The information center is for foreign nationals interested in studying in the United States and US nationals who wish to study abroad. Staffed primarily by volunteers, the center provides guidebooks, brochures, and university catalogs, as well as materials describing scholarships, internships, and teaching opportunities. ♦ Tu-Th. 809 UN Plaza (between E 45th and E 46th Sts). 984.5413

28 Palm ★★$$$$ Ranked among the city's best steak houses, this venerable dining room (opened in 1926) serves huge portions of aged prime cuts, lobsters, and very addictive cottage-fried potatoes. Caricatures of famous New York journalists are painted on the walls, but you're more likely to recognize faces at the next table. Across the street is its twin (23 years old), **Palm Too** (697.5198); unlike the original, here you can still find sawdust on the floor. ♦ Steak house ♦ M-F lunch and dinner; Sa dinner. Reservations required. 837 Second Ave (between E 44th and E 45th Sts). 687.2953

29 Captain's Table ★★$$ Come here for superb fresh fish offered in a variety of preparations—halibut with aioli, grilled red snapper, and breaded shrimp with hot peppers and mozzarella, for example. There's also a separate market section where you can buy fresh fish to take home. ♦ Seafood ♦ M-F lunch and dinner; Sa dinner. Reservations recommended. 860 Second Ave (at E 46th St). 697.9538

30 Sparks ★★$$$$ As at other great steak houses, excellent cuts of beef and fresh seafood are cooked to order here. But what makes this place different is the exceptional wine list—the extraordinary selection and fair prices make it a must for oenophiles. ♦ Steak house ♦ M-F lunch and dinner; Sa dinner.

Reservations required. 210 E 46th St (between Second and Third Aves). 687.4855

an American Restaurant

31 Colors ★$$$ Strange name for a beige room, but there are touches of color in the drapes, napkins and paintings. The name must refer to the colorful menu, which caters to the multicultural Midtown crowd with selections from everywhere, including some good fish dishes, like curried grilled swordfish, and an appealingly diverse wine list. ♦ International ♦ M-F lunch and dinner; Sa dinner. Reservations recommended. 237 Park Ave (entrance on E 46th St). 661.2000

32 The Helmsley Building Designed in 1929 by **Warren & Wetmore,** this fanciful tower was originally the **New York Central Building,** then **New York General.** An example of creative, sensitive urban design, it was a lively addition to the architects' own **Grand Central Terminal** and the hotels that surrounded it. Built above two levels of railroad tracks, it essentially "floats" on its foundations—those inside feel nary a vibration. The gold-leafed building is worth a special viewing at night. Pause to appreciate the distinct separation of automobile and pedestrian traffic in the street-level arcades, and stop for a look at the wonderful Rococo lobby. ♦ 230 Park Ave (entrance on E 46th St)

33 Metropolitan Life Building Formerly the **Pan Am Building,** this 59-story monolith set indelicately between the **Helmsley Building** and **Grand Central Terminal** started in 1963 as a purely speculative venture and became the largest commercial office building ever built, with 2.4 million square feet. Art in the lobby includes a mural by Josef Albers and a space sculpture by Richard Lippold. The shape of the tower is supposedly derived from an airplane wing section. The architects were **Emery Roth & Sons, Pietro Belluschi,** and **Walter Gropius.** Bauhaus founder and High Modernist, Gropius could have done better. High atop the building several peregrine falcons nest in its outdoor niches. ♦ 200 Park Ave (entrance on E 45th St, between Lexington and Vanderbilt Aves)

Within the Metropolitan Life Building:

Tropica ★★$$$ At lunchtime, it's a capacity crowd with a corresponding noise level. At night the hubbub recedes in this Caribbean-style "great house," and chef Franck Deletrian shows off

creative seafood preparations to an appreciative audience. Try the tuna *tartare* with ginger, miso and wasabi; Arctic char with roasted corn, pea leaves and hearts-of-palm salad; and Chilean sea bass with whipped taro root, sweet pepper relish, and lime-coconut sauce. Dessert highlights include orange-blossom–water crème brûlée and the Tropica Fantasy, which changes daily. ♦ Regional American/Tropical ♦ M-F lunch and dinner. Reservations required for lunch; recommended for dinner. Ground level. 867.6767 ♿

Cafe Centro ★★★$$$ This $5-million brasserie with marble inlay floors, gold-leaf columns, and etched Lalique-style chandelier is reminiscent of the grand cafes in European train stations. Among the superb entrées, don't miss the panseared calamari stuffed

Metropolitan Life Building

with basil and salmon; and monkfish *tagine* with sweet potatoes, artichokes, olives, and dates. Leave room for the rich vanilla crème brûlée–chocolate tart with caramel sauce. The beer bar offers over 20 selections, 10 of which are on draft. At the bar you can order hamburgers, chicken wings, and potato skins—sans reservations. ◆ American/French ◆ M-F lunch and dinner; Sa dinner. Reservations recommended. Ground level. 818.1222 &

34 The Yale Club In a neighborhood crowded with clubs waving the old school tie, this one boasts easy access to trains headed to New Haven for the over-nostalgic. The building was designed in 1913 by **James Gamble Rogers**. Only Yalies are allowed in; a handful of rooms are available for their overnight use. ◆ 50 Vanderbilt Ave (between E 44th and E 45th Sts). 661.2070

35 Worth & Worth Hat lovers know top quality when they see it, and it doesn't get any better in the city. The staff is knowledgeable, patient, and friendly, and the merchandise ranges from classic to cutting-edge. ◆ M-Sa. 331 Madison Ave (between E 42nd and E 43rd Sts). 867.6058 &

36 The Roosevelt Hotel $$$ Built in 1924 by **George B. Post and Sons**, this old hotel was prestigious when railroads were the main form of transportation and the location near **Grand Central** was highly valued. Now reopened after a $65-million renovation, it is managed by Interstate Hotels. All 1,033 rooms have received a much-needed facelift geared to the businessperson. Guests also enjoy a restaurant and bar. ◆ 45 E 45th St (between Vanderbilt and Madison Aves). 661.9600, 800/TEDDY.NY; fax 687.5064

37 Paul Stuart Classic, well-made clothing for the conservative gentleman (and woman) is the specialty. Look for jackets and suits in herringbone, Shetland, and tweed; handknit sweaters in alpaca, cashmere, and Shetland wool; and shirts of Sea Island cotton. Women have a reasonable niche to themselves on the mezzanine level, where there are tailored skirted suits, Shetland sweaters, and cotton shirts. If you're not the one shopping, a 17th-century Flemish tapestry and comfortable leather chairs make waiting quite pleasant. ◆ Daily. E 45th St (at Madison Ave). 682.0320 &

38 Brooks Brothers The home of the Ivy League look—the natural-shoulder sack suit, worn with an oxford-cloth shirt and silk rep tie—this store is an American institution. Founded in 1818, it is the country's oldest menswear shop, and continues to offer traditional, conservative clothing. Some styles have become classics, such as the trenchcoats, Shetland sweaters, oxford-cloth shirts, and bathrobes of soft wool and cotton. Boys can choose from shirts, slacks,

and sweaters; and women will find a feminine version of all the above on the fifth floor. ◆ M-Sa. 346 Madison Ave (at E 44th St). 682.8800 &

39 Chikubu ★★★$$$ This plainly decorated restaurant caters to a mostly Japanese clientele and is a good place for the delicate dishes of Kyoto. Specialties include *akabeko-ju* (rice with thin slices of grilled beef and broiled baby flounder) and *omakase* (a tasting menu of seven to eight courses, including appetizers, sashimi, steamed vegetables or fish, tempura, a noodle or rice dish, and dessert). ◆ Japanese ◆ M-F lunch and dinner; Sa dinner. Reservations recommended. 12 E 44th St (between Madison and Fifth Aves). 818.0715

40 Fred F. French Building The colorful glazed tiles in the tower call out from across the street. Answer the call; the lobby is a stunner. The building was designed in 1927 by **Fred F. French Company** and **H. Douglas Ives**. ◆ 551 Fifth Ave (at E 45th St)

Within the Fred F. French Building:

THE STEAKHOUSE

Morton's of Chicago ★★★$$$ With all the excellent steak houses in New York, especially in this part of town, this Chicago restaurant ranks along with the best. The extra-thick, extra-aged, extra-tender porterhouse is legendary. The lobster cooked in butter and sage is as good as the beef. ◆ Steak house ◆ M-F lunch and dinner; Sa-Su dinner. Reservations recommended. Entrance on E 45th St. 972.3315. Also at: 90 West St (between Albany and Cedar Sts). 732.5665

41 Century Association McKim, Mead & White designed this 1891 Palladian clubhouse for men of achievement in arts and letters (**McKim** and **Mead** were members), which is not open to the public. The large window above the entrance was originally a loggia. ◆ 7 W 43rd St (between Fifth and Sixth Aves). 944.0090

42 Mansfield $$$ The 131 rooms here are small—particularly their bathrooms—but big on style. A few steps off Fifth Avenue and an easy stroll to most Broadway theaters, location is an important draw but so is the quiet, sophisticated ambience. ◆ 12 W 44th St (between Fifth and Sixth Aves). 944.6050; fax 764.4477; www.uniquehotels.com

---

Restaurants/Clubs: Red   Hotels: Blue

Shops/ ♟ Outdoors: Green   **Sights/Culture:** Black

42 General Society Library of Mechanics and Tradesmen More than 140,000 books of fiction, nonfiction, and history are stocked in this private library. The comfortable, elegant surroundings are worth the low membership fee. Within the library are the **Small Press Center,** a nonprofit facility exhibiting books by independent publishers, and the *John M. Mossman Collection of Locks,* where 375 different locks—antique padlocks, powder-proof key locks, and friction locks—are on display. ♦ M-F; closed July. 20 W 44th St (between Fifth and Sixth Aves). 840.1840

43 The Harvard Club The interior of this 1894 Georgian-style building by **McKim, Mead & White** is much more impressive than its facade indicates. If you're not a **Harvard** alum, go around the block and see it through the magnificent window in back. If you are a club member, 60 rooms are available for your use. ♦ 27 W 44th St (between Fifth and Sixth Aves). 840.6600

43 The New York Yacht Club This unusually fanciful, sculptured work was the creation of **Warren & Wetmore** in 1899. The highlight of the eccentric facade are the sailing-ship sterns in the three window bays, complete with ocean waves and dolphins. The setback above the cornice used to be a pergola. This was the home of the America's Cup from 1857 to 1983, when it was lost to Australia (San Diego reclaimed it in 1987). ♦ 37 W 44th St (between Fifth and Sixth Aves). 382.1000

THE Algonquin HOTEL

44 The Algonquin $$$ Recently acquired by Camberley Hotels, this property was built in 1902 by **Goldwyn Starrett,** and was a gathering place for literary types even before the famous Round Table of such writers as Alexander Woollcott, Robert Benchley, and Dorothy Parker began meeting regularly in the **Rose Room.** What the Round Table members had in common, besides their razor-sharp wit, was that they were contributors to *The New Yorker,* whose offices at 25 West 43rd Street conveniently had a back entrance on West 44th Street. Few nearby places are as comfortable as the hotel's lobby, where you can summon a cocktail with the ringing of a bell. Guests find all the comforts and friendliness of a country inn here. A recent mural depicting the legendary Round Table writers was recently completed inside the hotel. (Of the 165 rooms, visiting writers favor Room 306, a suite whose walls are adorned with *Playbill* magazine covers.) ♦ 59 W 44th St (between Fifth and Sixth Aves). 840.6800, 800/548.0345; fax 944.1419 &

Within The Algonquin Hotel:

Oak and Rose Rooms ★$$$ The dark paneling in the **Oak Room** contrasts with the brighter **Rose Room.** But the menu is the same in both, and the quality doesn't vary. The plate-size apple pancake topped with tart lingonberries is a perfect after-theater snack. The Oak Room provides supper club entertainment after 8PM from Tuesday through Saturday. ♦ American ♦ Daily breakfast, lunch, and dinner. Reservations recommended. 840.6800

45 Hotel Royalton $$$$ This hotel's blocklong lobby is the setting for an ultradramatic space (cognac mahogany and green-gray slate) by French designer Philippe Starck. The front desk is discreetly tucked away, as is the bar, patterned after Hemingway's favorite at the Paris Ritz. The **Vodka Bar** is forever full of networking trendoids, and the 167 rooms, many with working fireplaces, are on the cutting edge of modern design and comfort. Amenities include daily newspaper delivery, Kiehl shampoos and bathcubes, and valet parking. The original structure, built in 1898 by **Ehrick Rossiter,** was renovated in 1988 by **Gruzen Samton Steinglass.** ♦ 44 W 44th St (between Fifth and Sixth Aves). 869.4400, 800/635.9013; fax 869.8965 &

Within the Hotel Royalton:

Restaurant 44 ★★$$$ Philippe Starck's minimalist decor—beige walls, furniture with clean modern lines, a hanging horizontal mirror—is just one of the draws at this dining room. Another is the American nouvelle cuisine: goat cheese tourine, mahimahi, scallop and shrimp ceviche, braised shank or seared loin of veal, slow-baked red snapper; and for dessert, celestine tart. ♦ American ♦ M-F breakfast, lunch, and dinner; Sa-Su brunch and dinner. Reservations required. 944.8844

46 Ipanema ★★$$ On what is known as Brazilian Row, this is a good back-up choice if the wait at **Via Brasil** is too long. All entrées at this modest little place come with rice, salad and beans, and you'll notice the clientele is mostly Brazilian, which is a good sign. Not as flamboyant as its neighbor, but still a good choice. ♦ Brazilian ♦ Daily lunch and dinner. Reservations recommended. 13 W 46th St (between Fifth and Sixth Aves). 730.5848

47 Via Brasil ★★$$ This is one of the best places to sample *feijoada,* the country's national dish, or you might want to try one of the lighter grilled meat or poultry dishes, such as *frango ma brasa* (charbroiled breast of chicken); sirloin steak cubed and marinated in garlic, tomatoes, and onions; or a mixed grill of pork, chicken, beef, and Brazilian sausage.

Down your meal with a *caipirinha,* the potent national drink made of rumlike *cachaça,* fresh lime juice, sugar, and ice. Diners are regaled with live music all evening, Wednesday through Saturday, and there's no cover charge. ♦ Brazilian ♦ Daily lunch and dinner. Reservations recommended. 34 W 46th St (between Fifth and Sixth Aves). 997.1158

48 Gotham Book Mart & Gallery Founded by Frances Steloff in 1920, this bookstore has long been a mecca for New York City's literati; Theodore Dreiser, Eugene O'Neill, George Gershwin, and Charlie Chaplin all shopped here. Today this New York equivalent to Paris's Shakespeare & Company is a bibliophile's heaven: a messy hodgepodge of books, mostly literature (especially 20th-century), poetry, drama, art, and literary journals as well as small press and used and rare books. Fans of illustrator/author Edward Gorey will find a large selection of his works. In the upstairs gallery, you'll find changing art exhibitions, including a summer show of vintage postcards from the extensive collection of the store's owner, Andy Brown. ♦ M-Sa. 41 W 47th St (between Fifth and Sixth Aves). 719.4448

49 Rockefeller Center This is the largest privately owned business and entertainment complex in the world, with 19 buildings covering 21 acres (see illustration below). It all began in 1928 when John D. Rockefeller Jr. secured leases on land in the area to provide a setting for the **Metropolitan Opera House,** which was going to move here from the Garment Center. The Great Depression changed the opera's plans and left the philanthropist with a long-term lease on 11.7 acres of Midtown Manhattan. He decided to develop it himself, and demolition of 228 buildings to make way for the project began in May 1931. The last of Rockefeller's original 14 buildings, the **Paramount Publishing Building** at 1230 Sixth Avenue, was opened in April 1940. Construction started again in 1957, when Marilyn Monroe detonated the first charge of dynamite to begin excavation for the **Time & Life Building,** designed by **Harrison & Abramovitz,** at 1271 Sixth Avenue. Since then, the building at 1211 Sixth Avenue and the **McGraw-Hill Building** at 1221 Sixth Avenue, also by **Harrison & Abramovitz,** have been added.

The original complex was designed by **Associated Architects,** a committee made up of **Reinhard & Hoffmeister; Corbett, Harrison and MacMurray;** and **Hood, Godley & Fouilhoux.** At its head, representing the Rockefeller interests, was John R. Todd of Todd, Robertson & Todd Engineering Corp. Their ideas included a north-south, midblock private street (Rockefeller Plaza) between West 48th and West 51st Streets, underground pedestrian and shopping passageways connecting all the buildings, and off-street freight delivery 30 feet underground, capable of handling a thousand trucks a day. The art that enhances the lobbies and exteriors is the work of 30 of the finest artists of the century. The crown jewel of the original **Rockefeller Center** complex is the 70-story **GE Building** at 1256 Sixth Avenue. Todd told the architects that no desk should be more than 30 feet from a window. They obliged him by placing all the rentable space no farther than 28 feet from natural light. About a quarter of the available space has been left open—unusual for an urban development—and much of it has been landscaped. The complex's gardeners keep busy with more than 20,000 flowering plants that are moved periodically, and two acres of formal gardens on the rooftops.

Almost inevitably, **Rockefeller Center** is as much a process as a place, continually changing in one way or another. At press time, a project to remake the blocks of

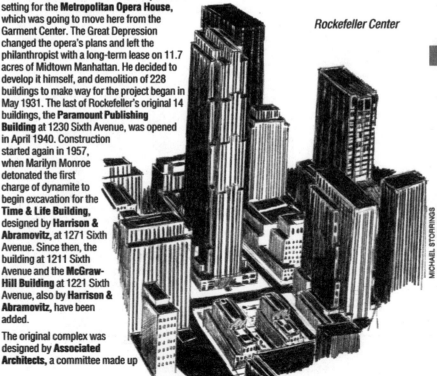

Rockefeller Center

MICHAEL STORRINGS

Rockefeller Plaza into pedestrian malls had just been completed, driving away the limousines that used to use the street as their own parking and pickup location, and two well-regarded restaurants—the **American Festival Cafe** and the **Sea Grill**—had closed down (both are to be replaced by new restaurants, scheduled to open in early 2000). A complete description of the buildings can be found in a walking tour guide available free at the information desk in the lobby at 30 Rockefeller Plaza. A free exhibition on the history of the center through photographs, models, a video presentation, and period memorabilia is located on the concourse level of 30 Rockefeller Plaza. Bounded by Fifth and Seventh Aves, and W 48th and W 52nd Sts. 632.3975

At Rockefeller Center:

Radio City Music Hall Since 1932, this Art Deco palace has maintained a tradition of spectacular entertainment. When it opened as a variety house operated by entrepreneur Roxy Rothafel, it was the largest theater in the world and included such features as a 50-foot turntable on the 110-foot stage, sections of which changed level, 75 rows of fly lines for scenery, a network of microphones, six motor-operated light bridges, a cyclorama 117 feet by 75 feet, and a host of other controls and effects. The scale was overwhelming. "What are those mice doing on stage?" someone asked on opening night. "Those aren't mice, those are horses," his neighbor replied.

The opening of the hall in December 1932 drew such celebrities as Charlie Chaplin, Clark Gable, Amelia Earhart, and Arturo Toscanini. The premiere performance had 75 stellar acts, including Ray Bolger, **The Wallendas**, and the **Roxyettes** (later known as the **Rockettes**).

The hall was soon turned into a movie house with stage shows, featuring the **Rockettes**, the **Corps de Ballet**, the **Symphony Orchestra**, and a variety of guest artists. The premiere feature film was Frank Capra's *The Bitter Tea of General Yen* with Barbara Stanwyck. From 1933 until 1979, more than 650 features debuted here, including *King Kong*, *It Happened One Night*, *Jezebel*, *Top Hat*, *Snow White and the Seven Dwarfs*, *An American in Paris*, and *Mister Roberts*. In 1979, a new format was introduced. Musical spectaculars and pop personalities in concert are the current bill of fare, with major names such as Frank Sinatra, Bette Midler, and Stevie Wonder performing to sold-out audiences. The 57 **Rockettes** still make an annual appearance during the traditional Christmas and Easter shows. Since the theater's opening night on 27 December 1932, nearly 2,000 **Rockettes** have high-kicked their way across the 144-foot stage.

The 5,882-seat hall was awarded landmark status and completely restored in 1979; a second, more ambitious restoration was completed in 1999, under the direction of **Hugh Hardy** of **Hardy Holzman Pfeiffer Associates.** The public areas, designed largely by **Donald Deskey,** are grand: A plush foyer rises 50 feet, overlooked by a sweeping stair and three mezzanine levels lined with gold mirrors and topped by a gold-leaf ceiling. The latest restoration has equipped the theater with state-of-the-art video and HDTV cabability (to meet the needs of Cablevision Systems Corp., the new owner) but also returned every visual detail (from the sign outside to the restrooms) to mint Art Deco condition. The auditorium is everything a theater should be: a plaster vault of overlapping semicircles lit from the inside edge in a rainbow of colors, it provides sunsets and sunrises as the lights go down and up. ♦ Tours: fee. Tours: M-Sa 10AM-5PM; Su 11AM-5PM. 1250 Ave of the Americas (at W 50th St). 247.4777

Rainbow by Cipriani ★★★★$$$$ First opened in 1934 to a reemerging New York society, the legendary Art Moderne restaurant/supper club on the 65th floor of Rockefeller Center was taken over by Cipriani International (which operates the famous Harry's Bar in Venice) in 1998. The new **Rainbow Room,** its famous revolving dance floor intact, is mostly used for private parties while the former **Promenade Bar** on the south side has been reincarnated as the **Rainbow Grill,** open seven days a week. The menu, which changes daily, is an inconceivably upscale take on the cuisine of Venice, under chef Giuseppe Marangi. ♦ Venetian ♦ Daily lunch and dinner. Reservations required; jacket and tie required. 49 W 49th St (between Rockefeller Plaza and Sixth Ave), 65th floor. 632.5000

NBC Studio Tours Tours of the radio and television facilities of the **National Broadcasting Co.** are offered. Children under six are not admitted. If you don't want to wait in line, walk over to West 49th and Rockefeller Plaza and see if you can catch sight of Katie Couric, Matt Lauer, and Al Roker who do the *Today Show,* live from their street level picture-window studio. ♦ Admission. Daily. 30 Rockefeller Plaza (between W 49th and W 50th Sts). 664.4000 &

The Rink at Rockefeller Center The summertime outdoor dining area of what used to be the **American Festival Cafe** becomes an ice-skating rink every October, staying slick and smooth right through April. Ice skates can be rented at the rink. ♦ Admission; additional fee for skate rental. Daily. Call for changing sessions. Lower plaza. 332.7654

Metropolitan Museum of Art Gift Shop At three floors and 6,000 square feet, this is the largest of the museum's nine gift shop outposts. The merchandise, for the most part inspired by the museum's permanent collections and special exhibitions, includes prints and posters, stationery, jewelry, tabletop accessories, sculpture reproductions, and educational gifts for children. Especially popular are the museum's signature items, which include *William,* a reproduction of the 12th-dynasty Egyptian hippo (the **Met**'s unofficial mascot); and Venus earrings, one black and one white teardrop, worn by the goddess in Rubens's *Venus Before the Mirror.* ♦ Daily. 15 W 49th St (between Fifth Ave and Rockefeller Plaza). 332.1380

Librairie de France and Librería Hispánica (French and European Publications) This bookstore provides one of the best—albeit expensive—selections of books in French and in English about France, with a smaller offering of Spanish books, and one of the world's great ranges of dictionaries and grammatical references for languages from all over the world. ♦ M-Sa. 610 Fifth Ave (south side of Promenade, between W 49th and W 50th Sts). 581.8810 ₤

Teuscher Chocolates of Switzerland Some of the city's best (and most expensive) chocolate bonbons are offered here. The spectacular window displays change with the season. ♦ M-Sa. 620 Fifth Ave (north side of Promenade, between W 49th and W 50th Sts). 246.4416. Also at: 25 E 61st St (at Madison Ave). 751.8482

Tuscan Square Tuscany comes to New York in this 11,700-square-foot, $45-million emporium, the brainchild of restaurateur Pino Luongo. The bilevel complex showcases everything that is Tuscan: clothing, porcelain and ceramics, herbed candles, bath oils, fragrances—and, of course, food and wine. The on-site restaurant—serving Northern Italian specialties, naturally, and pretty elegant for a department store, though not too pricey—seems to be getting larger and larger, threatening to take over the whole location. ♦ M-F 10AM-11PM; Sa 10 AM-10:30 PM; Su 11 AM-10:30 PM. 16 W 51st St (between Fifth Ave and Rockefeller Plaza). 977.7777

50 La Réserve ★★★$$$$ Handsome and spacious, with peach fabric banquettes and mirrors, this is the right place for a romantic dinner. The classic French menu features *coquillette d'escargot* (salted cod, mashed potatoes and garlic, with snails on the side); saddle of rabbit with wine sauce; and sliced duck breast with cabbage, honey, and balsamic vinegar. The chocolate basket filled with chocolate mousse and raspberries is an absolute must to round off the meal. ♦ French ♦ M-F lunch and dinner; Sa dinner. Reservations required. 4 W 49th St (between Fifth Ave and Rockefeller Plaza). 247.2993

50 The Goelet Building Ignore the ground-floor shops in this crisp, early-modern structure, built in 1932 by **E.H. Faile & Co.** But do stop in the elevator lobby: The highly ornamented space is a hidden Art Deco gem all the way to the paneling of the elevator cabs. Note the lighting in the pilasters and cornices. ♦ 608 Fifth Ave (at W 49th St)

51 Saks Fifth Avenue Fashionable and always in good taste, this New York institution has another asset few other stores can offer: service. Great designer collections throughout the store will please any woman's sense of style, and the men's department is legendary. The selection for children is heaven on earth for parents and grandparents who enjoy seeing the little ones turned out in style. The small luxury selection of candies, liqueur cakes, and chocolates includes beautiful truffles from Joseph Schmidt and decadent chocolate-and-caramel-covered apples from Mrs. Prindables. The airy **Cafe SFA** on the eighth floor is a great spot for lunch, particularly if you come early and secure a window table overlooking **St. Patrick's Cathedral** or **Rockefeller Center.** If it's Christmas time, the window displays are a must-see. ♦ Daily. 611 Fifth Ave (between E 49th and E 50th Sts). 753.4000 ₤

52 Hatsuhana ★★★$$$ Sushi lovers give this bar top ratings for the freshest sushi, creatively rolled. Sit at a table or the counter, but definitely try to find a spot where you can watch the sushi chef in action. In addition to the raw fare, good tempura and some skewered grilled dishes are also available. The à la carte items tend to add up quickly, so if you're on a budget, the prix-fixe lunch menu is a good buy. ♦ Japanese ♦ M-F lunch and dinner; Sa dinner. Reservations recommended. 17 E 48th St (between Madison and Fifth Aves). 355.3345

53 Crouch & Fitzgerald This store is an old New York institution for luggage, handbags, and business cases. The emphasis is on traditional styling. Don't miss their legendary seasonal sales. ♦ M-Sa. 400 Madison Ave (at E 48th St). 755.5888 ₤

54 Waldorf-Astoria Hotel $$$$ The incomparable grande dame has been home to permanent guests such as the Duchess of Windsor and the American representative to the **UN,** as well as temporary guests like King Faisal of Saudi Arabia and every US president (including Clinton) since 1931. It was moved here when the **Empire State Building** rose on its former site on lower Fifth Avenue. Taking up nearly the entire block between Lexington and Park Avenues and East 49th and East 50th Streets, it has 1,215 spacious guest rooms. Together with the adjacent and slightly more expensive **Waldorf Towers,** with 118 guest rooms and 77 suites, the hotel is now administered by the Hilton chain. Designed by **Schultze & Weaver,** the building is considered by many to be the best on this stretch of Park Avenue. The base is in proper relation to the surrounding buildings, while the unique twin towers are still noteworthy additions to the skyline.

The hotel epitomized the good life of New York in the 1930s, carrying on in the tradition of its fashionable predecessor at West 34th Street and Fifth Avenue. (The hotel's tony guests often arrived underground in their private railway cars on a specially constructed spur off the tracks under Park Avenue.) The luxurious Art Deco interiors have suffered some mistreatment and neglect over the years—the burled walnut elevator cabs, for example, were lined with brocade—but have been meticulously restored. Of particular interest are the Louis Rigel murals in the lobby and the *Wheel of Life* mosaic in the floor of the lobby. The **Bull and Bear** and the pretty **Peacock Alley** are popular dining spots. **Plus One** is a complete fitness and spa facility. ♦ 301 Park Ave (between E 49th and E 50th Sts). 355.3000, 800/445.8667; fax 872.7272 ♿

Within the Waldorf-Astoria Hotel:

Inagiku ★★★$$$$ Few rooms capture the cool and peaceful ambience as well as this recently renovated one with interiors by Adam Tihany. The design blends traditional Japanese with openness and theatricality, using yin-yang symbols and rice grains as recurring motifs. Chef Haruo Ohbu's menu does something similar with the glories of Japanese cooking, ranging from the traditional sushi, tempura, and sashimi (the latter may come in the form of a sculpted New York City skyline), or beef cooked in broth at the *shabu shabu* bar, through rare specialties like *hakata* (barbecued eel layered with shiitake mushrooms and spinach) or *kasuzake* (black cod marinated in sake lees and grilled), to an outrageous foie gras sushi. ♦ Japanese ♦ M-F lunch and dinner; Sa-Su dinner. Reservations required; jacket required. 355.0440

55 Chase Manhattan World Headquarters This 53-story monster was built in 1960 by **Skidmore, Owings & Merrill** for Union Carbide, which has since moved to the suburbs. Railroad yards under the building made it necessary to begin the elevator shafts on the second floor, which is why the ground-floor lobby looks forgotten. ♦ 270 Park Ave (at E 47th St). 270.6000

56 Hotel Inter-Continental New York $$$ Once known as the **Barclay,** this 692-room hotel designed by **Cross & Cross** in 1927 was the most luxurious of the hotels built by the **New York Central Railroad.** Now part of the Inter-Continental chain, it retains its elegance, with special amenities to make life easier for visiting businesspeople (24-hour room service, concierge, valet service, and health spa). The hotel's original name lives on in the **Barclay Bar and Grill.** ♦ 111 E 48th St (between Lexington and Park Aves). 755.5900, 800/327.0200; fax 644.0079 ♿

57 W New York $$$$ For the business traveler who appreciates both in-room Web surfing (via an infrared keyboard) and not just a respite but an all-out retreat from the concrete jungle, the new, David Rockwell–designed **W New York** is a great place to bed down. The former 722-room **Doral Inn** underwent a total transformation in 1998 to become the first in a new chain of stylish business hotels dubbed **W.** The nature theme—inevitably more Malibu than midtown Manhattan—is at its most dramatic in the uncommonly airy lobby, with its light, earth-toned colors and fabrics and huge columns decked out in swaying, silk-screened translucent fabrics. The result is dramatic and different, if not exactly cozy. Guest rooms are deliberately spare but comfortable, and feature such ostensibly restorative touches as sheets lined with inspirational sayings (such as "Dream with Lucidity" and "Sleep with Angels") and slender planters brimming with grass—along with watering cans.

You don't have to stay at the **W** to enjoy the cutting-edge establishments that call it home. First there's **Whiskey Blue,** Rande Gerber's chic watering hole with its rich brown and heather hues, sensual lighting and backlit mahogany bar. **Cool Juice** is a specialty sandwich shop as well as a juice and coffee bar. **Away,** a gym and full service spa, is located on the fourth floor. 541 Lexington Ave (at 49th St). 755.1200, 800/877.WHOTELS; www.whotels.com ♿

Within the W New York:

Heartbeat ★★$$$ Dining in restaurateur Drew Nieporent's theme restaurant is as much a conceptual as it is a culinary experience. The New Age/millennial decor is upbeat and bright, and the columns that grace the lobby get a multicolor treatment here that seems out of place. What merits closer inspection is executive chef Michel Nischan's innovative menu: New American meets spa cuisine in a style the management calls "Natural American." Try the roasted baby chicken with pear, apple, and goat cheese galette; grilled paillard of salmon with caramelized cauliflower; or arborio rice with butternut squash and wild mushrooms. Dessert is the domain of pastry chef George McKirdy; try his dome of chocolate mousse laced with cherries and almonds and served with homemade cherry sorbet or spiced sautéed pineapple and passion fruit with a lime-fennel sorbet and vanilla beet sauce. Top it off with tea of the gourmet variety—tea sommelier James Labe explains the brews on offer. ◆ Natural American ◆ Daily breakfast, lunch and dinner. Reservations recommended. 407.2900 ♿

58 New York Marriott East Side $$$ Originally the **Shelton**, a club/hotel for men, this 34-story tower designed by **Arthur Loomis Harmon** in 1924 was the first major building to reflect the 1916 zoning regulations. Its set-back massing is admirable, and the design became particularly famous as the winner of architectural awards and as the subject of many paintings by Georgia O'Keeffe. The hotel's 655 renovated rooms have character, but some are cramped. Within, the hotel has a coffee shop, the **Shelton Grill** for more serious dining, and the **Champion Sports Bar.** ◆ 525 Lexington Ave (between E 48th and E 49th Sts). 755.4000, 800/228.9290; fax 751.3440 ♿

59 Roger Smith Hotel $$$ This elegant hostelry offers 163 renovated rooms and suites and a spacious lobby that features mahogany and free-form bronze sculptures by hotel president/artist James Knowles. Rooms come with their own coffeemakers, and most rooms on the **Concierge Floor** have granite bathrooms with Jacuzzis and hair dryers. ◆ 501 Lexington Ave (at E 47th St). 755.1400, 800/455.0277; fax 319.9130 ♿

60 Helmsley Middletowne $$$ Part of the Helmsley chain, this 192-room hotel offers predominantly junior and large suites, some with kitchenettes, terraces, and fireplaces. ◆ 148 E 48th St (between Third and Lexington Aves). 755.3000, 800/221.4982; fax 832.0261 ♿

61 767 Third Avenue This squeaky-clean curved office tower designed in 1981 by **Fox & Fowle** is high-tech, clothed in brick and wood instead of aluminum and steel. The chessboard on the side wall of the building next door was provided by the developer, Melvyn Kauffman, so that guests would have something to look at. A new move is made on the board each week; ask the concierge at No. 767 for the bulletin and a short description of how to play the game. ◆ At E 48th St

62 Turtle Bay Gardens When planning began for the **UN** complex just east of here, these blocks were slated for demolition. Cooler heads prevailed, and this little development, dating from 1870 and remodeled in 1920 by architect **Clarence Dean,** was saved. The development, not open to the public, was created for Mrs. Walton Martin, who bought a back-to-back row of 10 houses on each street,

then ripped out all the walls and fences behind them to create a common garden. She left a 12-foot strip down the middle for a path, at the center of which she installed a fountain copied from the Villa Medici in Rome. She redesigned the 20 houses so that their living rooms faced the private garden rather than the street and began attracting such tenants as Tyrone Power and Leopold Stokowski. Katharine Hepburn still lives here. ◆ 227-247 E 48th St and 226-246 E 49th St (between Second and Third Aves)

63 Lescaze Residence Glass blocks, stucco, and industrial-pipe railings replaced the original brownstone front of this town house when modernist architect **William Lescaze** converted it to his combination office/residence in 1934. **Lescaze** is well known as the co-designer of Philadelphia's extraordinary PSFS Building with **George Howe.** He also participated in the design of **1 New York Plaza** overlooking the harbor, and the **Municipal Courthouse** at 111 Centre Street. ◆ 211 E 48th St (between Second and Third Aves)

64 780 Third Avenue This 50-story tower is clad in brick, but the cross patterns are the structure showing through—a sort of dressed version of Chicago's John Hancock Tower. A plaza on three sides is a relief in a crowded area. **Raul de Armas** was the partner in charge of the 1983 **Skidmore, Owings & Merrill** design. ◆ Between E 48th and E 49th Sts

65 Smith & Wollensky ★★$$$ Young corporate types favor this meat palace above all others. The decor is dramatic—black lacquered chairs, Chinese-lantern–style lights, and gargoyles perched on the sides of the banquettes—and the upstairs dining room has three skylights. The steaks and prime ribs are crowd pleasers, and such basic desserts as Austrian strudel don't disappoint. For more casual and less expensive fare, try **Wollensky's Grill** (205 East 49th St, between Second and Third Aves, 753.0444). Both restaurants offer an extraordinary American wine list. ◆ American ◆ M-F lunch and dinner; Sa-Su dinner. Reservations required. 797 Third Ave (at E 49th St). 753.1530

66 Chin Chin ★★$$$ Chinese cuisine takes an innovative turn in this handsome, sophisticated restaurant with beige walls and recessed lighting. Try the country-style chicken with spinach, crispy sea bass, steamed salmon with black-bean sauce, or sautéed leg of lamb with leeks. ♦ Cantonese ♦ M-F lunch and dinner; Sa-Su dinner. 216 E 49th St (between Second and Third Aves). 888.4555

67 Beekman Tower Hotel $$$ Originally called the **Panhellenic Hotel,** catering to women belonging to Greek-letter sororities, this is now an all-suite hotel (there are 171) favored by **UN** visitors looking for reasonably priced accommodations with fully equipped kitchens. **John Mead Howells** designed the building in 1928. For a wonderful view of the East River, have a drink in the newly renovated **Top of the Tower.** ♦ 3 Mitchell Pl (between Beekman Pl and First Ave). 355.7000, 800/637.8483; fax 753.9366

68 Wylie's ★★$$ Rib fans mightn't all agree, but many have called this place the best joint in town for almost 20 years. It's always crowded with a satiated-looking crowd of happy habitués. Specialties include juicy beef or pork ribs, moist barbecued chicken, and T-bone steak—with a side of onion rings, which call out for the restaurant's tasty hallmark dipping sauce. ♦ Barbecue/Ribs ♦ Daily lunch, dinner, and late-night meals. 891 First Ave (at E 50th St). 751.0700

69 Lutèce ★★★$$$$ Although Andre Soltner's presence is no longer felt, this decades-old bastion of Alsatian cooking still ranks at the top of every critic's list of special French restaurants. Today chef Eberhard Mueller is committed to retaining some of Soltner's traditions—the restaurant's famous onion tart, beef Wellington, roasted duck, rack of lamb, and soufflés, for example—while adding his own special touch to other creations. Seafood is emphasized on the lighter, seasonal menu—red snapper *tartare* cured in Riesling and crabmeat-and-potato salad with truffle vinaigrette are popular choices. Dessert selections—such as sautéed bananas in phyllo dough with banana-cashew ice cream and passion fruit sauce, or rhubarb pie—are hard to resist. ♦ French ♦ M, Sa dinner; Tu-F lunch and dinner. Reservations required. 249 E 50th St (between Second and Third Aves). 752.2225

70 Zarela ★★★$$ This place, decorated with antique Mexican masks, colorful paper cutouts, and very bright fabrics, maintains an ongoing party atmosphere. Don't miss the margaritas and Zarela's famous red snapper hash. Also try the grilled marinated skirt steak with salsa, guacamole, and flour tortillas. ♦ Mexican ♦ M-F lunch and dinner; Sa-Su dinner. Reservations required. 953 Second Ave (between E 50th and E 51st Sts). 644.6740

71 Pickwick Arms Hotel $ The 370 redecorated rooms (100 less expensive rooms share baths) in this hotel are popular for their Midtown location; other pluses are a roof garden, a cocktail lounge, and a gourmet deli. ♦ 230 E 51st St (between Second and Third Aves). 355.0300, 800/742.5945; fax 755.5729 &

72 Greenacre Park Another "vest pocket park," this one is slightly larger and more elaborate than its cousin, **Paley Park.** Designed in 1971 by **Sasaki, Dawson, DeMay Associates,** it was a gift to the city by Mrs. Jean Mauze, daughter of John D. Rockefeller Jr. ♦ 217-221 E 51st St (between Second and Third Aves)

73 Fu's ★★$$$ Decorated in a contemporary style in shades of gray, pink, and burgundy, this is a popular spot for gourmet Chinese food; the kitchen offers a variety of Hunan, Mandarin, Szechuan, and Cantonese specialties. Order the Grand Marnier shrimp (it's not on the menu, but regulars know to ask for it), lemon chicken, crispy orange beef, or panfried flounder. ♦ Chinese ♦ Daily lunch and dinner. Reservations recommended. 972 Second Ave (between E 51st and E 52nd Sts). 517.9670

74 Eamonn Doran ★★$$ Yes, it's the trendy spot where the young movers and shakers converge after hours. But it's the good country-style food that's the primary raison d'être. Straightforward meat and seafood dishes are served in generous portions along with salads, stews, and omelettes prepared to order. ♦ American/Irish ♦ M-F lunch, dinner, and late-night meals. Reservations recommended. 988 Second Ave (between E 52nd and E 53rd Sts). 752.8088. Also at: 224-232 E 39th St (between Second Ave and Tunnel Exit St). 687.7802; 136 W 33rd St (between Sixth and Seventh Aves). 967.7676; 174 Montague St (between Court and Clinton Sts), Brooklyn Heights. 718/596.4969

75 242 East 52nd Street Like the **Lescaze Residence,** this 1950 **Philip Johnson** design is a quintessentially modern composition in a row house lot. Commissioned by John D. Rockefeller Jr. as a guesthouse for the **Museum of Modern Art,** it was also used at one time by **Johnson** as a New York City pied-à-terre. The base is Wrightian brick, the top Miesian steel and glass, and the whole composition is almost Oriental in its simplicity and mystery. ♦ Between Second and Third Aves

76 Bridge Kitchenware Corp. Pros such as Julia Child pick up their copper pots, knife sets, and pastry tubes at this exceptional store, which stocks a large selection of expensive specialty utensils at more affordable prices. Kitchen novices are welcome here too; contrary to popular belief, the staff is both patient and knowledgeable. ♦ M-Sa. 214 E 52nd St (between Second and Third Aves). 688.4220

77 Nippon ★★$$$$ One of the first restaurants to introduce sushi and sashimi to New Yorkers, this gracious place maintains its overall high quality and continues to offer dishes unfamiliar to Western palates—*usuzukuri* (marinated fluke in very thin slices). There are also excellent versions of more familiar dishes, such as *shabu shabu* (beef and vegetables cooked at the table in a hot pot of soy broth) and tempura. ♦ Japanese ♦ M-F lunch and dinner; Sa dinner. Reservations recommended. 155 E 52nd St (between Third and Lexington Aves). 758.0226

77 Cosi Sandwich Bar ★★★$$ The prices aren't the cheapest in town, but the sandwiches, soups, and salads are delectable. Choose from a wealth of fresh ingredients—from smoked salmon with crème fraîche to tandoori grilled chicken with coriander-roasted tomatoes—when constructing your own super healthy sandwich on the signature pizza romana, a hearth-fired flat bread. ♦ Cafe ♦ M-F lunch and dinner; Sa dinner. No credit cards accepted. 165 E 52nd St (between Third and Lexington Aves). 758.7800

78 Rand McNally Map and Travel Center The well-stocked book department also has travel videos, road maps, wall maps, books, globes, travel games, map puzzles, beachballs, pillows, and geography games. Call 800/234.0679 for 24-hour mail-order service. ♦ Daily. 150 E 52nd St (between Third and Lexington Aves). 758.7488 ♿

79 San Carlos Hotel $$ Most of the 146 comfortably furnished rooms here have kitchenettes. ♦ 150 E 50th St (between Third and Lexington Aves). 755.1800, 800/722.2012; fax 688.9778

80 Tatou ★$$$ Opulent and slightly decadent-looking, this 1930s opera house sports lamps attached to Mephistophelian heads, a giant chandelier that looks borrowed from the set of *Phantom of the Opera,* statues and paintings of cherubs, and faux-antique windows set against yellow brocade walls. A band performs nightly on the stage where Edith Piaf and Judy Garland once sang. The creative fare includes grilled tuna with foie gras and porcini mushrooms in a Cabernet sauce, a Moroccan spiced salmon with artichokes, leeks, cured olives, and *harissa* sauce, venison with mustard spaetzle, apple-braised cabbage, and bacon-roasted Brussels sprouts. For dessert, sample such elegant creations as almond coconut flan, crème brûlée, or the chocolate *marquise* that's shaped like a piano. ♦ International ♦ M-F lunch and dinner; Sa dinner. Reservations recommended. 151 E 50th St (between Third and Lexington Aves). 753.1144

81 The Beverly $$$ Most of the 200 accommodations are suites or junior suites with kitchenettes in this homey and comfy hotel. **Kaufman Pharmacy** within the hotel is one of the few left in New York open 24 hours a day (but its prices are exorbitant). Decent steak can be had at **Kenny's Steak and Seafood House.** ♦ 125 E 50th St (at Lexington Ave). 753.2700, 800/223.0945; fax 753.2700 ♿

82 Loews New York Hotel $$$ **Morris Lapidus** and **Harle & Liebman**'s 1961 plastic modern design for this hotel is nonetheless cheery and comfortable inside. The lodging offers 722 rooms as well as an in-hotel garage, barbershop, beauty salon, and jewelry shop. There is also a coffee shop and the **Lexington Avenue Grill** for breakfast and dinner. ♦ 569 Lexington Ave (at E 51st St). 752.7000, 800/223.0888; fax 758.6311

83 General Electric Building This 51-story tower was designed in 1931 by **Cross & Cross** to harmonize with the Byzantine lines of **St. Bartholomew's Church,** and is still best seen with the church at its feet. But it's a beauty from any angle, lavishly decorated with what may have been intended to be stylized lightning bolts in honor of its first tenant, the Radio Corporation of America, which moved

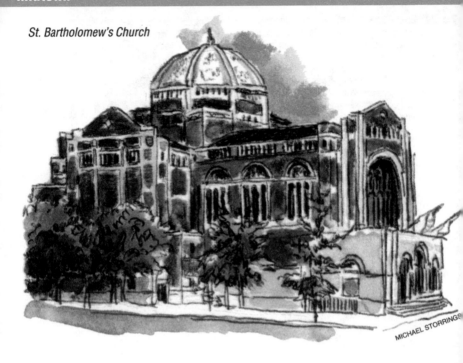

St. Bartholomew's Church

MICHAEL STORRINGS

soon after to the new **Rockefeller Center.**
Take a peek at the lobby. ♦ 570 Lexington Ave
(at E 51st St)

84 St. Bartholomew's Church This richly
detailed Byzantine landmark (shown above)
with a charming little garden is a breath of
fresh air on a high-rise–lined block. But it has
been the object of a long-running battle
between preservationists and church fathers,
who wanted to sell off the **Community House**
for commercial development (the plans were
eventually nixed). The portico was a
Vanderbilt-financed, **Stanford
White**–designed addition (1903) to a church
by **James Renwick Jr.** In 1919, **Bertram G.
Goodhue** inherited the portico and designed
the church—a confabulation handled with
style. The site was a Schaefer brewery in the
1860s. ♦ Park Ave (between E 50th and E 51st
Sts). 751.1616 ♿

85 Seagram Building The ultimate
representation of pure modernist reason, this
classically proportioned and exquisitely
detailed 1958 bronze, glass, and steel box by
Ludwig Mies van der Rohe and **Philip
Johnson** is the one everybody copied (see
Sixth Avenue and other parts of Park
Avenue)—but it's still the best. The
immutable object is a vestigial column set
back on a plaza that was an innovative relief
when it was conceived. ♦ 375 Park Ave (at E
53rd St)

Within the Seagram Building:

The Four Seasons ★★★★$$$$ Owners
Alex von Bidder and Julian Niccolini oversee
the two dining rooms at one of the world's
most celebrated restaurants. **The Bar Room
Grill** is power central at mid-day, when the t(
echelons of New York's publishing world
gather to exchange notes and gossip.
Featured in this casual space later in the day
one of the city's true fine dining bargains—a
under-$59.50 three-course meal, including
coffee or tea. The **Pool Room** next door, a
more formal spot, has been going strong
since 1958 and features such dishes as oxta
ravioli with sage, pumpkin bisque with
cinnamon, carpaccio of tuna and salmon wit
ginger, foie gras with figs, and sea bass in ar
herb crust. ♦ Continental ♦ M-F lunch and
dinner; Sa dinner. Reservations required;
jacket and tie required. 99 E 52nd St (betwee
Lexington and Park Aves). 754.9494

86 Racquet and Tennis Club A somewhat
uninspired Florentine palazzo, this 1918
McKim, Mead & White design is an
appropriate foil for the **Seagram Building**
across the street. Hard to believe as we
approach the 21st century, but "men only"
partake in tennis, squash, racquets (an
English game similar to squash but faster),
and swimming. ♦ Members only. M-F 7AM-

11PM. 370 Park Ave (between E 52nd and E 53rd Sts). 753.9700

87 Fresco ★★$$ This family affair owned by Marion Scotto and her children Anthony Jr., Elaina, and Rosanna (a famous local newscaster) is both elegant and cheery. Colors abound, on the ocher walls with bold paintings by SoHo artists, and in the complex floral displays. Try *spaghettini* with clams, garlic, basil, and roasted tomatoes; baked penne with pancetta (Italian unsmoked bacon), parmesan, and cream; one of the homemade ravioli specials; rib-eye steak and grilled veal chop. Desserts are irresistible— either the lemon tartlet or cinnamon ice- cream sandwich makes a perfect ending for the meal. ♦ Italian ♦ M-F lunch and dinner; Sa dinner. Reservations recommended. 34 E 52nd St (between Park and Madison Aves). 935.3434 ♿

88 Omni Berkshire Place $$$$ The old **Berkshire** has become one of the city's plushest European-style hotels. Its $50- million renovation added new life to the 396 generously proportioned rooms, which now boast faxes, two phone lines, and sitting areas; 44 spacious suites offer even more amenities. The face-lift also produced a new health club and fitness center. ♦ 21 E 52nd St (between Madison and Fifth Aves). 753.5800, 800/THE.OMNI; fax 755.2317

Within the Omni Berkshire Place:

Kokachin ★★★$$$ This has become a popular destination, thanks to talented chef Paul Voto's distinctive Asian-influenced menu. Choose from among such unusual but appealing pairings as mussels with curry rice paper; foie gras with green papaya salad; crispy quail with spicy greens in a mango vinaigrette; and taro-wrapped lobster with cèpes and chestnuts. Main courses are equally inventive, including marinated sturgeon with pickled plums and griddled rice cakes, miso-marinated cod with eggplant and tomato ginger sauce, and crispy whole sea bass with red seaweed salad and citrus. Desserts are memorable: Choose steamed chocolate pudding, passion fruit mousse topped with chopped mango, or coconut ice milk as a perfect finish to your meal. ♦ Asian/Seafood ♦ Daily lunch and dinner. Reservations recommended. 355.9300 ♿

89 Sushisay ★★$$$ The name means fresh sushi and that's exactly what you'll get at this branch of the Tokyo original, complete with white walls and *shoji* screens. At lunchtime it's filled with Japanese businessmen, so don't count on getting a seat at the sushi bar. ♦ Japanese ♦ M-F lunch and dinner; Sa dinner. Reservations required. 38 E 51st St (between Park and Madison Aves). 755.1780

89 Tse Yang ★★$$$ Like the original **Tse Yang** in Paris, this stateside outpost offers outstanding Beijing cuisine and European- style service in a stunning Imperial setting of black mirrors, rich wood paneling, and hammered copper and brass appointments. Chef Yang Kui-Fah serves a tasty crab-leg salad, tea-smoked salmon, hot-and-sour soup, orange beef (served cold), and pickled cabbage. ♦ Chinese ♦ Daily lunch and dinner. Reservations recommended; jacket required. 34 E 51st St (between Park and Madison Aves). 688.5447 ♿

90 The Villard Houses This collection of six houses was designed in 1884 by **McKim, Mead & White** to resemble a single Italian palazzo at the request of the original owner, publisher Henry Villard. They were later owned by the Archdiocese of New York, which sold them to Harry Helmsley. In a precedent- setting arrangement, Helmsley incorporated two of the landmark houses into his **Palace Hotel** and restored the interiors to their turn- of-the-century rococo splendor—although you might wonder if they ever looked as new as they do now. ♦ 451-459 Madison Ave (between E 50th and E 51st Sts)

Within The Villard Houses:

Urban Center The Municipal Art Society, Parks Council, **Architectural League of New York,** and the New York Chapter of the **American Institute of Architects** share the north wing of **The Villard Houses,** where they frequently host exhibitions that are open to the public. The Information Exchange, a service project of the Municipal Art Society that helps find answers to questions about New York City, "the built city," is also here. The service will, for example, field queries about the history of **Central Park** or how to clean brownstones and repair old plasterwork. ♦ M-F 10AM-1PM. 935.3960

Urban Center Books As you would expect, the emphasis is on books, periodicals, and journals about architecture, historic preservation, and urban design. ♦ M-Sa. 457 Madison Ave. 935.3595 ♿

91 The New York Palace Hotel $$$$ Thoroughly refurbished by its most recent owners, the royal family of Brunei, this elegant property incorporates part of the 110-year-old landmark **Villard Houses,** resulting in an uneasy but interesting marriage. The elaborate lobby in the old section (protected from alteration) is opulent—even excessively so—with the ornate woodwork, marble, frescoes, and fireplaces from the Gilded Age all intact. The 963 guest rooms, along with four triplex suites, are spaciously comfortable and thoughtfully appointed. Guests staying on the **Executive Floors** are afforded complimentary food and beverage lounges. A fitness center, the **Istana** restaurant, and **Le Cirque 2000** (see below) complete the picture. Don't miss the whimsical animal topiary on the Madison Avenue–side outdoor terrace area. ♦ 455 Madison Ave (entrance on E 50th St). 888.7000, 800/NYPALAC; fax 303.6000

Within The New York Palace Hotel:

Le Cirque 2000 ★★★$$$$ Sirio Maccioni of the legendary **Le Cirque** took his time before settling on this location for the reopening of his posh restaurant in 1997. Chef Sottha Khunn continues his culinary magic, producing many original dishes along with haute cuisine samplings. Best choices are foie gras ravioli in consommé, striped bass wrapped in lettuce with celery and carrots julienne, and blue prawns with halibut. Pastry chef Jacques Torres's spectacular desserts continue to dazzle diners—save room for the towering chocolate mousse cake and the house special crème brûlée. The wine list includes a good selection of vintage Bordeaux at surprisingly affordable prices. ♦ French ♦ M-Sa lunch and dinner; Su dinner. Reservations recommended; jacket and tie required. 303.7788

92 Maloney & Porcelli ★★$$$ New to Midtown is this restaurant whose hallmark is its tender, prime meats. Chef Patrick Vaccariello's most popular entrée, the crackling pork shank served on a bed of poppyseeded sauerkraut with firecracker applesauce, is simply terrific. Other specialties include London broil and grilled rib-eye, as well as such seafood dishes as lemon-crusted salmon steak and steamed lobster. Desserts are standard, with cheesecake topping the list. ♦ Steak house ♦ M-F lunch and dinner; Sa-Su dinner. Reservations recommended. 37 E 50th St (between Park and Madison Aves). 750.2233

93 St. Patrick's Cathedral Now dwarfed by its surroundings—particularly by the **Rockefeller Center**—this church was considered too far out of town when **James Renwick Jr.** built it in the 1880s. (**Charles T. Matthews** added **Lady Chapel** in 1906.) The 11th-largest church in the world, the structure is a finely detailed and well-proportioned but not very strict adaptation of its French-Gothic predecessors. There are no flying buttresses, for example, but there are pinnacles. The spires rise to 330 feet, and the rose window above the center portal is 26 feet in diameter. More than half of the 70 stained-glass

windows were made in Chartres and Nantes. **Renwick** also designed the high altar, presided over by New York's Roman Catholic archbishop. ♦ Fifth Ave (between E 50th and E 51st Sts). 753.2261 ♿

94 Olympic Tower This black glass box full of exclusive apartments was designed in 1976 by **Skidmore, Owings & Merrill.** The hospitable interior arcade is complete with a waterfall and a refreshment stand, plus a foreign currency exchange office. Reflections of **St. Patrick's** are a nice bonus. ♦ 645 Fifth Ave (at E 51st St)

95 Versace The late designer's newest boutique is a 28,000-square-foot renovated Vanderbilt mansion. The shop offers the popular—sometimes flamboyant—Couture collection for men and women. For those with limits on their Visa Golds, there are also the mid-priced Versus and Istante labels. ♦ M-Sa 647 Fifth Ave (between E 51st and E 52nd Sts). Also at, for men: 816 Madison Ave (between E 68th and E 69th Sts). 744.5572; for women: 817 Madison Ave (between E 68th and E 69th Sts). 744.6868

Cartier

95 Cartier Lovely baubles for the body and the home, mostly at astronomical prices, are this shop's stock in trade. The creator of the tank watch is always coming up with original designs, and there are all those rings of diamonds, emeralds, and pearls. Don't miss "Les Must," the more affordable boutique collection of gifts, such as cigarette lighters. Once the residence of businessman Morton F Plant, the Renaissance palazzo–style building is a rare survivor of the days when Fifth Avenue was lined with the private homes of such people as William Vanderbilt, who lived diagonally across the street. **Robert W. Gibson** designed the building in 1905; **William Welles Bosworth** supervised the conversion to a store in 1917. Note the detailing of the entrance and centralized composition on East 52nd Street. ♦ M-F; Sa June-August. 2 E 52nd St (at Fifth Ave). 753.0111 ♿

LA GRENOUILLE

96 La Grenouille ★★$$$$ The annual budget for flowers here is close to $100,000, and the fresh daily arrangements show it. Mirrors sparkle everywhere, and the lighting is nearly perfect, making the "beautiful people" who frequent this place look even more beautiful. There are wonderful traditional dishes on the menu such as Dover sole, rack of lamb, cheese soufflé, but be prepared to spend big time if you want a good wine to go with them. ◆ French ◆ Tu-Sa lunch and dinner; closed mid-July–August. Reservations required; jacket and tie required. 3 E 52nd St (between Madison and Fifth Aves). 752.1495

97 '21' Club ★★★$$$$ Settle down to a savory '21' Burger, onetime favorite of Aristotle Onassis, or for that matter black-mint–crusted antelope with roasted pearl onions, flageolet and fava beans, and soak up the atmosphere of what is one of only a handful of genuinely legendary New York restaurants. Actually *establishment* is the more apt word to describe **'21'**, which has been a magnet for the rich, famous and powerful almost since its inception as a speakeasy during the Prohibition years. There's an unmistakable and mildly intoxicating buzz in the air here, generated as much by the legions of devotees past (Humphrey Bogart, Ernest Hemingway, and Salvador Dalí, to name a few) and present (it's David Letterman's favorite place for a steak) as the uncommonly toothsome food. Executive Chef Erik Blauberg balances the classic and the contemporary with exceptional finesse, so whether you go for the "Speakeasy" steak *tartare* or crisp black sea bass with truffled potatoes and Champagne sauce, your palate is sure to be pleased. It will surely be overjoyed by dessert: all are champions, but the warm chocolate S'mores with chocolate peanut brittle ice cream should be declared a national institution. There are very reasonable prix-fixe lunch and pre-theater menus; if it's drinks and a lighter menu you're after, ask for a table in the fireplaced lounge. ◆ Continental ◆ M-F lunch and dinner; Sa dinner.

Reservations required; jacket required of men at lunch; jacket and tie at dinner. 21 W 52nd St (between Fifth and Sixth Aves). 582.7200 ♿

97 Museum of Television and Radio Originally called the **Museum of Broadcasting**, this gallery was established in 1965 by the late William S. Paley, the founder of **CBS**. Only the winners air here, such as a Hitchcock retrospective or a tribute to Henry Fonda or Barbra Streisand. You can choose TV and radio programs from the museum's vast archives—everything from Edward R. Murrow to "Mr. Ed"—and screen or listen for hours if you wish. The entire permanent collection consists of more than 60,000 recordings (from commercials to documentaries). In 1991, the museum (illustrated below) moved from its longtime home next to **Paley Plaza** on East 53rd Street into this $55-million, 17-story building designed by **John Burgee Architects** that more than doubled the museum's size and added two theaters, a screening room, a gallery space, an expanded library with computer access to catalogs, and a museum shop. Docent-led tours are usually held at 12:30PM on Tuesday. ◆ Admission. Tu-Su. 25 W 52nd St (between Fifth and Sixth Aves). 621.6600

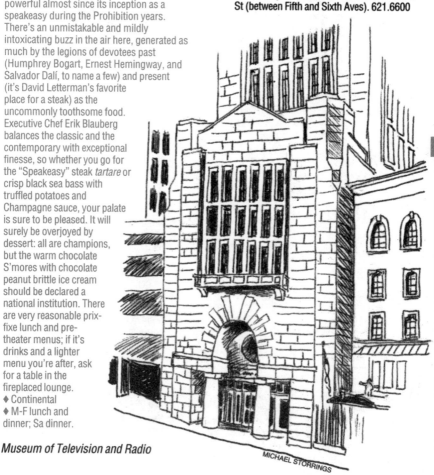

Museum of Television and Radio

MICHAEL STORRINGS

98 Hines Building In 1986, while designing this building, architects **Kevin Roche John Dinkloo & Associates** were also working on plans for the new zoo in **Central Park.** The zoo has covered walkways supported by columns with sliced edges, an effect called chamfering. The firm used the same idea here and put the building on similar columns. In 1989, with the support of neighboring cultural institutions, including the **American Craft Museum** and the **Museum of Television and Radio,** the occupants established the ground-floor **Lobby Gallery,** a nonprofit exhibition space that mounts about 12 shows a year. ♦ 31 W 52nd St (between Fifth and Sixth Aves). 767.2666 &

99 Bombay Palace ★★$$ The crisp and light Indian breads, such as the *nan* stuffed with cashew nuts and dried fruits, are delightful, the curries mild, and the tandoori chicken properly moist and tender at this pleasant, subtly lit Indian restaurant with friendly service. Try the lamb *vindaloo* (cooked in a fiery vinegar-flavored sauce), followed by mango ice cream or Indian rice pudding—subtly flavored with rose water—for dessert. Don't miss the daily buffet, it's a best-bet bargain. ♦ Indian ♦ Daily lunch and dinner. 30 W 52nd St (between Fifth and Sixth Aves). 541.7777

99 Artusi ★★$$$ Named in honor of the Italian who authored one of the premier cookbooks at the beginning of this century, the former **Cesarina** continues its tradition of friendly and efficient service. The risottos and pastas are superb, as are *vitello tonnato* (veal with tuna sauce, capers, and arugula); roasted pork loin with eggplant, sun-dried tomatoes, and potatoes; and panroasted striped bass with spinach. ♦ Northern Italian ♦ M-F lunch and dinner; Sa dinner. Reservations recommended for lunch. 36 W 52nd St (between Fifth and Sixth Aves). 582.6900

100 CBS Building This is **Eero Saarinen**'s only high-rise building, although he didn't live to see its completion in 1965. Known as "Black Rock," the dark gray granite mass is removed from the street, and its surface is given depth by triangular columns. With the top the same

as the bottom, the tower is the image of mystery—even the entrances are hard to identify—a replica of the monolith from *2001* right on Sixth Avenue. ♦ 51 W 52nd St (at Sixth Ave)

Within the CBS Building:

China Grill ★★$$$ Although this place is not related to Wolfgang Puck's Santa Monica landmark, Chinois on Main, the cuisine—an amalgam of Asian, French, and California influences—is similar. The modern, airy space is fairly dramatic, with dark gleaming walls and light fixtures that resemble flying saucers hovering overhead. The food is inventive and delicious; try the sake-cured salmon rolls with lemongrass vinaigrette or the grilled dry-aged Szechuan beef and chipotle mashed potatoes. Dishes are served family style, making it fun to share. And such desserts as pumpkin cheesecake and cream cheese mousse are also sure to please. ♦ Asian ♦ M-F lunch and dinner; Sa-Su dinner. Reservations required. 52 W 53rd St (between Fifth and Sixth Aves). 333.7788 &

101 The MoMA Design Store Design-sensitive merchandise is inspired by the **Museum of Modern Art** collections across the street, including educational toys (Colorforms, kaleidoscopes, architectural blocks), furniture (designs by **Frank Lloyd Wright** and Charles Eames, plus a reproduction of the famous butterfly chair by Antonio Bonet, Jorge Farrari and Juan Kurchen), housewares, desk accessories, and great gift ideas. ♦ Daily. 44 W 53rd St (between Fifth and Sixth Aves). 767.1050

101 American Craft Museum The appreciation of American crafts has grown in recent years, partly due to an interest in things that are not machine-made and partly due to the pioneering of the American Crafts Council and its New York City museum, built in 1986 by **Fox & Fowle.** Works in glass, fiber, wood, clay, metal, and paper by America's most talented craftspeople, either from the museum's collection (from 1900 to the present) or from changing loan exhibitions, are displayed. Sometimes the shows are amusing, sometimes serious, but the level of taste is always high. ♦ Admission. Tu-Su. 40 W 53rd St (between Fifth and Sixth Aves). 956.6047 &

102 New York Public Library, Donnell Library Center When he died in 1896, textile merchant Ezekiel Donnell left his estate to the New York Public Library to establish a place where young people could spend their evenings away from demoralizing influences. Thanks to Donnell's legacy, this library has one of the best collections of children's literature in the United States. ♦ Each department has its own hours; call for specific times. Main floor: daily. 20 W 53rd St (between Fifth and Sixth Aves). 621.0618

103 Museum Tower This prestigious apartment building, designed in 1983 by **Cesar Pelli & Associates,** was built to raise funds for the **Museum of Modern Art** next door. ♦ 15 W 53rd St (between Fifth and Sixth Aves)

MoMA

104 Museum of Modern Art (MoMA) When this museum was founded in 1929, a few days after the big stock market crash, the idea of a museum dedicated to the understanding and enjoyment of contemporary visual arts was novel. Founders Abby Aldrich Rockefeller (wife of John D. Jr.), Lillie P. Bliss, and Mrs. Cornelius J. Sullivan were joined by other collectors and philanthropists in the venture, and the collections have grown through the largesse of the early benefactors and others.

The original sleek white horizontal building with its marble veneer and tile-and-glass facade was designed in 1939 by **Philip L. Goodwin** and **Edward Durell Stone** in the International Style—a striking statement by an innovative institution, practicing what it preached in a row of brownstones. There was (briefly) a plan to cut a street through the two blocks from **Rockefeller Center** leading directly to the museum (the Rockefellers controlled the land in the vicinity). **Philip Johnson's** 1951 and 1964 additions, black glass wings to the east and west, not only expanded the gallery space and improved the **Sculpture Garden** (designed in 1953 by **Johnson** and **Zion & Breen**), but were an effective frame for the original front. The tower and addition by **Cesar Pelli** in 1984 replaced **Johnson's** west wing; **Pelli** also replaced the garden facade with a glassed-in **Garden Court** full of escalators. The then-controversial condominium tower rising above the base of the museum wing is an important source of income for the museum, though it is criticized by those who appreciated the sunny garden and low-rise side streets. The tower's cladding consists of 11 shades of glass. The expansion doubled the space available for loan shows and for the permanent collection.

One of the institution's most important contributions to the art world is its embracing of disciplines previously considered unworthy of museum status, resulting in a collection

that is not only strong in 20th-century painting and sculpture, but also photography, film, theater, music, industrial design, and architecture. When the museum's first director, Alfred H. Barr Jr., espoused this multidepartmental concept in 1929, the idea of including practical design and industrial objects was considered radical. At first the museum displayed only the traditional "fine arts" of painting, drawing, and sculpture, but soon began a slow and steady implementation of Barr's idea. Today, **MoMA** also includes a publishing house, movie theater, and film department.

The museum is strongest in art of the first half of the century—Impressionists, Cubists, and Realists such as Picasso, Matisse, Miró, and Hopper—but it also has good examples of post–World War II Abstract Expressionists through Conceptualists, including de Kooning, Rothko, Lichtenstein, di Suvero, and LeWitt. The photography galleries are worth seeing, as are the galleries of architecture and design, where you will find such 20th-century classics as Thonet bentwood chairs, Tiffany glass, Bauhaus textiles, and Marcel Breuer furniture. Among the most important paintings in the collection are van Gogh's *Starry Night,* Mondrian's *Broadway Boogie Woogie,* Matisse's *Dance,* Picasso's *Les Demoiselles d'Avignon,* Andrew Wyeth's *Christina's World,* and Jackson Pollock's *One (Number 31, 1950).* With its newfound spaciousness, the unrivaled multidepartmental museum has truly fulfilled Barr's dream. The lower level holds the **Roy and Niuta Titus Theaters,** showing off the Department of Film, the largest international collection of its kind. The ground floor leads to temporary exhibitions and the **Abby Aldrich Rockefeller Sculpture Garden.** Stretching across the second floor is the **Painting and Sculpture Collection,** with separate rooms allotted to Picasso and Matisse, among others. The **Drawing Collection** on the third floor has its own exhibition space. Acquisitions include Max Pechstein's *Reclining Nude with Cat* and Picasso's 1913 *Head.* The *Prints and Illustrated Books Collection* owns a 1968 self-portrait by Picasso, the first of a series of 347 intaglio prints. The **Architecture and Design Collection** on the fourth floor features two designs for houses by **Frank Lloyd Wright** and a Mindset Computer. ♦ Admission; members and children under 16 accompanied by an adult free; voluntary contribution Thursday and Friday evening. M-Tu, Th-Su. 11 W 53rd St (between Fifth and Sixth Aves). 708.9480; film schedule 708.9490 ᵴ

Within the Museum of Modern Art:

 The Sculpture Garden One of the most pleasant outdoor spaces in the city, the garden has sculpture by Rodin, Renoir, Miró,

Matisse, and Picasso, among others. Weather permitting, it's open the same hours as the museum and holds a variety of concerts in the summer. The **Garden Cafe** overlooks the garden and offers a variety of snacks and light meals. ♦ 708.9480

The MoMA Bookstore Be sure to peruse the bookstore's extensive assortment of books, posters, and cards relating to the museum's collection. **The MoMA Design Store** is located across the street. ♦ M-Sa. 708.9480

Sette MoMA ★$$$ The dining room is cool and contemporary, fitted with art from the museum's permanent collection, and in nice weather tables are set on the outdoor terrace, which has a lovely view of the sculpture garden. Best bets include the simple grilled vegetable plate, sautéed loin of lamb with juniper berries, or ravioli filled with goat cheese and eggplant. During museum hours, enter through the museum; after 5PM use the entrance on West 54th Street. ♦ Italian ♦ M-Tu, Th-Sa lunch and dinner. Reservations recommended. 708.9710 &

105 St. Thomas Church **Cram, Goodhue & Ferguson** designed this picturesque French Gothic edifice (illustrated at right) on a tight corner in 1914. You have to wonder why a second tower wasn't included; the single one is rather awkward in an otherwise symmetrical composition. A dollar sign next to the "true lover's knot" over the Bride's Door is presumably a sculptor's comment on the social standing of the congregation. The Episcopal church's world-renowned boys' choir celebrated its 75th anniversary in 1994; it makes the services here a memorable experience from October through May. Call in advance for a schedule. ♦ 1 W 53rd St (at Fifth Ave). 757.7013 &

106 University Club
Considered by many to be the finest work of **Charles Follen McKim** (of **McKim, Mead & White**), this 1899

building is an original composition with a bow to a half-dozen Italian palaces. When it was built, in the days before air-conditioning, it had striped awnings in the windows, which made the pink marble exterior even more interesting. The interior is just as lavish. For decades, this private club set the style for all the others that followed. Despite its name, it is not linked with any particular university and only recently has accepted female members. ♦ 1 W 54th St (at Fifth Ave). 247.2100

AQUAVIT

107 Aquavit ★★★$$$$ Although Nelson Rockefeller once lived in this town house, he probably wouldn't recognize the nine-story atrium, complete with birch trees and a two-story waterfall that constitutes the main dining room of this lovely, modern Scandinavian restaurant. The creative menu has such dishes as smoked salmon with buckwheat-potato blini and goat-cheese cream; gravlax

St. Thomas Church

with dill, flatbread, and espresso-mustard sauce; tea-smoked duck with citrus risotto and seared sweetbreads; rare beef in beer and beef *jus;* and sweet mustard-glazed Arctic char. Be sure to save room for the warm chocolate cake or hazelnut pancakes with blueberry ice cream. Don't forget to try the "Aquatini"—a martini made with Aquavit, the Scandinavian liqueur flavored with anise, caraway, fennel, or orange peel and typically served neat and very cold. ♦ Scandinavian ♦ M-F lunch and dinner; Sa dinner; Su brunch. Reservations recommended; jacket requested. 13 W 54th St (between Fifth and Sixth Aves). 307.7311

07 Rockefeller Apartments When John D. Rockefeller Jr. was assembling the site for **Rockefeller Center,** he lived on this block. By the end of 1929 he owned 15 of the block's houses, having joined his neighbors, most of whom were members of his family, in protecting the street from commercial use. But he wasn't above a little commercialism himself, and hired **Harrison & Fouilhoux** to design this building in 1936, a few months before he moved over to Park Avenue. Its bay-windowed towers overlook the garden of the **Museum of Modern Art.** ♦ 17 W 54th St (between Fifth and Sixth Aves)

08 Warwick Hotel $$$ Rich in history, this 1926 apartment hotel was publishing magnate William Randolph Hearst's dream as his elegant residential retreat for his Hollywood friends. At a cost of over $5 million, this building, designed by **George B. Post and Sons** and **Emery Roth,** was considered one of the two tallest apartment hotels in the world. It's still quite impressive with its graceful towers. Following a major renovation, all 424 spacious guest rooms boast brocade decor, marble bathrooms, two-line phones, and voice mail. The **Ciao Europa** is a lively spot with outdoor tables in warm weather. ♦ 65 W 54th St (at Sixth Ave). 247.2700, 800/522.5634; fax 957.8915

09 La Côte Basque ★★★★$$$$
Considered by many to be one of the finest dining establishments in New York, and certainly one of the prettiest, the restaurant—first opened by famed Henri Soule in 1941—is now the domain of chef/owner Jean-Jacques Rachou, whose classic French cooking is nothing short of masterful. The presentation of crisp potato with scallops and lobster in a parsley-lime sauce, and wild mushrooms sautéed with oxtail in cabbage leaves, is stunning and sure to please. For the finishing touch to an elegant meal try the warm chocolate cake or the passion fruit flan served with blood orange–and–passion fruit sauce. The wine list, boasting 385 international varieties and 40,000 bottles, is one of New York's most extensive. A vestige from the former location—the *St. Jean de Luz at La*

Côte Basque mural—continues to be a beloved favorite among many loyal **Côte Basque** fans. ♦ French ♦ M-F lunch and dinner; Sa-Su dinner. Reservations required; jacket and tie required. 60 W 55 St (between Fifth and Sixth Aves). 688.6525

109 J.P. French Bakery Croissant lovers take note: This shop may have the best croissants in town, as well as a panoply of excellent French breads—from *ficelle* (a thin baguette) to large, round loaves—all baked on the premises. ♦ Daily. 54 W 55th St (between Fifth and Sixth Aves). 765.7575

109 La Bonne Soupe ★★$$ Soups, omelettes, a variety of chopped beef dishes, and daily French specials such as filet au poivre are good at this popular longstanding bistro. For a really retro experience, have a fondue. ♦ French ♦ Daily lunch and dinner. 48 W 55th St (between Fifth and Sixth Aves). 586.7650

MICHAEL'S

110 Michael's ★★$$ Sleek and airy, this is a "the" place with Midtown business types for healthful breakfasts and lunches. The sunny, spare setting is punctuated with an impressive collection of modern art, and the light menu features imaginative California-style cuisine. Michael's free-range chicken with goat cheese, tomatoes, onions, and peppers is a favorite for lunch. The menu changes seasonally. Service, however, can be sometimes snooty and condescending to nonregulars. ♦ American/California ♦ M-F breakfast, lunch, and dinner; Sa dinner. 24 W 55th St (between Fifth and Sixth Aves). 767.0555

Since 1931, the Rockefeller Center Christmas tree has been one of New York City's most beloved traditions. Today, the chosen tree is decorated with more than 27,000 7.5-watt, multicolored bulbs on five miles of wire. Sitting atop the tree is the 45-inch plastic star that's been used for more than four decades. It takes 15 to 20 people and an 80-ton crane to erect and move the tree. Since 1971, all trees have been recycled: The mulch is used for trails at a Boy Scout camp in New Jersey.

Between March and August of 1946, 26 sessions of the United Nations Security Council were held in the Hunter College gymnasium in the Bronx. Other locations used included a building on the East River and another in Lake Success on Long Island.

111 Menchanko-tei ★$$ Japanese businessmen frequent this cozy noodle emporium for hearty soups filled with a variety of ingredients. As authentic as can be found in Midtown, this place is great to duck into for a steamy broth. ♦ Japanese ♦ M lunch, dinner, and late-night meals; Tu-Su breakfast, lunch, dinner, and late-night meals. 39 W 55th St (between Fifth and Sixth Aves). 247.1585 &

111 Shoreham Hotel $$ Most of the hotels in this neighborhood are far grander than this. But the 84-room hostelry's 1994 make-over brought the Moderne decor up several notches on the luxury scale. This plus its excellent location make it a favorite among denizens of the fashion world. Amenities include a complimentary breakfast and a CD library. ♦ 33 W 55th St (between Fifth and Sixth Aves). 247.6700, 800/553.3347; fax 765.9741; www.uniquehotels.com

111 La Caravelle ★★★$$$$ Owners Rita and Andre Jammet happen to be among the friendliest and most charming hosts in New York. Open since 1961, their dining room with pink banquettes and murals of Paris is gracious, subdued, and quiet—even at dinner time. Specialties include a light *chair de crabe Caravelle* (crabmeat in a delicate herb dressing), sautéed duck foie gras, grilled Dover sole in mustard hollandaise, and lobster in red wine and cardamom. The lemon meringue tarts and *tarte tiède à la banane* (warm banana tart) are especially good. Although pricey, the extensive French wine list offers many fine selections. ♦ French ♦ M-F lunch and dinner; Sa dinner. Reservations required; jacket and tie required. 33 W 55th St (between Fifth and Sixth Aves). 586.4252 &

The tradition of New York's Easter Parade is said to have begun in the 1870s when parishioners of St. Thomas Episcopal Church on Fifth Avenue walked up the avenue to deliver flowers to St. Luke's Hospital, which stood just a block to the north. The "parade" soon became an annual ritual of fashion.

Rockefeller Center, from West 47th to West 52nd Streets, is the world's largest privately owned business and entertainment complex. It is composed of 19 buildings and covers nearly 22 acres.

112 Fifth Avenue Presbyterian Church When society moved uptown, this church, which had been at 19th Street since 1855, moved with it to this 1875 building designed by **Carl Pfeiffer.** Future president Theodore Roosevelt was one of the original parishioners, along with the Auchinclosses, Livingstons, and Walcotts. It was called the most influential congregation in New York. ♦ 7 W 55th St (at Fifth Ave). 247.0490

113 The Peninsula New York $$$$ This hotel was built in 1905 by **Hiss & Weeks** and for many years, as the **Gotham Hotel,** was a favorite stopping place for movie stars. Then briefly became **Maxim's** and was completely restored in the Belle Epoque tradition of the original Maxim's in Paris. Extensive renovations to the opulent lobby and 241 guestrooms in 1998 imbued the grand property with contemporary accents, such as bedside panels that adjust lighting, TV, and stereo and can even turn on a Do Not Disturb light. Bathrooms in the larger rooms boast hand-free telephones and stereo speakers. Decorative touches are luxe throughout, from silk bedspreads to Art Nouveau headboards, welcome vestiges from the **Maxim's** days. ♦ 700 Fifth Ave (at W 55th St). 247.2200, 800/262.9467; fax 903.3943 &

114 The Disney Store This recent addition to the New York shopping scene is complete with four floors of merchandise. Classic Disney characters from Bambi to Tinkerbell can be seen on T-shirts, jewelry (real and faux), dolls, luggage, and sportswear (in all sizes). The lower level features a travel department for those with an urge to visit Mickey's favorite theme park. ♦ Daily. 711 Fifth Ave (at E 55th St). 702.0702. Also at: Numerous locations throughout the city

ChristianDior
PARIS

115 Christian Dior Boutique Reminiscent of Dior's Paris headquarters at 30 Avenue Montaigne, the luxurious 4,500-square-foot space is large enough to display Gianfranco Ferré's complete haute couture and ready-to-wear collections. ♦ Daily. 703 Fifth Ave (at E 55th St). 223.4646

15 **The St. Regis Sheraton** $$$$ When **Trowbridge & Livingston** built the **St. Regis** for John Jacob Astor in 1904, Astor said he wanted the finest hotel in the world, a place where guests would feel as comfortable as they did in a gracious private home. Today this is the only hotel in New York that offers 24-hour butler service. A three-year, $100-million renovation, completed by **Brennan, Beer Gorman** in 1991, produced one of New York's most elegant hotels—a jewel in the crown of ITT Sheraton's Luxury Collection. The capacity has actually been lowered, from more than 500 rooms to 322, 86 of them suites. The spectacular landmark exterior remains, with its stone garlands and flowers and its slate mansard roof. But now its traditionally styled rooms are complemented by state-of-the-art technology, computerized phones, and other comforts. The hotel contains the **Astor Court,** which serves light meals and tea, and the **King Cole Bar and Lounge.** ♦ 2 E 55th St (between Madison and Fifth Aves). 753.4500, 800/759.7550; fax 787.3447 ♿

Within The St. Regis Sheraton:

Lespinasse ★★★★$$$$ The formal dining room brings forth images of Louis XVI grandeur, with pink satin chairs and gilt-framed oil paintings. As prepared by Christian Delouvrier, the food is quite astounding. Each spunky bite is shaded with many different tastes—some sparkling, some even sublime. Try the sautéed foie gras with lentils, risotto with wild mushrooms, steamed black bass with string beans and caviar, rack of lamb with spinach and parsnip galette, and duck with black beans and red-currant sauce. There is also a six-course vegetarian prix-fixe meal (menu changes seasonally), which includes dessert. The wine list offers a well-chosen selection in a variety of price ranges. ♦ Fusion ♦ M-Sa breakfast, lunch, and dinner; Su breakfast. Reservations required; jacket required. 339.6719

16 **Takashimaya** Japan's largest retail conglomerate launched a unique venture in 1993 when it opened this elegant 20-story building designed by New York architect **John Burgee.** A distinctive array of East-meets-West design-sensitive products are sold on the third through fifth floors, ranging from home furnishings and fashion accessories to table and bed linens, specialty gifts, and objets d'art. The ground floor consists of a 4,500-square-foot gallery as well as a multilevel atrium, used as an exhibition space for contemporary Asian and American art and artisanal crafts. ♦ M-Sa. 693 Fifth Ave (between E 54th and E 55th Sts). 350.0115 ♿

Within Takashimaya:

Tea Box Cafe ★$ This soothing beige cafe in the store's basement is the perfect place for escaping the bustle of Midtown. Try one of the 40 varieties of tea, including apricot, lemongrass, and *hoiji-cha* (a wood-smoked green tea), and a delicate sandwich—shrimp or cucumber on pressed rice, smoked salmon, or chicken with wasabi. ♦ Japanese ♦ M-Sa lunch and afternoon tea. 350.0100 ♿

116 **Elizabeth Arden Salon** Redecorated by Clodagh, one of New York's best designers, the famous red door leads to a world apart, filled with designer fashions, lingerie, and sportswear, and a salon that has made pampering a fine art. The recently expanded salon offers exercise facilities, massages, facials, hair styling, and more, all calculated to make you look and feel terrific. ♦ Daily. 691 Fifth Ave (between E 54th and E 55th Sts). 546.0200 ♿

116 **Façonnable** Replicating the **Façonnable** store on Rue Royale in Paris, this shop has already become a destination for well-heeled and well-dressed professional men who like the grouping of items by color and pattern. Choose from more than 7,000 ties and shirts in some 200 patterns. ♦ Daily. 689 Fifth Ave (at E 54th St). 319.0111 ♿

117 **Indonesian Pavilion** This is one of the few remaining buildings from the time when 54th Street east and west of Fifth Avenue was called "The Art Gallery of New York Streets." It was designed in 1900 by **McKim, Mead & White** and built by W.E.D. Stokes, who sold it to William H. Moore, a founder of the United States Steel and American Can companies. Note the massive balcony and strong cornices—evidence of **Charles Follen McKim**'s interest in Renaissance architecture. It has recently been converted into the New York branch of the *Banco di Napoli.* ♦ 4 E 54th St (between Madison and Fifth Aves)

GUCCI

117 **Gucci** A staff that ranges from very pleasant to simply cool sells shoes and leather goods for men and women, exquisitely crafted by the generations-old Florentine family. Recently infused with a fresh breath of contemporary style, leather goods are now joined by suits, topcoats, dresses, ties, and scarves. The famed red and green stripe and internationally recognized double-linked Gs are omnipresent on handbags, boots, and luggage. ◆ M-Sa. 685 Fifth Ave (at E 54th St). 826.2600 ዿ

fortunoff, the source®

117 Fortunoff You would never expect to find a reasonably priced jewelry and silver store on Fifth Avenue, but here is one (complete with a glitzy facade) that offers good prices on strings of pearls, gold chains, hammered silver pitchers, urns, chalices, sterling silver, and silver plate flatware by Oneida and Towle, Reed & Barton, and stainless-steel flatware by Fraser and Dansk. The sales help is refreshingly courteous. ◆ M-Sa. 681 Fifth Ave (between E 53rd and E 54th Sts). 758.6660 ዿ

THE MUSEUM
C O M P A N Y

118 The Museum Company With the city's major (and sometimes minor) museums now offering handsomely stocked gift stores that are as much a draw as the permanent art collections, this store one-ups them with a vast selection of items, all of which have been inspired by the great art collections of museums around the world. The two-floor shop's stock in trade includes such global treasures as boxed notes and greeting cards, coffee-table books, frames, jewelry, and journals, together with a wide selection of games and toys. ◆ M-Sa. 673 Fifth Ave (at E 53rd St). 758.0976

118 Samuel Paley Plaza Named for the father of its benefactor, the late William S. Paley of **CBS,** this park is a spare, very welcome anomaly in the densest part of town. Good furniture and a wonderful waterfall provide the perfect spot to steal a moment's peace. The park was designed in 1967 by landscape architects Zion & Breen and consulting architect **Albert Preston Moore.** Just a few storefronts east on this side of the street is another tiny outdoor seating area, worth a visit to see the large graffiti-covered slabs from the Berlin Wall. ◆ E 53rd St (between Madison and Fifth Aves)

SERYNA

119 Seryna ★★$$$ Avoid the frenzied crowds at lunch and visit this handsome restaurant for dinner, when it becomes more sedate. At either meal, the food, and the presentations, are first-rate. Steaks are cooked on a hot stone at your table and served with garlic-soy and chili sauces; there's also excellent *shabu shabu,* and an array of fresh fish, including poached salmon, stuffed Dover sole, and eel teriyaki. The sushi and sashimi are also very fresh. ◆ Japanese ◆ M-F lunch and dinner; Sa dinner. Reservations recommended. 11 E 53rd St (between Madison and Fifth Aves). 980.9393

120 San Pietro ★★$$$ Sister restaurant to the Upper East Side's **Sistina,** this place features dishes from Italy's Amalfi Coast. Try the shrimp with peppers and herbs, black sea bass baked on crushed sea salt or made to order, or grilled tuna steak with garlic and lemon. The sunny yellow setting—with jars of olives and sun-dried tomatoes, silver platters stacked with ripening tomatoes, and paintings of outdoor markets—manages to feel simultaneously elegant and homey. ◆ Neapolitan ◆ M-Sa lunch and dinner. Reservations required; jacket and tie required. 18 E 54th St (between Madison and Fifth Aves). 753.9015 ዿ

120 Typhoon Brewery ★★$$ There are a lot of beer lovers here, which is why the brewing process goes on right under your nose; to true aficionados there is nothing more appetizing than the sight of beer being made. Upstairs, above the brewery, some great Thai specialties are paired with various types of home brews. Lots of late-night action comes with the participation of a young crowd. ◆ Thai ◆ Daily lunch and dinner. Reservations recommended. 22 E 54th Street (between Madison and Fifth Aves). 754.9006

121 Bice ★★★$$$ The long, curved white-marble bar, multilevel seating, bright lighting, and exquisite flower arrangements create a truly luxurious setting. The menu is just as pleasing. Try such main courses as roasted rack of veal with new potatoes; baby chicken; grilled salmon, swordfish, or sole; and a delicious seafood risotto. Be forewarned: During lunch the noise level is thunderous. ◆ Italian ◆ Daily lunch and dinner. Reservations recommended. 7 E 54th St (between Madison and Fifth Aves). 688.1999

122 Morrell & Company, The Wine Emporium A playground for oenophiles, this large, well-organized store carries practically every worthwhile label, including many direct imports. Service is knowledgeable but occasionally impatient. ◆ M-Sa. 535 Madison Ave (between E 54th and E 55th Sts). 688.9370

123 The Sony Building and Sony Plaza Known as the **AT&T Headquarters** until 1992, this pinkish granite building designed by **Philip Johnson** and **John Burgee** in 1984 continues to be recognized by its top, often referred to as "Chippendale" in style. At its base, the glass-enclosed building is a cross between a technology museum and an amusement park, open and free to the public. An authentic 1925 French mail plane hangs from the ceiling along with other props and klieg lights to create the impression of being backstage. On the main concourse you can spend hours in **Sony Style,** a hands-on interactive electronics boutique; **Sony Signatures,** licensed merchandise with familiar faces and logos on everything from T-shirts to baseball caps; and the most popular of them all, **Sony Wonder Technology Lab,** where you can design your own video, re-edit videos by rock's megastars, or operate a sonogram. Recuperate from it all at the enticing **Baked From Scratch.** The building's profile is one of the more recognizable elements in Manhattan's urban fabric. ♦ Free. 550 Madison Ave (at E 55th St). Information 833.8830

24 Friars Club This is the private club for actors who invented the famous roasts, in which members poke fun at celebrity guests. The building is not open to the public. ♦ 57 E 55th St (between Park and Madison Aves). 751.7272

25 Oceana ★★★$$$$ When Rick Moonen, formerly of **The Water Club,** took charge of this kitchen already known for fine seafood, he proceeded to bring it up another level. Now diners in this pretty pastel room can experience such extraordinary dishes as oven-steamed spaghetti squash with vegetables and tomato *concassée* (reduction), crab cake with chipotle sauce, house-cured salmon gravlax with spicy black-bean cakes and cilantro crème fraîche, and grilled salmon paillard with asparagus in ginger-soy vinaigrette. ♦ Seafood ♦ M-Sa lunch and dinner. Reservations required; jacket required. 55 E 54th St (between Park and Madison Aves). 759.5941

26 Hotel Elysée $$$ Tallulah Bankhead used to be a regular here, as was Tennessee Williams. Handsomely renovated, the hotel still retains its Old World atmosphere in spite of the modern buildings rising around it. Each of the 99 rooms has its own personality, and most go by names as well as numbers. ♦ 60 E 54th St (between Park and Madison Aves). 753.1066, 800/535.9733; fax 980.9278 ♿

Within the Hotel Elysée:

Monkey Bar ★★★$$$ The crowds at this ever-popular bar are so thick that it's often impossible to see the whimsical monkey murals or red bar stools that architect **David Rockwell** contrasted with the plush, drop-dead-glamorous dining room—burgundy suede pillars and velvet banquettes. It's a perfect setting for chef Kurt Gutenbrunner's rich, complex food. Try the salmon with white cabbage and apple balsamic sauce, Nova Scotia halibut and cucumbers with fava beans and tassis sauce. Leave room for the baked Alaska. ♦ American ♦ M-Sa lunch and dinner; Su dinner. Reservations recommended; jacket required. 838.2600

127 Lever House **Gordon Bunschaft** was the partner in charge of this 1952 **Skidmore, Owings & Merrill** design. The first glass wall on Park Avenue, built when Charles Luckman was president of Lever Brothers, has, after a long battle, been awarded landmark status and saved from possible destruction or disfigurement. The articulate building displays the tenets of orthodox Corbusian Modernism: It is raised from the ground on columns, it has a roof garden, and there is a free facade on the outside and free plan on the inside. With the **Seagram Building** across the street, this is a landmark corner that changed the face of the city. ♦ 390 Park Ave (between E 53rd and E 54th Sts)

128 Central Synagogue This 1872 Moorish Revival building designed by **Henry Fernbach** is the oldest continuously used synagogue in the city. The onion domes on the 222-foot towers and the brightly stenciled interior add a bit of fancy to the mottled brownstone facade. A fire raged through the structure in late 1998; restoration will take until at least 2001. ♦ 652 Lexington Ave (at E 55th St). 838.5122 ♿

The United Nations has a peace garden that boasts more than 1,000 rose bushes.

Articles for sale in the United Nations gift shop are duty-free because the UN is not officially in any country. The gift shop offers items from every member nation.

Restaurants/Clubs: Red   **Hotels:** Blue

Shops/ 🍴 Outdoors: Green   **Sights/Culture:** Black

129 Shun Lee Palace ★★★$$$$ Owner Michael Tong collaborated with designer Adam Tihany to renovate this landmark Chinese restaurant. The result includes blue-suede walls with gold-leaf panels, chandeliers of frosted glass, and mahogany cases displaying treasures of past dynasties. Try the unfortunately named dish *Ants Climb on Tree* (a combination of beef, Chinese broccoli, and cellophane noodles), steamed dumplings, orange beef, or whole poached sea bass with brown-bean sauce. The dessert menu includes such Western favorites as chocolate mousse cake in addition to Asian offerings. ♦ Chinese ♦ Daily lunch and dinner. Reservations required. 155 E 55th St (between Third and Lexington Aves). 371.8844. Also at: 43 W 65th St (between Central Park W and Columbus Ave). 595.8895

130 Citicorp Center Designed in 1978 by **Hugh Stubbins & Associates,** the rakish angle of the building's top was planned as a solar collector but is now nothing more than a vent for the cooling system, which provides a steamy effect for the night lighting. Also under the roof is a 400-ton computer-operated Tuned Mass Damper (TMD or "earthquake machine" to most of us). They don't expect an earthquake any time soon, but the building (shown at right) is cantilevered on 145-foot columns that allow it to sway in the wind. Those 10-story stilts also make it possible for the structure to be the world's only skyscraper with skylights; they brighten its sunken floors, where free concerts and other programs take place in the center of a gaggle of shops and restaurants. ♦ 153 E 53rd St (between Third and Lexington Aves). 559.1000

Within Citicorp Center:

St. Peter's Lutheran Church This church is a major reason for the engineering and formal antics of **Citicorp Center**'s design: The church refused to sell its air rights to Citicorp unless the bank agreed to build a new church clearly distinct from the tower with the skyscraper perched on 10-story stilts above it. In contrast to the high-tech tower, the church is granite, with wooden furnishings and interior detailing by Massimo and Lella Vignelli. Within the church, the **Erol Beaker Chapel** was created by sculptor Louise Nevelson. Watch for jazz vespers every Sunday at 5PM (the church is known as the city's jazz ministry). But the interior is well worth a look at any time. ♦ 619 Lexington Ave (at E 54th St). 935.2200 ♦

York Theatre Company at St. Peter's Church Two productions began in this excellent 165-seat space in the basement of **Citicorp Center** and went on to Broadway: *Tintypes* and *The Elephant Man*. ♦ 935.5820 ♦

The Market at Citicorp Center Accessible from the sunken plaza at the corner of East

53rd Street and Lexington Avenue, this international bazaar offers three levels of shopping and dining alternatives for Midtown office workers, who occupy tables to have a quick lunch or just sit and read a newspaper.

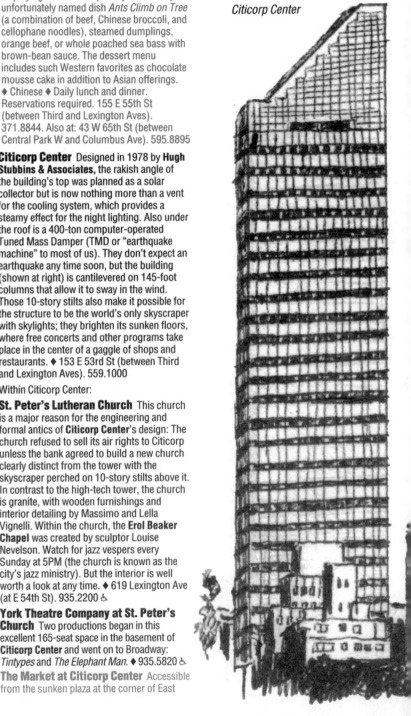

Citicorp Center

The Market Cafe, Barnes & Noble, City Sports, and Houston's restaurant are a few of the places to be explored here. Semiregular free entertainment enlivens the atrium (check the posted list of scheduled events): weeknight cabaret and pop concerts at 6PM, Saturday night jazz at 8PM, Sunday classical concerts at noon, and often Saturday programs for kids at 11AM. ♦ Concert information 559.1700

31 Fisher & Levy Caterers Chip Fisher (of **Mr. Chips** Upper East Side ice-cream parlor fame) and Doug Levy are the owners of this decidedly upscale food store that also does a huge catering and delivery business. For breakfast, try the homemade doughnuts and **Petrossian** smoked-salmon platters; for lunch, order a California-style pizza, grilled chicken with grilled vegetables on focaccia, or one of the classiest chef salads around—with filet mignon, Black Forest ham, hickory-smoked turkey, and parmesan dressing. ♦ M-F. 875 Third Ave (between E 52nd and E 53rd Sts), Concourse level. 832.3880

32 Solera ★★$$ Tapas and other Spanish delicacies top the list in this stylish town house. The soft lighting and colorful tiling create the ideal stage set for specialties that include empanadas (meat pies), organic duckling breast with juniper-rosemary sauce, fillet of trout with Serrano ham, and sliced Atlantic salmon. Desserts are heavenly— some favorites are coconut cheesecake with mango-pineapple salsa and vanilla poached pear with apple compote. ♦ Spanish ♦ M-F lunch and dinner; Sa dinner. Reservations recommended. 216 E 53rd St (between Second and Third Aves). 644.1166

33 Il Nido ★★★$$$ Owner Adi Giovannetti serves excellent Italian food in a rustic setting with timber beams and mirrors that are made to look like farmhouse windows. Try *malfatti* (irregularly shaped pasta squares filled with spinach and cheese), *linguine alla amatriciana* (in tomato sauce with onions and prosciutto), tortellini with four cheeses, baked red snapper with clams, and braised chicken in a white-wine sauce with mushrooms and tomato. ♦ Italian ♦ M-Sa lunch and dinner. Reservations required; jacket and tie required. 251 E 53rd St (between Second and Third Aves). 753.8450 &

"*La Mangeoire*"

34 La Mangeoire ★★$$$ The atmosphere of this warm, rustic Provençal spot is so inviting that it would be worth coming here even if the food were less appealing. The stucco walls are enlivened with pottery, and dried and fresh

flowers abound. The food more than complements the setting, with piquant spices and sunny flavors; try *pissaladière* (an onion, anchovy, and olive tart); penne with a sauce of tomato-olive puree; thyme-crusted rabbit; or beef *daube* with Swiss-chard ravioli. ♦ French ♦ M-F lunch and dinner; Sa-Su dinner. Reservations recommended. 1008 Second Ave (between E 53rd and E 54th Sts). 759.7086

135 Le Perigord ★★★$$$ A favorite haunt of **UN** ambassadors and celebrities, this formal but cozy French restaurant has been around for almost 35 years. But the romantic room, with its pink banquettes, is still pretty, and owner George Briguet is still a charming host. Best choices are the crisp sweetbreads in a Sauternes sauce, goat cheese and vegetable tart with arugula and black olive paste, grilled Dover sole with mustard sauce, and fillet of beef in red wine. Save room for one of the soufflés, or choose the chocolate mousse or lemon tart from the pastry cart. ♦ French ♦ M-F lunch and dinner; Sa-Su dinner. Reservations required; jacket and tie required. 405 E 52nd St (just east of First Ave). 755.6244

136 River House This 26-story, twin-towered, limestone-and-gray brick cooperative, built in 1931 by **Bottomley, Wagner & White,** has always been one of the most exclusive apartment buildings in the city (when there was a dock on the river, only the best yachts used it). The lower floors house the **River Club,** which includes squash and tennis courts, a pool, and a ballroom. The building is not open to the public. ♦ 435 E 53rd St (at Sutton Pl S)

137 Sutton Place and Sutton Place South Until colonized by Vanderbilts and Morgans moving from Fifth Avenue in the early 1920s, this elegant end of York Avenue was a run-down area. The town houses and apartment buildings are by such architects as **Mott B. Schmidt, Rosario Candela, Delano & Aldrich,** and **Cross & Cross.** Visit the park at the end of East 55th Street and the terrace on East 57th Street for views of the river and the Queensboro Bridge. Also peek in from East 58th Street, where Riverview Terrace, one of New York's last private streets, runs along the river lined with five ivy-covered brownstones. The secretary-general of the **United Nations** lives at **Nos. 1 to 3.** ♦ E 53rd to E 59th Sts

138 54th Street Recreation Center These turn-of-the-century enclosed public bathhouses built by **Werner & Windolph** in 1906 now offer an indoor running track, gymnasium facilities, and an indoor swimming pool open all year. ♦ M-F 3PM-10PM; Sa 10AM-5PM. 348 E 54th St (between First and Second Aves). 397.3154

139 Vong ★★★$$$ Superchef Jean-Georges
Vongerichten (of **JoJo, Lipstick Cafe,** and
Jean Georges fame) and chef de cuisine
Pierre Schutz weigh in with a wonderful
interpretation of Thai/French cuisine in an
elegant Eastern-influenced dining room. The
menu reflects the two years Vongerichten
spent in Bangkok: sautéed duck foie gras with
ginger sauce and mango, raw tuna, and
vegetables in rice paper with dipping sauce;
lobster with Thai herbs; roasted baby chicken
marinated with lemongrass and herbs; and
black bass with wok-fried cabbage, water
chestnuts, and hot chilies. The blend of
fresh local and exotic ingredients, and
an abundance of classic French ingenuity,
make this a truly unique dining experience.
♦ Thai/French ♦ M-F lunch and dinner; Sa-Su
dinner. 200 E 54th St (between Second and
Third Aves). 486.9592

139 Lipstick Cafe ★★$ In his "spare time,"
Jean-Georges Vongerichten throws a tasty
bone to hungry Midtown workers on a dining
budget. Delicious homemade soups, salads,
and sandwiches are served to stay or go. The
baked goods are a real treat. ♦ American ♦ M-
F breakfast and lunch. 885 Third Ave (between
E 53rd and E 54th Sts). 486.8664 &

140 900 Third Avenue The aluminum section at
the base of this brick-clad tower and the
silhouette of the greenhouse at the top are a
reference to the neighboring **Citicorp Center**
across East 54th Street. It was built in 1983,
five years after **Citicorp,** by **Cesar Pelli &
Associates** with **Rafael Vinoly.** ♦ At E 54th St

141 P.J. Clarke's ★$$ There are few better
places than this to witness rambunctious
young professionals of Midtown getting
slowly pickled during cocktail hour.
Mysteriously, the hamburgers are famous,
although habitués generally come here
looking to meet, not eat meat. ♦ American
♦ Daily lunch, dinner, and late-night meals.
915 Third Ave (at E 55th St). 759.1650

The
**MANHATTAN
ART & ANTIQUES
CENTER**

142 The Manhattan Art & Antiques Center
More than a hundred dealers spread their

quality wares over three large floors at
Manhattan's specialized antiques "mall."
One-stop shopping offers every imaginable
item from the affordable to the exorbitant,
from tiny pillboxes to magnificent chandeliers.
The variety is extensive, the prices are
competitive, and it's a fun place to browse.
♦ Daily. 1050 Second Ave (between E 55th
and E 56th Sts). 355.4400 &

143 Tapas Lounge ★★★$$ One of the best
places in town for martinis and tapas,
although if you want traditional sangria, that's
available too. Rotating decor makes this a
fresh place to come back to every four
months, and the laid-back, European crowd
usually goes easy on the eyes. Try Spanish
tortilla (omelet), *pulpo* (octopus), or paella to
get going. ♦ Spanish ♦ Daily dinner. 1078
First Ave (between E 58th and E 59th Sts).
421.8282

144 March ★★★$$$ Tucked away in a fin-de
siècle town house, this romantic restaurant–
co-owned by Joseph Salice, who oversees the
front, and Wayne Nish, who is in charge of the
multicultural kitchen—is fitted with elegant
banquettes and tapestries on the walls. The
eclectic menu (all dinners are prix-fixe)
changes monthly and is always exciting.
Appetizers have included ravioli of baby lamb
and crayfish with crispy artichokes; and rabbit
confit with foie gras and white beans. Five-
spice salmon with mushrooms, and a rack of
lamb with a sweet-mustard and herb crust
have been among some of the best entrées.
Make certain to save room for desserts like
crispy pancakes with vanilla ice cream,
mango, and berries. ♦ American ♦ M-Sa
dinner. Reservations recommended. 405 E
58th St (between Sutton Pl and First Ave).
754.6272

145 Rosa Mexicano ★★★$$$ Forget about
tacos and enchiladas; you won't miss them
because in their stead are complex regional
dishes—platters of fresh seafood, *carnitas*
(barbecued pork), shrimp in mustard-chili
vinaigrette, and chicken wrapped in
parchment. Be sure to sample the guacamole
prepared tableside—and spiced to your
pleasure. The frozen margaritas aren't bad,
either. ♦ Mexican ♦ Daily dinner. Reservations
recommended. 1063 First Ave (at E 58th St).
753.7407

**146 Iris Brown's Victorian Doll and
Miniature Shop** Since 1967 Brown has
been specializing in dolls and dollhouses,
miniature furniture and toys, and Christmas
ornaments of the Victorian era. ♦ M-Sa. 253
57th St (between Second and Third Aves).
593.2882

146 Les Sans Culottes ★$$ An overflowing
basket of charcuterie begins each meal at this
rustic, wood-beamed bistro, now more than
20 years old. Pace yourself, because most of

the food is just as rich. Dinners (all are prix-fixe) open with such traditional starters as onion soup or escargots. The main course, which changes daily, has been known to include baby rack of lamb, shell steak, chicken with tangerine sauce, or duck with Sherry sauce. ♦ French ♦ Daily lunch and dinner. Reservations recommended. 1085 Second Ave (between E 57th and E 58th Sts). 838.6660. Also at: 347 W 46th St (between Eighth and Ninth Aves). 247.4284

47 Felidia ★★★$$$$ Owners Felix and Lidia Bastianich preside over this magnificent brick and Tuscan-tiled namesake. Two stories of beautiful mahogany-paneled walls and authentic Italian floors await. Specialties from Lidia's native Istria (near Trieste) include *stinco di vitello* (roasted veal shank) in its own juices. Pastas are especially good, particularly the *pappardelle* (broad noodles) with porcini, or gnocchi with tomato sauce. The extensive wine list features some of Italy's top labels at equally high prices. ♦ Italian ♦ M-F lunch and dinner; Sa dinner. Reservations required; jacket required. 243 E 58th St (between Second and Third Aves). 758.1479

48 Dawat ★★★$$$ Actress and cookbook author Madhur Jaffrey is the guiding spirit behind this sophisticated Indian restaurant that's considered one of the best in town. Try *shami kabab* (finely ground lamb patty stuffed with fresh mint), *samosas,* or home-style *rogan gosh* (pieces of baby goat in a cardamom-flavored sauce). Desserts are first-rate. ♦ Indian ♦ M-Sa lunch and dinner; Su dinner. Reservations recommended. 210 E 58th St (between Second and Third Aves). 355.7555

49 Royal Athena Galleries Ancient, European, Oriental, pre-Columbian, and tribal works of art are sold here. Each object is labeled and has a price tag, but the staff enjoys answering questions from browsers as well as from serious collectors. ♦ M-Sa. 153 E 57th St (between Third and Lexington Aves). 355.2034 ᕗ

49 Le Colonial ★★★$$ A glamorized Vietnamese bistro with white, black, and brown shutters, potted palms, ceiling fans, and pictures of Indochina during the French colonial years, this place has been packing them in since the day it opened in 1993. Choice dishes include delicate spring rolls, ginger-marinated roasted duck with tamarind dipping sauce, crispy fried noodles with stir-fried vegetables, and a tasty beef salad with lemongrass and basil. The lemon tart and crème caramel ice cream are good dessert choices. A large after-work crowd convenes

for drinks in the lovely lounge upstairs. ♦ Vietnamese ♦ M-F lunch and dinner; Sa-Su dinner. Reservations required. 149 E 57th St (between Third and Lexington Aves). 752.0808

149 Hammacher Schlemmer Unintentionally one of the funniest stores in the city, it carries gadgetry to the limits of credibility with such items as a solar-powered ventilated golf cap, a seven-passenger bicycle, an electronic one-armed-bandit home casino, and an interactive talking chess game. They tend to get the last laugh, though, over the long run: this was the first store to introduce the steam iron, electric razor, and pressure cooker. The mail-order catalog is a kick, too. ♦ M-Sa. 147 E 57th St (between Third and Lexington Aves). 421.9000 ᕗ

150 The Fitzpatrick Manhattan Hotel $$$ One of the few hotels in this part of Midtown—and just two blocks from Bloomingdale's— this is the only US representation of a small Irish chain. A welcome attention to detail, 92 tastefully furnished rooms and public areas, marbled whirlpool baths, a smiling top-hatted bellman, and Irish-inspired hospitality make this a veritable oasis in the chaos of Midtown Manhattan. **Fitzers** serves an Irish grill including corned beef and cabbage. ♦ 687 Lexington Ave (between E 56th and E 57th Sts). 355.0100, 800/367.7701; fax 355.1371 ᕗ

151 Habitat Hotel $ This stylish yet inexpensive (by Manhattan standards) hostelry on the site of the former **Allerton Hotel** offers its guests modern furnishings, cable television and Internet access. Rooms have one or two twin-sized beds and there are shared and private baths. ♦ 130 E 57th St (at Lexington Ave). 753.8841, 888/649.6331

152 The Galleria This midblock tower, designed in 1975 chiefly by **David Kenneth Specter** and **Philip Birnbaum,** comprises luxury apartments above a health club, retail facilities, and a public through-block arcade. Also worthwhile is the individualistic silhouette created by a multigreenhouse quadriplex (considered one of Manhattan's most expensive apartments) custom-built for philanthropist Stewart Mott. Apparently Mott had such a passion for fresh milk that he wanted to keep cows on the roof, but the building's board turned him down. ♦ 117 E 57th St (between Lexington and Park Aves)

153 Ritz Tower **Emery Roth** and **Carrère & Hastings** built this 42-story tower in 1925 as part of the Hearst apartment-hotel chain. Its stepped spire is still a distinctive mark in the skyline. ♦ 465 Park Ave (at E 57th St)

154 Argosy Book Store Few places in the United States have a better selection of historical pictures: photographs, posters, playbills, maps, engravings, lithographs, etchings, and woodcuts. ♦ M-Sa. 116 E 59th St (between Lexington and Park Aves). 753.4455

155 Helene Arpels The pampered feet of Jacqueline de Ribes and Marie-Helene de Rothschild are among those sporting Helene Arpels designs. Shoes for both men and women can be custom-decorated with hand embroidery, bead appliqué, stone studding, or exotic leathers. ♦ M-Sa. 470 Park Ave (between E 57th and E 58th Sts). 755.1623

156 Four Seasons Hotel $$$$ The tallest in town, this 52-story (plus tower) world-class hotel was designed by **I.M. Pei**. The sparse limestone lobby with its 33-foot onyx ceiling and serene public areas has been compared to a soaring marble mausoleum, cool and Zen-like in its simplicity. But the 370 elegant and spacious (600-square-foot) rooms are considerably cozier and warmer, with Art Deco–influenced decor and wonderful views of the city and **Central Park**. Services befitting such a deluxe operation include 24-hour concierge, well-equipped fitness facilities, an executive business center, and a contemporary American grill/restaurant serving breakfast, lunch, and dinner. If you're not content with your room's 120-square-foot bathroom, look into the heart-stopping $7,000-a-night Presidential Suite. ♦ 57 E 57th St (between Park and Madison Aves). 758.5700, 800/332.3442; fax 758.5711 ♿

Within The Four Seasons Hotel:

Fifty Seven Fifty Seven ★★★$$$$ Marble walls, soaring ceilings that are twenty-two feet high, maple floors with walnut insets, and bronze chandeliers inlaid with onyx provide a sophisticated setting for the very sophisticated seasonal menus. Signature dishes available year-round include marinated swordfish and asparagus in a vinaigrette of sour cherry, ginger, and citrus; and black bass with corn and oyster mushrooms—one of the creative lower-fat and -calorie entrées on the

menu. Those willing to splurge, however, shouldn't miss the chocolate crème brûlée or caramelized banana cream pie with peanut ice cream and chocolate sauce. ♦ American ♦ M-F breakfast, lunch, and dinner; Sa-Su breakfast, brunch, and dinner. Reservations recommended. 758.5757 ♿

156 Louis Vuitton Luggage and leather accessories with the familiar LV signature fill the store. The designer's recent collections of leather goods in solid, bright colors present a more contemporary look. ♦ Daily. 49 E 57th St (between Park and Madison Aves). 371.6111 ♿

156 Prada The supple leather and industrial-nylon handbags and knapsacks sold here have become the accessories of choice for global customers who zealously follow this generations-old Milanese institution. Third-generation Miuccia Prada is responsible for the contemporary fashions displayed throughout the store, from shoes to separates. ♦ M-Sa. 45 E 57th St (between Park and Madison Aves). 308.2332. Also at: 841 Madison Ave (at E 70th St). 327.4200

157 Buccellati Silver Italy's most opulent hand-crafted silver, including flatware, is sold in this store. ♦ M-Sa. 46 E 57th St (between Park and Madison Aves). 308.2507

157 Guy Laroche The city's only outpost for the ready-to-wear collection of this French label carries everything from silk camisoles to full-length ball gowns. ♦ M-Sa. 36 E 57th St (between Park and Madison Aves). 759.2301

157 The Pace Gallery Among the heaviest of the city's heavy hitters, this gallery represents a formidable roster of artists and artists' estates, including Jim Dine, Chuck Close, Louise Nevelson, Mark Rothko, and Lucas Samaras. Housed in the same building are the gallery's many offspring—**Pace Prints, Pace Master Prints, Pace Primitive Art,** and **Pace/MacGill** for 20th-century photography ♦ Tu-Sa. 32 E 57th St (between Park and Madison Aves). 421.3292. Also at: 142 Greene St (between Prince and W Houston Sts). 431.9224 ♿

158 Suarez High-end designer bags—most of them European and all top-of-the-line—at 20 percent (and more) below standard retail are the specialty of this well-stocked boutique, which recently moved to larger quarters on Park Avenue. Some familiar labels are offered but most of them are the "big names" without the logos. There is now a small selection of classic shoes for women. This is a store for people who care more about quality than status. The staff has its priorities in place, too; they are friendly and helpful. ♦ M-Sa. 450 Park Ave (between E 56th and E 57th Sts). 753.3758

159 The Gazebo Hundreds of old and new quilts fill this airy shop, which also features baskets, charming white wicker indoor and outdoor furniture, appliquéd and patchwork pillows, and unusually wide (11 feet) rag rugs. New quilts are produced to the store's specifications with American fabrics in Haiti. Both quilts and rugs can be custom-made. ◆ Daily. 114 E 57th St (between Lexington and Park Aves). 832.7077

59 Universal Pictures Building This 1947 building by **Kahn & Jacobs** is noteworthy as the first office building on this previously residential section of Park Avenue and as the first to be built to the "wedding cake" outline of the then-current zoning regulations. It is perhaps the best example of pre–glass-curtain wall design. Compare it to its 1972 counterpart across the street at 450 Park Avenue. ◆ 445 Park Ave (between E 56th and E 57th Sts)

60 Lombardy $$$ Built in 1927 by **Henry Mandel,** this residential hotel has 100 transient suites and studios, each with a different decor and all with serving pantries and refrigerators. About a third of the accommodations are secured by long-term residents who call this home. ◆ 111 E 56th St (between Lexington and Park Aves). 753.8600, 800/223.5254; fax 754.5683 ♿

Within the Lombardy:

The Park ★★$$$ Breathtaking Baccarat chandeliers and rich furnishings in soft blues, yellows, and greens is the setting for John Scotto's (his mom and siblings own **Fresco**) new restaurant. Scotto has broken from family tradition; together with chef Fabrizzio Salerni, he has created an American menu with a French twist. Try crabmeat salad with bourbon tomato dressing or the terrine of spring vegetables with carrot-ginger emulsion to start. Follow with rack of lamb with fresh bean stew, seared Atlantic salmon with oyster mushrooms and fresh sorrel in Chardonnay reduction, or steak *frites.* Desserts are tempting—especially the Valrhona chocolate cake and freshly made sorbets. ◆ American ◆ Daily lunch and dinner. Reservations recommended. 750.5656

61 Mercedes-Benz Showroom One of New York City's rare works by **Frank Lloyd Wright,** this 1955 design is a curious exercise in glass, ramp, plants, and fancy cars in a too-tight space. ◆ M-Sa. 430 Park Ave (at E 56th St). 629.1666

62 The Drake Swissôtel $$$ Built by **Emery Roth** in 1927, this hotel was purchased by

real-estate entrepreneur William Zeckendorf in the 1960s and became the home of the city's first discotheque, **Shepheards.** It was restored in 1980 and again in 1995 by the Swissôtel chain to its original elegance, and is now more a setting for chamber music than rock. The **Drake Bar and Cafe** serves fresh seafood and grilled dishes with a Swiss flair. Amenities include refrigerators in all 494 rooms, 24-hour room service, concierge, a fitness center, and parking facilities. ◆ 440 Park Ave (at E 56th St). 421.0900, 800/372.5369; fax 688.8053

163 Fuller Building The identification over the entrance of this black-and-white Art Deco tower, designed in 1929 by **Walker & Gillette,** is graced by a pair of figures by sculptor Elie Nadelman. The building is home to many art galleries, including **Marisa del Re, André Emmerich,** and **Susan Sheehan.** ◆ 41 E 57th St (at Madison Ave)

163 Emporio Armani The Italian designer's complete avant-garde ready-to-wear and couture lines for men and women are now under one roof. If you're hungry (and if you have any money left), ask for a table at the cafe staffed by an army of beautiful people (what else?). ◆ M-Sa. 601 Madison Ave (at E 57th St). Also at: 110 Fifth Ave (at W 16th St). 727.3240 ♿

163 Maxwell Davidson Gallery This seasoned dealer, relocated from SoHo, hosts a variety of artists, with an emphasis on Realism. ◆ M-Sa. 41 E 57th St (at Madison Ave). 759.7555

164 Ronin Gallery This is the place to see Japanese art, including woodblock prints, ivory netsuke, and metalwork from the 17th through 20th centuries. The gallery offers free appraisals of Japanese art. ◆ M-Sa. 605 Madison Ave (between E 57th and E 58th Sts). 688.0188

There are 188 member states in the United Nations—the last being the Kingdom of Tonga, admitted 14 September 1999.

New York traffic engineers have not taken on the project of installing Walk/Don't Walk lights (a.k.a. "ped" lights) on Park Avenue between East 46th and East 56th Streets because of what lies barely eight inches below: the tunnels in and out of Grand Central Station.

In December 1968, an underground passageway was opened between the 42nd Street IND and the Fifth Avenue IRT subway stations. The pedestrian tunnel is unusual on many counts: It is not only well lighted, its walls are adorned with photographic images of nearby street scenes that have been transferred to porcelain enamel panels.

New York City in Print

Nonfiction

ACCESS New York City Restaurants (HarperCollins Publishers, 1997). The ultimate inside scoop on the city's best restaurants and fancy food shops, for gourmets and gourmands.

AIA Guide to New York City by Norval White and Elliot Willensky (Harcourt Brace Jovanovich, 1988). In this richly illustrated third edition, the authors give you an architectural insider's view of New York City's buildings and landscapes, from the familiar to the off-beat. Organized by neighborhoods.

The Best Guided Walking Tours of NYC by Leslie Gourse (The Globe Pequot Press, 1989). A directory and reference book for the institutions and the people to contact for a variety of specialized walking tours.

The Building of Manhattan by Donald Mackay (Harper & Row, 1987). This book answers the question: "How did they build that?" Hundreds of archival photos and drawings trace the history of construction in **Manhattan,** from the early Dutch homes to the giant skyscrapers and the latest innovations in architecture and construction techniques.

The Columbia Historical Portrait of New York by John A. Kouwenhoven (Harper & Row, 1972). A show-and-tell guide combining brief essays and 900 photographs accompanied by historical data.

The Encyclopedia of New York City by Kenneth T. Jackson (Yale University Press/The New York Historical Society, 1995). This massive illustrated volume contains encapsulated information, some of it highly detailed, on just about everything and everyone associated with New York City.

Ethnic New York: A Complete Guide to the Many Faces and Cultures of New York by Mark Leeds (Passport Books, 1991). A primer on the melting pot that is New York City. The histories of different neighborhoods are coupled with a guide to restaurants, shops, museums, and, of course, festivals.

The I Hate New York Guidebook by Warren D. Leight (Dell, 1983). This slim paperback may be going on 20 years in age, but the satirical observations about the city and its inhabitants are still right on target. You'll wonder why the author hasn't done an updated edition—there's so much more to laugh about now.

The Late, Great Pennsylvania Station by Lauren B. Diesel (The Stephen Green Press, 1987). This illustrated oversized paperback traces the history and tragic end of one of New York's architectural wonders.

Literary Neighborhoods of New York by Maraca Leisure (Satchel Press,

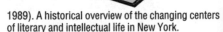

1989). A historical overview of the changing centers of literary and intellectual life in New York.

Lost New York: Pictorial Record of Vanished NYC by Nathan Silver (American Legacy Press, 1982). An illustrated history of the buildings and neighborhoods of New York.

New York, A Guide to the Metropolis: Walking Tour of Architecture and History by Gerald R. Wolf (McGraw-Hill, 1988). Three hundred photographs and 20 walking tours in Manhattan, **Brooklyn,** and **Queens** lead you through the history of New York by way of its architecture.

New York City Yesterday & Today: 30 Timeless Walking Adventures by Judith H. Browning (Corsair Publications, 1990). This book specializes in uncommon facts, personal observations, and novel perspectives on familiar sights all over New York.

New York Observed: Artists and Writers Look at the City, 1650 to the Present, edited by Barbara Coven, Seymour Chwast, and Steven Heller (Harry N. Abrams, 1988). New York City has long fascinated artists and writers. This collection presents some of those views over the ages.

The New York Theatre Sourcebook by Chuck Lawliss (Simon & Schuster, 1981). Although slightly dated, this reference book contains something for the novice as well as the pro, from the history of over 250 theaters to the search for cheap tickets.

Fiction

The Age of Innocence by Edith Wharton, originally published 1920 (Charles Scribner's Sons, 1968). An incisive but subtle attack on the mores and customs of upper-class society in turn-of-the-century New York. A richly detailed portrait of a world Wharton knew quite well, and disdained.

Catcher in the Rye by J.D. Salinger, originally published 1951 (Bantam Books, 1964). This controversial classic, about the adolescence of Holden Caulfield, a young runaway in New York, has been a touchstone for a generation or two.

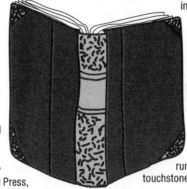

Diedrick Knickerbocker's History of New York by Washington Irving, originally published 1840 (Sleepy Hollow, 1981). A satirical and somewhat burlesque "history" of New York, written by Irving under the pseudonym Diedrick Knickerbocker (the same narrator as in Rip Van Winkle).

The House of Mirth by Edith Wharton (Charles Scribner's Sons, 1905). Wharton lets loose on New York society again in this novel, which is about a woman who rejects marrying for love in the hope of marrying for money. In the end, she gets neither.

This Side of Paradise by F. Scott Fitzgerald (Charles Scribner's Sons, 1920). A portrait of the "Lost Generation" in its college days, and yet another battle between true love and money-lust that ends in regret and cynicism.

Time and Again by Jack Finney (Simon & Schuster, 1970). If you could go back in time and change the world, what would you do? Finney offers some suggestions.

A Tree Grows in Brooklyn by Betty Smith, originally published 1943 (Harper & Row, 1968). A sensitive child grows up in a rough neighborhood with a drunk but lovable father and a determined but sweet mother. Tender and moving.

Washington Square by Henry James, originally published 1880 (New American Library, 1990). James grew up on **Washington Square,** the setting for this novel about the shy young daughter of a domineering and wealthy doctor who makes her life miserable. Made into a movie and a play titled *The Heiress* and, in 1997, a movie titled *Washington Square.*

165 Show Me New York Even the most diehard tourist finds it nearly impossible to see all the Big Apple has to offer. But in less than an hour, this film delivers an overview of the city that even has native New Yorkers viewing their hometown from a different vantage point. This three-dimensional journey is loaded with spectacular images and sounds, with views soaring high above skyscrapers, or sliding into **Yankee Stadium.** ♦ Admission. Daily. 42 E 58th Street (between Park and Madison Aves). 888.5200

166 James II Galleries Edwardian and Victorian jewelry, Spode pottery, ironstone, majolica, brass, silver plate, and Art Nouveau and Art Deco silver are featured. ♦ M-Sa. 11 E 57th St (between Madison and Fifth Aves). 355.7040

166 Hermès Saddlery, scarves, and silk shirts are sold at this quintessentially Parisian original, including the Hermès tie, the foolproof gift for the boss who has everything. ♦ M-Sa. 11 E 57th St (between Madison and Fifth Aves), Ground floor. 751.3181

166 Chanel Recently opened at this location, the spacious world-class boutique showcases the increasingly popular Chanel fashions and accessories. The scent of Coco remains, but it is Karl "the Kaiser" Lagerfeld who now calls the sartorial shots from his Paris atelier. Super-hairstylist Frederic Fekkai has opened his salon on the fifth through ninth floors. ♦ M-Sa. 15 E 57th St (between Madison and Fifth Aves). 355.5050 &

167 IBM Building This 43-story green granite building, designed in 1982 by **Edward Larrabee Barnes,** rises dramatically over a high atrium containing tables and chairs for relaxing and cool, modern sculptures to take your mind off Midtown's hectic pace. Now owned by a multinational corporation, the building houses many private companies.

♦ 590 Madison Ave (between E 56th and E 57th Sts)

168 Burberrys A recent redesign of the store mirrors the rejuvenated image this store hopes to project. Their classic raincoat has always possessed an incomparable style, but now the rest of the clothes for men and women—including hats, coats, jackets, trousers, and skirts—are striving to appeal to a less staid generation. ♦ Daily. 9 E 57th St (between Madison and Fifth Aves). 371.5010 &

WB Warner Bros. Studio Store

168 Warner Brothers Studio Store Smack in the middle of a tony enclave of luxury stores and sky-high real estate is this nine-story Hollywood-inspired shopping center that resembles a high-tech back lot, with TV screens playing old Warner Brothers movies. The gift-shop area is filled with watches, address books, posters, ties, mugs, and more. But if you're not in the mood to buy any of the 3,000 items (much of it apparel), just come for the experience of riding the glass elevator powered by a figure of Superman. ♦ Daily. 1 E 57th St (at Fifth Ave). 754.0300 &

169 David McKee Gallery This small but very smart gallery boasts an impressive list of youngish artists like sculptor Martin Puryear and painters Sean Scully and Jake Berthot, as well as the estate of the influential artist Philip Guston. ♦ Tu-Sa. 745 Fifth Ave (between E 57th and E 58th Sts). 688.5951

169 Forum Twentieth-century figurative American paintings and sculpture by names such as William Beckman and Gregory Gillespie are featured in this gallery. ♦ Tu-Sa. 745 Fifth Ave (between E 57th and E 58th Sts). 355.4545

169 Mary Boone A much publicized upstart among art dealers during the early 1980s heyday of Neo-Expressionism, Boone has settled into the establishment with a solid roster of American and mid-career European artists. Eric Fischl, David Salle, and Ross Bleckner are among her successes. ♦ Tu-Sa. 745 Fifth Ave. (between E 57th and E 58th Sts). 752.2929

169 Bergdorf Goodman Men According to department store's chairman, Ira Neimark, this store is "for the sort of men who dine at the best restaurants, stay at the best hotels, and join the best clubs." What do these men wear? Shirts from Turnbull & Asser and Charvet; suits from Zegna and Brioni, Luciana Barbera, and St. Andrews; sportswear from Willis & Geiger. The couture also leans toward the cutting edge with names like Romeo Gigli and Dolce & Gabbana. ♦ M-Sa. 745 Fifth Ave (between E 57th and E 58th Sts). 753.7300 ♿

170 Bergdorf Goodman In the most luxurious of the city's legendary department stores (although there is some moderately priced merchandise), the idea that living well is the best revenge reigns, partly because of the architecture (high ceilings, delicate moldings, arched windows) and partly because of the wares. It was the first store to promote the designers of Milan with a vengeance. And all the merchandise bears the stamp of luxury, whether it's the impeccable clothing by Donna Karan and Calvin Klein, the iridescent jewelry of Ted Muehling, the aromatic scents from London's Penhaligon, delicate candies from Manon Chocolates, or glove-leather bags by Paloma Picasso. There is also a top-of-the-line beauty salon **(John Barrett)** and a cafe. ♦ M-Sa. 754 Fifth Ave (between W 57th and W 58th Sts). 753.7300 ♿

171 Van Cleef & Arpels When the late Shah of Iran needed a tiara made for his Empress Farah, he came here. The boutique department, where jewelry ranges from moderate to expensive, is actually in **Bergdorf**'s main store next door, while gemstones that cost more are sold here. Jewelry can be custom-designed. Estate jewelry is also bought and sold. The guard is formidable, but the salespeople at least deign to acknowledge customers who make it past him. ♦ M-Sa. 744 Fifth Ave (at W 57th St). 644.9500 ♿

172 The Crown Building At 26 stories, this was once the tallest building on Fifth Avenue above 42nd Street. Originally called the **Heckscher Building,** it was designed by **Warren & Wetmore** and built in 1922 as a wholesale center for women's fashions. In 1929, the **Museum of Modern Art** opened its first gallery here. The gold leaf on the facade and tower is recent, as is the lighting of this entire intersection. ♦ 730 Fifth Ave (between W 56th and W 57th Sts)

Within The Crown Building:

Bulgari Elegantly nestled on the corner of one of the world's most expensive-per-commercial-square-foot intersections is this temple to the Rome-based jeweler of the privileged. Bold mountings offset the precious stones of vibrant colors for which this generations-old house is renowned. The intricate workmanship of some pieces is often an engineering and artisanal feat. ♦ M-Sa. 315.9000

Kennedy Galleries Works by American artists from the 18th century on, including John Singleton Copley, Edward Hopper, Georgia O'Keeffe, and John Marin, are shown at this gallery, founded in 1874. Its catalogs are wonderful, too. ♦ Tu-Sa. Second floor (enter at 9 W 56th St, between Fifth and Sixth Aves). 541.9600 ♿

173 NikeTown On a street with some of the most exclusive names in retailing, this five-story tower is what some consider the best entertainment in town. Everything you could possibly want in the way of athletic gear can be found here. From the amusing turnstile entrance on the street level to the rooftop garden, this is as much a high-tech amusement park as it is a merchandise mart. There are tons of sports memorabilia, interactive displays, big screen videos, and an overall feeling of fun. Of course, buying is the real name of the game, and the store never lets you forget why you came here: Footwear is displayed on racks in such a way as to give it the importance of fine art, and the brightly colored clothing catches the eye faster than a Michael Jordan slam-dunk. ♦ Daily. 6 E 57th St (between Madison and Fifth Aves). 891.6453

173 Tiffany & Co. Built in 1940 by **Cross & Cross,** this store has become so famous for quality and style that many of its well-designed wares have become classics: the all-purpose wineglass and Wedgwood china, to name just a couple. Given as gifts, these items are further enhanced by the cachet of the signature light-blue box. In addition to table appointments, the store also boasts a selection of fine jewelry, gems, stationery items, crystal, clocks, and watches in all price ranges. Salespeople are friendly and helpful. The window displays are worth going out of your way to see—especially at Christmas. ◆ M-Sa. 727 Fifth Ave (at E 57th St). 755.8000

174 Trump Tower Offices fill the lower floors, along with a glitzy six-story atrium replete with a vertical waterfall along a soaring pink granite wall. Stores such as **Ferragamo, Cartier, Tower Records,** and **Coach** are showcased. Cafes and restaurants are on the sunken ground level. Built in 1983, the tower was designed by **Der Scutt** of **Swanke, Hayden, Connell & Partners.** ◆ Daily. 725 Fifth Ave (between E 56th and E 57th Sts). 832.2000 &

175 Steuben More like a museum than a store, engraved sculptures featuring Chinese calligraphy, animals, or even a forest of spreading pine are highlighted here. All are displayed in backlit glass cases in a gray-walled sanctuary. The State Department buys its gifts for heads of state here, and the hoi polloi find crystal in the shape of dolphins, elephants, and hippopotamuses. ◆ M-Sa. 717 Fifth Ave (at E 56th St). 752.1441, 800/424.4240

176 Henri Bendel The windows are among the most imaginative in New York, but don't stop there. Shopping here is an experience no one should miss. This exclusive store is filled with unique merchandise at moderate to eye-popping prices, including tabletop wares by Frank McIntosh, and it's still fun to kick up your heels and announce you just got those stunning shoes at **Bendel's** (be sure to say *Ben*-dls, as the natives do). The second floor's **Petite Cafe** and **Salon de The** are pricey but delightful. Take a moment to appreciate the unique Lalique etched glass windows. ◆ Daily. 712 Fifth Ave (between W 55th and W 56th Sts). 247.1100

176 Harry Winston, Inc. The father of this world-famous seller of diamonds owned a little jewelry store on Columbus Avenue, but Harry went into business for himself while he was still a teenager and eventually established what may be the most daunting diamond salon in the city. It is the only store on Fifth Avenue that processes diamonds from rough stones to finished jewelry. ◆ M-Sa. 718 Fifth Ave (at W 56th St). 245.2000

177 D.C. Moore Milton Avery and other masters of 20th-century art and promising newcomers are shown here. ◆ Tu-Sa. 724 Fifth Ave (at W 56th St), Eighth floor. 247.2111 &

178 Felissimo Located within a turn-of-the-century town house built by **Warren &**

Wetmore in 1901, this store is the first US outlet of one of the most successful retailers in Japan. It carries men's and women's clothing, accessories, and gifts. The fourth-floor tearoom provides an oasis of calm. ◆ M-Sa. 10 W 56th St (between Fifth and Sixth Aves). 247.5656 &

179 OMO Norma Kamali Kamali is the designer who put many American women into high-fashion sweatshirt dresses, blouses, slit skirts, and cocoon wraps. The bottom floor of the shop carries shoes, less expensive cottons and lycra knits, and swimsuits, while the upstairs floor has one-of-a-kind eveningwear. Kamali is also known for her outerwear, particularly her talent for making down coats and jackets look fashionable. ◆ M-Sa. 11 W 56th St (between Fifth and Sixth Aves). 957.9797 &

180 Kiiroi Hana ★★$$ The simple but carefully selected menu at this popular spot offers other dishes besides sushi, including bacon-wrapped filet mignon, *negimaki* (steak wrapped around scallions), salmon teriyaki, and noodle dishes. For an extra treat, sit at the sushi bar and watch the deft assembly behind the counter, but be prepared for a manic lunchtime scene as everyone arrives and scrambles for seats seemingly all at once. ◆ Japanese ◆ M-Sa lunch and dinner; Su dinner. Reservations recommended for dinner. 23 W 56th St (between Fifth and Sixth Aves). 582.7499

181 L'Ermitage ★★$$ The cream-colored walls are hung with 19th-century Russian paintings, the lighting is subdued, and the menu reflects both the French and Russian nationals in the kitchen. Don't miss *pelmeni* (nicely spiced Siberian meat dumplings served with just a touch of sour cream), blini with caviar, and marinated lamb. Finish the meal off with a warm fruit tart, particularly if it's plum. ◆ Russian/French ◆ M-F lunch and dinner; Sa dinner. Reservations recommended. 40 West 56th St (between Fifth and Sixth Aves). 581.0777 &

The task of cleaning Rockefeller Center's rentable area of 15,000,000 square feet is equivalent to cleaning almost 11,000 six-room apartments. Some 65,000 people work in Rockefeller-owned or -operated buildings daily, and approximately 175,000 visit each day for business or pleasure, giving it a daily population of 240,000. Only 60 cities in the US exceed this total.

New York is the only American city to house an American embassy, the United States Mission, located across the street from the United Nations.

182 Harley-Davidson Cafe ★$$ Welcome to Harleywood. Inside, Harleys dangle from the ceiling in an atmosphere that's somewhere between Mardi Gras and mayhem. The menu features "great American road food," items such as Carolina pulled pork, blackened chicken, barbecued baby back ribs, burgers, and sandwiches (including a Harley Hog). There's also Mississippi mud and chocolate toll house pies for dessert. ♦ American ♦ Daily lunch, dinner, and late-night meals. 1370 Sixth Ave (at W 56th St). 245.6000 ♿

183 Frumkin/Adams Gallery The blue-ribbon stable of contemporary artists includes Jack Beal, Robert Arneson, and Luis Cruz Azaceta. ♦ Tu-Sa. 50 W 57th St (between Fifth and Sixth Aves), Second floor. 757.6655 ♿

183 Marlborough Gallery One of New York's old-line establishments represents some of the most important names in European and American art, including Larry Rivers, Fernando Botero, Red Grooms, and Magdalena Abakanowicz. ♦ M-Sa. 40 W 57th St (between Fifth and Sixth Aves), Second floor. 541.4900 ♿

184 J.N. Bartfield Galleries & Books Nineteenth-century American and European art, including works by Remington, Russell, and other masters of the American West, are displayed here, along with elegantly bound antiquarian books by classic authors such as Shakespeare and Dickens. ♦ M-F mid-October–May; M-Sa June–mid-October. 30 W 57th St (between Fifth and Sixth Aves), Third floor. 245.8890 ♿

184 William H. Schab Gallery Master prints and drawings by such artists as Delacroix, Dürer, Piranesi, and Rembrandt are showcased. ♦ Tu-Sa. 24 W 57th St (between Fifth and Sixth Aves). 410.2366 ♿

It is often said that the Chrysler Building was built to honor secretaries; the building and its stunning spire resemble an upturned pencil point.

More than 1,200 people were killed in riots near Tudor City in 1863, caused when the rich newcomers to the area were permitted to buy draft exemptions that the poor could not afford.

One of the waiting rooms in Grand Central Station was once known as the "Kissing Gallery" because it was there that travelers who had come long distances were met and kissed by kin and loved ones.

Restaurants/Clubs: Red
Hotels: Blue
Shops/ ♥ Outdoors: Green
Sights/Culture: Black

184 Marian Goodman Gallery The gallery's stark but generous space is devoted to a host of weighty imported talents, including the German painter Anselm Kiefer and British sculptor Tony Cragg. Don't miss the gallery's new space, where **Multiples,** the print-publishing arm, displays its wares. ♦ M-Sa. 24 W 57th St (between Fifth and Sixth Aves), Fourth floor. 977.7160 ♿

185 Blum Helman Gallery This unusually large space features contemporary American painting and sculpture. ♦ Tu-Sa. 20 W 57th St (between Fifth and Sixth Aves), Second floor. 245.2888 ♿

186 Rizzoli Bookstore The ultimate bookstore, it is reminiscent of an oak-paneled library in an opulent Italian villa, with classical music playing (records are for sale) and a hushed, unhurried atmosphere. Known for foreign-language, travel, art, architecture, and design books, the store also has an outstanding foreign and domestic general interest and design periodical department. The building dates from the turn of the century, and was restored in 1985 by **Hardy Holzman Pfeiffer Associates.** ♦ Daily. 31 W 57th St (between Fifth and Sixth Aves). 759.2424. Also at: 454 W Broadway (between Prince and W Houston Sts). 674.1616; World Financial Center (West St, between Liberty and Vesey Sts), Winter Garden Atrium. 385.1400

187 Brewster Gallery The graphics at this gallery are by such important European artists as Picasso, Miró, and Chagall. ♦ Tu-Sa. 41 W 57th St (between Fifth and Sixth Aves), Third floor. 980.1975 ♿

187 Hacker Art Books This store features in- and out-of-print art books and reprints, plus some excellent bargains on the literature of the visual arts. ♦ M-Sa. 45 W 57th St (between Fifth and Sixth Aves). 688.7600 ♿

188 Chateaubriand ★★$$$ This cozy Parisian-style neighborhood bistro in the heart of Manhattan is popular with the business crowd due to the $19.95 express lunch. It's a good deal for anyone who wants some quality food without having to wait hours. Other menu items are just as delectable, although not as quick. ♦ French ♦ M-F lunch and dinner; Sa-Su dinner. 68 W 58th St (between Fifth and Sixth Aves). 751.2323

189 Wyndham Hotel $$ This remarkably comfortable hotel is a favorite with stars appearing on Broadway, many of whom, such as Peter Falk and Carol Burnett, could easily afford to stay at the **Plaza.** Some stars, planning for a long Broadway run, have been known to arrive with their own furniture. Despite the 200-plus rooms, the atmosphere is that of a small, charming hotel. There is a restaurant serving breakfast, lunch, and dinner. ♦ 42 W 58th St (between Fifth and Sixth Aves). 753.3500, 800/257.1111; fax 754.5638 ♿

190 The Manhattan Ocean Club ★★★$$$
The excellent seafood at this extremely popular restaurant reflects an often overlooked fact—New York is still a port, with easy access to the treasures of the sea. Try appetizers of seared tuna with lattice potatoes and *salsa verde* or baked oysters with morel cream; follow with grilled swordfish with cream of lentil curry, salmon with tandoori spices, or red snapper with rosemary crust. The owner's personal collection of more than a dozen Picasso ceramics is on display. The wine list is extensive, well chosen, and well priced. ♦ Seafood ♦ M-F lunch and dinner; Sa-Su dinner. Reservations recommended; jacket and tie requested. 57 W 58th St (between Fifth and Sixth Aves). 371.7777

191 St. Moritz on the Park $$$ Designed in 1931 by **Emery Roth & Sons,** this park-side hotel has 680 small, refurbished rooms. Ask for park views; the least expensive rooms face the courtyard. Niceties include room service, a newsstand, and a gift shop. **Rumpelmayer's** serves only breakfast. ♦ 50 Central Park S (at Sixth Ave). 755.5800, 800/221.4774; fax 751.2952 ♿

192 Mickey Mantle's ★$$ It's not surprising that sports fans of all ages love this place. They get to watch the day's big game or memorable moments in sports history on huge video screens and they can study the restaurant's collection of uniforms and memorabilia. The basic American fare— gigantic burgers, ribs, hot-fudge sundaes— should please not-too-picky eaters; it's certainly a lot better than ballpark franks. ♦ American ♦ Daily lunch and dinner. 42 Central Park S (between Fifth and Sixth Aves). 688.7777

192 Helmsley Park Lane Hotel $$$ A relative newcomer to the neighborhood, this 46-story building designed by **Emery Roth & Sons** in 1971 has arches at the top that add interest to the block. The late Harry Helmsley and Leona (of scandalous tax-evasion fame), who owned several hotels and a lot of real estate in Manhattan, once picked this as their own home address. Its 640 rooms have undergone a refurbishing; marble and chandeliers abound, and the multilingual staff is eager to please. ♦ 36 Central Park S (between Fifth and Sixth Aves). 371.4000, 800/221.4982; fax 319.9065

193 The Plaza Hotel $$$ This hotel is a legend in its own time, a landmark that has hosted Teddy Roosevelt, the Beatles, and F. Scott Fitzgerald and his wife, Zelda (who, it's rumored, danced nude in the fountain out front). Solomon R. Guggenheim lived for years in the State Suite surrounded by fabulous paintings, and **Frank Lloyd Wright** made the grande dame his New York headquarters.

This stylish Edwardian/French pile dating from 1907 is considered one of architect **Henry J. Hardenbergh**'s masterpieces (he also did the **Dakota** apartments). **Warren & Wetmore** oversaw the 1921 addition. Located on a unique site with two sides of the building equally exposed, the dignified hotel has survived many years as the center of high social activity. Now managed by Fairmont Hotels, the decor, size, and location of the 806 rooms vary wildly (resultantly in price as well: from $$$ to $$$$). Many of the lovely high-ceilinged ones are still in top condition, but some face air shafts. Request an outside room—or better still, a park view. The 24-hour room service remains, and so do the flags outside representing countries of important foreign guests. Donald Trump bought the hotel in 1988; his now–ex-wife, Ivana, oversaw a major renovation and hired several of New York's top hotel personnel, but she has since left. Happily, the elegant dining options endure in high style: **The Oak Bar and Restaurant** is still in its original (woody, elegant, and comfortable) condition; the **Oyster Bar** still opens sparkling fresh clams and oysters to order; and the venerable, paneled **Edwardian Room** is still a fashionable spot for dining and dancing. The fabled **Palm Court** in the lobby is fine and festive, particularly as a choice for high tea. ♦ Fifth Ave (between W 58th St and Central Park S). 546.5493, 800/759.3000; fax 546.5324 ♿

194 Grand Army Plaza One of the city's few formal pedestrian spaces, the plaza (dissected by **Central Park South**) acts as both a forecourt to the **Plaza Hotel** to the south and as an entrance terrace to **Central**

Park to the north. Although the wall of the square has been weakened by the **GM Building,** the center has held strong, solidly anchored by the circular **Pulitzer Memorial Fountain,** built with funds provided in Joseph Pulitzer's will and designed by **Carrère & Hastings.** The sculpture on top is by Karl Bitter, and the equestrian statue of *General William Tecumseh Sherman* (by Augustus Saint-Gaudens) was displayed at the **World Exhibition** in Paris in 1900 and was erected here in 1903. Tradition still survives in the horse-drawn carriages that congregate here. They were the limousines of another era, and in the 1930s, Hollywood loved to send romancing couples off in them for jaunts in **Central Park.** You can still take a romantic ride through the park in a carriage, many with top-hatted drivers.

♦ Fifth Ave (between W 58th St and Central Park)

195 FAO Schwarz Because this is the best-stocked toy store in the United States, some parents never bring their kids here; the sight of so many toys can turn children into monsters of greed. The inexhaustible stock includes Madame Alexander dolls, Steiff stuffed animals, LGB electric trains, outdoor swings, magic tricks, video games, and hundreds of other amusements. At Christmastime you may have to wait in line just to go inside. ♦ Daily. 767 Fifth Ave (at E 58th St). 644.9400 &

196 Baccarat Newly expanded and more luxurious than ever, this is where to come for world-famous crystal, Limoges china, plus fine glassware and silver. ♦ M-Sa. 625 Madison Ave (at E 59th St). 826.4100, 800/777.0100

Bests

Chuck Scarborough
Broadcast Journalist, NBC

The **'21' Club.** When you visit this venerable old New York dining institution, be certain to ask the maître d' to give you a tour of the old Prohibition-era wine cellar. It was so cleverly hidden that the Feds never successfully raided **'21'** during Prohibition. Once you are shown the astonishing secret entrance, you will be allowed to browse through one of New York's most extensive wine collections, complete with the private stock of the rich and famous—past and present.

Linda Wells
Editor-in-Chief, *Allure* magazine

Madison Avenue, from East 60th to East 93rd Streets, is the greatest shopping, people watching, salon-stopping stretch in New York. Start at the **Calvin Klein** store for clean, modern, sleek clothes. Then go to **Barneys New York** for quirky, unusual beauty products, great children's gifts, stylish stationery, and a fashion-editor's wardrobe. **TSE Cashmere** for luxurious sweaters, **Prada** for three floors of delicious fashion, shoes, and handbags, and **Polo Sport–Ralph Lauren** for the best weekend gear. Also duck in to **Madison Avenue Bookshop** and **The Corner Bookstore**—great selections and advice from salespeople who actually read (the latter has a nice bunch of children's books, and welcomes dogs).

For a serious weekday breakfast, **The Carlyle Hotel** attracts the local moguls.

For a breather, duck into the **Frick Museum** and meditate by the fountain. The **Metropolitan Museum of Art** is wonderful for everything, especially the Frank Lloyd Wright room and the serene, hidden Chinese garden. I love **Nica's,** at the **Stanhope Hotel,** for a drink, a little Billie Holliday, and a quick dinner.

Run around the **Central Park** reservoir or skate at **Wollman Rink** at the southern end of the park. Both give an enchanted view of the city.

Donna Hanover
Broadcast Journalist/First Lady, City of New York

Go watch the inflating of the giant balloons at **West 77th Street** and **Central Park West** the Wednesday night before **Macy's** Thanksgiving Day Parade.

See the **Rockettes** perform in **Radio City Music Hall**'s Christmas and Easter Shows.

The American Museum of Natural History or **The Children's Museum of Manhattan.** Both are perfect for children on a rainy day.

Annette Green
President, The Fragrance Foundation

Jogging in or around **Gramercy Park.**

Soaking up ballet at the **Joyce Theater.**

Dining on seafood delights at **The Ocean Club.**

SoHo gallery crawling.

Plays, plays, and more plays—on, off, and around **Broadway.**

Enjoying the shows at **Fashion Institute of Technology.**

Visiting the sensory garden at the **Staten Island Botanical Garden.**

Hitting the books at the **Barnes & Noble Sales Annex** on Fifth Avenue at West 18th Street.

Ending the evening with **Bobby Short** in **Cafe Carlyle**

Visiting the rose garden at the **United Nations Park.**

Waterfront escape at **The Water Club.**

Betty Rollin
Author/News Correspondent, NBC

Walking, walking, walking—and soaking up the diversity that is New York.

Hopping on a cool city bus on a hot day for a ride up or down the avenues.

Fairway: great, fresh, abundant/cheap(!) produce.

Wandering around the streets of **Murray Hill** (where the action isn't); then stopping at the **Morgan Library** with its lovely courtyard.

Getting exhausted at **Bloomingdale's**.

Dinner at **The Union Square Cafe**, where the food is divine and you don't have to trip the waiters to get their attention.

Playing hooky from work on a weekday and going to the **Botanical Gardens.**

The New York Public Library, starting with the lions.

The range of odd, beautiful, quirky, and occasionally peaceful places—apartments—in which people live.

Elizabeth Tilberis
Former Editor-in-Chief, *Harper's Bazaar*

The view of Manhattan from the **Triborough Bridge** at dusk.

Driving down the **FDR Drive.**

Skating at **Wollman Rink.**

Eating outdoors on summer evenings as the sun sets at any restaurant with sidewalk cafes.

The shop windows at Christmastime.

The Egyptian rooms at the **Metropolitan Museum of Art.**

Circling Manhattan at sunset before the plane lands at **La Guardia Airport.**

Chinatown for Chinese food—the children love it here.

Little League baseball on Saturday in **Central Park.**

Knicks games on Sunday at **Madison Square Garden**—and the heavenly hot dogs.

Walter Cronkite
Newscaster Emeritus, *CBS Evening News*

South Street Seaport Museum.

Cable ride from Manhattan to **Roosevelt Island.** Exciting view of the **East River.**

Ellis Island. Where freedom began for many Americans.

Brooklyn Botanic Garden. Where bonsai and horticultural beauty abound.

Gracie Mansion.

P.J. Clarke's Bar. A saloon at the corner of East 55th Street and Third Avenue in the best tradition of the old New York City saloons before they tore down the el.

Zabar's, the deli supreme. However, almost any deli in New York should be visited for its smells and sights.

City Hall. A magnificent example of Federal architecture.

The **John Finley Walk** along the East River near where you can watch the ships coming down the river.

Merce Cunningham
Artistic Director, Merce Cunningham Dance Company

The **Union Square Greenmarket** on any market day, but particularly in the late spring through fall when the fresh produce and flowers and people are at their best. Beware the pickpockets, the signs say.

The vision of a large cruise ship through the windows of Westbeth, making a stately, steady progress down the Hudson to the open sea, when I am teaching a class of dancers. The ship's rhythm and movement is a delicious addition, however brief, to the bustle of the class, particularly in late afternoon, with the rays of the polluted sunset over New Jersey.

Being in the theater, backstage or out front, just before the curtain goes up.

Patricia Jean
Restaurant Owner, Provence

The Frick Collection, because it feels grand and special, and I can never walk by without going in.

The **Union Square Greenmarket,** where the city and country really meet. Because it's really seasonal produce from the region. Because you can't beat the bread from Boiceville or the tomatoes from Long Island (no, not New Jersey).

Horseback riding in **Central Park,** ice-skating at **Rockefeller Center,** and looking up at the buildings around and feeling a sense of solitude.

Restaurant Florent for onion soup and tripe at two in the morning. As close as you get to Paris without losing New York.

The food stores, especially **Dean & DeLuca** and **Jefferson Market.**

SoHo's streets before the stores and galleries open. It has the best neighborhood feeling in all New York, and it all changes after noon.

Dinner at the **River Café** at sunset because there's not a more beautiful and edifying view around!

Saturday afternoon gallery-hopping.

The flowers everywhere, but especially at the market on **West 28th Street.**

The feeling that anything is possible (it comes and goes, but I've only felt this in New York).

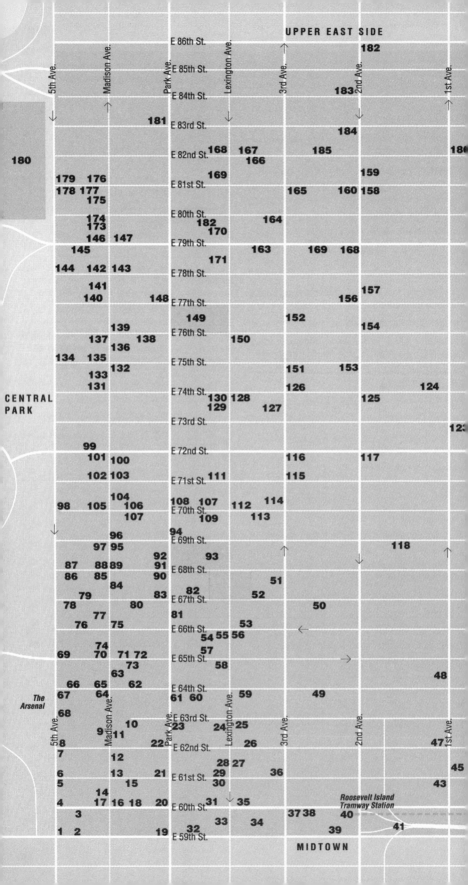

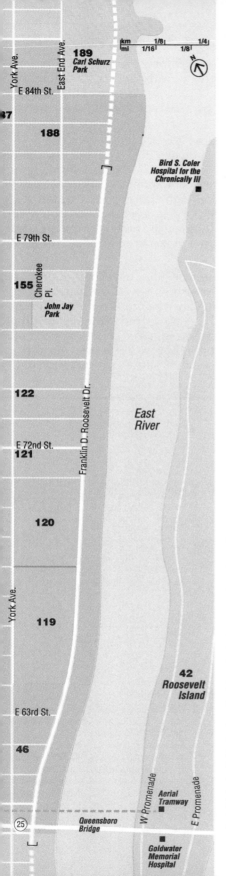

East Side

In the 1920s, *The New York Times* described the East Side as "a string of pearls: Each pearl is a double block of millionaires, and **Madison Avenue** is the string." Like everything else about New York, the East Side has been altered by time. But there are few places in the city where memory is as intact as in the blocks bounded by the **East River**, **Fifth Avenue**, and **East 59th** and **East 86th Streets**.

Until the close of the Civil War, this was the part of New York where the fashionable gathered to escape city summers—the counterpart of today's Hamptons on Long Island's South Shore. At the end of the 18th century, a necklace of mansions in parklike settings followed the shore of the East River all the way to Harlem. The **Boston Post Road**, now **Third Avenue**, made access to the city below Canal Street convenient, and summer residents with lots of leisure time traveled downtown on steamboats. By the late 1860s, the old summer houses were converted to year-round use for pioneering commuters, and, a few years later, the coming of elevated railroads on **Second** and Third Avenues opened the area to working-class people.

The improved transportation brought summer fun-seekers as well. The area bounded by the East River, Third Avenue, and **East 66th** and **East 75th Streets** became **Jones's Wood**. It included such attractions as a beer garden, a bathhouse, an athletic club, and a blocklong coliseum for indoor entertainment.

Society had its heyday on the East Side between 1895 and the outbreak of World War I. The state of American architecture was superb at the time, and the super-rich had the financial resources to hire the best. Technology was very much in vogue then, and it was a rare four-story house that didn't have at least one elevator. Nearly every house had an elaborate intercom system, and all installed dumbwaiters, usually electrically operated, to make life simpler for the servants. But the showplace was the bathroom—no New York house had indoor plumbing until the **Croton Aqueduct** began operating in 1842. Until the turn of the century, the style had been to bathe in dark, wood-paneled rooms designed to conceal their use.

Up until 1900, any family sharing a house with other families (except servants, of course) was labeled déclassé. But when the barrier fell, the "best of the best" apartment buildings appeared on the East Side, especially along Park Avenue, which after 1915 became what one contemporary called "a mass production of millionaires." The huge apartment houses created a kind of leveling effect among the wealthy, as well as a guarantee that this would remain *their* kind of neighborhood. They didn't even budge during the Great Depression, when armies of the unemployed took up residence across the way in **Central Park.**

The 1960s brought construction of uninspiring white and yellow brick apartment houses to the area; many of the elegant town houses had already been broken up into multiple-unit dwellings years before. Nevertheless, an air of privileged—often luxurious—lifestyle still prevails. And at the very mention of a stroll to the East Side, one still thinks of Madison Avenue and its roster of exclusive galleries and fashion boutiques brimming with European designer labels. The neighborhood continues to be what it has been for nearly a century: New York City's elite enclave.

1 Sherry-Netherland Hotel $$$$ One of the grandes dames rimming **Central Park,** this hotel, designed in 1927 by **McKim, Mead & White** and built by Louis Sherry of ice-cream fame, was once the centerpiece of an elegant trio, sitting between **The Pierre** and the **Savoy-Plaza** (whose site now hosts the **General Motors** tower). Its high-peaked roof sports gargoyles and chimneys like a Loire Valley confection. On the walls lining the entrance are panels rescued from a Vanderbilt mansion by **Richard Morris Hunt.** The 65-room hotel reopened in 1993 after a two-year total renovation that cost $18 million. Service is continental luxury class, and the rooms are large, many with park views. ♦ 781 Fifth Ave (at E 59th St). 355.2800, 800/247.4377; fax 319.4306

Within the Sherry-Netherland Hotel:

CIPRIANI

Harry Cipriani ★$$$$ If you can't get to the original Harry's Bar in Venice, don't think you can find it here. It's never been about the food—overpriced and consistently underwhelming—but rather the scene. Try one of the raviolis, with fillings that change daily, and swing back a Bellini—a blend of

peach nectar and dry Prosecco wine—while Ivana and Barbara Walters (possibly) do the same. ♦ Northern Italian ♦ Daily breakfast, lunch, and dinner. Reservations recommended; jacket required. 753.5566

IL TOSCANACCIO

2 Il Toscanaccio ★★$$$ The name means "naughty Tuscan" and that's the spirit restaurateur Pino Luongo is trying to achieve here. The colors are pure sunshine, with beige walls punctuated by orange and yellow. Don't miss the antipasto; baby octopus stewed in spicy tomato sauce; bowtie pasta with spring vegetables, herbs, tomato, and parmesan; homemade linguine with scallops, clams, mussels, and calamari; and lamb with olives and tomato served in a bread-crust shell. ♦ Tuscan ♦ M-Sa lunch and dinner; Su brunch and dinner. Reservations recommended. 7 E 59th St (between Madison and Fifth Aves). 935.3535 &

3 The Harmonie Club In 1852, wealthy German Jews, excluded from most other men's clubs, formed the *Harmonie Gesellschaft,* which was described at the time as "the most homelike of all clubs" because its members made it a practice to bring along their wives. Today, the home of this private club is located in a 1906 building designed by **McKim, Mead & White.** The building is not open to the public. ♦ 4 E 60th St (between Madison and Fifth Aves). 355.7400

Metropolitan Club

MICHAEL STORRINGS

4 Metropolitan Club Also designed by **McKim, Mead & White** in 1894, this is a good example of **Stanford White** in an enthusiastic mood. Note particularly the extravagant, colonnaded carriage entrance behind the gates of the château. An addition was built in 1912 by **Ogden Codman Jr.** The association was organized by J.P. Morgan for some of his friends who were not accepted at other clubs. ♦ 1 E 60th St (at Fifth Ave). 838.7400

5 The Pierre $$$$ Designed in 1930 by **Schultze & Weaver,** the architects of the **Sherry-Netherland,** this is another of the grand old European-style hotels with many permanent guests and a loyal following of the rich and the powerful. A stretched mansard roof clothed in weathered bronze at the top of the tower gives the structure a distinctive silhouette; it and the **Sherry** next door make a romantic couple. Though at first glance it all appears a bit intimidating, with all those limos in front and the miles of mural-lined lobby, the hotel offers the kind of luxury one could get used to: 202 enormous rooms (with dramatic **Central Park** views from the upper floors; you can actually see the seals in the **Central Park Wildlife Conservation Center**), and gleaming marble-and-tile bathrooms; 24-hour room

service; an attentive, multilingual staff; twice-daily maid service; complimentary shoe shine; even an unpacking service. Afternoon tea is served daily in the **Rotunda.** ♦ 2 E 61st St (at Fifth Ave). 838.8000, 800/743.7734; fax 826.0319 ₺

Within The Pierre:

Cafe Pierre ★★★$$$ This sophisticated dining room may be mistaken for a French chateau with its tones of pale yellow and gray, imported silks, and ceiling murals. But the elegance doesn't rest there. Indulge in an equally classic menu of risotto with wild mushrooms, asparagus, truffles, and chervil; and roasted rack of lamb in herb crust with sautéed artichokes. The appealing desserts are tempting, including the white-and-dark–chocolate terrine with ginger chips and caramelized orange sauce. There's a fine wine list as well. ♦ Continental ♦ Daily breakfast, lunch, and dinner. 940.8185

6 800 Fifth Avenue Until her death in 1977, Mrs. Marcellus Hartley Dodge, a niece of John D. Rockefeller Jr., lived here with her famous collection of stray dogs in a five-story brick mansion that was a mate to the nearby **Knickerbocker Club.** In 1978, **Ulrich Franzen & Associates** moved in, promising a tasteful building that would be a credit to the neighborhood. This 33-story building is how the promise was kept. The zoning law forced them to build a three-story wall along Fifth Avenue. Unfortunately, it isn't high enough to hide the building behind it. ♦ At E 61st St

7 The Knickerbocker Club In the 1860s, some members of the **Union Club** proposed that its membership be restricted to men descended from the colonial families of New York, known as the Knickerbockers. When their suggestion was rejected, they started their own club. But one of its most influential founders was August Belmont, a German immigrant. Today, the club is located in this 1914 building by **Delano & Aldrich,** which is not open to the public. ♦ 2 E 62nd St (at Fifth Ave). 838.6700

8 810 Fifth Avenue Former residents of this 13-story limestone building designed in 1926 by **J.E.R. Carpenter** include William Randolph Hearst and Mrs. Hamilton Fish, one of the last of the grandes dames of New York society. Before he moved to the White House in 1969, Richard M. Nixon lived here. His neighbor on the top floor was Nelson Rockefeller, who had New York's only fully equipped bomb shelter. ♦ The building is not open to the public. At E 62nd St

9 Nello ★$$$ There's an ample supply of models, debs and soap stars dangling designer shopping bags at this sleek trattoria, perfectly lit and covered with Peter Beard's magnificent photos of African fauna. As far as the menu's concerned, go for the arugula-and-fennel salad, grilled free range chicken, baby calamari stuffed with shrimps, scallops and salmon, or prime rib-eye steak. ♦ Italian ♦ Daily lunch and dinner. Reservations recommended; jacket required. 696 Madison Ave (between E 62nd and E 63rd Sts). 980.9099

9 Addison on Madison Subdued yet interesting men's shirts of fine French cotton are offered in appealing, gentle stripes and checks, with a few bolder stripes. Sleeves come short, regular, and extra long. ♦ M-Sa. 698 Madison Ave (between E 62nd and E 63rd Sts). 308.2660. Also at: 725 Fifth Ave (between E 56th and E 57th Sts). 752.2300 ઙ

THE
LOWELL

10 The Lowell $$$$ White-glove treatment is the norm in this small, charming hotel. Many of the 65 rooms and suites in the 1926 building by **Henry S. Churchill** have serving pantries and wood-burning fireplaces, and some can accommodate formal board meetings. Room-service meals arrive on a silver tray, or, if you prefer company, the second-floor dining room is both cheerful and serene. This is definitely one of New York City's best. ♦ 28 E 63rd St (between Park and Madison Aves). 838.1400, 800/221.4444; fax 319.4230

Within The Lowell:

The Post House ★★★$$$$ Many New York steak houses are strictly for red-meat eaters, but this gracious establishment has some alternate food choices and a softer touch—subdued lighting, peach walls, 18th-century American folk portraits, and models of ship hulls. The menu offers crab cakes and lemon-pepper chicken in addition to some of the best beef in the city. The extensive, well-priced wine list is one of New York's finest. ♦ American ♦ M-F lunch and dinner; Sa-Su dinner. Reservations required. 935.2888

11 Margo Feiden Galleries The specialty here is the work of caricaturist Al Hirschfeld, who has been capturing the essence of famous faces for *The New York Times* since the 1920s. The trick is to find all the "Ninas" in each drawing. Hirschfeld hides his daughter's name within folds of clothing, pompadours, wherever. One clue: The number of times "Nina" appears is indicated next to his sign-off. Original pen-and-ink drawings, limited editions, etchings, and lithographs are shown ♦ Daily. 699 Madison Ave (between E 62nd and E 63rd Sts). 677.5330

12 Georg Jensen Silversmiths Silver, including flatware and exquisite jewelry, is featured here: sleek, gleaming bangles and cuffs, Art Nouveau pins shaped like leaves and trimmed with precious stones. This is also a good source for crystal glassware and the entire collection of Royal Copenhagen china. ♦ Daily. 683 Madison Ave (between E 61st and E 62nd Sts). 759.6457 ઙ

13 Sherry Lehman One of the top wine merchants in the country, this place may have the most extensive retail inventory in the world. The store specializes in French, California, and Italian wines, but also stocks German, Spanish, South American, and kosher labels. Catalogues are published five times a year—one each season and an extra issue at Christmas—and the staff offers courteous, expert advice. It's also a handsome store for browsing. ♦ M-Sa. 679 Madison Ave (at E 61st St). 838.7500

14 Barneys New York This nine-story, 230,000-square-foot fashion temple designed by minimalist architect **Peter Marino** opened to much hoopla in 1993, three years—and $100 million—after the Pressman family decided to bring their (now defunct) downtown clothing mecca for men and women uptown. The largest specialty store to be built in Manhattan since the Depression, it's light and airy, with large stretches of loftlike space. The women's side measures more than twice the size of its quarters in the former flagship store in Chelsea. Don't miss the mesmerizing display of tropical fish in the main floor jewelry department. ◆ Daily. 660 Madison Ave (between E 60th and E 61st Sts). 826.8900. Also at: 2 World Financial Center (West St, between Liberty and Vesey Sts). 945.1600 ᶜ

Within Barneys New York:

Fred's at Barneys New York ★★$$$ Named for Fred Pressman, the late owner of **Barneys,** this bustling new restaurant is owned by chef Mark Strausmann (of **Campagna** fame). Try the assortment of marinated vegetables or a tasting of cheeses served with pears and Granny Smith apples. Also on hand are individual-size pizzas, and for hearty appetites, Baltimore crab cakes with homemade cole slaw and Belgian *pommes frites.* ◆ Eclectic ◆ M-Sa lunch and dinner; Su lunch. Reservations required. 833.2200 ᶜ

15 Aureole ★★★$$$$ This is one of the most charming dining rooms in town. Chef Charlie Palmer's complex food, given a praiseworthy architectural presentation, is also among the most admired; lately, though, the presentation seems to be overshadowing the flavor. Try the terrine of natural foie gras with pressed-duck confit, applewood-grilled salmon with basil-braised artichokes, or slow-basted breast of guinea fowl with melted savoy cabbage and a ragout of morels. The desserts are spectacular, particularly the tower of dark-chocolate and praline mousse. ◆ Continental ◆ M-F lunch and dinner; Sa dinner. Reservations required. 34 E 61st St (between Park and Madison Aves). 319.1660

16 Boyd's Madison Avenue Legions of well-known women, including Cher and the late Jackie Onassis, have come here to choose from a vast, international collection of feather powder puffs, rouges, combs, hairbrushes, and toothbrushes. ◆ Daily. 655 Madison Ave (at E 60th St). 838.6558 ᶜ

17 Calvin Klein The trend-setting designs of one of America's timeless fashion icons can be seen here at Madison Avenue's latest megastore. The 22,000-square-foot retail space, built in 1928 to house the **Morgan Guaranty Bank,** now offers shoppers his distinctive collection, accessories, and home furnishings. ◆ M-Sa. 654 Madison Ave (at E 60th St). 292.9000

18 Match ★★★$$ Minimalism with an uptown flair best describes this newly opened version of downtown's chic in-spot where dining doesn't take second place to decor. Beautifully appointed in a less-is-more fashion, it has polished hardwood floors, candlelit tables at dinner, and flower arrangements everywhere. Excellent dishes include eggplant and roasted–red pepper cannelloni served with spinach, corn-mushroom barley risotto, and seared pepper tuna with roasted pineapple. For dessert, don't miss the trio of mocha, cinnamon, and white chocolate mousse. ◆ International ◆ M-Sa lunch and dinner; Su brunch and dinner. Reservations recommended. 33 E 60th St (between Park and Madison Aves). 906.9177. Also at: 160 Mercer St (between Prince and W Houston Sts). 343.0020

19 Caviarteria This is one of the most reliable and fairly-priced places in town for the eggs of the beloved sturgeon. You can also sit down to enjoy your caviar on site at one of the tables, but despite an impressive array of exquisite caviar and a number of fine champagnes by the glass, it's hard to escape the ambience at this ostensibly ritzy retail shop and bar—somewhat reminiscent of a bus terminal. ◆ M-Sa 9AM-8PM; Su 11AM-4PM. 502 Park Ave (at E 59th St). 759.7410

19 Christie's The New York headquarters of the famous London auction house specializes in old masters, Impressionists, 19th- and 20th-century European and American art, and 22 other areas of art, including antiques and Chinese art. Tickets, available without charge a week or two before an auction, are required for evening auctions. Previews of items to be auctioned are held five days prior to the auction itself, and catalogs are available. ◆ Open to the public only during viewings before scheduled auctions; call first. Call 546.1007 for schedule. 502 Park Ave (at E 59th St). 546.1000 ᶜ

20 Christ Church Built in 1932 by **Ralph Adams Cram,** this is an interesting limestone-and-brick Methodist church. One of the best ecclesiastical structures of the 1930s, it was designed to look hundreds of years old. ◆ 520 Park Ave (at E 60th St). 838.3036

20 The Grolier Club Named for the 16th-century bibliophile Jean Grolier, this Georgian structure, designed by **Bertram G. Goodhue** in 1917, houses a collection of fine bookbindings and a specialized library open only to scholars and researchers. Regularly changing exhibitions display books, prints, and rare manuscripts. ◆ Free. M-Sa. 47 E 60th St (between Park and Madison Aves). 838.6690 ᶜ

21 The Regency $$$ This elegant hotel is the scene of some of New York's most important power breakfasts, at which the city's movers and shakers get together to start their business day. Guests can take advantage of

24-hour room service for their breakfast, but it isn't as exciting. Other advantages include a well-equipped fitness center and a large, multilingual staff. The hotel's recent $40-million refurbishment has added a new luxurious feel, enhanced by French antiques, to all 393 rooms. For added pleasure, **The Library** is a cozy spot for a drink or light meal. ♦ 540 Park Ave (at E 61st St). 759.4100, 800/23LOEWS; fax 826.5674 ♿

22 The Colony Club The building, which houses an exclusive club for society women, presents a solid, Neo-Georgian, Federal redbrick face, settled on a limestone base. It was designed in 1924 by **Delano & Aldrich** and is not open to the public. ♦ 564 Park Ave (at E 62nd St). 838.4200

23 Park Avenue Cafe ★★★$$$ Even when it's packed to the rafters—as it usually is—this whimsical, stylish room with blond wood and an American flag mural is a relaxed setting for chef David Burke's creative combinations. Try the tuna and salmon *tartare*, lobster dumplings, crabmeat ravioli in a seafood broth, gazpacho with a smoked-shrimp and jack-cheese quesadilla, baby lamb chops wrapped in pastry, or the signature "swordfish chop." But save room for Dan Budd's desserts. Among the standouts are milk-chocolate crème brûlée, chocolate-caramel cake with caramel ice cream, and Hawaii Vintage (a chocolate and banana tart). The wine list includes excellent French and American choices. ♦ American ♦ M-F lunch and dinner; Sa dinner; Su brunch and dinner. Reservations required. 100 E 63rd St (at Park Ave). 644.1900

24 Society of Illustrators Built in 1875, this museum of American illustration features changing exhibitions of advertising art, book illustration, editorial art, and other

contemporary work. ♦ Free. M-Sa. 128 E 63 St (between Lexington and Park Aves). 838.2560 ♿

24 Saint-Remy Produits de Provence Pale muted floral and paisley fabrics are sold here mainly by the yard (but can be ordered made up into napkins, lamp shades, and place mats). ♦ M-Sa. 818 Lexington Ave (between 62nd and E 63rd Sts). 486.2018 ♿

25 The Barbizon Hotel $$$ Its richly detailed brickwork and fine interiors have made this former residence for women—actresses Candice Bergen, Gene Tierney, and Grace Kelly stayed here at various times—one of the East Side's better-known buildings; it was designed in 1927 by **Murgatroyd & Ogden.** Until 1981—when it was converted to a hotel open to both sexes, with interiors by Milton Glaser—its upper floors were off-limits to men. But the rooftop arcades framed skyline views that were made famous by photographer Samuel Gottscho. The view also inspired painter Georgia O'Keeffe. Now under new ownership, the hotel features 310 refurbished rooms, 11 tower suites offering panoramic views of the city, a new bar and lounge, and a breakfast room. There's also a modern, multilevel **Equinox Fitness Club** on the premises, complete with pool and spa. ♦ 140 E 63rd St (at Lexington Ave). 838.5700 800/223.1020; fax 888.4271 ♿

26 Tender Buttons Featured here are millions and millions of buttons, new and antique, made of brass, stoneware, taqua nut, Lucite, wood, abalone, seashell, agate, plastic, silver—you name it. ♦ M-Sa. 143 E 62nd St (between Third and Lexington Aves). 758.7004

27 New York Doll Hospital Even if your doll isn't sick, don't miss this experience. They buy and sell antique dolls and toys here, but what makes it so much fun is the collection o spare parts. ♦ M-Sa. 787 Lexington Ave (between E 61st and E 62nd Sts), Second floor. 838.7527

28 Brio ★★$$ Thanks to its Italian-style home cooking, this attractive, wood-paneled trattori is almost always full. The hearty polenta with porcini or aromatic pesto-laden fusilli are two reasons to return again and again. ♦ Italian ♦ Daily lunch and dinner. Reservations recommended. 786 Lexington Ave (between E 61st and E 62nd Sts). 980.2300

29 Il Valletto ★$$$ If the owner, Nanni, is around when you visit, let him order for you. If not, here are some suggestions: bruschetta, tender baked clams, eggplant *siciliana* (with light ricotta and spinach), and linguine with tender clams in a light white sauce. For dessert, try the baked pear with zabaglione or fresh fruit salad. ♦ Italian ♦ M-F lunch and dinner; Sa dinner. Reservations required; jacket required. 133 E 61st St (between Lexington and Park Aves). 838.3939

30 The Pillowry Owner/designer Marjorie Lawrence sells kilims and Oriental rugs and makes pillows from antique rugs and textiles collected from all over the world. ♦ M-F. 132 E 61st St (between Lexington and Park Aves), Second floor. 308.1630

31 Le Veau d'Or ★★$$$ Longtime East Siders still flock to this great old bistro for such well-prepared, basic French fare as steak au poivre, baby chicken with tarragon, and chocolate mousse. The service is unpretentious and efficient. ♦ French ♦ M-Sa lunch and dinner. Reservations recommended. 129 E 60th St (between Lexington and Park Aves). 838.8133

32 The Lighthouse This is the headquarters of the New York Association for the Blind. The on-site gift shop, staffed by volunteers, sells items made by blind persons, and all proceeds benefit the blind. ♦ Hours vary; call ahead. 111 E 59th (between Lexington and Park Aves). 821.9200 ♿

33 The Original Levi's Store An icon in the annals of American fashion, the Levi's jean is here in every model, size, color, and interpretation imaginable. This spacious store is always filled with foreign shoppers having a field day. ♦ Daily. 750 Lexington Ave (between E 59th and E 60th Sts). 826.5957 ♿ Also at: 1492 Third Ave (at E 84th St). 249.5045 ♿ 3 E 57th St (between Madison and Fifth Aves). 838.2188

34 Bloomingdale's This store is show business. It caters to those who like to buy their clothes, food, and sofas in an atmosphere that is a cross between a designer showcase and a Middle Eastern *souk*. Once you get beyond the smiling and sometimes overzealous salespersons who threaten to squirt perfume at you, and TV screens showing endless tapes of designer fashion shows, you'll find the children's department, with layettes, strollers, Oshkosh overalls, and hand-knit sweaters. For women, there is slinky knitwear by Missoni, seductive knits by Sonia Rykiel, the American chic of Ralph

Lauren, and the luxe of Yves Saint Laurent and Chanel. For men, there are clothes by Donna Karan, Calvin Klein, and Armani. The sixth-floor **Main Course** is a cornucopia of kitchenware and gadgets. If it's all too much for you, special shopping services are extensive. ♦ Daily. 1000 Third Ave (between E 59th and E 60th Sts). 705.2000

Within Bloomingdale's:

Le Train Bleu ★$$ A re-creation of the dining car on the long defunct **Calais-Méditerranée Express (Le Train Bleu),** this welcome resting ground for worn-out shoppers has a spectacular view of the Queensboro Bridge and the **Roosevelt Island Tramway.** Not surprisingly, the food—such as steak au poivre, gemelli pasta with julienned fresh vegetables, and grilled chicken over Caesar salad—is simple and simply overpriced. ♦ Continental ♦ M-F lunch and afternoon tea; Sa lunch; Su brunch. Reservations recommended. Sixth floor. 705.2100

35 New York Women's Exchange Established in 1878 to help women support themselves without sacrificing their pride, this is an excellent source of handmade children's articles, lingerie, and gifts. ♦ M-Sa. 149 E 60th St (between Third and Lexington Aves). 753.2330 ♿

36 Trump Plaza You can easily pass this 1987 building by **Philip Birnbaum & Associates.** It is another attempt to immortalize the name of developer Donald Trump. The building is not open to the public, but don't pass up the waterfall or the open space to the left of the entrance that make it so pleasant. ♦ 167 E 61st St (at Third Ave)

36 Matthew's ★★★$$$ Talented young chef Matthew Kenney pushes the limits of American cuisine here. The changing seasonal menu may include such standout dishes as ahi (Hawaiian tuna) *tartare* with green-olive *tapenade* (a thick paste made from capers, anchovies, olives, olive oil, and lemon juice); marinated shrimp and yam salad with avocado, lime, and sweet onion; or lemon-glazed lobster with white corn, chanterelles, and asparagus. Rustic yet elegant—with white linen, rattan chairs, and ceiling fans—the setting is perfect for the beautiful people who flock here. ♦ American ♦ M-F lunch and dinner; Sa-Su brunch and dinner. 1030 Third Ave (at E 61st St). 838.4343 ♿

37 Contrapunto ★★$$$ This modern, recently renovated glassed-in room is great for watching the scene along Third Avenue. It's also a dependable spot for good pasta, including fresh squares filled with lobster, scallops, fresh fennel, and leeks in a lemon-cream sauce; and delicate angel-hair pasta with littleneck clams. There are also decent desserts, such as a rich chocolate torte, and a good, balanced wine list. ◆ American/Italian ◆ M-Sa lunch and dinner; Su dinner. 200 E. 60th St (at Third Ave). 751.8615

38 Bolivar ★★★$$$ The team behind the formerly fabulous, now closed **Arizona 206** is riding the crest of the latest culinary wave to hit Manhattan: Pan-Latin. If you're thinking twice-fried plantains, Cuban sandwiches, and lard-laden burritos, think Peruvian seviches and Argentine grills instead. Former **Sign of the Dove** chef Larry Kolar is determined to show off a Latin cuisine most of us didn't even know existed. ◆ New Latin ◆ Daily lunch and dinner. Reservations recommended. 206 East 60th St (between Second and Third Aves). 838.0440

39 Galleria Hugo Owner Hugo Ramirez is a master of restoration of 19th-century antique lighting. His work (which is all done by hand) can be found in **Gracie Mansion,** city museums, and historic homes around the country. ◆ By appointment only. Call for schedule. 233 E 59th St (between Second and Third Aves). 750.6877. Also at: 304 E 76th St (between First and Second Aves). 288.8444

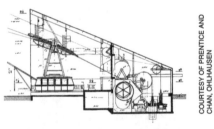

COURTESY OF PRENTICE AND CHAN, OHLHAUSEN

40 Roosevelt Island Tramway Station The Swiss-made tram (see diagram above), designed in 1976 by **Prentice and Chan, Ohlhausen,** would be more at home on a snow-covered mountain. It takes you across the East River's West Channel at 16mph and provides wonderful views of the East Side and the Queensboro Bridge. ◆ Nominal charge. M-Th, Su 6AM-2AM; F-Sa 6AM-3:30AM. Second Ave and E 60th St. 832.4543 ♿

41 Queensboro Bridge Designed by engineer Gustav Lindenthal and built in 1909 by **Palmer & Hornbostel,** the distinctive triple span of this bridge is the image of a machine, an intricate web of steel that speaks of power, if not finesse. Referred to by most locals, including Simon and Garfunkel, as the "59th Street Bridge." ◆ Between Queens Plaza, Queens and Second Ave

42 Roosevelt Island This island is separated from Manhattan by 300 yards and more than a few decibels, but politically it is very much a part of it. The community, built in the 1970s, is accessible from Manhattan by tramway and subway, and from Queens by a small bridge at 36th Avenue, Queens Plaza. The master plan for a series of U-shaped housing projects facing the river was designed by **Philip Johnson** and **John Burgee.** Only the southern section was built, and it's taller and denser than they recommended. Until the 1970s, when rental agents needed a name change, it was known as **Welfare Island** because of its many hospitals and sanitariums. Before 1921 it was **Blackwell's Island,** named for the family that farmed it for two centuries. A prison was built in 1828, and over the next several years, a workhouse, an almshouse, and an insane asylum were added. A century later those institutions were swept away and hospitals were substituted. The present city has reminders of each of the island's former lives. The ruin at the southern end was the **Smallpox Hospital,** designed in 1856 by **James Renwick Jr.** Just above it are the remains of the 1859 **City Hospital,** and under the Queensboro Bridge is **Goldwater Memorial Hospital.** Not far from the tramway station is the **Blackwell Farmhouse** (1796-1804). Nearby are the **Eastwood Apartments,** built for low- and middle-income tenants in 1976 by **Sert, Jackson & Associates.** On the Manhattan side are **Rivercross Apartments,** built in 1975 by **Johansen & Bhavnani,** for people who can afford to pay more. There are two more luxury complexes: **Westview,** built in 1976 by **Sert, Jackson & Associates,** and **Island House,** built in 1975 by **Johansen & Bhavnani,** which has a glassed-in swimming pool overlooking Manhattan.

Cars are not allowed on the island except in the garage complex known as **Motorgate.** Garbage is removed through vacuum tubes to the **AVAC (Automated Vacuum Collection) Building**—where it is sorted, sanitized, and packed for removal. Near this monument to a "Brave New World" is the **Chapel of the Good Shepherd,** originally built in 1889 by **Frederick Clarke Withers** and restored by **Giorgio Cavaglieri** in 1976, now used as a recreation center. Landmarks at the northern end include the **Octagon Tower,** an 1839 building by **Alexander Jackson Davis,** all that's left of the **New York City Lunatic Asylum,** and a 50-foot stone lighthouse designed in 1872 by **James Renwick Jr.** (According to an inscription on the lighthouse, it was constructed by John McCarthy, an asylum inmate who busied himself by building a fort to defend himself against the British but was persuaded to replace it with a more attractive lighthouse instead.) The hospital at the uptown end of the island is the 1952 **Bird S. Coler Hospital for** the **Chronically Ill.** A complex of 1,104 apartments, **Northtown II** was completed by Starrett Housing in 1989. Development continues on 15-acre **Octagon Park,** a multi-use park with sports facilities just south of the **Coler Hospital,** and **Southtown,** a complex that should eventually contain 2,000 mixed-income apartments. Transportation on the island is provided by bus, but probably the best way to enjoy it is by walking on its riverside promenades. ◆ East River

43 Darrow's Fun Antiques This is a place for grownups to become children: toy soldiers; cigar store Indians; antique windup monkeys, dogs, and bears; movie star memorabilia; and even the occasional funhouse mirror. ◆ M-Sa. 1101 First Ave (between E 60th and E 61st Sts). 838.0730

43 Chicago City Limits Established in New York in 1980, this is one of the oldest, and probably the only self-sustaining, comedy improvisation groups in the city. It was formed in Chicago in 1977 by George Todisco and actors participating in workshops at that city's renowned **Second City.** It then moved to Manhattan's Theater Row, then the **Jan Hus Church,** before moving here. ◆ Shows: W-Th 8:30PM; F-Sa 8PM, 10:30PM. 1105 First Ave (at E 61st St). 888.LAFF

44 Abigail Adams Smith Museum The daughter of John Adams, for whom this 1799 house-museum is named, never even slept here. But she and her husband, Colonel William Smith, did own the land it was built on. They bought 23 choice acres on the bank of the East River in 1796 with the idea of building a country estate called "Mt. Vernon" (Colonel Smith served under George Washington). Because of financial reverses, they sold the estate in 1796. The stone stable that is now the museum was remodeled as a country day hotel in the 1820s, then used as a private dwelling until the neighborhood fell on hard times. The Colonial Dames of America rescued it in 1924, furnished it in the style of the Federal period, planted an 18th-century garden, and opened the house as a museum. It has since then been refurbished to reflect the style of a 19th-century hotel. Colonial Dames members, well versed in the contents of the house (but not necessarily about antiques or the history of the period), show visitors the nine rooms. ◆ Admission. Tu-Su. 421 E 61st St (between York and First Aves). 838.6878

45 Dangerfield's This club, which showcases new and established comic talent, is owned

and operated by well-known comedian Rodney Dangerfield. It has a typical Las Vegas/Atlantic City atmosphere and caters to out-of-town convention goers and suburbanites. ◆ Cover. Shows: M-Th, Su 9PM, 12:30AM; F 9PM, 11:15PM; Sa 8PM, 10:30PM, 12:30AM. 1118 First Ave (between E 61st and E 62nd Sts). 593.1650

46 Bentley Hotel $$$ Impossible though it may be to truly escape Manhattan's madding crowds, you do come pretty close at this office tower-turned-hotel on island's edge. The 197 guest rooms in this 21-story tower overlooking the East River are sleek and surprisingly spacious. There's an expansive glass-enclosed rooftop restaurant where complimentary continental breakfast is served. Request a room ending in "04" and you'll be treated to nighttime views of the Triboro Bridge that make your knees wobble. ◆ 500 E 62nd St (at York Ave). 644.6000; fax 207.4800; www.nycityhotels.net

47 Il Vagabondo ★★$$ Robust Italian cooking, mostly Southern style, is one of the draws at this noisy, good-humored neighborhood trattoria. But the main reason to come here is to watch people play bocce at the city's only indoor court (ask for a courtside table). Specialties include homemade gnocchi, tuna steak, a fragrant veal stew, and fillet of sole. ◆ Italian ◆ M-F lunch and dinner; Sa-Su dinner. 351 E 62nd St (between First and Second Aves). 832.9221

48 Maya ★★★$$ Never mind the name—here is a Mexican restaurant unlike any other. Soft rosy walls, inlaid wood floors, and colorful glassware add a touch of elegance to this newly opened room. But that's just the beginning: Chef Richard Sandoval's native dishes are outstanding. Some of the best include *mole poblano* (grilled chicken breast with cilantro rice and mole sauce) and *chilaquiles* (sun-dried tomato tortillas served with grilled chicken, black bean puree, and tomatillo salsa). The sliced flambéed bananas with tequila and caramel sauce are the perfect ending to a satisfying meal. ◆ Mexican ◆ M-Sa dinner. 1191 First Ave (between E 64th and E 65th Sts). 585.1818

Rockefeller University, on York Avenue in the east sixties, has the lowest teacher-pupil ratio of any university in the United States.

One of the more colorful inmates at Roosevelt Island's New York City Lunatic Asylum was Mae West, who was locked up there for 10 days in 1926 and fined $500. She had been appearing locally in a lewd play called *Sex* that raised one too many eyebrows. Upon her request, she was permitted to wear her silk undergarments beneath her prison uniform.

On a Clear Day You Can See. . .

Everything looks better from a distance—and New York City's no exception. Unlike the aging actress whose left profile is better than her right, the Big Apple shines every which way, especially from the following vantage points:

Circle Line Cruises
Pier 83, 12th Ave and W 42nd St. 563.3200

Columbia Heights
Between Clark and Cranberry Sts, Brooklyn Heights

Empire State Observatory
Fifth Ave and W 34th St. 736.3100

Fort Tryon Park and The Cloisters
Washington Heights

Liberty State Park
Johnston Ave (east of Grand St), Jersey City, New Jersey

Promenade
Atop the Brooklyn-Queens Expressway, Brooklyn Heights

The Rainbow Room Restaurant and Bar
30 Rockefeller Plaza (between W 49th and W 50th Sts). 632.5000

River Café
1 Water St (at Old Fulton St, under the Brooklyn Bridge), Brooklyn. 718/522.5200

Riverside Church
490 Riverside Dr (at W 122nd St). 870.6700

Roosevelt Island Tramway Station
Second Ave and E 60th St. 832.4543

Spirit Cruises
Chelsea Piers, Pier 62, 11th Ave (between W 14th and W 23rd Sts). 727.2789

Staten Island Ferry
Battery Park, South St and Peter Minuit Plaza. 806.6940

Statue of Liberty
Liberty Island. 363.3200

The Terrace
400 W 119th St (at Morningside Dr). 666.9490

Triborough Bridge
Entrance at E 125th St and Second Ave

The View Restaurant
1535 Broadway (at W 45th St). 704.8900

Windows on the World Restaurant
1 World Trade Center, Church St (between Liberty and Vesey Sts), 107th floor. 524.7011

World Trade Center Observation Deck
2 World Trade Center, Church St (between Liberty and Vesey Sts), 107th floor. 323.2340

49 Jackson Hole ★$$ Delicious, juicy hamburgers approaching the size of Wyoming are the specialty of this restaurant. Any (or several) of 12 toppings can be requested to adorn the seven-ounce burgers; a side order of onion rings or french fries is an integral part of the experience. There's also a large selection of good omelettes. This place is a favorite with kids on weekends, and, as could be expected, the noise level increases dramatically. ♦ American ♦ Daily lunch, dinner, and late-night meals. 232 E 64th St (between Second and Third Aves). 371.7187. Also at: Numerous locations throughout the city

50 Solow Houses Developer Sheldon Solow, who built the innovative office building at 9 West 57th Street in 1983, created these 11 houses (designed by **Attia & Perkins**), the first new town house row in the city since the end of the 19th century. The granite facade, which binds them together between flat and slightly bowed fronts, barely articulates each individual house. The front is fortresslike, hiding luxurious interiors. ♦ 222-242 E 67th St (between Second and Third Aves)

51 Soleil ★★$$ The setting is bright and yellow; the fare, sunny Italian. Start with grilled portobello mushrooms served with arugula and tomato and move on to any of the pasta dishes, including rigatoni with tomatoes, prosciutto, and basil, or the vegetable lasagna. Delicious sandwiches (brie and arugula on Tuscan bread with pesto is a winner) come with salad and tasty french fries. ♦ Italian ♦ M-F lunch and dinner; Sa-Su brunch and dinner. Reservations required. 1160 Third Ave (between E 67th and E 68th Sts). 717.1177 &

52 Park East Synagogue Designed in 1890 by **Schneider & Herter,** this Moorish extravaganza has a more sedate Victorian interior. ♦ 163 E 67th St (between Third and Lexington Aves). 737.6900

53 131-135 East 66th Street The two apartment blocks, designed in 1905 by **Charles A. Platt,** are most noted for dignified

---

Restaurants/Clubs: Red   **Hotels:** Blue
Shops/ ♥ Outdoors: Green   **Sights/Culture:** Black

grandeur and Mannerist porticoes. ♦ Between Third and Lexington Aves

54 Cosmopolitan Club Cast-iron balconies give a New Orleans flavor to this 1932 Greek Revival building, designed by **Thomas Harlan Ellett**. It is the headquarters of a prestigious women's club for those interested in the arts and sciences. ♦ 122 E 66th St (between Lexington and Park Aves). 734.5950

55 The Forgotten Woman This unfortunately named store offers handsome designer clothing for the larger woman (sizes 14 to 24). There are tailored suits, pure cashmere sweaters, cocktail dresses, and leather skirts. The service is exceptionally good. ♦ Daily. 888 Lexington Ave (at E 66th St). 535.8848. Also at: 60 W 49th St (between Rockefeller Plaza and Sixth Ave). 247.8888 ♿

56 Church of St. Vincent Ferrer When New York's Roman Catholic elite make wedding plans, **St. Patrick's Cathedral** is their first choice. If the cathedral is booked, this is where they turn. It was designed by **Bertram G. Goodhue** in 1923. ♦ Lexington Ave and E 66th St. 744.2080

57 China House Gallery/China Institute in America This gift of publisher Henry R. Luce, the son of missionaries to China, reflects his lifelong interest in Sino-American cultural and political exchange. Along with changing exhibitions on Chinese fine arts and folk traditions, the institute, housed in a 1905 building by **Charles A. Platt**, conducts educational programs. ♦ Donation suggested. Daily. 125 E 65th St (between Lexington and Park Aves). 744.8181

58 Ségires à Solanée Classic Provençal designs—hand-painted wood furniture, iron furniture, faience from Moustiers-Sainte-Marie, and linen placemats and napkins abound in this sunny shop. ♦ M-Sa. 866 Lexington Ave (at E 65th St). 439.6109 ♿

59 JoJo ★★★$$$ Hailed as a creative genius, chef-owner Jean-Georges Vongerichten was a forerunner in the movement to replace cream- and butter-based sauces with more healthful infused oils and vegetable juices. His casual spot, simply decorated with ocher walls, plain wooden tables and chairs, and a few vivid oil paintings, has been a hit since the day the sign went up. The limited menu offers Vongerichten's interpretations of bistro fare, including shrimp in carrot juice with Thai lime leaves; chicken roasted with ginger, green olives, and coriander juice; foie gras with quince puree; and for dessert, a spectacular chocolate cake. The wine list spotlights good

French wines, some at affordable prices. ♦ French ♦ M-F lunch and dinner; Sa dinner. Reservations recommended. 160 E 64th St (between Third and Lexington Aves). 223.5656

60 Edward Durell Stone House Designed by **Edward Durell Stone** in 1956, the concrete grillwork covering the facade of the late architect's home is similar to the screen he used in his design for the American Embassy in New Delhi two years earlier. ♦ 130 E 64th St (between Lexington and Park Aves)

61 Central Presbyterian Church To build this former Baptist church, which was designed by **Henry C. Pelton** and **Allen & Collens** in 1922, John D. Rockefeller Jr. matched every contribution, dollar for dollar; he also taught Bible classes here. In 1930, the congregation moved to **Riverside Church**, also largely funded by Rockefeller. ♦ 593 Park Ave (at E 64th St). 838.0808

62 Hotel Plaza Athénée $$$$ Formerly the **Alrae Apartments**, designed by **George F. Pelham** in 1927, this intimate, ultraclassy hotel is modeled after the famous Paris original. Its moderate size (153 spacious rooms and 36 suites) and residential location attract guests in search of serenity rather than the hustle of Midtown. The lobby is a combination of French period furnishings, Italian marble floors, and hand-painted mural tapestry walls. Amenities include 24-hour concierge and room service, kitchenettes, in-room safes (the hotel itself is extremely secure, with only one entrance), and fax machines available upon request. Each of the four duplex penthouse suites includes a terrace and solarium. ♦ 37 E 64th St (between Park and Madison Aves). 734.9100, 800/447.8800; fax 772.0958 ♿

Within the Hotel Plaza Athénée:

Le Regence ★★★★$$$$ This glittery Louis XIV–style restaurant in a color scheme of aquamarine and shell is bedecked with mirrors, chandeliers, and a ceiling mural of a cloudy sky. Not surprisingly, this place excels in all categories: The service is impeccable, and chef Marcel Agnez's food is outstanding. At lunch, choose from an extensive à la carte menu that features lamb chops, veal, and various fruits of the sea. For dinner, consult the à la carte menu or choose between two elaborate prix-fixe meals. Duck-liver salad, Mediterranean seafood soup, and Dover sole are frequently offered. Come on Sundays for a sensational brunch. ♦ French ♦ M-Sa breakfast, lunch, and dinner; Su brunch and dinner. Reservations required; jacket and tie required. 606.4647

63 Walter Steiger This women's shoe salon features the newest silhouettes from Europe by one of the leading designers. ♦ M-Sa. 739 Madison Ave (between E 64th and E 65th Sts). 570.1212 ♿ Also at: 417 Park Ave (at E 55th St). 826.7171

63 Valentino In this hushed and lavish setting, you can see the designer's ready-to-wear collection, including classic pants, beautifully shaped jackets, and luxurious dresses for day and night. ♦ M-Sa. 747 Madison Ave (between E 64th and E 65th Sts). 772.6969

64 Chase Manhattan Bank A brick wall to the left of this Georgian bank, designed by **Morrel Smith** in 1932, conceals a colonial garden—a rarity on this busy street. ♦ 726 Madison Ave (at E 64th St)

64 Emilio Pucci This boutique for the Italian designer is in a house that was once owned by Consuela Vanderbilt Smith, daughter of William K. Vanderbilt. It was built in 1882 by **Theodore Weston**, with a 1920 facade by **Mott B. Schmidt.** Pucci, whose designs became popular in the 1950s, passed away in 1992. ♦ M-Sa. 24 E 64th St (between Madison and Fifth Aves). 752.4777

64 Biologique Recherche This luxurious but low-key full-service day spa, tucked away on the fourth floor of an elegant renovated brownstone, enjoys a solid reputation for the know-how of its polite staff and signature facial treatments, which include the Manual Face Lift and Remodeling Face, among others. The meticulous approach to skincare found here stems from French founder Yvan Allouche's work as a biologist, and is reflected in the pure bio-vegetal ingredients of the company's extensive (and expensive) corresponding range of products. Whether you choose to indulge in a high-powered facial, reflexology massage, or both, you're sure to emerge from this chic but sedate spot revitalized and renewed. ♦ M-Sa. 26 E 64th St (between Madison and Fifth Aves). 755.5270

65 Wildenstein & Co. In 1932, **Horace Trumbauer** designed the building housing this gallery, which is known for the depth of its collections of old and contemporary paintings and objets d'art. Exhibitions often rival museum shows. ♦ M-F. 19 E 64th St (between Madison and Fifth Aves). 879.0500 ♿

66 India House This unusually wide (65 feet) mansion, designed by **Warren & Wetmore** in 1903, would be right at home on the streets of Paris. It was built for banker Marshall Orme Wilson, whose wife was Carrie Astor, daughter of the Mrs. Astor who lived around the corner. It is now owned by the government of India. ♦ 3 E 64th St (between Madison and Fifth Aves)

67 Berwind Mansion This Venetian Renaissance mansion was the home of coal magnate Edwin J. Berwind, who was the sole supplier of coal for America's warships. Today, the building, which was designed in 1896 by **N.C. Melton,** contains cooperative apartments. ♦ 2 E 64th St (at Fifth Ave)

68 820 Fifth Avenue Designed in 1916 by **Starrett & Van Vleck,** this is one of the earliest luxury apartment buildings on Fifth Avenue. Among its first tenants was New York's governor Al Smith. ♦ At E 63rd St

69 Temple Emanu-El Designed by **Robert D. Kohn, Charles Butler,** and **Clarence Stein** in 1929, this impressive gray limestone edifice on the site of a mansion belonging to Caroline Schermerhorn Astor is the temple of the oldest Reform congregation in New York. Resembling only the nave of a cathedral, the structure has masonry-bearing walls. In style, it is Romanesque with Eastern influences; these are repeated on the interior with Byzantine ornaments. The hall is 77 feet wide, 150 feet long, and 403 feet high; it seats 2,500—more than **St. Patrick's Cathedral.** ♦ 1 E 65th St (at Fifth Ave). 744.1400 ♿

70 Cambridge Chemists Any top-of-the-line European product can be found here, including Cyclax of London, Innoxa, Roc, and Vichy. ♦ M-Sa. 21 E 65th St (between Madison and Fifth Aves). 734.5678 ♿

71 Ferrier ★$$ If you want to have dinner in relative peace at this dining spot, go early; otherwise it may be difficult to squeeze past the bar, so dense does the scene become here. Good bistro cooking is offered in the beige back room: Try the coq au vin, roasted salmon in a fennel-and-Champagne sauce, confit of duck marinated and cooked in red-wine sauce, or roasted monkfish with sautéed spinach. ♦ French ♦ M-F lunch and dinner; Sa-Su brunch and dinner. Reservations recommended. 29 E 65th St (between Park and Madison Aves). 772.9000

72 Sarah Delano Roosevelt Memorial House In 1908, when her son, Franklin, was married, Sarah Delano Roosevelt commissioned **Charles A. Platt** to design this pair of houses; one was for herself, the other for the newlyweds. The houses are identical, with a common entrance. Several of their rooms were connected by folding doors to make them larger when necessary, as well as to give interior access between the two houses. It was in the fourth-floor front bedroom of the house on the right that Roosevelt went through his long recovery from polio in 1921-22. The future president's mother wanted him to go to their estate in Hyde Park, New York, but his wife, Eleanor, persuaded him to stay in the city. She felt he had a future in politics and needed to be closer to the centers of power, even though he was bedridden. Her decision doomed her to live under the thumb of her mother-in-law, no one of her favorite people. The buildings are now a community center for **Hunter College** students. ♦ 45-47 E 65th St (between Park and Madison Aves)

72 American Federation of the Arts (AFA) Located in a 1910 building that was designed by **Trowbridge & Livingston,** this organization provides traveling exhibitions for small museums around the country. The interior of the building, designed by **Edward Durell Stone** in 1960 and now devoted to office space, is richly detailed. ♦ 41 E 65th St (between Park and Madison Aves). 988.7700

73 Daniel ★★★★$$$$ Believe the hype: New York's most talked-about four-star restaurant, the creation of power chef Daniel Boulud, offers one of the finest dining experiences to be had anywhere. Interior designer Patrick Naggar transformed the former ground floor of the **Mayfair Hotel** (onetime home to **Le Cirque**) into a rarefied and resplendent domain that unites Venetian, ancient Greek and Roman, and Art Deco elements. Boulud recognizes that good service is as essential an ingredient to an enjoyable evening as maximum flavor, and here it is as stellar as the food. For appetizers, try the Peekytoe crab salad in a green-apple gelée with celery-root remoulade or the risotto of wild trumpets and sweetbreads with scallions and *jus persillade.* Boulud's signature dish, black sea bass in a crisp potato shell with tender leeks and a Barolo wine sauce, is as divine as ever. Other star entrées include spiced sea scallops à la Plancha with creamy rosemary polenta, caramelized endive and a blood-orange glaze, and squab à la broche with Brussels sprouts, fricassee of wild mushrooms, and salsify with sweet garlic. If the Idaho potato baked in sea salt, crushed and covered with fresh white truffle, is on the menu, get it. Desserts come in both seasonal fruit and chocolate varieties. With flavors like raspberry-hibiscus and green apple, the sorbets are hard to resist. You could try to top the caramel-chocolate bombe with passion fruit crème brûlée and sweet mango chutney, but oh, an easy task it's not. **Daniel**'s wine list is, not surprisingly, superlative.♦ French ♦ M-Sa lunch and dinner. Reservations are strongly advised and are taken up to one month in advance. Jacket and tie required for men. 60 E 65 St (at Park Ave). 288.0033

GIORGIO ARMANI

74 Giorgio Armani Here's the top of the line for discerning shoppers with big dollars. The four-story white cube makes the nearby **Calvin Klein** store seem cozy by comparison. What you'll find within these spartan surroundings are stunning (read: expensive) clothes and accessories for men and women.

The staff is friendly and helpful. ♦ M-Sa. 760 Madison Ave (between E 65th and E 66th Sts). 988.9191

74 Julie: Artisans' Gallery Clothes conceived as art to wear: Julia Hill's jackets of hand-painted silk, Linda Mendelson's scarves and coats loom-knitted in geometrical patterns, and many other flights of fancy. ♦ M-Sa. 762 Madison Ave (between E 65th and E 66th Sts). 717.5959 ♿

75 45 East 66th Street Designed in 1900 by **Harde & Short,** this building displays a lacy pastry exuberance at an even higher level than the **Alwyn Court Apartments** (W 58th St and Seventh Ave) designed by the same firm. Note the Elizabethan and Flemish Gothic detailing and the sensuous ease of the round tower on the corner. ♦ At Madison Ave

76 The Lotos Club Designed by **Richard Howland Hunt** in 1900, this was once the home of William J. Schieffelin, head of a wholesale drug firm and a crusader for civil rights at the end of the 19th century. The rusticated limestone base supports a redbrick midsection and a double-story mansard roof. A vigorous Second Empire composite on the verge of being excessive, it is now headquarters to **The Lotos Club,** an organization of artists, musicians, actors, and journalists. ♦ 5 E 66th St (between Madison and Fifth Aves). 737.7100

77 Emanuel Ungaro Here is the new location for this designer's collection for women, including his opulently printed, jewel-toned fabrics—paisleys, stripes, florals, and checks. The shop also sells such accessories as boots, shoes, belts, and shawls. ♦ M-Sa. 792 Madison Ave (between E 66th and E 67th Sts). 249.4090 ♿

78 4 East 67th Street This is an ornate Beaux Arts mansion, built for banker Henri P. Wertheim in 1902 and designed by **John H. Duncan.** It is now the residence of the Consul General of Japan. ♦ Between Madison and Fifth Aves

79 13 and 15 East 67th Street This is a curious pair, particularly in contrast to the Modernist red-granite face at **No. 17. No. 13,** designed in 1921 by **Harry Allan Jacobs,** is an Italian Renaissance concoction that was built for theatrical producer Martin Beck. **No. 15,** a 1904 building by **Ernest Flagg,** now the **Regency Whist Club,** was the **Cortland Field Bishop House.** Concocted of stone and restrained ironwork, this rather Parisian house was designed by the man who did the marvelous **Scribner's Bookstore,** now a **Benneton** shop, at **597 Fifth Avenue.** ♦ Between Madison and Fifth Aves

80 Gallery of Wearable Art Everything here makes a statement. Whether it is a statement you'd care to make is something you'll have to decide. In addition to daily—though hardly quotidian—clothes, there's a unique collection of wedding gowns and bridal accessories. ♦ Tu-Sa. 34 E 67th St (between Park and Madison Aves). 425.5379 &

81 Seventh Regiment Armory Designed by **Charles W. Clinton** in 1880, this is a crenellated, almost cartoonish fort in an otherwise very proper neighborhood. The interiors were furnished and detailed by Louis Comfort Tiffany. The hall is immense: 187 feet by 290 feet. It is the site of the annual **Winter Antiques Fair** and other huge events. ♦ Park Ave (between E 66th and E 67th Sts). 744.4107 &

82 115 East 67th Street Designed in 1932 by **Andrew J. Thomas,** this building is a happy place with owls, squirrels, and other animals in the decorative panels and huge arched entry. ♦ Between Lexington and Park Aves

83 660 Park Avenue Architect **Philip Sawyer,** of **York & Sawyer,** carved a reputation for himself as a designer of banks, but his work on the rustication of this handsome 1927 apartment building is worthy of any of them. ♦ At E 67th St

84 Frette This sleek Italian shop features extravagant linens for bed and table, including piqué bedspreads, linen sheets, and damask tablecloths. ♦ M-Sa. 799 Madison Ave (between E 67th and 68th Sts). 988.5221 &

84 Les Copains Though not as well known as other labels on the avenue, this newcomer is already popular with professional women who prefer the tailored French look with a feminine slant. Prices are quite reasonable for top-quality dresses and suits. ♦ M-Sa. 807 Madison Ave (between E 67th and E 68th Sts). 372.3014

85 Joseph The latest knits from London are here—some simple, some romantic, all representing the world of street chic. Also for sale are hats and leather bags. ♦ M-Sa. 804 Madison Ave (between E 67th and E 68th Sts). 570.0077 &

85 Billy Martin's Western Wear Yes, it's the late Billy Martin who used to pace the dugout at **Yankee Stadium.** This one-stop source of cowboy boots, fancy belts, and other expensive duds will make you look at home on the range. ♦ Daily. 812 Madison Ave (at E 68th St). 861.3100 &

86 6, 8, and 10 East 68th Street These three houses, designed by **John H. Duncan** in 1900 were bought by financier Otto Kuhn, of Kuhn Loeb & Co., in 1916, and altered in 1919 with a French Renaissance limestone facade designed by **Harry Allan Jacobs.** ♦ Between Madison and Fifth Aves

87 9 East 68th Street Designed in 1906 by **Heins & LaFarge,** this was formerly the **George T. Bliss House.** Four giant columns hold up nothing but that little balcony and a brave front to the world. Remarkably out of scale, the house is noteworthy because it is engaging and not overly pretentious. ♦ Between Madison and Fifth Aves

88 Joan & David This is one of two Manhattan boutiques for the exclusive lines of shoes, clothing, and accessories by wife-and-husband team Joan and David Helpern. ♦ Daily. 816 Madison Ave (between E 68th and E 69th Sts) 772.3970. Also at: 104 Fifth Ave (between W 15th and W 16th Sts). 627.1780

malo

88 Malo If you have to ask how much these sumptuous cashmere items for men and women cost, you'd best not enter. This is the company's first American boutique, featuring their remarkably lightweight—if heavy-priced—items of ultimate luxury. ♦ M-Sa. 814 Madison Ave (between E 68th and E 69th Sts) 396.4721 &

MaxMara

89 MaxMara This upscale Italian women's clothing company purchased this six-story building and tastefully restored it to the tune of $1 million. Designed and built in 1882 in the Neo-Greco style with Federal elements, the first two floors provide elegant retail space for the well-known manufacturer's stylish collections. ♦ M-Sa. 813 Madison Ave (at E 68th St). 879.6100

89 Bogner You expect slick, well-made active sportswear from this Austrian manufacturer of ski clothing. The surprise is the line of leisurewear for men and women—jackets, coats, sweaters, pants, skirts, and shoes. ♦ M-Sa. 821 Madison Ave (between E 68th and E 69th Sts). 472.0266

90 Council on Foreign Relations This building, designed in 1920 by **Delano & Aldrich,** was built by **Harold I. Pratt,** son of Charles Pratt, a partner of John D. Rockefeller Jr. and founder of Brooklyn's **Pratt Institute.** The present owner is an organization that promotes interest in foreign relations and publishes the influential magazine *Foreign Affairs.* ♦ 58 E 68th St (at Park Ave). 734.0400

91 Americas Society In the late 1940s and early 1950s, this was the **Soviet Delegation to the United Nations,** which made this corner the scene of almost continuous anti-Communist demonstrations. Before the Russians arrived, it was the home of banker Percy Rivington Pyne. The building, designed in 1909 by **McKim, Mead & White** now houses a gallery specializing in Central, South, and North American art. ♦ Tu-Su noon-6PM. 680 Park Ave (at E 68th St). 249.8950 ♿

92 680-690 Park Avenue A lively but not exceptional collection of brick and limestone Neo-Georgian buildings, this ensemble is special because it is the only full block of town houses surviving on Park Avenue. No. 680: **Americas Society,** formerly the **Soviet Delegation to the UN,** originally the **Percy Pyne House,** was designed in 1909 by **McKim, Mead & White;** No. 684: **Spanish Institute,** the house of Pyne's son-in-law, Oliver D. Filey, was built in Pyne's garden in 1926, by **McKim, Mead & White;** No. 686: **Istituto Italiano di Cultura,** formerly the **William Sloane House,** was designed in 1918 by **Delano & Aldrich;** No. 690: **Italian Consulate,** originally the **Henry P. Davidson House,** was designed in 1917 by **Walker & Gillette.** ♦ Between E 68th and E 69th Sts

93 Hunter College Founded in 1870 as a school for training teachers, this is one of the colleges of the **City University of New York.** Today the school emphasizes such practical disciplines as science, premed and nursing, and education. The **Hunter College Theater** (772.4000), in the main building, is used for lectures, political forums, and music and dance programs. ♦ Bounded by Lexington and Park Aves, and E 68th and E 69th Sts. 772.4000 ♿

94 The Union Club Designed in 1932 by **Delano & Aldrich,** this limestone-and-granite structure is a rather dry palazzo composition (compare with the **University** or **Metropolitan Clubs**) and, no doubt, looks the way you would expect the oldest men's club in New York City to look. The building is not open to the public. ♦ 101 E 69th St (at Park Ave). 734.5400

95 TSE Cashmere This impressive minimalist fashion shop showcases its cashmere collection and also features silk and fine-gauged wool. Spacious and modern, it's the perfect backdrop for the natural and pure hues and lines of the designer collection. ♦ M-Sa. 827 Madison Ave (at E 69th St). 472.7790

96 Pratesi One of the more sybaritic bed-and-bath shops in town, sheets of linen, silk, and Egyptian cotton, as well as comforters filled with goose down or cashmere and covered in silk, are sold here. ♦ M-Sa. 829 Madison Ave (at E 69th St). 288.2315 ♿

96 Madison Avenue Bookshop It looks deceptively small, but the two no-nonsense floors are packed with a wide range of literary criticism, art, current fiction, and cookbooks. It stocks the full line of every major publisher, including a lot of first novels. ♦ M-Sa. 833 Madison Ave (between E 69th and E 70th Sts). 535.6130 ♿

96 Maraolo Italian-made shoes for men, women, and children can be found here at reasonable prices, considering the style, location, and the quality. If you're looking for a bargain, one location serves as an outlet for overstocked items and discontinued styles (131 W 72nd St, between Columbus and Amsterdam Aves, 787.6550). ♦ Daily. 835 Madison Ave (between E 69th and E 70th Sts). 628.5080. Also at: 782 Lexington Ave (between E 60th and E 61st Sts). 832.8182; 1321 Third Ave (between E 75th and E 76th Sts). 535.6225

97 MacKenzie-Childs Madison Avenue's newest purveyor of high-end home accessories is no place for the minimalist-minded. Designed and decorated with objets such as lamps, boxes, and frames that are hand-painted with spots, checks, stripes, and flowers, this charming three-level store is supplied by artisan workshops in upstate New York. Hand-painted dinnerware in myriad designs and mix-and-match possibilities is a particular strength. ♦ M-Sa. 824 Madison Ave (between E 68th and E 69th Sts). 570.6050

97 D. Porthault This shop can weave tablecloths that will go the entire length of a ballroom, sheets to fit the beds of private airplanes, and duvet covers of fine linen. Queen Elizabeth II has slept on **Porthault** sheets. ◆ M-Sa. 18 E 69th St (at Madison Ave). 688.1661

98 The Frick Collection When the old Lenox Library was torn down, Henry Clay Frick, chairman of the Carnegie Steel Corp., bought the site, wanting a place to display his art. He had **Thomas Hastings** design the Beaux Arts house in 1914—one of the last great mansions on Fifth Avenue—with apartments for the family and reception rooms for the art. In his will, Frick decreed that his wife could continue living there until her death, at which time it would be renovated and expanded as a museum (illustrated below). **John Russell Pope,** who later designed the National Gallery in Washington, DC, designed in 1935 what is now the museum. He is responsible for its unique character, especially the glass-covered courtyard, a rewarding retreat from city anxieties if ever there was one. The east wing was added in 1977, designed by **John Barrington Bayley** and **Harry Van Dyke;** the great landscape architect Russell Page designed the garden.

Visiting here is like being asked into the sumptuous private home of a collector who bought only the crème de la crème of the old masters. Treasures here include Rembrandt's *The Polish Rider,* Van Dyck's *Virgin and Child with Saints and Donor,* Bellini's *Saint Francis in the Desert,* Titian's *Man in a Red Cap,* El Greco's *Saint Jerome,* Piero della Francesca's *Saint Simon the Apostle,* and a whole room of Fragonard. There are occasional free lectures and chamber music concerts. (Call or write for ticket information.) Absolutely worth a visit. ◆ Admission. Tu-Su. Children under 10 not admitted. 1 E 70th St (at Fifth Ave). 288.0700 &

99 Lycée Français The French school now occupies two French Renaissance mansions: **No. 7,** designed in 1899 by **Flagg & Chambers,** was the **Oliver Gould**

Jennings House; No. 9, created in 1896 by **Carrère & Hastings,** was the **Henry T. Sloane House.** ◆ 7 and 9 E 72nd St (between Madison and Fifth Aves). 861.9400

100 Polo–Ralph Lauren If you like the Polo look, you'll love the exquisite wonderland Ralph Lauren has created here. Designed in 1898 by **Kimball & Thompson,** the French Renaissance building was commissioned by Gertrude Rhinelander Waldo, a descendant of one of New York's most influential families. She lived here for a few months, but preferred to live across the street with her sister. She offered it to her son, but he preferred to live elsewhere too, and the house stood empty until it was sold in a foreclosure in 1920. Before Lauren moved in it was the **Philips Auction Gallery.** Now it overflows with his designs for outerwear, sportswear, separates, and accessories for men, women, and children and an opulent home design section as well. It's well worth a visit even if you don't buy anything. ◆ M-Sa. 867 Madison Ave (between E 71st and E 72nd Sts). 606.2100 &

101 Polo Sport–Ralph Lauren Ralph Lauren has extended his fashion emporium across the street to this modern 10,000-square-foot activewear shop. There's a boutique featuring Lauren's Double RL division of weathered classics: jeans, motorcycle jackets, flannel shirts, and the like. ◆ M-Sa. 888 Madison Ave (at E 72nd St). 434.8000 &

102 Pierre Deux The French family Demery has spent 300 years creating richly colored paisley and floral fabrics that are quintessentially *Provençal,* and they sell their best designs— the **Souleiado** line—to this shop. ◆ M-Sa. 870 Madison Ave (between E 71st and E 72nd Sts). 570.9343. Also at: 369 Bleecker St (at Charles St). 243.7740

103 St. James Episcopal Church Originally designed in 1884 by **R.H. Robertson,** this church was established on the East Side

The Frick Collection

before the invasion of the millionaires, but its future was secured when families such as the Schermerhorns, the Rhinelanders, and the Astors became members of its vestry. In 1924, the church was rebuilt by **Ralph Adams Cram;** the steeple was added by **Richard Kimball** in 1950. ♦ 865 Madison Ave (at E 71st St). 288.4100

04 Yves Saint Laurent–Rive Gauche Neighboring stores combine to offer the entire Saint Laurent line for men and women. Together, they have the city's largest variety of his collections, including hats, umbrellas, shirts, slacks, dresses, suits, and ball gowns. ♦ M-Sa. 855-859 Madison Ave (between E 70th and E 71st Sts). 517.7400 ♿

05 Hirschl & Adler Top-quality shows of 18th-, 19th-, and 20th-century American and European art appear here. Also featured are American prints and contemporary paintings and sculpture. ♦ Tu-Sa. 21 E 70th St (between Madison and Fifth Aves). 535.8810 ♿

05 Knoedler Contemporary Art The oldest New York–based art gallery, founded in 1846, handles contemporary greats such as Richard Diebenkorn, Nancy Graves, Robert Motherwell, Frank Stella, and Robert Rauschenberg. Located in a 1910 building by **Thornton & Chard,** this gallery is always worth checking out. ♦ Tu-Sa. 19 E 70th St (between Madison and Fifth Aves). 794.0550

06 45 East 70th Street Originally the home of investment banker Arthur S. Lehman, this nondescript town house was designed by **Aymar Embury II** in 1929. His wife was the former Adele Lewisohn, a philanthropist and champion tennis player. It is now the home of Estee Lauder. ♦ Between Park and Madison Aves

07 46 East 70th Street This ornate Neo-Jacobean house, designed in 1912 by **Frederick Sterner,** was built for Stephen C. Clark, whose family owned the Singer Sewing Machine Co. Parts of his extensive art collection are in the **Metropolitan Museum of Art.** Among his many interests was baseball—he founded the Baseball Hall of Fame at Cooperstown, New York. The former residence is now the **Lowell Thomas Building of the Explorers Club.** ♦ Between Park and Madison Aves

ASIA SOCIETY

08 The Asia Society The permanent collection of Asian art assembled by John D. Rockefeller

III between 1951 and 1979 was moved in 1981 to this building designed by **Edward Larrabee Barnes.** It is known for its outstanding Southeast Asian and Indian sculpture, Chinese ceramics and bronzes, and Japanese ceramics and wood sculptures. Other galleries in this serene albeit extravagant building feature changing exhibits ranging from Chinese snuff bottles to Islamic books from the collection of Prince Aga Kahn. The society also sponsors lectures here on Asian arts and adventures, as well as films and performances. A large bookstore is well stocked with books, periodicals, and prints from or about Asia. ♦ Admission; free Thursday after 6PM. Tu-Su. Tours: Tu-Sa 12:30PM; Su 2:30PM. 725 Park Ave (at E 70th St). 288.6400 ♿

108 Visiting Nurse Service of New York This organization is in a Tudor Revival mansion, designed in 1921 by **Walker & Gillette,** that was once home to Thomas W. Lamont, chairman of J.P. Morgan & Co. ♦ 107 E 70th St (between Lexington and Park Aves). 794.9200

109 124 East 70th Street Built for financier Edward A. Norman in 1941 by **William Lescaze,** this International-style house was cited by the **Museum of Modern Art** for its innovative design. ♦ Between Lexington and Park Aves

110 123 East 70th Street Designer **Samuel Trowbridge,** whose works include the **St. Regis Hotel** and other Beaux Arts gems, built this house for himself in 1903. ♦ Between Lexington and Park Aves

110 Paul Mellon House This French Provincial town house, right at home in New York, was built for the industrialist and art collector in 1965 by **H. Page Cross.** ♦ 125 E 70th St (between Lexington and Park Aves)

111 131 East 71st Street America's first interior decorator, Elsie de Wolfe, lived here and used the house as a showcase. The house was built in 1867, but she designed the present facade in 1910 with **Ogden Codman Jr.** ♦ Between Lexington and Park Aves

112 Sette Mezzo ★★$$ Whitewashed walls and sandy polished wood floors and tables set the tone in this coolly understated trattoria. A neighborhood hangout known for its earthy, flavorful pastas: saffron ravioli, orechiette with butter peas and capers, and capellini with grappa-spiked puttanesca sauce. ♦ Italian ♦ Daily lunch and dinner. Reservations recommended. No credit cards accepted. 969 Lexington Ave (between E 70th and E 71st Sts). 472.0400

113 The Lenox School This Tudor house, built in 1907 by **Edward P. Casey** for Stephen H. Brown, governor of the New York Stock Exchange, was considered one of the area's showplaces before it was converted to a school in 1932. ◆ 154 E 70th St (between Third and Lexington Aves)

114 Gracious Home The ultimate neighborhood hardware store: TVs, woks, umbrellas, dishwashers, typewriters, radiator covers, mason jars, and all the expected basics. At the store across the street (No. 1217), you will find a complete bath shop—everything from sinks and faucets to shower curtains and bath mats. ◆ Daily. 1220 Third Ave (between E 70th and E 71st Sts). 517.6300

115 Grace's Marketplace It's no coincidence that this gourmet market resembles **Balducci's;** Grace is the daughter of that downtown institution's founding family. Similarly, this place has glorious produce, cheeses, breads, prepared foods, and cakes of the highest quality. But there's also a salad bar here and spectacular fresh pasta in colors seen only on tropical fish. ◆ Daily. 1237 Third Ave (at E 71st St). 737.0600

116 Evergreen Antiques Scandinavian country furniture and accessories as well as continental and Biedermeier furniture are available here. ◆ M-Sa. 1249 Third Ave (at E 72nd St). 744.5664

117 Cafe Greco ★$$ Lively and flower-filled, this restaurant offers fare inspired by the Mediterranean's various shores; French, Italian, Spanish, and Moroccan dishes all find their way onto a menu that includes grilled octopus and penne with black olives, tomatoes, and capers. ◆ Continental ◆ M-F lunch and dinner; Sa-Su brunch and dinner. 1390 Second Ave (at E 72nd St). 737.4300

118 First Reformed Hungarian Church Hungarian-born architect **Emery Roth** gave us a taste of the old country in 1915 when he designed this ornamented white stucco church topped by an 80-foot, conical-roofed bell tower. ◆ 344 E 69th St (between First and Second Aves). 734.5252

By 1643, 18 languages were spoken in New York City. More than 75 are spoken today.

There are nearly 17,000 restaurants dishing out everything from hamburgers to steak *frites* in the city that never sleeps.

119 Rockefeller University This collection of buildings was originally known as the **Rockefeller Institute for Medical Research.** The lovely site, which was a summer estate of the Schermerhorn family, was acquired in 1901; the first building, **Founder's Hall,** opened in 1903 as a laboratory. Most striking are the gray hemisphere of **Caspary Auditorium,** built in 1957, and the **President House,** built in 1958, both by **Harrison & Abramovitz.** It's worth a visit. Ask the guard for permission to enter, and while you're here stroll toward the river for a look at the gardens. ◆ York Ave (between E 63rd and E 70th Sts). 327.8000

120 New York Hospital/Cornell University Medical College What appears to be a singular, almost solid, well-balanced mass is actually 15 buildings, designed in 1932 by **Coolidge, Shepley, Bullfinch & Abbott.** The strong vertical lines are offset by Gothic arches. ◆ York Ave (between E 63rd and E 71st Sts). 746.5454

SOTHEBY'S

121 Sotheby's The London-based Sotheby's is the largest and oldest fine-arts auctioneer in the world. With its original Madison Avenue headquarters closed, it has relocated here in larger but less personal space, where there is a full round of important sales, exhibitions, and free seminars. Admission to the more important auctions is by ticket only, but all viewings are open to the public. ◆ Open for viewings before scheduled auctions. Call ahead for schedule. 1334 York Ave (at E 72nd St). 606.7000 ♿

122 Woodard and Greenstein American Antiques At the city's premier shop for high quality antique and early 20th-century quilts you'll find sizes ranging from crib to king. Designs include stars, postage stamps, and "drunkard's path." ◆ M-Sa. 506 E 74th St (between FDR Dr and York Ave), Fifth floor. 988.2906

123 Petaluma ★★$$$ This once-trendy cafe still attracts a decent crowd who flock to its bar or dine in the vast, pastel-colored postmodern space. The food includes spaghetti primavera; zesty baby chicken in light mustard sauce; osso buco; and swordfish with tomatoes, capers, and olive Dessert fans shouldn't miss the Belgian chocolate cake. ◆ Italian ◆ Daily lunch and dinner; Sa-Su brunch. Reservations required. 1356 First Ave (at E 73rd St). 772.8800 ♿

124 Jan Hus Church This 1914 Presbyterian church was founded by the Czech community whose presence in the neighborhood led it to be known as Little Bohemia in the 1920s and 1930s. The parsonage is furnished to resemble a Czech peasant's house. ♦ 351 E 74th St (between First and Second Aves). 288.6743

25 AccScentiques by Mahdavi This interior design studio features an extensive range of furniture, window treatments, and custom-decorated pillows, beds, and table dressings. ♦ M-Tu by appointment only; W-Sa; Su noon-5PM. 1418 Second Ave (at E 74th St). 988.3247 ♿

26 Mezzaluna ★$$ This tiny restaurant with a distinct Tuscan flavor is quite popular among East Siders for pizzas baked in a wood-burning oven, as well as carpaccio, salads, and pasta specials. Pumpkin *tortelloni* (large tortellini) are among the favorites. ♦ Italian ♦ Daily lunch, dinner, and late-night meals. 1295 Third Ave (between E 74th and E 75th Sts). 535.9600. Also at: 75 Fifth Ave (between E 15th and E 16th Sts). 633.9933 ♿

27 Lenox Room ★★$$$ Count on innovative New American dishes from the kitchen of this understated but stylish restaurant, where standouts among entrees include blackened mahimahi with basmati rice and coconut-mango sauce and braised lamb shank over gnocchi with a ragout of pine nuts. For dessert, try the caramelized banana parfait with coconut and vanilla sauce or the frozen praline soufflé with bittersweet chocolate sauce. There's an extensive raw bar. ♦ New American ♦ M-F lunch and dinner; Sa-Su brunch and dinner. 1278 Third Ave(between 73rd and 74th Sts). 772.0404

28 Paraclete Theological (mainly Christian) works are this bookstore's specialty. ♦ Tu-Sa. 146 E 74th St (at Lexington Ave). 535.4050 ♿

29 Payard Patisserie & Bistro ★★★$$$ Pastry chef François Payard owns this luxe East Side place with superchef Daniel Boulud—and the victuals on offer come with the attendant intensity of flavor. The bistro menu features updated takes on regional French dishes, but sweet stuff is without question the biggest draw here. Payard oversees the creation of a stunning array of toothsome French cakes, tarts, cookies, croissants and traditional breads made with imported French flour. Nibble on the premises or select an assortment to go. There are hand-made chocolates and macaroons too, available via overnight delivery for all your replenishment needs. ♦ French ♦ Bistro: M-Sa lunch, afternoon tea, and dinner. Pastry shop: M-Sa 7AM-11PM. 1032 Lexington Ave (between 73rd and 74th Sts). 717.5252.

130 Vivolo ★★$ This attractive trattoria features standard, well-prepared dishes that include eggplant rollatini, linguine with clam sauce, grilled panini sandwiches on homemade bread and a host of appetizing salads. For dessert, try the peach or coconut sorbettos. ♦ Italian ♦ M-F lunch and dinner; Sa dinner. Reservations required. 140 E 74th St (between Lexington and Park Aves). 737.3533. Also at: 222 E 58th St (between Second and Third Aves). 308.0112

131 Coco Pazzo ★$$$$ Now at the helm of a restaurant empire, Pino Luongo may have spread himself just a bit too thin. The formerly sublime and richly textured fare at this celebrity magnet is starting to taste, well, canned. A remaining bright note is the warm cinnamon-chocolate pudding with caramel sauce. ♦ Italian ♦ M-Sa lunch and dinner; Su brunch and dinner. Reservations required. 23 E 74th St (at Madison Ave). 794.0205

132 Whitney Museum of American Art Sculptor Gertrude Vanderbilt Whitney founded this museum in 1931 to support young artists and increase awareness of American art. The nucleus of its collection was 600 of the works she owned by Thomas Hart Benton, George Bellows, Maurice Prendergast, Edward Hopper, John Sloan, and other American artists of the era. The present building (shown on page 228), designed by **Marcel Breuer** with **Hamilton Smith** in 1966, is the museum's third home. Like the **Guggenheim,** the structure is more sculpture than building. A dark, rectilinear, Brutalist mass steps out toward the street, almost threatening those who want to enter. Only the drawbridge entrance seems protective. The museum, perched on the corner, is isolated from its surroundings by sidewalls. You can peer down into the sunken sculpture garden and see through to parts of the lobby. But otherwise, the interior's workings are a mystery, guarded by angled trapezoidal windows that refuse to look you in the eye.

A recent $13.5-million expansion added 7,600 square feet of space to the museum. The vast gallery spaces are surprisingly flexible, and can be quite appropriate for a variety of types of art—an important quality for a museum dedicated to temporary exhibitions of contemporary art. The permanent collection, which has been increased to 10,000 pieces through gifts and acquisitions, includes works by Alexander Calder, Louise Nevelson, Georgia O'Keeffe, Robert Rauschenberg, Ad Reinhardt, and Jasper Johns, among others, and a portion of it is always on display. Special exhibitions often concentrate on the output of a single artist. It could be video art of the 1980s Nam June Paik, or Realist of the 1930s Edward Hopper. The museum's regular invitational *Biennial,* which critics often pan, is a mixed bag of what's going on across the country. The museum has an aggressively independent series for American film and video artists and makes adventurous forays into the performing arts. For information on these and gallery lectures, check the information desk. Take a relaxing break in the museum's restaurant, a branch of **Sarabeth's Kitchen,** which features delicious pasta, salads, and sandwiches. The museum operates two branches, including one at Champion International Corp. in Stamford, Connecticut, and one at the **Philip Morris Building** (see page 167). ♦ Admission; free Th 6-8PM. W-Su. Madison Ave and E 75th St. 570.3676 &

133 The Chocolate Soup Charming children's clothes and accessories are crammed into this minuscule store. The most renowned item is the Danish Superbag, an imported schoolbag that's as popular with adults as with children. The best time to go is during the frequent great sales. ♦ M-Sa. 946 Madison Ave (between E 74th and E 75th Sts). 861.2210

134 Harkness House This 1905 building by **Hale & Rogers** was built for Edward S. Harkness,

Whitney Museum of American Art

MICHAEL STORRINGS

son of a Standard Oil Company founder. It is now headquarters of the Commonwealth Fund, a philanthropic foundation. ♦ 1 E 75th St (at Fifth Ave). 535.0400

135 Givenchy For women who want their haute couture brought to their doorsteps, this boutique sends fitters from the House of Givenchy in Paris to New York each spring and fall to measure their local clients. For others, there are blouses, skirts, sweaters, coats, suits, ball gowns, and hats from both ready-to-wear and couture adaptations, which feature the same styles as in the couture collection but in less expensive fabrics. ♦ M-Sa. 954 Madison Ave (at E 75th St). 772.1040

135 Delorenzo Top-drawer furniture of the Art Deco era, sometimes including pieces by such imminent designers as Emile Rouhlmann, Jean Dunand, and Pierre Chareau, is available here. ♦ M-Sa. 958 Madison Ave (between E 75th and E 76th Sts). 249.7575

135 Time Will Tell More than 1,000 antique watches and timepieces by such prestigious manufacturers as Rolex and Tiffany fill this specialty store. Pocket watches from the 1800s join more "modern" pieces from the turn of the century, a variety of Art Deco models, and even some of the early Mickey Mouse numbers. A full repair service is available. ♦ M-Sa. 962 Madison Ave (between E 75th and E 76th Sts). 861.2663 &

136 Minna Rosenblatt An enchanting collection of Tiffany lamps and other glass antiques are offered here. ♦ M-Sa. 961 Madison Ave (between E 75th and E 76th Sts). 288.0250 &

137 The Surrey $$$ This small apartment-hotel, part of the Manhattan East group, has 130 large and tastefully decorated rooms. The room service is from **Cafe Boulud,** favorite spot of the staff of the nearby **Whitney Museum** and other art-world movers and shakers. ♦ 20 E 76th St (between Madison and Fifth Aves). 288.3700, 800/637.8483; fax 628.1549 &

Within The Surrey:

Café Boulud ★★★$$$$ Executive chef Andrew Carmellini takes the helm at Daniel Boulud's casual (that is, no ties required) creation in the smallish space that the more formal **Daniel** (see page 221 for the new location) used to occupy. The food here is as delectable as the sky-high prices would imply, and it's refreshingly unpretentious, too. The menu—including dessert selections—is divided into four categories: Le Voyage, inspired by world cuisines; La Saison, featuring courses in tune with the season; Le Potager, offering vegetarian dishes; and La Tradition, where classic French cuisine shines brightly. Choice selections, respectively, include potato gnocchi with country lentils and black truffle; roasted beef rib with carrots fondant and red-wine shallots; root vegetable cassoulet; and chocolate-cinnamon mousse with a crisp red wine tuile. No matter what you order, make a point of trying one of the signature soups. Whether it's a curried cream of cauliflower and apple soup or chilled tomato soup with a basil guacamole, the combinations of ingredients are sure to be as unlikely as the results are light and delicious. ♦ French ♦ M, Su dinner; Tu-Sa lunch and dinner. Reservations recommended; taken up to one month in advance. 772.2600 ♿

38 William Secord Gallery William Secord, former director of the Dog Museum (now located in St. Louis), operates this gallery devoted to man's best friend. Exhibitions may also include cats and barnyard animals. ♦ M-Sa. 52 E 76th St (between Park and Madison Aves), Third floor. 249.0075

39 Carlyle Hotel $$$$ At 38 stories, this hotel, designed in 1929 by **Bien & Prince,** soars above the East Side. Decorous charm and easy elegance pervade the 180 guest rooms and public premises; it is always at the top of someone's list of best New York City hotels, and is one of the few hotels tolerated by those who are used to the grand European style. For them, the **Tower** apartments seem to fill the bill for short stays or as permanent residences. Pianist Bobby Short has made the **Cafe Carlyle** famous, but his frequent substitutes are popular, too. The more relaxed and less expensive **Bemelmans Bar,** named for illustrator Ludwig Bemelmans, who painted the murals here, features jazz singer/pianist Barbara Carroll. The **Gallery** is recommended for people watching at tea time. The **Carlyle Restaurant** serves an elegant dinner. ♦ 35 E 76th St (at Madison Ave). 744.1600, 800/227.5737; fax 717.4682 ♿

40 The Mark $$$$ This elegant and intimate luxury hotel boasts rooms with original 18th-century Piranesi prints, feather pillows, VCRs, marble bathrooms, terry cloth robes, and heated towel racks. Many of the 180 rooms and suites have their own kitchens. ♦ 25 E 77th St (between Madison and Fifth Aves). 744.4300, 800/843.6275; fax 744.4586 ♿

Within The Mark:

Mark's ★★★$$$$ Here's a versatile hotel restaurant that can hold its own with the East Side's best. Chef David Paulstich brings a deft gourmet hand to a menu that changes according to the season, as does the selection of vintage wines offered by the glass. Dinner entrées might include whole roasted black sea bass wrapped in sage and pancetta; panroasted veal medaillons with fettucine and chanterelles; and Moroccan crusted salmon with quinoa, dried-cherry vinaigrette, and sizzled zucchini. Appetizers are correspondingly excellent, from a playful beet carpaccio to salad of apples, walnuts and warm goat cheese. Desserts are sumptuous: bittersweet chocolate tart with passion fruit sorbet or Grand Marnier soufflé, for example. Try the surprisingly inexpensive three-course prix-fixe lunch. ♦ French ♦ M-Sa breakfast, lunch, afternoon tea, and dinner; Su breakfast, brunch, afternoon tea, and dinner. Reservations recommended. 879.1864

141 Sant Ambroeus ★★★$$$ Twenty-five dollars for a plate of pasta and tomatoes! But oh, it is simply the best plate of it you've ever tasted. This trendy Milanese restaurant serves up gorgeously simple and delicious food at prices to make you think twice. Don't. Seafood antipasto, grilled salmon, shrimp with mustard—how can such simple dishes taste so extravagant? For dessert, simply the best gelato in town. Be sure to get a pint to go. ♦ Italian ♦ M-Sa breakfast, lunch, and dinner; Su breakfast and lunch. Reservations required; jacket required. 1000 Madison Ave (between E 77th and E 78th Sts). 570.2211

142 La Maison du Chocolat For chocolates of unsurpassed quality New Yorkers in the know look no further than this understated temple to the cacao bean. French proprietor Robert Linxe treats chocolate with the earnestness and ardor of a true connoisseur. Try one of the dense ganaches, wedges of intense milk or dark chocolate with different fillings such as coconut and praline, or the pastries flown in fresh from Paris. The rear of the store is given over to a small tea room where you can experience true chocolate nirvana: a silky, ultrarich $7 cup of Guayaquil (mild) or Caracas (bittersweet) hot chocolate. In summer there are equally indulgent chocolate sorbets and ice creams. ♦ M-Su. 1018 Madison Ave (between 78th and 79th Sts). 744.7117

142 Stuyvesant Fish House Designed by **McKim, Mead & White** in 1898, this Renaissance palace was once the scene of the city's most lavish parties. It was owned by Stuyvesant Fish, who was president of the Illinois Central Railroad. He and his wife, Marion, were prominent social leaders. ♦ 25 E 78th St (at Madison Ave)

143 Missoni The whole store is devoted to the Missoni signature Italian knits on what is becoming "European Designers' Row." The recognizable blend of subtle color combinations and patterns is worked up in all kinds of dashing sportswear for men and women. ♦ M-Sa. 1009 Madison Ave (at E 78th St). 517.9339 &

144 James B. Duke House A copy of an 18th-century château in Bordeaux, this mansion, designed in 1912 by **Horace Trumbauer,** was built for the founder of the American Tobacco Company. It was given to **New York University** in 1959 by Duke's widow and her daughter, Doris (who, along with Barbara Hutton, was known as a "poor little rich girl" in the 1930s), and is now **NYU's Institute of Fine Arts.** Many of the original furnishings are still here, including a Gainsborough portrait in the main hall. ♦ 1 E 78th St (at Fifth Ave). 772.5800

144 French Embassy Created in 1906 by **McKim, Mead & White,** this Italian Renaissance mansion, built for financier Payne Whitney, is typical of upper Fifth Avenue at the turn of the century, before the arrival of massive apartment houses. ♦ 972 Fifth Ave (between E 78th and E 79th Sts). 439.1400

145 Acquavella One of the uptown heavy hitters, this gallery shows 19th- and 20th-century European masters and postwar American and European artists. ♦ M-F. 18 E 79th St (between Madison and Fifth Aves). 734.6300

145 Salander-O'Reilly Galleries Twentieth-century Modernist American painters of the Stieglitz group (Alfred Maurer, Arthur Dove, Stuart Davis) as well as bold, contemporary ones (Susan Roth, Dan Christensen, John Greifen) are shown here. ♦ Tu-Sa. 20 E 79th St (between Madison and Fifth Aves). 879.6606

146 Hanae Mori A striking balance of stucco front and off-center chrome cylinder, this slightly mysterious 1969 storefront is **Hans Hollein**'s first work in Manhattan. Inside is the retail outlet for the designer's sophisticated, Japanese-influenced women's clothing. ♦ M-Sa. 27 E 79th St (between Madison and Fifth Aves). 472.2352 &

THE NEW YORK SOCIETY LIBRARY

147 New York Society Library Often confused with the **New-York Historical Society,** this is New York City's oldest circulating library, founded in 1754 by a civic-minded group who believed that the availability of books would help the city to prosper. Housed since 1937 in a handsome Italianate town house built in 1917 by **Trowbridge & Livingston,** today it is a local landmark boasting a collection of more than 200,000 volumes, as well as first editions and rare books and manuscripts. The library's particular strengths are in English and American literature, biography, history, art history, and travel and exploration, as well as works relating to the Big Apple. There is also a children's section. ♦ M-Sa. 53 E 79th St (between Park and Madison Aves). 288.6900

148 870 Park Avenue This 1898 town house has been completely remodeled. The tripartite division of the facade alludes to that era's tradition and the scale of the surrounding buildings. In terms of styling, this is the next step after Modernism (see the **Lescaze Residence** on page 179), and it holds its own. This structure was designed in 1976 by **Robert A.M. Stern** and **John S. Hagmann.** ♦ At E 77th St

149 Lenox Hill Hospital A compound of modern buildings extends from the hospital's nucleus, the **Uris Pavilion,** built in 1975 by **Rogers, Butler, Burgun & Bradbury.** Ranked as one of the city's—and the nation's—best, this hospital is a forerunner in obstetrical and neonatal care (its **Prenatal Testing Center** is one of the most comprehensive in the country); cardiology (the first balloon angioplasty in the country was performed here in 1978); and sports medicine (the **Nicholas Institute of Sports Medicine and Athletic Trauma** was the first such hospital-based center in the US). ♦ Bounded by Lexington and Park Aves, and E 76th and E 77th Sts. 439.2345

150 St. Jean Baptiste Church This Roman Catholic church, designed by **Nicholas Serracino** in 1913, was founded by French Canadians in the area. It is a little overwrought, but charming nevertheless. Among its best features is the French-style organ, which is one of the finest in any New York church. ♦ Lexington Ave and E 76th St. 288.5082

151 Candle Cafe ★★$ Vegetarians rejoice: This cheerful purple and gold neighborhood haunt serves organic foods fresh from farm to table. Try the Paradise Casserole (layers of sweet potato, black beans and millet), the fat-free soy burger, or the charred seitan steak, complete with mashed potatoes and gravy. A delectable array of desserts includes wonderful fruit pies and one amazing organic brownie. Should you find yourself requiring even more fiber, there's also a superb juice bar. ◆ Vegetarian ◆ Daily lunch and dinner. 1307 Third Ave (at 75th St). 472.0970 ᗕ

152 Atlantic Grill ★★★$$$ The former **Jim McMullen** has been transformed into a palace of all things piscine. Fish here comes grilled, baked, broiled, poached or raw, with accents as varied as citrus vinaigrette, porcini crust, mango chutney and tamarind glaze. The menu offers a sweeping and tantalizing array of options, as the black-clad crowds that fill the two boisterous dining rooms nightly can attest. Enjoy one of the best by-the-glass wine lists in the city. ◆ Seafood ◆ Daily lunch and dinner. 1337 Third Ave (between 76th and 77th Sts). 988.9200 ᗕ

Baraonda

153 Baraonda ★★$$$ The cheery, fanciful room is fitted with primary-color lanterns, caricatures on the walls, and streamers. Late at night there's even dancing on the tables. Before running completely amok, line your stomach with a good, simple plate of pasta, such as *tagliolini* (thin noodles) with tomato and basil; shrimp risotto; or an entrée—grilled salmon with wild-mushroom sauce is a good bet. ◆ Northern Italian ◆ M-Sa lunch and dinner; Su brunch and dinner. Reservations required. 1439 Second Ave (at E 75th St). 288.8555

153 Pamir ★★$$ Ahmad Bayat's eatery gets good marks for both ambience and cuisine. Handsome plush carpets line the walls and add to the exotic decor. Stop by for such classic and savory Afghan treats as skewered-meat entrées—lamb and chicken—served with moist rice pilaf and side dishes of yogurt and sautéed eggplant. ◆ Afghan ◆ Tu-Su dinner. Reservations required. 1437 Second Ave (between E 74th and E 75th Sts). 734.3791

154 Il Monello ★★$$$ Those who like a little razzle-dazzle with their meal will enjoy the way most dishes are given finishing touches in the dining room; otherwise, the food is simple

and reliable. Try *spaghetti carbonara* (with cream, eggs, parmesan, peas, and bacon); breast of chicken with onion, tomato, and basil sauce; and red snapper with a pine-nut crust and balsamic sauce. The in-depth Italian wine list is not only laudable, it's applaudable. ◆ Italian ◆ Daily lunch and dinner. Reservations required. 1460 Second Ave (between E 76th and E 77th Sts). 535.9310 ᗕ

155 Cherokee Apartments Built as model housing for the working class, these apartments are distinguished by the amount of light and air admitted by large casements and balconies—an unusual commodity in the days of "dumbbell" tenements; these were designed in 1909 by **Henry Atterbury Smith.** ◆ Bounded by Cherokee Pl and York Ave, and E 77th and E 78th Sts

coconut grill

156 Coconut Grill ★$$ The social scene is always in high gear at this attractive, deep-yellow and royal-blue spot. The food is quite respectable, particularly such homemade pastas as rigatoni with smoked mozzarella, eggplant, and plum tomatoes; and basil linguine with shrimp, scallops, mussels, and clams in a spicy tomato sauce. Delectable Sunday brunch basics like eggs Benedict pack them in. ◆ American ◆ M-Sa lunch and dinner; Su brunch and dinner. 1481 Second Ave (at E 77th St). 772.6262

157 Vermicelli ★★$$ This sensuously designed spot features a wide-ranging menu that borrows freely from Malaysian, Thai, Vietnamese and even Indian cuisines. Crispy shrimp rolls, a fiery green-papaya salad and an assortment of satays make for pleasing starters. For a main course, try the yellow curry vegetables over vermicelli (cooked and served in a clay pot) or the silky grilled pork chop. ◆ Asian ◆ Daily lunch and dinner. Reservations recommended. 1492 Second Ave (between 77th and 78th Sts). 288.8868 ᗕ

157 Lusardi's ★★$$$ This is one of several informal, clublike uptown trattorie that attract a sleek, affluent crowd. The food here, however, is more reliable than at other places, and the service is more attentive. Try calamari with tomato sauce, sun-dried–tomato ravioli, pasta with white truffles (in season), or chicken with artichokes and sausage. ◆ Italian ◆ M-F lunch and dinner; Sa-Su dinner. Reservations recommended. 1494 Second Ave (between E 77th and E 78th Sts). 249.2020

158 Divino Ristorante ★★$$ Service and pasta are the high points of this unpretentious favorite of Italian expatriates. Specialties include good fettuccine with four cheeses, linguine with baby clams, breaded veal chop Milanese, and shrimp scampi. Top it all off with a wonderful cappuccino. ♦ Italian ♦ M-Sa lunch and dinner; Su brunch and dinner. Reservations required. 1556 Second Ave (between E 80th and E 81st Sts). 861.1096

159 The Comic Strip A showcase club for stand-up comics and singers. Eddie Murphy, Jerry Seinfeld, and Paul Reiser started here, and sometimes a big name will drop by. ♦ Cover, minimum. Shows: M-Th 9PM; F 8:30PM, 10:45PM; Sa 8PM, 10:30PM, 12:30AM; Su 8:30PM. 1568 Second Ave (between E 81st and E 82nd Sts). 861.9386

160 Sistina ★★$$$ Owned by brothers Giuseppe, Gerardo, Antonio, and Cosimo Bruno, this restaurant serves a pleasing mix of Northern and Southern Italian dishes. Try *pappardelle* (broad noodles) in veal sauce with mushrooms and tomatoes, grilled chicken with arugula salad, and sea scallops in a tarragon broth. For dessert, don't miss the almond cake with chocolate and vanilla sauces. ♦ Italian ♦ Daily dinner. Reservations required. 1555 Second Ave (between E 80th and E 81st Sts). 861.7660

161 Border Cafe ★★$$ Fajitas, nachos, chilis, chicken wings, and of course frozen margaritas are the main draw here. Late in the evening, especially during the weekends, this place becomes a crowded bar scene. ♦ Southwestern ♦ M-F lunch and dinner; Sa dinner; Su brunch and dinner. Reservations recommended. 244 E 79th St (between Second and Third Aves). 535.4347

162 New York Public Library, Yorkville Branch This rather academic Neo-Classical building, designed in 1902 by **James Brown Lord,** is the earliest of what are known as the "Carnegie Libraries." There are 65 of these small branch libraries throughout the city, established by a donation from Andrew Carnegie. Later ones, similar in style, were designed by **Lord** and other distinguished architects such as **McKim, Mead & White, Carrère & Hastings,** and **Babb, Cook & Willard.** ♦ M-Sa. 222 E 79th St (between Second and Third Aves). 744.5824

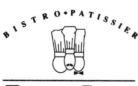

163 Trois Jean ★★★$$$ The three Jeans of the name refer to owners Jean-Luc Andriot

and chef Jean-Louis Dumonet, and the late pastry chef Jean-Marc Burillier. This is one of the finest French bistros in New York, turning out earthy, delicious food in a wood-paneled, candlelit setting with paintings of women adorning the walls and lace curtains on the windows. Nothing on the classic French menu disappoints: try the cassoulet or pot-au-feu. Desserts are spectacular: Try the warm chocolate cake, *frou-frou au café* (coffee and caramel mousse wrapped in a chocolate ribbon and served with cappuccino sauce), *pyramide au chocolat* (an iced chocolate cake made from three different types of chocolate), and a crème brûlée that sets the standard for others to follow. Pastries can be taken home and enjoyed later. The well-chosen and attractively priced wine list also offers a good selection of wines by the glass. ♦ French ♦ M-Sa lunch, afternoon tea, and dinner; Su brunch, afternoon tea, and dinner. Reservations recommended. 154 E 79th St (between Third and Lexington Aves). 988.4858

164 Parma ★★$$ Owner John Piscina greets everyone at the door of this popular East Side trattoria, and a more hospitable atmosphere you won't find outside your grandmother's kitchen. All the homey favorites—gnocchi, lasagna, chicken parmigiana—are deftly prepared and generously portioned. In between courses of his own harried meal in the corner, Piscina will make sure you want for nothing. An extensive wine list also features a number of good wines by the glass; the Montepulciano being particularly fine. ♦ Italian ♦ Daily dinner. Reservations recommended. 1404 Third Ave (between E 79th and E 80th Sts). 535.3520

165 Samalita's Tortilla Factory ★$ Within this small, bright, yellow-and-blue room with Mexican silver lamps, colorful tiles, and wicker chairs, diners are treated to fresh Mexican and Cal-Mex fare. Try the spicy guacamole; vegetarian burritos with char-grilled corn, red and green peppers, chilies, and broccoli; *carnitas* (grilled chunks of marinated pork); or any of the tacos. Wash it all down with a Corona, Pacifico, or Negro Modelo. ♦ Mexican ♦ Daily lunch and dinner. 1429 Third Ave (at E 81st St). 737.5070 &

166 Le Refuge ★★$$$ Bare wooden tables, kitchen towels for napkins, American stoneware, and etched stemware generate a mood of romantic, rustic elegance. The ever-changing menu is prepared with carefully chosen fresh ingredients, all cooked and seasoned by the sure hand of chef/owner Pierre Saint-Denis. Try the vegetable terrine bathed in tomato coulis or the bouillabaisse, considered the best this side of the Atlantic. For dessert, go for the airy raspberry cheesecake, chocolate soufflé cake, or heavenly crème brûlée. ♦ French ♦ M-F lunch and dinner; Sa-Su brunch, lunch, and dinner. Reservations required. 166 E 82nd St (between Third and Lexington Aves). 861.4505

67 Girasole ★★$$$ A local, conservative crowd of East Siders favors this dependable, noisy Italian restaurant located on the ground floor of a brownstone. Poultry and game dishes—such as chicken sautéed with lemon, and grilled organic Cornish hens with peppercorns—are standards. ♦ Italian ♦ Daily lunch and dinner. Reservations required. 151 E 82nd St (between Third and Lexington Aves). 772.6690

68 Big City Kite Co., Inc. More than 150 kinds of kites are sold here. They come in a variety of shapes, including tigers, teddy bears, sailboats, sharks, dragons, and bats. They will also guide you to nearby kite flights. ♦ M-Sa. 1210 Lexington Ave (at E 82nd St). 472.2623

69 Rosenthal Wine Merchant Here you'll find unique wines from California and Europe (particularly Burgundies). ♦ M-Sa. 1200 Lexington Ave (between E 81st and E 82nd Sts). 249.6650 &

70 Tiny Doll House All the teeny, tiny furniture and accessories it takes to make a doll's home, including mini Degas paintings, handmade English houses, and furniture, are here under one roof. If you think you can make something better yourself, all the supplies you need are available. ♦ M-Sa. 1146 Lexington Ave (between E 79th and E 80th Sts). 744.3719 &

Nara
FINE LEATHER GOODS

71 Nara This small but inviting shop that sells leather goods and costume jewelry is a good source for the increasingly hard-to-find labels such as Koret, as well as French handbags. There is also a selection of ladies' leather belts. The staff is polite and helpful. ♦ M-Sa. 1132 Lexington Ave (between E 78th and E 79th Sts). 628.1577

72 Junior League of The City of New York One of a trio of perfect neighbors, this sophisticated 1928 Regency-style mansion by **Mott B. Schmidt** was built for Vincent Astor. The other two are **Schmidt's** Georgian house for Clarence Dillon (1930) at 124 East 80th Street, and the Federal-style **George Whitney House** (1930) at 120 East 80th Street, by

Cross & Cross. ♦ 130 E 80th St (between Lexington and Park Aves). 288.6220

173 L'Occitane Although the company's sensual bath accessories—soaps, perfumes, and creams—can be found in upscale department stores and boutiques throughout the city, making your purchase at its flagship store is like stepping into a garden in Provence. No matter the weather outside: Inside, you'll find a sunny world redolent of herbs, fruits, and fragrant flowers. Prices are in the moderate range. Note that the essences are quite intense—a dab or two is all that's needed. ♦ M-Sa; Su noon-6PM. 1046 Madison Ave (between E 79th and E 80th Sts). 639.9185, toll-free 888/MAD.AT80. Also at: 146 Spring St (at Wooster St). 343.0109; 198 Columbus Ave (at W 69th St). 352.5146

174 Lobster Club ★★$$ This casual restaurant has a wide and varied menu, though many diners are happily drawn to its eponymous (and delicious) house sandwich. Don't let that stop you from trying the venison or the braised Maine lobster with truffles. Butterscotch pudding and an almond-crusted banana split will appease even the sweetest of sweet tooths. ♦ American ♦ M-Sa lunch and dinner; Su dinner. 24 East 80th St (between Fifth and Madison Aves). 249.6500

175 E.A.T. ★★$$$ Owned by Eli Zabar (of **Zabar's** fame), this informal eatery makes all its breads with a sourdough starter, including the famous *ficelle* (a supercrusty loaf, 22 inches long with a diameter barely larger than a silver dollar). Popular choices from the menu are linguine with broccoli rabe, the Three-Salad Plate (choose three from a list of 12 salads), lamb sandwich, crab cakes, pot roast, and grilled chicken. For dessert try the chocolate cake or raspberry tart. The prices are high, but so is the quality. Plus, the people watching is pretty good; celebrities occasionally drop in. ♦ American ♦ Daily breakfast, lunch, and dinner. 1064 Madison Ave (between E 80th and E 81st Sts). 772.0022

New York City is definitely the media giant, with headquarters for 90 book publishers, 125 consumer magazines, 100 ethnic and local newspapers, and 59 trade publications.

In 1882, Charles Henry Dow and Edward Jones, the namesakes of today's stock index, founded a financial news service that became the *Wall Street Journal* in 1902 when it was sold to C.W. Barron.

The *New York World* printed the first crossword puzzle in 1913. The first comic strip serial, *The Yellow Kid,* ran in an 1896 *New York Journal.*

East Side, West Side . . . Detours Around the Town

First-time visitors to the city frequently stick to the main avenues of **Fifth, Madison, Columbus,** or **Broadway.** For those with a bit more time, there are some unusual clusters of side streets scattered throughout Manhattan and other boroughs. Many of these streets are specialty-interest areas catering to certain industries—did you know New York boasts a button district and a ribbon district? Other detours afford glimpses into the lives and customs of many of the city's ethnic communities. Most commercial areas are livelier during weekday business hours; on weekends and evenings, the deserted streets can be somewhat intimidating—and not particularly interesting, though many downtown side streets tend to have more after-dark activity, especially in the **East** and **West Villages.** Here are some off-the-beaten-path destinations worth a detour or two.

East Village

Start with **St. Mark's Place.** Here you'll find the ghosts of the 1960s in hole-in-the-wall vintage record stores, clothing stores, and inexpensive restaurants serving counterculture cuisine. While a few chain stores are beginning to intrude, the atmosphere is still tinged with patchouli. The surroundings become more exotic the farther east you venture. **East Sixth** through **East 14th Streets** are chock-full of antique furniture and clothing stores, ethnic restaurants (East Sixth Street between **First** and **Second Avenues** has a large number of similarly priced Indian spots; rumor has it that they're all owned by the same person), and offbeat stores. Several spots cater to practitioners of the occult arts; you can buy herbs and charms to cast your own personal spells. This neighborhood is also home to Off-Off-Broadway theater companies, some of which operate out of small churches. Between **Avenues A** and **B,** the streets reflect the growing gentrification of the area.

Greenwich Village

West Eighth Street between Broadway and Sixth Avenue is another, though more commercial, time-warp tribute to the age of Jimi Hendrix and Sgt. Pepper. Clothing stores and smoke shops (a time-honored euphemism) have a distinct air of the Sixties and Seventies about them. If cutting-edge shoes and designer cowboy boots are your passion, this is the place to plant your feet. Nearby **Bleecker Street,** running roughly between the same avenues, cuts through the **NYU** campus and what's left of the old folk and rock clubs where people like Bob Dylan and Peter, Paul & Mary got

their starts. **West Fourth Street** is p*ositively* another good crosswalk to browse through on a Village stroll

A bit farther uptown, **9th** through **13th Streets,** from **Fourth Avenue** heading west, you'll find some of the most elegant and expensive antique furniture dealers this side of Paris or London. French Country, Louis XVI, and a smattering of European Retro are the primary styles. These are also some of the more genteel residential streets in the neighborhood. Crafts galleries and restaurants have made inroads, too.

Union Square & Chelsea

The teens—mainly **15th** through **19th Streets**— west of Union Square to **Ninth Avenue** are dotted with high-end vintage art poster galleries, photo and drafting supply stores, second-hand and specialty book stores, and a growing number of trendy restaurants and night spots. These streets cut through the new shopping areas of **Lower Fifth, Sixth,** and **Seventh Avenues.** Many of the side streets here sell discounted name-brand perfumes. Some are more reliable than others; it's best to be guided by your common scents!

Garment and Flower Districts

The side streets of the **West 30s** from **Eighth Avenue** to Fifth Avenue are the lifeblood of New York's growing Korean population. There are dozens of tantalizing barbecue restaurants (they can get rather smoky) where you grill your own meats and fire up your tongue with spicy pickled vegetables. The upper West 30s between Fifth and Sixth Avenues are dominated by trimming and notion stores. Bridal veils and beading are a specialty, as are buttons, bows, and fanciful borders. There are some non–brand name costume jewelry stores whose goods resemble those sold in better shops, but whose workmanship doesn't. Still, there's nothing wrong with a $5 knockoff to go with a certain outfit. Check the clips and clasps before you buy.

East Side

East 60th Street, between Second and **Third Avenues,** is an eclectic mix of elegant antiques shops, fabric stores, and men's Italian clothing boutiques. Designer Betsey Johnson has one of her larger branches here. There's a startling store window filled with wigs, and a graceful Episcopal church with a noteworthy stained-glass window that oddly resembles the Star of David. This block is also home to **Arizona 206, Yellowfingers,** and other popular restaurants. It's an exhilarating warm-up walk at the gateway to **Bloomie's** and the rest of the East Side.

West Side

The **West 60s** and **70s,** between **Central Park West** and **West End Avenue,** are rife with romantic restaurants like **Café des Artistes,** impressive buildings like **Christ and St. Stephen's Church,** and the **Pythian Temple,** where Buddy Holly recorded his later songs, and popular local shopping spots like **Acker-Merrall-Condit** (fine wines) and the **Maraolo** outlet (fine shoes at discount prices), located on opposite sides of the same busy block—**West 72nd** between Columbus Avenue and Broadway. While crosstown thoroughfares like West 72nd and **West 79th Streets** have the greatest density, don't ignore the less-explored and exploited streets in this thriving residential neighborhood.

Harlem

West 125th Street has regained its former status as the heart of **Harlem.** Cultural landmarks like the **Apollo Theater** and the **Studio Museum** are on this famous street, as is the **Cotton Club.** In between are a growing number of familiar chain outlets, African-American boutiques, and a number of food stores and restaurants. Other Harlem cross streets of note are **West 138th** and **West 139th Streets,** between **Adam Clayton Powell Jr.** and **Frederick Douglass**

Boulevards. Known as **Striver's Row,** these two blocks of elegant late-19th-century houses were (and still are) home to many noted African-American professionals. The **Mount Morris Park Historical District** has quite a few buildings of architectural and historical note. The most interesting run from **West 119th** to **West 124th Streets,** just west of **Mt. Morris Park**.

Queens

Jackson Heights is a heady mixture of Colombian, Argentine, Korean, and Indian cultures. At night, strolling outsiders may be viewed with suspicion, except at the area's many restaurants. The block of **74th Street** between **Roosevelt** and **37th Avenues** is replete with some very good—and relatively little known—Indian restaurants, as well as dazzling jewelry and sari stores.

Astoria's side streets, jutting off from either side of the elevated subway around **Broadway, Steinway Street, Astoria, Northern,** and **Ditmars Boulevards,** have rows of neat and tidy single-family homes, international and Mediterranean grocery stores, and lots of restaurants—especially **Elias Corner.**

Downtown **Flushing's Main Street,** running from **Sanford Avenue** to Northern Boulevard, mirrors Asian culture with herbal shops, greengrocers, and, best of all, some of the best Chinese, Korean, and Japanese restaurants in the city. This enclave of Oriental delights can be found at the end of the **No. 7** subway line.

176 Frank E. Campbell Funeral Chapel In this building, possibly the most prestigious funeral chapel in the world, we have said farewell to Elizabeth Arden, James Cagney, Jack Dempsey, Tommy Dorsey, Judy Garland, Howard Johnson, Robert F. Kennedy, John Lennon, J.C. Penney, Damon Runyon, Arturo Toscanini, Mae West, and Tennessee Williams, to name-drop just a few. ♦ 1076 Madison Ave (at E 81st St). 288.3500 ♿

177 Parioli Romanissimo ★★★$$$$ Located in a charming town house, this dining room is sedately decorated with beige walls and beige print fabric window shades and seat cushions. The delicate egg pasta and risotto with porcini (among others) are divine, and the entrées, including baked sea bass with tarragon sauce and baby chicken roasted with black truffles, are impeccable. For dessert, have the tiramisù or zabaglione. The wine list is extensive, well chosen, and expensive. Because the restaurant is run like a private club for regular patrons, it is often difficult to get a reservation. ♦ Italian ♦ M-Sa dinner. Reservations required; jacket and tie required. 24 E 81st St (between Madison and Fifth Aves). 288.2391

178 The Stanhope Hotel $$$$ Created in 1926 by **Rosario Candela,** this hotel is strategically located across the street from the **Metropolitan Museum of Art** and **Central Park.** Now under new ownership, the septuagenarian has been freshened up without great disturbance to its gentility. The 140 rooms (nearly all suites), decorated in the Louis XVI style with Asian accents, have such amenities as in-room safes and multiple telephones. Room service and valet service are available 24 hours a day, and limousine service is provided to Midtown and Wall Street. Rooms facing the museum and the park are particularly choice. **Cafe M** is a favorite escape from museum overload. ♦ 995 Fifth Ave (at E 81st St). 288.5800, 800/828.1123; fax 517.0088

179 998 Fifth Avenue This 1912 apartment building in the guise of an Italian Renaissance palazzo was built by **McKim, Mead & White** when the bulk of society lived in mansions up and down the avenue. The largest apartment here has 25 rooms; it was originally leased by Murray Guggenheim. ♦ At E 81st St

179 1001 Fifth Avenue Designed in 1978 by **Philip Birnbaum,** this average apartment tower has been upgraded with a limestone facade by **Philip Johnson** and **John Burgee.** Half-round ornamental molding relates horizontally to the neighboring **No. 998,** while the mullions struggle for a vertical emphasis, pointing at the mansard-shaped cut-out roof. ♦ Between E 81st and E 82nd Sts

180 Metropolitan Museum of Art The first, original section was built in 1880 by **Calvert Vaux** and **Jacob Wrey Mould.** Additions and renovations were as follows: southwest wing 1888, **Theodore Weston;** north wing 1894, **Arthur Tuckerman;** central facade 1902, **Richard Morris Hunt, Richard Howland Hunt,** and **George B. Post;** Fifth Avenue wings 1906, **McKim, Mead & White;** stairs, pool, **Lehman Wing,** and **Great Hall** renovations 1970, **Kevin Roche John Dinkeloo & Associates;** later additions 1975-87, **Kevin Roche John Dinkeloo & Associates; Andre Meyer Gallery** renovation 1993, **David Harvey,** and **Gary Tinterow,** with **Alvin Holm** and **Kevin Roche.** Ten years after the first section was finished at the edge of **Central Park,** Frederick Law Olmsted, the park's designer, said he regretted having allowed it to be built there. He should see it now. The museum (pictured on page 237) has grown to 1.4 million square feet of floor space (more than 32 acres), with some 3.3 million works of art, making it the largest art museum in the Western Hemisphere. It seems to be expanding and getting better every day (much of this growth must be credited to director **Philippe de Montebello**). Founded in 1870 by a group of art-collecting financiers and industrialists who were on the art committee of New York's **Union League Club,** the museum's original collection consisted of 174 paintings, mostly Dutch and Flemish, and a gift of antiquities from General di Cesnola, the former US consul to Cyprus.

The more recent additions, including the **Lila Acheson Wallace Wing** (20th-century art) with its beautiful roof garden, provide a dramatic contrast of high-tech glass curtain walls to the solid limestone Beaux Arts front. The interiors are spectacular, too, contrasting

but not fighting with **Richard Morris Hunt**'s equally spectacular **Great Hall,** just inside the main entrance.

The list of benefactors who have swelled the museum's holdings over the years reads like a *Who's Who* of the city's First Families—Morgan, Rockefeller, Altman, Marquand, Hearn, Bache, Lehman. The push to house the collection in style has produced the **Sackler Wing** (1979) for the *Raymond R. Sackler Far East Art Collection;* the entire Egyptian **Temple of Dendur** (1978), given to the people of the United States for their support in saving monuments threatened by the construction of the Aswan High Dam; the **Egyptian Galleries** (1983) for the museum's world-class permanent collection; the impressive **Michael C. Rockefeller Wing** (1982) for the art of Africa, the Americas, and the Pacific Islands; the **Douglas Dillon Galleries of Chinese Painting** (1983) and the **Astor Chinese Garden Court** (1980), with a reception hall from the home of a 16th-century scholar; an expanded and dramatically redesigned **American Wing** (1980); and the **Lehman Wing** (1975), which displays its collection of paintings, drawings, and decorative objects in rooms re-created from the original Lehman town house on West 54th Street. Don't miss the beautifully renovated **Andre Meyer Galleries** (1993), where you'll see the premier collection of 19th-century European paintings and sculpture in the world, rivaling the Musée d'Orsay in Paris.

The permanent collection (about a third of which can be displayed at any one time) is expanding in every department. The museum already has the most comprehensive collection of American art in the world, and excels in Egyptian, Greek and Roman, and European art. The list of priceless art and artifacts within these walls is almost impossible to comprehend. Everyone seems to have their favorite sections, but you won't want to miss the new **Greek Galleries,** seven completely renovated and re-installed rooms showcasing masterpieces from the museum's monumental collection of archaic and classical Greek art. Not new but always captivating is the colossal collection of historic arms and armor from around the world.

The **Costume Institute** displays its 35,000 articles of clothing in stylish themes, with special temporary blockbuster exhibits you won't want to miss.

The information desk in the center of the **Great Hall** has floor plans and a helpful staff to direct you. The staff also has information about concerts and lectures in the museum's **Grace Rainey Rogers Auditorium** and will help you arrange for a guided tour, available in

Metropolitan Museum of Art

MICHAEL STORRINGS

several languages. At the north end of the **Great Hall,** tape-recorded tours of most of the exhibits are available for rental. Just off the **Great Hall** is the justly famous and recently expanded book and gift shop.

The museum restaurant is a hectic, cafeteria-style arrangement with tables around a pool. A little-known resource is weekend brunch in the elegant upstairs dining room, which, during the week, is only open to sponsors. **The Iris and B. Gerald Cantor Roof Garden,** a lovely open-air sculpture garden with grand views from the roof of the museum, is open early May through late October and sells coffee, wine, and soft drinks.

The Friday and Saturday evening hours have added a touch of civility and grace to the busy city scene. Many of the museum's guests take advantage of the tranquil twilight hours, when, beginning at 5PM, a string quartet serenades from the **Great Hall** balcony, where a bar and candlelit tables are set up for relaxation. Evening educational offerings—art lectures and documentaries—coincide with the concerts in the **Grace Rainey Rogers Auditorium.** ♦ Admission. Tu-Th, Su 9:30AM-5:15PM; F-Sa 9:30AM-8:45PM. Fifth Ave (at E. 82nd St). 535.7710, 879.5500 ♿

181 Church of St. Ignatius Loyola The overscaled Vignoia facade on Park Avenue was designed by **Ditmars & Schickel** in 1898. Its flat limestone late-Renaissance style looks very comfortable here—and it's a welcome change from all that Gothic. ♦ 980 Park Ave (at E 83rd St). 288.3588 ♿

182 Schaller & Weber This incredible store is filled from floor to ceiling with cold cuts. Liverwursts, salamis, bolognas, and other savories are piled on counters, packed into display cases, and hung from the walls and ceilings. ♦ M-Sa. 1654 Second Ave (between E 85th and E 86th Sts). 879.3047

183 Elio's ★★$$$ Wall Streeters and bankers mix with media types and celebs at this trendy neighborhood eatery, a spin-off of the ever-popular **Elaine's.** It's always crowded and noisy, and the food is always good. Order one of the specials, which seem to inspire the kitchen even more than the regular menu does. But the pasta dishes and veal chops are also good picks. ♦ Italian ♦ Daily dinner. Reservations required. 1621 Second Ave (between E 84th and E 85th Sts). 772.2242 ♿

184 Erminia ★★$$$ The crowning achievements here are the lushly sauced *pappardelle* tossed with artichokes, tomato, sausage, and porcini, and the excellent Tuscan lamb grilled over a wood fire. There are also a number of other roasted dishes, including veal chops. The romantic candlelight atmosphere makes this restaurant a popular place, so be sure to reserve a couple of days in advance. ♦ Italian ♦ M-Sa dinner. Reservations required. 250 E 83rd St (between Second and Third Aves). 879.4284

185 King's Carriage House ★★$$ In a charming recreated Irish country cottage that lacks a proper sign you'll find well-prepared food in a setting that will melt away those city blues and have you dreaming of *Ryan's Daughter*. The menu might include a buttery smooth salmon napoleon, chicken paillard over grilled vegetables and greens, or first-rate Gulf shrimp. Chocolate cake and crème brûlée are dessert winners. For afternoon tea, try the genteel scarlet room upstairs. ♦ Irish ♦ M-Sa lunch and dinner; Su dinner. Reservations recommended. 251 East 82nd St (between Second and Third Aves). 734.5490 ᕐ

186 Primavera ★★$$$$ One of the great watering holes for the older, distinguished smart set, this sedate room has deep-colored wood paneling and upmarket, if not particularly attractive, oil paintings. The food is similarly dignified and usually of good quality. Try the chicken breast with Champagne sauce, pasta with truffles, or green-and-white pasta with peas and ham. ♦ Italian ♦ Daily dinner. Reservations required; jacket and tie required. 1578 First Ave (at E 82nd St). 861.8608

187 Wilkinson's 1573 Seafood Cafe ★★$$$ The interior of this little gem of a restaurant is relaxed and intimate, with pastel-colored murals adorning the bare brick walls. To complement the charming ambience **Wilkinson's** offers some first-rate fare. Try such creatively prepared seafood dishes as grilled John Dory (a white fish that is also known as St. Peter's fish) with Thai ginger broth, or panseared, spice-coated tuna. ♦ Seafood ♦ Daily dinner. Reservations recommended. 1573 York Ave (at E 83rd St). 535.5454

Sirabella's

188 Sirabella's ★★$$ Perpetually packed, this place makes fresh pasta *in casa*—and it

shows. Taste the difference it makes in such standard dishes as linguine with clam sauce. On cold winter nights the rich textured soups are a must; another winner is the crisp calamari. The osso buco is delectable, and the vegetables—cooked escarole, for example—are redolent of garlic and olive oil. ♦ Italian ♦ Daily dinner. Reservations recommended. 72 East End Ave (between E 82nd and E 83rd Sts). 988.6557

189 Carl Schurz Park Situated on land acquired by the city in 1891, the park was named in 1911 for the German immigrant who served as a general during the Civil War, was a senator from Missouri and secretary of the interior under President Hayes, and went on to become editor of the *New York Evening Post* and *Harper's Weekly*.

The park, which was remodeled in 1938 by Harvey Stevenson and Cameron Clark, is a delightful edge to the neighborhood of Yorkville. It is not very large, but its distinct sections and the varied topography make a walk here rewarding. The promenade along the East River above FDR Drive is named for John Finley, a former editor of *The New York Times* and an enthusiastic walker. **Gracie Mansion,** the residence of the mayor of New York City, occupies the center of the north end of the park.

Across the river is Astoria, Queens; spanning the river are the Triborough Bridge and Hell Gate railroad trestle; also visible are Wards Island and Randalls Island; the yellow building is **Manhattan State Mental Hospital,** and the little island that looks like an elephant's head is known as Mill Rock. This point of the river is a treacherous confluence of currents from the Harlem River, Long Island Sound, and the harbor—hence the name "Hell Gate." ♦ Bounded by the East River and East End Ave, and Gracie Sq and FDR Dr

Organized fire fighting began in New York in 1648 when the first Fire Ordinance was adopted by the Dutch Settlement of New Amsterdam.

Perhaps the most distinguishing feature of the city's streets in the 1880s was the mass of telephone and telegraph wires overhead. After the blizzard of 1888 they were placed underground.

Zarela Martinez
Owner, Zarela's restaurant

I love going to:

Copacabana on Tuesday evenings for Latin and ballroom dancing and their all-you-can-eat buffet. It's a great place to learn to dance and to see dancing's old-timers.

Roosevelt Avenue between 80th and 87th Streets in **Queens** to have really authentic Mexican tacos and to shop for Mexican and other Latin American products.

The **Isamu Noguchi Garden Museum** in **Long Island City** with its beautiful sculpture garden that changes with every season.

Catching first-run and hard-to-find movies at the **Film Forum, Walter Reade Theater, Museum of Modern Art,** and **Anthology Film Archives.**

Have a drink and watch the sunset from the top of the **Metropolitan Museum of Art** Thursday and Friday evenings.

Watch the roller skaters near the **Sheep Meadow** in **Central Park.**

Joan Juliet Buck
Novelist/Film Critic/Journalist

The **West 26th Street Flea Market** for relics from the 1920s.

E.A.T. on **Madison Avenue** for the deep-fried baby artichokes.

The **Fifth Avenue** bus all the way downtown.

Strand Bookstore, because you don't know what you don't know till you find it here, usually from the top of a ladder and slightly out of reach, definitely out of print.

Weekend lunch at **Petaluma** because it's bright and the *quattro stagioni* pizza is perfect.

André Emmerich
Owner, André Emmerich Gallery

Lunch midtown in the **Grill Room** of the **Four Seasons** with its unequaled spa cuisine and sparkling fellow guests.

Early, pre-theater dinner at **Le Bernardin**—the best food in the world that stays safely within Pritikin limits.

Sunday night dinner at **Elaine's,** the most relaxing setting for the tensest people in the world—New York's intelligentsia.

Shopping the gentleman's quarter-mile along **Madison Avenue** from **Brooks Brothers, Paul Stuart,** and on, ending at **Saks Fifth Avenue** on **East 49th Street.**

The antiques furniture shops around **Broadway** below **East 13th Street.**

The revived **Brooklyn Museum** —as the French guidebooks say, well worth the "detour" to see its spectacular exhibitions.

A harbor cruise on a party boat, especially when the ship sails close to the floodlit **Statue of Liberty,** still the grandest public sculpture in the world.

The galleries of ancient Greek and Roman art at the **Metropolitan Museum of Art.**

The drive into Manhattan from the north along the **Henry Hudson Parkway.**

Finally, New York at sunset seen from my apartment, 380 feet above the avenue right behind the **Guggenheim.**

Cindy Adams
Syndicated Columnist for the *New York Post*/ WNBC-TV *Today in New York* Correspondent

For jewelry watching: The **Diamond Center,** West 47th Street between Fifth and Sixth Avenues.

For people watching: Bench in front of the **Plaza Hotel** around noon.

For kid watching: **FAO Schwarz.**

For view watching: **Rainbow Room.**

For lox/bagel/pastrami/salami watching: **Stage Deli.**

For window shopping: **Madison Avenue** going uptown from East 57th Street.

For shopping: **Trump Tower.**

For culture: **Lincoln Center.**

For color: **Greenwich Village.**

For architecture: **Seagram's Building** (supermodern glass and chrome), **Chrysler Building** (Art Deco), **Guggenheim Museum** (Frank Lloyd Wright), **World Trade Center** (tallest).

For VIP high-rises, where people from Phil Donahue to me dwell: Walk **Fifth Avenue.**

For caviar: **Petrossian's.**

For seafood: **The Sea Grill.**

For steaks: **Gallagher's.**

For Chinese: **Fu's.**

For Japanese: **Inagiku** at the **Waldorf.**

For atmosphere: **The Water Club.**

For what's no place else in the whole world but in New York: **Statue of Liberty, Radio City Music Hall, United Nations, Rockefeller Center** skating rink, the **Theater District, Empire State Building.**

And read the *New York Post.*

Beverly Sills
Diva/Former Director of the New York City Opera

The **New York City Opera.**

The best restaurants in the world.

The greatest theater district in the world.

Brooklyn, where I was born.

Upper East Side

The upscale and largely residential Upper East Side, which is bounded by the **East River** and **Fifth Avenue**, and **East 86th** and **East 110th Streets,** has a heavy concentration of town houses, deluxe apartment buildings, elitist hotels, and elegant mansions, interspersed with churches, museums, restaurants, gourmet take-out stores, and its fair share of tenements and neglect. It is a mixed bag, where one of the city's most prestigious zip codes meets **Spanish Harlem** as you head north.

Most of the great mansions of **Park** and Fifth Avenues and the cross streets between them, the first constructions in this part of New York, were built between 1900 and 1920, when the classical tradition was in flower—they all exhibit Neo-Georgian, Neo-Federal, Neo-French, or Neo-Italian Renaissance styling. The original owners, families such as the Whitneys, the Astors, the Straights, the Dillons, the Dukes, the Mellons, the Pulitzers, and the Harknesses, all moved here from downtown.

Construction of apartment houses and hotels began in 1881 and ended in 1932. Almost all the churches were erected between 1890 and 1920. Although there are still isolated blocks of row houses that date from the late 1860s to

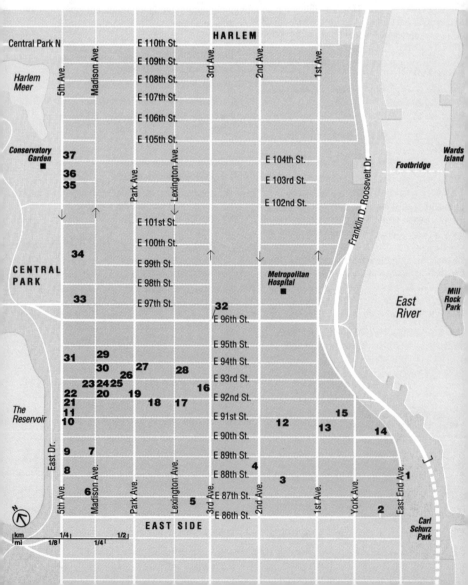

880s, as well as a few colonial relics and some contemporary buildings, the look, especially in the western part of the district, is generally more uniform than elsewhere in the city. The reason for the relatively late start in populating this area is that, except for the German village of **Yorkville** nestled along its eastern border, this was all open country. When work started on **Central Park** in 1857, the neighborhood consisted mainly of farms and squatters' shanties, and pigs grubbed on Fifth Avenue. Even after the park opened in 1863, steam trains chugging along Park Avenue made this an undesirable residential neighborhood. But in 1907, when the **New York Central Railroad** electrified the trains and covered the Park Avenue tracks, the Upper East Side became an attractive place for the well-to-do to live.

A few new buildings have been slipped into the otherwise unbroken frontage that progresses up Fifth Avenue north of **Grand Army Plaza** at **West 58th Street**. **Museum Mile** begins at the heroic **Metropolitan Museum of Art** on the park side of Fifth Avenue and ends with the **Museum of the City of New York** at **103rd Street**. In between are the **International Center of Photography**, the **Cooper-Hewitt Museum**, the **Solomon R. Guggenheim Museum**, and the **Jewish Museum**. The vertical palace on **East 92nd Street** that was the former home of Marjorie Merriwether Post is only one of the numerous outstanding apartment buildings and town houses in the neighborhood.

Among the many churches on the Upper East Side are the **Episcopal Church of the Holy Trinity** and **St. Christopher Home and Parsonage** at **East 88th Street**, which form a Neo-Gothic grouping around a courtyard built on land donated by Serena Rhinelander that had been in her family since 1798.

Madison Avenue has become largely a street of important art galleries, jewelry stores, antiques shops, clothing boutiques, and restaurants. Although the Saturday afternoon stroll is still a diversion for East Siders, Madison Avenue above East 86th Street now seems sedate compared to SoHo with its newer galleries and boutiques, or Columbus Avenue with its trendy shops.

Park Avenue, with its landscaped center island (covered with thousands of tulips in the springtime and a forest of evergreen trees in the winter months) and legions of dignified apartment houses and old mansions (most of which are now occupied by foreign cultural missions or clubs), is still an address to conjure with.

Lexington Avenue is a Madison Avenue without the cachet—and often without the quality. Shops, restaurants, and singles bars line **Third, Second, and First Avenues**, and, farther north, more high-rise "people boxes" border these thoroughfares. The side streets are a mix of tenements—some gentrified, some not—and modest town houses. A pocket neighborhood around Madison Avenue in the East Nineties called **Carnegie Hill** has become an increasingly attractive magnet for young couples choosing to raise families in Manhattan.

Yorkville, which extends from the East River to Lexington Avenue, from **East 77th** to **East 96th Streets**, continued to receive immigrants from Germany over the first half of the 20th century, but the ethnic heart is shrinking. At one time, East 86th Street was filled with German restaurants, beer gardens, and grocery, pastry, and dry goods stores. Now, although there still are inexpensive chain stores and fried chicken and pizza parlors, a new Eastern European presence can be felt, and only a few of the old restaurants, groceries, and record stores remain. Amidst it all sits **Gracie Mansion**, the official mayoral residence since the 1942 term of Fiorello La Guardia.

1 Gracie Mansion The site was known to the Dutch as "Hoek Van Hoorn"; when the British captured it during the Revolutionary War, the shelling destroyed the farmhouse that was there. The kernel of the present house was built in 1799 by Scottish-born merchant Archibald Gracie as a country retreat. Acquired by the city in 1887, it served, among its many uses, as the first home of the **Museum of the City of New York,** a refreshment stand, and a storehouse. In 1942, at the urging of Parks Commissioner Robert Moses, Fiorello La Guardia accepted it as the mayor's official residence. (The 98 men who preceded him in the office had lived in their own homes.) In 1966, an addition to the house was designed by **Mott B. Schmidt.** The **Gracie Mansion Conservancy** has restored the mansion to something better than its former glory, and conducts tours and special programs there. ♦ Voluntary contribution. Tours by appointment only W 10AM, 11AM, 1PM, 2PM mid-Mar–mid-Nov. East End Ave (between Gracie Sq and York Ave). 570.4751 &

2 Henderson Place These 24 Queen Anne houses were commissioned by John C. Henderson, a fur importer and hat manufacturer, and designed by **Lamb & Rich** in 1882 as a self-contained community with river views. Symmetrical compositions tie the numerous pieces together below an enthusiastic profusion of turrets, parapets, and dormers. There are rumors that some of these houses are haunted. The ghosts may be looking for the eight houses from the group that were demolished to allow for a yellow apartment block. ♦ Off E 86th St (between East End and York Aves)

3 Church of the Holy Trinity Built in 1897 by **Barney & Chapman,** this picturesque gold, brown, and red Victorian church modestly slipped into this side street encloses a charming garden. The sleek tower with its fanciful Gothic crown is rather nice, too. ♦ 316 E 88th St (between First and Second Aves). 289.4100

The first recorded owner of the property on which Gracie Mansion stands was a Dutch farmer named Sybout Claessen who acquired 106 acres and named it "Horn's Hook." In 1799, a subsequent owner, Archibald Gracie, built a handsome frame house on the property that he had acquired for $5,625.

Rockefeller University, on York Avenue in the east sixties, has the lowest teacher-pupil ratio of any university in the United States.

Restaurants/Clubs: Red   Hotels: Blue
Shops/ ♥ Outdoors: Green   Sights/Culture: Black

4 Elaine's ★$$$ Those whose idea of a good time is watching celebrities eat steamed mussels should be in heaven here. It's a kind of club for media celebrities, gossips, and literary types, but they don't necessarily come here for the food, although the spaghetti bolognese and grilled veal chops are decent. ♦ Italian ♦ Daily dinner and late-night meals. Reservations required. 1703 Second Ave (between E 88th and E 89th Sts). 534.8103

5 The Franklin Hotel $$ Built in 1931, this refurbished 47-room hotel offers high style for the price. The rooms are small but nicely decorated, the service is good, and the buffet breakfast is complimentary. East Side residents often book rooms for their guests here. ♦ 164 E 87th St (between Third and Lexington Aves). 369.1000, 800/600.8787; fax 369.8000

6 Au Chat Botté Expensive charm pervades this shop, which sells baby furniture—cribs, chairs, chests of drawers, clothes racks, and bumper guards—as well as children's clothes. ♦ M-Sa. 1192 Madison Ave (at E 87th St). 772.6474 &

ART & TAPISSERIE

7 Art & Tapisserie The young students from the prestigious private schools in the neighborhood are a captive audience for the personalized toys, toy chests, children's books, and frames sold here. ♦ M-Sa. 1242 Madison Ave (at E 89th St). 722.3222 &

8 Solomon R. Guggenheim Museum When Solomon R. Guggenheim wanted a museum that would "foster an appreciation of art by acquainting museum visitors with significant painting and sculpture of our time," he founded this repository, which has remained a testament to his personal taste. Guggenheim collected old masters at first, but in the 1920s he began acquiring the avant-garde work of painters such as Delaunay, Kandinsky, and Léger. Soon his apartment at **The Plaza** was bursting at the seams (the old masters were relegated to his wife's bedroom), and he began to look for other quarters for his burgeoning collection. During two sojourns in rented space, his new museum began to buy more of everything by both established and new talent. Finally, the need for a permanent home was realized in a building (shown on page 243) designed in 1959 by **Frank Lloyd Wright.** The museum is one of the architect's fantasies, first dreamed of in the mid-1940s. It is an extraordinary structure: A massive concrete spiral sits atop one end of a low horizontal base, expanding as it ascends, dominating not only its plinth and a counterweight block of offices at the other end, but the site itself and the blocks around it.

Solomon R. Guggenheim Museum

MICHAEL STORRINGS

The display of art was clearly not **Wright**'s main concern, however. The essence of architecture for the sake of architecture, the **Guggenheim** seems to evoke an opinion from most people who visit—some positive, many negative. To make matters worse, the first addition, built in 1968 by **Taliesin Associates,** was not up to snuff. That firm, **Wright**'s successors and keepers-of-the-flame, never had the touch of the master, who had personally handled all the details of the construction of the original building, right down to the Fifth Avenue sidewalk.

Construction of a second addition, by **Gwathmey Siegel & Associates,** was completed in 1992. Although it doubles the museum's gallery space and visitors have increased, controversy continues over its questionable aesthetics.

The newly restored **Frank Lloyd Wright**–designed **Museum Cafe,** open daily (even when the museum is closed) for breakfast and lunch, and most days for light dinner, makes for an excellent respite from museum trekking. ◆ Admission; voluntary contribution Friday 6-8PM. M-W, Su 10AM-6PM; F-Sa until 8PM. Cafe: M-W, F-Su breakfast, lunch, and light dinner; Th breakfast and lunch. Museum shop: M-Th; F-Sa 9:30AM-8:30PM. Fifth Ave and E 89th St. Museum: 360.3500. Shop: 423.3615; www.guggenheim.org. Annex at: 575 Broadway (at Prince St). 423.3500

9 National Academy of Design Since its founding in 1825 by Samuel F.B. Morse, painter and inventor of the telegraph, this academy has been an artist-run museum, a fine-arts school, and an honorary organization of artists. Headquartered in a town house that was remodeled in 1915 by **Ogden Codman Jr.,** and located around the corner from its **School of Fine Arts,** it is the second-oldest museum school in the country. In addition to an annual exhibition (alternately open to member artists and all artists), the academy presents special exhibitions of art and architecture. Painters, sculptors, watercolorists, graphic artists, and architects number among its members today. ◆ Admission. W-Th, Sa-Su noon-5PM; F noon-8PM. 1083 Fifth Ave (at E 89th St). 369.4880 &

10 Cooper-Hewitt National Design Museum, Smithsonian Institution After an extensive $20-million renovation to its galleries, the museum is more inviting than ever. This splendidly decorated mansion designed in 1903 by **Babb, Cook & Willard** was built on the northern fringe of the well-heeled stretch of Fifth Avenue mansions for industrialist Andrew Carnegie, who requested "the most modest, plainest, and most roomy house in New York City." The rather standard Renaissance-Georgian mix of red brick and limestone trim on a rusticated base is most noteworthy for the fact that it is freestanding in quite an expansive garden. The richly ornamented rooms of the sumptuous mansion, which was renovated in 1977 by **Hardy Holzman Pfeiffer Associates,** sometimes compete with the exhibitions; the conservatory is particularly pleasant. Also notice the very low door to what was once the library at the west end—Carnegie was a short man, and this was his private room.

243

The Cooper-Hewitt

MICHAEL STORRINGS

The permanent collection—based on the collections of the Cooper and Hewitt families and under the stewardship of museum director Diane Pilgrim—encompasses textiles dating back 3,000 years, jewelry, furniture, wallpaper, and metal-, glass-, and earthenware. It also includes the single largest group of architectural drawings in this country. The library is a design student's reference paradise of picture collections, auction catalogs, and 17th- and 18th-century architecture books. Lectures, symposia, summer concerts, and classes for school groups take place on a regular basis. A gift shop in the **Louis XV Music Room** sells design objects, catalogs, postcards, and museum publications. ♦ Admission; free Tuesday 5-9PM. Tu 10AM-9PM; W-Sa 10AM-5PM; Su noon-5PM. 2 E 91st St (between Madison and Fifth Aves). 849.8400 ♿

11 The Convent of the Sacred Heart
Originally built in 1918 by **C.P.H. Gilbert** and **J. Armstrong Stenhouse,** this extravagant Italian palazzo was one of the largest private houses built in New York City, and the last on "Millionaire's Row." It was the home of Otto Kahn, a banker, philanthropist, and art patron. Now it's a private school for girls. ♦ 1 E 91st St (at Fifth Ave). 722.4745

11 Mrs. James A. Burden House When Vanderbilt heiress Adele Sloane married James A. Burden, heir to a steel fortune, they moved into this freestanding mansion, which was built in 1902 by **Warren & Wetmore.** The spiral staircase under a stained-glass skylight is one of the city's grandest, and was called the "stairway to heaven." Not surprisingly, it is a favorite rental location for wedding receptions. ♦ 7 E 91st St (between Madison and Fifth Aves)

11 Mrs. John Henry Hammond House
When Hammond saw the plans for this house, designed in 1906 by **Carrère & Hastings,** he said that this gift from his wife's family made him feel "like a kept man." He moved in anyway, along with a staff of 16 full-time servants. The couple's musicales were legendary. Among the many noteworthy folk who visited, Benny Goodman came here frequently in the 1930s to play Mozart's clarinet works. ♦ 9 E 91st St (between Madison and Fifth Aves)

12 Playhouse 91 Plays that relate to the Jewish experience are given standard to excellent treatment here by the **Jewish Repertory Theatre,** which stages revivals (of Chekhov, Neil Simon), originals (*Crossing Delancey* premiered here), and musicals. ♦ 316 E 91st St (between First and Second Aves). 831.2000

13 El Pollo ★★$ What this tiny storefront lacks in atmosphere, it more than makes up fo with its chicken served with a side order of fried plantains. Wash it all down with an Inca Kola and top it off with an exotic pudding mad of raisins, cinnamon, and quinoa. ♦ Peruvian ♦ M-F lunch and dinner; Sa-Su dinner. No credit cards accepted. 1746 First Ave (betwee E 90th and E 91st Sts). 996.7810

14 Asphalt Green Housed in what was once a asphalt factory, the facility offers clients two pools, a fully equipped gym, and an outdoor running track. Since the pools are sometimes used for local team practice and competitions it's best to call in advance for swim periods. ♦ Fee. Daily. 555 E 90th St (at East End Ave). 369.8890

★ THE ★
VINEGAR FACTORY

15 Vinegar Factory Located in an old mustard-and-vinegar factory, this timely brainchild of **E.A.T.**'s owner Eli Zabar recycles unsold prepared foods in a most delicious way. Eli's famous focaccia, wonderful when fresh, is twice as good made into parmesan toast; dried-out loaves of brioche become a scrumptious bread pudding. Foods in their first incarnations are available here as well, at secondhand prices: breads baked fresh daily here are sold at a fraction above wholesale, and the cheese prices may be the lowest in town. There's also a full range of fresh produce and homemade pâtés. Weekend brunch is served until 4:30 PM on the balcony above the selling floor. ◆ Daily. 431 E 91st St (between York and First Aves). 987.0885

16 Yura and Company ★★$$ One of the neighborhood's best cafes, this place has excellent bouillabaisse, braised stuffed chicken breast with wild-mushroom ragout, and osso buco. For dessert, the fruit crisp and devil's-food cake are fine choices. Some of this gourmet fare is also available for takeout. Be sure to take a close look at the lighting fixtures; they look like Mexican silver designs, but are actually metal colanders. ◆ American/French ◆ M-F breakfast, lunch, and dinner; Sa-Su brunch and dinner. 1650 Third Ave (between E 92nd and E 93rd Sts). 860.8060 &

17 92nd Street Y This branch of the **Young Men's/Women's Hebrew Association** is one of the city's cultural landmarks. Its **Kaufman Concert Hall** has become one of New York's best places for chamber music and recitals, in the Chamber Music at the Y series directed by violinist Jaime Laredo and much more, including regular appearances by groups such as the **Guarneri, Cleveland,** and **Tokyo Quartets** and singers like Thomas Allen, Simon Estes, and Carol Vaness. The renowned **Poetry Center** has offered readings by every major poet in the world and a host of great prose writers as well since its founding in 1939, and the tradition continues with such writers as Kenneth Koch, Rachel Hadas, V.S. Naipaul, and Edwidge Danticat. The **American Jewish Theater** is sponsored by the organization, as are lectures, seminars, and workshops, and even unusual tours of the city. ◆ 1395 Lexington Ave (at E 92nd St). 427.6000 &

17 De Hirsch Residence $ Because of its affiliation with the well-known cultural and community center next door, this lodging tends to attract an interesting international crowd as compared to what you'd expect to find at a **Y.** Men and women are accommodated in 300 dorm-style rooms on separate floors with shared bathrooms and kitchens, or in simple private rooms for shorter stays (limited coed accommodations for couples do exist). Guests receive discounted admission to the cultural center's events. There is a three-night minimum stay requirement and a maximum stay of one year with special monthly rates; applications are needed in advance for long-term stay. ◆ 1395 Lexington Ave (at E 92nd St). 415.5650, 800/858.4692; fax 415.5578 &

18 120 and 122 East 92nd Street Because fire laws made the construction of wooden houses illegal in the 1860s, there are very few of them in Manhattan. This pair (and the frame houses at **160 East 92nd Street** and **128 East 93rd Street**), built in 1850, are a reminder of what this neighborhood was like in the mid–19th century. ◆ Between Lexington and Park Aves

19 Night Presence IV The intentionally rusty steel sculpture is by the late Louise Nevelson. The view down the avenue from here is picture-perfect. ◆ Park Ave and E 92nd St

Jacob Walton, the owner of the Gracie Mansion area in 1770, was loyal to the King of England. When the Revolution began, he built a tunnel leading to the East River so he could escape to a waiting ship if necessary. The tunnel wasn't discovered until 1913.

By the 1800s, Yorkville had become a haven for middle-class Germans, although the majority of Manhattan Germans still lived on the Lower East Side in an area around Tompkins Square Park called "Kleindeutschland." By the turn of the century, many German families were leaving the southern part of the island to resettle in Yorkville in order to avoid the waves of immigrants from Eastern Europe and Italy. The single greatest event that originally brought New York Germans to Yorkville was the General Slocum disaster of 1904. This excursion steamer was filled with passengers, mostly women and children from Kleindeutschland. It burned and sank in the East River, killing more than a thousand people. The men of these families, who had not been on board because they could not get away from work that day, found their empty homes unbearable. They moved to Yorkville to help themselves forget.

Jewish Museum

20 Wales Hotel $$ This small, moderately priced European-style hotel is ideally located if you plan to spend a lot of time on Museum Mile, shopping on Madison, or jogging every morning in **Central Park.** All of the 86 rooms have been tastefully renovated, but ask for a large, bright room or you may end up with the opposite. ♦ 1295 Madison Ave (between E 92nd and E 93rd Sts). 876.6000, 800/428.5252; fax 860.7000

20 Sarabeth's Kitchen ★★$$ Many a New Yorker has stood in line here for a weekend brunch of gourmet comfort foods: homemade waffles and pancakes crowned with fresh fruit; hot porridge; and warm-from-the-oven muffins (no reservations accepted for brunch). On your way out, pick up homemade brownies and cookies for a treat later. ♦ American ♦ M-F breakfast, lunch, and dinner; Sa-Su brunch and dinner. Reservations recommended for dinner. 1295 Madison Ave (between E 92nd and E 93rd Sts). 410.7335. Also at: 423 Amsterdam Ave (between W 80th and W 81st Sts). 496.6280; the Whitney Museum, Madison Ave (between E 74th and E 75th Sts). 570.3670

21 1107 Fifth Avenue Built in 1925 by **Rouse & Goldstone,** this was a perfectly ordinary apartment building except for a few anomalies on the facade—evidence of an era past. Marjorie Merriwether Post (at the time married to stockbroker E.F. Hutton)

purchased a 54-room apartment here. The Palladian window near the top center of the facade opened onto the main foyer of this apartment. ♦ At E 92nd St

22 Jewish Museum This renovated museum (illustrated above) holds the country's larges collection of Judaica. Besides permanent an rotating exhibits, it has classrooms, a delightful kosher cafe, and an attractive book and gift shop. Designed by **C.P.H. Gilbert** in 1908, the French Renaissance mansion was the home of financier Felix M. Warburg. Two annexes have been added: the first, in 1963, by **Samuel Glazer,** and the second, finished 1993, is by **Kevin Roche John Dinkeloo & Associates.** ♦ Admission; free Tu 5-8PM. M, W-Th, Su 11AM-5:45PM; Tu 11AM-8PM. 1109 Fifth Ave (at E 92nd St). 423.3230

23 Bistro du Nord ★★$$ This cozy little bistro with Parisian atmosphere serves haut versions of dishes you'd expect to find in thi kind of place—smoked salmon from **Petrossian** downtown, and baby rack of lamb with ratatouille. Steak *frites* and roasted codfish are among the more basic fare on the menu, but the high-quality preparation renders them extra special. ♦ French ♦ Daily lunch and dinner; Sa-Su brunch. Reservations recommended. 1312 Madison Ave (at E 93rd St). 289.0997

24 Corner Bookstore Featuring a wide selection of books, over a third of them for children, this store has an atmosphere conducive to browsing. Works on literature, art, and architecture are well represented. ♦ Daily. 1313 Madison Ave (at E 93rd St). 831.3554 ♿

24 Island ★$$$ You might expect to find this sort of place on the West Side—a room full of young people wolfing down good, if slightly overpriced, pasta and dishes from the grill, including chicken paillard and pepper-roasted tuna. ♦ Continental ♦ M-F lunch and dinner; Sa-Su brunch and dinner. Reservations recommended. 1305 Madison Ave (between E 92nd and E 93rd Sts). 996.1200 ♿

25 Smithers Alcoholism and Treatment Center This former home of showman Billy Rose was the last of the large, great mansions to be built in New York. It is in the delicate style of the 18th-century Scottish brothers **Lambert** and **Nicholas Adam,** who created some of the best houses in Edinburgh and London. This one, however, was designed in 1932 by **Walker & Gillette.** ♦ 56 E 93rd St (between Park and Madison Aves). 369.9566

25 60 East 93rd Street After Mrs. William K. Vanderbilt divorced her husband, she leased an apartment on Park Avenue, only to discover that her ex-husband had one in the same building. She broke the lease and had **John Russell Pope** build this beautiful French Renaissance mansion in 1930. ♦ Between Park and Madison Aves

26 Synod of Bishops of the Russian Orthodox Church Outside Russia Built in 1917 for Francis F. Palmer and renovated in 1928 by **Delano & Aldrich** for banker George F. Baker, this unusually large Georgian mansion has remained virtually unchanged, except for the introduction of exquisite Russian icons. A small cathedral occupies the former ballroom. ♦ 75 E 93rd St (between Park and Madison Aves). 534.1601

27 1185 Park Avenue Designed in 1929 by **Schwartz & Gross,** this is the only East Side version of the full-block courtyard apartment house typified by the **Belnord, Astor Court,** and **Apthorp** across town. The Gothicized entrance adds needed levity to the otherwise

traditional composition. ♦ Between E 93rd and E 94th Sts

28 Kitchen Arts & Letters Books on low-fat cooking, regional American cooking, cooking with flowers, and cooking on boats, along with more traditional cookbooks— approximately 9,000 in all, covering every aspect of food and wine—are displayed in this unique store. Paintings and photographs of food, and reproductions of tin biscuit boxes and other culinary memorabilia are on sale as well. ♦ M-Sa; summer hours are irregular, call first. 1435 Lexington Ave (between E 93rd and E 94th Sts). 876.5550

29 Squadron A and Eighth Regiment Armory/Hunter High School When the armory—a distinctly businesslike fortress built in 1895 by **John Rochester Thomas**—was on the verge of being torn down, community protest saved at least the facade on Madison Avenue. The school's architects, **Morris Ketchum Jr. & Associates,** did a marvelous task in 1971 of using it as both a backdrop to the playground and as a formal inspiration for the new building. ♦ Madison Ave (between E 94th and E 95th Sts)

30 Dollhouse Antics Here you'll find all the necessary Lilliputian accessories for dollhouse decorating: playpens, paint easels, overstuffed sofas, sterling silver knives and forks, copper pots and pans, and hundreds of other minute items. Houses can be custom-ordered and even wired for electricity. ♦ M-Sa; Tu-F July and August. 1343 Madison Ave (at E 94th St). 876.2288

31 International Center of Photography (ICP) Here you'll find the only museum in New York City—and perhaps the world— devoted entirely to photography. Designed in 1914 by **Delano & Aldrich,** the building is an ebullient and hospitable home for practitioners of the art, where the best and the brightest are given shows and encouragement. Every inch of the Georgian town house it occupies is used in the service of photography: four galleries for revolving shows; workshops and photo labs; a screening room; and a gallery for the permanent collection, which includes works by 20th-century photographers W. Eugene Smith and Henri Cartier-Bresson, among others. A gift shop sells books, catalogs, posters, and, of course, picture postcards. The center maintains additional gallery space at 1133 Sixth Avenue. ♦ Admission; voluntary contribution Tuesday 6-8PM. Tu 11AM-8PM; W-Su 11AM-6PM. 1130 Fifth Ave (at E 94th St). 860.1777. Also at: 1133 Sixth Ave (at W 43rd St). 768.4680 &

32 Islamic Center of New York A computer was used to ensure that this mosque faces Mecca, as Islamic law requires. Built in 1991 by **Skidmore, Owings & Merrill,** it is New York's first major mosque, and is intended as the spiritual home of the city's 400,000 Moslems and to serve diplomats from Islamic countries. ♦ 1711 Third Ave (at E 96th St). 722.5234

33 Russian Orthodox Cathedral of St. Nicholas Built in 1901-02, this church is unusual because, set above the polychromatic Victorian body, there are five onion domes. ♦ 15 E 97th St (between Madison and Fifth Aves). 289.1915

34 Mount Sinai Hospital The most recent construction project, completed in 1992 by **Pei Cobb Freed & Partners,** includes three hospital towers in one grand pavilion. These facilities replace 10 older buildings—some dating as far back as 1904 and all now demolished. Also of architectural interest is the **Annenburg Building,** a 436-foot Cor-Ten steel box that gets its color from a coating of rust that protects the steel from further corrosion. ♦ Bounded by Madison and Fifth Aves, and E 98th and E 101st Sts. 241.6500 &

35 New York Academy of Medicine Built in 1926 by **York & Sawyer,** this charming combination of Byzantine and Romanesque architecture contains one of the most important medical libraries in the country. The collection includes 4,000 cookbooks, a gift of Dr. Margaret Barclay Wilson, who believed that good nutrition was the key to good health. ♦ M-F. 2 E 103rd St (at Fifth Ave). 876.8200

36 Museum of the City of New York The story of New York City is told through historical paintings, Currier & Ives prints, period rooms, costumes, Duncan Phyfe furniture, Tiffany silver, ship models, and wonderful toys and dolls, all handsomely displayed in a roomy Neo-Georgian building.

The structure, red brick with white trim, designed by **Joseph Freedlander** in 1932, was built for the museum after it moved from **Gracie Mansion.** Puppet shows are staged for children, concerts and lectures for adults. ♦ Donation suggested. W-Sa; Su 1PM-5PM. 1220 Fifth Ave (between E 103rd and E 104th Sts). 534.1672

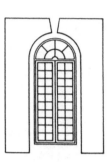

37 El Museo del Barrio This cultural center and showcase for the historic and contemporary arts of Latin America (especially Puerto Rico) began as a neighborhood museum in an East Harlem classroom. Video, painting, sculpture, photography, theater, and film are featured. Permanent collections include pre-Columbian art and hand-carved wooden saints, one of the region's most important art forms. ♦ Donation suggested. W-Su 11AM-5PM. 1230 Fifth Ave (between E 104th and E 105th Sts). 831.7272

New York is the only major city in the country that has an official residence for its mayor (Gracie Mansion).

"New York had all the iridescence of the beginning of the world."

F. Scott Fitzgerald, *The Crack-up*

"Gotham," a term for New York, was coined by Washington Irving in his satire *A History of New York* written in 1807. In it he also introduced the word "Knickerbockers" for New Yorkers. Also the author of *Rip Van Winkle* and *The Legend of Sleepy Hollow,* Irving's works garnered some of the first serious international recognition for American literature.

"If I live in New York, it is because I choose to live here. It is the city of total intensity, the city of the moment."

Diana Vreeland

Fred Ferretti
Columnist, *Gourmet* magazine

A bowl of fresh and thick barley soup with mushrooms in **Ratner's** dairy restaurant on the **Lower East Side.** With onion rolls.

The cooking, on any day, in the very best of the city's French restaurants—**Lutèce, La Réserve, and Montrachet.**

There is nothing better than a hot dog, boiled on a street cart, served with a lot of mustard and a bit of sauerkraut, and eaten while sitting with General Sherman at the entrance to **Central Park.**

Breakfast, lunch, or dinner, provided they have slabs of that rough country pâté, at **Café des Artistes,** just outside **Central Park's** western border.

The upper right-field stands of **Yankee Stadium** on a hot Sunday afternoon with a cold beer.

The best steak in the city at **Sparks** steak house, with a selection from what may well be New York's best list of American wines.

Corky Pollan
"Best Bets" Editor, *New York* magazine

The Frick Collection—this is probably on everyone's list of favorites, but where else in New York can you view some of the greatest works of art without having to jockey for position?

The **Seal Pond** at the renovated **Central Park Zoo.**

Lunch at the **Post House** for Old World elegance and service.

The **Conservatory Garden** any spring day.

The **Museum of the City of New York** for its enchanting collection of antique and vintage dolls, doll houses, and toys.

Lower **Broadway** on a Saturday or Sunday to catch the hottest and trendiest fashion looks.

Rizzoli, even when you're not looking for a book.

Drinks at the **Top of the Tower** at the **Beekman Tower Hotel** at sunset—one of the city's most romantic spots.

George Lang
Consultant and Author/Owner of Café des Artistes

Remi—I have rarely eaten Italian food as good as that served in this place, even in the Mother Country. Francesco Antonucci's dishes—like the roasted quail wrapped in bacon and served with warm lentil salad—remind me that a good chef is like a good fairy who dispenses happiness. Even the most knowledgeable Italian wine connoisseur will find surprises on the reasonably priced wine list.

Park Bistro—When I stepped through the lace-lined door into the packed, noisy 65-seat restaurant with its plain wood floors, banquettes, posters, and photos of France, it was almost like being in Paris.

One of my favorite dishes is lamb shank braised for seven hours with bits of dried apricots, currants, vegetables, and wild mushrooms.

Carmine's—I think Carmine's reflects the post-Reagan–era yearning for an America where the tables had four legs, the light source was not halogen, and the pasta of choice was spaghetti. My recommendations, based on serious soul- and stomach-searching: fried calamari, rigatoni with broccoli, or chicken Contadina.

Jimmy Breslin
Author/Former Columnist for *Newsday*

Sit at night on **Shore Road** and watch the **Queen Elizabeth II** slide under the **Verrazano-Narrows Bridge.** The ship at first seems to be part of another shore. Then you see it moving so quickly.

Coming from **Queens** to Manhattan at night over the **Queensboro Bridge.**

Living anywhere on the water in **Brooklyn Heights, Williamsburg, Long Island City,** or up on the hill in **Maspeth** and **Middle Village** in Queens and looking over at Manhattan. The people in Manhattan can only see Queens with its Pepsi-Cola signs. The smart people live in Queens and get a view that is unique in the world, even to photos, for the most sophisticated camera people don't know where these neighborhoods are.

The May Wave in the **Ramble** at **Central Park** and in the **Bird Sanctuary** at **Jamaica Bay.** The flocks come north again and on 10 May the same birds are in the same places. For decades the same type of bird is in the same spot, in the Ramble or at the bird sanctuary. So many types that even the best books cannot have them all cataloged. They are en route to Canada and as far as the North Pole.

Third Avenue and **East 42nd Street** and all the sidewalks in every direction at 5PM. Crowds of such size that it is hard to think that one place can hold them.

Florence Fabricant
Food Columnist/Cookbook Author

Manhattan from **96th Street** to **Wall Street**—walking, not driving as in most other cities.

Union Square—The bustle of the **Greenmarket** on Monday, Wednesday, Friday, and Saturday.

Oyster Bar and Restaurant—Sitting at the counter for oysters or pan roast.

Rainbow Room—The glamour! The view! The setting! An incomparable experience that's thoroughly New York.

Felissimo—Tea or a mid-afternoon snack in the lovely fifth-floor cafe—quiet, serene.

Madison Square Garden Center—New York **Knicks,** especially when they're winning.

Central Park

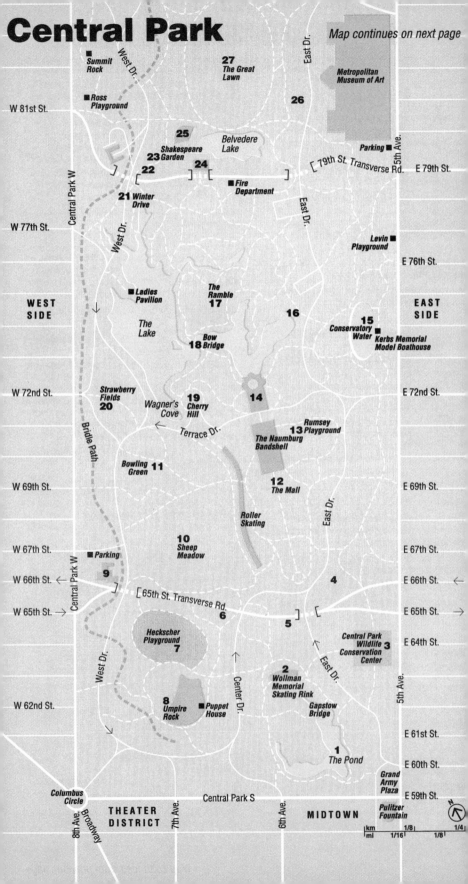

Map continues on next page

Summit Rock

Ross Playground

West Dr.

27 The Great Lawn

26

Metropolitan Museum of Art

25 Shakespeare Garden

Belvedere Lake

23
22
24

Parking

79th St. Transverse Rd.

5th Ave.

E 79th St.

W 81st St.

21 Winter Drive

Fire Department

East Dr.

Levin Playground

E 76th St.

W 77th St.

West Dr.

Central Park W

WEST SIDE

Ladies Pavilion

The Ramble
17

The Lake

16

EAST SIDE

Conservatory Water

15 Kerbs Memorial Model Boathouse

Bow Bridge
18

Strawberry Fields
20

Wagner's Cove

19 Cherry Hill

14

Rumsey Playground
13

E 72nd St.

W 72nd St.

Terrace Dr.

The Naumburg Bandshell

Bridle Path

Bowling Green
11

12 The Mall

E 69th St.

W 69th St.

Roller Skating

10 Sheep Meadow

East Dr.

Parking

9

4

E 67th St.

W 67th St.

Central Park W

65th St. Transverse Rd.
6

5

E 66th St.

W 66th St.

E 65th St.

W 65th St.

Heckscher Playground
7

Central Park Wildlife Conservation Center
3

E 64th St.

2 Wollman Memorial Skating Rink

West Dr.

Center Dr.

East Dr.

5th Ave.

W 62nd St.

8 Umpire Rock

Puppet House

Gapstow Bridge

E 61st St.

1 The Pond

E 60th St.

Columbus Circle

Grand Army Plaza

E 59th St.

8th Ave.

Broadway

THEATER DISTRICT

7th Ave.

Central Park S

6th Ave.

MIDTOWN

Pulitzer Fountain

N

km
ml

1/16

1/8

1/8

1/4

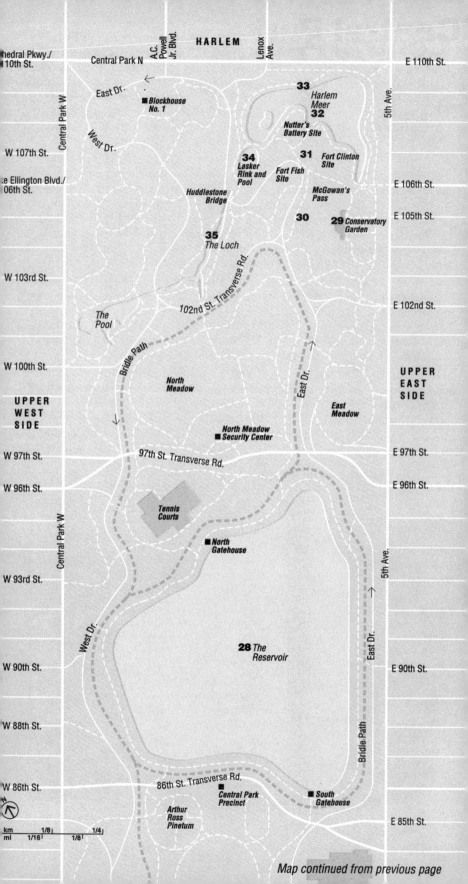

HARLEM

Central Park N

A.C. Powell Jr. Blvd.

Lenox Ave.

E 110th St.

hedral Pkwy./
10th St.

East Dr.

■ Blockhouse No. 1

West Dr.

33

Harlem Meer

32

Nutter's Battery Site

5th Ave.

W 107th St.

Central Park W

34
Lasker Rink and Pool

Fort Fish Site

31 Fort Clinton Site

e Ellington Blvd./
06th St.

Huddlestone Bridge

McGowan's Pass

E 106th St.

E 105th St.

30

29 Conservatory Garden

35
The Loch

102nd St. Transverse Rd.

W 103rd St.

The Pool

E 102nd St.

W 100th St.

Bridle Path

North Meadow

East Dr.

East Meadow

UPPER EAST SIDE

UPPER WEST SIDE

North Meadow
■ Security Center

W 97th St.

97th St. Transverse Rd.

E 97th St.

W 96th St.

E 96th St.

Tennis Courts

Central Park W

■ North Gatehouse

W 93rd St.

5th Ave.

28 The Reservoir

Bridle Path

East Dr.

W 90th St.

West Dr.

E 90th St.

W 88th St.

W 86th St.

86th St. Transverse Rd.

Central Park Precinct

■ South Gatehouse

E 85th St.

Arthur Ross Pinetum

km   1/8   1/4
mi   1/16   1/8

Map continued from previous page

Central Park

"This different and many smiling presence" is how Henry James once referred to **Central Park**, bounded by **Fifth Avenue, Central Park West, Central Park South,** and **Central Park North.** The completely man-made park, unlike any other urban park in the United States, certainly elicits smiles from the more than 14 million people who wander through it every year. It is obviously an equally pleasing place to sky-borne creatures: nearly 250 species of birds are sighted here, with the best birding at **The Ramble.**

Not long after work began to clear the site on 12 August 1857, a friend suggested to journalist Frederick Law Olmsted, whose avocation was landscaping, that he should compete for the job of superintendent of the new **Central Park.** He found backers in newspaper editors Horace Greeley and William Cullen Bryant, and when writer Washington Irving added his name to the list, Olmsted got the job. Later that same year, the Parks Commission announced a design competition for the new park, and Olmsted's friend, architect **Calvert Vaux**, suggested they join forces.

On 28 April 1858, after Olmsted and **Vaux** submitted what they called their "Greensward" plan, Olmsted wrote: "Every foot of the Park's surface, every tree and bush, as well as every arch, roadway, and walk, has been placed where it is with a purpose." In the years since, buildings and monuments have been added, and playgrounds, roads, even parking lots have been constructed. But the original purpose is still well served.

The groundswell of support for the park had begun in 1844 when William Cullen Bryant warned that commerce was devouring Manhattan inch by inch. He pointed out that there were still unoccupied parts of the island, but that "while we are discussing the subject, the advancing population of the city is sweeping over them and covering them from our reach." In 1853, the

The Dairy

MICHAEL STORRINGS

252

tate legislature authorized the city to buy the larger and much more central present site. The price tag was $5 million.

The land was no bargain. A swampy pesthole filled with pig farms and squatters' shacks, it was used as a garbage dump and served as a prime location for bone-boiling plants. But Olmsted succeeded in turning it into what New Yorkers today proudly call the "lungs of the city."

Actual work began in 1857, and by the time the park was considered finished 16 years later, nearly five million cubic yards of stone and dirt had been rearranged and almost five million trees planted. Before construction started, 42 species of trees grew on the site; by the time it was completed, 402 kinds of deciduous trees thrived, along with 230 species of evergreens and 815 varieties of shrubs. There were also 58 miles of pedestrian walks, 6.5 miles of roads, and a bridle path 4.5 miles long. A reservoir was created in 1862, covering 106 acres, and a sprawling lake occupied another 22 acres. A series of smaller lakes and ponds was also created and some 62 miles of pipe installed to carry off unwanted water.

Fortunately, **Central Park** is alive and well in spite of countless schemes to "improve" it. In 1918, someone in all seriousness suggested digging trenches in the **North Meadow** to give people an idea of what the doughboys were going through "over there." A year later, plans were submitted for an airport near the sheepfold that is now **Tavern on the Green.** There have been several proposals to use some of the space for housing projects, and plans for underground parking garages have been coming and going since the 1920s. Not only have the **Parks Department** and the **Central Park Conservancy** resisted encroachment, they've been working for a decade or more to restore the park to what it once was. The result is that one of the best things about New York is getting better every day.

Note: Although city officials claim that the park is safer due to increased patrol efforts, it is wise to avoid walking or jogging here at night; and even during daylight hours, be cautious, and don't wander into densely wooded areas.

---

1 The Pond A shot of the reflection of the nearby buildings, especially **The Plaza Hotel,** in this crescent-shaped haven for ducks and other waterfowl may be among the best pictures you'll take home. The view is from the Gapstow Bridge, which crosses the northern end of the pond. The water pocket was created to reflect the rocks in what is now a bird sanctuary on its western shore, as well as a favorite lunch spot for nearby office workers. From the time the park opened until 1924, swan boats like the ones still used in the Boston Garden dodged real swans here. The Pond was reduced to about half of its original size in 1951 when the **Wollman Memorial Skating Rink** was built. ♦ East Dr (between Grand Army Plaza and 65th St Transverse Rd)

2 Wollman Memorial Skating Rink The original rink lasted less than 30 years, and when the city attempted to rebuild it, the project became mired in so much red tape that it began to look as though it might take another 30 years to replace it. In 1986, real estate and casino tycoon Donald Trump took it upon himself to do the job—without the regulations the city imposes on itself—and finished it in record time. Ice-skating is generally from October to April, with roller-skating at other times. ♦ Admission; skate rental. M 10AM-5PM; Tu-Th, Su 10AM-9:30PM (classes offered W-Th 6-7:30PM); F-Sa 10AM-11PM. East Dr (between Grand Army Plaza and 65th St Transverse Rd). 396.1010

3 The Arsenal The 10 acres of land around this building were a park before **Central Park** was even a dream. Designed by **Martin E. Thompson** and completed in 1851, its original use as a storehouse for arms and ammunition accounts for the iconography of cannons and rifles around the Fifth Avenue entrance. It became the citywide headquarters of the **Parks and Recreation Department** in 1934, following use as a police precinct, a weather bureau, a menagerie, and the first home of the **American Museum of Natural History.** A third-floor gallery contains, among other exhibits, the original Greensward plan, whose results are all around you. ♦ Free. M-F. Fifth Ave (between Grand Army Plaza and 65th St Transverse Rd). 360.8141 ♿

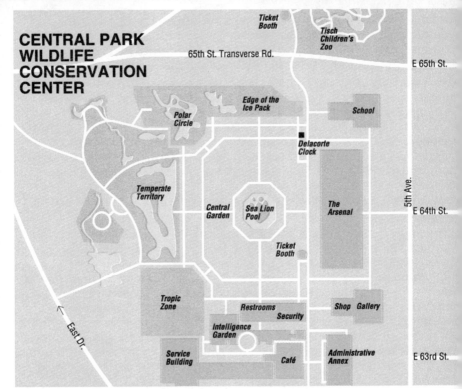

CENTRAL PARK
WILDLIFE
CONSERVATION
CENTER

Ticket Booth

Tisch Children's Zoo

65th St. Transverse Rd.

E 65th St.

Edge of the Ice Pack

School

Polar Circle

Delacorte Clock

Temperate Territory

Central Garden

Sea Lion Pool

The Arsenal

5th Ave.

E 64th St.

Ticket Booth

Tropic Zone

Restrooms

Security

Shop Gallery

East Dr.

Intelligence Garden

Service Building

Café

Administrative Annex

E 63rd St.

3 Central Park Wildlife Conservation Center (Central Park Zoo) This 5.5-acre complex is home to some 450 animals (not counting the 100,000 leaf-cutter ants) representing more than a hundred species. Opened a decade ago at the cost of $35 million, the zoo it replaced had elephants and other animals too large for such cramped quarters; they were given to other zoos with more hospitable facilities. The bears and sea lions have been given more natural homes here, and penguins cavort under a simulated ice pack in a pool with glass walls that allow you to watch their underwater antics. Monkeys swing in trees in a reproduction of an African environment, bats fly through a naturalistic cave, and crocodilians swim in the most comfortable swamp north of the Okefenokee. The center encompasses three climatic zones: tropical, temperate, and polar. In 1998 a new division geared to children 6 and under opened, the **Tisch Children's Zoo,** featuring naturalistic interactive animal habitats and a petting zoo, with lots of clambering opportunities and frequent musical and theatrical performances. A cafeteria and a gift shop at the southern entranceway are accessible without entering the grounds. The main zoo was designed by **Kevin Roche John Dinkeloo & Associates.** ♦ Admission. M-F 10AM-5PM; Sa-Su 10:30AM-5:30PM. Fifth Ave (between Grand Army Plaza and 65th St Transverse Rd). 861.6030

4 Balto One of the most popular monuments in the park, this 1925 bronze portrait by Frederick G.R. Roth represents the husky who led his team of dogs from Anchorage to Nome (a thousand miles) to deliver serum to stem a diphtheria epidemic. ♦ East Dr (just north of 65th St Transverse Rd)

5 The Dairy When this Gothic building (illustrated on page 252) was constructed in 1870, fresh milk was a relative luxury. The park's planners, following European models, added milkmaids and a herd of cows to enhance the sylvan setting and to provide children with a healthy treat. After the turn of the century, the cows were sent off to the country, the milkmaids retired, and the building became a storehouse. In 1981, it was restored and its wooden porch replaced and painted in Victorian colors. It is now the park's central **Visitors' Center,** with an information desk and exhibitions. Weekend walking tours led by the Urban Park Rangers, usually leave from here or from the **Dana Discovery Center.** ♦ Visitors' Center: Tu-Th, Sa-Su 11AM-5PM; F 1PM-5PM. 65th St Transverse Rd (between East and Center Drs). Urban Park Rangers (tour information) 427.4040

6 The Carousel There has been a merry-go-round here since 1871. The original was powered by real horses that walked a treadmill in an underground pit. The present one, built in 1908 at Coney Island, was moved here in

1951. Its 58 horses were hand-carved by Stein & Goldstein, considered the best woodcarvers of their day. Don't just stand there—climb up and go for the ride of your life. ◆ Nominal admission. Daily. 65th St Transverse Rd and Center Dr. 879.0244

7 Heckscher Playground The original park plan didn't include sports facilities, but this was one of three loosely connected areas for children who had secured the proper permits to play games like baseball and croquet. In the 1920s, adults wanted to get into the game and pressured the city into building them five softball diamonds with backstops and bleachers. At about the same time, the former meadow was converted into an asphalt-covered playground to give the kids something to do while the adults were running bases. It was the first formal playground in the park. The softball fields are available by permit only, and are used by teams from corporations, Broadway shows, and other groups. ◆ Call 794.6567 to see who's playing today; for a permit for your own team, call 397.3100. Off West Dr (between Center Dr and 65th St Transverse Rd)

8 Umpire Rock Central Park is laced with rocky outcrops like this one, left behind some 20,000 years ago by the Laurentian Glacier. The boulder on top is called an erratic, and was carried down with the ice from the Far North. The tracks on the face of the rock, called striations, were formed by the scraping of large stones embedded in the glacier as it moved southeast across Manhattan. Most of the rocky outcrops in the park are a type of mica-rich shale called Manhattan schist. About 400 million years ago, they formed the base of a mountain chain about as high as the present-day Rocky Mountains. ◆ Just south of Heckscher Playground

9 Tavern on the Green ★★★$$$$ Designed by **Jacob Wrey Mould**, the building housing this lovely dining spot was erected in 1870 by Boss Tweed and his corrupt Tammany Hall city government over the strenuous objection of Frederick Law Olmsted, landscape architect and designer of **Central Park.** Originally called the **Sheepfold**, the structure housed the herd of Southdown sheep that grazed in Central Park until 1934, when they were exiled to **Prospect Park** in Brooklyn. The **Sheepfold** then became a restaurant, and was completely redesigned in 1976 under the supervision of super-restaurateur Warner LeRoy. The outdoor garden is a wonderful place to spend a summer evening and is spectacularly lit by twinkling lights in the trees from November through May. But any time of year the **Crystal Room,** dripping with chandeliers, is an unforgettable experience, especially for Sunday brunch. Try the chef's warm house-smoked salmon with mushroom-and-potato salad in a chive aioli, grilled black

Angus fillet of beef with wild mushrooms in a red-wine sauce, grilled Port porterhouse with bacon and cabbage mashed potatoes, or the Moroccan-style barbecued salmon on savoy cabbage. Desserts are terrific—especially the napoleon filled with ginger crème brûlée. There's an extensive wine list. ◆ American ◆ M-F lunch and dinner; Sa-Su brunch and dinner. Reservations required. Central Park W (at 65th St Transverse Rd). 873.3200

10 Sheep Meadow The original park design called for a meadow here to enhance the view from the gentle hill to the north. The 15-acre hill was resodded in 1980 after concerts and other crowd-pleasing events had reduced it to hardpan. On the first warm day of the year, New Yorkers flock here for picnicking, sunbathing, and quiet recreation. The view from the hill with the city skyline in the background is in some ways more breathtaking than the park's architects ever envisioned. ◆ 1 April–30 Oct: Tu-F, Su 11AM-5PM; Sa 1-5PM. Closed November through April unless there are at least six inches of snow. West Dr (between 65th St Transverse Rd and Terrace Dr)

11 Bowling Green Lawn bowling and croquet were first played here in the 1920s. The folks who play today take their games very seriously, which explains why the greens are so well maintained. You can get a permit to join them by calling 360.8133. ◆ Games start at 1PM and 1:30PM Tu-Sa 1 May–1 Nov. West Dr (between 65th St Transverse Rd and Terrace Dr)

If you get lost in the park, find the nearest lamppost. The first two digits of the number on the post signify the nearest numbered (east-west) street.

Particularly evident from Central Park are a flurry of twin-towered buildings on Central Park West. Landmark luxury apartment complexes that are a favorite element in New York City's distinctive skyline, they were built from 1929 to 1931 during the peak of the Art Deco period when zoning laws allowed taller buildings if setbacks and towers were used. That period's prolific architect, the eminent Emery Roth, designed the San Remo at 145 Central Park West as well as the Eldorado at 300 Central Park West and Oliver Cromwell at West 72nd Street. The Art Deco gem at 55 Central Park West was featured in the film *Ghostbusters.*

Restaurants/Clubs: Red **Hotels:** Blue
Shops/ Outdoors: Green **Sights/Culture:** Black

12 The Mall This formal promenade was largely the work of Ignaz Anton Pilat, a plant expert who worked with Olmsted and **Vaux** on the overall design of the park. He deviated from the romantic naturalism of the plan by planting a double row of elm trees along the length of the promenade, but in the process created a reminder of what country roads and New England villages were like a century ago. The walkway was placed on a northwest angle to provide a sightline directly to a high outcropping above 79th Street known as **Vista Rock.** Vaux designed a miniature castle for the top of the rock to create an impression of greater distance. The bandshell at the north end was designed in 1923 by **William G. Tachau** and donated by Elkan Naumburg, who presented concerts here for many years. It replaced an 1862 cast-iron bandstand that included a sky-blue cupola dotted with gold-leaf stars. The current bandshell, which now sits vacant, was used for *Summer Stage* concerts and special events until recently; they're now held at **Rumsey Field** near the playground. ♦ East and Center Drs

13 Rumsey Playground A 1938 sculpture of *Mother Goose* by Frederick G.R. Roth and Walter Beretta provides a welcome to this walk-up playground with a wisteria-covered pergola at its western edge. Its location at the top of a hill and a less-than-inviting design make it unattractive to parents of small children. A recent decline in the number of children living near the park has reduced the use of all the park's playgrounds. This one is used primarily as an athletic field for nearby private schools. It was built on the site of the **Central Park Casino,** a cottage originally designed as a ladies' house of refreshment. In the 1920s, it was turned into a restaurant, designed by **Joseph Urban,** which became the most popular place in town for the likes of Gentleman Jimmy Walker, whose basic rule of life was that the only real sin was to go to bed on the same day that you got up. ♦ East Dr (between Center and Terrace Drs)

14 Bethesda Terrace Located between the Lake and the Mall, this terrace has always been considered the heart of **Central Park.** It was named for a pool in Jerusalem that the Gospel of St. John says was given healing powers by the annual visitation of an angel. The *Angel of the Waters,* Emma Stebbins's statue on top of the magnificent fountain (shown at right), re-creates the event. It was unveiled in 1873, but the terrace itself had opened in 1861. The basic design is the work of **Calvert Vaux.** But the arcade ceiling, tile floors, and elaborate friezes and other ornamentation are by **Jacob Wrey Mould,** whose early background was in Islamic architecture—which explains why the terrace is so much like a courtyard in a Spanish palace. ♦ Terrace Dr (between East and West Drs)

15 Conservatory Water The name for this pond comes from a conservatory that was never built. The space is occupied by the **Kerbs Memorial Model Boathouse,** designed by **Aymar Embury II** in 1954. It houses model yachts that race on the pond every Saturday in the summer. At the north end is José de Creeft's fanciful *Alice in Wonderland* group, given to the park in 1960 by publisher George Delacorte. At the western edge is George Lober's 1956 bronze statue of *Hans Christian Andersen,* a gift of the Danish people. During the summer, a storyteller appears here every Saturday at 11AM. A small snack bar with outdoor tables overlooks the water on the east side. ♦ Off Fifth Ave (between Terrace Dr and 79th St Transverse Rd)

16 Loeb Boathouse Besides rowboat and bicycle rentals, there is also an authentic Venetian gondola that holds six people. The Venetians gave a gondola to the park in 1862, but for lack of a gondolier, it rotted away. This one, a more recent gift, includes the services of an expert to pole it around the Lake. Bicycle

Bethesda Fountain

MICHAEL STORRINGS

rentals are also available (call 861.4137 for information). ♦ Fee for gondola rides. Rowboat rentals: Daily. Gondola rides: M-F 5PM-10PM; Sa-Su 3PM-10PM Mar-Oct. Reservations required. East Dr (between Terrace Dr and 79th St Transverse Rd). 517.2233

Within Loeb Boathouse:

Park View at the Boathouse ★★$$
This landmark restaurant has at long last been renovated and its menu updated. Thanks to chef John Villa there's now food to accompany the fantastic view of **Central Park**'s boating pond that goes well beyond the merely edible. Notable selections from the new Asian-influenced American menu include a tasty Indian-spiced salmon *tartare* and succulent Gulf shrimp wrapped in rice paper. A few technical improvements mean that the restaurant is now open year-round. After 7PM, a trolley at 72nd Street and Fifth Avenue will take you right to the restaurant. ♦ American ♦ W-F dinner; Sa brunch and dinner; Su brunch. 517.2233

17 The Ramble This 37-acre wooded section of the park was conceived as a wild garden preserve for native plants and was also intended as a foreground for **Vista Rock** as viewed from **The Mall**. The garden has seen better days, but it is still a wild place, with a brook meandering through and tumbling over several small waterfalls, and it's a perfect place for bird watching. One of the winding paths led to a man-made cave at the edge of the Lake, but the cave was walled up in the 1920s. There are few better places to get away from it all. Because this area can be relatively deserted, it may be best to share with a friend. ♦ Off East Dr (between Terrace Dr and 79th St Transverse Rd)

18 Bow Bridge **Calvert Vaux** designed most of the park's bridges, and no two are alike. This one, crossing the narrowest part of the Lake, is considered one of the most beautiful. When the cast-iron bridge was put in place, it was supposedly set on cannonballs to allow for expansion caused by temperature changes. But when it was restored in 1974, no cannonballs were found. ♦ The Lake (between Cherry Hill and the Ramble)

19 Cherry Hill Designed as a vantage point with a view of the Mall, the Lake, Bethesda Terrace, and the Ramble, this spot also provided a turnaround for carriages and a fountain for watering the horses. It was converted into a parking lot in 1934 but restored with 8,500 new trees and shrubs and 23,000 square feet of new sod in 1981. ♦ Terrace Dr (between East and West Drs)

20 Strawberry Fields This teardrop-shaped memorial grove has recently undergone some rehabilitation with funds provided by Yoko Ono in memory of her late husband, John Lennon. The former Beatle was assassinated in front of the **Dakota** apartment house, which overlooks this tranquil spot. You'll find many fans around the *Imagine* centerpiece mosaic. ♦ West Dr (at Terrace Dr)

21 Winter Drive Evergreens were originally planted in all parts of the park to provide color in the winter months, but the heaviest concentration is here, where 19th-century gay blades entered the park for ice-skating. When the ice on the Lake was hard enough, a red ball was hoisted on the flagpole above **Belvedere Castle,** and horsecars on Broadway carried the message downtown by displaying special flags. The parks commissioners estimated that as many as 80,000 people a day crowded the 20-acre frozen lake during the 1850s. The **Arthur Ross Pinetum,** added in 1971 at the north end of the **Great Lawn,** enhances the original plantings with unusual species of conifers from all over the world. ♦ West Dr (between Terrace Dr and 79th St Transverse Rd)

22 Swedish Cottage Moved here from Philadelphia after the 1876 Centennial Exposition, this building was used as a comfort station until Swedish-Americans mounted a protest. After many years, it was converted into a marionette theater in 1973. ♦ Admission. Call for show times. Reservations required. 79th St Transverse Rd and West Dr. 988.9093

23 Shakespeare Garden In this lovely secluded garden, you'll find a series of pathways, pools, and cascades among trees and plants mentioned in the works of William Shakespeare. ♦ West Dr (between 79th St Transverse and 86th St Transverse Rds)

There are 22 playgrounds, 26 ball fields, and 30 tennis courts in Central Park.

"In its influence as an educator, as a place of agreeable resort, as a source of scientific interest, and in its effect upon the health, happiness, and comfort of our people may be found its chief value."

Frederick Law Olmsted, *Report of the Commissioners of Central Park, 1870*

Before construction on Central Park began in 1856, Fifth Avenue from 59th to 120th streets was called "Squatters' Sovereignty," where poor people lived in shacks made of wooden planks and flattened tin cans. When construction on the park started, the poor were evicted and soon the area housed the city's richest and most powerful people.

Belvedere Castle

24 Belvedere Castle A scaled-down version of a Scottish castle (pictured above) was placed here to become part of the view. Its interior is just as impressive. The building houses a National Weather Service station and the **Central Park Learning Center.** ♦ W-Su 11AM-4PM. 79th St Transverse Rd (between East and West Drs). 772.0210

25 Delacorte Theatre A 1960 addition to the park provides a modern home for the late Joseph Papp's **New York Shakespeare Festival.** Obtaining one of the 2,000 tickets (which are given out to the general public only on the day of the performance) is a summer ritual that begins when would-be audience members queue up for tickets distributed at 1PM for that evening's performance. The line starts to form early, but with good friends and a picnic, it can be a pleasant experience. Tickets can also be picked up at the **Public Theater** (425 Lafayette St, between E Fourth St and Astor Pl) from 1-3PM only, on the day of the performance. Two plays, at least one of them by Shakespeare, are chosen for performance each summer. ♦ Free performances. Tu-Su at 8PM late June–early Sept. West Dr (between 79th St Transverse and 86th St Transverse Rds). 861.7277 &

26 Cleopatra's Needle The Khedive of Egypt gave this obelisk to New York in 1881 and presented its mate to Queen Victoria, who had it placed on the Thames Embankment in London. When the 200-ton granite shaft was delivered to New York, it was placed in a special cradle and rolled here from the Hudson River on cannonballs. Because it had stood for many centuries in front of a temple once believed to have been built by Cleopatra,

New Yorkers immediately dubbed it Cleopatra's Needle. It was, however, built by Egypt's King Thotmes III in 1600 BC. The hieroglyphics on its sides had survived for 3,500 years, but New York's air pollution has rendered them unreadable in fewer than a hundred. Movie producer Cecil B. De Mille thoughtfully provided plaques translating the tales they told of Thotmes III, Rameses II, and Osorkon I. ♦ East Dr (between 79th St Transverse and 86th St Transverse Rds)

27 The Great Lawn The largest field in the park was formerly a rectangular reservoir that was drained just in time to provide a location for a Depression-inspired collection of squatters' shacks known as a Hooverville. By 1936 it was cleared again, and the oval-shaped lawn, with Belvedere Lake at the south end and two playgrounds to the north, was fenced off to create a cooling patch of green. It didn't stay that way long. It was surrounded by ball fields with their backstops where the lawn was, and overuse almost completely eliminated the grass. In 1980, Elton John drew 300,000 people here for a concert; Simon & Garfunkel attracted 500,000 a year later; in 1982, an antinuclear rally brought out 750,000; in 1993, Pavarotti sang before an audience of 500,000; and in 1995 Disney's animated film *Pocahontas* was given its premiere here. The lawn recently underwent a much-needed restoration, which has made it a verdant space once more. As it has in the past, the **New York Philharmonic** and the **Metropolitan Opera** will continue to give several free performances here every summer, each of which attracts about 100,000 people who bring blankets and picnic dinners. ♦ Bounded by East and West Drs, and 79th St Transverse and 86th St Transverse Rds

28 **The Reservoir** Designed as part of the Croton Water System in 1862, this billion-gallon reservoir actively fed the city's thirst until 1994 when it was pulled out of service. Covering nearly 107 acres, it is better known for the soft-surface track that encircles it, providing a perfect amenity for serious runners—one of whom was the late Jacqueline Kennedy Onassis, after whom the reservoir has been unofficially renamed. Once around is 1.58 miles. ♦ Bounded by East and West Drs, and 86th St Transverse and 97th St Transverse Rds

29 **Conservatory Garden** A park nursery was replaced in 1899 by a glass conservatory, which was removed in 1934 to create this series of three formal gardens, one of which is planted with seasonal flowers, another with perennials, and a third with grass surrounded by yew hedges and flowering trees and featuring a wisteria-covered pergola. Each is enhanced by a fountain. ♦ Free. Daily 8AM-dusk. Fifth Ave (between 102nd St Transverse Rd and Central Park N). 860.1382

30 **The Mount** When General Washington's army was retreating through Manhattan in 1776, the British were held at bay here from a small fortress overlooking McGowan's Pass. **The Mount** was named for a tavern on top of the hill, which in 1846 became, of all things, a convent. The sisters moved out when the park was created, and the building was converted back into a tavern. It was one of the city's better restaurants in the late 19th century, but was demolished on orders of Mayor John Purroy Mitchel in 1917. ♦ East Dr (between 102nd St Transverse Rd and West Dr)

31 **The Forts** During the War of 1812, three forts were built on the future park site to fend off an anticipated British attack. None was actually used, but their now-barren sites are marked with plaques and are waiting for a history buff to re-create them. A little farther to the north, an 1814 blockhouse, the oldest structure in the park, is also waiting for renovation. These days, its thick walls, laced with gunports, look into groves of trees. But when they were placed there, men inside

could spot an enemy miles away. None ever came, and few people climb the hill to see the site today. ♦ East Dr (between 102nd St Transverse Rd and West Dr)

32 **Harlem Meer** The park's original northern boundary was at 106th Street until 1863, when it was extended another four blocks northward, at which time this 11-acre lake was created. It uses the Dutch word for lake, although it hardly qualified as a lake or a meer for a long time. In 1941, the **Parks Department** altered its shoreline to eliminate the natural coves and inlets the original designers had placed there, and the whole thing was rimmed and lined with concrete. Fortunately, this beautiful corner of the park, once desperately in need of loving care, has now been restored to its natural appearance. With a new playground just opened, work is also underway to rebuild the boathouse, create a discovery center for children, and build an esplanade for small concerts at Central Park North. ♦ Central Park N and Fifth Ave

33 **Charles A. Dana Discovery Center** This is the newest of the park's visitors' centers, opened in 1993, with exhibits and programs on environmental issues for all ages. Some of the park tours led by the Urban Park Rangers leave from here. ♦ Tu-Su. Central Park N (at Harlem Meer). 860.1370 ♿

34 **Lasker Rink and Pool** Built in 1964, this shallow swimming pool near the edge of the park doubles as an ice-skating rink from Thanksgiving through March. It gets considerably less traffic than the downtown **Wollman Rink,** even though it costs less to use. It was built at the mouth of the stream that feeds Harlem Meer. ♦ Pool: Daily 11AM-7PM July-Sept. Ice-skating: M-Th, Su 10AM-9:30PM; F-Sa 10AM-11PM Thanksgiving-Mar. East Dr (between 102nd St Transverse Rd and West Dr). 534.7639

35 **The Loch** This natural pond, undisturbed by the original designers, has been left alone to the point of being silted almost out of existence. A brook leading from the north end forms a small waterfall near the Huddleston Bridge, which carries East Drive over it. ♦ Off East Dr (between 102nd St Transverse Rd and West Dr)

West Side

Bisected by Broadway and its casual jumble of bookstores, delis, theaters, and restaurants, Manhattan's West Side is more relaxed and laid-back than its fashionable East Side counterpart across **Central Park**. The area was first settled by Eastern European Jews and other immigrants from the Lower East Side in the early part of the century. Today this vibrant neighborhood, bounded by **Central Park West**, the **Hudson River**, and **West 59th** and **West 86th Streets**, is characterized by in-line skaters zipping past patrons at sidewalk cafes, young mothers pushing baby carriages, and well-dressed crowds pouring in and out of the concert halls and restaurants. Highlights include **Lincoln Center for the Performing Arts**, the ever-changing mix of clothing stores and sidewalk

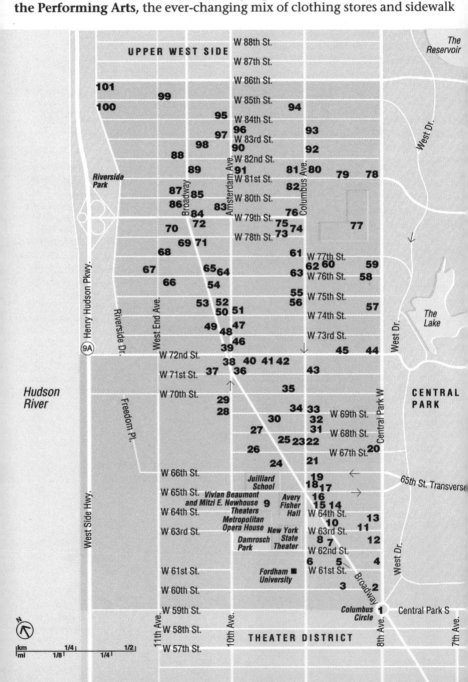

cafes on **Columbus Avenue** and **Broadway**, and numerous architecturally noteworthy buildings.

Riverside Drive, along the neighborhood's western edge, was originally a street of upper-middle-class town houses, and although it had spectacular river views, it lacked the cachet of Fifth Avenue, where "the 400" (Mrs. William Astor's most intimate circle, so called because her home could only accommodate that number) were erecting their palazzi and châteaux. Riverside Drive only had a few grand mansions, like the one Charles Schwab built in 1906 at **West 73rd Street** (now an apartment house). Many of the private homes were replaced in the 1920s by the 15-story apartment buildings of today, their faces sometimes curving to follow the shape of the street.

Some argue that **Central Park West**, skirting the neighborhood's eastern edge, is finer than Fifth Avenue, because the buildings are more distinguished and the street wider. Most of the buildings on Central Park West were originally built as apartments rather than houses, including the wonderfully chateaulike **Dakota** (the city's first luxury apartment house, built in 1884 by the same architect who would later design the **Plaza Hotel**) at **West 72nd Street**, and the Art Deco **Century** (built in 1931) at 25 Central Park West. A number of twin-towered Art-Deco apartment buildings, most notably the **San Remo** and **Eldorado**, make Central Park West's skyline unique.

The park blocks—the numbered streets between Central Park West and Columbus Avenue—contain interesting collections of brownstones and apartments. Particularly noteworthy are the six buildings with artists' studios on **West 67th Street**, including the **Hotel des Artistes** (site of the **Café des Artistes**), whose plush apartments have been home to many well-known artists, actors, and writers, among them Isadora Duncan, Noel Coward, and Fannie Hurst.

West End Avenue—once lined with Romanesque and Queen Anne–style row houses and now with apartment houses—was supposed to be the West Side's commercial street, while Broadway was slated to be the residential area; hence the avenue's generous width and the mall in the center. But the reverse happened, and Broadway became—and has remained—the neighborhood's "Main Street."

---

1 **Columbus Circle** This traffic circle (today a real runaround for pedestrians, though less daunting since a recent rerouting of the cars) was built after the commissioners of Central Park were empowered to develop the West Side from West 55th to West 155th Streets in 1887. Around the edges are the Moorish white block of the **New York City Department of Cultural Affairs,** designed in 1962 by **Edward Durell Stone** and originally built by A&P heir Huntington Hartford for his abortive **Gallery of Modern Art;** and the grayish lump of the **Coliseum,** designed in 1956 by **Leon & Lionel Levy**—all in all a dismal landscape in a difficult space that planners have been trying to solve for years. ♦ Central Park S and Central Park W

2 **Trump International Hotel & Tower** $$$$ Developer Donald Trump combined forces with noted architects **Philip Johnson** and **Costas Kondylis** to transform the former **Gulf + Western Building** into a gleaming combination of hotel and residential condominiums. The hotel section is relatively small—there are 168 rooms and suites, which occupy the first 17 floors. Lavish condos fill the rest of the skyscraper. Hotel accommodations feature a modern decor of wood accents, earthy tones of beige and brown, plush furnishings, marble bath, and a galley kitchen complete with appliances. In addition, there's a **Plus-One** health club on premises. ♦ 1 Central Park W (at Columbus Cir). 299.1000; fax 299.1150 ♿

Within the Trump International Hotel & Tower:

Jean Georges ★★★★$$$$ An elegant Adam Tihany–designed room is the setting for another of superchef Jean-Georges Vongerichten's ventures. Unlike his **Vong** and JoJo restaurants, this place is smallish (only 70 seats); it boasts a luxurious setting with marble and terrazzo floors with earthy shades of nutmeg, sage, and gray throughout. One factor remains constant: The food is uniquely prepared and beautifully presented. Look for such signature dishes as spit-roasted lobster with chanterelles and sautéed shrimp with orange zest and wild yarrow. Also, don't miss the broiled squab, rack of lamb, or Arctic char with potatoes and horseradish cream. Delicious endings include roasted pear spiked with vanilla beans and roasted apricot tart. There's an adjoining cafe, and in warm weather ask to sit on the terrace. ♦ French ♦ Main room: M-Sa dinner. Cafe: daily breakfast, lunch, and dinner. 299.3900

3 Gabriel's ★★$$$ Come here for arguably the best homemade pasta, risotto, grilled dishes, and desserts in the Lincoln Center area. Among the offerings are *pappardelle* (wide pasta) with braised artichokes and mint; wood-grilled trout with fresh sautéed tomatoes and roasted peppers; and fettuccine with tomato, basil, and buffalo-milk ricotta. If you need help deciding what to order, owner Gabriel Aiello is a great source for wine and food recommendations. ♦ Northern Italian ♦ M-F lunch and dinner; Sa dinner. Reservations recommended. 11 W 60th St (between Broadway and Columbus Ave). 956.4600

4 Mayflower $$$ Well located for **Lincoln Center,** this hotel offers 356 roomy accommodations, all with color TVs and most with serving pantries. There's also a fitness center. **The Conservatory Restaurant** serves breakfast, lunch, and dinner, plus an after-theater supper, often with classical music; it's a popular spot for Sunday brunch. ♦ 15 Central Park W (between W 61st and W 62nd Sts). 265.0060, 800/223.4164; fax 265.5098

5 Bible House/American Bible Society This society tries to make the Holy Scripture available in every language on earth. Its headquarters has a gallery for exhibitions from its collection of rare and unusual bibles, which includes pages from the Gutenberg Bible. ♦ Free. M-F. 1865 Broadway (at W 61st St). 408.1200

6 45 Columbus Avenue Designed by **Jardine, Hill & Murdock** in 1930, this 27-story building was originally the **Columbus Circle Automatic Garage.** It is a tremendous Art Deco sampler: All the walls are embellished with ornament. ♦ Between W 61st and W 62nd Sts

7 The Ballet Company This favorite shop of balletomanes specializes in dance

publications—in- and out-of-print—and records, videos, and souvenirs. ♦ Daily. 1887 Broadway (between W 62nd and W 63rd Sts) 246.6893

8 The Radisson Empire Hotel $$ Each of this hotel's 375 rooms is equipped with a cassette and CD player, VCR, and two-line telephone. Other highlights are the corporate lounge, the **West 63rd Street Steakhouse,** and its proximity to **Lincoln Center.** ♦ 44 W 63rd St (between Broadway and Columbus Ave). 265.7400, 800/333.3333; fax 315.0349 &

Within The Radisson Empire Hotel:

West 63rd Street Steakhouse ★★$$$ Contrary to what the name implies, there's neither sawdust on the floor nor red-and-white–checkered tablecloths. Instead, mahogany paneling, elaborately draped windows, handsome table lamps, and Australian Aboriginal art appoint this grand environment. The setting is made even more dramatic by the subdued noise level and a jazz pianist playing standard tunes. Shrimp cocktail is succulent and very fresh, and prime cuts of beef—including a 24-ounce T-bone—are enhanced by such excellent sauces as red wine shallot, herb butter, and Chardonnay-lemon. The french fries are hand-cut, and the wine list is well chosen and affordable. ♦ Steak house ♦ M-Sa breakfast and dinner; Su breakfast. Reservations recommended. 246.6363 &

8 Merlot ★★$$ Located in the former **Iridium** restaurant (a jazz club by that name is downstairs), this dining spot is noteworthy for its wine-inspired menu. Appetizers might include duck confit strudel with potatoes and wild mushrooms, baked clams, or brie *en croûte* (baked in puff pastry with wild loganberry jelly). Among the main courses try dry-aged sirloin steak *frites* (with french fries), farfel with sautéed jumbo shrimp in pink Champagne sauce, panseared fillet of Atlantic skate with ratatouille, or roasted prime rib with creamed spinach and oven-roasted potatoes. Leave room for the sinfully good chocolate *entremet* (rich chocolate mousse with custard served with fresh berries). ♦ California/French ♦ M-F dinner; Su brunch and dinner. 48 W 63rd St (between Broadway and Columbus Ave). 582.2121

9 Lincoln Center for the Performing Arts Robert Moses, urban planner and New York powerbroker, initiated the idea of a center for the city's major performing arts institutions in the 1950s, and this conglomeration of travertine halls came slowly into existence. Massed on a plaza above the street, the buildings have been called an Acropolis, but the arrangement around the fountain is actually a static version of Michelangelo's Capitoline Hill in Rome. Although the main theaters all take their formal cues from images of classical architecture, critics claim they never really come together as a whole, and remain, at best, individual *tours de* trite. Although **Wallace K. Harrison** coordinated the project and designed the master plan, individual architects designed the buildings in the 1960s. ♦ Bounded by Columbus Ave, Broadway, Amsterdam Ave, and W 62nd and W 66th Sts. 875.5000

At Lincoln Center for the Performing Arts:

Avery Fisher Hall Standing opposite the State Theater, this building was designed in 1966 by **Max Abramovitz.** Originally **Philharmonic Hall,** it has been reconstructed several times in the hopes of improving the sound, and a final touch-up in 1992 turned it into an acoustic gem. The stabile in the foyer is by Richard Lippold. **The New York Philharmonic** is in residence here from September through May. Music director Kurt Masur is the latest in an illustrious line that has included Zubin Mehta, the late Leonard Bernstein, Arturo Toscanini, and Leopold Stokowski. The informal *Mostly Mozart* concerts are held in July and August; *Great Performances* concerts are held September through May. Both are presentations of Lincoln Center Productions. **The Philharmonic**'s *Young People's Concerts* have been letting kids in on the motives behind the music since 1898; performances take place four times a year. Don't miss the orchestra's regularly scheduled open rehearsals, which usually occur on Thursday morning at 9:45AM. ♦ Broadway and W 65th St. 875.5030 ♿

Within Avery Fisher Hall:

PANEVINO
R I S T O R A N T E

Panevino ★$$ This is a pleasant place for dinner, a pastry and coffee, or just drinks. During the summer, this lobby cafe spills out onto the plaza. For dinner, try carpaccio, mozzarella with roasted tomatoes, rigatoni with eggplant and mozzarella, grilled chicken paillard with balsamic vinegar, or grilled salmon with seasoned olive butter. ♦ Italian ♦ Tu-Sa dinner. Reservations recommended. 132 W 65th St. 874.7000

Metropolitan Opera House Home to the **Metropolitan Opera Company,** the plaza's

magnificent centerpiece (designed by **Wallace K. Harrison**) opened in 1966 with Samuel Barber's *Antony and Cleopatra.* Behind the thin, 10-story colonnade and sheer glass walls, two wonderful murals by Marc Chagall beam out onto the plaza. The interior is filled with a red-carpeted lobby, a dramatic staircase lit by exquisite Austrian crystal chandeliers, and an equally plush auditorium. The opera season, from mid-September to April, leaves the stage available for visiting performers and companies, including the **American Ballet Theater,** during the rest of the year. ♦ Off Columbus Ave (between W 62nd and W 65th Sts). 362.6000 ♿

Within Metropolitan Opera House:

Metropolitan Opera Shop Imaginative opera- and music-related gifts and clothing are sold, most of them exclusive to this shop. Pick up hard-to-find books, records, posters, and libretti, with proceeds going to the **Metropolitan Opera.** ♦ M-Sa 10AM-second intermission (usually 9:30PM); Su noon-6PM. Next to the Met box office. 580.4090

New York State Theater Located on the plaza's south side, this theater was designed in 1964 by **Philip Johnson** and **Richard Foster.** At the culmination of a series of increasingly grand entrance spaces is a striking four-story foyer with balconies at every level, a pair of large white marble sculptures by Elie Nadelman, and a gold-leaf ceiling. The rich red and gold auditorium was designed for both ballet and musical theater. From 1964 to 1968, under the artistic directorship of Richard Rodgers of the **Music Theater of Lincoln Center,** revivals of musical classics were staged here. Now it's home to the famed dance company of the late George Balanchine, the **New York City Ballet,** and to the **New York City Opera.** The ballet's double season usually runs from late November through February and April through June. The annually sold-out *Nutcracker* season runs the entire month of December. The opera performs from July through November, with a schedule balancing warhorses and less familiar works than the **Met** normally risks, in often adventuresome productions with fresh, young singers. The acoustics, designed to muffle the thud of dancers' feet, have never been right for opera; in 1999, the company began to experiment with amplified sound—the purists were horrified, but it turned out to sound pretty good. Note the diamond-shaped floodlights surrounding the building. ♦ Columbus Ave (between W 62nd and W 65th Sts). 870.5570 ♿

Guggenheim Bandshell South of the **Met,** within **Damrosch Park** (site of the annual **Big Apple Circus**), the bandshell is a beautiful space for free concerts. It was designed by **The Eggars Partnership** in 1969 and seats 2,500. ♦ Damrosch Park, Amsterdam Ave (at W 62nd St). 875.5000

Vivian Beaumont Theater Located north of the **Met,** behind a tree-studded plaza and reflecting pool (with a sculpture by Henry Moore), this theater was designed by **Eero Saarinen & Associates** and first opened in 1965. It has had its share of trouble since the **Repertory Company of Lincoln Center** opened here under the direction of Robert Whitehead and Elia Kazan with Arthur Miller's apologia *After the Fall.* After several mediocre productions, there was a change of leadership. The new team, Jules Irving and Herbert Blau of the **Actor's Workshop** in San Francisco, produced some fine plays, including Bertolt Brecht's *Galileo,* Heinar Kipphardt's *In the Matter of J. Robert Oppenheimer,* and a revival of Tennessee Williams's *A Streetcar Named Desire.* The theater, however, was losing money, and after eight years, impresario Joseph Papp took over. His **New York Shakespeare Festival** at **Lincoln Center** presented many innovative productions here and at the **Mitzi E. Newhouse,** including David Rabe's *Streamers,* Brecht's *Threepenny Opera,* Miguel Pinero's *Short Eyes,* and, directed by André Serban, Anton Chekhov's *The Cherry Orchard.* After continued deficits and power struggles, however, Papp left in 1977. The **Beaumont** was dark for three years, until director Richmond Crinkley formed a group of famous entertainment-world personalities to chart a new course for the theater, including writer/actor/director Woody Allen, playwright Edward Albee, and directors Robin Phillips, Ellis Rabb, and Liviu Ciulei. ♦ 150 W 65th St (between Broadway and Amsterdam Ave). 239.6277 &

Mitzi E. Newhouse Theater Directly below the **Beaumont,** this smaller theater is for experimental and workshop productions, such as Mike Nichols's controversial *Waiting for Godot* starring Steve Martin, Robin Williams, and Bill Irwin. The 334-seat theater itself was designed by **Eero Saarinen & Associates** and opened in 1965. ♦ 150 W 65th St (between Broadway and Amsterdam Ave). 239.6277

Juilliard School Located across a large terrace/bridge over West 66th Street is one of the nation's most acclaimed performing arts schools, founded in 1905 by Augustus D. Juilliard. Enrollment is limited to fewer than a thousand, making acceptance in itself a career achievement for gifted students of music, dance, and drama. The building, a Modernist contrast to **Lincoln Center's** classicism, was designed by **Pietro Belluschi** with **Eduardo Catalano** and **Westerman & Miller,** and opened in 1968. Theaters: **Juilliard Theater** (seats 933); **Drama Theater** (seats 206); **C. Michael Paul Recital Hall** (seats 278). ♦ 60 Lincoln Center Plaza. 799.5000

Alice Tully Recital Hall East of **Juilliard,** this recital hall is the most intimate and best of the auditoriums at **Lincoln Center.**

Designed for chamber music and recitals by **Pietro Belluschi** in 1969, it is the home of the **Chamber Music Society of Lincoln Center** from October through May. It is also the main venue for the highly distinguished jazz performances of **Jazz at Lincoln Center** under the artistic direction of trumpeter/conductor/composer Wynton Marsalis, October through June. Students of the **Juilliard School** perform here, too, and films from around the world are shown every late September and October at the **New York International Film Festival.** ♦ 1941 Broadway (at W 65th St). 875.5050, Film Society 875.5610 &

New York Public Library/Library and Museum of the Performing Arts The two galleries at this popular library branch were part of the 1965 creation of **Skidmore, Owings & Merrill.** They exhibit costume and set designs, music scores, and other tools and tricks of the trade, as well as art. The 212-seat **Bruno Walter Auditorium** presents showcase productions and music recitals. In addition to the most extensive collections of books on the performing arts in the city (in a circulating library downstairs and research facilities on the second floor), the library is equipped with state-of-the-art audio equipment and a vast collection of recordings. A convenient entrance is in Lincoln Plaza next to the **Vivian Beaumont Theater.** The library has been closed since 1998 during major renovations and is not expected to reopen until early 2001; for information about the current whereabouts of the collections call, or consult the library's website. ♦ M, Th noon-8PM; Tu-W, F-Sa noon-6PM. 111 Amsterdam Ave (between W 62nd and W 65th Sts). 870.1630; www.nypl.org/research/lpa/ &

Lincoln Center Guided Tours Take a tour to see the physical plant, hear the legends and history, and peek at whatever else is going on, perhaps a rehearsal of **The Philharmonic** or *Rigoletto.* Another plus: the expertise and enthusiasm of the tour guides, who are often performers themselves. Backstage tours of the **Met** are also conducted by knowledgeable guides and provide a behind-the-scenes look at the opera. ♦ Fee. Hourly tours are offered daily; schedule varies, so call ahead. Main Concourse (accessible through the lobby of the Met). 769.7020 &

Performing Arts Gift Shop Records, music boxes, jewelry, clothing, and toys, all tuned into the performing arts, are sold here. Many items, such as the composer signature mugs and a belt with a music staff brass buckle, are designed for and sold exclusively at **Lincoln Center.** ♦ Daily. Main Concourse. 580.4356 &

Lincoln Center Poster Gallery This is the sales outlet for specially commissioned **Lincoln Center** prints and posters by such artists as Josef Albers, Marc Chagall, Robert

Indiana, and Andy Warhol. ♦ M-Sa. Main Concourse. 580.4673 ঙ

Samuel B. & David Rose Building
Tenants on the first 10 floors of this tower, designed by **Davis, Brody & Associates** and completed in 1990, include the Riverside branch of the **New York Public Library,** the **Walter Reade Theater,** the Film Society of **Lincoln Center,** and Lincoln Center, Inc. offices. Floors 12 to 29 are dormitories for students at **Juilliard** and the **School of American Ballet.** In order to finance construction of this building **Lincoln Center** sold $50 million worth of air rights to the developers of the neighboring condominiums at 3 Lincoln Plaza. ♦ 165 W 65th St (between Broadway and Amsterdam Ave)

10 Fiorello's ★★$$$ The location across from **Lincoln Center** is only one reason tables continue to fill up here. Pretheater, the place is a madhouse, but after 8PM, the wood-paneled room, decorated with burgundy banquettes and Mark Kostabi paintings, is a calm place to sample the antipasto bar; such pastas as lamb *bolognese* and linguine with clams, calamari, and mussels; and main courses that include clay-pot–roasted chicken with rosemary, roasted bass with olives and sun-dried tomatoes, and lamb osso buco. ♦ Italian ♦ M-F lunch and dinner; Sa-Su brunch and dinner. Reservations required. 1900 Broadway (between W 63rd and W 64th Sts). 595.5330

11 West Side YMCA $ In 1966, the city planned to raze this building—designed by **Dwight James Baum** and built in 1930—to clear the entire block up to Central Park West for a **Lincoln Center** mall. Plans fell through when the **YMCA** refused to sell out. This hostelry offers 550 single and double rooms to both men and women. In addition to a popular sports/fitness center, it has a family and youth services department. ♦ 5 W 63rd St (between Central Park W and Broadway). 787.4400, 800/FIT.YMCA; fax 580.0441 ঙ

12 Century Apartments Brother of the **Majestic (No. 115,** designed in 1930), this is the southernmost pair of the sets of twin towers designed by the office of **Irwin S. Chanin** that make the skyline of Central Park West so distinctive. The structure was built in 1931, when **Jacques Delamarre** was the director of **Chanin's** office. The apartment house occupies the site of the resoundingly unsuccessful (but magnificent) **Century**

Theater, a 1909 building by **Carrère & Hastings,** which first failed as a national theater, then as an opera house, and finally as a Ziegfeld vaudeville theater. ♦ 25 Central Park W (between W 62nd and W 63rd Sts). 265.1608

13 New York Society for Ethical Culture
It's refreshing to find this example of Art Nouveau in New York. **Robert D. Kohn,** who was also the architect of **Temple Emanu-El,** was the president of the society at the time he designed this building in 1910. ♦ 2 W 64th St (at Central Park W). 874.5210

14 Picholine ★★★$$$ Owner/chef Terrance Brennan pays homage to the sunny foods of the Mediterranean, especially Provence. His wife, Julie, designed the room with wallpaper checkered in white and green, the color of the olives that give the restaurant its name. From the kitchen come dishes of great imagination and very heady flavor. Don't miss the signature grilled octopus with fennel, potato, and lemon-pepper vinaigrette; carpaccio of tuna with vegetables *escabèche* (marinated in lemon juice) and *tapenade* aioli (an olive-based mayonnaise); tournedos of salmon with horseradish crust, cucumbers, and salmon caviar; and whole roasted fish (there's a different choice every day). Desserts are just as tempting, with homemade sorbets and mascarpone cannoli with roasted pear leading the list. There's an excellent wine list. ♦ Mediterranean ♦ M, Su dinner; Tu-Sa lunch and dinner. 35 W 64th St (between Central Park W and Broadway). 724.8585

O'NEALS'

15 O'Neals' ★$$$ The straightforward menu offers predictably decent fare ranging from hamburgers and Chicago-style ribs to tarragon chicken. The dining room is visibly calmer after 8PM, when the crowds empty out to catch the curtain at **Lincoln Center.** ♦ American ♦ Daily lunch, dinner, and late-night meals. 49 W 64th St (between Central Park W and Broadway). 787.4663

Jack Dempsey's 14-room apartment at 145 Central Park West included a huge kitchen where the fighter practiced his favorite hobby—cooking.

Congregation Shearith Israel at West 70th Street is the oldest Jewish congregation in the United States. The first house of worship was built in 1730 by descendants of 23 men, women, and children who arrived in Nieuw Amsterdam in 1654. It was moved uptown three times until the current synagogue at West 70th Street was built in 1897.

15 The Saloon ★$$ The service in this cavernous dining room and street cafe can vary. The enormous snack and dinner menu includes crab cakes, quesadillas, angel-hair pasta with prosciutto, various pizzas, grilled salmon, and veal scallops. The waiters are fast, if not always efficient; those who can zoom around on in-line skates. On warm, sunny days, the outdoor tables are great for people watching. **The Saloon Grill** (874.2082) next door serves the same food in a slightly calmer atmosphere. ◆ Continental ◆ M-F lunch and dinner; Sa-Su brunch and dinner. Reservations recommended. 1920 Broadway (at W 64th St). 874.1500 &

15 World Gym If you've taken advantage of one too many New York restaurants, this spacious facility with a view of Lincoln Center features a full range of weight training and cardiovascular equipment, exercise classes, steam rooms, juice bar, and pro shop. This is serious stuff, obvious from the pumped-up late-night workaholics who take advantage of the 24-hour schedule. The club offers mini memberships by the day, week, or month, as well as 10-visit cards. ◆ M-F open 24 hours, Sa-Su 7AM-9PM. 1926 Broadway (between W 64th and W 65th Sts), Second floor. 874.0942. Also at: 232 Mercer St (between Bleecker and W Third Sts). 780.7407 &

16 Coco Opera ★★$$ Specialties at this lively trattoria include *linguine alla pirata* (with seafood and fresh peas), *cacciucco* (mixed seafood cooked in spicy tomato sauce), and *stracotto di manzo* (braised beef braised in red wine and served with soft polenta). The sorbets are refreshing and the wine list affordable. ◆ Italian ◆ Daily lunch and dinner. Reservations recommended. 58 W 65th St (between Central Park W and Broadway). 873.3700

17 Shun Lee Dynasty ★★$$$ Long a favorite of the **Lincoln Center** crowd, the restaurant does many regional Chinese cuisines justice. Try the steamed dumplings, beggar's chicken (baked in clay), or prawns in black-bean sauce. The vast dining room is dramatic—black banquettes and brightly colored dragon lanterns—though not as fancy as the prices. In the second dining room the lower-priced **Shun Lee Cafe** features dim sum. ◆ Chinese ◆ Daily lunch and dinner. Reservations required. 43 W 65th St (between Central Park W and Columbus Ave). 595.8895. Also at: 155 E 55th St (between Third and Lexington Aves). 371.8844

18 Museum of American Folk Art/Eva and Morris Feld Gallery at Lincoln Square The best of American folk art from the 18th century to the present, including paintings, sculpture, textiles, furniture, and decorative arts, is displayed here. The museum holds regular lectures and workshops and has an adjacent gift shop that's worth a visit. ◆ Donation suggested. Tu-Su. 2 Lincoln Sq (between W 65th and W 66th Sts). 977.7298, gift shop 496.2966 &

19 First Battery Armory, New York National Guard Today, **ABC**'s TV studios hide behind this fortress facade, designed in 1901 by **Horgan & Slattery** and altered in 1978 by **Kohn Pederson Fox**. ◆ 56 W 66th St (between Central Park W and Columbus Ave)

20 Hotel des Artistes An early studio building designed by **George Mort Pollard** in 1913 specifically for artists—duplexes with double-height main spaces—this is now one of the more lavish co-ops around. It has always attracted noteworthy tenants, among them Isadora Duncan, Alexander Woollcott, Norman Rockwell, Noel Coward, and Howard Chandler Christy. ◆ 1 W 67th St (at Central Park W). 362.6700

Within the Hotel des Artistes:

Café des Artistes ★★★$$$ The West Side's most charming and romantic restaurant was originally, as the name suggests, intended for artists. Light streams through the leaded-glass windows by day, and the six colorful murals of capricious female nudes, painted in 1934 by Howard Chandler Christy, are an enduring visual feast. The restaurant's serene trappings and quality fare have always drawn a high-powered crowd—you might see Bill Clinton or Dustin Hoffman across the room. Owner George Lang updates the menu and the well-chosen and well-priced wine list daily as well as seasonally—his renowned asparagus festival occurs every May and June. But regular dishes you shouldn't miss include the salmon four ways (smoked, poached, gravlax, and *tartare*), duck confit, fresh Dover sole meunière, and rack of lamb with basil crust. Save room for the hot fudge napoleon, the great dessert plate, or "chocolatissimo for two." The famous weekend brunch is a must. ◆ French ◆ M-F lunch and dinner; Sa-Su brunch and dinner. Reservations required; jacket and tie required after 5PM. 877.3500 &

21 American Broadcasting Company Facilities (ABC) Fortunately, these two buildings don't intrude on this quiet, low-scale street: 30 West 67th Street, the technical center, is set back respectfully, and the limestone, tan brick, and glass are in harmony with the surroundings. In 1979, architects

Kohn Pederson Fox used a lot of glass to create an inviting lobby for the local television studios at 7 Lincoln Square; an open atrium with a flying staircase on the top three floors is illuminated at night. ♦ 30 W 67th St and 7 Lincoln Sq (between Central Park W and Columbus Ave)

22 Vince & Eddie's ★★$$ Locals pack this rustic-looking, intimate room—especially before a **Lincoln Center** performance—for chef Scott Campbell's earthy but elegantly prepared dishes. The menu changes seasonally, but such dishes as braised lamb shank with Michigan cherry sauce and panroasted chicken with spinach and lentils are available all year. Vegetable purees, including turnip and pumpkin, may sound humble but are silky and rich and not to be missed. ♦ American ♦ M-Sa lunch and dinner; Su brunch and dinner. Reservations recommended. 70 W 68th St (between Central Park W and Columbus Ave). 721.0068

22 67 Wine & Spirits With its extensive selection of wines and spirits, this store is well known for its diversity, fair prices, and knowledgeable staff. ♦ M-Sa. 179 Columbus Ave (at W 68th St). 724.6767

23 Reebok Sports Club/NY Outfitted on six levels, this megaclub is the most extravagant of urban country clubs. Over 140,000 square feet of tracks, courts, sun decks, pools, and locker rooms are outfitted with $55 million worth of state-of-the-art equipment. Membership is steep, but where else in town will you find a 45-foot rockclimbing wall or a downhill-skiing simulator? ♦ Daily. 174 Columbus Ave (at W 68th St). 362.6800

24 Tower Records This enormous multilevel emporium covers all the music bases with CDs and cassettes (including single recordings), and sells videos, too. You can also purchase tickets to most concerts at the store's Ticketmaster counter. A lot of late-night socializing goes on here. ♦ Daily until midnight. 1977 Broadway (between W 66th and W 67th Sts). 799.2500. Also at: 692

Broadway (at E Fourth St). 799.2500; Trump Tower, 725 Fifth Ave (between E 56th and E 57th Sts). 838.8118 &

25 Sony Theaters Lincoln Square The multiplex flagship of this Japanese-owned chain is a show in itself. Each of the 10 screening rooms is reminiscent of an old-time movie palace. Although ticket prices are high, the atmosphere and better-than-average concessions and conveniences (there's even an ATM in the lobby) almost make it worthwhile. The centerpiece of the lavish complex is the 3-D IMAX theater with an eight-story–high screen (the largest in the US); reclining chairs and a sleek wraparound headset guarantee virtual immersion. ♦ Daily. Broadway and W 68th St. 336.5000 &

26 Merkin Concert Hall Concert series are held here, including ensemble programs and contemporary and chamber music. The 457-seat hall is located in the **Abraham Goodman House**. ♦ 129 W 67th St (between Broadway and Amsterdam Ave). 501.3340 &

27 The Civilized Traveller This popular, well-stocked shop is dedicated to the serious globetrotter. Along with travel accessories, including bags in every color and description, there's an in-depth selection of travel books and guides. Browsing is not discouraged. This branch also features a well-informed travel agency. ♦ Daily. 2003 Broadway (between W 68th and W 69th Sts). 875.0306. Also at: 864 Lexington Ave (between E 64th and E 65th Sts). 288.9190

28 Lincoln Square Synagogue Designed in 1970 by **Hausman & Rosenberg**, this is a mannered, curved building with fins and rectangular block attached, all clad in travertine, à la neighboring **Lincoln Center**. It is one of Manhattan's most popular Orthodox synagogues. ♦ 200 Amsterdam Ave (between W 66th and W 70th Sts). 874.6100

To create Lincoln Center—six buildings devoted to theater, music, and dance in an area of 14 acres—it was necessary to demolish 188 buildings and relocate 1,600 people. These were the very slums in which Leonard Bernstein set his famous American musical *West Side Story*. He would later be instrumental in the development and creative organization of Lincoln Center.

Most shipping these days is done by air, but the Port of New York, which handles more than 150 million tons a year, is far and away the most important seaport in America. New York Harbor is at the apex of a triangle that extends more than 100 miles to the east and south like a giant funnel.

Restaurants/Clubs: Red	**Hotels:** Blue
Shops/ ♦ Outdoors: Green	**Sights/Culture:** Black

29 Cafe Luxembourg ★★$$$ A people watcher's Art Deco brasserie, this cafe is affiliated with TriBeCa's trendy **Odeon.** The zinc-topped bar here draws a stylish, international crowd, and the menu is a mélange of French, Italian, and regional American offerings. Order marinated octopus; lemon risotto with fresh asparagus and parmesan; *Provençale* vegetable tart; roasted leg of lamb; duck cassoulet; or striped bass with fresh herbs, garlic, and oil. For dessert, try the profiteroles with chocolate or vanilla ice cream. ♦ French ♦ M-F lunch, dinner, and late-night meals; Sa-Su brunch, dinner, and late-night meals. Reservations recommended. 200 W 70th St (at Amsterdam Ave). 873.7411 &

30 Christ and St. Stephen's Episcopal Church This charming country church, built in 1880 to the designs of **William H. Day** and altered in 1897 by **J.D. Fouguet,** is holding up well in the big city. ♦ 120 W 69th St (between Columbus Ave and Broadway). 787.2755

31 La Boîte en Bois ★★$$$ A few steps down and far from the madding crowd on Columbus Avenue, this charming French bistro with a country atmosphere and *Provençale* menu offers fine fish soup, roast chicken with herbs, and roasted salmon glazed with honey mustard. ♦ French ♦ M-Sa lunch and dinner; Su brunch and dinner. Reservations recommended. No credit cards accepted. 75 W 68th St (between Central Park W and Columbus Ave). 874.2705

32 Santa Fe ★★$$ This refurbished town house dining room is painted in flattering soft desert tones and fitted with fine Southwestern arts and crafts. All in all, it's a very pleasant place to dine on such fare as seviche, shrimp in a green tomatillo sauce, and crab cakes in a smoked tomato-and-chile sauce. ♦ Southwestern ♦ M-F lunch and dinner; Sa-Su brunch and dinner. Reservations recommended. 72 W 69th St (between Central Park W and Columbus Ave). 724.0822

33 World Cafe ★$$ The all-encompassing menu in this beige eatery with ceiling fans spans the globe from East to West. The Indian spiced yogurt-avocado dip is interesting, as is the grilled tuna in a carrot-ginger glaze. But the most successful item on the menu might well be the humble hamburger, given a jolt here with chipotle barbecue sauce. ♦ International ♦ M-F lunch and dinner; Sa-Su brunch and dinner. Reservations recommended. 201 Columbus Ave (at W 69th St). 799.8090

34 Rikyu ★$$ Predating the invasion of trendy spots along Columbus Avenue, this popular restaurant is a favorite with locals and the **Lincoln Center** crowd for good traditional dishes and fresh sushi. Another plus: Competition from the neighboring sushi bars keeps the prices reasonable. ♦ Japanese ♦ Daily lunch and dinner. Reservations recommended. 210 Columbus Ave (between W 69th and W 70th Sts). 799.7847

35 Epices du Traiteur ★★$$ This tiny, friendly French-Tunisian restaurant hits the West Side like a beam of Mediterranean sunshine. Menu offerings, while diverse, are uniformly light and delicious, from the signature *salade épice* (a tangy mélange of romaine lettuce, pine nuts, egg, orange slices, and Caesar-style dressing) to the flavorful pasta and seafood dishes. For dessert, opt for the homemade mousse au chocolat or a slice of the lighter but equally ambrosial mixed berry tart, flown in from France. ♦ French ♦ Daily dinner. 103 W 70th St (between Columbus Ave and Broadway). 579.5904

36 The Dorilton When this Beaux Arts masterpiece, designed by **Janes & Leo,** was completed in 1902, critic Montgomery Schuyler was so displeased with its design that he wrote the following in *Architectural Record:* "The incendiary qualities of the edifice may be referred, first to violence of color, then to violence of scale, then to violence of 'thingness,' to the multiplicity and importunity of the details." When the Landmarks Preservation Commission granted this apartment building its landmark status in 1974, they described it as "exceptionally handsome." ♦ 171 W 71st St (at Broadway)

37 Applause Theater Books For thespians, this is a good place to find an obscure play or movie scenario. Books on other performing arts are also sold. ♦ Daily. 211 W 71st St (between Broadway and West End Ave). 496.7511

38 Sherman Square Another one of those places where Broadway crosses the city grid to form a bow tie, not a square, this one is occupied by an **IRT Subway Control House,** which was designed by **Heins & LaFarge** in 1904. This is one of two surviving ornate entrances to the original **IRT** subway line (the other is at the **Battery Park Control House** in Lower Manhattan). Note the stylish detailing of the Neo-Dutch, somewhat Baroque shed. ♦ Broadway and Amsterdam Ave

39 Gray's Papaya $ Nowhere else does a dollar buy so much. A cast of characters frequents this supercheap round-the-clock hot dog stand that brags its tube steaks are "tastier than filet mignon" and its papaya drink is "a definite aid to digestion." Unless you've got a cast-iron stomach, you'll need all the help you can get. The fruit-flavored refreshments are definitely worth a stop here. ♦ Hot dogs ♦ Daily 24 hours. 2090 Broadway (at W 72nd St). 799.0243

40 Acker-Merrall-Condit Experts on Burgundy, these established liquor merchants boast a reputation for good service. The store design is nice, too. ♦ M-Sa. 160 W 72nd St (between Columbus Ave and Broadway). 787.1700 &

41 Fine & Schapiro ★$$ This long-established classic kosher delicatessen makes one nostalgic for the days before cholesterol counts. There's a salt-free corner on the menu, but if you need to consult it, you're probably in the wrong place. ♦ Jewish deli ♦ Daily lunch and dinner. 138 W 72nd St (between Columbus Ave and Broadway). 877.2874

42 Blades Boards & Skate Rent a pair of rollerblades and protective gear, then set off for a day of inline skating in the park. The blades—as well as ice skates, skateboards, snowboards, helmets, and accessories—are also for sale. ♦ Daily. 120 W 72nd St (between Columbus Ave and Broadway). 787.3911. Also at: 160 E 86th St (between Third and Lexington Aves). 996.1644

43 Harry's Burrito Junction ★$ If **Lincoln Center** tickets have busted your budget or if you happen to be in the market for some great nachos, this is the place. A young crowd that fills the three-level space decorated with memorabilia from the 1960s seems to have a special fondness for the footlong bay burrito, oozing with black beans and shredded beef. ♦ Mexican ♦ Daily lunch and dinner. 241 Columbus Ave (at W 71st St). 580.9494

43 Fishin Eddie ★★$$$ Courtesy of the folks behind **Vince & Eddie's** (see page 267), this restaurant specializing in seafood is ideal for a pre- or post-**Lincoln Center** meal. Given a stylized log-cabin design by interior decorator Sam Lopata, the room has paneling on the ceiling, barnsiding, antique wooden farmhouse tables, and Shaker furniture. However, the yellow-and-chartreuse color scheme and nautical props, including buoys, suggest nothing so much as the inside of a fish tank, an interesting setting for a high-quality fish dinner. Try the grilled black bass with thyme pesto, cioppino (a seafood stew in a spicy red broth), grouper sautéed with arugula and tomato sauce, or perfectly steamed lobster. For dessert there's an excellent lemon tart; the chocolate-walnut cake and apple-oat tart are also recommended. ♦ Seafood ♦ Daily dinner.

Reservations recommended. 73 W 71st St (at Columbus Ave). 874.3474

43 Café La Fortuna ★$ A mainstay of the neighborhood for years—and one of the late John Lennon's hangouts—this pleasant, unassuming cafe serves excellent Italian coffees and a mouthwatering array of traditional Italian pastries and other sweets. The garden in the back is an ideal respite from summer heat. Sandwiches, antipasti, and salads are also available. ♦ Cafe ♦ Tu-Su lunch, dinner, and late-night meals. No credit cards accepted. 69 W 71st St (between Central Park W and Columbus Ave). 724.5846

44 Dakota Apartments Built in 1884, this was one of the first luxury apartment houses in the city (along with the **Osborne** on West 57th Street and **34 Gramercy Park East**). The building (pictured on page 270) was christened when someone remarked to its owner, Edward Clark, president of the Singer Sewing Company, that it was so far out of town, "it might as well be in Dakota Territory." Clark, not without a sense of humor, went on to instruct the architect, **Henry J. Hardenbergh,** to embellish the building with symbols of the Wild West; arrowheads, sheaves of wheat, and ears of corn appear in bas-relief on the building's interior and exterior facades. (**Hardenbergh** later designed **The Plaza Hotel.**) The apartment building is a highly original masonry mass with echoes of Romanesque and German Renaissance architecture, and a facade of rich creamy brownstone. Victorian details and miscellaneous pieces sprout at every turn—turrets, gables, oriels, dormers, and pinnacles. The top three floors, once servants' quarters and a playroom and gymnasium for children, are now some of the most prized apartments in Manhattan. The building has gained notoriety not only as the setting for the film *Rosemary's Baby* but also as the home of Boris Karloff, Judy Garland, Lauren Bacall, Leonard Bernstein, Rex Reed, Roberta Flack, Yoko Ono and John Lennon, and Kim Basinger. ♦ 1 W 72nd St (at Central Park W)

America's first patent was issued in New York City on 31 July 1790. It was granted to Samuel Hopkins for a process that involved the making and purifying of potash, an ingredient used in soap making. The patent was signed by President George Washington and Secretary of State Thomas Jefferson.

The New York City Landmarks Preservation Commission was established in 1965, two years after the demolition of the original Pennsylvania Station. The commission protects buildings of historic, cultural, and esthetic value to the city.

Dakota Apartments

45 Dallas BBQ $ The barbecued ribs and chicken are well seasoned, tender, and juicy. But the big draw for many of the neighborhood fans of this large, informal, and noisy restaurant is the huge loaf of greasy onion rings. ♦ Barbecue ♦ M-Th, Su lunch and dinner; F-Sa lunch, dinner, and late-night meals. 27 W 72nd St (between Central Park W and Columbus Ave). 873.2004. Also at: Numerous locations throughout the city

46 Star Magic If you're in the market for crystals, New Age–inspired accessories, and trinkets for the astral traveler, stop by this shop. ♦ Daily. 275 Amsterdam Ave (at W 73rd St). 769.2020. Also at: 745 Broadway (between Waverly Pl and E Eighth St). 228.7770; 1296 Lexington Ave (at E 87th St). 988.0300 ♿

47 Vinnie's Pizza ★$ At this neighborhood favorite, the thin-crusted pizza is loaded with cheese and superfresh toppings. The parlor itself wouldn't win any design awards, so get your pie to go. ♦ Pizza ♦ Daily lunch and dinner. 285 Amsterdam Ave (between W 73rd and W 74th Sts). 874.4382

48 Apple Bank A Florentine palazzo seems like an appropriate model for a bank. This one, designed in 1928 by the masters **York & Sawyer** (who also designed the **Federal Reserve Bank of New York**), skillfully contains a proper rectangular banking hall within the trapezoidal building necessary on the site. ♦ 2100 Broadway (between W 73rd and W 74th Sts). 472.4545 ♿

49 Ansonia Hotel Designed by **Graves & Duboy** and built in 1904, this Belle Epoque masterpiece, bristling with ornament, balconies, towers, and dormers, is one of the great apartment buildings in New York. (As with the **Hotel des Artistes,** this was never a hotel at all; the appellation is from the earlier meaning of French *hôtel,* "mansion.") The thick walls and floors required for fireproofing have made the 16-story cooperative apartment building a favorite of musicians. Among those who have lived here are Enrico Caruso, Arturo Toscanini, Florenz Ziegfeld, Sol Hurok, Theodore Dreiser, and George Herman (Babe) Ruth. ♦ 2109 Broadway (between W 73rd and W 74th Sts). 724.2600

50 Josie's ★★$ Food for the health conscious is served at this popular place: The grains and produce are organic, the water filtered, and all dishes are dairy-free. But healthful doesn't mean boring here—the creative cuisine features such dishes as ginger-grilled calamari with pineapple–red pepper salsa; and sweet-potato ravioli with Gulf shrimp, sweet corn, and roasted peppers in white wine and leek sauce. There are a couple of unrepentantly sinful desserts, including lemon-ribbon ice-cream pie. ♦ American ♦ Daily dinner. 300 Amsterdam Ave (at W 74th St). 769.1212

51 Freddie and Pepper's Gourmet Pizza ★$ This no-frills pizza place makes a good tomato base for its myriad toppings. Try the unusual seafood smorgasbord pie. ♦ Pizza ♦ Daily lunch and dinner. No credit cards accepted. 303 Amsterdam Ave (between W 74th and W 75th Sts). No phone

51 Shark Bar ★$$ Within a swanky setting—dark, split-level, candlelit—is a beautiful and well-dressed crowd, including more than a few models and music-industry types. Among the inventive appetizers that shouldn't be missed is the soul roll (pastry filled with vegetables, chicken, and rice). Otherwise, skip the Cajun side of the menu and stick to classic soul food dishes—barbecued ribs, fried chicken, collard greens, black-eyed peas, macaroni and cheese, yams, and sweet potato pie. ♦ Soul food/Cajun ♦ M-Tu dinner; W-F lunch and dinner; Sa-Su brunch and dinner. Reservations recommended. 307 Amsterdam Ave (between W 74th and W 75th Sts). 874.8500

52 Beacon Theatre Special films, dance groups, and foreign performing arts groups, as well as mainstream soul and rock artists, are featured in this 2,700-seat theater. Some say the magnificent interior by **Walter Ahlschlager** is second only to **Radio City**'s. ♦ 2124 Broadway (between W 74th and W 75th Sts). 496.7070

53 Fairway Residents swear by this all-purpose market, which offers produce, excellent cheeses, charcuterie, coffee, chocolates, baked goods, breads, prepared foods, and smoked fish. Avoiding the crowds here is something of a local sport; the prevailing current strategy seems to entail arriving early in the morning or after 8PM. The newest location on 12th Avenue provides six square miles of shopping space, with fresh-baked pizza, a coffee bar, and a walk-in freezer featuring custom-cut meats and fish. ♦ M-Sa 24 hours; Su 8AM-midnight. 2127 Broadway (between W 74th and W 75th Sts). 595.1888 ♿ Also at: 2328 12th Ave (at W 132nd St). 234.3883 ♿

53 Citarella This retail fish store and and all-round gourmet shop sells prepared foods from oysters shucked while-you-wait and caviar to take-home pastas and soups for the neighborhood's microwave artists. The elaborate fish-sculpture displays take the art of window dressing to new heights. For those who are doing their own cooking, the range of fresh seafood and prime cuts of meat is simply dazzling. ♦ Daily. 2135 Broadway (at W 75th St). 874.0383. Also at: 1313 Third Ave (between E 75th St and E 76th St). 874.0383

54 Ernie's $$ Light wooden floors, white walls, and spotlights give a fresh, airy look to this barnlike restaurant. The menu features such favorites as angel-hair pasta with lobster, Caesar salad, grilled chicken, and "death by chocolate." But this place has always been more about chatting with friends than about food. ♦ Italian ♦ M-F lunch and dinner; Sa-Su brunch, lunch, and dinner. Reservations recommended. 2150 Broadway (between W 75th and W 76th Sts). 496.1588

55 Mughlai $$ For Indian food that never errs on the too-spicy side, this is the place. The tandoori here is best, and the mango chutney served with the curry is quite good. Desserts are uninspired, except for the highly recommended rice pudding with rose water. ♦ Indian ♦ M-F dinner; Sa-Su brunch and dinner. Reservations recommended. 320 Columbus Ave (at W 75th St). 724.6363

56 Pappardella ★$$ This is a popular destination for pasta and *secondi piatti* (second, or main, dishes) with a Tuscan accent. Try a thin-crusted pizza with a glass of Chianti, ravioli with mushrooms, or *bistecca fiorentina* (grilled T-bone steak marinated in olive oil, rosemary, and a touch of garlic, served with sautéed vegetables), and relish the escape from the bustle of Columbus Avenue. ♦ Italian ♦ M-F lunch and dinner; Sa-Su brunch and dinner. Reservations recommended. 316 Columbus Ave (at W 75th St). 595.7996

57 San Remo In contrast to the streamlined **Century** and **Majestic** apartments by **Irwin S. Chanin, Emory Roth**'s twin towers, constructed in 1930, are capped with Roman temples surmounted by finials. ♦ 145-146 Central Park W (between W 74th and W 75th Sts)

58 Central Park West/76th Street Historic District This district, designated a historic area in 1973, comprises the blocks on Central Park West between West 75th and West 77th Streets and about half of West 76th Street. It includes a variety of row houses built at the turn of the century; the Neo-Grecian **Nos. 21-31** by **George M. Walgrove** are the earliest, and the Baroque **Nos. 8-10** by **John H. Duncan** are the most recent. Of interest as well are the **Kenilworth** apartment building (151 Central Park W), designed in 1908 by **Townsend, Steinle & Haskell,** noteworthy for its convex mansard roof and highly ornamented limestone, and the Oxfordish **Universalist Church of New York** (W 76th St and Central Park W), designed in 1898 by **William A. Potter.** Also included in the designated area is **44 West 77th Street,** designed in 1909 by **Harde & Short,** a Gothic-style building used as artists' studios; much of the ornament was removed in 1944. ♦ Bounded by Central Park W and Columbus Ave, and W 75th and W 77th Sts

59 New-York Historical Society The society is housed in a fine Neo-Classical French building, the central portion of which was designed by **York & Sawyer** in 1908, with unimaginative 1938 additions by **Walker & Gillette.** Inside, the collection is rich with such Americana as wall-to-wall silver, rare maps, antique toys, splendid carriages, portraits by Gilbert Stuart and Benjamin West, watercolors by John James Audubon, and landscapes by again-popular Frederic Church and the rest of the Hudson River boys. The society also has stunning 17th-, 18th-, and 19th-century furniture arranged in chronological order. Changing shows touch on cast-iron stoves, American bands, or early women's magazines. There is also a permanent exhibition for children, **Kid City,** presenting a picture of New York at the turn between the 19th and 20th centuries, with a market, bakery, and apartment with toys and a book nook. The society's library is one of the major reference libraries of American history in this country. If you're wondering about the hyphen in "New-York Historical Society," it's a point of pride for the museum: When it was founded in 1804, everybody spelled New York that way. ♦ Admission. Museum: Tu-Su. Library closed Sunday, closed Saturday in summer. 2 W 77th St (at Central Park W). 873.3400 ♿

60 Scaletta ★★$$$ A large dinner menu, fast and efficient service, and excellent pasta and antipasto (especially the prosciutto) are highlights of this lovely Northern Italian restaurant. Try the specials of the day, which might include risotto with wild mushrooms, and veal *sorrentino* (sautéed with eggplant and mozzarella). Desserts are of the rich Italian variety, and the espresso is good, too. ♦ Northern Italian ♦ Daily dinner. 50 W 77th St (between Central Park W and Columbus Ave). 769.9191

61 Spazzia ★★$$ This hip Mediterranean eatery just across the street from the **American Museum of Natural History** and the **Hayden Planetarium** spent decades as the dismally mediocre **Museum Cafe;** under the ownership of Stephen Kalt and Cindy Smith, the decor is little changed—the old pink walls are now an equally odd shade of yellow, and a peculiar piece of wall art, from a 1930s stage set representing Central Park South, has been added—but the menu is another matter altogether. Try Ligurian fish soup with basil and saffron, Niçoise-style fried ravioli with caper-anchovy sauce, or chestnut-flour fettuccine with chicken, artichokes, and pine nuts; or one of the individual pizzas. Entrées include herb-crusted Catskill trout with roasted root vegetables and red-wine mushroom sauce, or veal three ways (osso buco, meat loaf, and braised) with potato croquettes and sautéed spinach. Desserts are not the strong point here, but a peach upside-down cake has received favorable notice. ♦ Mediterranean ♦ M-F lunch and dinner; Sa-Su brunch and dinner. 366 Columbus Ave (at W 77th St). 799.0150

62 Isabella ★$$ Well liked for its simple, pleasant decor and inviting sidewalk cafe, this place offers such homemade pasta as cheese-and-herb ravioli in tomato sauce, and a selection of grilled dishes, including veal chops and chicken, all of which are good. ♦ Italian ♦ M-F lunch and dinner; Su brunch, lunch, and dinner. 359 Columbus Ave (at W 77th St). 724.2100

62 Kenneth Cole Shoes and accessories by the witty, self-promoting designer are sold in this shop. Copies of his print ads, which address the political and social issues of the moment—one suggests that customers buy one fewer pair of shoes and, instead, donate the money to AIDS research—are displayed along the right-hand wall as you enter. ♦ Daily. 353 Columbus Ave (between W 76th and W 77th Sts). 873.2061. Also at: 95 Fifth Ave (at E 17th St). 675.2550

63 GreenFlea/IS 44 Market If you can't make the trek down to the larger weekend flea market at West 26th Street and Sixth Avenue, you'll fare well here, though the pickings aren't as extensive. The emphasis is on new, used, and vintage clothing and accessories, with a nice mix of antiques, collectibles, and furniture. ♦ Free. Su. Columbus Ave and W 76th St. 721.0900

64 Equinox Fitness Club Ideal for visitors, this cutting-edge megagym opens its doors for one-time-use admission. A huge success since its 1991 debut, this gym is as famous for its social scene as for its unsurpassed fitness programs. A killer 10-week program is available for those who plan to stay on in New York. ♦ M-Th 5:30AM-11PM; F 6AM-10PM; Sa-Su 8AM-9PM. 344 Amsterdam Ave (between W 76th and W 77th Sts). 721.4200. Also at: Numerous locations throughout the city

65 Promenade Theatre New plays and revivals of lesser-known plays by established playwrights are featured at this intimate 399-seat theater, often with big-name stars returning to the boards to hone their craft. ♦ 2162 Broadway (between W 76th and W 77th Sts). 580.1313

65 Ruby Foo's Dim Sum and Sushi Palace ★★$$ Basically, this fun new place is an updated version of the old **Trader Vic's** concept: Asian food geared openly to American palates in an Oriental-fantasy decor, but so well done that you can't keep your tongue in your cheek. The bar area and upstairs dining room feature lacquered tables and walls, gilt Buddhas and mahjong tiles, and a winding staircase out of a Hollywood opium den. The menu features sushi and dim sum with as many vegetarian and meat options as seafood items, and some extravagant fusion entrées: Thai basil–curried salmon with lemongrass risotto and Asian vegetables, wok-seared wasabi pork with stir-fried vegetables and black-bean sauce. West Siders can't get enough of it: If you don't like *very* thick crowds, go very late, when the noise level begins to diminish. ♦ Asian ♦ Daily lunch, dinner, and late-night meals. Reservations recommended. 2182 Broadway (between W 76th and W 77th Sts). 724.6700

66 Milburn Hotel $ Handsome prewar apartment buildings are common in this residential area, and the **Milburn** was one of them until a multimillion-dollar refurbishing converted it to a gracious 70-suite hotel. All the traditionally furnished rooms have fully equipped kitchens with microwaves, making this a good choice for families and long-term visitors. ♦ 242 W 76th St (between Broadway and West End Ave). 362.1006, 800/833.9622; fax 721.5476

67 343-357 West End Avenue Built in 1891 and designed by **Lamb & Rich,** this complete block-front on West End and around both corners is a lively, well-ordered collection typical of Victorian town houses, and the only West Side block without high-rises between West End Avenue and Riverside Drive. (Rumor has it that Mayor Jimmy Walker's mistress lived at West 76th Street and Broadway and the block was supposedly

zoned to protect his river view.) The variety of shapes and materials—gables, bays, dormers, and limestone, red, and tan brick—is clearly under control, resulting in a stylish, humorous energy with no dissonance. ♦ Between W 76th and W 77th Sts

68 West End Collegiate Church and School The school, established by the Dutch in 1637, is housed in a copy of the market building in Haarlem, Holland. Designed in 1893 by **Robert W. Gibson,** this is a particularly good example of Dutch detailing; note the stepped gables and the use of long bricks. ♦ 368 West End Ave (between W 77th and W 78th Sts). 787.1566 &

69 La Caridad $$ Expect a fairly long wait at this popular and inexpensive Cuban/Chinese beanery where such standards as roasted pork and shredded beef are the standouts. ♦ Cuban/Chinese ♦ Daily lunch, dinner, and late-night meals. No credit cards accepted. 2199 Broadway (at W 78th St). 874.2780

70 Apthorp Apartments Designed by **Clinton & Russell** and built in 1908, this is the best of the three big West Side courtyard buildings (the **Belnord** on West 86th Street and **Astor Court** on Broadway between West 89th and West 90th Streets are the others). The ornate ironwork here is especially wonderful. It was built by William Waldorf Astor, who owned much of the land in the area, and was named for the man who had owned the site in 1763. ♦ 2207 Broadway (between W 78th and W 79th Sts)

71 Stand-Up NY Up-and-coming and established merchants of the one-liner play this comedy club. ♦ Cover, minimum. Shows: M-Th, Su 6:30, 9PM; F 9, 11:30PM; Sa 7:30, 9:30, 11:30PM. Reservations required. 236 W 78th St (at Broadway). 595.0850 &

72 Two Two Two ★★★★$$$$ This skylit town house restaurant is *the* special occasion place on the upper West Side—the detailed oak paneling, classic oil paintings, and ornate crystal chandelier set the tone for the exquisite and sometimes very rich food. Owner Frank Valenza offers such tempting appetizers as the Two Two Two soup, a mélange of lobster, whitefish, and salmon in a thickened tarragon broth; and escargots baked in garlic with herbed crumbs. For a main course, don't miss the panseared fillet of Canadian salmon with potato scallion pancake, rack of Colorado lamb marinated in garlic and rosemary, or any of the daily pasta specials served with white or black truffles. For those who can still manage dessert, try the excellent warm chocolate cake, maple crème brûlée, or a fresh fruit sorbet assortment. The restaurant boasts two extensive wine lists, one American and one French, both with exceptional (and expensive) selections. ♦ Continental ♦ M, Sa-Su dinner;

Tu-F lunch and dinner. Reservations recommended. 222 W 79th St (between Amsterdam Ave and Broadway). 799.0400 &

73 121-131 West 78th Street Built in 1886 by **Raphael Gustavino,** an Italian mason famous for his vaults (see the **Oyster Bar** at **Grand Central Terminal**), these six red-and-white houses are unified by their symmetrical arrangement and cheery details. ♦ Between Columbus and Amsterdam Aves

74 Only Hearts Silky lingerie, sweet-smelling sachets, jewelry, books about hearts and kissing, and heart-shaped waffle irons and fly swatters are sold in this pretty shop for the shameless romantic. ♦ Daily. 386 Columbus Ave (between W 78th and W 79th Sts). 724.5608 &

75 Bag One Arts Named after the interviews that John Lennon and Yoko Ono gave from the inside of a black bag, this gallery sells limited-edition graphics by the ex-Beatle. ♦ By appointment only. 110 W 79th St (between Columbus and Amsterdam Aves). 595.5537 &

76 Laura Ashley Floral patterns, frilly trim, and classic understatement are the Laura Ashley trademark. Home furnishings and fashions are also available. It's as if Louisa May Alcott had gone into retailing a century later. ♦ Daily. 398 Columbus Ave (at W 79th St). 496.5110

77 American Museum of Natural History This preeminent scientific research institution is one of the top cultural draws in New York City. Its collections—more than 34 million artifacts and specimens—constitute a priceless record of life, illuminating millions of years of evolution from the birth of the planet through the present day.

Built in 1872 in the middle of a landscape of goats and squatters, the original building (designed by **Jacob Wrey Mould** and **Calvert Vaux**) can now be glimpsed only from Columbus Avenue. The body of the museum (built in 1899 by **J.C. Cady & Co.** and **Cady, Berg & See,** with later additions by **Charles Vos** and **Trowbridge & Livingston**), an example of Romanesque Revival at its grandest, can best be admired from West 77th Street. The building itself is nothing if not a piecemeal reflection of changing tastes in style. In between the turreted extensions, a massive carriage entrance passes under a sweeping flight of stairs: The heavy red-brown brick and granite add to the medieval aura and positive strength typified by the seven-arch colonnade. That welcoming entrance is now ignored (except by those arriving with strollers or wheelchairs), and the main facade of the museum has been shifted to the **Theodore Roosevelt Memorial** facing Central Park West—a Beaux Arts triumphal arch and terrace designed by **John Russell Pope** in 1936. On top of the four giant Ionic columns are statues of explorers *Boone, Audubon,* and *Lewis and Clark* (these and the attic frieze are by James Earle Fraser; the animal relief is by James L. Clark). Behind this facade is intimidating **Memorial Hall.** The museum is widely recognized as having the greatest collection of fossil vertebrates in the world.

MICHAEL STORRINGS

American Museum of Natural History

The dinosaur and fossil halls reopened in 1995 as part of an extensive $45-million remodeling restructured the entire 4th floor, adding 6 exhibition halls to tell the story of the evolution of vertebrates. Barosaurus, the world's tallest freestanding dinosaur exhibit, stands majestically in the **Theodore Roosevelt Hall.** The museum has returned the halls to their original splendor— expanding exhibition spaces, revealing architectural details that include grand arches and columns, and providing panoramic views of Central Park.

The **Wallace Wing,** housing two fossil halls, displays an extraordinary assemblage of fossil mammals, including saber-toothed cats, woolly mammoths, giant sloths, and bizarre reptilelike proto-mammals with three-foot sails on their backs. An interactive computer system allows visitors to explore different locations and time periods and the animals that inhabited them. Of the four exhibitions, two dinosaur halls showcase Tyrannosaurus rex and Apatosaurus, dramatically remounted to reflect new scientific thinking, along with Triceratops, a duck-billed dinosaur mummy, and dozens more.

New permanent exhibition halls in the same updated style, peppered with interactive video terminals and often visually spectacular, are continually being added. Recent examples include the **Hall of Human Biology and Evolution,** examining the heritage we share with other living things and tracing the patterns of human evolution; the **Hall of Biodiversity,** including an enormous and vivid mockup of a Central African rain forest, complete with authentic soundtrack and film projections in the background that you see through the trees; and the **Hall of Planet Earth,** featuring computer simluations speeding up the inversion of the earth's magnetic field or the process of continental drift so you can watch the eons hurtle by in a couple of minutes. There are also always two or three large-scale temporary exhibits, some focusing on currently hot scientific topics, most charging an additional fee, including the **Butterfly Conservatory**'s live insects, open early October through February.

The museum has an ongoing program of lectures, films, plays, workshops, and concerts. Free Museum Highlights Tours assemble at the second-floor information desk approximately every hour. Two gift shops, one just for children, and several more mini-stores all over the building, offer Mexican and Indian crafts, microscopes, puppets, books, petrified wood, and other surprises. There are three restaurants: the **Under the Whale** (cocktails and snacks), the **Garden Cafe** (lunch and dinner in a greenhouse setting), and **Dinersaurus** (cafeteria). Limited paid parking is available in the museum lot, on West 81st Street.
♦ Suggested admission. M-Th, Su 10AM-5:45PM; F-Sa 10AM-8:45PM. Central Park W (between W 77th and W 81st Sts). 769.5100

At the American Museum of Natural History:

IMAX Theater Superspectacular films are shown daily on a four-story screen that puts you right into the action. ♦ Admission. Call for schedule. 769.5000 ♿

77 Frederick Phineas and Sandra Priest Rose Center for Earth and Space
The beloved old **Hayden Planetarium,** first opened in 1935, has been demolished and rebuilt as an enormous white sphere, visible within the glass-and–wire mesh box of the new **Rose Center,** designed by **James Stewart Polshek & Partners** and set to open in early 2000. Star shows will be provided by the Museum-designed Zeiss Universarium MkIX projector, with 9,000 fiber-optically projected stars and 84 deep-space objects, and computer-manipulated imagery to create displays of the latest discoveries in planetary and space science from a wealth of unfamiliar perspectives (some of which can make you feel awfully small and marginal). ♦ Admission. Call for schedule. W 81st St (between Central Park W and Columbus Ave). 769.5200 ♿

78 The Beresford On a street of twin-towered landmarks, this deluxe 1929 apartment building designed by **Emery Roth** distinguishes itself by having three rather squat Baroque turrets that give it a double silhouette from two directions. Famous residents have included poet Sara Teasdale, underworld crime leader Meyer Lansky, Margaret Mead, and Rock Hudson. Tennis great John McEnroe and newscaster Peter Jennings are among the current residents. ♦ 211 Central Park W (between W 81st St and W 82nd Sts). 787.2100

79 Excelsior $ In a classy block across the street from the grounds of the **American Museum of Natural History,** this budget hotel caters to the convention crowd. Most of the 169 guest quarters are one-bedroom suites. Updated units are a bit higher in price, but still a bargain for this location. ♦ 45 W 81st St (between Central Park W and Columbus Ave). 362.9200, 800/368.4575; fax 721.2994

80 Maxilla & Mandible When they say you can find anything in this city, they mean it. This shop, specializing in all types of bones and fossils for students and collectors, is definitely worth a visit. ♦ Daily. 451 Columbus Ave (between W 81st and W 82nd Sts). 724.6173

Restaurants/Clubs: Red   Hotels: Blue
Shops/♥ Outdoors: Green   Sights/Culture: Black

275

81 Penny Whistle Toys The Pustefix teddy bear out front is forever blowing bubbles to get your attention. If he could talk, he'd tell you all about the quality classics inside: board games, stuffed animals, dolls, cars, indoor gyms, table soccer games, rattles for infants, and—surprise—no electronic video games! ♦ Daily. 448 Columbus Ave (between W 81st and W 82nd Sts). 873.9090. Also at: 1283 Madison Ave (between E 91st and E 92nd Sts). 369.3868

81 Greenstones & Cie European clothing for children, including brightly colored French sportswear from Petit Boy and Maugin and dressy duds from Italy's Mona Lisa, are sold. Happily, nothing is so extravagant that it's unwearable. ♦ Daily. 442 Columbus Ave (between W 81st and W 82nd Sts). 580.4322. Also at: 1184 Madison Ave (between E 86th and E 87th Sts). 427.1665

82 Pizzeria Uno $ The deep-dish, Chicago-style pizza at this chain outpost is a decent pie. This place also happens to be one of the very few near the **American Museum of Natural History** that is appropriate for children—the express lunch is ready in five minutes. ♦ Pizza ♦ Daily lunch, dinner, and late-night meals. 432 Columbus Ave (at W 81st St). 595.4700. Also at: Numerous locations throughout the city

83 Baci $$ Zippy but uneven Sicilian fare is served in this upbeat, handsome candlelit dining room. Pasta dishes are the best bets here, particularly the gnocchi with pesto and rigatoni with cauliflower, raisins, pine nuts, and tomato sauce. ♦ Italian ♦ M-F lunch and dinner; Sa-Su brunch and dinner. No credit cards accepted. 412 Amsterdam Ave (between W 79th and W 80th Sts). 496.1550

84 Dublin House Tap Room At night, the area's younger, newer residents take over this former worker's retreat, and the place gets very lively indeed. The brilliant neon harp over the door beckons you to have a lager, and the separate back room makes you wish you'd invited the whole team. ♦ M-Sa 8AM-4AM; Su noon-4AM. 225 W 79th St (between Amsterdam Ave and Broadway). 874.9528

FILENE'S BASEMENT

84 Filene's Basement This longtime Boston tradition came first to New York via Queens; the chain later added another store on Broadway. Known for selling perfect and slightly damaged clothing and shoes for men and women from the country's best department stores at bargain prices, this store gave rise to the expression "bargain basement." ♦ Daily. 2222 Broadway (at W 79th St). 873.8000 ♦ Also at: Numerous locations throughout the city

85 Gryphon Book Shop Used and rare books are sold at decent prices. Look for general humanities plus theater, performing arts, and children's books, especially the *Oz* series by L. Frank Baum. ♦ Daily 10AM-midnight. 2246 Broadway (between W 80th and W 81st Sts). 362.0706

86 H&H Bagels West This bakery turns out 60,000 bagels a day, some of which are shipped as far as London! Count on getting one fresh from the oven around the clock. This also happens to be one of the last Manhattan bastions of the "baker's dozen" (buy 12, get 13). While you're at it, check out the section of kosher and nonkosher deli products. ♦ Daily 24 hours. 2239 Broadway (at W 80th St). 595.8003, 800/692.2435 ♦ Also at: 639 W 46th St (at 12th Ave). 595.8000 ♦

87 Zabar's A food bazaar like no other in the world, this place evolved from a small Jewish deli, and is now a giant grocery and housewares store. Cookware and appliances, and packaged, prepared, and fresh foods from all over the world can be found here. On the weekend, a long line forms for the Western Nova Salmon (if you're lucky, the counter help will pass you a slice to nosh on). Though the crowded, narrow aisles can induce an attack of claustrophobia, take a deep breath and persevere: The reward is unrivaled quality at prices that beat the competition. ♦ Daily. 2245 Broadway (at W 80th St). 787.2000 ♦

Adjacent to Zabar's:

Zabar's Cafe ★$ Cappuccino as good as any that can be found on the West Side is served in the neighborhood's most undistinguished interior. Try a warm knish or pastry with your coffee for a superlative afternoon delight. An espresso may be just the restorative you need after a shopping trip to **Zabar's**. ♦ Cafe/Takeout ♦ Daily. 787.2000

88 Barnes & Noble One of 110 "superstores" throughout the US—this vast two-story space has late hours that encourage the

neighborhood's singles to socialize in an intelligent environment, and an interior designed to look like a library, with varnished wood, brass lighting fixtures, and Shaker-style chairs and tables where you can sit for hours. ♦ M-Th, Su 9AM-11PM; F-Sa 9AM-midnight. 2289 Broadway (at W 82nd St). 362.8835. Also at: Numerous locations throughout the city &

Within Barnes & Noble:

Barnes & Noble Cafe A popular singles bar, this cafe offers decent espresso with a selection of cookies, dainty sandwiches, and the like, and a sedate, literary atmosphere. ♦ Daily. 362.8835. Also at: Numerous locations throughout the city

89 The Yarn Co. In addition to being one of the best sources for yarn and expert knitting instruction in the city, this is one of the most pleasant yarn shops, with a big wooden farm table and chairs in the center of the room and an abundant stock of high-quality yarns. ♦ Tu-Sa. 2274 Broadway (between W 81st and W 82nd Sts), Second floor. 787.7878

90 Bath Island This is an oasis for stressed-out New Yorkers in search of biodegradable beauty and bath products—shampoo, essential perfume oils, and bubble bath. You can't miss the store; every morning they scent the sidewalk with hot sudsy water and one of the 75 available perfume oils. ♦ Daily. 469 Amsterdam Ave (between W 82nd and W 83rd Sts). 787.9415

90 Shoofly You may want to only admire, not buy, the adorable children's shoes and accessories here, as many cost more than parents spend on themselves. The European shoes are displayed on low shelves that children can reach (gulp!), and the hats, either from Europe or made by local artisans, are each hung on a different-shaped hook, ranging from a dinosaur to a crab to a corn cob. ♦ Daily. 465 Amsterdam Ave (between W 82nd and W 83rd Sts). 580.4390. Also at: 42 Hudson St (between Duane and Thomas Sts). 406.3270

90 Avventura Gorgeous hand-painted pottery imported from all over the world, particularly Italy, is on display at this handsome store. The one-of-a-kind platters, bowls, and plates are absolute knockouts. ♦ M-Th, Su; F until

sunset. 463 Amsterdam Ave (between W 82nd and W 83rd Sts). 769.2510

Louie's WESTSIDE CAFÉ

91 Louie's Westside Café ★$$ Grand yet casual, this cafe with peach walls, subdued lighting, and French rattan chairs offers a basic but well-prepared American menu, with something for everyone. Try the crab cakes, spinach linguine with turkey *bolognese,* herb-roasted chicken, hanger steak, lamb chops with Tuscan white-bean stew, or pasta primavera. For dessert, have the mocha torte, chocolate velvet cake, or carrot cake. Brunch may be the best meal to have here; try the pecan waffles or Southwestern-style eggs. ♦ American ♦ M-F breakfast, lunch, and dinner; Sa-Su brunch and dinner. Reservations recommended. 441 Amsterdam Ave (at W 81st St). 877.1900 &

FUJIYAMA MAMA

92 Fujiyama Mama ★$$ Not your ordinary Japanese restaurant, this place has loud rock music and waitresses dressed in traditional kimonos. There are some interesting offerings, especially the *yakitori* (broiled dishes). The delightfully weird old menu—in which chicken teriyaki used to be called "Chicken the Chicken" and sirloin with vegetables in a curry sauce was "Agony and Ecstasy"—has given way, alas, to one that just tells you what's to eat. ♦ Japanese ♦ Daily dinner. Reservations recommended. 467 Columbus Ave (between W 82nd and W 83rd Sts). 769.1144

93 Isola ★$$ The apricot-and-yellow walls, covered with wave-and-fish stencils, evoke an Italian island feeling. Good choices include delicious thin-crusted pizzas; pasta with sardines, pine nuts, fennel, and raisins; spaghetti in a puree of black olives; and a salad of oranges, olives, and fennel. The food is vibrant, and unfortunately so is the noise level. ♦ Italian ♦ Daily lunch and dinner. 485 Columbus Ave (between W 83rd and W 84th Sts). 362.7400 &

93 April Cornell For those who like the exotic look of handblocked fabrics, this is an oasis. The owners have asked their suppliers in India to make traditional patterns as well as totally untraditional ones, such as checks and *Provençale*-inspired florals, and to whip them up into pillowcases, duvet covers, tablecloths, placemats, and pillow shams. The fabrics themselves are not stocked. ◆ Daily. 487 Columbus Ave (between W 83rd and W 84th Sts). 799.4342 &

94 Down & Quilt Shop Reasonably priced quilts and down comforters are this store's specialty. ◆ Daily. 518 Columbus Ave (at W 85th St). 496.8980

94 Avenue ★★$$ Equal parts French bistro and New American haven, this spacious but cozy hot spot packs in the Upper West Side hoi polloi and a smattering of celebrities for chef/owner Scott Campbell's uniformly delicious and creative fare. Start with the calamari or the authentic *pommes frites* (french fries)—each fried to crispy perfection—before moving on to roast duckling, steak *frites,* or tuna with roasted beets and greens in a white wine caper sauce. Dessert treats include berry cobbler with crème Chantilly, and pear frangipane tartlet and caramel ice cream. An added plus (though this neighborhood isn't exactly starved for bakeries any more): oven-fresh French baked goods are sold every morning. ◆ New American/French ◆ M-F breakfast, lunch and dinner; Sa-Su brunch and dinner. Reservations recommended. 520 Columbus Ave (at W 85th St). 579.3194 &

95 Harriet's Kitchen Excellent chicken soup and straightforward family fare—roasted chicken with green beans and carrots, fudge layer cake—are available from this unpretentious take-out shop that opens its doors in late afternoon, just when hard-working parents and professionals decide they're not in the mood to cook. ◆ M-Sa 4:30-11PM; Su 4:30-10PM. 502 Amsterdam Ave (between W 84th and W 85th Sts). 721.0045

The oldest independent secondary school in the country is the Collegiate School on the Upper West Side (378 West End Ave).

Broadway, originating in Lower Manhattan at Bowling Green and ending in Albany, is one of the world's longest streets at 150 miles. It is officially designated as Highway 9.

96 Good Enough to Eat ★★$$ Breakfast or weekend brunch are the best bets at this tiny Vermont-style outpost. But be ready to wait in line for pecan-flecked waffles, cinnamon-swirl French toast, or the lumberjack breakfast— it's as big as it sounds. Lunch and dinner are prepared with a homey, if less inventive, touch. Popular picks include a turkey dinner with gravy, stuffing, and cranberry sauce; meat loaf; and turkey club sandwich. All breads, soups, and desserts are homemade, and pasta and pizza specials change daily. ◆ American ◆ M-Sa breakfast, lunch, and dinner; Su brunch and dinner. Reservations recommended for dinner. 483 Amsterdam Ave (between W 83rd and W 84th Sts). 496.0163

97 The Raccoon Lodge West Siders come to this bar for the pool table, friendly atmosphere, great jukebox, and cheap drinks. ◆ M-F 11AM-4AM; Sa-Su 3PM-4AM. 480 Amsterdam Ave (at W 83rd St). 874.9984. Also at: 59 Warren St (at W Broadway). 766.9656; 1439 York Ave (between E 76th and E 77th Sts). 650.1775

97 Cafe Lalo ★$ Long French-style windows open onto the street at this dessert-only cafe with brick walls, the scene of Meg Ryan's and Tom Hanks's first in-the-flesh meeting in *You've Got Mail.* During the day, it's quite pleasant to linger over a cappuccino and such desserts as cappuccino tart, Snicker's Bar cheesecake, lemon mousse cake, chocolate Vienna torte, and assorted fruit pies. At night, it tends to get crowded and loud. ◆ Cafe ◆ M-Th 8AM-2AM; F 8AM-4AM; Sa 9AM-4AM; Su 9AM-2AM. 201 W 83rd St (between Amsterdam Ave and Broadway). 496.6031

98 Children's Museum of Manhattan This educational playground of interactive exhibitions and activity centers is all built around the museum's theme of self-discovery. On the fourth floor is the **Time Warner Center for Media,** where children can produce their own videotapes, newscasts, and public affairs programs. Exhibition interpreters are always on hand to provide assistance, and entertainers are stationed at key points to provide further understanding through song, dance, or puppetry. There is an art studio where classes in book- and paper-making and other studio arts are held, and a theater where performances are given by theater groups, dancers, musicians, puppeteers, and storytellers, as well as children participating in the museum's education and video programs and workshops. ♦ Admission. W-Su. 212 W 83rd St (between Amsterdam Ave and Broadway). 721.1223 ♿

99 520 West End Avenue Neighborhood residents vehemently defended their many-gabled "castle" when, in 1987, a misled developer proposed building an apartment house on this site. This survivor was built in 1892 to the designs of **Clarence F. True.** ♦ At W 85th St

100 The Red House Designed and built in 1904, this six-story apartment building is a cross between an Elizabethan manor and a redbrick row house. Note the dragon and crown near the top. ♦ 350 W 85th St (between West End Ave and Riverside Dr)

101 The Clarendon In 1908, publisher William Randolph Hearst moved his family into a 30-room apartment on the top three floors of this 1903 building designed by **Charles Birge.** In 1913, when the landlord refused to ask the residents on the other nine floors to leave so that Hearst, his family, and his art collection could spread out, Hearst simply purchased the building and forced them out himself. Faced with financial woes, he sold the property in 1938. ♦ 137 Riverside Dr (at W 86th St)

Bests

George Page
Host, PBS *Nature* series

The **Hudson River.** One of the world's greatest and most beautiful estuaries—a natural wonder and a highway of American history. Rent a yacht for a cruise to **Bear Mountain State Park.** The **Circle Line** cruise around Manhattan is also recommended.

The **Metropolitan Museum.** Simply the world's most glorious museum.

The **Palm Court,** the **Oak Room,** and the **Oak Bar,** at **The Plaza Hotel.** All retain an ageless elegance and gentility that is quintessential Old New York.

Lutèce. Splurge. It's still the best restaurant in New York, if not the world.

Under no circumstances should you visit New York in July or August unless you enjoy walking around in the world's largest steambath.

Ed Levine
Author, *New York Eats*

The **Second Avenue Deli** is one of the last old-time Jewish delis in New York. Have mushroom-barley soup, a pastrami sandwich, and an order of fries.

Then wander around the East Village and the Lower East Side. There you'll find what's left of our melting pot. Ukrainian shops coexist peacefully with Muslim meat markets, Polish bakeries, and pasta stores.

Have a meal at the **Union Square Cafe.** They're serious about food without being in the least bit pretentious. It's one of the few great restaurants in New York that treats everyone like a regular.

Go to **Madison Avenue** and window shop at the **Valentino** and the **Armani** boutiques. Don't even think about buying anything, unless you plan on taking out a second mortgage on your home.

Fairway market has a wonderful selection of produce, cheese, bread, and coffee. Next, wander up **Broadway** to **Zabar's** and check out the smoked fish

and the cookware. Then walk over to the **Museum of Natural History** and see the dinosaurs.

Wander around **SoHo** checking out the shops and galleries. Then go to **Melampo Imported Foods** for the best focaccia sandwich you've ever eaten. Take your sandwich next door to the playground and sit at one of the booths the city has conveniently constructed for **Melampo** sandwich buyers.

Betsy Carter
Editor-in-Chief, *New Woman* magazine

Central Park: In the winter, walking through the brambles hearing the ice crunch beneath your feet and seeing the frozen lake.

The Conservatory Garden: In the spring and summer when the lilies and the roses bloom and doll-like brides get married under the trellis.

The surprise and solitude of the **Shakespeare Garden** any time of year. (It's particularly fun with a dog.)

The walk through **Fort Tryon Park** to **The Cloisters.** The herb garden in spring and summer is a treat.

Sitting outside **Da Silvano** eating pasta with truffles and watching the large dogs lie at their owners' feet.

A warm, fresh pretzel bagel with mustard anywhere in the city.

"In Manhattan, there are gardens on roofs, gardens outside basement apartments, and minigardens on miniterraces. How do the gardens grow? Expensively. And what do they grow? Almost anything. Apparently, even cash crops. Wildflowers have been tamed on tiny balconies, and families fed on vegetables nurtured in the alien soil bordered by sidewalks."

Ralph Caplan, writer and design consultant

Upper West Side

A neighborhood in transition, the Upper West Side (the area bordered by **Central Park**, the **Hudson River**, **West 86th Street**, and **Cathedral Parkway/West 110th Street**) is undergoing the same kind of gentrifying process that has taken place farther south. The commercial zone is extending north along **Broadway** and **Amsterdam** and **Columbus Avenues**, and the residential zone that surrounds **Columbia University** is moving south along those same streets. While the **Central Park** blocks (the numbered streets between Columbus Avenue and **Central Park West**) contain brownstones and apartments that are in excellent condition as far north as **West 95th Street**, even the blocks of tenements and middle-income apartments between Amsterdam Avenue and Broadway, in disrepair for years, have become desirable residences—if only for their proximity to the burgeoning shopping and dining strips. The residential **West End Avenue** and **Riverside Drive** remain staunchly unchanged, except perhaps for the parade of new windows in the grand old high-rises, most of which have been converted to co-ops as far north as **Duke Ellington Boulevard/West 106th Street**.

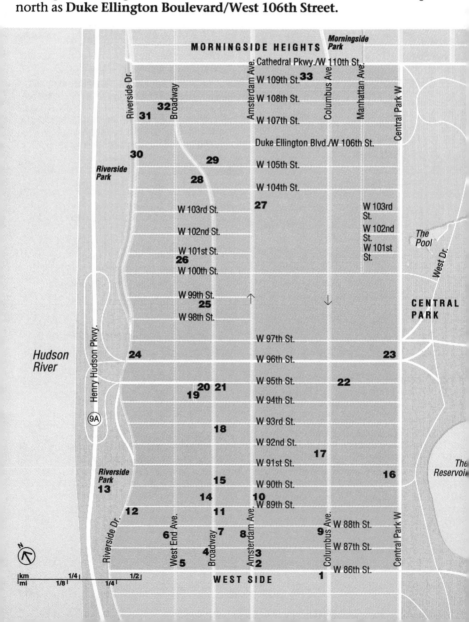

Whereas only a few years ago it seemed to be a fading reminder of the Old World, the West Side north of West 86th Street is now a thriving cosmopolitan mix that feels like the best of both worlds. New high-rise buildings fronted by sidewalk cafes and attractive retail stores are graceful and stabilizing elements to a rapidly changing upper Broadway. Columbus Avenue buzzes with life spilling in and out of its restaurants, bars, antiques shops, and clothing stores. Even the area from **West 96th** to West 110th Streets is sprucing up, particularly east of Broadway, where what was once considered the periphery of Harlem has been given a name of its own—**Manhattan Valley**—and is now more readily associated with the Upper West Side. And while there's easy access to **Central Park** on the eastern side of this area, to the west is **Riverside Park**, a 50-block oasis along the Hudson River, designed by Frederick Law Olmsted, creator of **Central Park.**

1 La Mirabelle ★$$$ A fresh, inviting decor, efficient service, and food that is a notch above the ordinary keep this French bistro busy. Good choices are escargots, soft-shell crabs cooked with lots of garlic and tomatoes, a pink, spicy rack of lamb, and the best steak *frites* (with french fries) on the West Side. However, we recommend going elsewhere to satisfy your sweet tooth. ♦ French ♦ Daily dinner; Su brunch and dinner. Reservations recommended. 102 W 86th St (at Columbus Ave). 496.0458

2 West Park Presbyterian Church Originally the **Park Presbyterian Church,** this church was built in 1890 to the designs of **Henry F. Kilburn.** The rough-hewn red sandstone of the Richardsonian Romanesque mass is enlivened by the lightness of the almost Byzantine details of the capitals and doorways and the fineness of the colonettes in the tower. The church's boldness is emphasized by the asymmetrical massing, with the single tower holding the corner between two strong facades. ♦ 165 W 86th (at Amsterdam Ave). 362.4890 ᴌ

2 Barney Greengrass (The Sturgeon King) ★★$$ Supplying the West Side with appetizing since 1908, this place, run by Barney's son Moe and grandson Gary, includes a retail shop that is folksier than **Zabar's,** though not as complete. On one side is a smoked-fish counter with perfect smoked salmon, sturgeon, pickled herring, and chopped liver. On the other is an earthy dining room furnished with brown vinyl seats, fluorescent lighting that makes everyone look as if they need to be hospitalized, and, inexplicably, a mural of New Orleans. It's well worth the wait for a table. ♦ Deli ♦ Tu-Su breakfast and lunch. No credit cards accepted. 541 Amsterdam Ave (between W 86th and W 87th Sts). 724.4707

3 Popover Café ★$$ A cozy spot with white brick walls and plaid banquettes, this place has teddy bears scattered around the room for company. Breakfast is a popular meal here— the neighborhood piles in for freshly made popovers served with strawberry butter, raspberry jam, or apple butter; omelettes; and scrambled eggs with smoked salmon, cream cheese, and chives. There are also good salads and sandwiches at lunchtime, and at dinner, more serious food is offered, including grilled prime rib, blackened swordfish, and duck breast with raspberry sauce. ♦ American ♦ M-F breakfast, lunch, and dinner; Sa-Su brunch and dinner. 551 Amsterdam Ave (between W 86th and W 87th Sts). 595.8555 ᴌ

4 Starbucks The Seattle-based chain, with more than 600 coffee bars across the country, entered the New York market with a vengeance at this location—the largest in the city. Sit back and catch up on your favorite reading while sipping a cappuccino and munching a *biscotto.* ♦ Daily. 2379 Broadway (at W 87th St). 875.8470. Also at: Numerous locations throughout the city

5 Church of St. Paul and St. Andrew Built in 1897 and designed by **R.H. Robertson,** this church has overtones of the manners of Boulee, particularly in the octagonal tower. Note the angels in the spandrels. ♦ 263 W 86th St (at West End Ave). 362.3179 ᴌ

6 565 West End Avenue Designed by **H.I. Feldman** in 1937, this is a Neo-Renaissance building in Art Deco fabric—brick instead of stone, corner windows instead of quoins. At the bottom, banded brick represents the shadow of a traditional plinth, and the cornice is stainless steel. ♦ Between W 87th and W 88th Sts

7 Boulevard $ The wide-ranging menu at this big, comfortable place with a nice outdoor cafe includes so-so barbecue brisket, ribs, roasted chicken, burgers, burritos, and angel-hair pasta primavera. The Monday dinner special, all-you-can-eat chicken and ribs, is a good deal. ♦ American ♦ M-Th lunch and dinner; F lunch, dinner, and late-night meals; Sa-Su brunch, dinner, and late-night meals. 2398 Broadway (at W 88th St). 874.7400 &

8 Ozu ★$ This simple, earthy room with exposed brick walls and wooden furniture serves good salmon teriyaki, and such macrobiotic fare as *soba* (buckwheat) noodle dishes; salads; a variety of grains, steamed vegetables, and seaweeds; and soups that include miso, pea, and carrot ginger. ♦ Japanese ♦ Daily lunch and dinner. 566 Amsterdam Ave (between W 87th and W 88th Sts). 787.8316 &

8 Pandit ★$ Save yourself the trek down to the East Village's Little India and have a memorable meal here in this cozy brick-walled room. Try any of the curries, chicken saag (cooked with spinach in a spicy sauce), or chicken biryani (curried and served on a mound of fragrant rice). The Goanese ownership makes authentic vinegar-scented vindaloos—a wonderfully subtle flavor, completely unlike what you'll find under that name elsewhere in the city, though just as fiery. ♦ Indian ♦ Daily lunch and dinner. 566 Amsterdam Ave (between W 87th and W 88th Sts). 724.1217

8 Les Routiers ★$$ This quaint French bistro with wooden beams and baskets of dried flowers has a fairly classic menu that features such items as onion soup; *boeuf bourguignon;* braised lamb shank with tomato, lentils, and *Provençale* herbs; roasted duck with raspberry and green-peppercorn sauce; lemon tart; and chocolate mousse. The wine list is well chosen and reasonably priced. ♦ French ♦ Daily dinner. 568 Amsterdam Ave (between W 87th and W 88th Sts). 874.2742

9 East West Books This New Age bookstore also is home to the **Himalayan Institute of New York,** which offers instruction in many areas, including yoga, meditation, relaxation and breathing techniques, homeopathy, and stress management. ♦ Daily. 568 Columbus Ave (between W 87th and W 88th Sts). 787.7552 & Also at: 78 Fifth Ave (between W 13th and W 14th Sts). 243.5994 &

10 Claremont Stables Though not actually in **Central Park,** the stables are very much a part

of it. Riders experienced with English saddles rent horses here and enjoy the park from its bridle path. ♦ M-F 6:30AM-10PM; Sa-Su 6:30AM-5PM. Reservations required. 175 W 89th St (between Columbus and Amsterdam Aves). 724.5100/1

11 Westside Judaica Religious articles and a large stock of fiction and nonfiction covering all aspects of the Jewish experience are sold, along with cassette tapes, videos, and holiday decorations for children's parties. ♦ M-Th, Su F 10:30AM-2PM. 2412 Broadway (between W 88th and W 89th Sts). 362.7846 &

12 Yeshiva Chofetz Chaim Isaac L. Rice had this house built in 1901 and named it **Villa Julia** for his wife, the founder of the now defunct Society for the Suppression of Unnecessary Noise. This and the former **Schinasi Residence** (351 Riverside Drive) are the only two mansions left from the days when Riverside Drive was lined with them. Note the slightly askew porte cochere (a porch large enough for wheeled vehicles to pass through). The architects, **Herts & Tallant,** also designed the **Lyceum Theater.** ♦ 346 W 89th St (at Riverside Dr). 362.1435

13 Riverside Park Originally designed by Frederick Law Olmsted (of **Central Park**) from 1873 to 1910, this welcome strip of greenery stretches for three miles (blessedly covering a rail line below), with space for jogging, tennis, and baseball. When there's snow, people actually sleigh ride and cross-country ski here. Additions were made to the park in 1888 by **Calvert Vaux** and Samuel Parsons Jr., and in 1937 by Clinton F. Lloyd.

Not a monument in itself, as is **Central Park,** this piece of land is spattered with a few little memorials—most notably the *Soldiers' and Sailors' Monument* designed in 1902 by **Stoughton & Stoughton** and **Paul E.M. Dubo** at West 89th Street, modeled after the *Choragic Monument of Lysicrates* in Athens; the *Firemen's Memorial* at West 100th Street, designed in 1913 by sculptor Attilio Piccirilli and architect **H. Van Buren Magonigle,** and graced by statues of *Courage and Duty;* and the easy-to-overlook but not-to-be-forgotten *Carrère Memorial* (1916), a small terrace and plaque at West 99th Street honoring the great architect **John Merven Carrère,** designed by his partner **Thomas Hastings.** Carrère died in an automobile accident in 1911. ♦ Bounded by Riverside Dr and the Hudson River, and W 72nd and W 145th Sts

14 Docks Oyster Bar and Seafood Grill ★★$$ Fresh seafood is featured in this lively black-and-white–tiled neighborhood haunt. The catch of the day varies, but fried oysters coated in cornmeal are a sure bet anytime, and the french-fried yams are an inspiration. Also worth trying are the crab cakes, grilled snapper, and fried calamari. Dessert specials include mud cake and Key lime pie. Stop in on Sunday or Monday night for a full New England clambake. ♦ Seafood ♦ M-Sa lunch and dinner; Su brunch and dinner. Reservations recommended. 2427 Broadway (between W 89th and W 90th Sts). 724.5588. Also at: 633 Third Ave (between E 40th and E 41st Sts). 986.8080

14 Murray's Sturgeon For more than a half-century, the ultimate Jewish appetizing store has continued to live up to its reputation for high-quality sturgeon, herring, lox, whitefish, and other smoked fish items. The store also carries caviar, coffee beans, and dried fruit. ♦ Daily. 2429 Broadway (between W 89th and W 90th Sts). 724.2650

15 The Hero's Journey This shop carries all the latest crystals, New Age books, trinkets, and paraphernalia. ♦ Daily. 2440 Broadway (at W 90th St). 874.4630

16 The Eldorado The northernmost of the twin-towered silhouettes on Central Park West, this apartment building, which was designed by **Margon & Holder** and built in 1931, is characterized by its Art Deco detailing. ♦ 300 Central Park W (at W 90th St)

17 Trinity School and Trinity House The main building was built in 1894 to the designs of **Charles C. Haight;** the east building was designed by **William A. Potter** in 1892; and the apartment tower and school addition were designed by **Brown, Guenther, Battaglia, Seckler** in 1969. Straight, wonderful Romanesque Revival, now locked to an intricate 1960s tower, it is much better than average. ♦ House: 100 W 92nd St; School: 101 W 91st St (between Columbus and Amsterdam Aves). House: 724.1313. School: 873.1650

18 Murder Ink. The grandmother of all mystery bookstores, this is just the way you picture it: cozy and English, with fat fuzzy cats and an intriguing clutter of new and out-of-print mysteries, references, and periodicals. Most major mystery authors do signings here. ♦ Daily. 2486 Broadway (between W 92nd and W 93rd Sts). 362.8905. Also at: 1465 Second Ave (between E 76th and E 77th Sts).

517.3222; 1 Whitehall St (at Stone St). 742.7025 ♿

19 Pomander Walk A surprising little enclave, this double row of mock-Tudor town houses was named after a play that was produced in London and played on Broadway in 1911. The houses, designed in 1922 by **King & Campbell,** were meant to look like the stage set for the New York production. Tenants have included Rosalind Russell, Humphrey Bogart, and Lillian and Dorothy Gish. The buildings are not open to the public. ♦ Between W 94th and W 95th Sts

SYMPHONY SPACE

20 Symphony Space Constructed during the first decade of this century, this building began as the **Crystal Carnival Skating Rink** and was converted into a movie house in the 1920s. Under the guidance of artistic director Isaiah Sheffer, it has become a performing arts center that has contributed to a cultural renaissance on the Upper West Side, with an incredibly wide-ranging program (at outstandingly low prices, too) of music, dance, theater, film, and the "Selected Shorts" series of short-story readings by distinguished actors like William Hurt, Jane Curtin, and Jerry Stiller. Every year, usually in March, they present a free-of-charge 12-hour "Wall to Wall" musical marathon celebrating the work of a single composer, anyone from J.S. Bach through Kurt Weill or George Gershwin to John Cage. Notable supporters include violinists Itzhak Perlman and Pinchas Zukerman, jazz pianist Dr. Billy Taylor, the late composer John Cage, actor Fritz Weaver, and actresses Estelle Parsons and Claire Bloom. Every 16 June they present *Bloomsday on Broadway,* during which James Joyce's novel *Ulysses* is read aloud. At press time, work had begun on a 22-story apartment building around and over the theater and the beloved **Thalia** movie house next door, to be completed by 2001, until which it will be possible to have the unique experience of going to a first-rate concert in the middle of a large construction site. With the money garnered from the air rights, **Symphony Space** hopes to seed an endowment for major renovations to its space and the **Thalia** as well. ♦ 2537 Broadway (between W 94th and W 95th Sts). 864.5400

21 Key West Diner $ The salmon-and-turquoise decor is straight out of the Sunshine State, just as the name suggests. Nevertheless, this place is just a basic New York coffee shop with standard fare such as decent burgers, sandwiches, salads, omelettes, bagels, and challah French toast. ♦ Diner ♦ Daily breakfast, lunch, dinner, and late-night meals. 2532 Broadway (between W 94th and W 95th Sts). 932.0068

22 West 95th Street These blocks of diverse row houses represent one aspect of the ongoing Upper West Side urban renewal effort. Between the housing projects on the avenues, side streets such as this one, which provide unique and charming character, are being gradually restored. ♦ Between Central Park W and Amsterdam Ave

23 First Church of Christ, Scientist This building is, surprisingly, not particularly Beaux Arts, but more in the style of the English Renaissance, with a touch of Hawksmoor revealed in the energetic facade and steeple. The marble interiors are quite impressive. **Carrère & Hastings,** who designed this structure in 1903, were also responsible for the **New York Public Library** and the **Frick Residence.** ♦ 1 W 96th St (at Central Park W). 749.3088

24 The Cliff Dwellers' Apartments The facade is decorated with a frieze of mountain lions, snakes, and buffalo skulls—symbols of the Arizona cliff dwellers. Designed in 1914 by **Herman Lee Leader,** this is an unusual example of Art Deco interest in prehistoric art and culture. ♦ 243 Riverside Dr (at W 96th St)

25 Health Nuts Hypoallergenic vitamins, natural breads, and organic goods—grains, nuts, herbs, and honey—are sold here. ♦ Daily. 2611 Broadway (at W 99th St). 678.0054. Also at: numerous locations throughout the city

26 838 West End Avenue Covered with terra-cotta decoration, both in geometric patterns and stylized natural forms, this structure was designed by **George Blum** and **Edward Blum** in 1914. ♦ At W 101st St

There are approximately 504 miles of sidewalk in New York City.

Before the Ninth Avenue El was pushed uptown in 1879, the only "rapid" means of transportation on the Upper West Side were the Eighth Avenue horsecar line and a stage coach on the Bloomingdale Road (now Broadway).

Restaurants/Clubs: Red **Hotels:** Blue
Shops/ 🌳 Outdoors: Green **Sights/Culture:** Black

27 New York International American Youth Hostel (AYH) $ Clean, safe, and inexpensive accommodations come in the form of 90 dorm-style rooms that sleep from 4 to 12; there is no curfew, and the hostel stays open all day long. Like other hostels, this one requires that guests be members of AYH (nonmembers can join here) and bring a sleeping bag or rent sheets. The building—designed by **Richard Morris Hunt,** and once a home operated by the Association for the Relief of Respectable Aged Indigent Females— is a Designated Landmark of the City of New York. The maximum stay is seven days, but you can apply for an extension. Bathrooms are shared. ♦ 891 Amsterdam Ave (between W 102nd and W 104th Sts). 932.2300 &

28 Positively 104th Street Cafe ★$ Simple and cozy, this cafe offers a range of fare. Try one of the well-prepared salads— spinach with goat cheese and sun-dried tomatoes, or Cobb—or such sandwiches as roast beef with coleslaw. More ambitious entrées include turkey meat loaf and salmon with caper, tomato, basil, and balsamic vinaigrette sauce. For a light dessert, try the angel food cake with raspberry puree. ♦ American ♦ M-F breakfast, lunch, and dinner; Sa-Su brunch, lunch, and dinner. 2725 Broadway (between W 104th and W 105th Sts). 316.0372

Metisse

29 Metisse ★★★$$ Since the day it opened this cozy bistro has been wowing the neighborhood. But that shouldn't be surprising considering the pedigree of its principal: Chef-owner Claude Waryniak learned the ropes working with Jean-Georges Vongerichten at **Lafayette** and **JoJo,** and simple, perfect French food is the result of his efforts; try sautéed sweetbreads with beurre blanc, the signature potato and goat-cheese terrine with arugula juice, duck breast with *pommes délices,* mushroom sauce, and confit of plum, or the ultimate steak *frites.* Desserts are also exceptional, particularly crème brûlée and a warm chocolate *gâteau* (cake) with vanilla ice cream. The wine list is small but well chosen and affordable. ♦ French ♦ Daily dinner. Reservations recommended. 239 W 105th St (between Amsterdam Ave and Broadway). 666.8825

30 Riverside Drive/West 105th Street Historic District Riverside Drive between West 105th and 106th Streets (plus some of

New York Speak

New Yorkers have cultivated unique phrases that, once understood, speak volumes. Here is a guide to some of the more trenchant vocabulary:

Greetings and Such

Yo Could mean "Pardon me," "Watch it, you," or "Pleased to see you, my good man."

Cuisine

Appetizing Mostly smoked fish—lox, whitefish, sturgeon—yummy!

Grab a slice To purchase and consume pizza.

The Original Ray's Refers to a famed establishment on Sixth Avenue at 11th Street, whose name has since been used by dozens of imitators.

A schmear Refers to a small portion of cream cheese to be smeared upon a bagel.

A regular A cup of coffee with milk, which may or may not automatically come with sugar. Ask.

A black A cup of coffee, no milk, often with sugar.

Wait on them Contrary to popular practice, something that waiters tell customers to do, as in "You're gonna have to wait on them fries."

Geography

The Island (Long Island). Not used to refer to Staten Island. Never used to refer to Manhattan.

Uptown When used in Greenwich Village or points south, refers to the area north of 14th Street.

Upstate Refers to anywhere north of New York City, within New York State.

Over there New Jersey.

Consumerism

Bloomie's Bloomingdale's department store, as in "I saw her in Bloomie's."

Standing on line Known everywhere else in the world as "standing in line."

Fashion victim Someone whose clothes and makeup are too trendy to wear anywhere but at a photo shoot.

East Village type The flip side of "fashion victim"; someone whose clothes and makeup are too urban funky to wear anywhere but on **Avenue D.**

Sample sales Sales of leftover or sample merchandise held by manufacturers in the Garment District.

Lotto fever An affliction that compels people to wait "on line" for hours for a one-in–26-million chance at wealth.

Two-fer A theater coupon that entitles the bearer to two tickets for the price of one (plus a surcharge). Available at the **Convention and Visitors Bureau.**

Our Fair Streets

Don't block the box Anti-gridlock warning to drivers meaning "Do not drive into the intersection until there is room to cross it."

Gridlock The traffic jam that results when someone "blocks the box."

Don't even THINK of parking here Courteous street sign provided by the city. Usually ignored.

Alternate parking When the side of the street one may park on depends on the hour and day of the week.

Bridge-and-tunnel people Commuters from New Jersey and Long Island. See "Over there."

BBQs Those who commute into Manhattan from the boroughs of Brooklyn, the Bronx, and Queens.

No radio Posted on car windows as an appeal to thieves who might be tempted to break in without checking to see that the radio has been removed.

West 105th Street) has an excellent collection of turn-of-the-century French Beaux Arts town houses. Of special interest is **No. 331,** designed in 1902 by **Janes & Leo,** formerly Marion Davies's residence and now part of the **New York Buddhist Church** and **American Buddhist Academy.**

31 Nicholas Roerich Museum Roerich was well known in his native Russia and throughout the world as an artist, philosopher, archaeologist, and founder of an educational institution to promote world peace through the arts. This beautiful old town house, one unit of his **Master Institute,** overflows with his landscapes, books, and pamphlets on art, culture, and philosophy. Lectures and concerts take place here.
♦ Donation suggested. Tu-Su 2-5PM. 319 W 107th St (between Broadway and Riverside Dr). 864.7752

32 107 West ★$$ A mostly young, upscale crowd keeps this three-room establishment bustling. The overall tone is Cajun, but the menu throws a few Mexican and pasta specialties into the mix. Try the jambalaya, which is some of the best to be had in the city. The wine list offers decent selections at affordable prices. ♦ American ♦ Daily dinner; Sa-Su brunch. 2787 Broadway (between W 107th and W 108th Sts). 864.1555

33 Cathedral Parkway Houses These two massive apartment towers were carefully articulated in an attempt to accommodate them to the much smaller scale of the neighborhood. They were built in 1975 and designed by **Davis, Brody & Associates** and **Roger Glasgow.** ♦ 125 W 109th St (between Columbus and Amsterdam Aves). 749.1100

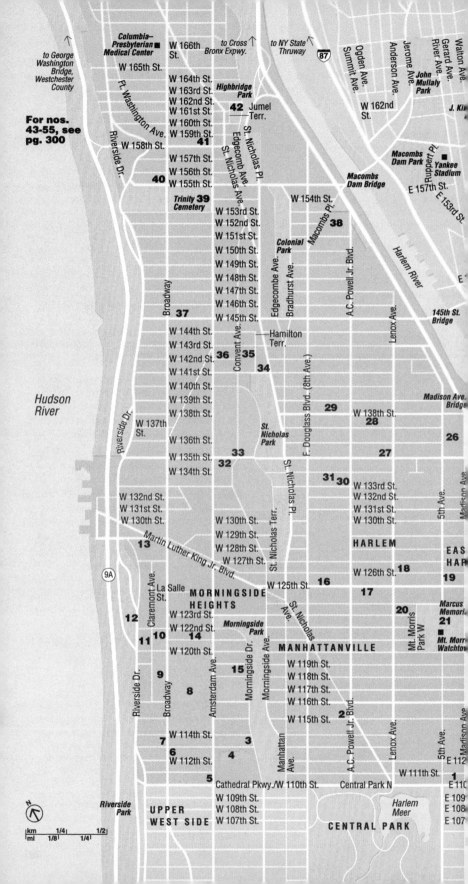

to George
Washington
Bridge,
Westchester
County

Columbia–
Presbyterian
Medical Center ■

W 166th
St.

to Cross
Bronx Expwy.

to NY State
Thruway

87

Walton Ave.
Gerard Ave.
River Ave.
Grand Ave.

Jerome Ave.
Anderson Ave.
John Mullaly
Park

W 165th St.

Ogden Ave.
Summit Ave.

W 164th St.
W 163rd St.
W 162nd St.
W 161st St.
W 160th St.
W 159th St.

Highbridge
Park

42 — Jumel
Terr.

W 162nd
St.

J. Ki

Ft. Washington Ave.

41

For nos.
43-55, see
pg. 300

W 158th St.

Riverside Dr.

St. Nicholas Pl.

Macombs
Dam Park

Ruppert Pl.

■
Yankee
Stadium

W 157th St.
W 156th St.
W 155th St.

40

St. Nicholas Ave.

E 157th St.

E 153rd St.

Edgecomb Ave.

Macombs
Dam Bridge

Macombs
Dam Bridge

Harlem River

Trinity 39
Cemetery

Broadway

W 154th St.

Macombs Pl.

E

38

W 153rd St.
W 152nd St.
W 151st St.
W 150th St.
W 149th St.
W 148th St.
W 147th St.
W 146th St.
W 145th St.

Colonial
Park

Edgecombe Ave.
Bradhurst Ave.

A.C. Powell Jr. Blvd.

Lenox Ave.

145th
St.
Bridge

37

Hudson
River

W 144th St.
W 143rd St.
W 142nd St.
W 141st St.
W 140th St.
W 139th St.
W 138th St.

36 35

Convent Ave.

34

— Hamilton
Terr.

F. Douglass Blvd. (8th Ave.)

29

Madison Ave.
Bridge

28

W 138th St.

26

Madison Ave

Riverside Dr.

W 137th
St.

W 136th St.
W 135th St.
W 134th St.

St. Nicholas
Park

27

33

32

31 30

W 133rd St.
W 132nd St.
W 131st St.
W 130th St.

5th Ave.

Madison Ave

9A

W 132nd St.
W 131st St.
W 130th St.

13

Martin Luther King Jr. Blvd.

St. Nicholas Terr.

W 130th St.
W 129th St.
W 128th St.
W 127th St.

St. Nicholas Pl.

HARLEM

EAS
HAR

18

16

17

19

Claremont Ave.

La Salle
St.

MORNINGSIDE
HEIGHTS

W 123rd St.
W 122nd St.

W 126th St.

St. Nicholas
Ave.

20

Marcus
Memoria

12

10

11

14

Morningside
Park

Morningside Dr.

Morningside Ave.

21

Mt. Morris
Park W

Mt. Morri
Watchtow

W 120th St.

MANHATTANVILLE

9

Riverside Dr.

Broadway

Amsterdam Ave.

15

W 119th St.
W 118th St.
W 117th St.
W 116th St.
W 115th St.

8

2

A.C. Powell Jr. Blvd.

Lenox Ave.

5th Ave.

Madison Ave

E 112

7

W 114th St.

3

6

4

W 112th St.

Manhattan
Ave.

W 111th St.

1

5

Cathedral Pkwy./W 110th St.

Central Park N

E 110

W 109th St.
W 108th St.
W 107th St.

UPPER
WEST SIDE

Riverside
Park

N

km   1/4   1/2
mi   1/8   1/4

CENTRAL PARK

Harlem
Meer

E 109
E 108
E 107

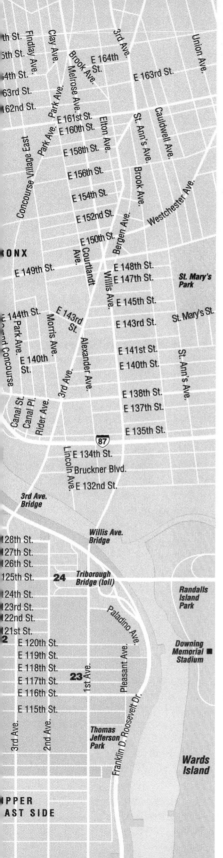

Heights/ Harlem

Located north of **Cathedral Parkway/West 110th Street**, the geographical peaks and valleys of the Heights and Harlem more or less define neighborhood boundaries all the way up to **Spuyten-Duyvil**, where the **Hudson** and **East Rivers** join.

Morningside Heights, the hilly terrain between Cathedral Parkway and **West 125th Street,** was largely undeveloped until the opening of **Morningside Park** in 1887 and of **Riverside Drive** in 1891. World-renowned scholars began to settle in shortly thereafter, and today the area is dominated by educational giants. **Union Theological Seminary, Jewish Theological Seminary, Columbia University,** and **Barnard College** form the cornerstone of this outstanding academic community. Two other structures stand out in the landscape: the massive work-in-progress of the **Cathedral Church of St. John the Divine,** and the **Riverside Church,** an important religious and cultural center in its own right. While you're in the neighborhood, don't forget **Grant's Tomb,** set high on a hill above the river. **Broadway** is the main drag, just as it is on the **Upper West Side,** but here it's less prettied up, although **Columbia University,** a major property owner in the area, has been bringing in more chic—and consequently more expensive—stores and restaurants.

Hamilton Heights, from West 125th Street north to **Trinity Cemetery** (West 153rd Street), is a former factory and ferry-landing town named for Alexander Hamilton, who built a country estate here in 1802. Other 19th-century buildings survive, but most of the development occurred after 1904, when the **Broadway IRT** subway opened. The area has remained primarily residential, and today some of the most desirable residences are the turn-of-the-century row houses in the

Hamilton Heights Historic District. City College of New York (CCNY), the northernmost Manhattan outpost of the **City University of New York (CUNY)** system, moved into the former campus of **Manhattanville College** (now located in Riverdale) in 1950.

Harlem, which becomes **East Harlem** east of **Fifth Avenue,** is Manhattan's foremost residential black neighborhood, where immigrants from the Caribbean and Africa and economic refugees from the American states live, oftentimes in less than adequate conditions. Many people of Hispanic origin, mostly from Puerto Rico, have settled in East Harlem, renaming it *El Barrio* ("the neighborhood" in Spanish), while the later wave of Dominicans and Cubans has settled along upper Broadway (Broadway in the 140s is known as "Little Dominica"), and on the east side of Broadway as far north as **Inwood (207th Street).** The two Harlems are older than most black urban communities in this country, as well as larger, taking up six square miles from West 110th Street north to the **Harlem River** and bounded on the east by the East River. Unlike in many other inner city districts throughout the United States, housing stock was once excellent, and although much of it has deteriorated, it's still worth renovating—which is what increasing numbers of middle-class families are doing.

This section of the island was covered with wooded hills and valleys inhabited by Indians when the Dutch started the settlement of **Nieuw Haarlem** in 1658. Black slaves owned by the West India Company helped build a road, later called Broadway, and the **Haarlem** outpost grew. In the early 19th century, affluent Manhattanites, including James Roosevelt, built estates and plantations here. It was also a haven for the poor, with Irish immigrants among those who built shantytowns on the East River, where they raised free roaming hogs, geese, sheep, and goats.

Harlem began to develop as a suburb for the well-to-do when the **New York and Harlem Railroad** started service from Lower Manhattan in 1837. More railway lines followed, and as handsome brownstones, schools, and stores went up, immigrant families who had achieved some degree of success, many of them German Jews, moved up from the Lower East Side.

The announcement that work was starting on the **IRT Lenox** subway line touched off another round of development, but this time the boom went bust. When the subway was completed in 1905, most of the buildings were still empty. Blacks began renting, often at inflated rates, after having been squeezed out of other parts of the city by commercial development. Eventually the only whites who remained were poor and lived on the fringes, and Harlem became *the* black community in the United States. The subsequent waves of blacks that poured in were often in need of jobs while lacking in skills and education.

Although many blacks in Harlem were existing at poverty level in the 1920s and 1930s, black culture blossomed here—in dance, drama, literature, and music. Speakeasies flourished in the area during Prohibition, and the smart set came uptown to the **Sugar Cane Club** and the **Cotton Club** to hear Count Basie, Duke Ellington, and other jazz legends. Lena Horne got her start here, and literary giants Langston Hughes and James Baldwin were native sons.

In the 1950s, urban renewal made a dent in the declining housing stock by clearing blocks of slums and replacing them with grim housing developments. Gentrification began in Harlem in earnest in the 1970s and continues today, as middle-class families move into **Striver's Row** in the **St. Nicholas District** and to the **Mount Morris Park Historic District,** where the brownstones are among the city's finest. Still, certain sections of Harlem are less than ideal places to visit at night and, in some neighborhoods, during the day. (Try not to go alone, and always take taxis to and from your destination.) On the brighter side, venues for jazz are beginning to come into their own again, as well as family-style restaurants. In 1995, Harlem became one of nine zones in the US chosen as the recipient of $100 million in federal aid for job training and social services programs.

Washington Heights, starting at **Trinity Cemetery** and going north to **Dyckman Street,** was once an Irish neighborhood. In addition to the descendants of the Irish, the area now has an ethnic mix of blacks, Puerto Ricans and other Latins, and Greeks and Armenians.

Audubon Terrace, a turn-of-the-century Beaux Arts museum complex, seems out of place at **West 155th** and Broadway, where it's surrounded by housing projects and tenements. But the complex is easy to reach by subway and worth a visit. North and east of Audubon Terrace is the **Jumel Terrace Historic District.**

Another important Heights landmark is **Fort Tryon Park** (pronounced *Try-on*), the site of **Fort Tryon,** the northernmost defense of **Fort Washington.** Its crowning jewel is **The Cloisters,** which houses the medieval collection of the **Metropolitan Museum of Art.** Just south of **The Cloisters** is a little-known shrine, the **St. Frances Cabrini Chapel.** Here, under the altar in a crystal casket, lies the body of Mother Cabrini, the patron saint of all immigrants. It is recorded that shortly after her death in 1917, a lock of her hair restored an infant boy's eyesight; he later became a priest.

Inwood Hill Park, where Indian cave dwellers once lived, caps the northern end of the island with a rural flourish. Playing fields and open parkland with views over the Hudson and the **George Washington Bridge** and as far as the **Tappan Zee Bridge** are highlights, along with a wilderness of hackberry bushes, maples, Chinese white ash, and Oriental pine trees that stretches to the end of the island, where you can wander the trails and imagine what it was like when the Algonquin Indians had this forest paradise all to themselves.

---

1 Arthur A. Schomburg Plaza These 35-story octagonal apartment towers, completed in 1975 by **Gruzen & Partners** and **Castro-Blanco, Piscioneri & Feder,** are distinguished markers at the corner of **Central Park.** The pairing of the balconies creates an original rhythm in moderating the scale. ♦ 1295 Fifth Ave (between E 110th and E 111th Sts). 289.4465

2 New York Public Library, 115th Street Branch This 1908 Renaissance composition in limestone, a style favored by architects **McKim, Mead & White,** is one of the finest of the branch libraries. ♦ Call for seasonally changing hours. 203 W 115th St (between St. Nicholas Ave and Frederick Douglass Blvd). 666.9393

3 St. Luke's–Roosevelt Hospital At least the central entrance pavilion and east wing remain of **Ernest Flagg**'s Classical/Baroque composition. The 1896 building is charming, dignified, slightly busy, and certainly original. ♦ Morningside Dr (between W 113th and W 114th Sts). 523.4000

4 The Cathedral Church of St. John the Divine Begun in 1892 under the sponsorship of Bishop Henry Codman Potter to designs by **Heins & LaFarge,** this giant, slightly rough

Byzantine church (illustrated on page 289) with Romanesque influences is still a work in progress. By 1911, the apse, choir, and crossing were done, the architects and the bishop were dead, and fashions had changed. Gothic enthusiast **Ralph Adams Cram** of **Cram & Ferguson** drew up new plans to complete the church. The nave and western facade are, therefore, fine French Gothic. Work was discontinued in 1941, but resumed in the 1980s in an effort to complete the cathedral, particularly the towers. In the stone yard in operation next to the church, two dozen artisans, many of them neighborhood youths, worked under a master mason from England to carve blocks in a centuries-old tradition until declaring bankruptcy in 1994; the cathedral is launching a major fund-raising campaign to resume building.

When it is finished (a project that will carry over well into the new millennium), this will be the largest cathedral in the world. The nave is 601 feet long and 146 feet wide; when completed, the transepts will be just as wide and span 320 feet. The floor area is greater than Chartres and Notre Dame together, and the towers will be 300 feet high. Although not entirely complete, four of the five portals have been fitted with Burmese teak doors; the bronze door of the central portal was cast in Paris by M. Barbedienne, who cast the *Statue of Liberty*. The interior is spectacular, with seven apsidal chapels in a variety of styles by a collection of prominent architects. The finest is that of St. Ambrose, a Renaissance-inspired composition by **Carrère & Hastings**. The eight granite columns that ring the sanctuary are 55 feet high and weigh 130 tons each. The dome over the crossing, intended to be temporary, was erected in 1909. Master woodworker George Nakashima's massive heart-shaped *Altar for Peace,* cut from a 125-foot English walnut tree from Long Island and finished with his trademark rosewood inlays, is the site of monthly meditations for peace. The Episcopal church, under the direction of its dean, the Very Rev. James Parks Morton, hosts the visiting Dalai Lama as well as an impressive schedule of concerts, art exhibitions, lectures, and theater and dance events. ◆ 1047 Amsterdam Ave (between Cathedral Pkwy and W 113th St). 316.7540; box office 662.2133

All that remains of Revolutionary War–era Fort Washington is the outline of the foundation, marked by paving stones, in Bennett Park. Here at Fort Washington Avenue, between West 183rd and West 185th Streets, is the highest point in Manhattan, 267.75 feet above sea level.

Restaurants/Clubs: Red   **Hotels:** Blue

Shops/ 🍷 **Outdoors:** Green   **Sights/Culture:** Black

5 V&T Pizzeria ★$ Its fans maintain that this place has the best pizza on the Upper West Side—hefty, thick-crusted, with fresh tomato sauce, whole-milk mozzarella, and flavorful toppings, such as sausage. ◆ Pizza ◆ Daily lunch and dinner. No credit cards accepted. 1024 Amsterdam Ave (between Cathedral Pkwy and W 111th St). 663.1708

6 Symposium $ Greek specialties such as moussaka, spinach pie, and *exohiko* (lamb, feta cheese, artichoke hearts, and peas wrapped in phyllo dough) are featured at this popular and comfortable spot. During spring and summer, the garden is available for dining. ◆ Greek ◆ Daily lunch and dinner. 544 W 113th St (between Amsterdam Ave and Broadway). 865.1011

PAPYRUS

7 Papyrus Booksellers The paperbacks here are geared to Columbia students, and the fine periodical section leans toward politics and the arts. ◆ M-Sa 9:30AM-10PM; Su 11AM-9PM. 2915 Broadway (at W 114th St). 222.3350

8 Columbia University Founded in 1754, this historic Ivy League school has an enrollment of nearly 20,000. Now less politically outspoken than they were in the 1960s, the students have settled down to their studies in the university's three undergraduate schools: **Columbia College, School of General Studies,** and **School of Engineering and Applied Science.**

On the site of the **Bloomingdale Insane Asylum** (of which **Buell Hall** is a remnant), the original design and early buildings of the campus (the third one the university has occupied) were planned by **Charles Follen McKim** of **McKim, Mead & White** in a grand Beaux Arts tradition. Although only a segment of his plan was completed in 1897, most of its elements can be discerned. The Italian Renaissance–inspired institutional buildings— in red brick with limestone trim and copper roofs—are arranged around a central quad on a terrace two stories above the street. There were to be six smaller side courts like the one between **Avery** and **Fayerweather Halls** (somewhat changed now due to the extension of **Avery Library**).

McKim's dominant central element is the magnificent **Low Memorial Library** (1897), a monumental pantheon named after the father of university president Seth Low (who was also mayor of New York City from 1902 to 1903). No longer used as a library, Low remains the administrative and ceremonial center of the university. The statue of the *Alma Mater* on the front steps—made famous during the riots of

Map labels:
International House, W 123rd St., Manhattan School of Music, Morningside School, W 122nd St., Corpus Christi Church, Grant, Sarasota, Union Theological Seminary, Bancroft, The Fairholm, W 121st St., Riverside Church, Thorndike, Grace, Dodge, Plimpton, Seth Low, Horace Mann, Teachers College, Whittier, Barnard, Thompson, Russell, W 120th St., Interchurch Center, Milbank, Brinkerhoff, Fiske, Pupin, Schapiro Research Center, Seeley W. Mudd, MacIntosh Center, Dodge Fitness Center, Sherman Fairchild Center, W 119th St., Butler Hall, Altschul, Morningside Park, Riverside Park, Uris, Lehman, Havemeyer, W 118th St., East Campus Residence Hall, Fayerweather, Avery, School of International Affairs, Barnard College, Mathematics, Low Memorial Library, St. Paul's Chapel, Faculty House, Sulzberger, Earl, Visitors' Center, Buell Hall, Wien, Brooks, Miller Theatre, Alma Mater, Law School, President's House, W 116th St., College Walk, W 116th St., Journalism, Hamilton, King's Crown, Woodbridge, Schapiro Hall, Post Office, W 115th St., St. Hilda's and St. Hugh's School, Ferris Booth, Butler Library, Women's Hospital, Notre Dame Church, Broadway Presbyterian Church, Carman, John Jay, Eli White, River, W 114th St., Hogan, Ruggles, St. Luke's Hospital, Watt, W 113th St., McVickar, McBain, Cathedral Church of St. John the Divine, Armstrong, W 112th St.

Avenues: Riverside Dr., Claremont Ave., Broadway, Amsterdam Ave., Morningside Dr.

km/mi scale: 1/16, 1/8, 1/8, 1/4

1968—was unveiled by Daniel Chester French in 1903.

Other noteworthy buildings on the campus include **Butler Library,** a colonnaded box facing **Low,** completed in 1934 by **James Gamble Rogers.** The **Sherman Fairchild Center for the Life Sciences,** a 1977 **Mitchell/Giurgola** creation, is an interesting contextual essay in which a glass-and-metal building has been hidden behind a screen of quarry tile that resembles the ground pavers. The **Law School** and the **School of International Affairs** extension, built in 1963 and 1971 by **Harrison & Abramovitz,** forms a great white mass beyond a blocklong bridge that spans Amsterdam Avenue. Charming and modest, the Byzantine/Renaissance **St. Paul's Chapel,** a 1907 work by **Howell & Stokes,** has a lovely, vaulted, and light interior. Tours of the campus, which originate at **Low Library** (854.4900), are conducted according to interest and the availability of guides. The main entrance is at Broadway and West 116th Street. ◆ Bounded by Morningside Dr and Broadway, and W 114th and W 121st Sts. 854.1754 ♿

9 Barnard College The 2,200-student women's school, an undergraduate college of **Columbia University,** offers bachelor's degrees in 27 majors, with an emphasis on liberal arts. Across Broadway from the elegant expanse of Columbia, the sister school's campus appears crowded but somehow more lively. The older buildings at the north end— **Milbank, Brinkerhoff,** and **Fiske Halls**—were designed by **Lamb & Rich** in the 1890s in a sort of New England academic style. More interesting is the heart of the campus today: the limestone counterpoints of **MacIntosh Center** and **Altschul Hall,** both built by Philadelphia architect **Vincent G. Kling** in 1969. In 1989, 400 students moved into **Sulzberger Hall,** a 17-story tower at the southern end of campus, designed by **James Stewart Polshek & Partners.** ◆ Bounded by Broadway and Claremont Ave, and W 116th and W 120th Sts. 854.5262

10 Union Theological Seminary Bookstore This bookstore, affiliated with the seminary, stocks any and all in-print books and periodicals that concern theology. ♦ M-F. 3041 Broadway (between W 120th and W 122nd Sts). 280.1554

10 Union Theological Seminary In a landscape studded with institutions, this is one of the few that truly manage to keep the city at bay. Designed by **Allen & Collens** in 1910 with alterations by **Collens, Willis & Beckonert** in 1952, the building is an example of collegiate Gothic borrowed from Oxbridge and, in that tradition, it has a secluded interior courtyard. ♦ Bounded by Broadway and Claremont Ave, and W 120th and W 122nd Sts. 662.7100

11 Riverside Church This church (shown above) was built in 1930 by **Allen & Collens, Henry C. Pelton,** and **Burnham Hoyt,** with a south wing added in 1960 by **Collens, Willis & Beckonert.** Funded by John D. Rockefeller Jr., it is a steel frame in a thin, institutional Gothic skin. The fine nave is almost overpowered by the tower, which rises 21 stories, and the 74-bell carillon is the largest in the world. Visit the **Observation Deck** in the tower, not only to look at the bells on the way up but for a splendid view of the Hudson, **Riverside Park,** and the surrounding institutions. Forty-five-minute guided tours are offered Sunday, after services. ♦ Daily 9AM-5PM. Carillon bell concerts: Su 10:30AM, noon, 3PM. Tours: Su 12:30PM. Observation deck: Su 12:30-4PM. Riverside Dr (between W 120th and W 122nd Sts). 870.6700

Within Riverside Church:

Theater at Riverside Church For more than a decade, dancers and choreographers tested their mettle on this tiny stage as part of the Riverside Dance Festival. These days, the church no longer sponsors performances, but still opens its doors to various theater, music, video, and dance productions. ♦ 864.2929

12 Grant's Tomb/General Grant National Memorial Now's the time to pose the infamous college exam question: Who is buried in **Grant's Tomb?** The massive granite mausoleum, designed in 1897 by **John H. Duncan,** is set on a hill overlooking the river, thereby dominating its surroundings. The walk to the tomb is impressive: You pass along the terrace, up the stairs, through the colonnade and bronze doors, and find yourself under a high dome looking down on the identical black marble sarcophagi of the general and his wife in the center of a rotunda—an open crypt similar to Napoleon's tomb at the Hôtel des Invalides in Paris. It's surrounded by bronze busts of the general's comrades-in-arms and by allegorical figures between the arches representing scenes from his life. Photographs in two flanking rooms fill in with more realistic details. More fun, however, are the benches on the outside, created in 1973 by Pedro Silva of the Cityarts Workshop. The bright mosaic decorations were done by community residents. Make this trip in daytime only, as the tomb attracts some unsavory characters at night. Oh, yes, the answer: Ulysses S. Grant and his wife, Julia. ♦ Free. Daily. Riverside Dr E (just north of Riverside Dr W). 666.1640

Grant's Tomb

13 **The Cotton Club** ★$$ The legendary Harlem nightclub (at this location since 1978) is becoming almost as well known for its food as for its entertainment. The earthy Southern fare is served in a white-walled dining room with white leather banquettes. Try the ribs or fried chicken, and don't forget the greens and ham hocks. For dessert have a piece of cheesecake or the light chocolate cake. The original home of the weekend gospel brunch (seatings at noon and 2:30PM), it offers a prix-fixe buffet, with dishes ranging from scrambled eggs and grits to meat loaf and rice pilaf. ♦ Southern ♦ W-F dinner; Sa-Su brunch and dinner. Reservations recommended. 656 W 125 St (at St. Clair Pl). 663.7980

14 **Teachers College, Bancroft Hall** A stew of abstracted details—basically Beaux Arts Renaissance but with a touch of Spanish and a pinch of Art Nouveau—enliven the facade of this apartment house, designed in 1911 by **Emery Roth.** ♦ 509 W 121st St (between Amsterdam Ave and Broadway)

15 **The Terrace** ★★$$$$ The sparkling wraparound views of the George Washington Bridge to the northwest and skyscrapers to the south are made even more romantic by the reflection of tabletop candles in the windows and harp music wafting in from the bar area. If only the food were as completely wonderful as the ambience. Stick to classic French dishes— *feuilletée* (puff-pastry shell) of seafood with lobster sauce and herb-crusted rack of lamb that are superb. Although pricey, the wine list is very well chosen. ♦ Continental ♦ Tu-F lunch and dinner; Sa dinner. Reservations recommended. 400 W 119th St (at Morningside Dr). 666.9490

16 **The Apollo Theater** This former vaudeville house, designed by **George Keister** and built in 1914, became the entertainment center of the black community in the 1930s, and by the 1950s it was *the* venue for black popular music. A decade later, however, the theater fell on hard times as big-name acts began playing larger downtown houses. It wasn't until the early 1980s, when it was rescued by **Inner City Broadcasting,** that the faded theater was given a much-needed face-lift and turned into a showplace for black television productions as well as live entertainment. It is now a National Historic Landmark run by a not-for-profit foundation. Stars who have performed here include such legends as B.B. King, Stevie Wonder, and James Brown. Wednesday amateur nights are always fun and packed with budding talents. ♦ No credit cards accepted. 253 W 125th St (between Adam Clayton Powell Jr. and Frederick Douglass Blvds). 749.5838

17 **Studio Museum in Harlem** Changing exhibitions of black art and culture from Africa, the Caribbean, and America are featured in this small museum of black fine arts. Year-round education programs, including the well-known "Vital Expression in American Art," offer lectures, concerts, and poetry readings. ♦ Admission. Wed-Su. 144 W 125th St (between Lenox Ave and Adam Clayton Powell Jr. Blvd). 864.4500 &

18 **Sylvia's** ★★$$ The most renowned soul-food restaurant in Harlem and perhaps in New York City has expanded into a second dining room, and during the warmer months, into an open patio next door. Southern-fried and smothered chicken are standouts, as are the dumplings, candied sweets (yams), greens, and desserts—especially the cinnamony sweet-potato pie. The atmosphere is homey and relaxed; there's a snow-scene mural on the wall and one of the best-stocked jukeboxes in town. ♦ Southern ♦ M-Sa breakfast, lunch, and dinner; Su gospel brunch and dinner. 328 Lenox Ave (between W 126th and W 127th Sts). 996.0660

19 **National Black Theater** Courses, readings, performance workshops, and productions all take place at this 99-seat theater. ♦ 2033 Fifth Ave (between E 125th and E 126th Sts), Second floor. 722.3800

20 **Mount Morris Park Historic District** The charming Victorian character of this district, designated historic in 1971, was established during the speculative boom at the end of the 19th century, when it was urbanized by descendants of Dutch, Irish, and English immigrants. After 1900, it became a primarily German-Jewish neighborhood. The houses on Lenox Avenue between 120th and 121st Streets, designed by **Demeuron & Smith** in 1888, are particularly captivating. The **Morris Apartments** at 81-85 East 125th Street, built just a year later by **Lamb & Rich,** now house the **Mount Morris Bank and Safety Deposit Vaults.** The building is distinguished by Richardsonian Romanesque arches and stained glass.

The district also has a fine collection of religious buildings. Dating from 1907, the Neo-Classical **Mount Olivet Baptist Church,** at 201 Lenox Avenue, was originally designed by **Arnold W. Brunner** as **Temple Israel,** one of the most prestigious synagogues in the city. **St. Martin's Episcopal Church,** on Lenox Avenue at 122nd Street, is a bulky, asymmetrical Romanesque 1888 composition by **William A. Potter** with a carillon of 40 bells, second in size only to that of **Riverside Church.** Built in 1889 by **Lamb & Rich,** the **Bethel Gospel Pentecostal Assembly,** at 36 West 123rd Street, used to be the **Harlem**

Club. The **Greater Bethel AME Church,** built in 1892 by **Lamb & Rich,** was originally the **Harlem Free Library.** Originally the **Dwight Residence,** Frank H. Smith's 1890 building at 1 West 123rd Street is now the home of the **Ethiopian Hebrew Congregation.** It is a Renaissance mansion with an unusual round- and flat-bayed front that is a strong addition to the block of fine brownstones on West 123rd Street. ♦ Bounded by Mt. Morris Park W and Lenox Ave, and W 119th and W 124th Sts

21 Marcus Garvey Memorial Park When the city purchased this craggy square of land in 1839, it was named **Mount Morris Park.** It was renamed in 1973 for Garvey, who was a brilliant orator and the founder of the Universal Negro Improvement Association and of the now-defunct newspaper *Negro World.* The highland in the center supports an 1856 fire watchtower, the only one surviving in the city. Its steel frame and sweeping spiral stairs, once practical innovations, are now nostalgic. ♦ Bounded by Madison Ave and Mt. Morris Park W, and W 120th and W 124th Sts

22 Harlem Courthouse Constructed with a mix of brick and stone, the Romanesque edifice was built in 1891 to the designs of **Thom & Wilson.** With its gables, archways, and corner tower, the dignified and delicate mass represents the American tradition of great "country" courthouses. ♦ 170 E 121st St (between Third and Lexington Aves)

23 Patsy's Pizzeria ★$ It's worth making the trip uptown for what connoisseurs say is the most delicious thin-crust pizza in the city. ♦ Pizza ♦ Daily lunch, dinner, and late-night meals. No credit cards accepted. 2287 First Ave (between E 117th and E 118th Sts). 534.9783

24 Triborough Bridge A lift span connects Manhattan and Randalls Island, a fixed roadway springs from Randalls Island to the Bronx, and a suspension span crosses the Hell Gate. The impressive connector-collection was designed by **Othmar Ammann** (already recognized for his design of the George Washington Bridge) and **Aymar Embury II** in 1936. ♦ Between Grand Central Pkwy, Queens, Bruckner Expwy, the Bronx, and E 125th St &

New York City boasts more than 2,700 traffic signals.

Billie Holiday called her home at 108 West 193rd Street "a combination YMCA, boardinghouse for broke musicians, soup kitchen for anyone with a hard luck story, community center, and after-hours joint where a couple of bucks would get you a shot of whiskey and the most fabulous fried chicken."

25 All Saints Church This fine group of buildings shows the Gothic influence of architect **James Renwick Jr.** The firm he founded, **Renwick, Aspinwall & Russell,** buil the church in 1894 and the rectory in 1889, and the school was built by **W.W. Renwick** in 1904. Some say this work is more pleasing than **St. Patrick's Cathedral,** also a **Renwick** creation. Especially worthwhile is the harmony of the terra-cotta tracery and buff, honey, and brown brick. ♦ 47 E 129th St (at Madison Ave). 534.3535

26 Riverbend Houses The complex of 625 apartments for moderate-income families is respectful of context and use of material, whil assembled with great style and imagination. Built in 1967 by **Davis, Brody & Associates,** the complex is a landmark in the recent tradition of publicly subsidized housing. ♦ Fift Ave (between E 135th and E 138th Sts)

27 Schomburg Center for Research in Black Culture The largest library of black and African culture in the United States, collected by Puerto Rican black Arthur Schomburg (1874-1938), is housed in this research center. As a young man, Schomberg was disturbed by the absence of information available on black heritage and history. The center hosts revolving exhibits and shows by African and black American artists. The gift shop offers items from the worldwide African diaspora, from hand-carved statues to postcards by Harlem's own African-American artists. ♦ Free. Daily. 515 Lenox Ave (at W 135th St). 491.2200

28 Abyssinian Baptist Church Built in 1923 by **Charles W. Bolton,** this bluestone Gothic Tudor building is renowned for its late pastor, US Congressman Adam Clayton Powell Jr. Founded in 1808, it is New York's oldest blacl church. ♦ Services: Su 9AM, 11AM. 132 W 138th St (between Lenox Ave and Adam Clayton Powell Jr. Blvd). 862.7474

29 St. Nicholas Historic District/King Model Houses In an unusual and highly successful 1891 venture, speculative builder David King chose three architects to design the row housing on these three blocks. **Nos. 202** to **250 West 138th Street** and **2350** to **2354 Adam Clayton Powell Jr. Boulevard** are by **James Brown Lord,** all in simple Georgian red brick on a brownstone base. **Nos. 203** to **271 West 138th Street, 2360** to **2390 Adam Clayton Powell Jr. Boulevard,** and **Nos. 202** to **272 West 139th Street** are by **Bruce Price** and **Clarence S. Luce. Nos. 203** to **267 West 139th Street** and **1380** to **1390 Adam Clayton Powell Jr. Boulevard** are the finest— elegantly detailed, Renaissance-inspired designs by **McKim, Mead & White.** The harmony of the ensemble, achieved through similarity of scale and sensitive design, despite the variety of styles and materials, is extraordinary. The area came to be known as

"Striver's Row," the home of the area's young and professionally ambitious. It was designated a historic district in 1967. ♦ Bounded by Adam Clayton Powell Jr. and Frederick Douglass Blvds, and W 138th and W 139th Sts

30 Jamaican Hot Pot ★★$ Owned by Yvonne Richards and Gary Walters, this place turns out fabulous Jamaican specialties—fried chicken, oxtail stew, garlic shrimp, jerk chicken, curried goat, and pepper steak, to name just a few. Understandably, it is loved by locals and visitors. ♦ Jamaican ♦ Daily lunch, dinner, and late-night meals. 2260 Adam Clayton Powell Jr. Blvd (at W 133rd St). 491.5270

31 P.S. 92 This 1965 work of **Percival Goodman** is elegantly articulated and warmly detailed. ♦ 222 W 134th St (between Adam Clayton Powell Jr. and Frederick Douglass Blvds). 690.5915

32 135th Street Gatehouse, Croton Aqueduct Built in 1890, this brownstone-and-granite watchtower, with a Roman echo, was the end of the aqueduct over High Bridge. From here, water was taken in pipes to West 119th Street, by an aqueduct under Amsterdam Avenue, to West 113th Street and then by pipe again to the city. Finely crafted gatehouses still stand at West 119th and West 113th Streets. ♦ At Convent Ave

33 City College/City University of New York Nearly 12,000 students—75 percent of them minorities—attend classes at this 34-acre campus. Bachelor's and master's degrees are offered in liberal arts, education, engineering, architecture, and nursing. The science programs are also noteworthy. The campus is an ornately costumed, energetic collection of white-trimmed, Neo-Gothic buildings constructed of Manhattan schist excavated during the construction of the **IRT** subway. The old campus, completed in 1905 by **George B. Post,** is especially wonderful in contrast to the more recent buildings that have grown up around it. The Romanesque south campus used to be **Manhattanville College of the Sacred Heart,** originally an academy and convent. ♦ Convent Ave (between Convent Hill and W 140th St). 650.7000

Within City College:

Aaron Davis Hall at City College This multiarts theater is home to, among others,

the **Dance Theater of Harlem** and the **City Opera National Company.** ♦ W 135th St and Convent Ave. 650.6900 &

34 Harlem School of the Arts (HSA) In 1965, soprano Dorothy Maynor began teaching piano in the basement of the **St. James Presbyterian Church Community Center.** From that modest beginning, it has grown to 1,300 students, and has gained national prominence as a performing arts school. Several former students and teachers now have active Broadway careers. With world-famous mezzo-soprano Betty Allen as president, the school now teaches musical instrument study (piano, orchestral string, percussion), ballet and modern dance, and visual and dramatic arts. (The orchestral string department is especially noteworthy; the 23-member **Suzuki Ensemble,** made up of 8- to 17-year-olds, is known throughout the city.) Through the "Opportunities for Learning in the Arts" program, students from other schools are brought in to take classes during the day. The "Community and Culture in Harlem" program hosts concerts, art exhibitions, and readings. The school's award-winning building, a 1977 work of **Ulrich Franzen & Associates,** is a complex marriage of classrooms, practice studios, three large dance studios, auditoriums, offices, and an enclosed garden. An adjacent building holds the 200-seat **Harlem School of the Arts Theater.** ♦ 645 St. Nicholas Ave (at W 141st St). 926.4100 &

35 Hamilton Heights Historic District The Hamilton Heights area, designated historic in 1974, was once the country estate of Alexander Hamilton. His house, the **Grange,** stands at Convent Avenue and West 141st Street next to **St. Luke's Hospital.** The district has a generally high-quality collection of row houses dating from the turn of the century and exhibiting a mixture of styles and a wealth of ornament. **West 144th Street** is exemplary. The row at **Nos. 413** to **423,** designed in 1898 by **T.H. Dunn,** has Venetian Gothic, Italian, and French Renaissance elements. Because there is very little through traffic, the neighborhood has always been slightly secluded and desirable. It is occupied primarily by faculty from nearby **City College.** ♦ Bounded by Hamilton Terr and Convent Ave, and W 141st and W 145th Sts

295

Studio Shoo-Ins: How to Get TV Tickets

New York is headquarters for a variety of major TV shows and talk shows that the public can attend without charge. Although most tickets must be obtained in advance, many programs offer standby seats (policies vary, so call ahead). Lines for standby seats often form hours in advance, particularly when well-known guests are booked.

The following addresses for written ticket requests do not always reflect the location of the studio or the place where standby tickets are distributed. Audience members must be 18 or older. Request tickets by postcard unless otherwise indicated, and specify which show you want to see and the number of seats.

Asking for a certain day or week is discouraged. But if you will only be visiting New York for a short time and you send in your request a few months in advance, most studios will try to accommodate you, usually permitting two to four tickets per postcard. Even if you don't stipulate a specific date, it can take a few months to receive tickets for the more popular shows.

Late Night with Conan O'Brian (NBC)
NBC
30 Rockefeller Plaza
New York, NY 10112
212/644.3056

David Letterman's successor accepts postcards requesting no more than two tickets and will not accommodate specific dates. The show is taped Monday to Friday at 5:30PM; a limited number of standby tickets (one per person) are distributed at 9AM in NBC's main lobby; entry isn't guaranteed.

The Late Show with David Letterman (CBS)
Dave Letterman Tickets
1697 Broadway
New York, NY 10019
212/975.2476

"The Late Show," taped Monday through Friday at 5:30PM, is one of the hottest tickets in town—expect a three- to four-month wait. One hundred standby tickets are distributed weekdays at noon, though the line forms as early as 9AM on days when important guests are scheduled. Two tickets are allotted for each postcard.

Live with Regis and Kathie Lee (ABC)
"Live" Tickets
Ansonia Station
PO Box 777
New York, NY 10023
212/456.3537

This talk show broadcasts Monday through Friday at 9AM. Request up to four tickets per postcard, but be prepared to wait—about 8 to 10 months. Standby tickets are available after ticket-holders are seated each weekday; the line usually starts forming around 7:30AM at the studio, 7 Lincoln Square (West 67th St and Columbus Ave).

The Rosie O'Donnell Show (ABC)
Tickets, The Rosie O'Donnell Show
30 Rockefeller Plaza
New York, NY 10112
212/506.3288

This is the audience to join at the moment. Taped at 2PM on weekdays, you'd better put in your bid months in advance. Standbys should wear comfortable shoes and be prepared to wait for hours. Requests are given out first come, first served.

Sally Jessy Raphael (NBC)
"Sally Jessy Raphael" Tickets
PO Box 1400
Radio City Station
New York, NY 10101
212/582.1722

Tapings are scheduled Monday through Thursday at 11AM. Each request can yield up to six tickets, with a usual two- to three-month wait. For standby, show up at 10AM at the studio at 515 West 57th Street (between 10th and 11th Aves).

Saturday Night Live (NBC)
"Saturday Night Live" Tickets
NBC
30 Rockefeller Plaza
New York, NY 10112
212/664.3056

A ticket lottery is held each year at the end of August; only postcards (two tickets each) sent in August will be accepted. Since the majority of each audience fills up with network associates, advertisers, and their families and friends, few seats make it to the lottery. Winners are seated on Saturday at 8PM for a dress rehearsal and 11:30PM for the live taping. On Saturday morning, 50 standby tickets for each seating are distributed at 9:15AM at NBC at the 49th Street entrance of Rockefeller Plaza. One person is admitted per ticket, although holding a ticket does not guarantee admission. Fans have been known to camp out overnight for tickets. If you're a fan of Britney, Christina, 'N Sync and others of that ilk, your best bet would be to start lining up the afternoon before.

Other popular shows taped in New York City:

Montel Williams (Fox)
356 W 58th St
New York, NY 10019
212/560.3003

Ricki Lake Show
401 Fifth Ave, Fifth floor
New York, NY 10016
212/889.7091

36 **Our Lady of Lourdes Church** Truly a scavenger's monument, this 1904 church by the **O'Reilly Brothers** is composed of pieces from three other buildings: the Ruskinian Gothic gray-and-white marble and bluestone facade on West 142nd Street is from the old **National Academy of Design,** built in 1865 by **P.B. Wight,** that stood at East 23rd Street and Park Avenue South; and the apse and part of the east wall were once the Madison Avenue end of **St. Patrick's Cathedral**—removed for the construction of the Lady Chapel. The pedestals flanking the steps are from A.T. Stewart's palatial department store, which stood on 34th Street at Fifth Avenue when it was built by **John Kellum** in 1867. ◆ 467 W 142nd St (between Convent and Amsterdam Aves). 862.4380

37 **Copeland's** ★$$ Although the dining room is gussied up with linens and fresh flowers, the food here couldn't be any earthier; try the oxtails, corn fritters, Louisiana gumbo, and barbecued jumbo shrimp. Come on a Friday or Saturday night and be treated to live jazz; the first set starts at 7:30PM (no cover charge). Every Sunday is one of the city's finest gospel brunches. ◆ Southern/Continental ◆ M-Sa breakfast, lunch and dinner; Su brunch, lunch, and dinner. Reservations recommended for brunch and dinner. 547 W 145th St (between Amsterdam Ave and Broadway). 234.2356.

38 **Harlem River Houses** This exemplary complex consisting of nine acres of public housing developed by the **Federal Administration of Public Works** was built in 1937 by **Archibald Manning Brown** with **Charles F. Fuller, Horace Ginsberg, Frank J. Forster, Will Rice Amon, Richard W. Buckley,** and **John L. Wilson.** Michael Rapuano was the landscape architect. An energetic variety of building shapes are arranged in three groups around a central plaza and landscaped courts, becoming less formal nearer the river. The sculpture inside the West 151st Street entrance is by Paul Manship, who also did the *Prometheus* at **Rockefeller Center.** ◆ Bounded by Harlem River Dr and Macombs Pl, and W 151st St and Colonel Charles Young Triangle

39 **Trinity Cemetery** This hilly cemetery used to be a part of the estate of naturalist J.J. Audubon, who is among those buried here. Others include many members of families that made New York, such as the Schermerhorns, Astors, Bleeckers, and Van Burens. The grave of Clement Clarke Moore draws special attention—he wrote *A Visit from St. Nicholas.* The boundary walls and gates date from 1876; the gatehouse and keeper's lodge were designed in 1883 by **Vaux & Redford;** and the grounds were laid out in 1881 by Vaux & Co. ◆ Daily 8AM-dusk. Bounded by Amsterdam Ave and Riverside Dr, and W 153rd and W 155th Sts. 602.0787

At Trinity Cemetery:

Chapel of the Intercession Built in 1914 by **Cram, Goodhue & Ferguson,** this chapel is essentially a large country church set in the middle of rural **Trinity Cemetery.** The cloister at the West 155th Street entrance is particularly nice, and the richly detailed interior is marvelous, highlighted by an altar inlaid with stones from the Holy Land and sites of early Christian worship. The ashes of architect **Bertram G. Goodhue** are entombed in a memorial in the north transept. ◆ Broadway and W 155th St. 283.6200

40 **Audubon Terrace** This collection of classical buildings was first planned in 1908, and bankrolled by poet and scholar Archer M. Huntington. The master plan was created by **Charles Pratt Huntington,** his nephew, who also designed five of the buildings: the **Museum of the American Indian, Heye Foundation,** built in 1916; the **American Geographic Society,** built in 1916; the **Hispanic Society of America** (north building, constructed in 1916; south building, constructed between 1910 and 1926); the **American Numismatic Society,** built in 1908; and the **Church of Our Lady of Esperanza,** built in 1912. The green-and-gold interior of the church is rather nice; the stained glass, skylight, and lamps were gifts of the king of Spain, who also knighted the architect. The two buildings of the **American Academy and Institute of Arts and Letters** are by **William M. Kendall** (administration building, constructed

in 1923) and **Cass Gilbert** (auditorium and gallery, built in 1930). ◆ Broadway (between W 155th and W 156th Sts)

At Audubon Terrace:

Hispanic Society of America The museum of the **Hispanic Society** is in a lavishly appointed building lined with the paintings of old masters—El Greco, Goya, Velásquez— archaeological finds, ceramics, and other decorative arts of the Iberian Peninsula. The library in the building across the terrace is an important research center. ◆ Free. Tu-Sa 10AM-4:30PM; Su 1-4PM. 613 W 155th St (between Broadway and Riverside Dr). 926.2234

American Numismatic Society Downstairs are rotating examples of the world's coinage—past and present—and a display of medals and decorations. On the second floor is the most comprehensive numismatic library in America. For collectors, a Public Inquiry Counter is staffed by a curator to answer questions. Write or call in advance for help with investigating a specific type of coinage in the collection. ◆ Free. Tu-Sa 9AM-4:30PM; Su 1-4PM. 617 W 155th St (between Broadway and Riverside Dr). 234.3130

American Academy and Institute of Arts and Letters View annual exhibitions of the work of members and nonmembers of this honor society for American writers, artists, and composers. ◆ Free. M-F. Call for schedule. 368.5900

41 Wilson's Bakery & Restaurant ★★$$ The menu changes daily, but no matter what's listed, you'll be assured of a satisfying meal any day of the week at this Harlem institution.

When they're available, don't miss the chicken and dumplings, barbecued ribs, fried chicken, smothered steak, ham hocks, and meat loaf. Save room for dessert, particularly the peach cobbler, coconut cake, or sweet-potato pie, all of which come from the excellent bakery adjoining the restaurant. ◆ Bakery/Southern ◆ Daily breakfast, lunch, and dinner. 1980 Amsterdam Ave (at W 158th St). 923.9821 &

42 Morris-Jumel Mansion Built in 1765 by **Roger Morris** as a summer residence on an estate that stretched from river to river, the mansion's two-story portico (illustrated below) became the model for many houses built in Canada and the United States at the turn of the century. During the Revolution, George Washington *did* sleep here, and even briefly used it as a headquarters, until New York City was taken over by the British. After housing a tavern, the mansion was bought and remodeled by French merchant Stephen Jumel. The exterior of the house is Georgian Palladian, with some details added in the Federal period; note the conceit of the quoins—a stone form mimicked in wood.

Inside, the elegant home is decorated with excellent Georgian, Federal, and French Empire–style furnishings, silver, and china. Some draperies were woven by master fabric-maker Franco Scalamandre using period patterns, and some of Napoleon's furniture is here. In 1833, Aaron Burr and the newly widowed Madame Jumel were married in the front parlor room (some accounts claim that her spirit still lingers about the place). Museum educators and volunteers now conduct guided tours of the house, and lectures and concerts

Morris-Jumel Mansion

are held here as well. Picnickers are welcome to use the colonial herb and rose gardens. Around the mansion is the **Jumel Terrace Historic District,** designated in 1970, a charming neighborhood of well-kept 19th-century row houses. ♦ Admission. W-Su. 65 Jumel Terr (between W 160th and W 162nd Sts). 923.8008

43 Columbia-Presbyterian Medical Center Affiliated with **Columbia University,** this enormous hospital complex continues to grow. The hospital enjoys a reputation as a top-notch teaching facility and working hospital, and it has stabilized the neighborhood it serves. ♦ 622 W 168th St (between Broadway and Ft. Washington Ave). 305.2500

44 High Bridge Originally an aqueduct as well, this footbridge is the oldest bridge extant connecting Manhattan to the mainland. Construction lasted from 1839 to 1849. The architect, **John B. Jervis,** also designed the **Highbridge Tower** in 1872, which was used to equalize pressure in the Croton Aqueduct. ♦ Between University Ave, the Bronx and Highbridge Park ♿

45 The United Church When it was erected in 1930 by **Thomas W. Lamb,** this building was **Loew's 175th Street Theater.** The Miami-Egyptian concoction is movie palace architecture at the height of its glory. It's one of the few remaining movie palaces in Manhattan *not* to suffer from the sixplex syndrome, but the stage has been given over to Reverend Ike, the "positive-thinking" preacher. ♦ 4140 Broadway (at W 175th St). 568.6700

46 George Washington Bridge Bus Station This concrete butterfly is a noteworthy attempt at celebrating the bus station in the shadow of a grand bridge. It was constructed in 1963 by the Port Authority of New York in collaboration with architect/engineer **Pier Luigi Nervi.** ♦ Broadway (between W 178th and W 179th Sts). Bus information 564.1114

47 Little Red Lighthouse Now overshadowed by the eastern tower of the George Washington Bridge, this lighthouse was built in 1921 to steer barges away from Jeffrey's Hook. Because navigation lights were put on the bridge, the lighthouse went up for auction in 1951, but the community's support saved it. The pair is the subject of a well-known children's book by Hildegarde Hoyt Swift entitled *The Little Red Lighthouse and the Great Gray Bridge.* ♦ Fort Washington Park (beneath the George Washington Bridge)

48 George Washington Bridge In 1947, French architect and master of Modernism **Le Corbusier** said this spectacularly sited and magnificently elegant suspension bridge with its 3,500-foot span was "the most beautiful bridge in the world . . . it gleams like a reversed arch. It is blessed." If the original plans had been completed, architectural

consultant **Cass Gilbert** would have encased the towers in stone. The work of **Othmar Ammann,** the bridge took four years to build and was completed in 1931. In 1962, it was expanded to become the world's first 14-lane suspension bridge. The roadway peaks at 212 feet above the water and the towers rise 604 feet. Today the CMI Engineering landmark is the world's busiest bridge, with a hundred million vehicles crossing it yearly. For pedestrians, there is a good view of the bridge from West 181st Street, west of Ft. Washington Avenue. But the real heart-thumper is a walk across the bridge. ♦ Between Ft. Washington Ave and Fort Lee, New Jersey

49 Yeshiva University The oldest Jewish studies center in the country, this independent university celebrated its centennial in 1986. Offered here are both undergraduate and graduate degrees in programs ranging from Hebraic studies to biomedicine, law, and rabbinics. Also part of the university are the **Albert Einstein College of Medicine** in the Bronx; **Brookdale Center–Cardozo School of Law** in Greenwich Village; and **Stern College for Women** in Midtown. The main building of its Washington Heights campus was built in 1928 by **Charles B. Meyers Associates.** It's characterized by a fanciful, romantic composition of institutional underpinnings overlaid with a Middle Eastern collection of turrets, towers and tracery, minarets, arches, and balconies—all in an unusual orange, with marble and granite striping. The light in the auditorium is especially extraordinary, with mirrored chandeliers and orange and yellow windows. ♦ W 186th St (at Amsterdam Ave). 960.5400

50 Shrine of Saint Frances Xavier Cabrini The remains of St. Frances Cabrini are enshrined in the glass altar here (above her neck is a wax mask; her head is in Rome). There is also a display of personal items belonging to the saint, the first American citizen ever to be canonized (in 1946) and patron saint of all immigrants. Mother Cabrini was born in Italy in 1850, became an American citizen in 1909, and died in the US in 1917. ♦ 701 Ft. Washington Ave (at W 190th St). 923.3536 ♿

Harlem's best-known dance hall during the Great Depression was the Savoy Ballroom, located at Lenox Avenue and West 140th Street. Notable talents, including Duke Ellington, Louis Armstrong, and Ella Fitzgerald, were regular performers.

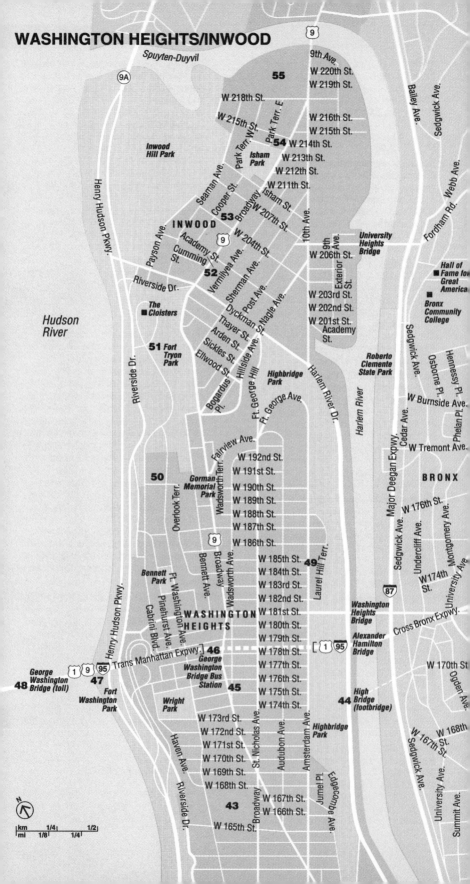

WASHINGTON HEIGHTS/INWOOD

Spuyten-Duyvil

Hudson River

55

9th Ave.
W 220th St.
W 219th St.

W 218th St.

W 215th St.

W 216th St.
W 215th St.

54 W 214th St.

Inwood Hill Park

Isham Park

W 213th St.
W 212th St.
W 211th St.

Broadway W 207th St.

Isham St.

53

INWOOD

W 206th St.

W 204th St.

University Heights Bridge

52

W 203rd St.
W 202nd St.

W 201st St. Academy St.

The Cloisters

Academy St.
Cumming St.

Seaman Ave.
Park Terr. W.
Park Terr. E

Cooper St.
Vermilyea Ave.
Sherman Ave.
Post Ave.
Nagle Ave.

10th Ave.
9th Ave.
Exterior St.

Payson Ave.

Riverside Dr.

Dyckman St.

Thayer St.
Arden St.
Sickles St.
Ellwood St.

Hillside Ave.
Ft. George Hill

51 Fort Tryon Park

Hall of Fame for Great America

Bronx Community College

Roberto Clemente State Park

Fordham Rd.

Bailey Ave.
Sedgwick Ave.
Webb Ave.

Bogardus Pl.

Highbridge Park

Ft. George Ave.

Harlem River Dr.

Harlem River

Sedgwick Ave.
Cedar Ave.
Osborne Pl.
Phelan Pl.
Hennessy Pl.

W Burnside Ave.

W Tremont Ave.

BRONX

W 176th St.

Sedgwick Ave.
Undercliff Ave.
University Ave.
Montgomery Ave.

Major Deegan Expwy.

Riverside Dr.

Fairview Ave.

W 192nd St.
W 191st St.
W 190th St.
W 189th St.
W 188th St.
W 187th St.
W 186th St.

50

Gorman Memorial Park

Wadsworth Terr.

Overlook Terr.

W 174th St.

87

W 185th St.
W 184th St.
W 183rd St.
W 182nd St.
W 181st St.
W 180th St.
W 179th St.
W 178th St.
W 177th St.
W 176th St.
W 175th St.
W 174th St.

49

Laurel Hill Terr.

Washington Heights Bridge

Bennett Park

Ft. Washington Ave.

Bennett Ave.

Broadway
Wadsworth Ave.

WASHINGTON HEIGHTS

Pinehurst Ave.
Cabrini Blvd.

Alexander Hamilton Bridge

1 95

Cross Bronx Expwy.

W 170th St.

Trans Manhattan Expwy.

46 George Washington Bridge Bus Station

1 9 95

47

Fort Washington Park

48 George Washington Bridge (toll)

45

Wright Park

W 173rd St.
W 172nd St.
W 171st St.
W 170th St.
W 169th St.
W 168th St.

Haven Ave.

Riverside Dr.

43

W 167th St.
W 166th St.

W 165th St.

Broadway
St. Nicholas Ave.
Audubon Ave.
Amsterdam Ave.

Highbridge Park

Jumel Pl.

Edgecombe Ave.

44 High Bridge (footbridge)

W 168th St.

Ogden Ave.
Sedgwick Ave.
University Ave.
Summit Ave.

W 167th St.

N

km 1/4 1/2
mi 1/8 1/4

51 Fort Tryon Park This 62-acre park, with its sweeping views of the Hudson River, is beyond exquisite. Originally the C.K.G. Billings estate (whose entrance was the triple-arched driveway from Riverside Drive), the land was bought by John D. Rockefeller Jr. in 1909 and given to the city in 1930. (As part of the deal, the city had to agree to close off the ends of several streets above East 60th Street to create the site for **Rockefeller University**.) There are still signs of **Fort Tryon**, a Revolutionary War bulwark. Don't miss the magnificent flower gardens. The landscaping is by Frederick Law Olmsted Jr., who gave us **Central Park**. ♦ Bounded by Broadway and Riverside Dr

Within Fort Tryon Park:

The Cloisters Both the building and the contents of this branch of the **Metropolitan Museum of Art** were a gift of the munificent John D. Rockefeller Jr. Arranged among cloisters and other architectural elements from monasteries in southern France and Spain, this is very much a medieval ensemble, incorporating both Gothic and Romanesque elements dating from the 12th to 15th centuries. The complex was designed in the mid-1930s by **Charles Collens** to house the **Met**'s medieval collection, and the **Fuentidueña** chapel was added in 1962 by **Brown, Lawford & Forbes**. The best way to see the pastiche of architectural and art fragments is in chronological sequence—discover romantic gardens, ancient stained-glass windows, altar pieces, sculpture, and tapestries along the way. Highlights include the **Treasury,** where precious enamels, 13th- to 15th-century manuscripts, and ivories are on display, and the pièce de résistance, the celebrated *Unicorn Tapestries* from the late 15th and early 16th centuries. Recorded medieval music sets the mood. Special programs, including gallery talks, musical performances, and demonstrations, are scheduled on Saturday at noon and 2PM. A special place to relax is the herb garden (in the **Bonnefont Cloister**), with a view of the Palisades as Henry Hudson might have seen it. (Rockefeller protected the view by also buying the land on the Palisades opposite and restricting development.) Visiting **The Cloisters** is an absolute must. ♦ Voluntary contribution. Tu-Su. Free tours Tu-F 3PM; Su noon. Margaret Corbin Rd (off Ft. Washington Ave). 923.3700

52 International Gourmet and Gift Center China, cutlery, crystal, appliances, food, and cosmetics imported mainly from Germany can be found in this well-stocked store. ♦ M-Th, Su; F until 2PM. 4791 Broadway (between Cumming and Academy Sts). 569.2611

53 Dyckman House The only 18th-century Dutch farmhouse in Manhattan survives despite the inroads of 20th-century apartment houses and supermarkets. Built in 1783 and given to the city as a museum in 1915, the house has been restored and filled with original Dutch and English family furnishings, and gets high marks for authenticity and charm. An herb garden, smokehouse, and reproduction of a Revolutionary hut are further reminders of life on a farm in the colonies. It's worth a visit. ♦ Free. Tu-Su 11AM-4PM. 4881 Broadway (at W 204th St). 304.9422

54 Carrot Top Pastries Owner Renee Allen Mancino bakes the single best carrot cake in New York, as well as delicious pecan, sweet-potato, and pumpkin pies. Devoted customers can also enjoy the light cafe menu. Its downtown branch is much bigger and also serves pasta dishes, and chicken, eggplant, and meatball parmigiana. ♦ M-Sa; Su until 4PM. 5025 Broadway (between Isham and W 215th Sts). 569.1532. Also at: 3931 Broadway (between W 164th and W 165th Sts). 927.4800

55 Baker Field Fieldhouse/Lawrence Wein Stadium **Columbia University**'s uptown athletic facility features Manhattan's only college football stadium. The views from the stadium (**Inwood Hill Park** is just to the west, **Spuyten-Duyvil** just beyond the northern end zone) are a treat. There's also a soccer field closer to Broadway. ♦ Call for a schedule. W 218th St (just west of Broadway). 567.0404

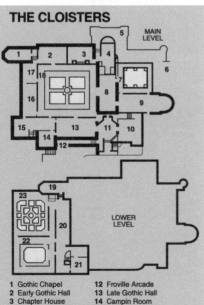

THE CLOISTERS

MAIN LEVEL

LOWER LEVEL

1 Gothic Chapel
2 Early Gothic Hall
3 Chapter House from Pontaut
4 Langon Chapel
5 West Terrace
6 Ramparts
7 St. Guilhem Cloister
8 Romanesque Hall
9 Fuentidueña Chapel
10 Books and Reproductions
11 Main Hall
12 Froville Arcade
13 Late Gothic Hall
14 Campin Room
15 Boppard Room
16 Unicorn Tapestries
17 Nine Heroes Tapestries
18 Cuxa Cloister
19 Gothic Chapel
20 Glass Gallery
21 Treasury
22 Trie Cloister
23 Bonnefont Cloister

Boroughs

While Manhattanites refer to **Brooklyn, Queens,** the **Bronx,** and **Staten Island** as the "outer" boroughs, residents of these boroughs refer to Manhattan as "the city." A great deal of attitude is implied therein. They are outside the skyline's media limelight and inevitably play supporting roles to Manhattan. Their main contribution to the city is work force—there just isn't room for all those commuters to live in Manhattan—but they hold their own on many fronts, with their own high-caliber restaurants, theaters, parks, and architecture.

Brooklyn

With over 300 years of history and more than 75 square miles of land, Brooklyn has always been a city in its own right. It has also been a step up the ladder for immigrant groups, an oceanfront resort, a shipping capital, a cultural mecca, a teeming slum, and the front-runner of an urban renaissance.

Its national reputation is built on vaudeville jokes, an imitable accent, urban conflict, and a host of famous and often comedic natives—George Gershwin, Woody Allen, Mel Brooks, Barbra Streisand, and Beverly Sills among them. Impressive as it may be, this esteem doesn't begin to do justice to the diverse immensity of what would be, were it still autonomous, America's fourth-largest city. Independent until its annexation into New York City in 1898 (Brooklyn-born author Pete Hamill calls this the "great mistake"), Brooklyn has all the earmarks of a major metropolis.

The borough is divided into many ethnic diversities, among them the Middle Eastern development along **Atlantic Avenue,** the Russian section of **Brighton Beach,** and the Italian enclave in **Bensonhurst.** On any day, you'll see locals and visitors cramming the markets and stores in these vibrant communities—much of the charm of the Old Country can still be found in the heart of Brooklyn.

1 **River Café** ★★★$$$$ The backdrop of this lovely dining spot—the towering, glittering Manhattan skyline seen from the foot of the Brooklyn Bridge—is unequaled. The menu is just as exciting, with such dishes as salmon and tuna *tartare* with wasabi, ragout of grilled octopus and Manila clams, sautéed yellowfin tuna with fennel and hundred-year-old balsamic vinegar, grilled cumin and black-pepper–rubbed squab, and charred saddle of venison. And don't miss dessert. The chocolate mousse layer cake, shaped like the Brooklyn Bridge, will put a smile on your face—and a few inches around your middle. The wine list features the most

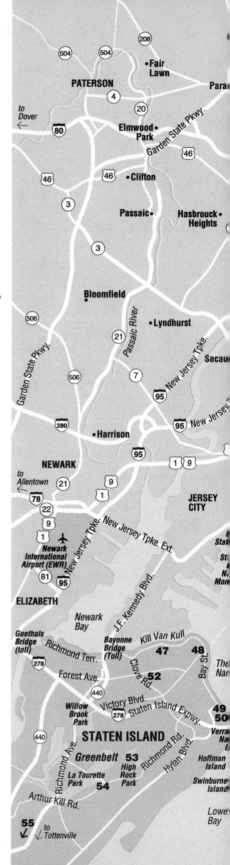

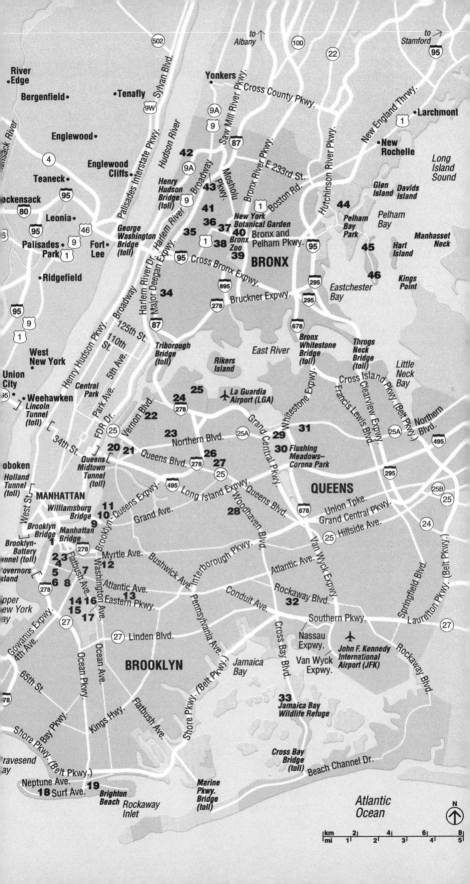

extensive selection of California labels you'll find this side of the Golden Gate Bridge. ♦ American ♦ M-F lunch and dinner; Sa-Su brunch and dinner. Reservations required; jacket required. 1 Water St (at Old Fulton St), Brooklyn Heights. 718/522.5200

1 Patsy's Pizza ★★$ Patsy Grimaldi learned the art of pizza making from his late uncle (also named Patsy), owner of the famed Patsy's pizzeria in East Harlem. Fans of the pizza here say that it has surpassed even Uncle Patsy's. The fresh dough is charred in a brick oven and the mozzarella is made fresh, as is the tomato sauce. This may be as close to pizza heaven as you can get. It's also Sinatra heaven, with that most famous of the Grimaldi family friends heavily represented on the jukebox and in photos adorning the walls. ♦ Pizza ♦ M, W-Su lunch and dinner. No credit cards accepted. 19 Old Fulton St (between Front and Water Sts), Brooklyn Heights. 718/858.4300 &

2 Montague Street Saloon ★$$ A friendly, casual atmosphere fills this local hangout. The basic pub fare is good, and the quaint outdoor cafe is open during the warmer months. Try fried calamari, steamed mussels, Cajun catfish, steak Delmonico, grilled steak topped with fried onions, chicken piccata, or tomato-basil chicken. Finish the meal with mud cake, Key lime pie, or peanut butter pie. ♦ American ♦ Daily lunch, dinner, and late-night meals. 122 Montague St (between Henry and Hicks Sts), Brooklyn Heights. 718/522.6770

3 Brooklyn Borough Hall A palatial sweep of stairs rises to the entrance of this Greek Revival hall of government, designed by **Gamaliel King** and built in 1851. The building, originally fashioned after **Dr. William Thornton**'s competition-winning design, was supposed to mimic Manhattan's **City Hall,** but subsequent design changes dulled the effect. ♦ 209 Joralemon St (at Court St), Downtown. 718/802.3700 &

Flushing Meadows–Corona Park's Unisphere is the world's largest globe at 140 feet high and 120 feet in diameter. Constructed for the 1964-1965 World's Fair, it was given landmark status by the Landmarks Preservation Commission.

The Grand Central Parkway, which connects Long Island to Queens, was designed by Robert Moses as part of a network of parkways that was constructed in the 1940s and 1950s.

The Bronx is the only borough that is part of mainland New York. Manhattan and Staten Island are islands, and Brooklyn and Queens are on the western end of Long Island. New York City is, in fact, an archipelago.

NEW YORK TRANSIT MUSEUM

4 New York Transit Museum Popular with young and old transportation buffs, this small museum takes you back in time with one of the world's finest collections of mass transit artifacts, including vintage cars, signal equipment, turnstiles, mosaics, photographs, and an extensive collection of engineering drawings dating to the beginning of the century. ♦ Admission. Tu-F 10AM-4PM; Sa-Su noon-5PM. Schermerhorn St (at Boerum Pl), Downtown. 718/243.3060

5 Tripoli ★★$$ Atlantic Avenue is the city's center for Middle Eastern cuisine, and among the numerous small restaurants, this bilevel place, in business for almost 25 years, is probably the best and most authentic. Order any of the Lebanese dishes, including falafel, hummus, lamb kabobs, stuffed grape leaves, lamb stew, and one of the heavily honeyed desserts. There's live music and entertainment Saturday nights. ♦ Middle Eastern ♦ Daily lunch and dinner. Reservations required Friday and Saturday nights. 156 Atlantic Ave (at Clinton St), Brooklyn Heights. 718/596.5800

6 Casa Rosa ★$$ Good—and inexpensive—home-style cooking is this unpretentious trattoria's trademark. Have pork chops with broccoli rabe; *zuppa di pesce a la Rosa* (fish soup); clams, shrimp, and calamari in a light tomato sauce; or lobster *fra diavolo* (half of a lobster with mussels, clams, and shrimp on a bed of linguine). Be forewarned: The service can be extremely slow. ♦ Italian ♦ Tu-Su lunch and dinner. Reservations recommended. 384 Court St (at Carroll St), Carroll Gardens. 718/625.8874 &

7 Brooklyn Academy of Music This organization, affectionately known as "BAM," was founded in 1859 on Montague Street and is housed in a 1908 **Herts & Tallant**–designed building. Among the superlative performers who have appeared here are Edwin Booth as *Hamlet* and Sarah Bernhardt as *Camille.* Pavlova danced and Caruso sang in the **Opera House. BAM** is the home of the **Brooklyn Philharmonic.** Over the last decade, impresario Harvey Lichtenstein has introduced many innovative programs in music and dance. His annual Next Wave Festival has been the launching pad for artists like Philip Glass, Laurie Anderson, and choreographer Mark Morris. In 1987, the organization reopened the **Majestic,** an 83-year-old theater-turned-movie house that had been lying dormant for nearly 20 years. Interestingly, the shell of the theater was left intact—the wear and tear of the years showing—while two semicircular tiers of seats around a large stage were built, creating an intimate amphitheater-like space with an exciting medieval feel. The interior was designed by **Hardy Holzman Pfeiffer**

Associates. Successful engagements at the **Majestic** (located on Fulton Street, a block away from the main structure) have included choreographer-director Martha Clarke's *Endangered Species* and the musical *Township Fever,* from Mbongeni Ngema, the director of *Sarafina!* Theaters: **Opera House** (seats 2,100); **Helen Carey Playhouse** (seats 1,078); **Lepercq Space** (seats 550); **Majestic** (seats 900). ♦ A shuttle bus coordinated with scheduled performances at Opera House or Majestic departs from Lexington Avenue at East 51st Street in Manhattan; call BAM for a schedule. 30 Lafayette Ave (between St. Felix St and Ashland Pl), Downtown. 718/636.4100 &

8 Junior's ★★$$ Some say the cheesecake here is the best in New York, and it just may be true. The rest of the food is standard deli/diner fare, however, including pastrami sandwiches and roasted chicken, distinguished only by the large portions. Weekend evenings the place jumps, and the cars are double- and triple-parked out front. ♦ Deli ♦ Daily breakfast, lunch, dinner, and late-night meals. 386 Flatbush Ave (at DeKalb Ave), Downtown. 718/852.5257

9 Peter Luger ★★★★$$$ One of the oldest and still one of the better, more colorful steak houses in the city, this place is great for one thing only: well-charred porterhouse steak made from prime, aged, Iowa corn-fed beef. These hefty heifer parts, for two or more, are always cooked perfectly to order and come presliced unless you request otherwise. Potato side dishes are serviceable, but skip the other vegetables. For dessert, try cheesecake or ice cream. ♦ Steak house ♦ Daily lunch and dinner. Reservations required. No credit cards accepted. 178 Broadway (at Driggs Ave), Williamsburg. 718/387.7400 &

10 Architectural Salvage Warehouse If you want to recycle some of the charm and detail of old New York into your new home, try this warehouse, which is stocked with authentic architectural artifacts and elements rescued from the city's condemned buildings. Established in 1980 by the New York City Landmarks Preservation Commission, its purpose is to supply New Yorkers who are restoring their homes with bits and pieces of the past. Architects and interior designers come here looking for old woodwork, shutters, doors, mantels, pedestal sinks, and exterior ironwork; you'll need to arrange the transportation of your acquisitions. ♦ By appointment. 337 Berry St (at S Fifth St), Williamsburg. 718/388.4527

11 Plan Eat Thailand ★$ Owners David and Anna Popermhem add pizzazz to the menu using fresh ingredients for their flavorful salads, lemony and tender squid, or charred beef with onions, chilies, and basil. The food contains just the right amount of spices to make it popular with Western palates. Best entrées include chicken in a fragrant coconut curry and the grilled, moist, marinated chicken. ♦ Thai ♦ Daily lunch and dinner. 184 Bedford Ave (at N 7th St), Williamsburg. 718/599.5758

12 Pratt Institute Architecture, business, science, and fine arts are the strong suits of this 3,200-student school established in 1887. The 25-acre campus has a satellite in Manhattan. ♦ Bounded by Taaffe Pl and Hall St, and DeKalb and Willoughby Aves (between Classon Ave and Hall St), Clinton Hill. 718/636.3600

13 Brooklyn Children's Museum In this museum, which was built in 1976 to the designs of **Hardy Holzman Pfeiffer Associates,** children visit a greenhouse, work with butterflies and fossils, and learn about how animals get energy from food. They can also participate in a dream sequence inside a 25-foot model of a sleeping head and use their five senses to unlock the mystery of objects, using as tools 20,000 cultural artifacts and natural history specimens from the museum's collection. Special events include films, workshops, field trips, concerts, and storytelling sessions. ♦ Donation suggested. W-F 2PM-5PM; Sa-Su, holidays noon-5PM. 145 Brooklyn Ave (at St. Mark's Ave), Crown Heights. 718/735.4432

14 Santa Fe Grill ★$ At this popular spot for the young after-work crowd, the bar offers a variety of fancy concoctions and thirst-quenching margaritas. The serene Southwestern setting, rich in New Mexican artifacts, is lovely; the noise level, however, makes for a less-than-peaceful mood. The food is quite respectable for this far north—try the vegetable quesadilla, any of the burritos and enchiladas (including a spinach-and-cheese variety), or one of the decent burgers. ♦ Tex-Mex ♦ Daily dinner. 62 Seventh Ave (at Lincoln Pl), Park Slope. 718/636.0279

14 Leaf & Bean Approximately 50 types of coffee beans and 20 types of loose tea are offered here, along with other gourmet items, including truffle candies, fancy jams, and white cocoa. There's also a large supply of kitchen accessories—wine glasses, cookie jars, place mats, Italian ceramic plates, candles, cloth napkins, and of course a variety of coffeemakers and teapots. ◆ Daily. 83 Seventh Ave (between Union St and Berkeley Pl), Park Slope. 718/638.5791

14 Cucina ★★★$$ This warm, inviting place has a stylish decor—maple tables and Art Deco chairs, dried flowers, a vibrant mural, and a colorful antipasto table featuring platters of marinated vegetables, grilled shiitake mushrooms, various tarts including an onion-and-olive variety, eggplant and roasted pepper terrine, grilled marinated shrimp with white beans and escarole, and *soppressata* (a mild sausage). Pasta dishes and entrées are also earthy and alluring: try *linguine nostra* (with clams, mussels, shrimp, lobster, and calamari); *fusilli puttanesca* (with capers, olives, diced tomatoes, garlic, and olive oil); fillet of red snapper; grilled Cornish hen; or osso buco served with *pappardelle* (broad noodles). Save room for the chocolate tasting plate or richly fruity sorbets. Reasonably priced wines from Italy, France, and California are available. ◆ Italian ◆ Tu-Su dinner. No credit cards accepted. 256 Fifth Ave (between Garfield Pl and Carroll St), Park Slope. 718/230.0711 占

Bed & Breakfast on the Park

15 Bed & Breakfast on the Park $$ Former antiques-store owner Liana Paolella has meticulously restored this landmark 19th-century home-turned-inn. Her guests enjoy eight spacious, beautifully furnished rooms (two with shared baths) replete with wood-burning fireplaces, canopied beds, stained-glass windows, Oriental rugs, and an extensive collection of museum-quality paintings. A scrumptious breakfast further complements the inn's grand style. ◆ 113 Prospect Park W (between Sixth and Seventh Sts), Park Slope. 718/499.6115; fax 718/499.1385

16 Grand Army Plaza Monuments have been added since the plaza was first laid out in 1870 by Frederick Law Olmsted and **Calvert Vaux**. The Roman-style *Soldiers' and Sailors' Arch* was raised as a tribute to the Union Army in 1892 and was later encrusted with Frederick MacMonnies's massive sculptures and some less exuberant

bas-relief forms. The **Bailey Fountain** was added in 1932 by architect **Edgerton Swarthwout** and sculptor Eugene Savage. **Morris Ketchum Jr. & Associates** designed the 1965 **John F. Kennedy Memorial**.
◆ Flatbush Ave (between Prospect Park and Plaza St), Park Slope–Prospect Heights

16 Prospect Park The Grand Army Plaza is the official entrance to this 526-acre park, as loved by Brooklynites as the larger **Central Park** is by Manhattanites. In fact, these two parks share designers (landscape architects Frederick Law Olmsted and **Calvert Vaux**), and—not surprisingly—landscaping characteristics (meadowlands, footpaths, skating rink, boating lake, and carousel). The recipient of a multimillion-dollar renovation, the park is being returned to its original bucolic state. Among other sites, an 18th-century Dutch farmhouse was relocated here to be used as a museum, and an old Quaker cemetery contains Montgomery Clift's tomb. Other highlights include the famous **Brooklyn Botanic Garden** (see below) and the **Prospect Park Wildlife Center** (718/399.7339), one of the world's largest children's zoos, featuring sea lions, wallabies, and a baboon enclosure where it's the humans that are encased in glass while the primates run free. ◆ Bounded by Ocean Ave, Flatbush Ave, Prospect Park SW, Prospect Park W, and Parkside Ave. 718/965.8900

17 Brooklyn Museum of Art This museum (formerly the **Brooklyn Museum**) always seems to be undergoing construction, which began in 1893 and continued until 1924 by **McKim, Mead & White. Prentice and Chan, Ohlhausen** designed the next addition in 1978, and **Joseph Tonetti** designed the next in 1987. The most recent addition of this massive five-story museum, part of a major $31-million renovation completed in 1993, was designed by **Arata Isozaki** and **James Stewart Polshek & Partners**. It includes three floors of new galleries in the **West Wing**, the 460-seat **Iris and B. Gerald Cantor Auditorium** (which will serve as the museum's first formal gathering place since the original auditorium was converted into the **Grand Lobby** in the early 1930s), and two floors of additional art storage space. Excellent collections include the arts of Egypt, the classical Middle East, and Asia. Exhibitions of primitive arts come from Africa, the South Pacific, and the Americas; other displays feature Greek and Roman antiquities. Costumes, textiles, decorative arts, and period furniture dating from the late 17th century are all beautifully laid out for viewing. The permanent collection includes works by Rodin, Modigliani, Cassatt, Degas, Monet, Chagall, Gauguin, Toulouse-Lautrec, Homer, Sargent, and Bierstadt. The continuing series of exhibitions by contemporary artists has included Joseph Kosuth, Alfredo Jarr, and Reeva Potoff. ◆ Donation suggested. W-Su. 200 Eastern Pkwy (at Washington Ave), Prospect Heights. 718/638.5000 &

Within Brooklyn Museum of Art:

Cafe at Brooklyn Museum of Art ★$ Rest your tired feet after viewing the museum's exhibits in this bright, cheery room decorated with prints on the walls and fresh flowers on the tables. The small gourmet sandwich menu includes roasted eggplant with mozzarella, tomato, and basil on focaccia, vegetable tuna on a croissant, and grilled chicken with pesto sauce. For dessert try raspberry cheesecake or carrot cake. ◆ Cafe ◆ W-Su breakfast, lunch, and afternoon snacks. No credit cards accepted. 718/638.5000 &

17 Brooklyn Botanic Garden Although not as large or as famous as the **New York Botanical Garden** in the Bronx, this one has such celebrated plantings as a Japanese hill-and-pond garden, an herb garden with over 300 specimens, and one of the largest public rose collections in America. A conservatory houses the largest bonsai collection in the country. The 50 acres of flora include a fragrance garden for the blind. The master plan for the garden was designed by the Olmsted brothers and laid down in 1910; the landscaping was completed in 1912 by Harold Caparn; and the **Steinhardt Conservatory,** which was designed by **Davis, Brody & Associates,** was completed in 1988. ◆ Parking fee. Admission, free Tuesdays. Tu-Su. 1000 Washington Ave (between Empire Blvd and Eastern Pkwy), Prospect Heights. 718/622.4433

18 Coney Island Rattling over the tracks since 1927, the wooden *Cyclone* roller coaster still provides thrills, and a **Nathan's** hot dog with everything on it is still a genuine treat, but the golden days of Coney Island are over. The beach has survived somewhat intact, and it sure beats the tar beaches many Brooklynites settle for on the roofs of their apartment buildings on hot summer weekends. In the 1920s, however, this was the Riviera, the "World's Largest Playground" for generations of hard-working immigrants and native New Yorkers. It has since faded into neglect, though it provides a certain nostalgia with a glimpse of other times, ocean views, and a visit to nearby Brighton Beach for a peek into Little Russia. ◆ Surf Ave (between Ocean Pkwy and W 37th St)

At Coney Island:

Nathan's Famous ★$ Indeed, this is probably the most famous and elaborate hot-dog stand in the world, having served spicy franks and fabulously greasy, crinkle-cut fried potatoes for nearly a century. Nowadays, there are branches all over, but this was the first. ◆ American ◆ Daily 8AM-4PM. Surf and Stillwell Aves. 718/946.2202. Also at: Numerous locations throughout the city

18 Aquarium for Wildlife Conservation Native creatures of the *Hudson River Display* and dramatic denizens of the shark tank are on exhibit in the **Native Sea Life** building. Penguins and sea lions provide comic relief, and **Aquatheater** shows provide great entertainment: dolphins in the summer and whales, walruses, and sea lions in the winter. There's also a **Discovery Cove,** where kids can touch sea stars and horseshoe crabs. ◆ Admission; parking fee. Daily. Surf Ave (between Ocean Pkwy and W 10th St). 718/265.3400 &

19 National Restaurant ★★$$$ Known for its boisterous good times and late-night bonhomie, this Russian restaurant is the place to come with friends; the rivers of vodka and the live band will have you singing tunes from the motherland before you know it. The set dinners are huge, featuring a parade of cold appetizers, such as herring with potatoes or beet salad, and five main courses, including shish kebab or roasted chicken. ◆ Russian ◆ Daily dinner and late-night meals. Reservations recommended. 273 Brighton Beach Ave (between Third and Second Sts), Brighton Beach. 718/646.1225

19 Odessa ★★$$$ Make a night of it with the decked-out Eastern European regulars indulging in vodka on ice and an endless parade of "appetizers" (here indistinguishable from the entrées). Try the herring, eggplant caviar, baked salmon, or any of the many other dishes that will come your way. There's dancing and live music nightly. All in all, this is an extraordinary experience. ◆ Russian ◆ Daily lunch and dinner. Reservations required. 1113 Brighton Beach Ave (between 12th and 11th Sts), Brighton Beach. 718/332.3223

George Washington lost Queens to British troops during the Battle of Long Island in 1776. This was the first of several significant battles that led to the British occupation of New York City during the American Revolution.

Queens

This sprawling borough has always been a conglomeration of towns, villages, model communities, and real-estate developments. Suburban in spirit and design, it has grown far too dense to be anything but urban in essence, the type of immigrant staging ground that Manhattan, Brooklyn, and the Bronx used to be. Next to Athens, Queens has the world's largest Greek community in **Astoria,** while **Flushing** is home to an ever-growing Asian population. But unlike the older boroughs, Queens is oriented toward the highways that lace it together, toward the airports (**Kennedy** and **La Guardia**) that sit on either shore, and the suburban reaches of Nassau County. Things have changed considerably since the area of Queens was created in 1683 as one of the 12 counties in the province of New York. It was named for Queen Catherine of Braganza, the Portuguese-born wife of King Charles II of England.

20 Water's Edge ★★★$$$ Surrounded by glass walls on three sides, the tables in this swank riverside restaurant all have spectacular west-looking views of Midtown and Lower Manhattan. In the kitchen, the creative touch of chef Joel Somerstein (formerly of **Cafe Pierre**) is evidenced with delicious Oriental crab and lobster dumplings with enoki mushrooms and pea shoots in carrot-lobster broth; spinach fettuccine with artichokes, escargots, and parsley in a Pernod-lemon sauce; black bass with arugula vinaigrette; and red snapper in crust of *tapenade* (a thick paste of anchovies, capers, olives, olive oil, and lemon juice). Manhattanites need not fret about transportation to and from Queens—the restaurant runs a complimentary dinner ferry from East 34th Street every hour between 6 and 11PM, Monday through Saturday (except during January and February, when it runs only Tuesday through Saturday). ◆ Seafood ◆ M-F lunch and dinner; Sa dinner. Reservations required; jacket and tie required. 44th Dr (between Vernon Blvd and the East River), Long Island City. 718/482.0033

21 Manducatis ★★$$ Family atmosphere and a cozy fireplace give this place an authentic trattoria feeling. Chef Ida's fine, straightforward touch with fresh ingredients brings people from all over town to this out-of-the-way spot. One of the best dishes on the menu is *pappardelle* with garlic and white beans, but most regulars don't even look at the menu. They simply ask Vincenzo what looks good that day. ◆ Italian ◆ M-F lunch and dinner; Sa-Su dinner. Reservations recommended. 13-27 Jackson Ave (between 21st St and 47th Ave), Long Island City. 718/729.4602

21 P.S. 1 An alternative space of the **Institute for Contemporary Art,** this 19th-century school, under the directorship of Alanna Heiss, is used for exhibitions of new and established artists. An extensive renovation and expansion, designed by **Frederick Fisher,** was completed in 1997. ◆ Donation suggested. W-Su noon-6PM. 22-25 Jackson Ave (at 46th Ave), Long Island City. 718/784.2084 &

21 Silvercup Studios In 1983, the **Silvercup Bakery** was converted into a movie studio. Eighteen soundstages are contained within a mammoth three-block–long building. In addition to providing space for work on movies (*Garbo Talks, Street Smart, The Purple Rose of Cairo*), commercials (which account for most of the activity), and music videos, the studio rents screening rooms and production offices; some of the lucky tenants have windows overlooking the New York skyline. ◆ 42-22 22nd St (between 43rd Ave and Queens Plaza S), Long Island City. 718/784.3390

22 Isamu Noguchi Garden Museum Completed in 1985, this is one of the few museums dedicated to the work of a single artist, created by that artist. Isamu Noguchi (1904-88) had a controversial career filled with projects that ranged from immense sculpture gardens to *akari* lamps to set designs for choreographers Martha Graham and George Balanchine. Some of the greatest examples of Noguchi's work are on display in the museum's 12 galleries and outdoor sculpture garden. ◆ Donation suggested. W, Sa-Su 11AM-6PM Apr-Nov. 32-37 Vernon Blvd (at 33rd Rd), Long Island City. 718/204.7088

23 American Museum of the Moving Image Designed by **Gwathmey Siegel & Associates** and built in 1988, this museum is all that its name advertises and more, with extensive archives, special showings, and exhibitions. There are no snobbish distinctions between film and TV or technology and art, but it's not about junk culture, either. The artifacts displayed leave the visitor with an indelible impression of Pop history. ◆ Admission. Tu-F noon-5PM; Sa-Su noon-6PM. 36-01 35th Ave (at 36th St), Astoria. 718/784.0077; tours 718/784.4520 &

23 Kaufman Astoria Studio/U.S. Army Pictorial Center Rudolph Valentino and Gloria Swanson starred in silent films made here in the heyday of New York City's motion picture boom. Edward G. Robinson made the early talkie *Hole in the Wall* here, and the Marx Brothers used the studio for the filming of *The Cocoanuts.* After the studio's 1932 bankruptcy, the property passed through several hands. During World War II, it was used by the army for training and propaganda films done by Frank Capra. Now a historic landmark—not open to the public—the studio is back in business. It has been a favorite location of director Sidney Lumet. ♦ 34-12 36th St (between 35th and 34th Aves), Astoria. 718/392.5600.

24 Elias Corner ★★$$ When this simple taverna moved across the street to a bigger, glassed-in space—complete with guitars and stuffed fish on the walls—the crowds obligingly followed. Make a selection from among the day's catches on the ice-laden counter and have it grilled over charcoal. While you wait, try one of the traditional and richly flavored appetizers, such as *taramasalata* served with crackers, or stuffed grape leaves. ♦ Greek/Seafood ♦ Daily dinner. No credit cards accepted. 24-02 31st St (at 24th Ave), Astoria. 718/932.1510

25 Steinway Mansion William Steinway was a great friend of President Grover Cleveland and presented him with a grand piano as a wedding gift. The Steinway home, built in 1856, was once a lively setting for fairy tale social events. The building is not open to the public. ♦ 18-33 41st St (at 19th Ave), Astoria

26 Little India Known as Jackson Heights, this area is a solid, family-oriented neighborhood of Argentines, Thais, Spaniards, Koreans, Italians, and Pakistanis. But the bold colors and pungent smells of India make it the most foreign and exotic to the curious visitor. Some 60,000 Indian immigrants in the New York City area either live on this one block of 74th Street north of Roosevelt Avenue, or flock here regularly to shop, eat, and visit. Sari shops, aromatic grocery stores, jewelry stores whose windows are laden with 22K-gold wedding jewelry, and about a dozen authentic restaurants are part of the lively scene. ♦ 74th St (between Roosevelt and 37th Aves), Jackson Heights

In Little India:

Delhi Palace ★★$$ This is Queens's most elegant "Little India" dining choice, with crisp white tablecloths, fresh flowers, attentive service, and quiet background music. In addition to selections from the menu, choose from the extensive buffet that appears at both lunch and dinner. Don't miss the chicken with creamy cashew sauce or tandoori shrimp with *masala* (a mild creamy) sauce. ♦ Indian ♦ M-F lunch and dinner; Sa-Su brunch and dinner. 37-33 74th St. 718/507.0666

27 Jaiya Thai Oriental Restaurant ★★$$ The extensive, original menu at this Thai eatery includes more than 300 choices. Try the excellent spicy chicken and coconut soup; spicy shredded jellyfish; pork with very hot chili peppers and onions; pad thai; naked shrimp (rare shrimp with lime, lemongrass, and chili); and pork with string beans, red chili, and basil. ♦ Thai ♦ Daily lunch and dinner. Reservations recommended for dinner Friday through Sunday. 81-11 Broadway (between Britton Ave and Pettit Pl), Elmhurst. 718/651.1330. Also at: 396 Third Ave (between E 28th and E 29th Sts), Manhattan. 212/889.1330

28 London Lennie's ★$$ As befits the name of this place, prints of palace guards grace the dining room wall; otherwise, it's a basic, wood-paneled, nautically decorated fish house. Try the chowder, panfried oysters, big pots of steamers, Maryland crab cakes, and fried soft-shell crabs. There's also an extensive wine list. ♦ Seafood ♦ M-F lunch and dinner; Sa-Su dinner. 63-88 Woodhaven Blvd (between 64th Rd and Penelope Ave), Rego Park. 718/894.8084

29 Shea Stadium Home of the **New York Mets,** this 55,300-seat stadium, built in 1963 and designed by **Praeger-Kavanagh-Waterbury,** also hosted Pope John Paul II in 1979 and the history-making 1965 Beatles concert. The stadium opened for the **Mets'** 1964 season, which coincided with the **World's Fair** next door at **Flushing Meadows–Corona Park.** For its 25th anniversary in 1988, the stadium underwent a modest renovation and now features large neon figures on the outside, new plastic seating to replace old wooden benches, and a "DiamondVision" video screen. Traffic around the stadium is quite congested before and after games; call for directions by public transportation. ♦ 126th St (between Roosevelt Ave and Northern Blvd, Flushing. 718/507.8499 ♿

30 Flushing Meadows–Corona Park Once a garbage dump, this triumph of reclamation, smack dab in the geographic center of New York City, was later chosen for the **1939-40** and **1964-65 New York World's Fairs.** ♦ Bounded by Van Wyck Expwy and 111th St, and Union Tpke and the Port Washington Branch of the Long Island Railroad, Flushing

Within Flushing Meadows–Corona Park:

Hall of Science Designed by **Wallace K. Harrison** and built as a science pavilion for the **1964-65 World's Fair,** this is New York's only hands-on science and technology museum. The sophisticated collection includes 150 interactive exhibits focusing on color, light, microbiology, structures, feedback, and quantum physics. ♦ Admission; free W-Th 3PM-5PM. W-Su. 47-01 111th St (between Corona and 44th Aves). 718/699.0675

At the Hall of Science:

Science Playground Kids can exercise both minds and bodies in this recently opened 30,000-square-foot outdoor lab–playground. Try the water play area, construction zone, and the oversized teeter-totter that will balance 25 children at once. Science is made fun for youngsters, who learn centrifugal force on the **Standing Spinner** and kinetic energy from the enormous **Pinball Machine.** ♦ Free. W-Su. 718/699.0005

Queens Wildlife Center This lush habitat is devoted to North American wildlife, including mountain lions, bison, bobcats, coyotes, American black bears, and Roosevelt elks. There's a petting section in the domestic area. ♦ Free. Daily. 53-51 111th St (between Corona and 44th Aves). 718/271.7761

Queens Museum of Art Highlights include excellent art and photography shows and the world's largest scale model—a 9,335-square-foot *Panorama of New York City* that has recently been brought up to date and now includes just about every street, building, bridge, and park at a scale of one inch to 100 feet. ♦ Donation requested. Tu-F; Sa-Su noon-5PM. Off Grand Central Pkwy (between Long Island Expwy and Northern Blvd). 718/592.5555

USTA National Tennis Center Home to the **US Open** tennis championships since 1978, it now boasts the newly opened **Arthur Ashe Stadium,** the site of the August tournament. And for those who want to feel like champions, there are 27 outdoor courts and 9 indoor courts. Call to reserve play times. ♦ Fee. 718/592.8000

31 Jade Palace ★★$ This modern dining room gets absolutely mobbed at night, but regulars patiently wait for what many feel is the best Chinese seafood in the area. Try shark's-fin soup; steamed, live shrimp; and any of the evening's specials—often striped or sea bass, eel, shrimp, or crab. The dim sum selection is also a standout. If your mood dictates meat instead of fish, you'll have plenty to choose from, as well—lamb baked in a clay pot is a winner. ♦ Cantonese/Seafood ♦ Daily lunch and dinner. 136-14 38th Ave (between 138th and Main Sts), Flushing. 718/353.3366 &

31 Joe's Shanghai ★★$ Don't ask for the usual Chinese fare here. This medium-size restaurant doesn't fit the mold of eateries that are now located in the area dubbed "New Chinatown." Among connoisseurs this place is known for its crabmeat steamed dumplings, which are filled with a delicious savory crab-pork filling. Other tempting starters are shredded pork noodle soup, pork-and-chive fried dumplings, and scallion pancake. Among the best main dishes are crispy whole yellowfish, panfried noodles with chicken, fresh shiitake mushrooms with hearts of cabbage, and calamari with spicy black bean sauce. ♦ Chinese ♦ Daily lunch and dinner. 136-21 39th Ave (between 138th and Main Sts), Flushing. 718/539.4429. Also at: 9 Pell St (between Bowery and Doyers St), Manhattan. 212/233.8888; 24 W 56th St (between Fifth and Sixth Aves), Manhattan. 333.3868

32 Aqueduct Thoroughbred racing takes place here. ♦ Oct-May. Rockaway Blvd (between 114th and 108th Sts), Ozone Park. 718/641.4700 &

33 Jamaica Bay Wildlife Refuge Within the **Center Gateway National Recreation Area,** these vast man-made tidal wetlands and uplands have become a haven for hundreds of species of birds and plants. The fall migratory season, starting in mid-August, is a particularly good time to come. Dress appropriately. ♦ Free. Daily. Visitor Center: Cross Bay Blvd (at First Rd), Broad Channel. 718/318.4340

The Bronx

The Bronx not only stands as a study in contrasts, but also typifies the rapid succession of growth and decline experienced throughout New York City—a microcosm of American urban change squeezed into just over half a century. Today it is a mélange of devastated tenements, suburban riverfront mansions, seaside cottages, massive housing superblocks, and fading boulevards of grand Art Deco apartment towers. Although in recent years the Bronx has become a synonym for urban decay, some of the borough remains stable (even elegant and pastoral), and heavy philanthropic and governmental investment as well as the energetic efforts of community-based groups are helping to restore some of the more run-down areas.

34 Yankee Stadium In 1973, the **Yankees** celebrated their 50th anniversary in this 57,545-seat horseshoe arena designed in

1923 by **Osborn Engineering Co**. Remodeling has kept the home of the frequent World Series champs one of the most modern baseball facilities in the country. It was almost completely rebuilt in 1976 by **Praeger-Kavanagh-Waterbury.** The park is 11.6 acres, 3.5 of which are taken up by the field itself. Within the park are monuments to such Yankee greats as Lou Gehrig, Joe DiMaggio, Casey Stengel, and, of course, Babe Ruth. It is advised that you exercise caution when visiting the area surrounding the stadium—especially at night. ♦ E 161st St and River Ave, High Bridge. 718/293.6000 ♿

35 **Hall of Fame for Great Americans**
Bronze busts of nearly a hundred of America's greatest scientists, statesmen, and artists are on display in this handsome building designed in 1901 and 1914 by **McKim, Mead & White.** Sculptures are by Daniel Chester French, Frederick MacMonnies, and James Earle Fraser. Note the classic arcade by **Stanford White.** ♦ Free. Daily. Bronx Community College, Hall of Fame Terr (between University and Sedgwick Aves), University Heights. 718/289.5100

36 **Edgar Allan Poe Cottage**
From 1846 to 1848 the writer and his dying wife lived in this house, which dates back to 1812. *Annabel Lee* was among the works written here. The museum displays many of Poe's manuscripts and other memorabilia. ♦ Nominal admission. Sa 10AM-4PM; Su 1-5PM. Grand Concourse and E Kingsbridge Rd, Fordham. 718/881.8900

37 **Fordham University**
Site of one of the nation's foremost Jesuit schools, **Rose Hill Campus** comprises 85 acres and has over 13,000 students enrolled in a traditional arts and sciences curriculum. **Rose Hill Manor** (1838), which now forms part of the **Administration Building,** was the home of the original school, **St. John's College,** begun in 1841 by John Hughes. Hughes later became New York State's first Catholic archbishop. This beautiful campus has a classic collection of Collegiate Gothic structures, most notably **Keating Hall,** designed in 1936 by **Robert J. Reiley.** The university has two satellite campuses in Manhattan, the **Law School** and **Graduate School of Business** at West 62nd Street (212/636.6000). ♦ 441 E Fordham Rd (between Bathgate and Webster Aves), Fordham. 718/817.1000

38 Arthur Avenue Retail Market
This covered market is packed with stalls selling everything from high-quality Tuscan virgin olive oil to wheels of parmigiano reggiano, fresh eggs, thinly sliced veal, baby eggplant, and zucchini. For the best cheese, stop by **Mike & Sons'** stall. ♦ M-Sa. 2344 Arthur Ave (between Crescent Ave and E 186th St), Fordham. 718/367.5686

38 Calabria Pork Store
Choose, if you can, among the 500 kinds of sausage dangling from the ceiling; all are delicious, many studded with peppercorns or garlic. ♦ M-Sa. 2338 Arthur Ave (between Crescent Ave and E 186th St), Fordham. 718/367.5145

38 **Belmont Italian-American Playhouse**
In a cramped loft above a supermarket in a neighborhood where the newspapers are still read in Italian and social clubs are crowded with old men discussing soccer scores, this 70-seat theater draws crowds from Manhattan for classic and contemporary Italian works, Shakespearean productions, and works by local playwrights of all ethnic backgrounds. The three young Italian-American owners knew their theater would make it when Robert DeNiro used their space to audition for his 1993 film *A Bronx Tale.* ♦ Shows Th-Sa 8:30PM; Su matinee 2:30PM. Call for a schedule. 2385 Arthur Ave (between E 184th and E 187th Sts), Fordham. 718/364.4700 ♿

38 Dominick's ★★$
Don't let the lines outside dissuade you from eating at this noisy and chaotic restaurant. Once inside, you'll be greeted with terrific home-style Southern Italian fare and a solicitous staff. ♦ Italian ♦ M, W-Su lunch and dinner. No credit cards accepted. 2335 Arthur Ave (between E 184th and E 187th Sts), Fordham. 718/733.2807

39 **Bronx Zoo/Wildlife Conservation Center**
The most important of the zoos and aquarium managed by **NYZS/The Wildlife Conservation Society,** the zoo is home to almost 4,000 animals—650 species—on 265 acres, making it the largest metropolitan zoo in the United States. On its northern side is **Astor Court** (built from 1901 to 1922 to the design of **Heins & LaFarge**), a collection of formal zoo buildings that contains the **Zoo Center** (old elephant house), the renovated **Monkey House,** and the **Sea Lion Pool.** These structures, influenced by the **1893 Chicago World's Fair,** were built as part of the original plan, which envisioned a formal central court area surrounded by natural park settings. The balance of the zoo's acreage is designed to re-create naturalistic habitats where African and Asian wildlife roam. ♦ Admission; free Wednesday. Daily. Bounded by Bronx River Pkwy and Southern Blvd, and Bronx Park S and E Fordham Rd. 718/367.1010

Within the Bronx Zoo:

Paul Rainey Memorial Gate Images of bears and deer decorate these imaginative Art Deco gates, which open onto a 200-year-old Italian fountain donated by William Rockefeller. The gate was designed by **Charles A. Platt** in 1934, and the sculpture is by Paul Manship. ♦ E Fordham Rd (at Bronx and Pelham Pkwy)

World of Birds Visitors can observe more than 500 birds in the 25 environments of this well-designed aviary, with no bars or fences to obscure the view. It was designed in 1972 by **Morris Ketchum Jr. & Associates.** The recently opened **Aitken Aviary** is home to more than 100 Southern American sea birds (some were lost when the old aviary collapsed in 1995), including Inca terns and Magellanic penguins. ♦ Nominal admission Wednesday. Daily

Children's Zoo Children can explore prairie dog tunnels or hop like a wallaby in this hands-on zoo. Kids must be accompanied by an adult. ♦ Nominal admission. Last visitors admitted one hour before zoo closes

Jungle World This award-winning indoor rain forest has four habitats, five waterfalls, giant trees, and Asian animals separated from humans by bridges and small rivers. Look out for proboscis monkeys, silver-leaf langurs (monkey family), white-cheeked gibbons (ape family), and Indian gharials (a crocodilian relative that is believed to have lived 180 million years ago). ♦ Nominal admission Wednesday. Daily

World of Darkness Day and night are reversed for the nocturnal animals who live here, so they are awake and active for daytime visitors. This fascinating exhibit was designed by **Morris Ketchum Jr. & Associates** in 1972. ♦ Nominal admission Wednesday. Daily

Congo Gorilla Forest The most recent and most spectacular of the zoo's redeveloped areas is a 6.5-acre habitat for Central African rain forest species including DeBrazza's monkeys, okapi, mandrills, red river hogs, and especially the two large troops of Western lowland gorillas, the largest breeding group of these wonderful apes in North America, who can be watched for hours carrying on their gorilla social life with no interest in the *homo sapiens* population on the other side of the glass. ♦ Admission. Daily

40 **New York Botanical Garden** One of the world's outstanding botanical gardens, its 250 acres include a 40-acre virgin hemlock forest, formal gardens, and the **Enid A. Haupt Conservatory** (built in 1902 and restored in 1978 by **Edward Larrabee Barnes**), which was modeled after the Great Palm House at Kew Gardens in England. A museum houses an herbarium, accessible only to members, of 5.5 million dried plants, and a shop that sells plants and gardening books and supplies. The **Lorillard Snuff Mill** (built in 1840) was converted into a cafe in the 1950s. A massive renovation project with an

The New York Botanical Garden's conservatory is the largest Victorian glasshouse in the world.

New York Botanical Garden

estimated $165-million price tag is under way and is expected to be completed in the year 2001. The following projects are in the planning stages: a new library and herbarium, a renovated lecture hall, a restoration of the museum exterior, a new visitors' center, and a new restaurant. In addition, extensive renovations to the **Enid A. Haupt Conservatory** have included a computerized temperature/humidity/water/ventilation system. Within the Victorian glasshouse are more than 3,000 exotic species. ♦ Gardens: admission. Conservatory: admission. Tu-Su. Bounded by Bronx River Pkwy, Dr. Theodore Kazimiroff Blvd, and E Fordham Rd. 718/817.8705

41 **City University of New York, Herbert H. Lehman College** More than 10,000 students attend this school, founded in 1931 as **Hunter College.** The campus's Gothic buildings were designed by **Thompson Holmes & Converse** and **Frank Meyers** in 1928. The **Lehman Center for the Performing Arts,** designed in 1980 by **David Todd & Associates** and **Jan Hird Pokorny,** includes a 2,300-seat concert hall, experimental theater, recital hall, library, dance studio, and art galleries. The complex has become for the Bronx a kind of scaled-down **Lincoln Center,** attracting many of the same events that normally would play Manhattan only. ♦ Bedford Park Blvd W (between Jerome and Goulden Aves), Bedford Park. 718/960.8000

42 **Wave Hill** The 28-acre Hudson River estate of financier George W. Perkins was given to the city in 1965. Arturo Toscanini, Theodore Roosevelt, and Mark Twain each lived here for a short time. The 19th-century mansion hosts a chamber music series and family-arts projects and presents vintage recordings of Toscanini concerts. The dazzling gardens and greenhouses put on an impressive display each season. ◆ Admission Sa-Su. Tu-Su. 675 W 252nd St (at Sycamore Ave), Riverdale. 718/549.2055 &

43 Van Cortlandt House Museum This Georgian-Colonial mansion is one of those where George Washington actually slept—it was his military headquarters on several occasions. Built in 1748, the mansion has been restored with Dutch, English, and Colonial furnishings. ◆ Nominal admission. Tu-F 10AM-3PM; Sa-Su 11AM-4PM. Van Cortlandt Park, Broadway (between Van Cortlandt Park S and Henry Hudson Pkwy). 718/543.3344

44 Bartow-Pell Mansion Museum This Federal home on beautifully manicured grounds, with views of Long Island Sound and outstanding formal gardens, was built from 1836 to 1842. Run by the **International Garden Club**, it's a rare treat. ◆ Nominal admission. W, Sa-Su noon-4PM or by appointment. Pelham Bay Park, Pelham Bridge Rd (between City Island Rd and Park Dr). 718/885.1461

45 City Island A New England atmosphere persists on this small island that served as a US Coast Guard station in World War II. Located in the northeast reaches of the Bronx in Pelham Bay and attached to mainland New York by only one bridge, this picturesque 230-acre island is four blocks across at its widest point. It has the flavor of an island off the coast of Maine, not the Bronx, with marinas (four America's Cup yachts were built here), seagulls, seafood restaurants, antiques shops, and atmosphere. The **New York Sailing School** (231 Kirby St, off King Ave, between Ditmars and Bowne Sts, 800/834.SAIL) offers boat rentals and sailing instruction from April through October. Like the island, the only museum is both charming and quirky. The **North Wind Museum and Sea Institute** (610 City Island Ave, between Kilroe St and City Island Bridge, 718/885.0701), a nautical museum located in an old sea captain's house, traces the history of the island while offering a cache of old nautical curiosities. ◆ Over City Island Bridge

45 Le Refuge Bed & Breakfast $ Pierre Saint-Denis, proprietor/chef of Manhattan's East Side's extremely popular **Le Refuge** restaurant, has opened this ultracharming eight-room inn in a restored 19th-century sea captain's house. Replete with widow's walk, chamber music concerts, and the best

croissants in town, this is the only spot of its kind in the Bronx or New York City. While it's only a half-hour by subway to Midtown Manhattan (and Pierre's must-visit East Side eatery), it will seem light-years away. With a host who's one of Manhattan's premier chefs, you can count on a wonderful breakfast. ◆ 620 City Island Ave (between Kilroe St and City Island Bridge), City Island. 718/885.2478; fax 212/737.0384

46 Lobster Box ★★$$$ The Masucchia family turned this small white 1812 house into a restaurant more than 50 years ago. Over the years the popular spot has grown and now serves up to 2,000 pounds of fresh lobster a week. Pick from almost two dozen variations on the lobster theme—beginning with the simple steamed-and-split (lobsters here are never boiled), or any of the fresh seafood, and watch the fleet of local boats glide by. ◆ Lobster/Seafood ◆ Daily lunch and dinner Apr-Dec. 34 City Island Ave (between Belden and Rochelle Sts), City Island. 718/885.1952

Staten Island

Geographically distant from the rest of New York, Staten Island seems to be more a spiritual cousin to New Jersey, only a narrow stretch of water away. In fact, Staten Island's political ties to New York City are a historical accident: The island was ceded to Manhattan as a prize in a sailing contest sponsored by the Duke of York in 1687. Before 1964, access was possible only by ferry from Manhattan or by car through New Jersey. In 1964, the **Verrazano-Narrows Bridge** opened, tying Staten Island to Brooklyn. With a new frontier so close at hand, modern-day settlers poured over the bridge and changed the rugged face of the island forever. In 1990, tired of being ignored, residents of the "forgotten borough" voted to create a charter commission to provide for the separation of Staten Island from the rest of New York City. In 1993, residents voted two to one in favor of secession. Final approval rested, though, with the state legislature in Albany and the governor, which declined to act. If they ever did grant independence to Staten Island, it would become the second-largest city in New York.

Before the 1850s, immigrants afflicted with diseases were kept on a remote spot on Staten Island. Many local residents became sick and died as a result, and others retaliated by setting fire to the quarantined buildings. This action prompted the state to build Hoffman and Swinburne Islands to house the afflicted. The islands are in Lower New York Bay off Staten Island and date from 1872. They were abandoned in the 1920s following the new immigration laws and serve no purpose today.

47 Snug Harbor Cultural Center This 83-acre center for the performing and visual arts—a retirement village for sailors from 1833 until the mid-1970s—is composed of 28 historic buildings, many of which are fine examples of Greek Revival, Beaux Arts, Italianate, and Victorian architecture. Stop by the **Visitors' Center** for historical exhibitions and information on current and upcoming events, including indoor and outdoor classical, pop, and jazz concerts. A historical tour is held every Saturday and Sunday at 2PM. ♦ Daily dawn to dusk. 1000 Richmond Terr (between Tysen St and Snug Harbor Rd), Livingston. 718/448.2500

Within Snug Harbor Cultural Center:

The Newhouse Center for Contemporary Art New and emerging artists not often seen in Manhattan galleries are shown here. The center also hosts an indoor/outdoor sculpture exhibition in the summer. ♦ Donation suggested. W-Su noon-5PM. 718/448.2500 &

Staten Island Children's Museum Hands-on exhibits and related workshops and performances for five- to 12-year-olds are featured. A recent program gave children the opportunity to study bugs from both the scientist's and the artist's perspective. ♦ Admission. Tu-Su noon-5PM; call for extended summer hours. 718/273.2060 &

Staten Island Botanical Garden Located here are an English perennial garden; an herb and butterfly garden; a "White Garden" (all blooms in shades of gray and white) patterned after the famous English garden in Sissinghurst; and a greenhouse with a permanent display of tropicals, including the **Neil Vanderbilt Orchid Collection.** It's best to visit from May to October, when the flowers are in bloom. ♦ Free. Daily dawn to dusk. 718/273.8200

48 Cargo Cafe ★★★$$ This laid-back spot is just a five-minute walk from the Staten Island Ferry and worth the cross-harbor trip from Manhattan. Like the ambience the menu is casual but a cut above what you might expect out here. Sandwiches and salads are varied but uncommonly toothsome; try the blackened-tuna spinach salad with roasted tomato and garlic dressing. Entrées are imaginatively conceived and executed, and include the likes of panfried sea bass with roasted red pepper, green beans, and bacon; and grilled chicken breast with cranberry-walnut cornbread stuffing and wild mushrooms. If the weather's warm, eat or just chill out with an iced tea in the funky, loungey open-air space in the back. At press time there was an unbeatable $4.75 lunch special. ♦ American ♦ M-F lunch and dinner; Sa-Su brunch and dinner. 120 Bay St (between Staten Island Ferry and Victory Blvd). 718/876.0539

49 The Alice Austen House This is one of the finest records of turn-of-the-century American life from Alice Austen, a photographer whose work was first discovered in *Life* in 1949. ♦ Suggested donation. Th-Su noon-5PM. 2 Hylan Blvd (at Edgewater St), Rosebank. 718/816.4506

49 Aesop's Tables ★$$ Emblematic of how Staten Island sees itself—closer at heart to the country than the city—this rustic restaurant has country-garden wicker furniture, lots of dried flowers, and a patio for alfresco dining. The eclectic food can be a little uneven, but most dishes are interesting and flavorful; try the smoked mozzarella with portobello mushrooms, jerk chicken and beef, pork chops with a chili crust, or grilled catfish over greens. ♦ Eclectic ♦ Tu-F lunch and dinner; Sa dinner. No credit cards accepted. 1233 Bay St (between Fingerboard Rd and Hylan Blvd), Rosebank. 718/720.2005

50 Fort Wadsworth One of the oldest military installations in the US opened in 1997 as New York's newest National Park site. Now a part of the **Gateway National Recreation Area,** a 226-acre facility near the Verrazano-Narrows Bridge, this vital fortification played a major role in American history. There are exhibits, a visitors' center, remaining fortifications with panoramic views, and guided tours by rangers. ♦ Free. Call for information about days open and exhibits. Wadsworth Ave (at Bay St). 718/354.4500

51 Verrazano-Narrows Bridge Built in 1964 and designed by **Othmar Ammann,** this exquisite 4,260-foot minimalist steel ribbon is the world's longest suspension bridge (San Francisco's Golden Gate comes in a close second). It flies across the entrance to New York Harbor and is especially beautiful when seen from the Atlantic, against the city's skyline. It is named for Giovanni da Verrazano, the first European explorer to see New York (1524). The bridge has become familiar as the starting point for the **New York City Marathon** every November. ♦ Between Gowanus Expwy, Brooklyn and Staten Island Expwy

Queens is the largest of New York City's five boroughs and covers 109 square miles.

Before 1929, the site now occupied by La Guardia Airport was once an amusement park.

Seventy-five percent of New York City's restaurants change hands or close before they are five years old.

Restaurants/Clubs: Red   **Hotels:** Blue
Shops/ ♥ Outdoors: Green   **Sights/Culture:** Black

STATEN ISLAND ZOOLOGICAL SOCIETY, INC.

52 Staten Island Zoo Popular attractions at this zoo, beloved by many for its small (8.5 acres) scale, include an animal hospital, a re-created tropical rain forest, African savannah natural habitat, aquarium, and an outstanding reptile collection, which features the country's largest collection of rattlesnakes. Children can feed domestic animals daily at the **Children's Center,** and there's also a special Saturday-morning program (requiring reservations) called "Breakfast with the Beasts." ♦ Admission. Daily 10AM-4:45PM. 614 Broadway (between Glenwood Pl and W Raleigh Ave), West New Brighton. 718/442.3100

53 The Greenbelt Even New Yorkers are amazed when told that the sprawling 843-acre **Central Park** is not the largest in the city. Measuring in at a remarkable 2,500 acres, the park located on Staten Island offers locals little-known proximity to a variety of landscapes, from shaded woodlands and freshwater swamps to hardwood forests with hiking trails and cross-country skiing in winter. Regular programs, talks, and walking tours are organized by the park service. Call for information and schedules. ♦ Daily. Visitors' Center: High Rock Park, 200 Nevada Ave (off Rockland Ave, between Richmond and Manor Rds), Egbertville. 718/667.2165

54 Historic Richmond Town New York City's answer to Williamsburg is a continuing restoration of 27 buildings that show a picture of 17th- through 19th-century village life. Fourteen are currently open to visitors, including the **Voorlezer House** (1695),

the oldest surviving elementary school; the **General Store** (1840); and the **Bennet House** (1839), which is home to the **Museum of Childhood.** There are ongoing demonstrations of Early American trades and crafts, and working kitchens with cooking in progress. The **Museum Store** (in the **Historical Museum**) sells reproductions made by village craftspeople. ♦ Admission. W-Su 1PM-5PM. 441 Clarke Ave (at Old Mill Rd), Richmondtown. 718/351.1611

55 The Conference House/Billopp House Built in the 1670s, this was the scene of the only peace conference held to try to prevent the Revolutionary War. Admiral Lord Howe, in command of the British forces, hosted the parley on 11 September 1776 for three Continental Congress representatives—Benjamin Franklin, John Adams, and Edward Rutledge. The house is now a National Historic Landmark. ♦ Nominal admission. F-Su afternoon May-Nov. 7455 Hylan Blvd (at Satterlee St), Tottenville. 718/984.2086

Brownstones

L.L. BRENGELMAN

History

1524 Italian explorer Giovanni da Verrazano sails into New York Harbor.

1609 British captain Henry Hudson, in search of a shortcut to India for the Dutch West India Company, sails up the river that will bear his name.

1621 The city's history begins with a permanent Dutch settlement named Nieuw Amsterdam.

1625 The first black settlers are brought as slaves to build the city.

1626 Peter Minuit, the first governor, buys **Manhattan Island** from the Indians for a trunkful of relatively worthless trinkets.

1664 Nieuw Amsterdam becomes New York when Stuyvesant cedes control to Charles II of England and his brother, James, Duke of York.

1765 The British impose taxes, the harshest of which is the Stamp Act.

1774 The New York Tea Party takes place when the Sons of Liberty board the *London* and dump 18 cases of tea into the **East River.**

1776 The American Revolution starts, and General George Washington sets up quarters in **Lower Manhattan.** . . . As the Declaration of Independence is adopted by Congress, the Revolutionary forces are driven out of **Manhattan** by Lord Howe.

1789 New York City becomes capital of the United States. George Washington is inaugurated in front of **Federal Hall.**

1804 Aaron Burr, the vice president of the US, kills Alexander Hamilton, the first secretary of the treasury, in a duel.

1812 War is declared when the British blockade Manhattan. The new **City Hall** opens.

1830 With the arrival of new German immigrants throughout the previous decade, the population rises to 202,000.

1835 Newspaper editors William Cullen Bryant and Horace Greeley found *The New York Evening Post* and *The New York Tribune.* . . . Samuel F.B. Morse develops the telegraph.

1850 Irish immigrants, escaping the famine in their homeland, arrive in the city.

1851 *The New York Times* publishes its first edition.

1858 Calvert Vaux and Frederick Law Olmsted design **Central Park**.

1869 Infamous Black Friday rocks the financial world.

1870 A city charter approved by the state legislature gives the notorious William Marcy "Boss" Tweed financial control over New York City. Incredible sums of money disappear from city coffers.

1873 Wall Street panics as banks fail.

1883 The **Brooklyn Bridge,** considered the structural wonder of the age, opens.

1885 Southern Europeans, including large numbers of Italians, begin to arrive.

1886 The **Statue of Liberty** is unveiled. . . . Samuel Gompers organizes the American Federation of Labor (AFL).

1890 Jewish immigrants begin to arrive from Eastern Europe, many settling on the **Lower East Side.**

1891 Carnegie Hall opens with a concert featuring Peter Ilyich Tchaikovsky as conductor.

1892 Ellis Island becomes the city's immigration depot.

1898 The five boroughs unite to form **Greater New York.** The population is now over three million, making New York City the largest city in the world.

1904 The first subway system begins operation.

1911 The **New York Public Library** opens at **42nd Street** and **Fifth Avenue.** . . . Triangle Shirtwaist Company sweatshop fire leads to new labor laws and public safety measures.

1925 Playboy James Walker is elected mayor by popular vote.

1927 Charles A. Lindbergh returns to New York City after his solo flight to France. . . . Babe Ruth becomes baseball's home-run king, scoring 60 homers in one year. . . . The **Holland Tunnel,** the first **Hudson River** vehicular tunnel, opens and connects Manhattan with Jersey City.

1929 The stock market crashes as banks fail. . . . The **Chrysler Building** and the **Museum of Modern Art** open.

1931 The **Empire State Building,** the **George Washington Bridge,** and the new **Waldorf-Astoria Hotel** are completed.

When the first burials took place in St. Paul's and Trinity churchyards, at the end of the 17th century, they provided employment for gentlemen licensed by the city as Inviters to Funerals. Dressed in somber black, with long black streamers attached to their stovepipe hats, they marched in pairs from house to house extolling the virtues of the recently deceased. As they walked through the streets, one tolled a bell and the other pounded the pavement with a long black pole. They served as masters of ceremonies at the funeral itself, and their fee was determined by the turnout. At the gravesite the 12 pallbearers were given souvenir spoons engraved with figures of the 12 apostles, which were usually so badly cast they were known as monkey spoons. Female relatives were given a mourning brooch or ring, which had a compartment containing strands of the deceased's hair. (If they were burying a bald man, it was the hair of his nearest male relative.) Spoons, brooches, and rings were all sold by the Inviters, who also earned a fee for supervising the party that followed every funeral. The quality of the wine served was a tribute in itself, and many people stored away the best they could afford to be used at their own funerals. When a person became mortally ill, a different pair of licensed professionals, known as Comforters of the Sick, were hired by relatives to spend as many hours as were needed reading Scriptures, singing hymns, and otherwise preparing the doomed soul for an easy entry into Heaven.

932 Mayor James Walker resigns after it is learned that he and his administration are involved in municipal corruption.

933 Fiorello La Guardia is elected mayor.

937 The **Lincoln Tunnel** opens, connecting Midtown with Weehawken, NJ.

940 The **Queens-Midtown Tunnel** opens. . . . After the fall of France, New York City becomes home to many European artists—Mondrian, Léger, Ernst, Moholy-Nagy, and Breton among them.

941 Mayor Fiorello La Guardia initiates work on a giant air terminal in **Queens** (later named **John F. Kennedy International Airport**).

945 William O'Dwyer is elected mayor. . . . On 28 July, a US Army plane strikes the 79th floor of the **Empire State Building,** causing 14 deaths and a million dollars' worth of damage.

946 The **United Nations** establishes headquarters in Manhattan on 17 acres donated by the Rockefeller family.

950 The **Brooklyn Battery Tunnel** and the **Port Authority Bus Terminal** open. . . . William O'Dwyer resigns as mayor after disclosures of scandal and fraud in his administration.

953 Robert F. Wagner is elected mayor.

956 Ebbets Field is sold for a housing site after the **Brooklyn Dodgers** leave for Los Angeles.

959 The **Guggenheim Museum** opens.

964 The **Verrazano-Narrows Bridge** connects **Staten Island** and **Brooklyn.** . . . The **World's Fair** opens in **Flushing Meadow–Corona Park.**

965 New York City is paralyzed by a power blackout. . . . John V. Lindsay is elected mayor.

970 The **World Trade Center** is topped off and its first tenants move in.

973 Abraham D. Beame is elected mayor.

977 Ed Koch is elected mayor. . . . A four-month strike deprives New Yorkers of their newspapers.

981 A ticker-tape parade salutes 52 American hostages held captive in Iran for 444 days. . . . Former Beatle John Lennon is killed outside the **Dakota** apartments.

1982 Over half a million demonstrators against nuclear arms march to **Central Park.**

1986 Developer Donald Trump revamps **Wollman Rink** in **Central Park.** . . . The **Statue of Liberty** renovation is completed.

1987 The stock market crashes on 19 October. . . . Andy Warhol, the Father of Pop, dies in **New York Hospital.**

1989 David Dinkins wins the mayoral campaign to become the first black mayor in New York City history.

1990 Ellis Island reopens after a \$156-million renovation.

1991 Carnegie Hall celebrates its 100th anniversary.

1993 On 26 February, a terrorist bombing in the parking garages at **One World Trade Center** kills six people and injures thousands more. . . . Democrat David Dinkins is ousted in a bitter mayoral race by Rudolph Giuliani, a former Federal prosecutor. Giuliani becomes the first Republican to defeat an incumbent mayor in 60 years and the first Republican to head City Hall since 1974.

1995 New York City helps commemorate the 50th anniversary of the **United Nations** on 24 October.

1997 *Cats* becomes the longest running show on **Broadway,** with 6,138 performances.

1998 The City of New York celebrates its 100th birthday.

1999 As new term limit laws sent politicians scrambling for new jobs, Rudolf Giuliani seems set to tangle with Hillary Rodham Clinton in a celebrity food fight over the US Senate seat of retiring Daniel Patrick Moynihan. . . . On New Year's Eve, more than two million people gather in **Times Square** for the 96th dropping of the world-famous ball to welcome the new millennium.

Liberty Island

MICHAEL STORRINGS

Index

Index

Restaurants

Only restaurants with star
ratings are listed below. All
restaurants are listed
alphabetically in the main
(preceding) index. Always
call in advance to ensure a
restaurant has not closed,
changed its hours, or
booked its tables for a
private party. The
restaurant price ratings are
based on the average cost
of an entrée for one person,
excluding tax and tip.

★★★★ An Extraordinary
Experience
★★★ Excellent
★★ Very Good
★ Good

$$$$ Big Bucks ($30 and up)
$$$ Expensive ($20–$30)
$$ Reasonable ($10–$20)
$ The Price Is Right
(less than $10)

Index

NEW YORK CITY SUBWAYS

○○ Transfer Station
① Route Identifiers

Wakefield

① ⑨
242 St/
Van Cortlandt Park

238 St

231 St

225 St

Marble Hill

**Henry
Hudson
Bridge**

215 St

Spuyten-
Duyvil

Ⓐ
207 St/
Inwood

207 St

Dyckman
St/200 St

Dyckman
St

190 St

191 St

Harlem River

Metro North Hudson Line

181 St

181 St

George Washington
Bridge Bus Terminal

175 St

168 St/
Washington
Heights

Ⓑ

163 St/
Amsterdam
Ave

Ⓐ

157 St

155 St

155 St

① ⑨

Hudson River

St. Nicholas Ave

145 St

145 St

148 St/
Lenox
Terminal

③

145 St

137 St/
City
College

135 St

135 St

Broadway

125 St

125 St

125 St

HARLEM

116 St/
Columbia
University

116 St

116 St

Cathedral
Pkwy/
110 St

Cathedral
Pkwy/
110 St

110 St/
Central
Park
North

103 St

103 St

③

② ③

① ⑨

Lenox Ave

**Central
Park**

④
Woodlawn

Mosholu Pkwy

Bedford Park Blvd/
Lehman College

Kingsbridge
Rd

Fordham
Rd

Jerome Ave

183 St

Burnside
Ave

176 St

Mt. Eden
Ave

170 St

167 St

④

Grand Concourse

161 St/
Yankee Stadium

149 St/
Grand Concourse

②

138 St/
Grand
Concourse

⑥

125 St

116 St

110 St

103 St

Lexington Ave

②
241 St

Woodlawn

Williamsbridge

Ⓓ 205 St

Ⓒ
Bedford
Park Blvd

Kings-
bridge Rd

Fordham
Rd

182-
183 Sts

Tremont
Ave

174-
175 Sts

170 St

167 St

BRONX

Melrose

⑤
3 Ave/
149 St

138 St/
3 Ave

Brook
Ave

Cypress
Ave

Nereid
Ave/
238 St

⑤

233 St

225 St

Botanical
Gardens

219 St

Gun Hill
Rd

Burke
Ave

Gun Hill
Rd

Fordham
Rd

Allerton
Ave

Pelham
Pkwy

Pelham
Pkwy

Bronx
Park
East

Morris
Park

⑤

E 180 St

E Tremont Ave/
West Farms Sq

Tremont

174 St

Elder Ave

Freeman
St

Whitlock
Ave

Simpson
St

Intervale
Ave

Hunts
Point
Ave

⑥

Prospect
Ave

Longwood
Ave

Jackson
Ave

E 149
St

E 143 St/
St. Mary's St

Metro North Harlem and New Haven Lines

Triborough
Bridge

**Randalls
Island
Park**

**Wards
Island
Park**

Triborough
Bridge

Map continues on next page

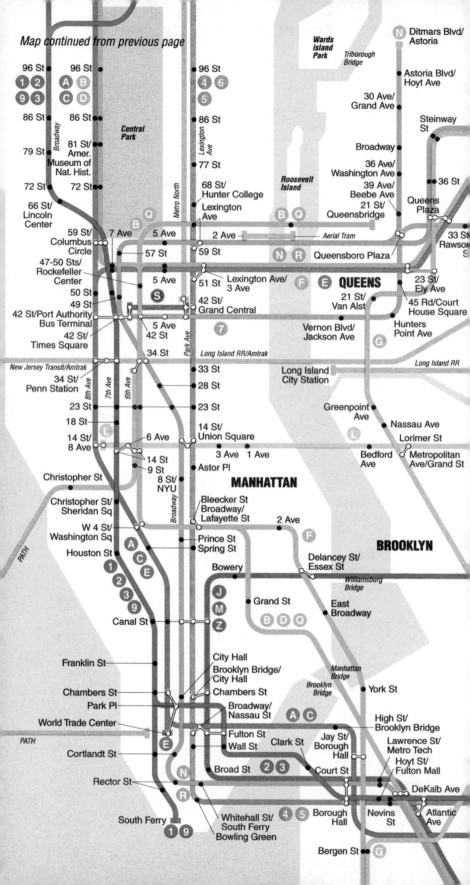

Map continued from previous page

Wards Island Park
Triborough Bridge

Ⓝ Ditmars Blvd/ Astoria

96 St
Ⓐ Ⓑ Ⓒ Ⓓ

96 St
Ⓐ Ⓑ
Ⓒ Ⓓ

Astoria Blvd/ Hoyt Ave

Central Park

96 St
Ⓐ Ⓑ

30 Ave/ Grand Ave

86 St
86 St

86 St

Steinway St

79 St
81 St/ Amer. Museum of Nat. Hist.

77 St

Broadway

Washington Ave

36 St

72 St
72 St

68 St/ Hunter College

39 Ave/ Beebe Ave

66 St/ Lincoln Center

Lexington Ave

Roosevelt Island

21 St/ Queensbridge

Queens Plaza

Ⓑ Ⓠ

Ⓑ Ⓠ

59 St/ Columbus Circle

7 Ave   5 Ave

2 Ave   Aerial Tram

33 St Rawson

57 St

59 St

Ⓝ Ⓡ   Queensboro Plaza

47-50 Sts/ Rockefeller Center

5 Ave

51 St

Lexington Ave/ 3 Ave

Ⓔ   QUEENS

23 St/ Ely Ave

50 St

Ⓢ

42 St/ Grand Central

21 St/ Van Alst

45 Rd/Court House Square

49 St

Metro North

Lexington Ave

42 St/Port Authority Bus Terminal

5 Ave

42 St/ Times Square

42 St

Ⓕ

Vernon Blvd/ Jackson Ave

Hunters Point Ave

Ⓖ

34 St

Long Island RR/Amtrak

Long Island RR

New Jersey Transit/Amtrak

33 St

Long Island City Station

34 St/ Penn Station

28 St

Greenpoint Ave

Nassau Ave

23 St

23 St

18 St

14 St/ Union Square

Lorimer St

Ⓛ

14 St/ 8 Ave

6 Ave

Ⓛ

Bedford Ave

Metropolitan Ave/Grand St

14 St

3 Ave   1 Ave

9 St

Astor Pl

Christopher St

8 St/ NYU

MANHATTAN

Christopher St/ Sheridan Sq

W 4 St/ Washington Sq

Bleecker St/ Broadway/ Lafayette St

2 Ave

Ⓕ

BROOKLYN

Houston St

Ⓐ
Ⓒ
Ⓔ

Prince St
Spring St

Delancey St/ Essex St

Ⓐ

PATH

Bowery

Williamsburg Bridge

Ⓑ Ⓓ Ⓠ

1
2
3
9

Ⓙ
Ⓜ
Ⓩ

Grand St

East Broadway

Canal St

Franklin St

Manhattan Bridge

York St

City Hall

Brooklyn Bridge/ City Hall

Chambers St

Park Pl

Chambers St

Brooklyn Bridge

Broadway/ Nassau St

Ⓐ Ⓒ

High St/ Brooklyn Bridge

World Trade Center

Ⓔ

Fulton St

Wall St

Clark St

Jay St/ Borough Hall

Lawrence St/ Metro Tech

PATH

Cortlandt St

Broad St

2 3

Court St

Hoyt St/ Fulton Mall

Rector St

Ⓝ

4 5

Borough Hall

DeKalb Ave

Ⓡ

Nevins St

Atlantic Ave

South Ferry

Whitehall St/ South Ferry Bowling Green

1 9

Bergen St

Ⓖ

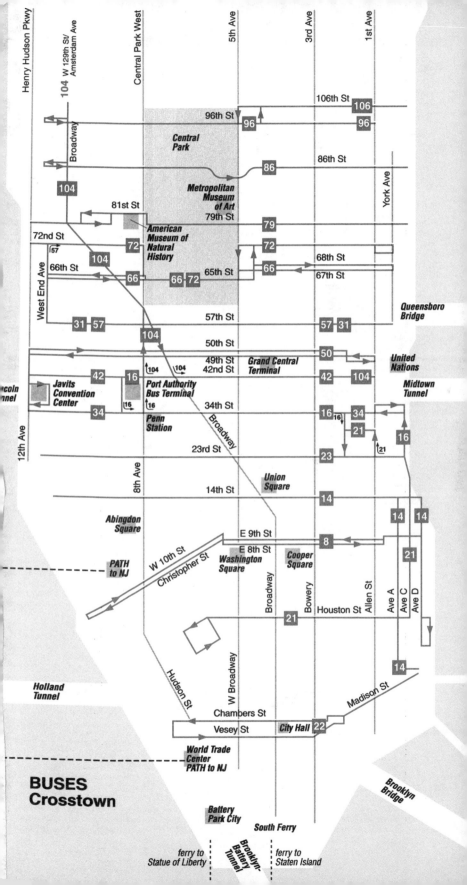

BUSES
Crosstown

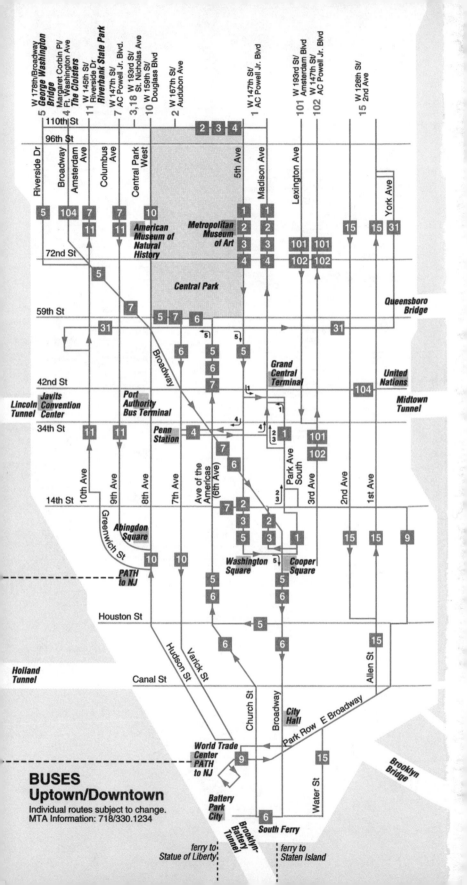

BUSES
Uptown/Downtown

Individual routes subject to change.
MTA Information: 718/330.1234